Animal Theologians

Animal Theologians

Edited by

ANDREW LINZEY AND CLAIR LINZEY

OXFORD
UNIVERSITY PRESS

Oxford University Press is a department of the University of Oxford. It furthers
the University's objective of excellence in research, scholarship, and education
by publishing worldwide. Oxford is a registered trade mark of Oxford University
Press in the UK and certain other countries.

Published in the United States of America by Oxford University Press
198 Madison Avenue, New York, NY 10016, United States of America.

CIP data is on file at the Library of Congress
ISBN 978–0–19–765555–9 (pbk.)
ISBN 978–0–19–765554–2 (hbk.)

DOI: 10.1093/oso/9780197655542.001.0001

Paperback printed by Marquis Book Printing, Canada
Hardback printed by Bridgeport National Bindery, Inc., United States of America

By the same editors

Animal Ethics for Veterinarians
The Ethical Case against Animal Experiments
The Palgrave Handbook of Practical Animal Ethics
The Routledge Handbook of Religion and Animal Ethics
Ethical Vegetarianism and Veganism
An Ethical Critique of Fur Factory Farming

This book is dedicated to Julius Kristoff Ormiston
for his faith, generosity, and love for animals

Contents

X CONTENTS

About the Contributors

A. W. H. Bates is medical director of Convit House Pathology Ltd. and honorary associate professor at University College London. His books include *Emblematic Monsters* (Rodopi, 2005), *The Anatomy of Robert Knox* (Sussex Academic Press, 2010), and *Antivivisection and the Profession of Medicine* (Palgrave Macmillan, 2017). His research interests include the history of the antivivisection movement and medical ethics.

Justin Begley is a Humboldt fellow at Ludwig-Maximilians-Universität München. He received his DPhil from the University of Oxford and has previously held research fellowships at the University of Helsinki, the Folger Shakespeare Library, the University of Bucharest, the Herzog August Bibliothek, the Gotha Research Centre, and the University of Bayreuth. Justin has a book forthcoming with Palgrave Macmillan, and he has published articles in journals including *Intellectual History Review*, *Annals of Science*, *Seventeenth Century*, *Review of English Studies*, and *Perspectives on Science*. Justin's research explores the intersections of literature, science, and philosophy during the early modern period, and he has a particular interest in what was thought to separate humans, animals, and plants at this time.

Ryan Brand is a PhD candidate in religion at Vanderbilt University. His area of study is the history and critical theories of religion, with a minor in philosophy. He is currently working on his dissertation, titled "Bear Traps: (Un)doing Human–Animal Entanglements in the Study of Religion." His areas of specialization encompass method and theory in religious studies, Buddhist traditions, critical animal studies, and animals and religion. He is studying Japanese; his research includes religion in Japan and the role of animals in the formation of what gets to count as religious behavior and who gets to inhabit religious categories.

Idan Breier is a senior lecturer in the Department of Jewish History and Contemporary Jewry at Bar-Ilan University (Ramat-Gan, Israel), where he gained his graduate and postgraduate degrees. His primary fields of interest are biblical and ancient Near Eastern history in the light of modern international relations theories on the one hand, and cultural history of the period on the other hand. Another field of his research is the Bible in modern and contemporary rabbinical thought. His publications deal with, inter alia, the history of the extended El Amarna period and the end of the First Temple period and the mutual relationship between human and animals in the Bible and ancient Near Eastern cultures. He is a fellow of the Oxford Centre for Animal Ethics.

Adam Bridgen is Fleeman Research Fellow in Eighteenth-Century Literature and Culture at the University of St Andrews, and an Associate Fellow of the Oxford Centre for Animal Ethics. He gained a DPhil in English from the University of Oxford in 2020 and has previously received fellowships from the Huntington Library and the Royal Historical Society. He has published in the *Huntington Literary Quarterly* and is a contributor to *Hannah More in Context* (2022) and *Romantic Environmental Sensibility: Nature, Empire and Class* (2022). His research concerns the influence of social class and religion on writing about slavery, empire, and the natural world during the long eighteenth century, as well as the theological and transatlantic contexts of animal rights thinking in Britain.

Alice Crary is University Distinguished Professor at the New School for Social Research in New York, where she is also a member of the Department of Liberal Studies and a founding codirector of the graduate program in gender and sexuality studies. She is also a visiting fellow at Regent's Park College, Oxford. Her books include *Beyond Moral Judgment* (Harvard University Press, 2007); *Wittgenstein and the Moral Life: Essays in Honor of Cora Diamond* (editor; MIT Press, 2006); and *Inside Ethics: On the Demands of Moral Thought* (Harvard University Press, 2016). Her research interests include normative and metaethics, philosophy and literature, Wittgenstein/Austin speech act theory, social epistemology, feminist theory, cognitive disability, and animal ethics.

Daniel A. Dombrowski is a professor of philosophy at Seattle University. He is the author of twenty books and over 180 articles in scholarly journals in philosophy, theology, classics, and literature. Among his books are *Rethinking the Ontological Argument: A Neoclassical Theistic Perspective* (Cambridge University Press, 2006), *Contemporary Athletics and Ancient Greek Ideals* (University of Chicago Press, 2009), and *Process Philosophy and Political Liberalism: Rawls, Whitehead, Hartshorne* (Edinburgh University Press, 2019). His main areas of intellectual interest are metaphysics and philosophy of religion from a neoclassical or process perspective. He is the editor of the journal *Process Studies*.

Carl Tobias Frayne is a PhD candidate in divinity at St John's College, Cambridge. He graduated first in philosophy with First Class Honours from the University of Melbourne and spent a year at St Peter's College, Oxford, reading philosophy and theology. He holds a master of arts in divinity from the University of Chicago, where he pursued his interest in philosophical and theological ethics, as well as ecclesiastical history. His recent academic work on nonhuman animals includes a comparative study of the place of creatures and creation in Islam and Christianity. He also wrote a brief history of abstinence from meat in the Christian tradition, which was published in the *Journal of Animal Ethics* 6, no. 2 (Fall 2016).

Nuri Friedlander is a faculty member in the Department of Religion and Philosophy department at the Lawrenceville School, where he teaches courses on religious studies, Islam, bioethics, and religion and ecology. In addition to his teaching responsibilities, he serves as the Director of Equity and Inclusion. His dissertation, titled "Sharpen Your Blade and Put Your Animal at Ease," addresses questions of law, ethics, and ritual in relation to practices of animal slaughter and sacrifice.

Michael J. Gilmour is an associate professor of New Testament and English literature at Providence University College in Manitoba, Canada, where he regularly offers an undergraduate course on animal ethics in biblical and theological perspective. Publications include *Eden's Other Residents: The Bible and Animals* (Cascade, 2014), *The Gospel according to Bob Dylan: The Old, Old Story for Modern Times* (Westminster John Knox Press, 2011), and *Gods and Guitars: Seeking the Sacred in Post-1960s Popular Music* (Baylor University Press, 2009). He is also editor (with Mary Ann Beavis) of the *Dictionary of the Bible and Western Culture* (Sheffield Phoenix Press, 2012). His most recent work is *Creative Compassion, Literature and Animal Welfare* (Palgrave Macmillan, 2020).

Robyn Hederman is the Principal Court Attorney for a New York State Supreme Court justice. She is a fellow of the Oxford Centre for Animal Ethics and the cochair of the Animal Law Committee of the New York City Bar Association. Her publications include "Gender and the Animal Experiments Controversy in Nineteenth-Century America" in *The Ethical Case against Animal Experimentation* (University of Illinois Press, 2018) and "The Cost of Cruelty: Henry Bergh and the Abattoirs" in *Ethical Vegetarianism and Veganism* (Routledge, 2019). She has a master of arts in history and is a member of the Phi Alpha Theta History Honor Society. Her research interests include gender and the history of the antivivisection movement in the United States.

Serenhedd James is the author of *George Errington and Roman Catholic Identity in Nineteenth-Century England* (Oxford University Press, 2016) and *The Cowley Fathers: A History of the English Congregation of the Society of St John the Evangelist* (Canterbury Press, 2019). He is an associate member of the Faculty of Theology and Religion at the University of Oxford, where he teaches ecclesiastical history at St Stephen's House, a fellow of the Royal Historical Society, and a contributing editor of the *Catholic Herald*.

Linda M. Johnson is Curator of Hancock Shaker Village, a living history museum in Pittsfield, MA. Johnson's research and teaching focus has been in American and European art history at the University of Michigan–Flint and the Massachusetts College of Liberal Arts. She is a Fellow of the Oxford Centre for Animal Ethics. Publications include "Increase Mather: A Pre-millennial Portrait during the Revocation of the Massachusetts Charter" in *American Literature and the New Puritan Studies* (Cambridge University Press, 2018). Her recent book *Art, Ethics and the Human-Animal Relationship* was published by Palgrave Macmillan (2021). Research interests include European and American art history, environmental humanities, and animal ethics.

Chien-hui Li is an associate professor in the Department of History, National Cheng Kung University, Taiwan. She has coedited and introduced *William Drummond's Rights of Animals and Man's Obligation to Treat Them with Humanity (1838)* (Mellen Animal Rights Library, 2005) and has published journal articles in the areas of animal protection, political radicalism, and relations between religion and science in nineteenth-century Britain. Her most recent book is *Mobilizing Traditions in the First Wave of the British Animal Defense Movement* (Palgrave Macmillan, 2019). Research interests include the history of human–animal relations, Victorian social and cultural history, and Western historiography.

Andrew Linzey is director of the Oxford Centre for Animal Ethics and has been a member of the Faculty of Theology in the University of Oxford for twenty-eight years. He is a visiting professor of animal theology at the University of Winchester and a professor of animal ethics at the Graduate Theological Foundation. He is the author or editor of more than thirty books, including *Animal Theology* (SCM Press / University of Illinois Press, 1994); *Why Animal Suffering Matters* (Oxford University Press, 2009); *The Global Guide to Animal Protection* (University of Illinois Press, 2013); and *The Palgrave Handbook of Practical Animal Ethics* (Palgrave Macmillan, 2018).

Clair Linzey is the deputy director of the Oxford Centre for Animal Ethics. She is a professor of animal theology at the Graduate Theological Foundation. She gained her doctorate in theology from the University of St Andrews, and is coeditor of the *Journal of Animal Ethics* and coeditor of the Palgrave Macmillan Animal Ethics Series. She is the author of *Developing Animal Theology* (Routledge, 2021). She is coeditor with Andrew Linzey of *Animal Ethics for Veterinarians* (University of Illinois Press, 2017); *The Ethical Case against Animal Experiments* (University of Illinois Press, 2018); *The Routledge Handbook of Religion and Animal Ethics* (Routledge, 2018); *The Palgrave Handbook of Practical Animal Ethics* (Palgrave Macmillan, 2018); and *Ethical Vegetarianism and Veganism* (Routledge, 2018).

Kathleen Long is a professor of French in the Department of Romance Studies at Cornell University. Author of two books, *Another Reality: Metamorphosis and the Imagination in the Poetry of Ovid, Petrarch, and Ronsard* and *Hermaphrodites in Renaissance Europe*, and more than fifty articles and book chapters, Kathleen Long now focuses her work on early modern theories of gender and of nonnormative corporealities. Her particular interests are in the relationship between gender, bodily, and behavioral norms and early modern theories of political order, as well as the circulation of very different ideas concerning natural variation's crucial role in human survival and thriving. She teaches courses on disability studies, religious violence in literature from the crusades to the Algerian War of Independence, and monsters. She is the editor of three volumes: *High Anxiety: Masculinity in Crisis in Early Modern France*, *Religious Differences in France*, and *Gender and Scientific Discourse in Early Modern Europe*, and coeditor for the series Monsters and Marvels: Alterity in the Medieval and Early Modern Worlds (Amsterdam University Press). Her current projects include a translation into English of *The Island of Hermaphrodites* (*L'isle des hermaphrodites*), a monograph on literature in the wake of the French Wars of Religion (*Bringing up the Dead*), and a study of early modern theories of disability and gender difference, *The Premodern Postnormal*.

Ryan Patrick McLaughlin is an assistant professor of religious studies at Saint Elizabeth University and is an associate fellow of the Oxford Centre for Animal Ethics. He also serves as the assistant editor for the *Biblical Theology Bulletin*. He has published two books: *Christian Theology and the Status of Animals: The Dominant Tradition and Its Alternatives* (Palgrave Macmillan, 2014) and *Preservation and Protest: Theological Foundations for an Eco-Eschatological Ethics* (Fortress Press, 2014). His areas of research include environmental ethics, animal ethics, and the problem of evolutionary evil.

Wesley T. Mott is a professor of English emeritus at Worcester Polytechnic Institute. Founder of the Ralph Waldo Emerson Society (1989), he has served on the advisory boards of the Louisa May Alcott Society, the Walden Woods Project, and the Thoreau Society, for which he also was vice president of publications. Author of *"The Strains of Eloquence": Emerson and His Sermons* (Penn State University Press, 1989), he edited *Bonds of Affection: Thoreau on Dogs and Cats* (University of Massachusetts Press, 2005) and *Ralph Waldo Emerson in Context* (Cambridge University Press, 2014). He has edited several reference books about transcendentalism and has written about that movement's religious, aesthetic, educational, geographical, and musical contexts. He is textual editor of volume 4 of Emerson's *Complete Sermons* (University of Missouri Press, 1992) and volume 9 of Thoreau's *Journal* (Princeton University Press, forthcoming).

Abbey Smith completed her PhD in philosophical theology and animal ethics at Winchester University. Her doctoral thesis was published as *Animals in Tillich's Philosophical Theology* (Palgrave Macmillan, Animal Ethics Series, 2017). She has also had two essays on animal welfare published in *The Global Guide for Animal Protection* (University of Illinois Press, 2013) and has a chapter in *The Routledge Handbook of Religion and Animal Ethics* (2018). She is a qualified veterinary anesthetist who has been involved in practical animal welfare for over two decades.

Kenneth R. Valpey (Krishna Kshetra Swami) completed his DPhil at the University of Oxford with a study of Vaishnava temple liturgical practices and theology (published by Routledge in 2006 as *Attending Kṛṣṇa's Image: Caitanya Vaiṣṇava Mūrti-sevā as Devotional Truth*). As a research fellow of the Oxford Centre for Hindu Studies, he codirects the Bhāgavata Purāṇa Research Project. In this capacity, he and Professor Ravi M. Gupta have edited a volume of articles and translated a volume of selections from the Bhāgavata Purāṇa, both volumes published by Columbia University Press (2013 and 2016, respectively). Drawing on classical Indic sources, he has written and lectured on nonviolence and environmentalism and, more recently,

as a fellow of the Oxford Centre for Animal Ethics, on the application of yoga principles and practices to thought on animal-human relationships and animal protection.
His latest book is *Cow Care in Hindu Animal Ethics* (Palgrave Macmillan, 2020).

Beruriah Wiegand is the Woolf Corob Lector in Yiddish at the University of Oxford.
She also teaches Yiddish classes for the Oxford School of Rare Jewish Languages and
for the Paideia Folkshögskola in Stockholm, as well as privately. She holds a BA and
MA in Hebrew and Jewish Studies from Leo Baeck College, London, and a PhD from
University College London. Her doctoral thesis looks at Jewish mystical motifs in the
works of Isaac Bashevis Singer. She is also a Yiddish poet and has published two bilingual collections of her poetry with the H. Leyvik-farlag in Tel Aviv under the titles *Tsi
hot ir gezen mayn tsig? un andere lider—Have You Seen My Goat? And Other Poems*
(2012) and *Kales-breyshis un andere lider—Kalat Bereshit and Other Poems* (2018).
As a translator from Yiddish she has published a bilingual edition of A. N. Stencl's
early verse, cotranslated with Stephen Watts (*All My Young Years: Yiddish Poetry from
Weimar Germany*, Five Leaves, 2007), as well as a translation of a book of memoirs by
the Grodno writer Leib Reizer (*In the Struggle: Memoirs from Grodno and the Forests*,
Yad Vashem, 2009).

Introduction

Before *Animal Theology*

Andrew Linzey and Clair Linzey

Defining Theology

Karl Barth famously described theology as "a *logia*, logic, or language bound to *the theos*, which makes it possible and also determines it."[1]

> We are speaking here of the God of the Gospel, his work and action, and of the Gospel in which his work and action are at the same time his speech. This is his Word, the Logos in which the theological *logia*, logic, and language have their creative basis and life.[2]

This is, of course, a Christian definition of theology, since the "Word" in question is the incarnate Logos, the Christ, who is the center of all Christian theology. But despite offering a specifically Christian definition of theology, Barth provides a useful starting point for understanding theology in a broader sense. The key is in the word "logia," which Barth describes as the "logic" of theology itself.

From this wider perspective, we may define theology as an understanding of the inner logic of a faith position. Theology in this sense must be sharply distinguished from knowledge of religion per se or the study of religion itself. Regrettably, many university departments of theology have now changed their names, to become departments of religion or religious studies, or have supplemented the word "theology" with one of these other appellations (including, sadly, what is now the Faculty of Theology and Religion at the University of Oxford). But there is a difference between *knowing about* and

---

[1] Karl Barth, *Evangelical Theology: An Introduction* (London: Collins, 1969), 20.
[2] Barth, *Evangelical Theology*, 23.

Andrew Linzey and Clair Linzey, *Introduction* In: *Animal Theologians*. Edited by: Andrew Linzey and Clair Linzey, Oxford University Press. © Oxford University Press 2023. DOI: 10.1093/oso/9780197655542.003.0001

understanding of. The psychology, the sociology, the philosophy, and the history of religion are all excellent fields of study and can be useful adjuncts to study of theology. They can illuminate theological positions and help us to contextualize them. But they are not theology. And neither do they by themselves fulfill the aim of theology, which is an understanding of its inner logic. There can be Jewish, Muslim, Hindu, and Christian theologies (to name but a few), but the aim should always be the same—not just to know about the faith position, but to grasp the inner logia of it.

Even this is not entirely satisfactory. Faith is often contrasted with reason or evidence, whereas in fact there are few religious positions devoid of both. Moreover, there is an unfortunate tendency to define faith as a private affair (like personal likes and dislikes) wholly or largely unrelated to society as a whole. Indeed, some have seen the attempt to define religion as faith as a way of marginalizing religion in contemporary society.[3] Perhaps, then, it is best to define theology as an understanding of the inner logic of a religious or spiritual stance or position.

But we need to go further. Religious perspectives are not just a set of intellectual propositions to which believers may give assent. Of course, religious perspectives invariably consist of intellectual positions, sometimes of a very complicated kind, and it is certainly important to have an appreciation of a religion's ideas and official statements, including its normative scriptures that enable us to have some insight into what a tradition holds to be true. But that is not all that is required to understand a religious perspective. Theology requires as much an understanding of the rites, symbols, and practices of what are (in most cases) living religions as it does an understanding of their intellectual affirmations. That is why we need to go further and speak of an understanding of the inner *moral* theo-logic that encompasses the values of the perspectives themselves. Indeed, so vital is the ethical dimension of religious belief that we might define all theology as moral theology, in the sense that it is lived theology with implicit and explicit moral values.[4] The mind we need here is not that of an anthropologist who seeks to be a neutral observer (if there can be such a thing) of people, events, and phenomena, but rather that of an open participant who treats religious practices seriously and seeks to grasp their inner logia.

[3] See, for example, Frances Margaret Young, *Dare We Speak of God in Public?* (London: Mowbray, 1995).

[4] This view is formulated in Andrew Linzey, "Theology," in *Dictionary of Ethics, Theology and Society*, ed. Paul Barry Clarke and Andrew Linzey (Abingdon, England: Routledge, 1996), 819–26.

When at least 85 percent of the world's population is religious, under-standing how people believe, practice, and live within religious traditions is a tremendously important goal if we want genuine intercultural and interfaith dialogue. It is difficult to see how there can be any possibility of overcoming conflict and mutual antagonisms, and establishing enduring mutuality without that understanding. Theology, then, as we see it, is a much more de-manding undertaking and far more important than is commonly supposed. It does not of itself require a religious belief (as many have previously sup-posed), but it does require people who can think beyond familiar boundaries and be open to insight into new layers of meaning and value in the world.

It is important to distinguish between understanding and agreement. Intellectual understanding is not the same as intellectual assent—almost the opposite. The deeper the understanding, the deeper the ability to see how the tradition can be developed and improved. John Macquarrie famously described theology as the attempt to think through the Church's faith into a coherent whole.[5] While this book is not limited to the specifically Christian approach that Macquarrie takes, the word "coherent"[6] is relevant. One idea or practice must relate to another, and there needs to be inner intellectual co-herence in doctrine and ethics. Not everything that has accrued within a tra-dition is necessarily essential to the main beliefs of that tradition. This means that theology is necessarily a critical discourse requiring understanding, en-gagement, and also the fullest use of one's critical faculties. The inner logic must not be shortchanged or unexamined.

The Neglected Creature

The question might not be unreasonably asked: Why should theo-logic be concerned with animals? Rather obviously, if God is by definition the Creator of all things, it follows that animals are fellow creatures. Humans are not God. It follows that we do not own other creatures, and they do not belong to us.[7] It also necessarily follows that their worth and value to God is an entirely separate thing from their worth and value to human beings. It is difficult to

---

[5] John Macquarrie, *Principles of Christian Theology* (London: SCM Press), 3.

[6] Macquarrie, *Principles of Christian Theology*, 3.

[7] See a discussion of this in Andrew Linzey and Clair Linzey, "Introduction," in *The Routledge Handbook of Religion and Animal Ethics*, ed. Andrew Linzey and Clair Linzey (London: Routledge, 2018), 1–20.

imagine that God would create millions of species but care for only one of them. The key point is that a true theo-logia must be able to provide a full account of the worth and value of creation, including and in particular fellow creatures, in order to be what it claims to be.

Perhaps the bigger and more important question, then, is why have these elementary but fundamental insights been lost in many, if not most, expositions of theo-logic? They haven't been entirely lost, of course. While religious traditions are often characterized by forgetting, it is also true that remembering can be a source of further enlightenment.[8] Perhaps that is why tradition may be characterized as the seedbed of creativity.

But there is no way to get around the general point that theistic traditions have been largely anthropocentric. Karl Barth writes that "in practice the doctrine of creation means anthropology—the doctrine of man."[9] Later, Barth writes, "He who in the biblical message is called God is obviously not interested in the totality of things and beings created by Him, nor in specific beings within this totality, but in man."[10] Hinduism is an exception to this anthropocentrism, of course, as are nontheistic traditions such as Buddhism and Jainism, but Christianity, which centers on the doctrine of the incarnation, has always been particularly susceptible to the charge of anthropocentrism. The concentration on humanity in most theistic traditions always carries with it the danger of idolatry—that is, of presuming that the needs and wants of human beings are the primary, or even the exclusive, concern of the Creator. Ludwig Feuerbach famously argued that Christianity is nothing other than the self-aggrandizement, even deification, of the human species.[11]

It follows even from this briefest of sketches that theology has a distinctive contribution to make to animal ethics. In the words attributed to Hans von Baltasaar, "the whole point of creation is for us to know that we are not Creator." Because we are not God, there has to be a limit to what we can justifiably do to animals or the use we can make of them. Human interest, however vital or important, cannot be the sole basis on which we judge the morality of our relations with other creatures. The big issue always is whether

[8] We are grateful for this point made in Maurice Wiles's essay in *Christian Believing: The Nature of the Christian Faith and Its Expression in Holy Scripture and Creeds: A Report* (London: SPCK, 1976).

[9] Karl Barth, *Church Dogmatics: The Doctrine of Creation*, vol. 3, part 2, *The Creature*, ed. G. W. Bromiley and T. F. Torrance, trans. H. Knight, G. W. Bromiley, J. K. S. Reid, and R. H. Fuller (Edinburgh: T. & T. Clark, 1960), 3.

[10] Karl Barth, *Church Dogmatics: The Doctrine of Creation*, vol. 3, part 4, ed. and trans. A. T. Mackay, T. H. L. Parker, H. Knight, H. A. Kennedy, and J. Marks (Edinburgh: T. & T. Clark, 1961), 337.

[11] Ludwig Feuerbach, *The Essence of Christianity*, trans. George Eliot, introd. Karl Barth (New York: Harper Torchbook, 1957), sec. 2, 12.

God's own interest as Creator is being properly reflected in what humans do with what God has created.

Christianity's historical anthropocentricity can be summed up in the words of St. Thomas Aquinas, who held that

> dumb animals and plants are devoid of the life of reason whereby to set themselves in motion; they are moved as it were by another, by a kind of natural impulse, a sign of which is that they are naturally enslaved and accommodated to the uses of others.[12]

Aquinas states his perspective even more directly in his "Summa Contra Gentiles": "By divine providence, they [animals] are intended for man's use according to the order of nature. Hence it is not wrong for man to make use of them, either by killing *or in any other way whatever*."[13]

Some eco-theologians have sought to put a gloss on St. Thomas so that his words might not appear as harsh as they seem.[14] But what they cannot dispute is that what has been perceived—and continues to be perceived—as the Catholic, if not the only Christian, view of animals that has been expounded in generation after generation in theological textbooks. For example, in his 1946 book *Moral and Pastoral Theology*, Henry Davis writes, "Animals have no rights; they can give us nothing freely nor understand our claims. We have no duties of justice or charity towards them."[15] This is a view that continues in the *Dictionary of Moral Theology*, published in 1962: "Zoophilists often lose sight of the end for which animals, irrational creatures were created by God, viz., the service and use of man. . . . In fact, Catholic moral doctrine teaches that animals have no rights on the part of man."[16] Notice how the inner moral theo-logic, to which we referred earlier, of these statements is morally and spiritually impoverished in relation to God's other creatures.

It is not, however, just the Catholic tradition that has a lacuna when it comes to animals. The Protestant tradition has largely followed suit. To give one recent illustration, Colin Gunton and other distinguished theologians

---

[12] Thomas Aquinas, "The Lawful Treatment of Animals," in *Animals and Christianity: A Book of Readings*, ed. Andrew Linzey and Tom Regan (New York: Crossroads, 1990), 125.

[13] Thomas Aquinas, "Summa Contra Gentiles," in *Basic Writings of Saint Thomas Aquinas*, trans A. C. Pegis (New York: Random House, 1945), 2:220–24; emphasis added.

[14] See, for example, Michael S. Northcott, *The Environment and Christian Ethics* (Cambridge: Cambridge University Press, 1996); and Celia Deane-Drummond, *The Ethics of Nature* (Oxford: Blackwell, 2004).

[15] Henry Davis, "Animals Have No Rights," in Linzey and Regan, *Animals and Christianity*, 130.

[16] P. Palazzini, ed., *Dictionary of Moral Theology* (London: Burns and Oates, 1962), 73.

published a reader for up-and-coming theologians in 2001 titled *The Practice of Theology*, which is still widely used in seminaries and theological colleges. It contains sections on sources for theology, the authority of the Christian tradition, creeds and confessions, the place of reason in theology, and the nature of theological claims, and a final section on doing theology today. This latter part contains discussions of modernity and postmodernity and "local theologies"—namely, liberation theology, feminist theology, and "Christian theology in a multi-faith world."[17] Notice how this admirable comprehensive work includes no mention of nonhuman beings or even of creation care. It is written as though the world of creatures has no theological import or does not exist at all.

The Publication of "*Animal Theology*"

Animal theology has now become a serious topic of theological discussion. But this was not always the case. As detailed in the preceding section, animals have been largely neglected in the Christian tradition. However, Andrew Linzey (hereafter "AL") saw that although the Christian tradition has been anthropocentric and has marginalized animals, it did not have to be interpreted in an animal-blind way.

As a reaction to the negative tradition, in 1994 AL penned his now seminal *Animal Theology*.[18] This work put animals firmly on the academic agenda as a topic for theological discussion. This was in many ways a watershed moment, and like all watershed moments, it was the subject of great criticism and discussion.

The book in particular challenged the traditional anthropocentrism of the Christian tradition and argued that Christianity had championed many negative ideas about animals that were theologically unsupportable. AL called on Christians to break through the negative barrier and draw on better and more authentic elements within the tradition. He wrote:

> My overall intention is to question the all too comfortable assumption that if theology is to speak on this question, it must do so only on the side of the oppressors of animals. . . . I question the timidity of those who hold fast

---

[17] Colin Gunton, Stephen R. Holmes, and Murray A. Rae, *The Practice of Theology: A Reader* (London: SCM Press, 2001).

[18] Andrew Linzey, *Animal Theology* (London: SCM Press, 1994).

to a Trinitarian faith and at the same time seemingly oppose, as a matter of principle, any exploration of its relevance beyond familiar boundaries. I propose that it has to be a matter of regret, even repentance, that the community of faith, which holds to the objective truth of the self-revelation of God in Christ should have advanced its world-affirming doctrine without much more than a passing thought for the millions of non-human inhabitants within creation itself. What are we to say of a theology which has so proceeded on the basis of a moral neglect of God's creatures?[19]

Animal Theology attracted both praise and criticism. On the positive side, Mark Rowlands kindly suggested that "Andrew Linzey is virtually synonymous with the discipline of animal theology: a discipline that he has legitimate claim to have single-handedly invented."[20] Bishop John Austin Baker claimed him as "the greatest living writer on theology and animals."[21] And amazingly, in 2006, AL was recognized by *The Independent*'s "Good List" as one of fifty people who have changed the world "for the better," for his animal-related work challenging both the churches and academia at some personal cost.

Interestingly enough, some of the strongest critical reactions to the animal issue came from within the Christian churches. AL's position had already attracted criticism, but the publication of *Animal Theology* crystallized the debate even further. For example, the Anglican and Roman Catholic bishops in Canada defended the trapping of "wild" animals for fur.[22] In 1995, the archbishop of York, John Habgood, publicly criticized rights language in relation to animals in response to the debate about live animal exports. He argued that the protesters were misguided, writing, "Talk of 'rights' seems to imply an absoluteness that is unsustainable in theory and dangerous in practice, in that it inflates moral claims to the point of inducing some protesters to disregard the legitimate claims of their fellow human beings."[23] Habgood

---

[19] Linzey, *Animal Theology*, vii–viii.

[20] Mark Rowlands, quoted from his endorsement of Linzey, *Why Animal Suffering Matters* (New York: Oxford University Press, 2007), back cover.

[21] John Austin Baker, quoted in "Launch of *Creatures of the Same God*," Oxford Centre for Animal Ethics, June 14, 2007, https://www.oxfordanimalethics.com/2007/06/launch-of-creatures-of-the-same-god/.

[22] See Bishops of Northern Canada, "In Defence of Fur-Trapping," in Linzey and Regan, *Animals and Christianity*, 167–70; and Andrew Linzey, "A Reply to the Bishops," in Linzey and Regan, *Animals and Christianity*, 170–73.

[23] John Habgood, "Claiming Animal 'Rights' Devalues Cases of Basic Human Need," *The Times*, February 11, 1995, 9. See Andrew Linzey's reply in Andrew Linzey, "Animals and the Churches: A Case of Theological Neglect," *Reviews in Religion and Theology*, August 3, 1995, 3–7.

subsequently defended hunting with dogs in the House of Lords. He argued that part of the reason "why people are fascinated lies in the kind of competitive encounter that one has with a wild animal."[24] In the same debate, twelve bishops supported the continuance of hunting. Previously, there had been a motion before the General Synod of the Church of England (the governing body) to ban hunting on church land. This motion was neutralized by the archbishops of Canterbury and York through their support for a wrecking amendment.[25] Afterward, AL was reported in *The Guardian* as saying, "I am deeply ashamed to be a member of the Church of England."[26]

The rejection of animal issues by the Church of England has continued into the twenty-first century. For example, in an astonishing departure from his predecessors, the present archbishop, Justin Welby, declined to become vice patron of the Royal Society for the Prevention of Cruelty to Animals.[27]

We could continue with further examples, but in fairness to the church, it should be pointed out that AL was able to garner the support of forty-two bishops against the wearing of fur.[28] In addition, archbishop George Carey awarded AL a Lambeth Doctor of Divinity for his "unique and massive pioneering work at a scholarly level in the area of the theology of creation with particular reference to the rights and welfare of God's sentient creatures."[29] Finally, in 2013, archbishop Desmond Tutu wrote a forthright foreword to AL's *The Global Guide to Animal Protection*, arguing that "churches should lead the way by making clear that all cruelty—to other animals as well as human beings—is an affront to civilized living and a sin before God."[30]

Animal Theology was not AL's only or even first effort to alter the course of Christian thinking. He had already written two previous books on animals that critiqued Christianity.[31] More especially, in order to introduce

[24] Lord Habgood, Hunting Bill, House of Lords, *Hansard*, March 12, 2001, https://api.parliament.uk/historic-hansard/lords/2001/mar/12/hunting-bill.

[25] General Synod, *General Synod Report of Proceedings July 1990*, vol. 21, no. 2 (London: Church House Publishing, 1990).

[26] As reported in Walter Schwarz, "Synod Rejects Hunting Ban on Church Land," *The Guardian*, July 9, 1990, 3. For a narrative of these events, see the chapter "Cruelty in the Church's Own Backyard," in Andrew Linzey, *Animal Gospel* (London: Hodder and Stoughton, 1998), 130–39.

[27] For a critique of the archbishop's decision, see Andrew Linzey, "Lambeth Folly," *The Tablet*, August 24, 2014, 11.

[28] Andrew Linzey, ed., *Cruelty and Christian Conscience: Bishops Say No to Fur* (Nottingham, England: Lynx, 1992).

[29] Statement by archbishop George Carey at the conferring of the doctorate of divinity, Lambeth Palace, 2001, https://www.oxfordanimalethics.com/who-we-are/director/.

[30] Desmond Tutu, "Extending Justice and Compassion," foreword to Andrew Linzey, *The Global Guide to Animal Protection* (Urbana: University of Illinois Press, 2013), xv.

[31] Andrew Linzey, *Animal Rights: A Christian Assessment* (London: SCM Press, 1976); and Andrew Linzey, *Christianity and the Rights of Animals* (London: SPCK, 1987).

new generations of theological students to alternative views of animals, he produced anthologies such as *Animals and Christianity: A Book of Readings*[32] and *Animals on the Agenda: Questions for Ethics and Theology*.[33] But *Animal Theology* has been his most successful and influential book and is still cited and discussed in both the academic and nonacademic literature. Perhaps one of the happiest outcomes is the way the book has encouraged Christians to consider animals within their own church traditions.[34] In addition, his work has been published in twelve different languages worldwide.[35]

Animal Theology's achievement was moving the subject of animals from the periphery to the almost mainstream. Although this present book demonstrates that there have been theological prophets concerned with animals throughout the tradition, those voices have been marginalized. This work seeks to reclaim lost voices within theological traditions that highlight concern for animals. Elizabeth Schüssler Firoenza, in her *Searching the Scriptures*, writes of how feminist theologians need both a "hermeneutics of suspicion" that seeks to investigate the tradition for women and a "hermeneutics of re-vision" that searches the tradition for lost voices on women.[36] If AL's *Animal Theology* was a work of "suspicion" in this sense, then *Animal Theologians* is a work of "re-vision," searching the tradition for different prophetic voices on animals.

In this volume, we have brought together Jewish, Unitarian, Christian, transcendentalist, Muslim, Hindu, Dissenting, deist, and Quaker voices, all offering unique theological perspectives. Some of the theologians are widely known (though seldom for their perspectives on animals), others less so. The key in all cases has been to understand the inner dynamic of what led them to

---

[32] Linzey and Regan, *Animals and Christianity*.

[33] Andrew Linzey and Dorothy Yamamoto, eds., *Animals on the Agenda: Questions about Animals for Theology and Ethics* (London: SCM Press, 1998).

[34] See, for example, Deborah M. Jones, *The School of Compassion: A Roman Catholic Theology of Animals* (Leominster, England: Gracewing, 2009); Philip Sampson, *Animal Ethics and the Nonconformist Conscience* (Basingstoke, England: Palgrave Macmillan, 2018); and Christina Nellist, *Eastern Orthodox Christianity and Animal Suffering* (Newcastle upon Tyne, England: Cambridge Scholars Publishing, 2018).

[35] For example, *Animal Theology* has subsequently been translated into Spanish (Barcelona: Herder, 1996); Italian (Turin: Edizione Cosmopolis, 1998); Japanese (Tokyo: Kyobunkan Publishing, 2001); French (Paris: One Voice, 2010); Polish (Kraków: Wydawnictwo Wam, 2010); and Croatian (Stubicke Toplice: Edukacijski centar NOVA ARKA, 2013). In addition, other works by Linzey have been translated into Korean, German, Czech, Chinese, Taiwanese, and Dutch.

[36] Elizabeth Schüssler Firoenza, ed., *Searching the Scriptures* (London: SCM Press, 1993), 1:11. See also Ann Loades, *Searching for Lost Coins: Explorations in Christianity and Feminism* (London: SPCK, 1987).

their beliefs. In some cases, in addition to rational analysis, this has required historical or contextual background.

Some of the featured theologians need greater historical contextualization as an introduction to their thought on animals. Although there is not sufficient space to explore all aspects of the subjects' lives in this volume, many of these thinkers were pioneers of ethical living in relation to animals, founding movements in their own right, such as Leo Tolstoy and Humphry Primatt. Sadly, their work in these areas has been all but marginalized along with their theology on animals.

Without disrupting our historical chronology, we can discern three stages of sensibility. Part I deals with "Prophets and Pioneers," Part II is called "Social Sensibility," and Part III is "Deeper Probing."

Part I: Prophets and Pioneers

The first chapter in Part I ("Pierre Gassendi [1592–1655]: Vegetarianism and the Beatific Vision") may seem puzzling. Why would we select a mathematician, historian, and philosopher as one of the first theologians of animals? The general answer is that thinking about God is certainly not reserved for academic theologians. The specific answer is that Gassendi's historic plea for vegetarianism was bracketed by a biblical context in which God made us vegetarian at the beginning of creation and will restore all creatures at the end of time. Thus, Gassendi believed that a vegetarian diet helped people "to reclaim the fullness of their God-given natures," writes chapter author Justin Begley.[37] It is striking that while many remember the granting of the image to human beings and the idea of dominion, few recall the subsequent command that humans follow a vegetarian, indeed vegan, diet (Gen. 1:29–30). The import of this one line relativizes the notion that humans have untrammeled power over animals and shows that the inner logic of Genesis 1 is God's will to create a peaceful world. As one of us has said elsewhere, herb-eating dominion is hardly a license for tyranny.[38]

But what do we know of the inner life of animals and their relations with the divine? A major blast against anthropocentrism is described in Kathleen Long's chapter, "Michel de Montaigne (1533–1592): Elephant Theologians."

---

[37] See p. 27 in this volume.
[38] Linzey, *Animal Theology*, 126.

And what precisely do elephant theologians do? Montaigne is clear that elephants have their own inner lives, even their own religion:

> We can also say that the elephants have some participation in religion, since after many ablutions and purifications we see them, raising their trunks like arms and keeping their eyes fixed toward the rising sun, stand still a long time in meditation and contemplation at certain hours of the day, by their own inclination, without instruction and without precept. But because we do not see any such signs in other animals, we cannot thereby prove that they are without religion and cannot grasp any part of what is hidden from us.[39]

Montaigne's comments are perceptive in the light of what we now know about the complexity of elephant awareness,[40] but the key point is that there exist lives beyond our comprehension, which may be more closely connected with the divine than we appreciate. In that sense, Montaigne also may be prophetic in pointing to a new field of theological inquiry.

Many people suppose that the notion of "animal rights" is somehow a modern invention, akin to the liberation movements that emerged in the post-1970s. In fact, there is a long history of ethical discussion of animals going back to early Greek thought.[41] Adam Bridgen, in his chapter ("Thomas Tryon [1634–1703]: A Theology of Animal Enslavement"), shows the aforementioned supposition to be a mistaken one. Many will be surprised to learn that the first use of the term "rights" actually arose in a specifically theological context based on the idea of the generosity of God the Creator, who bestows creatures with an inner life. From this insight follows a rejection not only of flesh-eating but also of slavery. Accordingly, Tryon is to be celebrated because he was the first to see that connection between the two forms of domination—namely, animal enslavement and human slavery. He was a protester no less of speciesism, racism, and colonialism. He may have been the first to espouse a theologically based veganism.

---

[39] Michel de Montaigne, "Apology for Raymond Sebond," in *Essays*, vol. 2, chapter 12, trans. Donald Frame (Stanford, CA: Stanford University Press, 1965), 343. See pp. 47–48 in this volume.

[40] See, for example, Marc Bekoff, *The Emotional Lives of Animals: A Leading Scientist Explores Animal Joy, Sorrow, and Empathy and Why They Matter* (Novato, CA: New World Library, 2007); Barbara King, *How Animals Grieve* (Chicago: University of Chicago Press, 2013); and Jeffrey Masson, *When Elephants Weep: The Emotional Lives of Animals* (New York: Vintage, 1996).

[41] See Andrew Linzey and Paul Barry Clarke, eds., *Animal Rights: A Historical Anthology* (New York: Columbia University Press, 2004).

There is no greater name in Methodism than John Wesley himself (indeed, the first Methodists were known as Wesleyans). Yet few appreciate that he also was a pioneer of the moral treatment of animals, was opposed to blood sports, and was—for at least a period—a vegetarian.[42] Ryan Patrick McLaughlin ("John Wesley [1703–1791]: The Tension between Theological Hope and Biological Reality") shows how the prelapsarian ideal of a nonviolent world inspired Wesley's belief that creation would one day be restored by the Creator and that humans needed to approximate that restoration through acts of compassion. But did such a prelapsarian state ever exist? McLaughlin is clear that it didn't. But the insight that the world is not as it should be is part of a metanarrative of loss and recompense that is not easily done away with. Plato himself anticipated this thought when he wrote of the Golden Age from which we have departed through our own selfishness.[43]

McLaughlin concludes that "perhaps Wesley's greatest contribution to animal theology is his refusal to reconcile the notion of God willing animal suffering with God's goodness."[44] In this way, Wesley has bequeathed to future theologians the problem of theodicy, which remains one of the greatest obstacles to theistic belief.

Thomas Tryon subsequently inspired one of the greatest animal theologians of the eighteenth century, if not of all time. Hardly known today, Humphry Primatt (examined by Adam Bridgen in "Humphry Primatt [1735–1777]: Animal Protection and Its Revolutionary Contexts") was a leading voice of Christian concern for animals who anticipated some of the later, more modern voices. His one publication was *The Duty of Mercy and the Sin of Cruelty*, published in 1776.[45] The central argument went as follows: Since the "religion of Jesus Christ originated in the mercy of God," it follows that "a cruel Christian is a monster of ingratitude, a scandal to his profession and beareth the name of Christ in vain." Specifically, Primatt writes, "We may pretend to what religion we please, but cruelty is atheism. We may make our boast of Christianity, but cruelty is infidelity. We may trust to our orthodoxy, but cruelty is the worst of heresies."[46]

---

[42] See Hilda Kean, *Animal Rights: Political and Social Change in Britain since 1800* (London: Reaktion Books, 1998), 20; and Andrew Linzey, "John Wesley: An Early Prophet of Animal Rights," *Methodist Recorder*, April 10, 2003, 15.

[43] Plato, "The Golden Age," extract in Linzey and Clarke, *Animal Rights*, 53–55.

[44] See p. 91 in this volume.

[45] Humphry Primatt, *A Dissertation on the Duty of Mercy and the Sin of Cruelty* (London: T. Cadell, 1776).

[46] Primatt, *Duty of Mercy*, 321–22.

Thus, Primatt centralizes cruelty as the one intolerable sin that makes or breaks true discipleship. Here we face a litmus test of true faith, of true moral theo-logic. Needless to say, Primatt's work aroused great debate in his day but had one long-lasting consequence: the creation of the Society for the Prevention of Cruelty to Animals in 1824. Anglican priest Arthur Broome founded the society after reading Primatt's work, and in 1822, 1831, and 1834 he arranged for Primatt's work to be republished.

The next two chapters should be examined together, since they focus on naturalists and explorers. Some people find God, or at least the transcendent, in contemplating creation itself. In "William Bartram (1739–1823): A Quaker-Inspired Animal Advocacy," Michael J. Gilmour introduces such a person who found spiritual solace in his long travels, after which he extolled what he believed was something close to an Edenic state. This reinforced his belief in the great Author and especially his sense of the God-given inner worth of sentient creatures. Not wholly dissimilarly, Wesley Mott illustrates Thoreau's quest to "find God in nature—to know his lurking places" in his chapter, "Henry David Thoreau (1817–1862): Capturing the Anima in Animals."[47] Thoreau was convinced that the "most important part of an animal is its *anima*, its vital spirit."[48] Thoreau was ambivalent about the treatment of animals, however. Although he extolled the animal, he was a failed vegetarian and hunted animals for food, although this often occasioned remorse.

Part II: Social Sensibility

This book's second part looks, inter alia, at the ways in which some of the ideas of the prophets and pioneers have led to social sensibility and indeed social embodiment.

The first three chapters need to be taken together because they share a common concern—namely, the use of animals in scientific research. Interestingly, the subject of the next chapter, by Linda M. Johnson ("John Ruskin [1819–1900]: 'Beholding Birds': A Visual Case against Vivisection") would have approved of Thoreau's conception of the inner "anima" in animals.

---

[47] See p. 137 in this volume.
[48] Henry D. Thoreau, *Journal*, in *The Writings of Henry David Thoreau*, ed. Bradford Torrey and Francis H. Allen (Boston: Houghton, Mifflin, 1906), 13:154.

For Ruskin, what was required both in our dealings with animals and in art was a "spiritual sight." Poignantly, he writes, "You do not see *with* the lens of the eye. You see *through* that, and by means of that, but you see with the soul of the eye."[49] When properly seen, nature and animals teach reverence for life because of the Author of life. Unsurprisingly, Ruskin opposed the vivisection of animals and resigned his Slade chair in fine art after the establishment of the first post in experimental physiology at Oxford. Ruskin was not alone. The individual who gave birth to the British antivivisection movement and its chief champion, Frances Power Cobbe (profiled by Chien-hui Li in "Frances Power Cobbe [1822–1904]: Theology, Science, and the Antivivisection Movement"), was also deeply opposed to vivisection on theological grounds. Since cruelty could never be in accordance with the will of a holy, loving deity, it could never, *never* be countenanced. As Chien-hui Li comments:

> Darwinism especially, with all its moral implications, signaled a world in which science had usurped religion and set itself up as the new deity, with its own moral system and order of priests—physiologists. So Cobbe parodied the credo held by scientists: " 'Blessed are the merciless, for they shall obtain useful knowledge.' —*New Gospel of Science*, Chapter First."[50]

Serenhedd James introduces us in "Frank Buckland [1826–1880] and Henry Parry Liddon [1829–1890]: *Vivisection in Oxford*" to two individuals who foregrounded the emerging sensitivity to nonhuman creatures. However, one ought to use the word "sensitivity" in appropriate question marks because, as James's account shows, Buckland was more of a menagerie collector than a humane regarder of animals. Nevertheless, it does seem that his fascination with other creatures, however insensitive his treatment of them seems to modern readers, provided a basis for a kind of fellow feeling among dons, such as Lewis Carroll (Charles L. Dodson) and Henry Parry Liddon, that culminated in a public protest against animal experiments at Oxford. The fly sheet *Vivisection in Oxford* included the signatures of many distinguished scholars of the Oxford Movement, including Ruskin, Dodson, Edward King, and S. R. Driver. Addressing their fellow academics, they

[49] John Ruskin, *The Eagle's Nest: Ten Lectures on the Relation of Natural Science to Art, Given before the University of Oxford in Lent Term, 1872* (New York: John Wiley & Sons, 1880), lecture 6, sec. 98, p. 90.

[50] See p. 185 in this volume. See also Frances Power Cobbe, "The New Morality," in *The Modern Rack: Papers on Vivisection* (London: Swan Sonnenschein, 1889), 65.

remonstrate, "Will you then allow it to go forth to the world that Oxford sanctions the doctrine of the Physiologists that knowledge may justly be acquired at the cost of torturing God's creatures?"[51]

The next person in our sequence, Leo Tolstoy, the subject of Alice Crary's chapter ("Leo Tolstoy [1828–1910]: Literature and the Lives of Animals"), began what became known as the "Tolstoyan revolution," which included people committed to nonviolence, simple living, purity of heart, and unsurprisingly, a vegetarian diet. Leo Tolstoy became an icon of a moral counterculture that attracted hundreds of people.[52] Crary analyzes Tolstoy's first visit to a slaughterhouse and champions the notion of sight or seeing that should be central not only to Christian ethicists but to all ethicists. Another influential writer and antivivisectionist crusader is celebrated by Robyn Hederman in "Elizabeth Stuart Phelps [1844–1911]: Preacher and Reformer." Phelps's religious convictions drove her to take on the mantle of an animal defender in her novels. She celebrated fellow creatures and argued that it was the task of the novelist to tell the truth about the world. In her case, it was primarily the truth about what happens to animals in laboratories. She lobbied for legislative reform in the United States until her death in 1911.

The subject of the following chapter, "Muḥammad ʿAbduh [1849–1905]: The Transvaal Fatwa and the Fate of Animals," might seem to be hardly an animal theologian at all. And chapter author Nuri Friedlander agrees up to a point. ʿAbduh's Transvaal fatwa allows other religious groups to slaughter animals according to their own rules, thus permitting animal slaughter by methods other than those prescribed by the Qur'an. A ramification of this decree is that it "opens the door for permitting pre-slaughter stunning as part of the process of halal slaughter."[53] Since so much anxiety has been generated by throat-slitting without pre-stunning, this fatwa enables a new dialogue between animal advocates and observant Muslims. Elsewhere, Friedlander describes ʿAbduh's regard for nonhuman animals and his belief that they possess emotional and rational faculties. In fact, Islam holds that animals are communities like our own and accepts that they will also go to heaven,[54] and

[51] *Vivisection in Oxford*, a fly post distributed ahead of the convocation of the university on Tuesday, March 10, 1885, box 2/5/3, Pusey House, Oxford. For a discussion, see Andrew Linzey and Clair Linzey, "Oxford: The Home of Controversy about Animals," in *The Ethical Case against Animal Experiments* (Urbana: University of Illinois Press, 2018), 1–3.
[52] For a discussion of Tolstoy and his ethics, see A. N. Wilson, *Tolstoy* (London: Penguin, 1988), especially p. 6.
[53] See p. 250 in this volume.
[54] See Tim Winter, "'Nations like Yourselves': Some Muslim Debates over Qur'an 6:38," in Linzey and Linzey, *Routledge Handbook*, 163–72.

the Prophet himself maintained that "kindness to any living creature will be rewarded."[55] In the light of these and other doctrines, it seems that Islamic theology has much to contribute to animal theology, and we await this further development.[56]

Whether the subject of the next chapter knew Tolstoy or corresponded with him is unknown, but there is a striking similarity to their views, apparent in A. W. H. Bates's "Josiah Oldfield (1863–1953): Vegetarianism and the Order of the Golden Age in Nineteenth-Century Britain." As a British kind of Tolstoyan, Oldfield also argued that nonviolence to animals was a necessary step toward building God's kingdom of peace on earth. He extolled a diet excluding fish, flesh, and fowl, and also alcohol. And in a link back to the Oxford Movement, he argued that the saving work of Christ extends to the whole of creation, holding even that, in Bates's words, "animal suffering [was] a reflection of, or even contributory to, the sufferings of Christ."[57] How different is this from the view of John Henry Newman, who extolled his congregation on Good Friday, "Think then, my brethren of your feelings at cruelty practised upon brute animals, and you will gain one sort of feeling which the history of Christ's Cross and Passion ought to excite within you"?[58] In other words, there is a Christlike character to the sufferings of animals.

Weighty contributions to vegetarianism are explored by the following two chapters. The concept of peace is developed by Idan Breier's chapter, "Abraham Isaac Kook (1865–1935): Biblical Ethics as the Basis of Rav Kook's *A Vision of Vegetarianism and Peace.*" Rav Kook's is the first systematic Jewish treatise on human–animal relations, and he views the tradition as being in a process of transition from meat-eating to a universal peace with other creatures that requires vegetarianism. The permissive dietary laws (Gen. 9) were intended at first to limit human violence to animals until the fullness of God's truth in the Torah became fully known. Kook invokes the notion of progressive revelation whereby the wholeness of God's plan "must be revealed to them [the Jewish people] gradually," writes Breier.[59] No less visionary is

---

[55] *SB* 8.11, Abū Hurayra, cited in *The Sayings of Muhammad*, select. and trans. Neal Robinson (London: Duckworth, 1991), 48.

[56] For a pioneering study, see Richard C. Foltz, *Animals in Islamic Tradition and Muslim Cultures* (Oxford: Oneworld Publications, 2006).

[57] See p. 264 in this volume.

[58] John Henry Newman, "The Crucifixion," in *Parochial and Plain Sermons*, 8 vols. (London: Rivington, 1868), 3:138. See also a discussion of the implications for animals in Andrew Linzey, *Why Animal Suffering Matters: Philosophy, Theology, and Practical Ethics* (Oxford: Oxford University Press, 2009), 37–40.

[59] See p. 279 in this volume.

the subject of the following chapter: "Mohandas K. Gandhi (1869–1948): In the Service of All That Lives" by Kenneth Valpey (Krishna Kshetra Swami). Gandhi offers nothing less than a vision of humans sacrificing themselves in the service of all God's creation. It is important to note that both visionaries have influenced their respective traditions: Kook is widely acknowledged as representing an ideal deep within Judaism, and Gandhi is known for his widespread dissemination of the concept of *ahiṁsā* in Hinduism and beyond.

Part III: Deeper Probing

The third part brings us virtually up to date. It comprises some of the deeper theologies of animals that influenced twentieth-century thought.

Special place among them must go to the subject of our first chapter in this part: "Albert Schweitzer (1875–1965): The Life of Reverence." Carl Tobias Frayne shows the range and depth of Schweitzer's conceptualization of the moral in what may be called a theo-logia of a virtue ethic or "ethical mysticism." Rejecting all past ethical theories of the East and West, Schweitzer locates the one principle of the moral based on the inner worth of all creatures to the Creator. The notion of "reverence for life" (*Ehrfurcht vor dem Leben*) is, however, more than just a principle (although Schweitzer describes it as that). It is more properly described as an experience, a revelation, given by God.

Not unrelatedly, the next chapter, "Martin Buber (1878–1965): Encountering Animals, a Prelude to the Animal Question," also addresses the nature of spiritual encounter and relationship with other-than-human creatures. While Buber claimed that such experiences could properly happen only between humans, Ryan Brand shows how Buber's "contact with other animals, that call into question his own hierarchical divide."[60] Thus, Buber opens up the possibility of an "I-Thou" (rather than an "I-It") relationship with animals, as his famous (if disputed) description of his meeting with a horse amply demonstrates:

When I was eleven years of age, spending the summer on my grandparents' estate, I used, as often as I could do it unobserved, to steal into the stable and gently stroke the neck of my darling, a broad dappel-grey horse

[60] See p. 335 in this volume.

[*Apfel-schimmel*]. It was not a casual delight but a great, certainly friendly, but also deeply stirring happening. If I am to explain it now, beginning from the still very fresh memory of my hand, I must say that what I experienced in touch with the animal was the Other, the immense otherness of the Other [*ungeheure Anderheit des Anderen*], which, however, did not remain strange like the otherness of the ox and the ram, but rather let me draw near and touch [*Berührung*] it. When I stroked the mighty mane, sometimes marvelously smoothcombed, at other times just as astonishingly wild, and felt the life beneath my hand, it was as though the element of vitality [*Vitalität*] itself bordered on my skin, something that was not I, was certainly not akin to me, palpably the other, not just another, really the Other itself; and yet it let me approach, confide itself to me, placed itself elementally in the relation of *Thou* and *Thou* with me.[61]

Paul Tillich, one of the most distinguished theologians of the twentieth century ("Paul Tillich [1886–1965]: The Method of Correlation and the Possibility of an Animal Ethic"), also was fascinated with animals. He famously preached the sermon "Nature, Also, Mourns for a Lost Good," in which he grasped only too well the suffering of nature, especially animals, and the theological challenge it represents to the notion of a holy Creator.[62] His answer, at least in part, is that where there is estrangement in the cosmos, so there must be cosmic redemption through a Savior figure.[63] But overall, Tillich's systematic theology remains firmly anthropocentric. Abbey Smith seeks to explore how through his "method of correlation" Tillich can still provide a solid basis for a progressive animal ethic.

But it should be noted that there was during this period a metaphysician who resolutely rejected anthropocentrism and embraced the idea that sentient animals are not only moral patients but also "persons" ("Charles Hartshorne [1897–2000]: Animals in Process Thought"). According to Charles Hartshorne, the traditional doctrine of God—impassible and unchanging—must be rejected. Rather, God is a dynamic being acting within and without the universe, evolving alongside creatures. Anthropocentrism is essentially hubristic, claims Hartshorne. By rejecting it, we can see

[61] Martin Buber, *Between Man and Man*, trans. Ronald Gregor Smith (London: Routledge, 2002; first published 1947), 26–27.
[62] Paul Tillich, *The Shaking of the Foundations* (Harmondsworth, England: Penguin, 1949), 82–92.
[63] See Paul Tillich, "Redemption of Other Worlds," in Linzey and Regan, *Animals and Christianity*, 106–7.

ourselves as animals (albeit special ones) alongside other animals. Daniel A. Dombrowski explains how Hartshorne's viewpoint also pioneered an ethical approach to animals that rejects killing animals when killing is avoidable and insists that we have a duty to reduce actions that cause suffering. Process lays the ground for the awareness of a new unity between God and the universe and especially between fellow sentient animals.

The notion that humans have a God-given dominion over animals—and therefore can use them as they wish—has influenced a great deal of specifically Jewish and Christian thinking about animals. But an Oxford don who stood against this view has left a distinguished legacy of writing that was as controversial then as it is now. C. S. Lewis's essay on vivisection absolutely rejected the practice on the ground that the deliberate infliction of pain is an intrinsically evil act.[64] But it was his earlier book, *The Problem of Pain*,[65] that raised the fundamental question of theodicy for animals and treated animal pain with especial seriousness. In "C. S. Lewis (1898–1963): Rethinking Dominion," Michael J. Gilmour shows how Lewis's views are expounded over the wide canvas of his fictional works, which reject dominion as despotism and insist on human responsibility to animals. Humans' failure to care for creation is egregious in the sight of God. Only an eschatologically renewed human species can provide the ultimate corrective to human depravity toward animals.

Similarly, a celebrated Jewish voice provided a landmark literary contribution. In "Isaac Bashevis Singer [1904–1991]: 'Myriads of Cows and Fowls . . . Ready to Take Revenge,'" Beruriah Wiegand introduces two of Singer's most famous and contrasting works: "The Slaughterer" (1967, English translation) and *The Slave* (1962, English translation). The former is a grim picture of a small Jewish community in Eastern Europe in which animal slaughter is part of people's daily life and where there is little sensitivity to animal suffering. *The Slave*, in contrast, offers a very positive vision of Jewish life in harmony with nature and animals, so much so that it could almost be characterized as eschatological in anticipating the Isaianic vision of a peaceful world (Isa. 11:1–9).The title of Wiegand's chapter echoes the passage from the Second Book of Enoch where animals are called upon to

---

[64] C. S. Lewis, *Vivisection* (Boston: New England Anti-Vivisection Society, 1947).

[65] C. S. Lewis, *The Problem of Pain* (London: Fontana, 1957; originally published in 1940). See also Andrew Linzey, "C. S. Lewis's Theology of Animals." *Anglican Theological Review* 80, no. 1 (1998): 60–81; and Michael J. Gilmour, *Animals in the Writings of C. S. Lewis* (Basingstoke, England: Palgrave Macmillan, 2017).

pass judgment on human beings for the humans' failure to show justice to them (2 Enoch 58–59).

One major theologian, Jürgen Moltmann, pushed the animal issue to theological center stage ("Jürgen Moltmann [1926–]: Creation and Sabbath Theology"). His *Theology of Hope* is unusually inclusive of animals. Ryan Patrick McLaughlin explains how, while light on concrete application, Moltmann's theology provides a framework for vegetarianism and opposition to abusive practices as anticipation of the promised future. The Sabbath is the key here as a symbol of what was or could be, where humans and all creatures coexist together in peace and harmony (Gen. 2:1–4). Moltmann explores the theological significance of the Sabbath in his *God in Creation*. He argues that the Sabbath is an "ecological day of rest,"[66] and "when the Sabbath is sanctified, a time is sanctified which is there for the whole creation. When the Sabbath is celebrated, it is celebrated for all created being."[67]

In the last chapter of the book, Ryan Patrick McLaughlin focuses on Andrew Linzey's work ("Andrew Linzey [1952–]: Animal Theology"). Much has already been said of AL's work in this introduction, so we will not discuss it in detail here. The point of this chapter is to explore some of the theological themes of Linzey's work, for example, the Jesus-shaped ethic of inclusive moral generosity, humans as the servant species, the Theos-rights of animals, and progressive disengagement from injury to animals. McLaughlin explores Linzey's Trinitarian and Christological focus, before considering the ethical implications for our daily use of animals for food, for research, and for "sport."

Purpose of the Book

We have come to love these chapters, not only because they are examples of fine scholarship, but also because they are original, pioneering, and morally engaging. They draw upon the long animal-friendly intellectual tradition that has frequently been ignored or overlooked. They push the "animal issue"—as it has been called—into mainstream theology or at least help others to do so. They show that there is so much in these traditions for others to explore, criticize, and engage with. This volume contributes to the reclaiming of the

---

[66] Jürgen Moltmann, *God in Creation: A New Theology of Creation and the Spirit of God*, trans. Margaret Kohl (Minneapolis: Fortress Press, 1993), 296.
[67] Moltmann, *God in Creation*, 284.

hidden or lost theological voices within different traditions that embrace an alternative view of creation.

We like the line from William Temple that "theology is still in its infancy"—and this is probably nowhere truer than in the case of mainstream thinking about animals. As one of us has written elsewhere, animals can help liberate theology from its own anthropocentric ghetto and enable a fuller and more convincing theological perspective on fellow creatures.[68] We look forward to the day when animal theology as well as Black theology, feminist theology, gay theology, and ecological theology are all unnecessary because religious communities have incorporated them into the theological mainstream. We believe and hope that this might one day happen, as theology grows into a deeper understanding of the potential of its own tradition.

In the meantime, specifically, this book focuses on some perennial underlying themes that can and should be addressed from a different, animal-sensitive perspective. These include

- the diet prescribed by God for humans;
- the state of nature, and to what extent, if at all, it represents God's will;
- the nature and significance of animal sentience;
- the meaning of human dominion or power over animals;
- the theological basis of animal protection; and
- eschatology and God's end for creatures.

Clearly, a huge amount of work still needs to be done.

Our special thanks to Cynthia Reid, senior editor at Oxford University Press, for seeing the merit in this act of re-visioning theology. Also thanks to Theodore Calderara and Paloma Escovedo for their expert help in seeing the book into publication. We are also grateful to Stephanie Ernst for her invaluable work on the text.

---

[68] See Andrew Linzey and Dan Cohn-Sherbok, *After Noah: Animals and the Liberation of Theology* (London: Continuum, 1997), 118–19.

PART I
PROPHETS AND PIONEERS

1

Pierre Gassendi (1592–1655)

Vegetarianism and the Beatific Vision

Justin Begley

Introduction: A Learned Vegetarian

The French priest, professor of mathematics, historian, and philosopher Pierre Gassendi was one of the most influential and well-respected thinkers of his day, and the learned scholar and divine Meric Casaubon even dubbed him "the most accomplished general scholar we have had of late."[1] Gassendi's groundbreaking rehabilitation of Epicurean philosophy of 1649, *Animadversiones in decimum librum Diogenis Laertii*, served as the basis for the popular 1654 *Physiologia* on atomism by the prominent English physician Walter Charleton, and his erudite critique of Aristotelian thought spurred on the efforts of early Royal Society fellows.[2] Although the density of Gassendi's Latin tomes consigned him to relative obscurity for much of the period from the late eighteenth century to the end of the twentieth, historians of philosophy, literature, science, and theology are now beginning to appreciate just how central his ideas were to early modern intellectual life. But studies of Gassendi in recent years have consistently bypassed a major component of his thought: his defense of a vegetarian diet.[3] Conversely,

---

[1] Meric Casaubon, *Generall Learning: A Seventeenth-Century Treatise on the Formation of the General Scholar*, ed. R. Serjeantson (Cambridge: RTM, 1999), 149.

[2] On some aspects of Gassendi's reception in England, see Dmitri Levitin, *Ancient Wisdom in the Age of the New Science: Histories of Philosophy in England, c. 1640–1700* (Cambridge: Cambridge University Press, 2015), 330–97.

[3] The most notable studies of Gassendi include Lynn Joy, *Gassendi the Atomist: Advocate of History in the Age of Science* (Cambridge: Cambridge University Press, 1987); Barry Brundell, *Pierre Gassendi: From Aristotelianism to a New Natural Philosophy* (Dordrecht: Reidel, 1987); Antonia Lolordo, *Pierre Gassendi and the Birth of Early Modern Philosophy* (Cambridge: Cambridge University Press, 2007); Margaret Osler, *Divine Will and the Mechanical Philosophy: Gassendi and Descartes on Contingency and Necessity in the Created World* (Cambridge: Cambridge University Press, 1994); and Lisa Sarasohn, *Gassendi's Ethics: Freedom in a Mechanistic University* (Ithaca, NY: Cornell University Press, 1996). But on Gassendi and animals, do see the discussion in Guido Giglioni, "Life and Its Animal Boundaries: Ethical Implications in Early Modern Theories of Universal Animation," *Ethical*

Justin Begley, *Pierre Gassendi (1592–1655)* In: *Animal Theologians*. Edited by: Andrew Linzey and Clair Linzey, Oxford University Press. © Oxford University Press 2023. DOI: 10.1093/oso/9780197655542.003.0002

because it is no small task to identify and translate the relevant passages from Gassendi's oeuvre, historical surveys of vegetarianism have mostly neglected his contributions to this topic.

There are two principal reasons that such a state of affairs is unfortunate, and this chapter takes steps toward remedying both oversights. First, with regard to the history of vegetarianism, there has been an overwhelming emphasis on "radical" sectarians such as Thomas Bushnell, Roger Crab, and Thomas Tryon.[4] While Gassendi was a fierce critic of the Scholastic tradition in his own right, he nonetheless remained thoroughly embedded in the institutions of his day, and channeled the full gamut of humanist apparatuses in his mission to replace one ancient philosophy with another. It was to this end that he labored to cleanse Epicurus of his popular association with excess and debauchery, and to resuscitate his philosophy as one that promoted not only frugality but also a plant-based diet.[5] By looking at Gassendi's arguments for vegetarianism, this chapter accordingly seeks to demonstrate that defending abstention from meat consumption was not simply a peripheral reaction to the intellectual mainstream that could be written off as either a fad or a narrow, sectarian position.

Second, in terms of the history of philosophy, Gassendi has frequently been deemed an unsystematic or "eclectic" thinker. As Richard Westfall once framed it in a witty conceit, "Gassendi was the original scissors and paste man, and his book contains all the inconsistencies of eclectic compilations."[6] His historical and philological approach is one of the reasons that he has been dismissed as less significant to philosophical developments than his supposedly more innovative and methodical contemporaries, such as René Descartes. Yet Gassendi's reflections on abstention from meat underscore how the ethical, natural philosophical, and theological facets of his thought could unite in his struggle to unravel the tightly interwoven structure of the

Perspectives on Animals in the Renaissance and Early Modern Period, ed. C. Muratori and B. Dohm (Florence: SISMEL edizioni del Galluzzo, 2013), 111–37 (especially 114–23).

[4] See Tristram Stuart, *Bloodless Revolution: Radical Vegetarians and the Discovery of India* (London: HarperPress, 2006); Diane Kelsey McColley, *Poetry and Ecology in the Age of Milton and Marvell* (Aldershot: Ashgate, 2007), 171–96; Anita Guerrini, "A Diet for a Sensitive Soul: Vegetarianism in Eighteenth-Century Britain," *Eighteenth-Century Life* 23, no. 3 (1999): 34–42; and Colin Spencer, *The Heretic's Feast: A History of Vegetarianism* (London: University Press of New England, 1995), 201–51.

[5] For the background to Gassendi's undertaking, see Don Cameron Allen, "The Rehabilitation of Epicurus and His Theory of Pleasure in the Renaissance," *Studies in Philology* 41, no. 1 (1944): 1–15.

[6] Richard Westfall, *The Construction of Modern Science: Mechanism and Mechanics* (Cambridge: Cambridge University Press, 1977), 39.

corpus aristotelicum. Gassendi made three key arguments, which were rooted in scripture, history, and medicine respectively: he considered Adam and Eve to have been vegetarians in their prelapsarian state; he interpreted many of the Greek sects, especially the "Garden Philosophers," as encouraging or demanding abstention from meat; and he called on comparative anatomy to buttress the view that humans were designed as herbivores.

This chapter homes in on the two places in Gassendi's *Opera Omnia*—which was posthumously published in 1658—that most explicitly tackle the issue of vegetarianism. The main body of his *Opera Omnia* is known as the *Syntagma Philosophicum*, but this six-volume work also houses material from Gassendi's manuscripts, including the preponderance of his letters. In its first section, then, this chapter grapples with a segment of *Syntagma Philosophicum*, "On the Faculties and Organs That Carry Nutrition," which consists of a protracted deliberation on abstention from meat.[7] It then turns to how two early Royal Society affiliates, John Wallis and Edward Tyson, took Gassendi's ideas as a foundation upon which to build their own anatomical insights, and ultimately to oppose the Frenchman's conclusion about the herbivorous nature of humans. The last section explores Gassendi's epistolary attempt to persuade the famous Flemish physician and medical reformer Jan Baptista van Helmont that vegetarianism had its virtues.[8] Taken as a whole, I display that Gassendi not only hoped to reinvigorate the universities by pushing for a shift in their philosophical orientations, but also strove to convince his contemporaries that a vegetarian diet could help them to reclaim the fullness of their God-given natures.

The Virtue of Pleasure

In *Syntagma Philosophicum*, Gassendi made the case that just as every species has a unique shape and structure, each species likewise has its proper sustenance.[9] Setting aside the fact that humans had long been accustomed to

---

[7] See Pierre Gassendi, "De facultatibus, ac organis quibus Nutritio peragatur," in *Opera Omnia* (Lyon, 1658), vol. 2, 296–302.

[8] Gassendi, "Viro Clarissimo, & Philosopho, ac Medico expertissimo *Joanni Baptistæ Helmontio* amico suo singulari," in *Opera Omnia*, vol. 6, 19–24.

[9] "Dicendum heic aliquid foret de varietate alimentorum, quibus Animalia nutriuntur; verùm res manifesta est, cùm & constet non posse eadem idonea esse omnibus, propter varietatem temperamentorum, ex qua est, ut quæ his gratissima sunt, illis nauseam pariant, neque ab ipsis attingantur." Gassendi, *Opera Omnia*, vol. 2, 301.

feasting on a wide variety of foodstuffs, he thus returned to the fundamental question: what is the appropriate diet for the beings made in God's image? Although he later summoned scriptural authority, Gassendi supposed that nature itself contained the key.

Taking his cue from Plutarch's seminal essay "On the Eating of Flesh," Gassendi specifically recognized that carnivores such as lions and wolves are outfitted with long and sharp teeth, and that human teeth are, by contrast, short and flat, akin to those of herbivorous horses, oxen, and sheep.[10] For all of his dissatisfaction with Aristotle, it is noteworthy here that Gassendi embraced the Scholastic precept that God did not create any superfluity in nature, but rather devised everything to fulfill its purpose. As an outgrowth of this premise, he maintained that God formed humans with teeth that are perfectly suited to the food that they are meant to consume.[11] God, according to Gassendi, would have furnished humans with claws or a beak that could tear flesh if He had intended for them to eat other animals.[12] Humans instead had to invent tools and train species with superior senses such as dogs to help with hunting, all to sustain a diet that was unnecessary for continued existence. Additionally, Gassendi noted that meat is "a burden to the stomach" and can hardly "be distributed through the parts of our bodies," necessitating the arduous task of cooking.[13] Based on these considerations, he concluded that humans would be very different animals were they designed to feed on flesh. Responding to claims that vegetables could not afford the requisite energy for manual or intellectual labor—an argument that still circulates today— Gassendi further observed that the "strength of the bull and the swiftness of the deer" must be attributed to their plant-powered diets.[14] Putting a positive

---

[10] "Siquidem cùm inter terrestreis, gressileisque animanteis constituerit nos; non taleis nobis tribuit denteis, qualeis iis, quæ ex sua natura vesci debuerunt carnibus, ut sunt leones, lupi, & aliæ, ideò vocatæ carnivoræ; sed qualeis iis, quæ vesci herbis, variisque fructuum generibus, ut sunt equi, oues, & aliæ, quæ non carnivoræ habentur." Gassendi, *Opera Omnia*, vol. 2, 301. See Plutarch, *Moralia*, vol. 12, trans. H. Cherniss and W. Helmbold (Cambridge, MA: Harvard University Press, 1957), 551–53.

[11] See Aristotle, *Parts of Animals* 1.1.639b and *Physics* 2.3.195a. For the persistence of teleological accounts in contemporary discussions of animal ethics, see Bernard Rollin, "Animal Pain: What It Is and Why It Matters," *Journal of Ethics* 15, no. 4 (2011): 425–37.

[12] Gassendi, *Opera Omnia*, vol. 6, 21. For a brief synopsis of Gassendi's arguments for vegetarianism, see Justin Begley, "Animals in Early Modern Thought," in *Encyclopedia of Early Modern Philosophy and the Sciences*, ed. D. Jalobeanu and C. T. Wolfe (Cham: Springer, 2021), https://doi.org/ 10.1007/978-3-319-20791-9_628-1.

[13] "Potest insuper *tum* ex eo, quòd non est herbarum, fructuúmque usus ita stomacho onerosus, ut caro: siquidem cibus levior est; cùm caro Animalium ex parte ipsorum pinguiore facta, compactáque, difficiliùs longè exsolui, ac distribui per parteis nostri corporis possit." Gassendi, *Opera Omnia*, vol. 2, 302.

[14] "taurorum robur, & ceruorum pernicitas, & dotes aliorum Animalium similes, ex alio victu non deducantur." Gassendi, *Opera Omnia*, vol. 2, 302.

spin on dietary needs, he noted that "grains, honey, and especially wine" contain the sharp *aqua vitae* that can vivify the spirits of individuals with cold constitutions who might be tempted to turn to meat.[15] These, Gassendi insisted, were the victuals that humankind was always intended to consume.

A belief that it is possible to strip back layers of societal baggage to arrive at an image of a truly "natural" human underpinned Gassendi's vindication of vegetarianism.[16] Generating a line of reasoning that Jean-Jacques Rousseau later recycled in *Emile*, Gassendi contended that young children, with bodies that are physically purer than those of adults, consistently prefer fruit to meat.[17] Less optimistic than Rousseau, however, he proposed that the milk of a mother who regularly consumed meat might, in its own right, condition carnivorous inclinations in her child.[18] Indeed, a far cry from Romantic notions of innocence, Gassendi's appeal to infant predilections was derived from Epicurus's argument that a newborn, by instinct, pursues pleasure and evades pain.[19] In Gassendi's broader effort to Christianize Epicurus, he presented the pleasure principle as what allowed God to direct the natural world in such a way as to render His constant intrusion within it unnecessary. While this endowed cognizance of what it is natural to enjoy with the utmost ethical and even theological import, it also suggested that humans were not dissimilar to other animals (or natural objects, for that matter) in their possession of certain desires or inclinations. Harboring an Aristotelian outlook on the "will," Gassendi was of the opinion that inasmuch as a rock that is dropped from a high place falls spontaneously, it could properly be said that the rock "wills" or "desires" to go downward, just as a child of a certain age naturally reaches, without conscious self-reflection, for fruit instead of meat.[20] To provide a more proximate example, it is morally

---

[15] "Indicio porrò maximo est, quòd res unaquæque tanto sit magis alimentitia, quantò ex ea elicere maiorem huiusmodi aquæ, sive spiritus aquam licet; indéque sit, cur omnia grana, cur mel, cur vinum maximè nutrient." Gassendi, *Opera Omnia*, vol. 2, 301.

[16] For a relevant discussion, see Lynn Joy, *Gassendi the Atomist*, 83–105.

[17] On Rousseau and vegetarianism, see David Boonin-Vail, "The Vegetarian Savage: Rousseau's Critique of Meat Eating," *Environmental Ethics* 15, no. 1 (1993): 75–84.

[18] "Quodammodo, inquam; nam si puer foret & formatus ex semine, & nutritus lacte parentum, qui ipsi abstinuissent à carnibus; aut si saltem dimisso lacte pastus carnibus, jusculisque carneis, non esset, serretur haud-dubiè in fructus impensiùs." Gassendi, *Opera Omnia*, vol. 2, 302.

[19] Plutarch, *Moralia*, vol. 14, trans. B. Einarson and P. de Lacy (Cambridge, MA: Harvard University Press, 1967), 283. For Gassendi's adaptation, see *Opera Omnia*, vol. 2, part 701.

[20] See Gassendi, *Opera Omnia*, vol. 2, 824. For differing discussions of this issue, see Margaret Osler, "From Immanent Natures to Nature as Artifice: The Reinterpretation of Final Causes in Seventeenth-Century Natural Philosophy," *Monist* 79, no. 3 (1996): 388–407; and Veronica Gventsadze, "Aristotelian Influences in Gassendi's Moral Philosophy," *Journal of the History of Philosophy* 45, no. 2 (2007): 223–42.

acceptable for a lion to chase, kill, and consume a gazelle since the lion's pursuit of her prey is a natural act of self-preservation that occurs almost as spontaneously as the falling of a rock. But adult humans differ from both of the previous cases for Gassendi in their possession of reason in addition to will. It is this faculty that was thought to instigate an incessant tussle between the spontaneous pursuit of natural desires and the ability either to control and suppress yearnings or to conjure ever more innovative ways to obtain pleasure.

Far from espousing a Benthamite equality of pleasures, Gassendi posited a four-tiered hierarchy. First was the instinctive desire for instantaneous physical gratification, which humans shared with other animals, and then came the calculated search for increased pleasure that goads rational but unenlightened individuals.[21] Gassendi conceived of the latter as the level on which most historical actors (especially nonphilosophers) operated, and it was at this stage, he held, that humans began to delight in meat eating, having outstripped their childish preference for fruits, herbs, and vegetables. The other two kinds of pleasure, however, reinstated a vegetarian diet. Taking a cue from Epicurus, Gassendi promoted tranquility or lack of pain as the ultimate pleasure that could be achieved in this lifetime, and he averred that this goal animated all wise individuals. Finally, he described the sublime pleasure of the beatific vision of God, which is only fully attainable in the afterlife. Putting the latter to one side for the moment, Gassendi's understanding of pleasure as tranquility requires more attention, given that it was the instantiation that he discussed at the greatest length.

Gassendi affirmed the essential point of Epicurus's moral philosophy that virtue is a necessary adjunct to pleasure, and, with a stress on temperance and prudence, he followed Aristotle in defining virtue as a habit of the mind that inclines humans toward just and honorable actions. It was in the course of fitting Epicurus's ethical injunction against killing and consuming animals to an Aristotelian framework that Gassendi established the criterion that made meat eating unnatural. In the tradition of virtue ethics, each virtuous act is a mean between two extremes. If humans are natural omnivores, then the mean is to consume meat in moderation. By contrast, if a study of the human body leads one to classify humans as herbivores, then eating any meat at all

---

[21] See Gassendi, *Opera Omnia*, vol. 2, 659–735. This discussion of Gassendi's notion of pleasure relies on Sarasohn, *Gassendi's Ethics*, 51–75.

is gratuitous and should be avoided. Drawing the latter conclusion, Gassendi conceived of a vegetarian diet as not only natural and pleasurable but also virtuous. On this score, another possible source for his thought is Erasmus of Rotterdam's treatise on abstention from meat, *De interdicto esu carnium*, which similarly vocalized the notion that "sobernesse & temperaune of meat / maketh ye mynde more free & at lybertie / to gyve attedaunce to suche studies whiche helpeth move nere to vertue."[22]

Gassendi periodically expressed sympathy toward animals, but, as the preceding discussion indicates, he was not predominantly concerned with the suffering of other species in the Singerian sense that the pain caused by killing animals outweighs the maximum amount of pleasure that could be gained by eating them.[23] Rather, the pleasure that Epicurus and Gassendi advocated was known as *katastematic*, which is a passive pleasure that includes not only absence of pain but also resistance to surplus physical effort.[24] For Gassendi, the energy that an activity such as hunting required inevitably detracted from an individual's pursuit of more noble and virtuous undertakings—chiefly, philosophizing.[25] At least analogically, the stance that God created humans to calculate pleasure and avoid overexertion accorded with Gassendi's physical principle that each atom is infused with the necessary vitality to keep it in uniform motion.[26] Yet, in stark contrast to atoms, he pointed out that the gift of volition that God granted humans left most individuals enslaved to unnatural and detrimental desires, with meat consumption foremost among them.[27] After the Fall, meat began to appear, on Gassendi's account, as the fruit of a tree from which humans were all too easily lured into eating.

---

[22] See Erasmus, *De interdicto esu carnium* (Cologne, 1522). The quotation is from an early English translation: Erasmus, *An Epystell of ye Famous Doctor Erasm of Roterdam . . . cocernyng the Forbedynge of Eatynge of Flesshe* (London, 1534).

[23] See Peter Singer, *Practical Ethics* (Cambridge: Cambridge University Press, 1993), 55–82.

[24] See Peter Preuss, *Epicurean Ethics: Katastemic Hedonism* (Lampeter, Wales: Mellen, 1994); and David Wolfsdorf, *Pleasure in Ancient Greek Philosophy* (Cambridge: Cambridge University Press, 2012), 144–81.

[25] As regards the view that hunting and cooking is unnatural and unnecessary, Gassendi writes: "Potest item tum ex eo, quòd cùm nobis arma, seu instrumenta naturalia dilacerandis, dissecandisque carnibus non suppeterent, excogitare, usurpatéque artificialia oportuerit, cultros scilicet, quibus animantes carnibus alioquin vescentes non egent: tum ex eo, quòd cùm carneis crudas auersêmur, oportuerit variè illas coquere, ut suauiores efficerentur, quem apparatum quæ animantes carne vescuntur, non requirunt." Gassendi, *Opera Omina*, vol. 2, 302.

[26] See Lolordo, *Pierre Gassendi*, 174–79.

[27] On Gassendi and freedom, the best discussion remains Osler, *Divine Will*, especially 80–101.

The Anatomical Challenge

A later generation of medics and natural philosophers came to reject Gassendi's conception of naturalness, despite their profound debts both to his anatomical reflections and to his anti-Scholastic arguments. The implications of this deviation for debates about vegetarianism are palpable in an exchange between John Wallis, the Savilian Professor of Geometry at Oxford and founding member of the Royal Society, and the younger (and less well-known) physician and anatomist Edward Tyson.[28] Their correspondence on the topic took place between 1700 and 1701 and was published in the *Philosophical Transactions of the Royal Society*. At the outset of this exchange, Wallis drew attention to Gassendi's deliberations in *Syntagma Philosophicum* and the "Printed Epistles" to van Helmont that are housed in the *Opera Omnia* (which this chapter turns to in the next section). In doing so, he announced that Gassendi "thought it not (originally) Natural to *Man* to feed on *Flesh*; though by long usage (at least ever since the Flood) we have been accustomed to it."[29] Wallis went on to affirm, in agreement with Gassendi, that human teeth are ill-designed to break up the raw flesh of other animals, but, for Wallis, the implication was simply that meat needs "a preparative *Coction*, by boiling, roasting, baking, &c."[30] Wallis's divergence from Gassendi thus lay in his contention that the "natural" not only includes the immediate physical state of bodies but also the actions that they are able to perform, from producing weapons to lighting fires.[31]

The notion of the natural that the likes of Wallis advanced was premised on the denunciation of both teleology and the broader Aristotelian-Galenic understanding of experience, and was rather wrapped up with the

[28] On Tyson, see Anita Guerrini, "Edward Tyson," *Oxford Dictionary of National Biography*; and Ashley Montagu, *Edward Tyson, M.D., F.R.S., 1650–1708, and the Rise of Human and Comparative Anatomy in England; a Study in the History of Science* (Philadelphia: American Philosophical Society, 1943). On Wallis, see Philip Beeley and Christoph J. Scriba, Introduction to *Correspondence of John Wallis (1616–1703)*, vol. 1, *1641–1659* (Oxford: Oxford University Press, 2003); and Domenico Bertoloni Meli, "John Wallis," *Oxford Dictionary of National Biography*.

[29] John Wallis and Edward Tyson, "A Letter of Dr Wallis to Dr Tyson, concerning Mens Feeding on Flesh," *Philosophical Transactions (1683–1775)* 22 (1700–1701): 769–70. For slightly later physiological debates of a similar nature, see James Whorton, "'Tempest in a Flesh-Pot': The Formulation of a Physiological Rationale for Vegetarianism," *Journal of the History of Medicine and Allied Sciences* 32, no. 2 (1977): 115–39.

[30] Wallis and Tyson, "A Letter of Dr Wallis," 711.

[31] For an overview of ways to understand the "natural" during the early modern period, see A. J. Close, "Commonplace Theories of Art and Nature in Classical Antiquity and in the Renaissance," *Journal of the History of Ideas* 30, no. 4 (1969): 467–86. For an analysis of the Wallis-Tyson debate in the context of early modern animal ethics, see Begley, "Animals in Early Modern Thought."

post-Baconian emphasis on the power of microscopes, telescopes, and air pumps to provide fuller, more accurate, and ostensibly useful descriptions of the natural world.[32] To justify their experimental methodologies, figures in the Royal Society began to conceive of artificial instruments as auxiliaries to human nature. Thus humans were not only defined as rational language-users, but, increasingly, as tool-using animals. Wallis explicitly connected rationality to humankind's superior capacity to control environmental factors when he wrote that "Man's being indu'd with Reason, doth supply the want of many things, which, to other Animals may be needful."[33] Shifting the terms of the debate—and forwarding an argument that is usually attributed to the twentieth-century anthropologist Claude Lévi-Strauss—this was the reason that Wallis was only willing to affirm that human bodies were not designed to feast on "raw flesh."[34] In this sense, dining on roast beef or a fried duck, say, was not only acceptable; it was even "natural."

More fundamentally, Wallis alighted upon Gassendi's argument from the structure of the teeth, but he proceeded to pass it off as arbitrary, and hoped that Tyson, as the most renowned comparative anatomist of his day, could better elucidate the physiological similarities and differences between carnivores and herbivores either to support or complicate the Frenchman's broader verdict. Priming Tyson in his initial letter, Wallis observed that most quadrupeds that feed on plant matter (such as pigs, sheep, and oxen) have long colons, whereas carnivores (such as dogs, foxes, and wolves) have short and slender ones.[35] Unlike Gassendi, Wallis worked with the presupposition that humans are carnivores. But he realized that if only carnivores have short and slender colons, whereas humans have long ones, then it would follow that humans are naturally herbivorous. To Wallis's mind, it was perfectly clear that teeth can break down cooked and cut flesh (which undermined Gassendi's argument from anatomy), but he was aware that it would be truly

---

[32] The most important study of early modern "experience" remains Peter Dear, *Discipline and Experience: The Mathematical Way in the Scientific Revolution* (Chicago: University of Chicago Press, 1995). Also see Charles Schmitt, "Experience and Experiment: A Comparison of Zabarella's View with Galileo's in *De Motu*," *Studies in the Renaissance* 16 (1969): 80–138; and Didier Deleule, "Experientia-experimentum ou le mythe due culte de l'expérience chez Francis Bacon," in *Francis Bacon: Terminologia e fortuna nel XVII secolo: Seminario internazionale, Roma, 11–13 marzo 1984*, ed. M. Fattori (Rome: Edizioni dell'Ateneo, 1984), 59–72.

[33] Wallis and Tyson, "A Letter of Dr Wallis," 772–73.

[34] Wallis and Tyson, "A Letter of Dr Wallis," 771. See Claude Lévi-Strauss, *The Raw and the Cooked*, trans. John Weightman and Doreen Weightman (Chicago: University of Chicago Press, 1983).

[35] Wallis and Tyson, "A Letter of Dr Wallis," 771–72.

problematic if the colon was found to be wholly incapable of properly absorbing nutrients from animal flesh.

In his response, Tyson agreed with the thrust of Wallis's anatomical observations, and itemized twenty additional animals that accorded with his parallel dichotomies between herbivore/carnivore and long/short colons. Even so, he concluded by reeling off a number of exceptions—which have been labeled "omnivores" since the nineteenth century—such as opossums that have long colons yet eat poultry and birds, and hedgehogs that have short colons yet feed on fruits, roots, and herbs. Furthermore, he drew attention to the fact that hungry pigs would readily devour animal flesh, starving mice might nibble on bacon, and Ælian, the Roman rhetorician, mentions horses and sheep who were known to have eaten only fish.[36] Tyson was, however, aware that he was resorting to some special pleading after his long list of positive examples, adding that he had taken these examples "from the Indian Historians" and "shall therefore lay no stress upon them." Wallis similarly recognized that incidents such as "the *Horse* (you mention) that *Eats Oysters*" and "the *Rat* eating *Bacon*, for want of other Food" were highly aberrant. With this said, it was common for associates of the early Royal Society to take the anomalous seriously, and, as such, Tyson's aim was only to show that Wallis's insight about the colon "may hold for the most part true, yet it is no Universal."[37] Determined to call Gassendi's diagnosis into question, Tyson assumed that humans, with their manifold unrivaled capabilities, were another exceptional case.

In general, it was by no means obvious that any ethical responsibilities followed from the observation that humans anatomically resemble other animals, just as arguments for or against vegetarianism from shared DNA or common ancestry remain largely unpersuasive.[38] It is notable in this regard that Tyson's 1699 *Ourang-Outang* pinpointed numerous anatomical similarities between orangutans and human beings. Since the supposed superiority of humans had long rested on their ability to use language, he was struck, in particular, by the fact that human and orangutan vocal cords were virtually identical. But he proceeded to note that using language was not a capability of these great apes.[39] Such incongruity between bodily composition

---

[36] Wallis and Tyson, "A Letter of Dr Wallis," 782.

[37] Wallis and Tyson, "A Letter of Dr Wallis," 783.

[38] See James Rachels, *Created from Animals: The Moral Implications of Darwinism* (Oxford: Oxford University Press, 1990); and Rod Preece, "Darwinism, Christianity, and the Great Vivisection Debate," *Journal of the History of Ideas* 64, no. 3 (2003): 399–419.

[39] For the contours of this debate, see Richard Serjeantson, "The Passions and Animal Language, 1540–1700," *Journal of the History of Ideas* 62, no. 3 (2001): 425–44.

and capabilities, for Tyson, served to corroborate a certain reading of Aristotle according to which the rational soul, understood as a unifying principle, rather than the organization of the body as such, is what endows humans with their unique attributes.[40] It might have been tempting for Tyson to seize upon anatomical correspondences in order to narrow the gap between humankind and other species, but, on the contrary, they prompted him to view humans as all the more exceptional, with orangutans appearing as strange, deficient versions of humans to whom ethical considerations did not necessarily apply. Relatedly, if humans were perfectly capable of digesting meat yet appeared, in comparison to other species, ill-suited to the task on an anatomical level, then this might simply serve as another sign of human superiority over the rest of nature. Gassendi's repetition of his point concerning the teeth suggests that he found it convincing or at least likely to persuade his contemporaries. Its reception by the likes of Tyson and Wallis, however, indicates that Gassendi's other arguments based on an understanding of nature but grounded in ancient literature and theology in fact had more teeth than those from anatomy.

The Chemical Challenge

Gassendi first framed many of the arguments that made their way into *Syntagma Philosophicum* in the aforementioned epistle to van Helmont. Whereas Gassendi's reflections on teeth stimulated anatomical discussions in the early Royal Society, nutritional considerations (for which van Helmont's ideas were key) proved more pervasive and lasting sites of debates about meat consumption, both because abstention from meat was frequently construed as a dietary issue and due to the fact that medicine, diet, and ethics were thoroughly entangled during the early modern period. Before diving into the nature of van Helmont's intervention into this discourse, it is notable that doctors working within the established Galenic tradition typically advised their patients to abstain from overindulging on animal flesh, especially when ill. Nicholas Culpeper's 1652 translation of Galen's *Ars medica*, for instance, states that melancholics, phlegmatics, choleric-melancholics,

---

[40] On Tyson's *Ourang-Outang*, see Robert Wokler, "Tyson and Buffon on the Orang-utan," *Studies on Voltaire and the Eighteenth Century* 155 (1976): 2301–19; and Erica Fudge, "Bad Manners at the Anatomist's Table: Edward Tyson and the Naturalisation of Truth," in *The Political Subject: Essays on the Self from Art, Politics and Science*, ed. W. Wheeler (London: Lawrence & Wishard, 2000), 14–30.

melancholic-cholerics, phlegmatic-sanguines, and phlegmatic-cholerics should all "beware of overfilling themselves with meat."[41] Only straightforward cholerics were not warned against the dangers of animal flesh. Even Wallis's letter to Tyson drew attention to the fact that "we forbid it [meat] to persons in a Fever, or other like distempers, as of too hard digestion."[42] Although Gassendi did not dwell on the colon as such, he adhered to the standard position that meat is far more difficult to digest than vegetable matter, and he even reckoned that if humans habitually adhered to a vegetarian diet, then there would be less illness in the first place.[43] In early modern medicine, there was an entrenched distinction between therapy (the cure of disease) and hygiene (the prevention of disease).[44] By shifting vegetarianism from a therapeutic treatment to a hygienic prevention, Gassendi aspired to integrate a plant-based diet more fully into seventeenth-century life.

In the process of uprooting traditional medical practices, Helmontians sought to discredit the Galenic physician's hands-on approach to balancing individual humors, and especially the long-standing *regimen sanitatis* that was centrally concerned with dietary regulation. As a rule of thumb, learned medics holistically attended to individual patients, whereas empirics and chymists aimed to combat diseases directly, as they were manifested in shared symptoms.[45] Largely indifferent to dietary matters, van Helmont and his fellow chymists commonly advised patients to eat what they pleased, supposing that whatever satisfied the palate must be suitable, and that a content patient was more likely to experience a swift recovery than one who was forced into a strict and often unpleasant regimen. The Irish Helmonian Thomas O'Dowde thus urged a patient "to be kind to himself, and (without regard to Dietory Prescriptions) to eat Roast Beef and drink Sack."[46]

Gassendi denounced the abandonment of dietary considerations as a dangerous course, not least because it could clear the way for cannibalism. Addressing travelers tales about the anthropophagy of indigenous

---

[41] Nicholas Culpeper, *Galen's Art of Physick* (London, 1652), 64.

[42] Wallis and Tyson, "A Letter of Dr Wallis," 771.

[43] Gassendi, *Opera Omnia*, vol. 2, 302. For relevant discussions of early modern digestion, see the essays in *Studies in History and Philosophy of Biological and Biomedical Sciences* 43, no. 2 (2012), especially Justin Smith, "Diet, Embodiment, and Virtue in the Mechanical Philosophy," 338–48, and Antonio Clericuzio, "Chemical and Mechanical Theories of Digestion in Early Modern Medicine," 329–37.

[44] See Heikki Mikkeli, *Hygiene in the Early Modern Medical Tradition* (Helsinki: Academia Scientiarum Fennica, 1999), especially 125–40.

[45] See Andrew Wear, *Knowledge and Practice in English Medicine, 1550–1680* (Cambridge: Cambridge University Press, 2000), 399–434.

[46] Thomas O'Dowde, *The Poor Man's Physician, or The True Art of Medicine* (London, 1665), 22–23.

Brazilians—and recapitulating a sentiment found in Michel de Montaigne's essay "On Cannibals"—Gassendi surmised that they supposed themselves "to be following nature as their guide" as much as Europeans who feasted on animals.[47] While it may now seem like a stretch to link the consumption of human flesh with that of other species, this comparison was firmly grounded in seventeenth-century conceptions of digestion and nutrition.[48] Galenic physicians on the whole maintained that foods and drinks that were most dissimilar to the matter making up the human body were best assimilated, meaning that plants were widely deemed more salubrious than animals. If, by contrast, food that was most similar to the human body (such as animal flesh) was best assimilated—or simply if assimilation was passed off as irrelevant to human health—then there would have been less reason to consider anthropophagy taboo. Insofar as transgressing other ethical norms could be attributed to humoral imbalances that a diet of human flesh might serve to neutralize, cannibalism could even be ethically justifiable in some cases.

All of this is not to say that van Helmont was a champion of dietary decadence as such (never mind cannibalism). On the contrary, he frequently recycled the biblical dictum that "abstinence and sparingness, are the best meanes in the Dietary part."[49] Moreover, it is not clear in the letter itself whether van Helmont wholeheartedly embraced the conceits that he defended, since Gassendi implied that his letters were the resumption of a friendly spar, in which van Helmont had been pleased to play devil's advocate.[50] In any case, Gassendi recognized that the Flemish physician was at the forefront of medical reform, and he undoubtedly discerned that convincing van Helmont of vegetarianism's advantages for human health could have extensive and concrete effects on the diets of his contemporaries and subsequent generations. Since there was at least one solid reason within the

---

[47] "tum ex eo, quòd non est opponendum inventos esse Brasilianos, Hurones, aliósque feros Homines carnibus vescenteis; quasi illi Naturam ducem insequuti esse videantur; cùm ex hoc capite natura tam in illis potuerit, quàm in cæteris depravari, ac tantò magis, quantò minùs humanitatis retinuerunt, ut pote, qui non carnivori simpliciter, sed etiam Anthropophagi specialiter evaserint." Gassendi, Opera Omnia, vol. 2, 302.

[48] For fuller discussions of early modern ideas about cannibalism, see Cătălin Avramescu, An Intellectual History of Cannibalism (Princeton: Princeton University Press, 2009), especially 162–82. Also see Louise Noble, Medicinal Cannibalism in Early Modern English Literature and Culture (New York: Palgrave Macmillan, 2011); and Cecilia Muratori, "Animals in the Renaissance," in Animals: A History, ed. P. Adamson and G.F Edwards (Oxford: Oxford University Press, 2018), 163–86.

[49] See Jan Baptista van Helmont, Van Helmont's Works: Containing His Most Excellent Philosophy, Physick, Chirurgery, Anatomy, trans. J. Chandler (London, 1664), 70.

[50] "Tenuisti tu oppositam viam, sicque mutuis oppositisque contendentes rationibus, jucundissimas exegimus horas." Gassendi, Opera Omnia, vol. 6, 20.

framework of Helmontian medicine to suppose that meat eating could harm both body and soul, Gassendi had further reason to be hopeful. According to van Helmont, the chief agent of digestion was the divine *archeus*, understood as an immaterial principle that was suffused throughout the natural world and especially concentrated in the human body.[51] Yet he held that the *archeus* had lost much of its power to assimilate food at the Fall (which is why humans began to produce feces) and was particularly inept at absorbing rich or fatty foods such as meat. There was reason enough, in this regard, for him strongly to discourage the habit of meat consumption.

But, unwilling to enforce dietary strictures, van Helmont instead focused on the radical possibility of restoring humankind to prelapsarian perfection through a mithridate or universal remedy. In his more optimistic moments, he even appealed to an elixir or a "modern tree of life" that would extend the human life-span and preserve health for upwards of three hundred years.[52] With this in mind, Gassendi attempted to convince van Helmont that vegetarianism was a more historical and gradual way to restore the human body to some of its former excellences.[53] In doing so, the Frenchman made it clear that the most "natural" bodies were not those of children but rather of Adam and Eve in their pristine state. This sentiment was widespread at the time, with Wallis relaying to Tyson that it is "the Opinion of many Divines, that before the Flood, Men did not use to feed on Flesh," even if he admitted to holding "some doubt therein" because "we find, very early, that *Abel* was a *Keeper of Sheep*, as well as *Cain* a *Tiller of the Ground*."[54] For Gassendi, it was one thing to dispute interpretations of Genesis, but it was quite another to emphasize medicinal perfectibility and the prolongation of life, not least by stripping the prevailing conviction that antediluvian (or at least prelapsarian) humans were vegetarians of its practical import. This is one sense in which radical or positivistic modes of thought belied arguments for abstention from meat. In contrast to such millenarian inclinations, Gassendi saw

---

[51] See Walter Pagel, *Joan Baptista van Helmont: Reformer of Science and Medicine* (Cambridge: Cambridge University Press, 1982), 96–101.

[52] See van Helmont, *Van Helmont's Works*, 645–47. Also see Georgiana Hedesan, *An Alchemical Quest for Universal Knowledge: The "Christian Philosophy" of Jan Baptist van Helmont (1579–1644)* (London: Routledge, 2016), 172–92.

[53] "Etsi enim fieri videmus, ut ex usu vulgarium ciborum vix Homines possint propagare vitam ad sæculum usque, aut aliquid ampliùs, nihilominus certum esse paratam fuisse arborem in Paradiso terrestri, ex cuius esu homo potuisset immortalis euadere: & aliunde in hac naturæ corruptione probabile fieri, parari posse Elixir, cuius usu homo possit, nisi æternum tempus vivere, tot certè sæcula durare, ut duratio homini possit videri quædam æternitas." Gassendi, *Opera Omnia*, vol. 6, 20–21.

[54] Wallis and Tyson, "A Letter of Dr Wallis," 770–71.

ancient philosophy and the Bible as blueprints for behavior, in keeping with the humanist preoccupation with reading for action.[55]

Conclusion: The Beatific Vision

Working with a broadly Augustinian understanding of fallen humanity, Gassendi believed that the ultimate pleasure of human communion with God should be continually sought even if it could not be altogether realized in this lifetime.[56] He saw the consumption of flesh as a significant obstacle on the road to actualizing this beatific vision, since the natural world supported the Bible in suggesting that humankind would not eat meat after the restoration of paradise, when "men are no longer ignorant of God's ways."[57] In many regards, this insight can be seen as the culmination of Gassendi's eclectic endeavor to baptize the ancient heathens. Not only did Gassendi mobilize arguments from medicine, scripture, Epicurus, and Aristotle, but his focus on eventual unity with God was also derived from the stress on purity as a path to godliness among vegetarians of a Neoplatonic bent, including Porphyry and Plotinus, along with church fathers such as Tatian and John Chrysostom.[58] As a Catholic priest, Gassendi naturally considered decisions in this lifetime to be of paramount importance in preparing body and mind for the next. Rather than primarily shaping abstinence from meat as dutiful preparation for the hereafter, however, he grounded his acceptance of vegetarianism in a whole gamut of arguments that included the historical virtue and excellence of its practitioners.

In his letter to Wallis, Tyson pronounced that "had Man been design'd by Nature not to have been a Carnivorous Animal, no doubt there would have been observed, in some part of the World, Men which did not at all feed upon Flesh."[59] He took the paucity of evidence for vegetarian civilizations

---

[55] The classic work on this topic is Lisa Jardine and Anthony Grafton, "'Studied for Action': How Gabriel Harvey Read His Livy," *Past & Present* 129, no. 1 (1990): 30–78.

[56] Gassendi, *Opera Omnia*, vol. 2, 662 and 717.

[57] "Quid quòd etiam post primam labem, cum homines adhuc tam multa superarent sæcula, carnium usum nullum audimus; sed tum demum ille est inductus, cùm iam corruptis hominum viis Deus illum, ut permulta alia, ob duritiem cordis concessit?" Gassendi, *Opera Omnia*, vol. 6, 21.

[58] On the symbiotic relationship between these pagan writers and early Christian ones, see Gillian Clark, "Fattening the Soul: Christian Asceticism and Porphyry on Abstinence," in *Ascetica, Gnostica, Liturgica, Orientalia: Studia Patristica*, vol. 2, ed. M. F. Wiles and E. J. Yarnold (Leuven: Peeters, 2001), 41–51.

[59] Wallis and Tyson, "A Letter of Dr Wallis," 775.

as fodder for his conclusion that humans were designed as meat-eaters. By contrast, Gassendi lauded advocates of abstention from meat as some of the most enlightened and godly citizens in their societies. Far from endorsing radical egalitarianism, his argument for vegetarianism was accordingly founded on his methodological precept that thinkers should study, extract, and fuse the best ideas from the history of philosophy, medicine, and theology. Recognizing the widespread practice of vegetarianism among writers whom he and many of his contemporaries most admired—not least the Epicureans—Gassendi was adamant that if not all humans, then at least all *humanists* should be herbivores.[60]

Bibliography

Allen, Don Cameron. "The Rehabilitation of Epicurus and His Theory of Pleasure in the Renaissance." *Studies in Philology* 41, no. 1 (1944): 1–15.

Aristotle. *Parts of Animals; Movement of Animals; Progression of Animals.* Translated and edited by E. S. Forster and A. L. Peck. Cambridge, MA: Harvard University Press, 2014.

Aristotle. *Physics.* Translated and edited by F. M. Cornford and P. H. Wicksteed. Cambridge, MA: Harvard University Press, 2014.

Avramescu, Cătălin. *An Intellectual History of Cannibalism.* Princeton, NJ: Princeton University Press, 2009.

Beeley, Philip, and Christoph J. Scriba. Introduction to *Correspondence of John Wallis (1616–1703),* vol. 1, *1641–1659.* Oxford: Oxford University Press, 2003.

Begley, Justin. "Animals in Early Modern Thought." In *Encyclopedia of Early Modern Philosophy and the Sciences,* edited by D. Jalobeanu and C. T. Wolfe. Cham: Springer, 2021. https://doi.org/10.1007/978-3-319-20791-9_628-1.

Boonin-Vail, David. "The Vegetarian Savage: Rousseau's Critique of Meat Eating." *Environmental Ethics* 15, no. 1 (1993): 75–84.

Brundell, Barry. *Pierre Gassendi: From Aristotelianism to a New Natural Philosophy.* Dordrecht: Reidel, 1987.

Casaubon, Meric. *Generall Learning: A Seventeenth-Century Treatise on the Formation of the General Scholar.* Edited by R. Serjeantson. Cambridge: RTM, 1999.

Clark, Gillian. "Fattening the Soul: Christian Asceticism and Porphyry on Abstinence." In *Ascetica, Gnostica, Liturgica, Orientalia: Studia Patristica,* vol. 2, edited by M. F. Wiles and E. J. Yarnold, 41–51. Leuven: Peeters, 2001.

Clericuzio, Antonio. "Chemical and Mechanical Theories of Digestion in Early Modern Medicine." *Studies in History and Philosophy of Biological and Biomedical Sciences* 43, no. 2 (2012): 329–37.

---

[60] For the sense of humanism used here, see Nicholas Mann, "The Origins of Humanism," in *Cambridge Companion to Renaissance Humanism,* ed. J. Kraye (Cambridge: Cambridge University Press, 1996), 1–19.

Close, A. J. "Commonplace Theories of Art and Nature in Classical Antiquity and in the Renaissance." *Journal of the History of Ideas* 30, no. 4 (1969): 467–86.

Culpeper, Nicholas. *Galen's Art of Physick*. London, 1652.

Dear, Peter. *Discipline and Experience: The Mathematical Way in the Scientific Revolution*. Chicago: University of Chicago Press, 1995.

Deleule, Didier. "Experientia-experimentum ou le mythe due culte de l'expérience chez Francis Bacon." In *Francis Bacon: Terminologia e fortuna nel XVII secolo: Seminario internazionale, Roma, 11–13 marzo 1984*, edited by M. Fattori, 59–72. Rome: Edizioni dell'Ateneo, 1984.

Erasmus. *De interdicto esu carnium*. Cologne, 1522.

Erasmus. *An Epystell of ye Famous Doctor Erasm of Roterdam. . . cocernyng the Forbedynge of Eatynge of Flesshe*. London, 1534.

Fudge, Erica. "Bad Manners at the Anatomist's Table: Edward Tyson and the Naturalisation of Truth." In *The Political Subject: Essays on the Self from Art, Politics and Science*, edited by W. Wheeler, 14–30. London: Lawrence & Wishard, 2000.

Gassendi, Pierre. *Opera Omnia*. Lyon, 1658.

Giglioni, Guido. "Life and Its Animal Boundaries: Ethical Implications in Early Modern Theories of Universal Animation." In *Ethical Perspectives on Animals in the Renaissance and Early Modern Period*, edited by C. Muratori and B. Dohm, 111–37. Florence: SISMEL edizioni del Galluzzo, 2013.

Guerrini, Anita. "A Diet for a Sensitive Soul: Vegetarianism in Eighteenth-Century Britain." *Eighteenth-Century Life* 23, no. 3 (1999): 34–42.

Guerrini, Anita. "Edward Tyson (1651–1708)." *Oxford Dictionary of National Biography* (2004). Accessed April 24, 2019. https://ezproxy prd.bodleian.ox.ac.uk:4563/10.1093/ref:odnb/27961.

Gventsadze, Veronica. "Aristotelian Influences in Gassendi's Moral Philosophy." *Journal of the History of Philosophy* 45, no. 2 (2007): 223–42.

Hedesan, Georgiana. *An Alchemical Quest for Universal Knowledge: The "Christian Philosophy" of Jan Baptist van Helmont (1579–1644)*. London: Routledge, 2016.

Jardine, Lisa, and Anthony Grafton. "'Studied for Action': How Gabriel Harvey Read His Livy." *Past & Present* 129, no. 1 (1990): 30–78.

Joy, Lynn. *Gassendi the Atomist: Advocate of History in the Age of Science*. Cambridge: Cambridge University Press, 1987.

Lévi-Strauss, Claude. *The Raw and the Cooked*. Translated by John Weightman and Doreen Weightman. Chicago: University of Chicago Press, 1983.

Levitin, Dmitri. *Ancient Wisdom in the Age of the New Science: Histories of Philosophy in England, c. 1640–1700*. Cambridge: Cambridge University Press, 2015.

Lolordo, Antonia. *Pierre Gassendi and the Birth of Early Modern Philosophy*. Cambridge: Cambridge University Press, 2007.

Mann, Nicholas. "The Origins of Humanism." In *Cambridge Companion to Renaissance Humanism*, edited by J. Kraye, 1–19. Cambridge: Cambridge University Press, 1996.

McColley, Diane Kelsey. *Poetry and Ecology in the Age of Milton and Marvell*. Aldershot: Ashgate, 2007.

Meli, Domenico Bertoloni. "John Wallis (1616–1703)." *Oxford Dictionary of National Biography* (2004). Accessed April 24, 2019. https://ezproxy-prd.bodleian.ox.ac.uk:4563/10.1093/ref:odnb/28572.

Mikkeli, Heikki. *Hygiene in the Early Modern Medical Tradition*. Helsinki: Academia Scientiarum Fennica, 1999.

Montagu, Ashley. *Edward Tyson, M.D., F.R.S., 1650–1708, and the Rise of Human and Comparative Anatomy in England; a Study in the History of Science.* Philadelphia: American Philosophical Society, 1943.

Muratori, Cecilia. "Animals in the Renaissance." In *Animals: A History*, edited by P. Adamson and G. F. Edwards, 163–86. Oxford: Oxford University Press, 2018.

Noble, Louise. *Medicinal Cannibalism in Early Modern English Literature and Culture.* New York: Palgrave Macmillan, 2011.

O'Dowde, Thomas. *The Poor Man's Physician, or The True Art of Medicine.* London, 1665.

Osler, Margaret. *Divine Will and the Mechanical Philosophy: Gassendi and Descartes on Contingency and Necessity in the Created World.* Cambridge: Cambridge University Press, 1994.

Osler, Margaret. "From Immanent Natures to Nature as Artifice: The Reinterpretation of Final Causes in Seventeenth-Century Natural Philosophy." *Monist* 79, no. 3 (1996): 388–407.

Pagel, Walter. *Joan Baptista van Helmont: Reformer of Science and Medicine.* Cambridge: Cambridge University Press, 1982.

Plutarch. *Moralia.* Vol. 12. Translated by H. Cherniss and W. Helmbold. Cambridge, MA: Harvard University Press, 1957.

Plutarch. *Moralia.* Vol. 14. Translated by B. Einarson and P. de Lacy. Cambridge, MA: Harvard University Press, 1967.

Preece, Rod. "Darwinism, Christianity, and the Great Vivisection Debate." *Journal of the History of Ideas* 64, no. 3 (2003): 399–419.

Preuss, Peter. *Epicurean Ethics: Katastemic Hedonism.* Lampeter, Wales: Mellen, 1994.

Rachels, James. *Created from Animals: The Moral Implications of Darwinism.* Oxford: Oxford University Press, 1990.

Rollin, Bernard. "Animal Pain: What It Is and Why It Matters." *Journal of Ethics* 15, no. 4 (2011): 425–37.

Sarasohn, Lisa. *Gassendi's Ethics: Freedom in a Mechanistic University.* Ithaca, NY: Cornell University Press, 1996.

Schmitt, Charles. "Experience and Experiment: A Comparison of Zabarella's View with Galileo's in *De Motu*." *Studies in the Renaissance* 16 (1969): 80–138.

Serjeantson, Richard. "The Passions and Animal Language, 1540–1700." *Journal of the History of Ideas* 62, no. 3 (2001): 425–44.

Singer, Peter. *Practical Ethics.* Cambridge: Cambridge University Press, 1993.

Smith, Justin. "Diet, Embodiment, and Virtue in the Mechanical Philosophy." *Studies in History and Philosophy of Biological and Biomedical Sciences* 43, no. 2 (2012): 338–48.

Spencer, Colin. *The Heretic's Feast: A History of Vegetarianism.* London: University Press of New England, 1995.

Stuart, Tristram. *Bloodless Revolution: Radical Vegetarians and the Discovery of India.* London: HarperPress, 2006.

van Helmont, Jan Baptista. *Van Helmont's Works: Containing His Most Excellent Philosophy, Physick, Chirurgery, Anatomy.* Translated by J. Chandler. London, 1664.

Wallis, John, and Edward Tyson. "A Letter of Dr Wallis to Dr Tyson, concerning Mens Feeding on Flesh." *Philosophical Transactions (1683–1775)* 22 (1700–1701): 769–85.

Wear, Andrew. *Knowledge and Practice in English Medicine, 1550–1680.* Cambridge: Cambridge University Press, 2000.

Westfall, Richard. *The Construction of Modern Science: Mechanism and Mechanics.* Cambridge: Cambridge University Press, 1977.

Whorton, James. "'Tempest in a Flesh-Pot': The Formulation of a Physiological Rationale for Vegetarianism." *Journal of the History of Medicine and Allied Sciences* 32, no. 2 (1977): 115–39.

Wokler, Robert. "Tyson and Buffon on the Orang-utan." *Studies on Voltaire and the Eighteenth Century* 155 (1976): 2301–19.

Wolfsdorf, David. *Pleasure in Ancient Greek Philosophy*. Cambridge: Cambridge University Press, 2012.

2

Michel de Montaigne (1533–1592)

Elephant Theologians

Kathleen Long

Most scholars and theorists writing about animal rights describe them in relation to human rights, human functions, and human thinking. They argue that animals should have rights because, like us, they suffer[1] or because, like us, they are capable of reason or work or companionship.[2] We co-constitute each other's existence; or rather, animals are the ground upon which humans define themselves as human. Or humans are animals, and their lives are not so easily distinguishable from animal existence. Catharine Randall suggests that for Michel de Montaigne, animals serve as models for living in harmony with nature.[3] This attitude contrasts with that of many of Montaigne's contemporaries.[4] Theological arguments have been made, particularly by Andrew Linzey, to support animal rights and to correct the mistaken notion that dominion means despotism, with calls for a different relationship between humans and animals.[5] But what if animals had existences that had nothing to do with humans (something that is hard to imagine in the Anthropocene)? What if animals had their own religions and their own culture, not dependent on our own and not a reflection of ourselves? We have a hard time imagining animal lives without recourse to human terms, and yet,

---

[1] Peter Singer, *Animal Liberation: A New Ethics for Our Treatment of Animals* (New York: Harper, 2009). See also Martha Nussbaum, *Frontiers of Justice: Disability, Nationality, Species Membership* (Cambridge, MA: Belknap Press, 2007). Most recent, and most pertinent to this chapter, is Andrew Linzey's study *Why Animal Suffering Matters: Philosophy, Theology, and Practical Ethics* (Oxford: Oxford University Press, 2009).

[2] Donna Haraway, *When Species Meet* (Minneapolis: University of Minnesota Press, 2007). See also Singer, *Animal Liberation*.

[3] Catharine Randall, "Sixteenth-Century Animal Avatars in Montaigne and His Contemporaries," in Randall, *The Wisdom of Animals: Creatureliness in Early Modern French Spirituality* (Notre Dame, IN: University of Notre Dame Press, 2014), 15–37.

[4] Hassan Melehy makes this contrast clear in his essay "Silencing the Animals: Montaigne, Descartes, and the Hyperbole of Reason," *symplokē* 13, nos. 1–2 (2005): 263–82.

[5] See Andrew Linzey, *Animal Theology* (London: SCM Press, 1994).

Kathleen Long, *Michel de Montaigne (1533–1592)* In: *Animal Theologians*. Edited by: Andrew Linzey and Clair Linzey, Oxford University Press. © Oxford University Press 2023. DOI: 10.1093/oso/9780197655542.003.0003

as Montaigne himself argues, we should try, even if that attempt is futile and even if the knowledge of that aspect of animal existence not related to human interests and human self-understanding remains beyond our grasp. In his extensive discussion of animal culture and animal knowledge in his "Apology for Raymond Sebond," Montaigne offers glimpses of a world beyond human relationality and therefore beyond our understanding.[6] He links this world to the divine, equally inscrutable and ungraspable to human imagining, in the context of a critique of human presumption of mastery and centrality in the world.

Montaigne owes a great deal of his knowledge of animals to Pliny, who structures his *Natural History* in such a way as to juxtapose the monstrous humans of the work's seventh book with the more humanlike animals of the eighth book. This comparison puts animals in an advantageous light and underscores human cruelty both to humans and to animals—the theme that mostly closely links the last chapters of the seventh book to the first of the eighth. In the seventh book of his *Natural History*, Pliny gives detailed accounts of monstrous races found in foreign lands and exceptional or unusual humans found in Rome. The most exceptional of these is Caesar, who is praised for his mental vigor but criticized for his mass destruction of over a million people.[7]

Pliny begins the eighth book of *Natural History* by comparing elephants to humans, suggesting that their intelligence is closest to that of man and that they engage in religious practices:

> The largest land animal is the elephant, and it is the nearest to man in intelligence: it understands the language of its country and obeys orders, remembers duties that it has been taught, is pleased by affection and by marks of honour, nay more it possesses virtues rare even in man, honesty, wisdom, justice, also respect for the stars and reverence for the sun and moon. Authorities state that in the forests of Mauretania, when the new moon is shining, herds of elephants go down to a river named Amilo and

---

[6] This possibility is hinted at in some of the essays in the collection *Divinanimality: Animal Theory, Creaturely Theology*, ed. Stephen D. Moore (New York: Fordham University Press, 2014), particularly Jacob J. Erickson, "The Apophatic Animal: Toward a Negative Zootheological *Imago Dei*," 88–99. Erickson notes that "the human delineates the value of the animal creature, a creature that oddly exceeds him" (91). What Montaigne is hinting at, however, is that animals might have their own theories about themselves and perhaps also about humans.

[7] Pliny, *Natural History*, trans. H. Rackham (Cambridge, MA: Harvard University Press, 1942), vol. 2, bk. 7, pp. 566–67.

there perform a ritual of purification, sprinkling themselves with water, and after thus paying their respects to the moon return to the woods carrying before them those of their calves who are tired. They are also believed to understand the obligations of another's religion in so far as to refuse to embark on board ships when going overseas before they are lured on by the mahout's sworn promise in regard to their return.[8]

This opening passage suggests that although elephants engage skillfully with human culture, learning what they are taught and understanding human languages, they have their own rituals, a fact that hints at their own culture. Pliny suggests that their character actually surpasses that of humans, who, after all, use religion to trick them into servitude.

In subsequent chapters, humans' cruelty to elephants becomes even more evident, and the elephants' refusal to engage in such cruelty themselves is striking: "King Bocchus tied to stakes thirty elephants which he intended to punish and exposed them to a herd of the same number, men running out among them to provoke them to the attack, and it proved impossible to make them perform the service of ministering to another's cruelty."[9] This example is followed by the tale of a senseless massacre of elephants at Rome.

Elephants, on the other hand, demonstrate a great capacity for gentleness, such as when they carefully move sheep aside with their trunks when walking through a flock, so as not to step on any of them. They also defend their weak by placing them in the middle of their column, and when one elephant falls into a pit dug by humans to trap the animals, others in the herd will construct a ramp and pull out their companion.[10] In Pliny's accounts the examples of elephant kindness and loyalty are always matched by stories of human brutality toward these animals. Furthermore, by juxtaposing his representation of elephant religion and ethics with an assessment in the previous book of the devastation that human behavior imposes on the world, he seems to be suggesting that elephant morals are in fact superior to those of humans. Already in Pliny, we see animals who have their own knowledge and their own behavior, independent of human intervention, although inevitably described in human terms. Human–animal relations, in his depiction of them, are characterized by great cruelty on the part of humans and a range

---

[8] Pliny, *Natural History*, trans. H. Rackham (Cambridge, MA: Harvard University Press, 1940), vol. 3, bk. 8, p. 3.

[9] Pliny, *Natural History*, vol. 3, bk. 8, p. 13.

[10] Pliny, *Natural History*, vol. 3, bk. 8, p. 19.

of emotions on the part of elephants, from fear and violent self-defense to kindness and even love.

This aspect of Pliny's depiction of animals, as a critique of human behavior, resonates with Montaigne's views. Erica Fudge sees the essayist's representation of animals as unusual, if not unique, in the early modern period, although she limits her analysis mostly to Montaigne's essay "Of Cruelty." She observes in his work "a turning away from assertions of human superiority and the significance of the rule of reason that is rare in this period."[11] But Montaigne surpasses this assessment of his engagement with animals and, seeming to anticipate René Descartes's demotion of them to the realm of automata, ascribes to them a range of human qualities, intellectual and affective. His catalog of the capacities of animal knowledge is so extensive that the scope of this chapter allows for careful examination of only one example, that of elephants.

Montaigne revisits elephant intelligence and even religion in his essay "Apology for Raymond Sebond," concerning human knowledge and the human capacity to comprehend the divine. He explores this issue by examining the limitations of human knowledge in a wide range of contexts. The essay contains a long discussion of animal knowledge and its potential superiority to that of humans, given that human knowledge has been distanced from the understanding of natural phenomena as a result of humankind's arrogant presumption of mastery over the natural world and over animals in particular.[12] Elephants figure prominently in this discussion. They share human characteristics, helping their fellow animals and taking revenge on mean or stingy humans, as well as showing the capacity for courage and complex strategy in battle[13] and even for falling in love.[14] They also seem to have some religious practices:

> We can also say that the elephants have some participation in religion, since after many ablutions and purifications we see them, raising their trunks like arms and keeping their eyes fixed toward the rising sun, stand still a long time in meditation and contemplation at certain hours of the day, by their

---

[11] Erica Fudge, *Brutal Reasoning: Animals, Rationality, and Humanity in Early Modern England* (Ithaca, NY: Cornell University Press, 2006), 79.

[12] Michel de Montaigne, "Apology for Raymond Sebond," *Essays*, vol. 2, chap. 12, trans. Donald Frame (Stanford, CA: Stanford University Press, 1965), 330–58; "Apologie de Raimond Sebond," *Essais*, vol. 2, chap. 12, ed. Pierre Villey (Paris: Presses Universitaires de France, 1965), 452–86.

[13] Montaigne, "Apology," *Essays*, 342; "Apologie," *Essais*, 466.

[14] Montaigne, "Apology," *Essays*, 347; "Apologie," *Essais*, 472.

own inclination, without instruction and without precept. But because we do not see any such signs in other animals, we cannot thereby prove that they are without religion and cannot grasp any part of what is hidden from us.[15]

[Nous pouvons aussi dire que les elephans ont quelque participation de religion, d'autant qu'après plusieurs ablutions et purifications on les void, haussant leur trompe comme des bras et tenant les yeux fichez vers le Soleil levant, se planter long temps en meditation et contemplation à certaines heures du jour, de leur propre inclination, sans instruction et sans precepte. Mais, pour ne voir aucune telle apparence és autres animaux, nous ne pouvons pourtant establir qu'ils soient sans religion, et ne pouvons prendre en aucune part ce qui nous est caché.][16]

Montaigne takes up Pliny's description and places it in a different context, thus transforming its lesson. Just because we cannot imagine animal religion does not mean that it does not exist.[17] He then suggests that we perceive animal behavior only when it resembles human actions, thus returning to the idea stated earlier that the lack is to be found in our understanding of the world, not necessarily in the animals themselves: "This defect that hinders communication between them and us, why is it not just as much ours as theirs?" ("Ce defaut qui empesche la communication d'entre elles et nous, pourquoy n'est il aussi bien à nous qu'à elles?").[18] Montaigne applies his earlier argument to language: just because we cannot understand or discern animal language does not mean that animals are not communicating. He gives the examples of ants negotiating the return of a dead comrade, asserting that "we see something in this action which the philosopher Cleanthes observed, because it resembles our own" ("nous voyons quelque chose en cette action que le philosophe Cleanthes remerqua, par ce qu'elle retire aux nostres").[19] The limitations of man's knowledge do not limit nature, and nature continues on its way with or without us: "creatures who have no voice nevertheless have mutual intercourse and communication, in which it is our fault that we

---

[15] Montaigne, "Apology," Essays, 343.
[16] Montaigne, "Apologie," Essais, 468.
[17] Hassan Melehy makes a similar argument regarding Montaigne's depiction of reason in animals in his essay "Montaigne and Ethics: The Case of Animals," L'Esprit Créateur 46, no. 1 (2006): 96–107. But where Melehy recenters the focus on humans, I would make a slightly different argument, one that decenters the human.
[18] Montaigne, "Apology," Essays, 331; "Apologie," Essais, 453.
[19] Montaigne, "Apology," Essays, 343; "Apologie," Essais, 468.

cannot participate" ("celles qui n'ont point de voix, ne laissent pas d'avoir pratique et communication mutuelle, de laquelle c'est nostre defaut que nous ne soyons participans").[20] Animal language and behavior remain outside the scope of human knowledge, just as does the divine; humans clothe these aspects of the world that they cannot fully grasp with human qualities, but these qualities, which may seem to link us to the animal or the divine, actually prevent our fully understanding either.

Montaigne's discussion of elephant religion is placed at the center of a long discussion of animal capacities and their superiority to human ones, which begins with the following statement: "Presumption is our natural and original malady. The most vulnerable and frail of all creatures is man, and at the same time the most arrogant" ("La presomption est nostre maladie naturelle et originelle. La plus calamiteuse est fraile de toutes les creatures, c'est l'homme, et quant et quant la plus orgueilleuse").[21] The declared subject of this discussion is the resemblance between humans and animals, so many pages are spent enumerating qualities that humans and animals have in common. Yet Montaigne frequently gives animals the advantage in these comparisons—for example, when he presents tales of animal medicine. He points out that elephants can remove javelins and darts from their own and others' bodies with less pain than humans can and asks,

> Why do we not say likewise that that is science and wisdom? For to assert, to disparage them, that it is solely by the instruction and tutelage of nature that they know this, is not to take away from them the claim to science and wisdom; it is to attribute it to them by a better reason than to ourselves, because of the honor of so sure a schoolmistress.[22]

> [Pourquoy ne disons nous de mesmes que c'est science et prudence? Car d'alleguer, pour les deprimer, que c'est par la seule instruction et maistrise de nature qu'elles le sçavent, ce n'est pas leur oster le tiltre de science et de prudence: c'est la leur attribuer à plus forte raison que à nous, pour l'honneur d'une si certaine maistresse d'escolle.][23]

---

[20] Montaigne, "Apology," *Essays*, 343–44; "Apologie," *Essais*, 468.
[21] Montaigne, "Apology," *Essays*, 331; "Apologie," *Essais*, 452.
[22] Montaigne, "Apology," *Essays*, 339.
[23] Montaigne, "Apology," *Essays*, 463.

Natural knowledge is thus not inferior to human knowledge and reason; in fact, it seems to function better in many circumstances.

Animals are not inferior to humans but are at the very least their equals. They have their own perspective on the world. The opening lines of Montaigne's discussion of animals are followed closely by Montaigne's famous observation about his cat: "Quand je me jouë à ma chatte, qui sçait si elle passe son temps de moy plus que je ne fay d'elle" ("When I play with my cat, who knows if I am not a pastime to her more than she is to me?").[24] This perspective is presented as having its own value as well. Montaigne proceeds to give multiple examples of animal language, reason, and memory, citing the work of honeybees, swallows, and spiders as examples of natural knowledge that humans would do well to emulate.[25] After the example of the fox who can determine whether the ice is thick enough to walk on, he asserts that humans delude themselves when they think that this is merely instinct rather than "reason or inference."[26] So far, this argument has established that "there is more difference between a given man and a given man than between a given animal and a given man" ("il se trouve plus de différence de tel homme à tel homme que de tel animal à tel homme").[27] Montaigne presents a wide range of animals as equal to humans in reason, language, and skill, and he underscores these and other similarities between animals and humans.

But the suggestion of elephant religion takes us to a different place, even while Montaigne uses human forms of representation to discuss the inscrutability of animals' inner lives. As noted previously, Montaigne argues against the assumption that our lack of knowledge reflects a lack in animals themselves: "because we do not see any such signs in other animals, we cannot thereby prove that they are without religion and cannot grasp any part of what is hidden from us." This argument moves in two directions. As in "Of Cannibals,"[28] where Montaigne suggests that Europeans cannot even look upon the inhabitants of the Western Hemisphere without overlaying their culture upon indigenous culture, thereby occluding that which they seek to know, so he hints here that humans make assumptions about animals based on their own limited knowledge; these assumptions misrepresent that which

---

[24] Montaigne, "Apology," *Essays*, 331; "Apologie," *Essais*, 452. Note that Jacques Derrida echoes this exchange in his essay "The Animal That Therefore I Am (More to Follow)," *Critical Inquiry* 28, no. 2 (Winter 2002): 369–418. But he is very much focused on his situation as a philosopher, rather than on what his cat's perspective might be.

[25] Montaigne, "Apology," *Essays*, 332–33; "Apologie," *Essais*, 455.

[26] Montaigne, "Apology," *Essays*, 337; "Apologie," *Essais*, 460.

[27] Montaigne, "Apology," *Essays*, 342; "Apologie," *Essais*, 466.

[28] Montaigne, "Apology," *Essays*, 150–59; "Apologie," *Essais*, 202–17.

cannot be represented in the animals, creating an illusion of knowledge about something we cannot possibly know. The image of grasping (*prendre* in the French) is a crucial element of this point; this image will return at the end of the essay in an assessment of humans' potential for knowledge and for rising above their own limitations:

> Nor can man raise himself above himself and humanity; for he can see only with his own eyes, and seize only with his own grasp.
>
> He will rise, if God by exception lends him a hand; he will rise by abandoning and renouncing his own means, and letting himself be raised and uplifted by purely celestial means.[29]

> [Ny que l'homme se monte au dessus de soy et de l'humanité: car il ne peut voir que de ses yeux, ny saisir que de ses prises. Il s'eslevera si Dieu lui preste extraordinairement la main; il s'eslevera, abandonnant et renonçant à ses propres moyens, et se laissant hausser et soubslever par les moyens purement celestes.][30]

In Augustinian fashion, Montaigne sees the world (and God) as beyond human understanding, requiring humans to seek divine aid in order to grasp the world around them. This aid is not certain (hence the hypothetical "si Dieu lui preste extraordinairement la main"), but without it humans cannot have comprehensive knowledge of the world.

This view of nature can serve as a corrective to notions of relationality that focus on the entwinement of human and animal existence and that mostly use examples of domesticated animals or animals deemed worthy of conservation to illustrate the concept. Much of animal studies is dominated by the human perspective, focusing on animals who are of use or interest to us. It is hard, if not impossible, to untangle our understanding of animals from those uses and interests. For Montaigne, it seems crucial for humankind to understand that animals have an existence that plays out well beyond our knowledge of them. Nature is certainly profoundly affected by humanity's presence—and was even in the early modern period—but in the absence of humans, Montaigne suggests, nature would continue to exist and to function in ways that we cannot imagine. By linking this nature that exists beyond

---

[29] Montaigne, "Apology," *Essays*, 457.
[30] Montaigne, "Apologie," *Essais*, 604.

human interests, desires, use, and knowledge to the divine, Montaigne suggests the value of the animal natures that we cannot grasp, even while underscoring the impossibility of understanding God. If humans were not to see themselves as the measure of all things, if they were to decenter themselves from creation, perhaps they would better understand the nature of that creation and treat it with greater care. Elephant theologians could teach us much, if we were capable of listening.

Bibliography

Derrida, Jacques. "The Animal That Therefore I Am (More to Follow)." *Critical Inquiry* 28, no. 2 (Winter 2002): 369–418.

Erickson, Jacob J. "The Apophatic Animal: Toward a Negative Zootheological Imago Dei." In *Divinanimality: Animal Theory, Creaturely Theology*, edited by Stephen D. Moore, 88–99. New York: Fordham University Press, 2014.

Fudge, Erica. *Brutal Reasoning: Animals, Rationality, and Humanity in Early Modern England*. Ithaca, NY: Cornell University Press, 2006.

Haraway, Donna. *When Species Meet*. Minneapolis: University of Minnesota Press, 2007.

Linzey, Andrew. *Animal Theology*. London: SCM Press, 1994.

Linzey, Andrew. *Why Animal Suffering Matters: Philosophy, Theology, and Practical Ethics*. Oxford: Oxford University Press, 2009.

Melehy, Hassan. "Montaigne and Ethics: The Case of Animals." *L'Esprit Créateur* 46, no. 1 (2006): 96–107.

Melehy, Hassan. "Silencing the Animals: Montaigne, Descartes, and the Hyperbole of Reason." *symplokē* 13, nos. 1–2 (2005): 263–82.

Montaigne, Michel de. *Essais*. Edited by Pierre Villey. Paris: Presses Universitaires de France, 1965.

Montaigne, Michel de. *Essays*. Translated by Donald Frame. Stanford, CA: Stanford University Press, 1965.

Moore, Stephen D., ed. *Divinanimality: Animal Theory, Creaturely Theology*. New York: Fordham University Press, 2014.

Nussbaum, Martha. *Frontiers of Justice: Disability, Nationality, Species Membership*. Cambridge, MA: Belknap Press, 2007.

Pliny. *Natural History*. Vols. 2 and 3. Translated by H. Rackham. Cambridge, MA: Harvard University Press, 1940–42.

Randall, Catharine. "Sixteenth-Century Animal Avatars in Montaigne and His Contemporaries." In Randall, *The Wisdom of Animals: Creatureliness in Early Modern French Spirituality*, 15–37. Notre Dame, IN: University of Notre Dame Press, 2014.

Singer, Peter. *Animal Liberation: A New Ethics for Our Treatment of Animals*. New York: Harper, 2009.

3

Thomas Tryon (1634–1703)

A Theology of Animal Enslavement

Adam Bridgen

> Thus all of us live in great slavery most part of our Lives, far below that generous Liberty wherein our great and good *Creator* had estated us by his *grand Charter of Nature*, and at last we dye both untimely and unwillingly, many of us cut off in Youth, or in the prime of our strength, to please the Pallates of extravagant People, whose Lusts nothing but *Flesh* can satisfie.
>
> —Thomas Tryon[1]

Introduction: An "Unlearned" Vegetarian

Born in rural Gloucestershire in 1634, the son of a building craftsman, Thomas Tryon was an unlikely but important thinker in the tradition of animal theology. Although one might consider his background an encumbrance, his working experiences—both in England and abroad—and the eclecticism of his influences contributed to a perspective that was quite different from the more traditionally learned individuals who were writing in the seventeenth century. Tryon was sent to work at the age of six spinning and carding wool, and he spent his teenage years managing a small flock of sheep, so it was only through constant industry that he managed to gain the most basic literacy.[2] As Tryon recalls in his autobiography, he scraped together

---

[1] Thomas Tryon, "The Complaint of the Cows and Oxen," in Thomas Tryon [Philotheos Physiologus, pseud.], *The Way to Health, Long Life, and Happiness* (London: Andrew Sowle, 1683), 502. In my transcriptions of Tryon's works, I have maintained the characteristic spelling, grammar, capitalization, and italicization of the originals. Any clarifying additions or alterations are indicated with square brackets, and abridgments with ellipses.

[2] For an account of Tryon's self-education and economic background, see Margaret Spufford, "First Steps in Literacy: The Reading and Writing Experiences of the Humblest Seventeenth-Century Spiritual Autobiographers," *Social History* 4, no. 3 (1979): 415–17; and Spufford, *Small*

money to buy primers and spelling books and even traded one of his sheep for writing lessons; eventually outgrowing this settled existence, at eighteen years of age he sold his flock for three pounds and set out for London.[3] He apprenticed himself to an Anabaptist hatmaker in Bridewell Dock and subsequently converted and joined his master's conventicle. He continued to combine work and study, voraciously reading books of "Astrology, . . . Physick, and several other Natural Sciences and Arts."[4]

At the age of twenty-three, Tryon experienced something that would change the course of his life and subsequently lead him to become one of the most prolific vegetarian activists of the early modern period.[5] He recalls, "the Voice of Wisdom continually and most powerfully called upon me for Separation and Self-denial," and "flying all Intemperance . . . I betook my self to Water only for Drink, and forbore eating any kind of Flesh or Fish."[6] Perceiving the connectedness of bodily and spiritual purity, moreover, he believed that this "abstemious clean way of living in Innocency mightily . . . fit and qualifie[d] [him] for the contemplation of our great Creator, and of his wonderful Works in Nature."[7] Having married "a sober young Woman, but of a contrary sentiment to [Tryon's], as to Diet, and [his] method of living,"[8] Tryon left for Barbados in 1663 and established a successful hatmaking business, remaining there for nearly six years in total.[9] On returning to his family in London, he continued to ply his trade and to study. He also continued to have "Dreams and Visions,"[10] and in 1682 he was reportedly gripped by "an inward Instigation to Write and Publish something . . . recommending to the World Temperance, Cleanness, and Innocency of Living; and admonishing

---

Books and Pleasant Histories: Popular Fiction and Its Readership in Seventeenth-Century England (London: Methuen, 1981), 41n40.

[3] Thomas Tryon, Some Memoirs of the Life of Mr. Tho. Tryon (London: T. Sowle, 1705), 7–17. The biography occupies pages 1–56, including eighteen additional pages, numbered 1–18, inserted between pages 34 and 35 detailing Tryon's philosophy. None of my citations are to these pages.

[4] Tryon, Memoirs, 25.

[5] Not that they would have recognized the term "vegetarian." This term was not coined until 1847, with the formation of the first vegetarian society, before which such a diet was most often referred to as "Pythagorean."

[6] Tryon, Memoirs, 26–27.

[7] Tryon, Memoirs, 30.

[8] Tryon, Memoirs, 39.

[9] Tryon, Memoirs, 40–42. Although Tryon says little about his colonial ventures in his biography, other sources reveal that soon after his return he established himself as a commissions agent, which involved securing alternative forms of credit for West Indian planters and finding markets for their goods. Richard B. Sheridan, Sugar and Slavery: An Economic History of the British West Indies, 1623–1775 (Barbados: Caribbean University Press, 1974), 287–88.

[10] Tryon, Memoirs, 53.

Mankind against Violence, Oppression, and Cruelty, either to their own Kind, or any inferior Creatures."[11] The apparent suddenness of his transformation into a writer notwithstanding, Tryon was hugely successful. His magnum opus, *The Way to Health, Long Life, and Happiness* (1683), was reprinted at least five times before 1700 and gained a substantial following, famously inspiring the Restoration playwright Aphra Behn to forbear wearing fur and Benjamin Franklin to give up meat.[12] Going to press "on average . . . once every four months,"[13] Tryon published at least twenty-seven books on a vast array of subjects—from brewing, cooking, domestic management, and medicine to dream interpretation, mystic philosophy, education, and trade. Nevertheless, he returned continually to the topic of vegetarianism, remaining committed to this peaceful dietary panacea until the end of his life.

Tryon continued to be published and read after his death in 1703, but was most notably rediscovered by a new wave of vegetarian campaigners at the end of the eighteenth century, and as late as 1883, he was acknowledged as "one of the best known of the seventeenth-century humane Hygienists," whose arguments were deemed "worthy of the most advanced thinkers of the present day."[14] Among twentieth-century scholars, Andrew Linzey led the charge in recognizing Tryon not only as a vegetarian but also for his explicit argument for animal rights, based on theological principles.[15] Much discussed by critics since, Tryon espoused a form of ethical vegetarianism that emphasized the sanctity of all beings created by God and the clear admonitions against violence and flesh-eating in scripture; his advocacy of

[11] Tryon, *Memoirs*, 54–55.

[12] Aphra Behn (c. 1640–89) composed a short poetic epistle in praise of Tryon, "On the Author of That Excellent Book Intituled The Way to Health, Long Life, and Happiness," first published in her *Miscellany, Being a Collection of Poems by Several Hands Together with Reflections on Morality* (London, 1685), 252–56. The same poem, signed "A. Behn," is prefixed to Tryon's *The Way to Make All People Rich* (1685) and also to the third edition of *The Way to Health* (1697). Benjamin Franklin (1706–90) read *The Way to Health* when he was sixteen and immediately became an adherent of the lifestyle recommendations of "Master Tryon." See Tristram Stuart's excellent chapter, "'This Proud and Troublesome Thing, Called Man': Thomas Tryon, the Brahmin of Britain," in his book *The Bloodless Revolution: Radical Vegetarians and the Discovery of India* (London: HarperPress, 2006), 63–64, 71, 244. Stuart speculates that Tryon may have met Behn in the Caribbean in the 1660s. A "Tryonist" sect is included among a list of forty different sects extant in England in Charles Gildon's *The Post-Boy Robb'd of His Mail: or, The Pacquet Broke Open*, 2nd ed. (London: B. Mills, 1706; first published 1692), 430.

[13] Stuart, *Bloodless Revolution*, 63.

[14] Howard Williams, *The Ethics of Diet: A Catena of Authorities Deprecatory of the Practice of Flesh-Eating* (Urbana: University of Illinois Press, 2003; first published 1883), 309–14. See also Stuart, *Bloodless Revolution*, 64.

[15] Andrew Linzey, *Animal Theology* (London: SCM Press, 1994), 20.

vegetarianism was further supported by his convictions about the ill effects of meat consumption on human health.[16] One of his central (and more esoteric) influences was the German mystic Jakob Böhme (1575–1624), whose belief in the continuous conflict between good and evil forces found expression in Tryon's "particularly gastronomic Beheminism,"[17] whereby foods contained transferable spiritual energies.[18] While maintaining the Edenic notion that "The eating of Flesh was not allowed or practised in the first and purer Ages," Tryon also described at length the physical and spiritual dangers of humans' defiling their being with "all kind of Beastial [sic] Passions, as Anger, Revenge, Covetuousness, Love and Hate, which dispositions and Passions of the Flesh, but especially the Blood, doth retain after such Animals are Killed."[19] For him flesh-eating was a patent violence that broke the Golden Rule—to do unto others as you would be done unto—and by "simpathetical Operation"[20] it awoke a "wrathful savage Nature" in humankind.[21]

Religiously motivated vegetarianism was not uncommon among sectarians after the English civil war, but Tryon presented a significant "intensification" of this ethos, placing it at the center of his millenarian worldview.[22] As Alan Rudrum notes, unlike previous thinkers, Tryon drew on both "Judaeo-Christian and . . . classical streams of influence."[23] He was particularly interested in the "Brahmins," or Hindu high priests, as Tristram Stuart explains. Believing that Pythagoras had inspired their vegetarianism, and thereby passed down the sacred vegetarian philosophy of the ancients, Tryon saw the Brahmins as "the purest remnants of the paradisal tradition left on

[16] Anita Guerrini, "A Diet for a Sensitive Soul: Vegetarianism in Eighteenth-Century Britain," Eighteenth-Century Life 23, no. 2 (1999): 34–36. For another overview of Tryon's vegetarianism, see Rod Preece, Sins of the Flesh: A History of Ethical Vegetarian Thought (Vancouver: University of British Columbia Press, 2008), 172–73. Tryon maintained the absolute sufficiency and salubriousness of a vegetarian diet, arguing that fruits and vegetables have beneficial nature and that milk and honey are—as the spontaneously produced "Fruit" of animals—particularly nourishing. Tryon, The Way to Health, 80.

[17] B. J. Gibbons, Gender in Mystical and Occult Thought: Behmenism and Its Development in England (Cambridge: Cambridge University Press, 1996), 115.

[18] Tryon maintained that "Food is the Substance of Each Man[']s Body and Spirit"—a more philosophically and spiritually inflected notion of the modern maxim "You are what you eat." Thomas Tryon, Tryon's Letters, Domestic and Foreign (London: Geo. Conyers, 1700), 5.

[19] Thomas Tryon, Healths Grand Preservative (London, 1682), 13, 15.

[20] Tryon, The Way to Health, 98.

[21] Tryon, The Way to Health, 348.

[22] Andrew Bradstock, Winstanley and the Diggers, 1649–1999 (London: Frank Cass, 2000), 56–57.

[23] Alan Rudrum, "Ethical Vegetarianism in Seventeenth Century Britain: Its Roots in Sixteenth Century Theological Debate," Seventeenth Century 18, no. 1 (2003): 80. Rudrum's article is a welcome exception to the common misconception that vegetarianism arose somewhat spontaneously and mysteriously in the seventeenth century, as a "radical" departure from philosophical and theological traditions.

earth," and accordingly "bowed down to them as the pre-eminent guardians of divine law."[24] In *The Way to Health*, Tryon recommended the Brahmins' model explicitly, explaining that "for many Ages have they led peaceable and harmless Lives, in *Unity* and *Amity* with the whole Creation, shewing all kind of *Friendship* and *Equality*, not only to those of their own *Species*, but to all other Creatures."[25] Viewing the blessed lives of the Brahmins, Tryon argued, "The very same, and far greater Advantages would come to pass amongst *Christians*, if they would cease from Contention, Oppression, and (what tends and disposes them thereunto), the killing of Beasts, and eating their Flesh and Blood, and in a short time humane [*sic*] Murders, and devilish Fewds and Cruelties amongst each other would abate, and perhaps scarce have a being."[26] Just as Tryon perceived flesh-eating as the source of humankind's "wrathful savage Nature," Brahminism fueled his belief that vegetarianism was, contrariwise, the way to humans' return to a more peaceful, even paradisal, state on earth.[27]

Most recent studies, however, have focused on Tryon's early antislavery tract, *Friendly Advice to the Gentlemen Planters of the East and West Indies* (1684).[28] Based on his experience in Barbados in the 1660s, this work consists of a "Brief Treatise" upon the "Principal Fruits and Herbs" of the island, followed by two chapters on slavery: "The Negro's Complaint of their *Hard Servitude*, and the Cruelties Practised upon them by divers of their Masters Professing *Christianity* in the *West-Indian Plantations*" and "A Discourse, in way of *Dialogue*, Between an *Ethiopean* or *Negro-Slave* And a Christian,

---

[24] Stuart, *Bloodless Revolution*, 65–66. See also 53, 58, and 68–69 for evidence of the praise of Brahminism among Tryon's contemporaries.

[25] Tryon, *The Way to Health*, 353–54.

[26] Tryon, *The Way to Health*, 354.

[27] Tryon, *The Way to Health*, 348. Tryon further elaborated these points in a pamphlet he published in the same year, *A Dialogue between an East-Indian Brackmanny or Heathen Philosopher, and a French Gentleman concerning the Present Affairs of Europe* (London: Andrew Sowle, 1683), which staged a Socratic debunking of the superiority of European culture. "Brackmanny" was a variant of "Brahman" that remained in use until the nineteenth century. See *Oxford English Dictionary*, s.v. "Brahmin/Brahman."

[28] Nigel Smith, "Enthusiasm and Enlightenment: Of Food, Filth, and Slavery," in *The Country and the City Revisited*, ed. Donna Landry, Gerald McLean, and Joseph P. Ward (Cambridge: Cambridge University Press, 1999), 106–18; Timothy Morton, "The Plantation of Wrath," in *Radicalism in British Literary Culture, 1650–1830*, ed. Timothy Morton and Nigel Smith (Cambridge: Cambridge University Press, 2002), 64–85; Daniel Carey, "Sugar, Colonialism, and the Critique of Slavery: Thomas Tryon in Barbados," *Studies on Voltaire and the Eighteenth Century* 9 (2004): 303–21; Philippe Rosenberg, "Thomas Tryon and the Seventeenth-Century Dimensions of Antislavery," *William and Mary Quarterly*, 3rd ser., 61, no. 4 (2004); 609–42; Kim F. Hall, "'Extravagant Viciousness': Slavery and Gluttony in the Works of Thomas Tryon," in *Writing Race across the Atlantic World*, ed. P. Beidler and G. Taylor (Basingstoke: Palgrave Macmillan, 2005), 93–111.

that was his *Master* in *America*."[29] These evocative disquisitions, articulated from the standpoint of enslaved persons, sought to emphasize the great evil of slavery, the abusiveness and even apostasy of the "Christian" masters, and the illogic of their denial of Africans' equality. Although steadier critiques of plantation slavery had been published in the late seventeenth century, Tryon's intervention was unparalleled in its force of argument and highly stylized, even dramatic approach—and also in its prescient perception of the connections between overconsumption and cruelty.[30] Several scholars have underlined the positive contribution of Tryon's vegetarian philosophy to his antislavery arguments: whether calling it his "extended trope" of "Carnage,"[31] his "vegetarian rhetoric of *macellogia*,"[32] or his "simile" of "carnivorous consumption,"[33] they have illuminated Tryon's representation of plantation labor as a kind of "vast Consumption or Destruction" in which enslaved African persons were transformed, metonymically, into "piece[s] of raw Flesh"— being effectively "Butcher'd" by their profit-seeking masters amid the intensive sugar-making process.[34] These readings have done much to illustrate the capaciousness of Tryon's ethical thinking and the important insights into other forms of exploitation that his vegetarian philosophy could offer. That said, such readings share an unfortunate tendency to oversimplify the relationship between his vegetarian and antislavery views, forgetting that Tryon's experience of Barbados occurred some twenty years before his writing about it. As literary analyses, often focused on one text, they suffer from a disciplinary and methodological isolation that prevents an understanding of the *theological* complexity of Tryon's outlook and how, conversely, colonial slavery also might have shaped his vegetarian philosophy.

This chapter is different and takes a more thoroughly theological approach to recover Tryon's unique conception of the carnivorous origins of both human *and* animal bondage and the consequent codependence of his antislavery and vegetarian views. I explore a much wider range of Tryon's works from across his publishing career, giving particular attention to his little-discussed husbandry manual, *The Country-Man's Companion* (1684).

---

[29] Thomas Tryon [Philotheos Physiologus, pseud.], *Friendly Advice to the Gentlemen Planters of the East and West Indies* (London: Andrew Sowle, 1684), 1–74, 75–145, 146–222.

[30] For another response to colonial slavery that may have been directly influenced by Tryon, see Jane Spencer, *Aphra Behn's Afterlife* (Oxford: Oxford University Press, 2000), 225–26.

[31] Smith, "Food, Filth, and Slavery," 114.

[32] Morton, "Plantation of Wrath," 73–74.

[33] Carey, "Sugar, Colonialism, and the Critique of Slavery," 315. For discussion of Tryon's suggestion of the "cannibalism" of consumers of sugar, see also Hall, "Slavery and Gluttony," 102–3.

[34] Respectively, these quotations are from Tryon, *Friendly Advice*, 142, 109, 111.

As I argue, Tryon conceived of a biblical model of animal enslavement that perceives humans' proud postlapsarian dissociation from their "fellow-creatures" and subsequent destruction of those beings for consumption as a quite literal prefigurement of racial slavery. While Tryon drew a parallel between the plantation system and carnivorism, I contend that his experience of colonial slavery also incited some of his most powerful arguments against the *particular* perfidiousness of humankind's anthropocentric divorcement from and domination over the animal kingdom. Drawing increasingly on a language of colonialism and slavery to indict humans' unthinking invasion of and injustice toward other creatures, Tryon eventually came to encapsulate the enslavement of nonhuman animals as, in fact, the "highest Bondage"— not only in the sense of the extremity of the injustice animals suffered under voracious, sinful humankind, but also because, as Tryon saw it, humans' own descent into enslaving their fellow people was a direct consequence of the carnivorous consumption that slavery so uncomfortably resembled.

The Bondage of the Flesh

The first research article dedicated exclusively to Thomas Tryon was published in 2004. In it, Philippe Rosenberg argued for the importance of understanding Tryon's antislavery views in a seventeenth-century intellectual context, in contrast to the conventional teleological representation of him as a "religious eccentric" or a "'radical' who either anticipated or failed to properly anticipate a mature form of abolitionism."[35] While Rosenberg's admirable analysis of *Friendly Advice* covers much new ground, establishing the congruence of Tryon's antislavery arguments with the writings of his contemporaries, the Puritan Richard Baxter, the Quaker George Fox, and the Anglican Morgan Godwyn, his strategic evasion of Tryon's own theological particularity is a conspicuous limitation. As I contend, it is impossible to appreciate the visionary complexity of Tryon's views on colonial slavery without first comprehending the much longer—and fleshier—biblical conception of human and animal bondage that he formulated in his early works.

With enslaved people "sold (like Beasts) to the Merchant,"[36] cursed like "*Damn'd Doggs*"[37] by their owners, and forced to work until their "Hands and

---

[35] Rosenberg, "Seventeenth-Century Dimensions of Antislavery," 614.
[36] Tryon, *Friendly Advice*, 82.
[37] Tryon, *Friendly Advice*, 85.

Arms are crusht to pieces"[38] in the sugar mills and "fierce boyling Syrups"[39] devour them whole—or else beaten until their "Bodies become like a piece of raw Flesh"[40]—the comparison to be drawn between colonial slavery and animal slaughter was made apparent by Tryon. Prefiguring these carnivorous parallels in *Friendly Advice*, however, is an enslaved person's own plaintive self-questioning as to how he and his countrymen arrived at such a sorry state. In a series of counterfactuals, the character indicates a much longer, more biblical history of slavery's genesis:

> We had never been snatcht from the Lands of our Nativity, never travers'd Liquid Mountains, nor journied through the Hazards of vast Seas, to be cast away on Land; never been brought in Fetters into new Worlds, nor made perpetual Slaves in Regions which neither we nor our fore-Fathers ever heard of before, if we had not first forsaken and violated that Law of our Creator which he had planted in us, and entred with our Wills into the Root of *Bitterness* and the *fierce Wrath*, whereby the *Savage Nature* got the dominion in the hearts of us, and our Ancestors, so that *Fury, Revenge, Covetousness, Pride, vain Glory* and *Intemperance* is never satisfied.[41]

With that cataclysmic "if," Tryon attributes the cause of African slavery to Africans' violation of the "Law of the Creator" and the entering of their "Wills into the Root of *Bitterness* and the *fierce Wrath*, whereby the *Savage Nature* got the dominion in [their] hearts." From this, the enslaved character argues, developed the infighting and instability of his homeland, which in turn rendered Africans vulnerable to the so-called Christians who purchased captives from their shores (and who had the "chiefest Crime in them, since they are the Tempters and Occasioners of it").[42] In his brief overview of *Friendly Advice* in 1966, David Brion Davis claimed that Tryon's equation of slavery with sin was a straightforward colonialist obfuscation, which unfairly blamed African enslavement on Africans' own "savage nature."[43] However, Tryon opposes precisely the stance that Davis charges him with. He not only sees renegade Christians as the drivers of transatlantic slavery

---

[38] Tryon, *Friendly Advice*, 89.
[39] Tryon, *Friendly Advice*, 90.
[40] Tryon, *Friendly Advice*, 109.
[41] Tryon, *Friendly Advice*, 80–81.
[42] Tryon, *Friendly Advice*, 83.
[43] David Brion Davis, *The Problem of Slavery in Western Culture* (Ithaca, NY: Cornell University Press, 1966), 373–74.

but also debunks the other popular religious justification for slavery, which was that Africans were the cursed "Lineage" of Ham and hence destined to be slaves.[44] Understanding Tryon's theological vegetarianism allows us to see that the "*Savage Nature*" he refers to in *Friendly Advice* is not any culturally specific sin but relates to the violent turn in all humankind's behavior—what he had termed the "wrathful savage Nature of Beasts"—that resulted from eating flesh.[45]

Of course, the notion that carnivorism led to human bloodshed was not unique to Tryon. As Diane McColley explains, Aristotle's justificatory connection of "human dominion over all nature" to "dominion over women, slaves, and nations"[46] had been roundly responded to by Pythagoras, who similarly linked "animal slavery and slaughter . . . to human slavery and slaughter, but as unjust practices."[47] Tryon's intellectual innovation, however, was to explain this association *biblically* and, in so doing, to create a more direct and historicized connection between violence to animals and violence to other humans. In his debut work, *Healths Grand Preservative*, Tryon uses scripture to establish the original, peaceful vegetarianism of Edenic man and also to explain the postlapsarian events that led to the gradual normalization of flesh-eating. Having cited Genesis 1:29 ("the fruit of a Tree yielding Seed, to you it shall be for Meat"), he argues that flesh-eating followed humankind's Fall and—proceeding unchecked—perpetuated humans' captivation to sin and their descent into ever greater violence against creation.[48] Tryon substantiates this claim with an extended reading of Exodus. Reinterpreting God's temporary allowance of flesh-eating amongst the wandering Israelites

[44] Tryon, *Friendly Advice*, 114. Tryon had earlier questioned, in a passage condemning the violent usurpation involved in the formation of heritable distinctions of "*Gentility* and *Nobility*," "are not all those Millions of Men and Women scattered over the Face of the whole Earth, descended from this one Man [Adam]? . . . Are we not then all [our] *own Couzens*? Our *Pedigree* the same, and equally Antient?" (*The Way to Health*, 387).

[45] Tryon, *The Way to Health*, 348. In this description of man's beastliness, Tryon did not mean to defame animals. As he subsequently states, "'tis no fit comparison to liken some sorts of cruel Men to savage Beasts, for thereby the poor dumb Creatures are abused; they do according to their kind, but Man was made for another Life, *viz*, to live in the power and operation of the divine Principle of God's eternal *Light* and *Love*, but he has degenerated from his first state of Innocency, and many men by giving way to Cruelty and Violence are become so bad, that they cannot be compared to any Creature in Nature, but merely to *Devils*" (*The Way to Health*, 383–84).

[46] Diane Kelsey McColley, *Poetry and Ecology in the Age of Milton and Marvell* (Aldershot: Ashgate, 2007), 172.

[47] McColley, *Poetry and Ecology*, 174. Pythagoras was an acknowledged influence on Tryon. In the appendix to *A Dialogue between an East-Indian Brackmanny . . . and a French Gentleman*, he extracts from Book XV of George Sandy's translation of Ovid's *Metamorphoses* (7th ed., 1678), which offered a summary of Pythagoras's philosophy. The extract ends, "When limbs of *slaughtered* Beasts become your Meat, / Then think and know, that you your *Servants Eat*" (22).

[48] Tryon, *Healths Grand Preservative*, 13.

as a direct response to their "Murmur[s]" (that under the Egyptians they had had plenty of meat), Tryon suggests that the Israelites remained enslaved to their appetite for flesh after they were freed from Egypt.[49] As he states, having thus "awakened the dark wrathful powers" in themselves by eating meat, humans entered a vicious cycle of self-brutalization: "the more ignorant and sottish people are, the more they desire to eat Flesh, and the more Flesh they eat, the more Sottish, Ignorant, and Brutish they become."[50] By adopting a vegetarian diet, therefore, humankind "avoid[s] those many torturing diseases of Body, and distracting perturbations of Mind, to which the rest of the world necessarily enslave themselves."[51] In this nexus, the slaughter of animals for their flesh precipitates the enslavement of humankind's will to their own fleshly desires. Unsurprisingly, therefore, Tryon clearly links vegetarianism to human liberation in his revisitation of Exodus in *The Way to Health*:

> for the *Wilderness* represents this *World*, which all must pass through and deny themselves the *Vanities, Oppression* and *Violences* thereof, or else they cannot enter the *Holy Land*, but must fall in the Wilderness; for those that have, through the divine Power of the Lord, escaped the hands of the *Aegyptians*, and are got clear of the *Land of Bondage*, and have left *Pharaoh* and his Host swallowed up in the Red-Sea, ought not to *long* or *lust* after the *Violences* and *Flesh-Pots* of the *Land of Vanity*, but to continue in the *Spirit of Meekness, Love, Humanity, Self-denial,* and *to do unto all Creatures as a man would be done unto himself.*[52]

While offering in the shape of temperance a present remedy for humans' physical/spiritual corruption, Tryon illustrates the unfortunate biblical fact: following their escape, the Israelites' enslavement to the luxurious Egyptians was transformed into a more internalized captivity to their similarly corrupted, fleshly appetites.[53] What then connects this flesh-eating to

[49] Tryon, *Healths Grand Preservative*, 14.

[50] Tryon, *Healths Grand Preservative*, 20–21. For a comparable reading of Exodus, see Norm Phelps, *The Dominion of Love: Animal Rights according to the Bible* (New York: Lantern Books, 2002), 102.

[51] Tryon, *Healths Grand Preservative*, 22.

[52] Tryon, *The Way to Health*, 352.

[53] In this innovative location of humans' descent into carnivorism as a result of the Exodus, Tryon subtly differs from other sectarian thinkers, such as Roger Crab (1621–80), who took the more straightforward view that "meat-eating was the cause rather than a consequence of the Fall," as Alan Rudrum notes in "Ethical Vegetarianism," 80. As a London hatmaker, vegan, and fellow Boehminist, Crab, it has been suggested, may have been Tryon's "vegetarian guru"; Stuart, *Bloodless Revolution*,

humankind's more worldly enslavement is the flood of violence that extends beyond carnivorism to corrupt human relations also. As Tryon repeats, "all kinds of Violence, whether towards our own kind or inferior Creatures, arises from the *awakened Wrath* in *Nature.* . . . the same does by *Simile* excite the fierce Wrathful principle in the man that kills and eats [animals], and renders him prompt and ready for any Acts of Cruelty, or Oppression."[54] The exploitation of animals for their flesh sets off a domino effect by which the bodily labor of the multitude is extracted in order to satiate the extravagant tastes of a powerful elite, such as on the Sabbath, when "*English* Belly-Slaves and Gluttons make their Servants do more work then [*sic*] any other day of the Week, as to dressing of Food."[55] Requiring significant labor and land for its support, the continual eating of animal flesh aggravates various human inequalities: further attacking English "*Belly-Slaves*," Tryon states that "most or all those good Creatures which they spend on their Lusts, and to gratify their wicked Inclinations, are gotten by their oppressing both Man and Beast, [and] eating and drinking the blood of the poor."[56] Humans' proud assumption of the disposability of animals thus gives birth to the powerful, acquisitive drives that justify the similar exploitation of their fellow people. In short, the human species' inward slavery to its appetites enslaves the "whole Creation."[57]

This connection is made quite explicit in *Friendly Advice*. In one of many statements directly comparing human and animal suffering, the enslaved character articulates precisely Tryon's view that it is through humans' presumption of superiority over "inferior Beings" that "Man" becomes, by extension, "A *Tyrant*, a *Plague*, a *professed Enemy, Hunter, Betrayer, Destroyer* and *Devourer of all the Inhabitants of Earth, Air* and *Water*, and to those of his own kind no less fierce and cruel."[58] Not apprehending the significance of Tryon's unusual, biblical conception of the way in which humankind's cruelty in fact proceeded from its violence to animals, twentieth-century critics have

---

61. For other thinkers connecting the eating of flesh to postlapsarian violence, see McColley, *Poetry and Ecology*, 181. As I explore later in this discussion, Tryon's view of humans' *prior* divorcement from animals through their loss of the original, Adamic language (described in the Tower of Babel story) adds another layer to his etiology of the origins of humans' carnivorism and violence.

54 Thomas Tryon [Philotheos Physiologus, pseud.], *The Way to Make All People Rich: or, Wisdoms Call to Temperanae [sic] and Frugality* (London: Andrew Sowle, 1685), 46.
55 Tryon, *Healths Grand Preservative*, 22.
56 Tryon, *The Way to Health*, 384-85.
57 Tryon, *The Way to Health*, 385.
58 Tryon, *Friendly Advice*, 79.

often been puzzled by the "confusing jumble of inconsistencies" that *Friendly Advice* apparently posed—specifically in view of the author's principled rejection of slavery and yet his ultimate suggestion that it could be reformed by instilling temperance and humility in planters.[59] While this criticism has been sensitively responded to by Rosenberg, I suggest that taking a more theological view of Tryon's vegetarianism further corroborates the in fact *consistent* nature of his suggested reforms.[60] It was congruent with his Boehminist-influenced ideas about human sin and perfection—as an ongoing consequence of *diet*—to imagine that inculcating "Moderation and Compassion" in planters was a means of removing the root cause of violence and inspiring, from the ground up, harmonious relations in the New World colonies.[61] This perspective has advantages and disadvantages, of course. Tryon's conception of slavery's carnivorous origins offered him a powerful language with which to expose and attack the loathsome way in which African peoples were used as if mere "Beasts"; however, his literalization of this connection within a much broader, historical, Judeo-Christian framework—of humanity's sinful captivity to its fleshly appetites—led Tryon to approach slavery in a manner that homogenizes its various actors and tends toward an idealistically theo-centric solution.

Speciesism through the Lens of Colonial Slavery

Tryon's vegetarian philosophy undoubtedly contributed to the distinctive style of his arguments against colonial slavery. What is strikingly absent in scholarship, however, is an account of how his experience of colonial slavery also influenced his arguments against violence to animals. Even prior to the publication of *Friendly Advice*, Tryon's biblical account of humans' carnivorism and the subsequent plight of nonhuman creatures frequently

---

[59] Davis, *The Problem of Slavery*, 372.

[60] Rosenberg makes sense of the apparent incongruence of Tryon's more emancipatory arguments and his allowance of certain forms of bonded labor, explaining that in early modern understandings of slavery, by analogy to domestic service, "one could be dependent, and therefore unfree, while still not being a slave." Rosenberg, "Seventeenth-Century Dimensions of Antislavery," 635–36. In Tryon's *Friendly Advice*, the slave indeed appears to isolate cruelty, rather than unfreedom, as the defining characteristic of slavery, protesting to the planters: "You practise all sorts of *Cruelty*, not only on the inferior Creatures, but also on those of your *own Kind*, else what makes us your *Slaves*, and to be thus Lorded and Tyrannized over by you?" (162).

[61] Tryon, *Friendly Advice*, 141. Tryon's dietary advice was directed at consumers as much as planters, as Kim Hall explores in her discussion of his arguments against sugar-eating. Hall, "Slavery and Gluttony," 99–100.

drew upon a language of slavery; this was mainly metaphorical but also often literal, as in the "great slavery"[62] to "*Egyptian* Masters"[63] protested in "The Complaint of the Cows and Oxen" in *The Way to Health*. Though this language was drawn from the Bible—the primary source for popular ideas about slavery until the seventeenth century—in 1684 Tryon began to incorporate a more contemporary, colonial idiom when referring to the suffering of animals, which had a vastly different significance as a rhetorical mode. In the same year as *Friendly Advice to the Gentlemen Planters*, Tryon published a husbandry manual, *The Country-Man's Companion*.[64] There are clear parallels between the two works: while *Friendly Advice* presented itself as a guide to the good management of West Indian plantations, *The Country-Man's Companion* was purportedly concerned with the care of domestic livestock. Tryon also concludes *The Country-Man's Companion* with essays of a more moralizing nature, the last of which is "*The Complaints of the Birds and Fowls of Heaven to their Creator, for the Oppressions and Violences most Nations on the Earth do offer unto them, particularly the People called* Christians, *lately settled in several Provinces in* America."[65] Immediately following "The Planter[']s Speech To his Neighbours & Country-men . . . And to all such as have Transported themselves into *New-Colonies* for the sake of a quiet Life"—which included a vegetarian recommendations—this final chapter stages Tryon's argument against violence to animals within an explicitly anticolonialist framework.[66] Bearing evident similarities to "The Negro's Complaint," "The Complaints of the *Birds*" sought to persuade settlers, but also Anglophone audiences more generally, of the sheer irrationality, injustice, and perfidy of humankind's wanton destruction of their fellow creatures.

Jennifer Clement has recently discussed *The Country-Man's Companion* as the culmination of a theological "re-evaluation" of humankind's presumed self-importance in the early modern period. In compelling readings of Tryon's theorization (and subsequent dramatization) of animal language, she

---

[62] Tryon, *The Way to Health*, 502.

[63] Tryon, *The Way to Health*, 500.

[64] References within the text of *Friendly Advice* indicate it was published shortly after *The Country-Man's Companion*. See Geoffrey Plank, "Thomas Tryon, Sheep and the Politics of Eden," in *Cultural and Social History* 14 (2017): 12, 16 n. 81.

[65] Thomas Tryon [Philotheos Physiologus, pseud.], *The Country-Man's Companion, or a New Method of Ordering Horses & Sheep* (London: Andrew Sowle, 1684), 141–73.

[66] Tryon, *Country-Man's Companion*, 100–141. As a matter of fact, these two chapters were subsequently published together, as [Thomas Tryon], *The Planter's Speech to His Neighbours & Country-Men of Pennsylvania, East & West-Jersey and to all such as have Transported themselves into New-Colonies for the sake of a quiet retired Life. To which is added, The Complaints of Our Supra-Inferior Inhabitants* (London: Andrew Sowle, 1684).

argues that he extends this emphasis on humility into the sphere of human–animal relations and hence calls for a significant reconceptualization—and reconfiguration—of the hierarchies that had previously relegated animals to an inferior and even alternate plane to human beings.[67] While this positioning of Tryon in an existing and less stolidly anthropocentric tradition is salutary, avoiding his customary characterization as a religious "radical" or "eccentric," Clement's analysis nevertheless falls into the trap of isolating his vegetarian views from his experience of colonial slavery. It is not that Clement is unaware of Tryon's use of "terms that link tyranny over animals with tyranny over other humans," but she limits this to an "implicit connection between absolutist political philosophy and abuses of animals"[68]—which was a topical, though not uncontroversial, strategy at the time. Less implicit, I suggest, is Tryon's inventive use of a colonial idiom in his arguments against violence to animals. As I argue, in "The Complaints of the *Birds*" in particular, Tryon seeks to draw a direct comparison between European domination over animals and New World colonization.

Simply put, *The Country-Man's Companion* attempts for animals what *Friendly Advice* seeks to do for enslaved persons, taking on a supremacist ideology that was based on falsely construed physical and mental differences. Tryon first subverts notions about the inferiority of animals, foregrounding their marked similarity to humans before offering a biblical account of how humans' own sinful arrogance prevented them from appreciating this important similitude. His chapter entitled "Sheep, *their Natures, and the best way to secure them from the* Rot *and other Inconveniences, and preserve them Healthy*" includes a section on the "*Language of Sheep*," in which Tryon (drawing on his days as a shepherd) describes the sophistication of ovine communication and attributes this to their possession of a divine, original language—which post-Fall and post-Babel "Man," by contrast, "hath fooled away by suffering his Mind and Desires to enter into the evil, unclean, violent, savage, wrathful Nature."[69] As Clement concludes, "by representing sheep as, potentially, speaking subjects capable of forming communities, Tryon pushes his readers to also see themselves as part of a wider community of God's creatures, stressing what sheep share with humans rather than how they differ."[70] Moreover, by crediting animals with language, Tryon opposed

---

[67] Jennifer Clement, "Thomas Tryon's Reformed Stewardship," in *Reading Humility in Early Modern England* (London: Farnham: Ashgate, 2015), 108.

[68] Clement, "Reformed Stewardship," 117–18.

[69] Tryon, *The Country-Man's Companion*, 61.

[70] Clement, "Reformed Stewardship," 116.

the traditional philosophical view that asserted that speech, and by association reason, was unique to humankind; revealing himself instead as an early
"theriophilist" who sought to subvert this egotism, he insisted that animals
possessed perfections that humans had squandered.[71] While a handful of
thinkers in this period had begun to consider animal communication, one
of the most pressing concerns of Tryon's contemporaries was the establishment of a universal language scheme that would overcome the degraded
and scattered nature of human tongues post-Babel.[72] With his perception of
the perfections of *animal* language and its basis in simplicity, cooperation,
and fellow-feeling, Tryon's contribution is thus more moral than mathematical, suggesting that it is only through humans' renewed attention to other
creatures that they may recover the natural language they have lost.

This emphasis on the intelligent, inner lives of animals is a theme that
preoccupies *The Country-Man's Companion*. In the preface Tryon describes
the actual fallaciousness of humankind's denial of the language and reason of
animals, rebuking those who with

> *a proud disdainful Scorn call [them]* Dumb Creatures *and* Brute Beasts,
> *though yet they will have a Voice to cry against their Oppressions; and if all
> things were rightly weighed, the* former ["Man"] *would appear much more*
> Brutish *(that is, more Absurd, and acting more contrary to the pure Dictates
> of unbyass'd and indepraved [sic] Nature) than the* latter . . . [being] *grave*
> Bearded Animals *that pride themselves with the empty Title of* Rational
> Souls, *whilst the whole bent of their Lives and Actings is Diametrically oppo-
> site to all the Precepts of* Reason, *and even of* common Sense.[73]

Much like the approach taken in "The Negro's Complaint," Tryon exposes
the hypocrisy of humans' violent dominion over other intelligent beings,

---

[71] Clement, "Reformed Stewardship," 117. Following in the footsteps of numerous philosophers—
perhaps most prominently, Aristotle—Descartes had provided the most recent location of human
exceptionality in language, stating, "Nor should we think, as did certain of the ancients, that the
beasts speak, although we do not understand their language; for if this were true, then since they have
many organs related to ours, they could also easily make themselves understood by us as well as by
others like themselves." René Descartes, *Discourse on Method, Optics, Geometry, and Meteorology*,
trans. P. J. Olscamp, rev. ed. (Indianapolis: Hackett, 2001), 47.

[72] McColley, *Poetry and Ecology*, 185–89; see also Richard Serjeantson, "The Passions and Animal
Language 1540–1700," *Journal of the History of Ideas* 62, no. 3 (2001): 425–44. For an interesting
account of the ubiquity of "Babel reversal" schemes in the second half of the seventeenth century,
see Robert Markley, *Fallen Languages: Crises of Representation in Newtonian England, 1660–1740*
(Ithaca, NY: Cornell University Press, 1993), 63–94.

[73] Tryon, *The Country-Man's Companion*, A3r.

which he perceived as proceeding, ironically, from the corruption of humankind's *own* rational capacities. Reflecting the imagined dumbness and brutality of beasts back upon their accusers, Tryon deftly invalidates the purported basis of humans' superiority over animals. In "The Negro's Complaint," the enslaved character begins, "*Complaints* and *Lamentations* are the natural Language of the *Miserable*,"[74] explaining that they are both irrepressible overflowings and attempts to ease suffering by bringing the suffering to the attention of others. The enslaved character laments, however, that despite this inborn communicativeness, the "Extremity of [enslaved people's] *Calamities*" nevertheless "surpass[es] all belief," and any complaint, struggling to find sympathetic listeners, falls ultimately on the deaf ears of planters, who rather deem it "sufficient cause for addition of *Stripes*."[75] In this, and likewise in his description of humankind's resistance to imagining the sentient, subjective states of animals, Tryon was in fact formulating an early notion of the *differend*, a form of epistemic injustice whereby an injured party is "divested of the means to argue" and hence is given no "means to prove the damage."[76] Thus, while in "The Negro's Complaint" the persona concludes that "our Masters have built their *Babel*, and fortified themselves,"[77] here Tryon uses this Old Testament etiological myth as a means of directly attributing humans' unwarranted divorcement from animals to their own errant pride.

While the framing of *The Country-Man's Companion* bears only an incidental resemblance to the structure and approach of *Friendly Advice*, it is in the "Complaints of the *Birds*" that Tryon's anticolonialist conception of animal abuse becomes most apparent. As I argue, Tryon's understanding of the ideological structures of racial slavery contributes significantly to his attempt to destabilize the anthropocentric assumptions underpinning humankind's dominion over animals. While Clement provides an excellent close reading of this chapter, it is also clear that Tryon's argument gained rhetorical power through its colonial frame of reference, considering the skepticism with which transatlantic slavery was generally thought of at the time.[78] Overall, by

---

[74] Tryon, *Friendly Advice*, 75.

[75] Tryon, *Friendly Advice*, 77. For a good discussion of Tryon's "question[ing] the validity of sign systems," see Morton, "Plantation of Wrath," 72–73.

[76] Jean-François Lyotard, *The Differend: Phrases in Dispute*, trans. Georges Van Den Abbeele (Minneapolis: University of Minnesota Press, 1988), 5–9.

[77] Tryon, *Friendly Advice*, 136.

[78] Not only was there significant opposition to slavery in the late seventeenth century, but its relative newness as an institution also meant that certain categories we now considered fixed were in fact more fluid. Rosenberg, "Seventeenth-Century Dimensions of Antislavery," 614.

a direct comparison to Christian humans' violence toward their own species and to brutalized African slaves in particular, "The Complaints of the *Birds*" sought to denaturalize humans' presumptive dominion over animals and reveal it as a blatant injustice. Asking "What *Law*" they could have broken to deserve such treatment, the birds make a comparison of their own innocence relative to sinful humankind:

> Sure we are, we have not made our selves more *Rich* than our Neigbours, nor endeavour'd to establish to our selves a *Tyranny* over them: We have not taken away their *Priviledges*, nor laid *Cities* and *Countries* waste: We are not guilty of Burning of *Towns*, nor Deflowring of *Virgins*, nor Ravishing *Matrons*, nor of Slaying *Old Men*, or carrying away Captive the *Young*: We do not gather our selves into Troops to destroy those of our own kind; nor have we at any time *Plundered* them, or haled them into loathsom *Prisons*: Nor are we offended with each other, because our *Feathers* are not all of a *length* or of the same *colour*.[79]

It is no coincidence that Tryon ends on a subtle reference to discrimination based on color. In "The Negro's Complaint" he articulated expertly the workings of racism, which he would have perceived firsthand in midcentury Barbados.[80] In alluding to color, Tryon brings to mind the kind of artificial distinctions thrust between different cultures and ethnicities that became the basis of discriminatory and dominating treatment. Tryon also employs an additional, more popular language of enslavement in referring to bird-hunters as "Trepan[s]"—a term that described the notorious people-stealers who tricked, harried, and even forced children and young adults onto boats bound for America to sell them as indentured servants (or "bond-slaves," as they were more soberly known).[81]

---

[79] Tryon, *The Country-Man's Companion*, 146–47.

[80] Tryon's stay in Barbados from 1663 to 1669 makes him an important witness to the development of a specifically race-based form of slavery. Barbados was one of the first places to rely almost exclusively on slaves taken from Africa, whose term was perpetual and whose progeny became the chattel property of their owners. In 1661 the Master and Servant Act of Barbados was passed, which was the first of a number of laws that accorded specific privileges to white indentured servants in an attempt to disrupt the "potential axis of solidarity between them . . . and growing numbers of black slaves." Robin Blackburn, *The Making of New World Slavery: From the Baroque to the Modern, 1492–1800* (New York: Verso, 1997), 322–26. Accordingly, as this system developed, ideas about African subhumanity increasingly served the interests of planters.

[81] Tryon, *The Country-Man's Companion*, 148, 153. See John Wareing, "'Violently Taken Away or Cheatingly Duckoyed': The Illicit Recruitment in London of Indentured Servants for the American Colonies, 1645–1718," *London Journal* 26, no. 2 (2001): 1–22; Matthew Pursell, "'That Odious Name

While Tryon makes a comparison between the plight of animals and the plight increasingly of the poor, uneducated, and "uncivilized" peoples of the world, swept up into the transcontinental violence that was European colonization, he also seems to indicate the greater *embeddedness* of anthropocentric assumptions and hence suggests a difference, or intensification, in the silencing and suffering imposed upon animals.[82] In "The Negro's Complaint" the enslaved character wonders how planters could "extend no Compassion to us, who are of the same Species with themselves."[83] While meaning no harm by this statement, the character inadvertently speaks of a kind of contract or special privilege agreed to between humans—they were of a different order from animals and therefore deserved protective treatment. The enslaved character's hope, though ultimately confounded, inadvertently belies the plight of the absent "other"—the "Beasts" to whom enslaved people were so often contemptuously compared. Explicating this logic, in "The Complaints of the *Birds*," the interlocutors are, by contrast, not at all surprised by their treatment. They elegiacally lament, "But why should we wonder at this Violence and Unnaturalness of depraved men, seeing that they do not scruple to do almost the same to those of their own Species?"[84] Evidently, colonial slavery—more so than other, less explicit forms of socioeconomic oppression—revealed not only the similar structure of animal oppression but also its greater profundity. In Tryon's view, encapsulated within "The Complaints of the *Birds*," the only hope is urging humankind to "cease from Cruelty, first against those of thine own kind, and then thou mayst come to see and abhor the Error of oppressing thy Inferiors."[85] It is precisely this process, in fact, that Tryon's seeks to promote through his comparative, anticolonialist approach.

Sold': Narratives of the Servant Trade," *Coriolis: Interdisciplinary Journal of Maritime Studies* 5, no. 1 (2015): 37.

[82] In 1685 the Quaker John Field published a point-by-point rebuttal to Tryon's vegetarian philosophy and practical recommendations in *The Absurdity & Falseness of Thomas Trion's Doctrine* (London: Tho. Hawkins, 1685). Although he does not mention the comparable "Negro's Complaint," Field took particular issue with the "Feigned or fictitious Complaint of the Birds to their Creator," (21) quoting or writing (through an assumed persona, "B. A."): *"Did Thomas e're dumb Creatures hear complain / And speak as Balaam's Ass? or did he feign / The Jack-daw's Story, and the many cries? / They're either true, or else fictitious Lies"* (A4v).

[83] Tryon, *Friendly Advice*, 88.

[84] Tryon, *The Country-Man's Companion*, 150.

[85] Tryon, *The Country-Man's Companion*, 170.

Conclusion: Articulating Animal Enslavement

'Tis Man only that hath violated all Goodness and Sobriety, and by the Ministration of the Evil Powers has destroyed the Laws and Privileges of all other Creatures as well as his own, enslaving them in the highest Bondage.

—Thomas Tryon[86]

Tryon was an important precursor to an increasingly intersectional discussion of animals, servants, and slaves in ensuing decades and proves wrong the notion that "the most sustained works advocating humane treatment [of animals] were produced in the last quarter of the eighteenth century."[87] While the movement to abolish the slave trade in the late eighteenth century influenced a range of other humanitarian concerns, in particular the anticruelty movement, the importance of race-based slavery to reconsidering humans' treatment of animals reached back much further—indeed to the institution's earliest emergence. Tryon's experience of slavery in the 1660s seems to have been decisive both in his conception of humans' treatment of animals and in his emphasis on the necessity of designating animals *rights* in order to protect them from the "unparallel'd Barbarity" of humankind.[88] In Tryon's mocked-up *Transcript of Several Letters* (1695), in his "First Letter to the Indian King," Pythagoras begins, "The Gods have made your Majesty a King, Soveraign of a Numerous People, committed to your care, to be Preserved and Maintain'd, not to be Pillaged and Destroyed. So it is with the Universe, if the Creatures are our Subjects, they are not our Slaves."[89] Tryon extends the notion of *jus regium* in political relationships to humankind's relationship with nonhuman animals. As the Indian king later states, animals must be protected from humans' violence either because of a "natural Right of being exempted from our Power, or from some mutual Contract and Stipulation agreed to betwixt Man and them."[90] Melding the language of social contract theory with antislavery rhetoric, Tryon broaches one of the curious and uncomfortable paradoxes of the early English empire—the

---

[86] [Thomas Tryon], *Averroeana: Being A Transcript of Several Letters from Averroes . . . Also Several Letters from Pythagoras to the King of India* (London: T. Sowle, 1695), 89.

[87] Ingrid H. Tague, "Companions, Servants, or Slaves? Considering Animals in Eighteenth-Century Britain," *Studies in Eighteenth-Century Culture* 39 (2010): 115.

[88] Tryon, *The Country-Man's Companion*, 151.

[89] Tryon, *Transcript of Several Letters*, 83.

[90] Tryon, *Transcript of Several Letters*, 149.

emergence of racial slavery in the New World colonies at the same time as the development of a powerful ideology of individual liberty in England itself.[91] Perceiving humans' historical "Invasion" of free-living animals' environments and humans' "Injustice" toward those animals once domesticated, Tryon articulates a reformed view of human–animal relations that is indissociable from his egalitarian, anticolonialist views.[92]

Tryon must be situated among the various strands of "natural theology" or "phyisco-theology" that were developing in late seventeenth-century England, which broadly maintained that the study of the natural world *alongside* scripture would lead to a true knowledge of God.[93] However, while his engagement with contemporary theological and philosophical thinking is evident, Tryon's working-class, artisanal background and experiences should not be lost from view. Previously, scholars have attributed Tryon's "free[ing] himself from Christianity's anthropocentric value system and ma[king] a leap into another moral dimension"[94] to his Brahminist influences or, alternatively, to his emphasis on Christian humility,[95] but it is clear that Tryon's firsthand encounter with colonial slavery fed into, as well as fed off, his pacifist animal theology. Few individuals who worked in the vicinity of slaves in this period would have had the time, inclination, or opportunity to write about enslaved people's experiences; fewer still would have been spurred to think about the customary plight of animals in the light of this extraordinary modern abuse of fellow humans. Tryon was a shepherd at heart, touched simultaneously by the innocence of animals and by their powerlessness and inability to protest against humankind's violence toward them, and his vegetarian views were not balked but emboldened by slavery. Perceiving the continuity between these forms of violent consumption, Tryon devised the superlative conception of the "highest Bondage" of animals, which reflects

[91] For an excellent overview of the paradox of the exclusionary ethos of modern state formation and political rights, see Derek O'Brien, "Magna Carta, the 'Sugar Colonies' and 'Fantasies of Empire,'" in *Magna Carta and Its Modern Legacy*, ed. Robert Hazell and James Melton (Cambridge: Cambridge University Press, 2015), 99–122, esp. 107–18.

[92] Tryon, *Averroeana*, 150.

[93] See Scott Mandelbrote, "The Uses of Natural Theology in Seventeenth-Century England," *Science in Context* 20 (2007), 451–80, esp. 460–61. Tryon represents a more spiritualist wing of natural theology, emphasizing not only the importance of theology but also inward inspiration for the understanding of sense-experience. For example, Tryon lambasts those "*Hear-say-men*, or *Book-Philosophers*, called, *The Learned*," who boast their knowledge of "what *Aristotle* held, what *Galen* taught, what *Hippocrates*, or St. *Augustine*, or *Tho. Aquinas*," but who remain as "blind as *Bats*" as to the nature of the world and "as ignorant as any (nay, commonly more than any others) of the true knowledge of God in themselves" (*The Way to Health*, 361).

[94] Stuart, *Bloodless Revolution*, 71.

[95] Clement, *Reading Humility*, 125–26.

his dual understanding of its biblical dimensions: not only as the *prefiguring* form of slavery from which other slaveries descended but also as the most *pernicious*, an enslavement humans barely know they are committing.

Bibliography

Behn, Aphra. "On the Author of That Excellent Book Intituled The Way to Health, Long Life, and Happiness." In *Miscellany, Being a Collection of Poems by Several Hands Together with Reflections on Morality*, 252–56. London: J. Hindmarsh, 1685.

Blackburn, Robin. *The Making of New World Slavery: From the Baroque to the Modern, 1492–1800*. New York: Verso, 1997.

Bradstock, Andrew. *Winstanley and the Diggers, 1649–1999*. London: Frank Cass, 2000.

Carey, Daniel. "Sugar, Colonialism, and the Critique of Slavery: Thomas Tryon in Barbados." *Studies on Voltaire and the Eighteenth Century* 9 (2004): 303–21.

Clement, Jennifer. "Thomas Tryon's Reformed Stewardship." In Clement, *Reading Humility in Early Modern England*, 107–26. Farnham, UK: Ashgate, 2015.

Davis, David Brion. *The Problem of Slavery in Western Culture*. Ithaca, NY: Cornell University Press, 1966.

Descartes, René. *Discourse on Method, Optics, Geometry, and Meteorology*. Translated by P. J. Olscamp. Rev. ed. Indianapolis: Hackett, 2001.

Field, John. *The Absurdity & Falseness of Thomas Trion's Doctrine*. London: Tho. Hawkins, 1685.

Gibbons, B. J. *Gender in Mystical and Occult Thought: Behmenism and Its Development in England*. Cambridge: Cambridge University Press, 1996.

Gildon, Charles. *The Post-Boy Robb'd of His Mail: or, The Pacquet Broke Open*. 2nd. ed. London: B. Mills, 1706. First published 1692.

Guerrini, Anita. "A Diet for a Sensitive Soul: Vegetarianism in Eighteenth-Century Britain." *Eighteenth-Century Life* 23, no. 2 (1999): 34–42.

Hall, Kim F. "'Extravagant Viciousness': Slavery and Gluttony in the Works of Thomas Tryon." In *Writing Race across the Atlantic World*, edited by P. Beidler and G. Taylor, 93–111. Basingstoke: Palgrave Macmillan, 2005.

Linzey, Andrew. *Animal Theology*. London: SCM Press, 1994.

Lyotard, Jean-François. *The Differend: Phrases in Dispute*. Translated by Georges Van Den Abbeele. Minneapolis: University of Minnesota Press, 1988.

Mandelbrote, Scott. "The Uses of Natural Theology in Seventeenth-Century England." *Science in Context* 20 (2007): 451–80.

Markley, Robert. *Fallen Languages: Crises of Representation in Newtonian England, 1660–1740*. Ithaca, NY: Cornell University Press, 1993.

McColley, Diane Kelsey. *Poetry and Ecology in the Age of Milton and Marvell*. Aldershot: Ashgate, 2007.

Morton, Timothy. "The Plantation of Wrath." In *Radicalism in British Literary Culture, 1650–1830*, edited by Timothy Morton and Nigel Smith, 64–85. Cambridge: Cambridge University Press, 2002.

O'Brien, Derek. "Magna Carta, the 'Sugar Colonies' and 'Fantasies of Empire.'" In *Magna Carta and Its Modern Legacy*, edited by Robert Hazell and James Melton, 99–122. Cambridge: Cambridge University Press, 2015.

Phelps, Norm. *The Dominion of Love: Animal Rights according to the Bible.* New York: Lantern Books, 2002.

Plank, Geoffrey. "Thomas Tryon, Sheep and the Politics of Eden." *Cultural and Social History* 14 (2017), 1–17.

Preece, Rod. *Sins of the Flesh: A History of Ethical Vegetarian Thought.* Vancouver: University of British Columbia Press, 2008.

Pursell, Matthew. "'That Odious Name Sold': Narratives of the Servant Trade." *Coriolis: Interdisciplinary Journal of Maritime Studies* 5, no. 1 (2015): 34–39.

Rosenberg, Philippe. "Thomas Tryon and the Seventeenth-Century Dimensions of Antislavery." *William and Mary Quarterly*, 3rd ser., 61, no. 4 (2004): 609–42.

Rudrum, Alan. "Ethical Vegetarianism in Seventeenth Century Britain: Its Roots in Sixteenth Century Theological Debate." *Seventeenth Century* 18, no. 1 (2003): 76–92.

Serjeantson, Richard. "The Passions and Animal Language 1540–1700." *Journal of the History of Ideas* 62, no. 3 (2001): 425–44.

Sheridan, Richard B. *Sugar and Slavery: An Economic History of the British West Indies, 1623–1775.* Barbados: Caribbean University Press, 1974.

Smith, Nigel. "Enthusiasm and Enlightenment: Of Food, Filth, and Slavery." In *The Country and the City Revisited*, edited by Donna Landry, Gerald McLean, and Joseph P. Ward, 106–18. Cambridge: Cambridge University Press, 1999.

Spencer, Jane. *Aphra Behn's Afterlife.* Oxford: Oxford University Press, 2000.

Spufford, Margaret. "First Steps in Literacy: The Reading and Writing Experiences of the Humblest Seventeenth-Century Spiritual Autobiographers." *Social History* 4, no. 3 (1979): 407–35.

Spufford, Margaret. *Small Books and Pleasant Histories: Popular Fiction and Its Readership in Seventeenth-Century England.* London: Methuen, 1981.

Stuart, Tristram. *The Bloodless Revolution: Radical Vegetarians and the Discovery of India.* London: HarperPress, 2006.

Tague, Ingrid H. "Companions, Servants, or Slaves? Considering Animals in Eighteenth-Century Britain." *Studies in Eighteenth-Century Culture* 39 (2010): 111–30.

[Tryon, Thomas]. *Averroeana: Being A Transcript of Several Letters from Averroes . . . Also Several Letters from Pythagoras to the King of India.* London: T. Sowle, 1695.

Tryon, Thomas [Philotheos Physiologus, pseud.]. *The Country-Man's Companion, or a New Method of Ordering Horses & Sheep.* London: Andrew Sowle, 1684.

Tryon, Thomas. *A Dialogue between an East-Indian Brackmanny or Heathen Philosopher, and a French Gentleman concerning the Present Affairs of Europe.* London: Andrew Sowle, 1683.

Tryon, Thomas [Philotheos Physiologus, pseud.]. *Friendly Advice to the Gentlemen Planters of the East and West Indies.* London: Andrew Sowle, 1684.

Tryon, Thomas. *Healths Grand Preservative.* London: Printed for the Author, 1682.

[Tryon, Thomas]. *The Planter's Speech to His Neighbours & Country-Men of Pennsylvania, East & West-Jersey and to all such as have Transported themselves into New-Colonies for the sake of a quiet retired Life. To which is added, The Complaints of Our Supra-Inferior Inhabitants.* London: Andrew Sowle, 1684.

Tryon, Thomas. *Some Memoirs of the Life of Mr. Tho. Tryon.* London: T. Sowle, 1705.

Tryon, Thomas [Philotheos Physiologus, pseud.]. *The Way to Health, Long Life, and Happiness.* London: Andrew Sowle, 1683.

Tryon, Thomas [Philotheos Physiologus, pseud.]. *The Way to Make All People Rich: or, Wisdoms Call to Temperanae [sic] and Frugality.* London: Andrew Sowle, 1685.

Tryon, Thomas. *Tryon's Letters, Domestic and Foreign*. London: Geo. Conyers, 1700.
Wareing, John. "'Violently Taken Away or Cheatingly Duckoyed': The Illicit Recruitment in London of Indentured Servants for the American Colonies, 1645–1718." *London Journal* 26, no. 2 (2001): 1–22.
Williams, Howard. *The Ethics of Diet: A Catena of Authorities Deprecatory of the Practice of Flesh-Eating*. Urbana: University of Illinois Press, 2003. First published 1883.

4

John Wesley (1703–1791)

The Tension between Theological Hope and Biological Reality

Ryan Patrick McLaughlin

John Wesley is best known for inspiring the Methodist movement. Scholars often identify Wesley with his teachings on love, on Christian perfection, and on the work of the Spirit in the pursuit of sanctification; his emphasis on evangelization; and his deep concern for social justice. This focus is due in large part to the dominant presence of these themes in the fifty-two (or fifty-three) "standard sermons" that Wesley included in his 1771 collection of sermons.[1]

However, significant themes of Wesley's theology fade into the background if one focuses *only* on the "standards." For example, his later sermons, including "The General Deliverance" (1781) and "The New Creation" (1785), reveal Wesley's expansive understanding of soteriology and the atonement.[2] In these sermons, Wesley maintains that there is no real salvation without the creation—not just creation as generally understood, but particular instantiations of life, including nonhuman animals.

---

[1] Often, scholars speak of the fifty-two standard sermons because they exclude Wesley's "Eulogy for George Whitefield." See the introduction in Kenneth J. Collins and Jason E. Vickers, eds., *The Sermons of John Wesley: A Collection for the Christian Journey* (Nashville, TN: Abingdon Press, 2013), xiv–xv. Collins and Vickers maintain that Wesley clearly approved forty-four sermons for a standard rule, based on his publication of these sermons in 1762. In 1770–71, Wesley added nine more sermons (including the eulogy for Whitefield), bringing the total to fifty-three. Wesley's final version of his standard sermons (1777–78) reverted back to the forty-four sermons of the 1762 edition. This publishing history helps make sense of the variation between British and American lists of Wesley's standards. See Collins and Vickers, *Sermons*, xii–xv.

[2] "The General Deliverance" is thus excluded from compilations of Wesley's works. For example, it does not appear in Alice Russie, ed., *The Essential Works of John Wesley: Selected Books, Sermons, and Other Writings* (Uhrichsville, OH: Barbour, 2011). Albert Outler and Richard Heitzenrater included more than the standard sermons in their edited volume, *John Wesley's Sermons: An Anthology* (Nashville, TN: Abingdon Press, 1991). "The General Deliverance," however, remains absent. Both "The General Deliverance" and "The New Creation" appear in some later anthologies. See Collins and Vickers, *The Sermons of John Wesley*.

Ryan Patrick McLaughlin, *John Wesley (1703–1791)* In: *Animal Theologians*. Edited by: Andrew Linzey and Clair Linzey, Oxford University Press. © Oxford University Press 2023. DOI: 10.1093/oso/9780197655542.003.0005

Drawing on these later sermons, I argue that Wesley's theology provides an important contribution to animal theology and ethics. This contribution, however, is complicated. On the one hand, certain elements of his theology—particularly his understanding of protology and the Fall—are no longer scientifically viable. On the other hand, the problem he addresses regarding divine goodness in relation to animal suffering remains a legitimate issue. In this manner, Wesley forces contemporary readers to address a theological impasse at the intersection of God's goodness and biological reality. This impasse is positive inasmuch as it highlights the troubling (and perhaps irresolvable) tension between the hope Christians place in God's love and the troubling state of our cosmos.

John Wesley and Nonhuman Animals

Wesley argues that scripture presents God as one who cares for all creatures. However, Wesley is well aware of the terrors of nature. This tension leads Wesley to the following question: "How are these Scriptures [that present God as one who cares for *all* creatures] reconcilable to the present state of things?"[3] More specifically, "if the Creator and Father of every living thing is rich in mercy towards all; if he does not overlook or despise any of the works of his own hands; if he wills even the meanest of them to be happy, according to their degree; how comes it to pass, that such a complication of evils oppresses, yea, overwhelms them?"[4] For Wesley, these questions require recourse to revelation. Natural theology alone cannot answer them.[5] In "The General Deliverance," Wesley approaches these questions by depicting the biblical narrative of the nonhuman creation in its original state, as well as the nonhuman creation's present condition and its future hope.

[3] John Wesley, "The General Deliverance," in *The Sermons of John Wesley: A Collection for the Christian Journey*, ed. Kenneth J. Collins and Jason E. Vickers (Nashville, TN: Abingdon Press, 2013), sec. 2.

[4] Wesley, "General Deliverance," sec. 2. Note here that Wesley refers to harms as evils. On this point, see also John Wesley, "On the Fall of Man," in *The Sermons of John Wesley*, 1872 edition, ed. Thomas Jackson, sec. 2, accessed June 22, 2016, http://wesley.nnu.edu/john-wesley/the-sermons-of-john-wesley-1872-edition/sermon-57-on-the-fall-of-man/.

[5] Wesley, "General Deliverance," sec. 2.

The Original Creation

Two points stand out as particularly potent for animal theology in Wesley's protology. First, he understands the image of God in part as a responsibility that humans must embody vis-à-vis the nonhuman creation. Second, he understands the original state and constitution of nonhuman animals to be vastly different from their current state and constitution.

The Human Being as the Image of God

Wesley maintains that humanity's original state was one of impassibility and immortality. There was neither suffering nor death. Hence, in 1782, Wesley writes, "Had there been no sin, there would have been no pain."[6] In addition to these features of human existence, Wesley suggests that humans bore the image of God in a unique manner in their original state.

In his 1748 sermon "The New Birth," Wesley delineates three facets to the image of God: the "natural image," which entails capacities such as "understanding, freedom of will, and various affections"; the "political image," in which humans are "the governor of this lower world, having 'dominion over the fishes of the sea, and over all the earth'"; and what is for Wesley the central aspect of the image of God, the "moral image," in which God calls humans to emulate the divine character (e.g., love and justice).[7] Hence, Wesley envisions the image of God as multifaceted (natural, political, and moral).

The image of God in all its facets suggests that the human "was God's vice-gerent upon earth."[8] The unique qualities of humans entail a unique responsibility to become the image of a particular (moral) God in and for the world. In other words, humans bear the *natural* image of God in order to fulfill the *political* image of God as they continuously grow in the *moral* image of God.[9] And as humans grow in the *moral* image of God, they learn how to use their *natural* faculties in good ways—ways that enable humans to exercise the *political* image of God such that creation experiences, through humans, the

---

[6] Wesley, "On the Fall of Man," sec. 1.
[7] John Wesley, "The New Birth," in *The Sermons of John Wesley: A Collection for the Christian Journey*, ed. Kenneth J. Collins and Jason E. Vickers (Nashville, TN: Abingdon Press, 2013), 157–64, sec. 1.1.
[8] Wesley, "General Deliverance," sec. 1.3.
[9] See Theodore Runyan, *The New Creation: John Wesley's Theology Today* (Nashville, TN: Abingdon Press, 1998), 13–14.

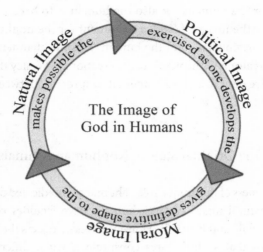

Figure 4.1 The cyclical development of the image of God in the theology of John Wesley

good and loving God in a unique manner. There is thus a circular pattern to the image of God in Wesley's thought, as Figure 4.1 suggests.

Wesley develops a reciprocal relationship between the human and non-human. Human beings must live into their status and role as the image of God for the nonhuman creation. Nonhuman creation, in turn, provides a sacramental vision of God for humans. Original humans had the ability to see "with unspeakable pleasure, the order, the beauty, the harmony, of all the creatures."[10] Wesley here speaks from a perspective similar to the Eastern Orthodox notion of cosmic sacramentality.[11] The creation is more than the space where humans and God meet; rather, the creation opens the space for humans, nonhumans, and God to meet. Wesley also echoes Orthodox theology (not to mention modern and contemporary biblical scholars) in parsing humanity's uniqueness at least partly in terms of responsibility.[12] This responsibility suggests that not only is the nonhuman creation

[10] Wesley, "General Deliverance," sec. 1.2.
[11] See John Chryssavgis, "The Earth as Sacrament: Insights from Orthodox Christian Theology and Spirituality," in *The Orthodox Handbook of Religion and Ecology*, ed. R. D. Gottlieb (New York: Oxford University Press, 2006), 92–114.
[12] On Orthodox theology, see Nonna Verna Harrison, "The Human Person as the Image and Likeness of God," in *The Cambridge Companion to Orthodox Christian Theology*, ed. M. B. Cunningham and E. Theokritoff (New York: Cambridge University Press, 2008), 78–91. On biblical scholarship, see J. Richard Middleton, *The Liberating Image: The Imago Dei in Genesis 1* (Grand Rapids, MI: Brazos Press, 2005).

a sacrament for the human, but also the human is to become, through the embodiment of the image of God, a sacrament for the nonhuman creation. Indeed, in the original creation the human "was the channel of conveyance between his Creator and the whole brute creation."[13] Wesley thus champions what I elsewhere refer to as a "sacramental reciprocity" between humans and nonhumans.[14]

The Original State of Nonhuman Animals

The appropriateness of the unique role of humans is predicated on their uniqueness. As the natural image of God, humans have faculties of "self-motion, understanding, will, and liberty."[15] However, Wesley rejects the common philosophical claim that such features constitute *essential* differences between humans and nonhumans.[16] Theodore Runyan notes that in Wesley's view, original animals also bore the natural image of God, albeit to a lesser degree than humans.[17] They had both reason and freedom. Furthermore, they still retain these features to some degree. Wesley writes: "What then is the barrier between men and brutes the line which they cannot pass? It was not reason. Set aside that ambiguous term: Exchange it for the plain word, understanding: and who can deny that brutes have this? We may as well deny that they have sight or hearing."[18]

Wesley's notion that animals had (and continue to have) features that philosophers and theologians so often associate with personhood is significant, both theologically and morally. More shocking still, however, is Wesley's claim that before the Fall humans were not even unique in their impassibility and immortality. Nonhuman animals experienced neither suffering nor death in Wesley's Eden.[19] In their original state, animals knew only "pleasure unmixed with pain; for pain was not yet; it had not entered into

---

[13] Wesley, "General Deliverance," sec. 1.3.

[14] See Ryan Patrick McLaughlin, *Christianity and the Status of Animals* (New York: Palgrave Macmillan, 2014), chap. 7.

[15] Wesley, "General Deliverance," sec. 1.1.

[16] See John B. Cobb Jr., *Grace & Responsibility: A Wesleyan Theology for Today* (Nashville, TN: Abingdon Press, 1995), 52–53.

[17] Runyan, *The New Creation*, 17.

[18] Wesley, "General Deliverance," sec. 1.5.

[19] Wesley, "On the Fall of Man," sec. 1.

paradise. And they too were immortal: For 'God made not death; neither hath he pleasure in the death of any living.' "[20]

Thus, for Wesley, original nonhuman animals bore the natural image of God. They existed in an immortal state, completely free from harm. The difference between the human and the nonhuman animal is that the former "is capable of God" whereas animals are not "in any degree, capable of knowing, loving, or obeying God."[21] By this claim Wesley seems to mean that humans can know God directly, as it were, while animals experience God *through humans*, who are "the great channel of communication" between God and the cosmos.[22] Here again Wesley sketches the sacramental role of humans in (or more properly *for*) the cosmos.

The Once Very Good Creation

This particular order, in which humans and animals experienced a death- and harm-free existence and humans carried a special responsibility for bearing God's love, goodness, and justice to the nonhuman creation, is the image of the "very good" creation according to Wesley. "But how far is this from being the present case," exclaims Wesley. "In what a condition is the whole lower world!"[23] All of this disarray, Wesley traces back to a cause: the original rebellion of humans. Because the human is the sacrament of divine love for the nonhuman creation, the rebellion of humans facilitates cosmic chaos, what we today call "nature." In short, human sin is the "origin of evil, whether natural or moral."[24]

The Present Creation

It is significant that Wesley links *all* creaturely suffering and death to the Fall. Humanity's failure to be the sacrament for the cosmos is the reason all its

---

[20] Wesley, "General Deliverance," sec. 1.5. Wesley is here quoting the deuterocanonical Wisdom of Solomon 1:13.

[21] Wesley, "General Deliverance," sec. 1.5.

[22] Wesley, "General Deliverance," sec. 1.7.

[23] Wesley, "General Deliverance," sec. 1.6.

[24] Wesley, "On the Fall of Man," sec. 2. Wesley also notes that evil angels have a role in creation's disorder. John Wesley, "Of Evil Angels," in *The Sermons of John Wesley*, 1872 edition, ed. Thomas Jackson, accessed June 22, 2016, http://wesley.nnu.edu/john-wesley/the-sermons-of-john-wesley-1872-edition/sermon-72-of-evil-angels/.

creatures are subjected "to sorrow, to pain of every kind, to all manner of evils."[25] God *permits* this "temporary evil" because out of it God will draw "eternal good."[26] The creation is the once and future very good cosmos. In the meantime, however, it is disrupted.

The nature of cosmic distortion is in part speculative for Wesley. He muses that the loss of understanding among nonhuman creatures might have been to the degree that worms originally had the intelligence of chimps. He suggests that the liberty of animals might have been "totally destroyed," to leave them now "utterly enslaved to irrational appetites."[27] Definitively, he maintains that nonhuman animals lost a degree of understanding, will, and liberty.[28] He also maintains that humanity's disobedience to God became mirrored in animals' disobedience to humans. Indeed, Wesley writes that dominion rests now with the animal's appetite, not with the human. The loss of human dominion corresponds to two attitudes in the animal: hateful fear and "open defiance."[29] Only domesticated animals "retain more or less of their original disposition."[30] But most creatures are in rebellion. I quote Wesley at length:

> How little shadow of good, of gratitude, of benevolence, of any right temper, is now to be found in any part of the brute creation! On the contrary, what savage fierceness, what unrelenting cruelty; are invariably observed in thousands of creatures; yea, is *inseparable from their natures*! Is it only the lion, the tiger, the wolf, among the inhabitants of the forest and plains—the shark, and a few more voracious monsters, among the inhabitants of the waters,—or the eagle, among birds,—that *tears the flesh, sucks the blood, and crushes the bones of their helpless fellow-creatures*? Nay; the harmless fly, the laborious ant, the painted butterfly, are treated in the same merciless manner, even by the innocent songsters of the grove! The innumerable *tribes of poor insects are continually devoured by them.*[31]

[25] Wesley, "General Deliverance," sec. 2.1.
[26] Wesley, "General Deliverance," sec. 2.1.
[27] Wesley, "General Deliverance," sec. 2.2.
[28] Wesley, "General Deliverance," sec. 2.2.
[29] Wesley, "General Deliverance," sec. 2.2.
[30] Wesley, "General Deliverance," sec. 2.3.
[31] Wesley, "General Deliverance," sec. 2.3. See also John Wesley, "The New Creation," in *The Sermons of John Wesley: A Collection for the Christian Journey*, ed. Kenneth J. Collins and Jason E. Vickers (Nashville, TN: Abingdon Press, 2013), 647–54, sec. 17.

It is noteworthy that Wesley acknowledges that the *nature* of some creatures is predatory. While his theology is difficult to reconcile with modern science, Wesley was well aware of that state of nature in his day.[32] There is room here for an aspect of "original sin" in the nonhuman creation. Sin has so deeply scarred the nonhuman creation that this creation has become something *different by nature*. Also notable is that cosmic disarray is an issue not only for sentient creatures but for all creatures, including insects.

Such is, for Wesley, the "the miserable constitution of the world."[33] It is one in which "an immense majority of creatures, perhaps a million to one, can no otherwise preserve their own lives, than by destroying their fellow-creatures!"[34] Again, hinting at his understanding of nature, Wesley notes that creatures are unable to avoid these forms of harm. In other words, they are inevitable outcomes of our current state of existence. Adding other phenomena such as natural disasters and disease to this picture of nature, Wesley struggles to find good in wild nature.[35] Furthermore, all creatures are now "exposed to the violence and cruelty of him that is now their common enemy—man."[36] Humans kill not out of necessity, but for pleasure. Wesley laments this distortion of human dominion.

The New Creation

Wesley's understanding of the original and present creation leads logically to the question of cosmic destiny. Will creation "always remain in this deplorable condition?" Wesley's response is vivid: "God forbid that we should affirm this; yea, or *even entertain* such a thought!"[37] This statement suggests how important a cosmic eschatology is for Wesley. To even entertain the idea that creation might remain under its current condition is a theological

---

[32] See John Wesley, *A Survey of the Wisdom of God in the Creation, or A Compendium of Natural Philosophy*, 4th ed., 4 vols. (London: Paramore, 1784). On Wesley's engagement with the sciences, see Margaret G. Flowers, "A Wesleyan Theology of Environmental Stewardship," in *Inward and Outward Health: John Wesley's Holistic Concept of Medical Science, the Environment and Holy Living*, ed. Deborah Madden (Eugene, OR: Wipf and Stock, 2008), 51–93; Randy Maddox, "John Wesley's Precedent for Theological Engagement with the Natural Sciences," *Wesleyan Theological Journal* 44, no. 1 (Spring 2009): 23–54.

[33] Wesley, "General Deliverance," sec. 2.3.

[34] Wesley, "General Deliverance," sec. 2.3.

[35] Wesley, "General Deliverance," sec. 2.4.

[36] Wesley, "General Deliverance," sec. 2.6.

[37] Wesley, "General Deliverance," sec. 3.1; emphasis added.

travesty. He therefore laments that the new creation is "little thought of or understood by the generality of Christians."[38]

But what will the new creation be? In his sermon "The New Creation"—which, according to Kenneth Collins and Jason Vickers, "represents Wesley's mature judgment in terms of the height, depth, and extent of salvation"[39]—Wesley acknowledges that human knowledge of the new creation is "exceedingly short and imperfect."[40] Because it is "remote from all our natural apprehensions,"[41] its content is necessarily "a point of mere revelation."[42]

Drawing upon scriptures—in particular, Isaiah 11, Romans 8, and Revelation 21—Wesley concludes: "The whole brute creation will . . . undoubtedly, be restored, not only to the vigour, strength, and swiftness which they had at their creation, but to a far higher degree of each than they ever enjoyed."[43] This claim highlights an Irenaean streak to Wesley's cosmology. The original creation is not the new creation. Neither is the new creation a return to Eden. The cosmos needs to grow into its eschatological destiny—toward a "more beautiful Paradise than Adam ever saw."[44]

In this destiny, the earth itself will experience a transformation. There will be no more extreme temperatures or earthquakes or volcanoes.[45] Indeed, the elements themselves will exist with completely different properties.[46] But animals will receive a special transformation because

in the living part of the creation were seen the most deplorable effects of Adam's apostasy. The whole animated creation, whatever has life, from leviathan to the smallest mite, was thereby made subject to such vanity, as the inanimate creatures could not be. They were subject to that fell monster, DEATH, the conqueror of all that breathe. They were made subject to its fore-runner, pain, in its ten thousand forms.[47]

All animals "will be delivered from all irregular appetites, from all unruly passions, from every disposition that is either evil in itself, or has any

---

[38] Wesley, "The New Creation," sec. 1.
[39] Collins and Vickers, *The Sermons of John Wesley*, 647.
[40] Wesley, "The New Creation," sec. 2.
[41] Wesley, "The New Creation," sec. 1.
[42] Wesley, "The New Creation," sec. 2.
[43] Wesley, "General Deliverance," sec. 3.3.
[44] Wesley, "The New Creation," sec. 16.
[45] Wesley, "The New Creation," secs. 14–15. Of course, "extreme weather" is a relative notion.
[46] See Wesley's reflection on fire in "The New Creation," sec. 10.
[47] Wesley, "The New Creation," sec. 17.

tendency to evil. No rage will be found in any creature, no fierceness, no cruelty, or thirst for blood."[48] The image is that of the end of suffering, of predation, and of all death. "On the new earth, no creature will kill, or hurt, or give pain to any other."[49] Wesley here draws on Isaiah's peaceable kingdom in which the wolf and the lamb live together in harmony. In this harmony, all animals "will suffer no more, either from within or without."[50] Wesley even conjectures that in the future animals might be raised to the station of the human in terms of faculties. It follows that they may become capable of God in themselves.

For Wesley, this future is *required* by God's justice. The animals are, in some sense, *owed* this recompense because of their innocent suffering.[51] An animal-inclusive eschaton is not a matter of gracious theology; it is a matter of justice. Here Wesley is also constructing a theodicy. The sin of humans explains the origin of innocent animal suffering. The recompense for suffering creatures provides "a full answer to a plausible objection against the justice of God."[52]

Wesley's Eschatological Ethics

Jürgen Moltmann, in line with his hope-based theology, writes, "Christian ethics are eschatological ethics."[53] Wesley's position is a forerunner to Moltmann's. For Wesley, eschatological considerations ultimately shape ethical reflection. These considerations

> may encourage us to imitate Him whose mercy is over all his works. They may soften our hearts towards the meaner creatures, knowing that the Lord careth for them. It may enlarge our hearts towards those poor creatures, to reflect that, as vile as they appear in our eyes, not one of them is forgotten in the sight of our Father which is in heaven. Through all the vanity to which

---

[48] Wesley, "General Deliverance," sec. 3.3.

[49] Wesley, "The New Creation," sec. 17.

[50] Wesley, "General Deliverance," sec. 3.4; see also Wesley, "The New Creation," sec. 17.

[51] David Clough is critical of Wesley's reduction of eschatological redemption to recompense. See David Clough, *On Animals* (New York: Bloomsbury, 2014), 133–36.

[52] Wesley, "General Deliverance," sec. 3.9. Of course, this theodicy is subject to a number of criticisms.

[53] Jürgen Moltmann, "The Liberation of the Future and Its Anticipations in History," in *God Will Be All in All: The Eschatology of Jürgen Moltmann*, ed. Richard Bauckham (Minneapolis: Fortress Press, 2001), 289.

they are now subjected, let us look to what God hath prepared for them. Yea, let us habituate ourselves to look forward, beyond this present scene of bondage, to the happy time when they will be delivered therefrom into the liberty of the children of God.[54]

Humans should look toward God's promise of peace for the cosmos and habituate our characters in a manner that, to whatever extent possible, embodies that promise even in the present.

The phrase "to whatever extent possible" requires qualification. Wesley is adamant that the new creation does not burgeon out of the natural flow of history but is rather an eschatological event that transforms history.[55] He acknowledges that harms such as suffering and death will persist "till the consummation of all things."[56] Thus, one must not overstate Wesley's eschatological ethics. But creation's groaning should nonetheless drive humans toward efforts to witness to redemption by nonviolent living, even as we recognize, as Wesley himself did, that victimization and violence are inevitable features of nature as we know it. Humans should live into the future hope that "all will be . . . light, fair, serene—a lively picture of the eternal day."[57]

Wesley's claims regarding eschatological ethics are significant. However, it is also important to note that Wesley cautions against what we today would call biocentric egalitarianism (in which all life shares equal dignity and value). He writes, "I dare not affirm that [God] has an equal regard for [nonhuman animals] as for the children of men."[58] The human remains superior in terms of God's favor—if only because humans are capable of receiving this favor in ways that animals cannot. At any rate, the unique station of the human—what I refer to as humans' sacramentality—here becomes essential. The value of humans and the value of nonhumans is not a zero-sum game. The increase of one does not necessitate a decrease in the other. In fact, the more valuable the human (as a sacramental conduit of God's love), the more valuable the nonhuman to whom the human is meant to reveal that love.

Based on Wesley's theology, it may not be too much to say that if humans do not love nonhumans, they are not functioning as sacraments of the divine love. In this case, they lose their essential place in the order of creation. They

[54] Wesley, "General Deliverance," sec. 3.10.
[55] See Wesley, "The New Creation," sec. 4.
[56] Wesley, "On the Fall of Man," sec. 3.7.
[57] Wesley, "The New Creation," sec. 9.
[58] Wesley, "General Deliverance," sec. 3.5.

become "beasts," as it were. So Wesley concludes: "So much more let all those who are of a nobler turn of mind assert the distinguishing dignity of their nature. Let all who are of a more generous spirit know and maintain their rank in the scale of beings."[59] The twist is that acknowledging this unique dignity in the human ascribes *more* value to nonhumans, not less. Creation is *not* all for us. Indeed, there is some sense in which, by God's gracious design, humans exist for everything else. As Randy Maddox notes, God intends humans to be in unique relationships with God, other humans, animals, and ourselves. And "the proper relationship to all . . . animals is loving protection."[60]

Wesley's Theology and Contemporary Science

Wesley's vision of protological harmony, cosmic disorder, and eschatological redemption is beautiful. At the heart of his message, I argue, are two fundamental points. First, scripture is authoritative in its portrayal of God's character. Second, scripture, at least in some grand sense, portrays God as the merciful and loving Creator of all things. For Wesley, as well as for the authors of the primeval creation narratives and the eschatological visions of many prophets, the present experience of reality cannot reflect God's will or desire for the cosmos. Nor can it be the final word for the victims of nature.

It is here that Wesley's vision presents a problem. Wesley died in 1791. Charles Darwin was born eighteen years later. Over the next century, the very meaning of science would shift dramatically.[61] Today, dominant cosmological pictures do not in the slightest cohere with Wesley's protology.[62] We live in a world in which, in the words of Denis Edwards, "loss and death on an unthinkable scale are built into the way things are."[63] This is the way things are

[59] Wesley, "General Deliverance," sec. 3.12.

[60] Randy Maddox, *Responsible Grace: John Wesley's Practical Theology* (Nashville, TN: Kingswood Books, 1994), 68.

[61] See Maddox, "John Wesley's Precedent," 30–35.

[62] Michael Northcott, *The Environment and Christian Ethics* (New York: Cambridge University Press, 1996), 174. Wesley writes of the history of the humans since Adam spanning six thousand years. Wesley, "On the Fall of Man," sec. 3.4. In his earlier writings (1730), Wesley writes that he is "ashamed" that people in his time were suggesting that humans "were not made in the image of the living God, but of the beasts that perish." John Wesley, "The Image of God," in *The Sermons of John Wesley: A Collection for the Christian Journey*, ed. Kenneth J. Collins and Jason E. Vickers (Nashville, TN: Abingdon Press, 2013), sec. 3.

[63] Denis Edwards, "Every Sparrow That Falls to the Ground: The Cost of Evolution and the Christ-Event," *Ecotheology* 11, no. 1 (2006): 104. See also Lisa Sideris, *Environmental Ethics, Ecological Theology, and Natural Selection* (New York: Columbia University Press, 2003), 19.

and the way things have always been, as long as there has been life. As John Polkinghorne notes, if by "fallenness" we intimate the harmful aspects of the cosmos, then "the universe is everywhere 'fallen' and it has always been so."[64] Life has always been, as Holmes Rolston III writes, "an uphill climb against the downhill tug of entropy."[65] There was no predation-free historical Eden.[66]

Of course, nature has positive qualities—instances of cooperation and mutual enrichment, for example. But these values are balanced by disvalues. Life is possible because of death. The good that Wesley treasures is inconceivable, biologically speaking, without the harms he laments.[67]

The necessity and inevitability of suffering and death have led many philosophers and theologians to embrace them as part of the good creation. J. Baird Callicott argues, "If nature as a whole is good, then pain and death are also good."[68] Rolston suggests that the "groaning in travail" of creation "is the Creator's will, productive as it is of glory."[69]

To a lesser extent, some also express incredulity regarding eschatological hopes for harmony among animals and humans. Lisa Sideris writes, "Although the desire to heal environments whose health has been compromised by human actions points to a worthy imperative, natural processes themselves cannot be seen as wrong, evil, or in need of redemption in an eschatological sense."[70]

And so science dismantles Wesley's protology. Many who embrace the findings of science would also decry Wesley's distaste for the current state of nature. Furthermore, they would raise questions about his image of eschatological hope. In the eyes of many scientists and theologians, the most promising path forward is to embrace even the darker mechanisms of evolutionary existence as part of God's good creation.[71]

---

[64] John Polkinghorne, *Reason and Reality: The Relationship between Science and Theology* (London: SPCK, 1991), 98.

[65] Holmes Rolston III, "Does Nature Need to Be Redeemed?," *Zygon* 29 (1994): 212.

[66] See Silvester de Nooijer, Barbara R. Holland, and David Penny, "The Emergence of Predators in Early Life: There Was NO Garden of Eden," *PLoS ONE* 4, no. 6 (2007): e5507, https://doi.org/10.1371/journal.pone.0005507.

[67] See Nancey Murphy, "Science and the Problem of Evil: Suffering as a By-product of a Finely Tuned Cosmos," in *Physics and Cosmology: Scientific Perspectives on the Problem of Natural Evil*, ed. Nancey Murphy, Robert John Russell, and William R. Stoeger (Notre Dame: University of Notre Dame Press, 2007), 131–52.

[68] J. Baird Callicott, "Animal Liberation: A Triangular Affair," *Environmental Ethics* 2 (Winter 1980): 333.

[69] Holmes Rolston III, "Naturalizing and Systematizing Evil," in *Is Nature Ever Evil? Religion, Science, and Value*, ed. Willem B. Drees (London: Routledge, 2003), 85.

[70] Sideris, *Environmental Ethics*, 200. See also Willis Jenkins, *Ecologies of Grace: Environmental Ethics and Christian Theology* (New York: Oxford University Press, 2008), 73–74.

[71] For notable exceptions, see Christopher Southgate, *The Groaning of Creation: God, Evolution, and the Problem of Evil* (Louisville, KY: Westminster John Knox Press, 2008); Robert John

A Theological Impasse: Wesley's Contribution

This aforementioned embrace sounds easy enough. But we must remember Wesley's earlier question: "If the Creator and Father of every living thing is rich in mercy towards all . . . how comes it to pass, that such a complication of evils oppresses, yea, overwhelms them?"[72] Science, it seems, has taken a large part of Wesley's answer away. He did not know that the very appeals he made to protological harmony would be all but obsolete in less than two centuries. But what then becomes of God? What is the answer to Wesley's question?

David Hull writes, "The God of Galapagos is careless, wasteful, indifferent, and almost diabolical."[73] James Rachels adds to this poignant remark: "Countless animals have suffered terribly in the millions of years that preceded the emergence of man, and the traditional theistic rejoinders do not even come close to justifying *that* evil."[74] If God is the author of evolution (or if God lured the world toward the particular lawlike structure we witness in the cosmos), then we must acknowledge that God authored a system of life in which countless individuals would inevitably pay incalculable prices for the sake of the whole. This God appears as unconcerned with individuals as is nature itself.

I wonder what Wesley would have said if he had become aware of the inevitability and necessity of suffering and death in the very structure of the cosmos—if he had become aware that features of existence such as predation, parasitism, disease, and death were all foregone conclusions billions of years prior to human sin. We have only speculation here, of course. But I suspect his response would at the very least include the claim that we cannot, as many environmental theologians have done, abandon a vision of protology without at the same time casting a large shadow of doubt on the character of God. Sideris recognizes this point when she writes, "Something must be given up: either the traditional understanding of God must be altered or the processes of evolution must be reinterpreted along less Darwinian lines."[75]

Russell, *Cosmology: From Alpha to Omega* (Minneapolis: Fortress Press, 2008), 173–93; and John Polkinghorne, *The God of Hope and the End of the World* (New Haven: Yale University Press, 2002), 113–23.

[72] Wesley, "General Deliverance," sec. 2.
[73] David L. Hull, "God of the Galapagos," *Nature* 352 (August 1992): 486.
[74] James Rachels, *Created from Animals: The Moral Implications of Darwinism* (New York: Oxford University Press, 1990), 105.
[75] Sideris, *Environmental Ethics*, 279n19.

Something must be given up. Are we at an impasse? Is it possible to maintain faith in Wesley's merciful God while at once dismissing the harmonious protological state of that God's creation? Aside from the polar options of a rejection of evolution and a full embrace of its goodness, there are other proposals on the table. However, I am not convinced that any of them satisfy completely the tension between biological reality and theological hope in God's goodness.[76] Some—including C. S. Lewis and, more recently, Gregory Boyd—appeal to an angelic fall to explain nature's disvalues.[77] But how can such an appeal account for the reality that these mechanisms are built into the very laws of the universe?[78] Unless fallen angels are the *actual* creators of *this* world—a rather Gnostic solution—appeals to an angelic fall appear to be inadequate.[79]

Others maintain that God ordains evolution because it is the only way to bring about greater goods, such as biodiversity or intelligent life, all of which are pointed toward some eschatological redemption.[80] This route makes God something of a consequentialist—and a rather harsh one at that. In Fyodor Dostoevsky's *The Brothers Karamazov*, Ivan Karamazov discusses the problem of evil (focusing on the suffering of children) with his brother, Alyosha. Ivan, who challenges the goodness of God's creative project, asks his faithful brother a question: "Imagine you yourself are building the edifice of human destiny with the object of making people happy in the finale, of giving them peace and rest at last, but for that you must inevitably and unavoidably torture just one tiny creature [Ivan proposes that this creature is an innocent child] ... Would you agree to be the architect on such conditions?"[81] Alyosha answers that he could not accept the cost. And yet, based on these greater-good arguments, we are to accept the torturous sufferings of all human and nonhuman innocents for the sake of God's kingdom. Ivan's lament is poignant here: "Too high a price is asked for harmony."

[76] For a detailed exploration, see my upcoming manuscript, *Celebration and Lament: Divine Goodness and Natural Evil* (currently under contract with Fortress Press).

[77] See C. S. Lewis, *The Problem of Pain* (New York: Macmillan, 1962), 135; Gregory Boyd, *Satan and the Problem of Evil: Constructing a Trinitarian Warfare Theodicy* (Downers Grove, IL: Intervarsity Press, 2001).

[78] On this critique, see Southgate, *The Groaning of Creation*, 33.

[79] On this criticism, see Richard Bauckham, *The Bible and Ecology: Rediscovering the Community of Creation* (Waco, TX: Baylor University Press, 2010), 160.

[80] Southgate's *The Groaning of Creation* provides one of the best examples of this approach.

[81] Fyodor Dostoevsky, *The Brothers Karamazov*, trans. Richard Pevear and Larissa Volokhonsky (New York: Farrar, Straus, and Giroux, 2002), 245.

Others appeal to a free-process defense, which is to natural evil what the free-will defense is to moral evil.[82] God gives creation its own integrity even though doing so entails the risk that horrendous harms will come to fruition. But the parallel with the free-will defense seems forced. Free will makes evil a *potentiality*. The structure of our cosmos in conjunction with biological evolution renders horrendous harms an *inevitability*.[83] The God who creates such a world does not risk evil; God renders it nearly inevitable that horrendous harms will befall countless individuals.

Still others suggest rethinking the doctrine of God in a manner that takes more seriously the so-called anthropomorphisms (e.g., descriptions of God with human categories) of scripture.[84] These approaches suggest that God lacks the ability to create an Edenic existence *ex nihilo* (from nothing). God is essentially limited by either internal (i.e., God's nature) or external (i.e., metaphysical principles) factors. This approach may exonerate God in the face of the horrendous harms of our cosmos, but it effectively obliterates any realistic hope in the kind of eschaton Wesley imagines. A God who is so thoroughly unable to prevent evil in the face of God's own limitations would be equally (if not more) unable to bring about an evil-free eschaton.

In short, unless we sacrifice God's concern for individual creatures (i.e., God's character) or God's ability to see God's eschatological promise through to fruition (i.e., our hope), we *are* at an impasse. Again, as Sideris says, "Something must be given up." But what? Perhaps Wesley's greatest contribution to animal theology is his refusal to reconcile the notion of God willing animal suffering with God's goodness. Embracing this impasse does not allow for an easy theodicy—one that downplays God's concern for individual creatures or purchases God's exoneration at the cost of reasonable hope for creaturely redemption. Wesley reminds us that God's goodness sits in an uneasy tension with creation's current state. Perhaps we ought to allow this tension to linger indefinitely rather than rushing to resolve it.

Living within this tension permits one to resist the temptation to glorify victimization and violence by declaring it part of God's good creation. God's creation is, frankly, *not* very good for many individuals who experience it.

---

[82] See John Polkinghorne, *Science and Providence: God's Interaction with the World* (West Conshohocken, PA: Templeton Foundation Press, 2005).

[83] Polkinghorne is aware of this point. His response is to claim BLAH!!!

[84] See David Ray Griffin, "Creation out of Nothing, Creation out of Chaos, and the Problem of Evil," in *Encountering Evil: Live Options in Theodicy*, ed. Stephen T. Davis (Louisville, KY: Westminster John Knox Press, 2001), 108–24; Thomas Jay Oord, *The Uncontrolling Love of God: An Open and Relational Account of Providence* (Downers Grove, IL: IVP Academic, 2015).

The groaning of these creatures should echo throughout our theodicies, constantly shaking their foundations. Even though the eschaton is ultimately a matter of God's work, it is nonetheless the province of humans to witness to this eschaton in our current practices. Virtue is, after all, directed toward the telos of creatures. The human telos is one that is shared with the other creatures we encounter. Our character and actions should therefore reflect this teleology. Wesley highlights this point in his sermon "On the Education of Children," in which he encourages the development of virtue in children by way of compassion for animals.[85]

> Truly affectionate parents will not indulge them in any kind or degree of unmercifulness. . . . They will not allow them to hurt, or give pain to, anything that has life. They will not permit them to rob birds' nests; much less to kill anything without necessity,—not even snakes, which are as innocent as worms, or toads, which, notwithstanding their ugliness, and the ill name they lie under, have been proved over and over to be as harmless as flies. Let them extend in its measure the rule of doing as they would be done by, to every animal whatsoever.[86]

Note here that Wesley acknowledges the possibility that harming and killing may be a necessity. Even so, the default position is to embrace an enlarged golden rule: Do to animals what you would have done to you.

Our practices of peace function as sacraments of the eschatological redemption for which Wesley hopes and scripture witnesses. Wesley calls us to ethical concern for both the whole and the individual, even though absolute concern for both is impossible. We must preserve the whole. But we can also, to a much greater degree than many of us do, witness to the eschatological peace by promoting the well-being of the many nonhuman individuals from whose sufferings we currently profit. Wesley reminds us that humans cannot justify the many harms we cause for individuals by appealing to nature.

[85] On this point, see Runyan, *The New Creation*, 203–4.
[86] John Wesley, "On the Education of Children," in *The Sermons of John Wesley*, 1872 edition, ed. Thomas Jackson, accessed June 22, 2016, http://wesley.nnu.edu/john-wesley/the-sermons-of-john-wesley-1872-edition/sermon-95-on-the-education-of-children/.

Conclusion

Wesley's theology provides a powerful contribution to animal theology. Humans must live into their status as the image of God by mediating God's love and justice to the nonhuman creation. The current relationship between humans and animals falls well short of this ideal on account of the Fall. However, humans bear the imperative to become witnesses to the animal-inclusive eschaton by engaging in practices of peace where such practices are possible. These claims, if taken seriously from an ethical perspective, would radically change the way the vast majority of humans currently relate to nonhuman animals. Even so, Wesley's theology—particularly his protology and notion of the Fall—is problematic in the face of modern science. There was no historical Eden. This issue notwithstanding, his refusal to downplay the harms that creatures suffer in order to exonerate God highlights the severity that this suffering casts upon faith. It furthermore challenges many responses to natural evil. While we cannot hold fast to a historical Eden absent of predation, we should not embrace suffering, predation, and death as unambiguously good pillars of God's created order.

Acknowledgment

The author would like to thank Gerard Chiusano for providing editorial assistance with the completion of this chapter.

Bibliography

Bauckham, Richard. *The Bible and Ecology: Rediscovering the Community of Creation.* Waco, TX: Baylor University Press, 2010.

Boyd, Gregory. *Satan and the Problem of Evil: Constructing a Trinitarian Warfare Theodicy.* Downers Grove, IL: Intervarsity Press, 2001.

Callicott, J. Baird. "Animal Liberation: A Triangular Affair." *Environmental Ethics* 2 (Winter 1980): 311–38.

Chryssavgis, John. "The Earth as Sacrament: Insights from Orthodox Christian Theology and Spirituality." In *The Orthodox Handbook of Religion and Ecology*, edited by R. D. Gottlieb, 92–114. New York: Oxford University Press, 2006.

Clough, David. *On Animals.* New York: Bloomsbury, 2014.

Cobb, John B., Jr. *Grace & Responsibility: A Wesleyan Theology for Today.* Nashville, TN: Abingdon Press, 1995.

Collins, Kenneth J., and Jason E. Vickers, eds. *The Sermons of John Wesley: A Collection for the Christian Journey*. Nashville, TN: Abingdon Press, 2013.

de Nooijer, Silvester, Barbara R. Holland, and David Penny. "The Emergence of Predators in Early Life: There Was NO Garden of Eden." *PLoS ONE* 4, no. 6 (2007): e5507. https://doi.org/10.1371/journal.pone.0005507.

Dostoevsky, Fyodor. *The Brothers Karamazov*. Translated by Richard Pevear and Larissa Volokhonsky. New York: Farrar, Straus and Giroux, 2002.

Edwards, Denis. "Every Sparrow That Falls to the Ground: The Cost of Evolution and the Christ-Event." *Ecotheology* 11, no. 1 (2006): 103–23.

Flowers, Margaret G. "A Wesleyan Theology of Environmental Stewardship." In *Inward and Outward Health: John Wesley's Holistic Concept of Medical Science, the Environment and Holy Living*, edited by Deborah Madden, 51–93. Eugene, OR: Wipf and Stock, 2008.

Griffin, David Ray. "Creation out of Nothing, Creation out of Chaos, and the Problem of Evil." In *Encountering Evil: Live Options in Theodicy*, edited by Stephen T. Davis, 108–24. Louisville, KY: Westminster John Knox Press, 2001.

Harrison, Nonna Verna. "The Human Person as the Image and Likeness of God." In *The Cambridge Companion to Orthodox Christian Theology*, edited by M. B. Cunningham and E. Theokritoff, 78–91. New York: Cambridge University Press, 2008.

Hull, David L. "God of the Galapagos." *Nature* 352 (August 1992): 485–86.

Jenkins, Willis. *Ecologies of Grace: Environmental Ethics and Christian Theology*. New York: Oxford University Press, 2008.

Lewis, C. S. *The Problem of Pain*. New York: Macmillan, 1962.

Maddox, Randy. "John Wesley's Precedent for Theological Engagement with the Natural Sciences." *Wesleyan Theological Journal* 44, no. 1 (Spring 2009): 23–54.

Maddox, Randy. *Responsible Grace: John Wesley's Practical Theology*. Nashville, TN: Kingswood Books, 1994.

McLaughlin, Ryan Patrick. *Christianity and the Status of Animals*. New York: Palgrave Macmillan, 2014.

Middleton, J. Richard. *The Liberating Image: The Imago Dei in Genesis 1*. Grand Rapids, MI: Brazos Press, 2005.

Moltmann, Jürgen. "The Liberation of the Future and Its Anticipations in History." In *God Will Be All in All: The Eschatology of Jürgen Moltmann*, edited by Richard Bauckham, 265–89. Minneapolis: Fortress Press, 2001.

Murphy, Nancey. "Science and the Problem of Evil: Suffering as a By-product of a Finely Tuned Cosmos." In *Physics and Cosmology: Scientific Perspectives on the Problem of Natural Evil*, edited by Nancey Murphy, Robert John Russell, and William R. Stoeger, 131–52. Notre Dame, IN: University of Notre Dame Press, 2007.

Northcott, Michael. *The Environment and Christian Ethics*. New York: Cambridge University Press, 1996.

Oord, Thomas Jay. *The Uncontrolling Love of God: An Open and Relational Account of Providence*. Downers Grove, IL: IVP Academic, 2015.

Outler, Albert, and Richard Heitzenrater, eds. *John Wesley's Sermons: An Anthology*. Nashville, TN: Abingdon Press, 1991.

Polkinghorne, John. *The God of Hope and the End of the World*. New Haven: Yale University Press, 2002.

Polkinghorne, John. *Reason and Reality: The Relationship between Science and Theology*. London: SPCK, 1991.

Polkinghorne, John. *Science and Providence: God's Interaction with the World*. West Conshohocken, PA: Templeton Foundation Press, 2005.

Rachels, James. *Created from Animals: The Moral Implications of Darwinism*. New York: Oxford University Press, 1990.

Rolston, Holmes, III. "Does Nature Need to Be Redeemed?" *Zygon* 29 (1994): 205–29.

Rolston, Holmes, III. "Naturalizing and Systematizing Evil." In *Is Nature Ever Evil? Religion, Science, and Value*, edited by Willem B. Drees, 67–86. London: Routledge, 2003.

Runyan, Theodore. *The New Creation: John Wesley's Theology Today*. Nashville, TN: Abingdon Press, 1998.

Russell, Robert John. *Cosmology: From Alpha to Omega*. Minneapolis: Fortress Press, 2008.

Russie, Alice, ed. *The Essential Works of John Wesley: Selected Books, Sermons, and Other Writings*. Uhrichsville, OH: Barbour, 2011.

Sideris, Lisa. *Environmental Ethics, Ecological Theology, and Natural Selection*. New York: Columbia University Press, 2003.

Southgate, Christopher. *The Groaning of Creation: God, Evolution, and the Problem of Evil*. Louisville, KY: Westminster John Knox Press, 2008.

Wesley, John. "The General Deliverance." In *The Sermons of John Wesley: A Collection for the Christian Journey*, edited by Kenneth J. Collins and Jason E. Vickers, 624–34. Nashville, TN: Abingdon Press, 2013.

Wesley, John. "The Image of God." In *The Sermons of John Wesley: A Collection for the Christian Journey*, edited by Kenneth J. Collins and Jason E. Vickers, 1–9. Nashville, TN: Abingdon Press, 2013.

Wesley, John. "The New Birth." In *The Sermons of John Wesley: A Collection for the Christian Journey*, edited by Kenneth J. Collins and Jason E. Vickers, 155–64. Nashville, TN: Abingdon Press, 2013.

Wesley, John. "The New Creation." In *The Sermons of John Wesley: A Collection for the Christian Journey*, edited by Kenneth J. Collins and Jason E. Vickers, 647–54. Nashville, TN: Abingdon Press, 2013.

Wesley, John. "Of Evil Angels." In *The Sermons of John Wesley*, 1872 edition, edited by Thomas Jackson. Accessed June 22, 2016. http://wesley.nnu.edu/john-wesley/the-sermons-of-john-wesley-1872-edition/sermon-72-of-evil-angels/.

Wesley, John. "On the Education of Children." In *The Sermons of John Wesley*, 1872 edition, edited by Thomas Jackson. Accessed June 22, 2016. http://wesley.nnu.edu/john-wesley/the-sermons-of-john-wesley-1872-edition/sermon-95-on-the-education-of-children/.

Wesley, John. "On the Fall of Man." In *The Sermons of John Wesley*, 1872 edition, edited by Thomas Jackson. Accessed June 22, 2016. http://wesley.nnu.edu/john-wesley/the-sermons-of-john-wesley-1872-edition/sermon-57-on-the-fall-of-man/.

Wesley, John. *A Survey of the Wisdom of God in the Creation, or A Compendium of Natural Philosophy*. 4th ed. London: Paramore, 1784.

5

Humphry Primatt (1735–1777)

Animal Protection and Its Revolutionary Contexts

Adam Bridgen

> We may pretend to what Religion we please, but Cruelty is Atheism.
> We may make our boast of Christianity, but cruelty is Infidelity. We
> may trust to our Orthodoxy, but Cruelty is the worst of Heresies.
> —Humphry Primatt[1]

Introduction: A Revolution in Animal Rights?

Humphry Primatt was an Anglican clergyman who left the Church of England in 1774 and shortly after published one of the foundational works of animal ethics, *A Dissertation on the Duty of Mercy and the Sin of Cruelty to Brute Animals* (1776). His only known publication, this 326-page anticruelty manifesto was the first book wholly dedicated to the protection of non-human animals, seeking to rectify the "mistaken notion" that "*Man alone of all Terrestrial animals is the only proper object of Mercy and Compassion, because he is the most highly favored and distinguished,*" while other creatures were, by contrast, thought "*Brutes . . . mere Excrescencies [sic] of Nature, beneath our notice, and infinitely unworthy of the care and cognisance of the Almighty.*"[2] Arguing against the prejudice that acted to "limit [justice] to our own species only" (i), Primatt emphasized the unlimited and universal

---

[1] Humphry Primatt, *A Dissertation on the Duty of Mercy and the Sin of Cruelty to Brute Animals* (London: T. Cadell, 1776), 321–22.

[2] Primatt, *Dissertation on the Duty of Mercy*, ii–iii. I will refer to this work as *Duty of Mercy* henceforth, and further references to this edition will be from this edition and cited parenthetically in the text by page number. Transcriptions are my own and preserve the spelling, grammar, capitalization, and italicization of the original text. The outmoded convention of block capitalization for emphasis, however, has not been preserved. Any clarifying additions or alterations are indicated with square brackets, and my own abridgments with ellipses.

Adam Bridgen, *Humphry Primatt (1735–1777)* In: *Animal Theologians*. Edited by: Andrew Linzey and Clair Linzey, Oxford University Press. © Oxford University Press 2023. DOI: 10.1093/oso/9780197655542.003.0006

extent of God's love and argued that true Christianity required care toward *all* created beings, "whether Beast, or Bird, or Fish, or Fly, or Worm," from the "highest rational to the lowest sensitive" (ii–iii). To ignore this requirement was, in fact, apostasy. Primatt warned that God "*will undoubtedly require of Man, superior Man, a strict account of his conduct to every creature entrusted to his care, or coming in his way; and who will avenge every instance of wanton cruelty and oppression*" (iv). Reasoning deductively from "the Principles of Nature" (1–78) before vindicating his conclusions through an in-depth analysis of scripture (78–326), Primatt reflected a naturalistic, rationalistic shift in early modern theological thinking on animals and also in didactic writing more broadly. Addressing himself to both ordained ministers and laymen, Primatt sought to provoke a simple but consequential reformation of the principles and practices of Christians—of all denominations.

Duty of Mercy occupies a pivotal place in histories of the animal rights movement. James Turner refers to 1776 as "that revolutionary *annus mirabilis*,"[3] which saw not only the American Declaration of Independence but also this declaration of the value of the lives of nonhuman animals. Primatt's view was pioneering, Turner argues, because he sidestepped abstruse theological discussions about animal souls, speech, or reason and focused on sentience.[4] Primatt, who wrote that "Pain is pain, whether it be inflicted on man or on beast; and the creature that suffers it, whether man or beast, being sensible of the misery of it whilst it lasts, suffers *Evil*" (7–8), is said to have anticipated the central argument of animal rights thinking, providing the "original"[5] of Jeremy Bentham's utilitarian maxim regarding animals: "The question is not can they *reason*? Nor, can they *talk*? But can they *suffer*?"[6] Primatt thus offered one of the earliest explicit critiques of what we would now know as speciesism—the prejudicial favoring of the interests of individuals belonging to humankind over the interests of members of other species—and he argued, accordingly, for the extension of welfare concerns to animals as well as humans.

Late eighteenth-century Britain saw a range of reform movements, the most prominent being the nationwide campaign to abolish the slave trade,

---

[3] James Turner, *Reckoning with the Beast: Animals, Pain, and Humility in the Victorian Mind* (Baltimore: Johns Hopkins University Press, 1980), 11.

[4] Turner, *Reckoning with the Beast*, 11.

[5] Aaron Garrett, *Animal Rights and Souls in the Eighteenth Century*, 6 vols. (Bristol: Thoemmes Press, 2000), 1:xix. Some of the biographical details about Primatt in this work are inaccurate.

[6] Jeremy Bentham, *Introduction to the Principles of Morals and Legislation* (London: T. Payne and Son, 1789), chap. 17, para. 4, footnote.

which reached its acme in 1788–89 under the MP William Wilberforce and the evangelical Clapham Sect. As Richard Ryder notes, Primatt was "active in attacking the slave trade and frequently drew the analogy between racism and the exploitation of nonhumans."[7] In parallel with the growth of humanitarianism, therefore, Primatt provided the intellectual foundations for the organized animal welfare movement that would emerge in the early nineteenth century.[8] Overall, *Duty of Mercy* sought to reorient ideas about humankind's place within the Chain of Being (4–7), a model that imagined creation as a hierarchical system with God and the angels at the top, followed by humankind and then animals, plants, and minerals below. While this concept was often cited as a justification for humankind's right to use lower beings as they wished, the chain could also suggest the connectedness of humans to other animals, as well as their own subordination to God's will.[9] In a distinctively legalistic articulation of this more animal-friendly theocentric viewpoint, Primatt argued that by virtue of the superior moral, rational, and spiritual capacities bestowed upon humankind, humans owed *greater* consideration to animals, and by the same logic "cruelty of Men to Brutes is more heinous (in point of injustice) than the cruelty of Men unto Men" (35)—a considerable elevation of the rights of animals over humans, in consideration of animals' innocence, vulnerability, and limited nature.[10]

While the aforementioned analyses have done much to establish Primatt's importance within the modern development of animal protectionism, there has been little interrogation of how exactly Primatt came to his views, of what drove him to publish those views when and in the form that he did, and of the impact they had in the "revolutionary" year of 1776 and shortly thereafter. Critical consideration of the contexts in which *Duty of Mercy* was written is not only lacking but also, in some cases, misleading. In a highly driven

[7] Richard D. Ryder, *Animal Revolution: Changing Attitudes towards Speciesism* (Oxford: Berg, 2000; first published 1989), 62.

[8] As has long been said, "Dr. Primatt's book may be considered the foundation-stone" of the first animal protection agency, the (Royal) Society for the Prevention of Cruelty to Animals (est. 1824). Edward G. Fairholme and Wellesley Pain, *A Century of Work for Animals* (London: J. Murray, 1924), 10.

[9] For an excellent discussion of the surprising conduciveness of the "Great Chain of Being" to animal rights, see James P. Carson, "The Great Chain of Being as an Ecological Idea," in *Animals and Humans: Sensibility and Representation, 1650–1820*, ed. Katherine M. Quinsey (Oxford: Oxford University Press, 2017), 99–118.

[10] See Andreas-Holger Maehle, "Cruelty and Kindness to the 'Brute Creation': Stability and Change in the Ethics of the Man–Animal Relationship, 1600–1850," in *Animals and Human Society: Changing Perspectives*, ed. Aubrey Manning and James Serpell (London: Routledge, 1994), 89; Aaron Garrett, "Animals and Ethics in the History of Modern Moral Philosophy," in *The Oxford Handbook of Animal Ethics*, ed. T. L. Beauchamp and R. G. Frey (Oxford: Oxford University Press, 2011), 80–81.

thesis isolating the rise of pro-animal sentiments to the eighteenth century, Nathaniel Wolloch claims that a "new libertine attitude towards religion" in the 1770s "enabled" Primatt to "present new opinions which would have been severely attacked two hundred, or even one hundred years earlier."[11] Overlooking the prior development—even preponderance—of theology concerned with the welfare of animals and human duties toward them, Wolloch demonstrates the narrowness of eighteenth-century historiography on this subject.[12] Another related view that needs complicating is that Primatt's "distinction" in the history of animal protectionism "was that he approached the subject from the standpoint of a clergyman of the Established Church," as a "retired Anglican vicar" or "loyal cleric."[13] In reality, Primatt left the Church of England in 1774—at just thirty-nine years old—due to his growing discontentment with it and his fellow clerics' doctrinalism, and out of a conviction that he could do more good outside of the church than within it. While his premature death in 1777 helped to preserve his reputation as an Anglican clergyman, his activities in the 1770s point in a different direction.

This chapter brings together a range of overlooked biographical sources, such as letter collections, contemporary accounts, reviews, reader responses, and marginalia, in an attempt to recover not only Primatt's growing disaffection with the church but also the radical atavism of *Duty of Mercy* as a tool of reform that rebuked the moral laxity of religious *and* social authorities, insisting that animal protection was an intrinsic part of the Christian faith. Despite Primatt's recognition as a "Latitudinarian clergyman" in historical studies, an awareness of his participation in clerical protest and his attendant views and influences has yet to be brought into discussions of his animal

[11] Nathaniel Wolloch, *Subjugated Animals: Animals and Anthropocentrism in Early Modern European Culture* (Amherst, NY: Humanity Books, 2006), 62. While claiming that Primatt's arguments were radically new, Wolloch suggests that his theological approach was nevertheless "anachronistic" and "not generally illustrative of the intellectual climate of the eighteenth century" (61). This progressivist view of the inevitable collapse of religious authority in the face of empirical science is misleading; specifically, it overlooks the continuing importance of theological discourse in moral arguments about animals well into the late eighteenth century.

[12] For a useful corrective, see Robert N. Watson, "Protestant Animals: Puritan Sects and English Animal-Protection Sentiment, 1550–1650," *English Literary History* 81, no. 4 (2014): 1111–48, esp. 1139–41.

[13] Jan Morris, "On the Animal Revelation Front: 'The Duty of Mercy,'" review of *Duty of Mercy*, by Humphry Primatt, *The Independent*, March 20, 1993, accessed February 28, 2019, http://www.independent.co.uk/arts-entertainment/books/book-revi.ew-on-the-animal-revelation-front-the-duty-of-mercy-humphrey-primatt-centaur-press-899-1498795.html. This common mistake has not been corrected by scholars, who typically describe Primatt as a "Cambridge graduate and retired clergyman," without qualification. See David Perkins, *Romanticism and Animal Rights* (Cambridge: Cambridge University Press, 2003), 2.

advocacy.[14] As I argue, while Primatt's break with the church was indicative of a desire for greater religious freedom, its more practical implication was his integration into leading circles of Rational Dissent in England. Tracing Primatt's involvement in the establishment of the first Unitarian chapel in London, on Essex Street, and the various personages he encountered in this new cosmopolitan setting, there is reason to believe that Primatt was introduced to the natural theology of both Benjamin Franklin (1706–1790) and his progenitor, the "divine physiologist" Thomas Tryon (1634–1703). Franklin has not previously been thought of as an influence on Primatt, and though Primatt has often been compared with Tryon, no direct connection between them has yet been attempted.[15] By considering Franklin's *A Dissertation on Liberty and Necessity, Pleasure and Pain* (1725) and Tryon's magnum opus, *The Way to Health* (1683), among other works, I will present a range of illuminating analogues for *Duty of Mercy* that suggest Primatt's engagement with and development on a much earlier tradition of theological discussion of animals. In this way, I seek to nuance our traditional account of Primatt as a singular or "revolutionary" adherent of the established church. As I contend, Primatt instead occupied a moderate and mediating position, and his importance in the tradition of animal theology was not so much his singularity as his ability to *incorporate* some of the more esoteric ideas of a wide range of theologians, Anglican and Dissenting, into the religious and public mainstream.

The 1770s Religious Context: From Latitudinarianism to Dissent

As Ryder's short entry in the *Oxford Dictionary of National Biography* attests, "little is known of [Humphry] Primatt's life."[16] Primatt was born in London in 1735, the younger son of the Reverend William Primatt, and received a BA from Clare College, Cambridge, in 1757, followed by an MA in 1764. Once

---

[14] G. M. Ditchfield, introduction to *The Letters of Theophilus Lindsey (1723–1808)*, by Theophilus Lindsey, ed. G. M. Ditchfield, 2 vols. (Woodbridge: Boydell Press, 2007), 1:lvi.

[15] John Simons, *Animal Rights and the Politics of Literary Representation* (Basingstoke: Palgrave Macmillan, 2002), 42; Richard D. Ryder, *The Political Animal: The Conquest of Speciesism* (London: McFarland, 1998), 16–17; Andrew Linzey, *Animal Theology* (London: SCM Press, 1994), 15–17, 20.

[16] Richard D. Ryder, "Primatt, Humphry (bap. 1735, d. 1776/7)," *Oxford Dictionary of National Biography*, January 2008, accessed March 17, 2017, http://dx.doi.org/10.1093/ref:odnb/47020.

ordained, he became vicar of Higham in Suffolk in 1760 and then also rector for Brampton and Swardeston, in Norfolk, in 1761 and 1766, respectively. He married in 1769. Inheriting half of his late father's estate in 1770, he appears to have lived comfortably—until his own untimely death on February 23, 1777.[17] In addition, Ryder notes that Primatt was "a signatory of the (unsuccessful) Feathers tavern petition" of 1771–72, was then made doctor of divinity by Marischal College, Aberdeen, in September 1773, and subsequently "resigned his living in 1774" and moved to Kingston upon Thames, in London.[18] Unfortunately, this is all the context we have for the publication of *Duty of Mercy*, which seems to have emerged somewhat miraculously from the pen of this inconspicuous ex-clergyman. There are few primary sources that tell us anything about Primatt, and *Duty of Mercy* contains—surprisingly for a debut work—no foreword or autobiographical note. Given this paucity (or even purposeful self-effacement) a much wider range of sources is needed to contextualize *Duty of Mercy*.

Our starting point is Primatt's involvement in the Feathers Tavern petition in 1771–72. This petition sought to end the requirement that Oxbridge graduates and those seeking to enter holy orders subscribe to the Thirty-Nine Articles—a regulatory post-Reformation statement of the codes and doctrines of the Church of England. Yet this only gets us so far in terms of the intellectual background of *Duty of Mercy*. Of course, we might suppose that Primatt distanced himself from the church because he deemed it complicit in humankind's cruelty toward animals. As G. H. Toulmin (1754–1817) noted in 1780, contemporary thinking was that "everything is created for our practical use,"[19] and such an exclusionary notion of human importance had typically gone unchallenged in the High Church. However, there is no evidence

---

[17] Although critics have seemed unsure whether Primatt died in 1776 or 1777, the *London Chronicle* confirms that Primatt died in Kingston-upon-Thames on February 23, 1777. "Country News," *London Chronicle*, February 25–27, 1777, 195.

[18] Ryder, "Primatt, Humphry." Ryder's chronology of Primatt's career does not quite agree with contemporary sources, local historians, or Primatt's own statement in 1773 that he had *already* resigned from his Norfolk livings (in 1771). See John Chambers, *A General History of the County of Norfolk*, 2 vols. (Norwich: John Stacy, 1829), 2:813; Tony Copsey, *Suffolk Writers from the Beginning until 1800: A Catalogue of Suffolk Authors with Some Account of Their Lives and a List of Their Writings* (Ipswich: Book Company, 2000), 394; John Nichols, *Illustrations of the Literary History of the Eighteenth Century: Consisting of Authentic Memoirs and Original Letters of Eminent Persons*, 6 vols. (London: Nichols, Son, and Bentley, 1822), 5:841.

[19] Quoted in Ryder, *Animal Revolution*, 63; see also Watson, "Protestant Animals," 1112–13. Toulmin was an Edinburgh graduate and doctor who wrote *The Antiquity and Duration of the World* (1780). For an excellent contextualization of his radical theories and influence, see Roy S. Porter, "Philosophy and Politics of a Geologist: G. H. Toulmin (1754–1817)," *Journal of the History of Ideas* 39 (1978): 435–50.

that Primatt yet held strong views about animals or, even if he did, that they drove his opposition to subscription. Rather, Primatt was expressing a view not uncommon at the time—particularly among the more robust wing of latitudinarianism—that compulsory conformity to the church's institutional norms frustrated a more individual, rational understanding and elaboration of Christian principles. The latitudinarian position preferred "the use of reason, rather than coercion, to convert theological opponents and a willingness to make compromises in ecclesiology, if not in matters of doctrine, in order to live in charity within a single Church and alongside as broad a group of Christians as possible."[20] Although latitudinarians "did not form a clearly-defined party," increasingly over the eighteenth century the term was used "to designate an important, and increasingly influential, body of opinion within the Established Church."[21] Further studies have argued that under the pressure of intellectual and political developments, by the 1760s there was growing coherence between latitudinarian and Dissenting positions, and subsequently new affiliations arose as once-compliant clergymen began to rebel against the Church of England's continuing inflexibility and isolationism.[22]

Cambridge, Primatt's alma mater, was the principal center of resistance to the Thirty-Nine Articles, particularly under the sway of the latitudinarian priests Edmund Law, master of Peterhouse from 1756 to 1768, and Francis Blackburne, who launched a decisive attack on subscription in *The Confessional, or a Full and Free Enquiry into the Right, Utility, and Success of Establishing Confessions of Faith and Doctrine in Protestant Churches* in 1766. The subsequent Feathers Tavern petition drew some 250 signatures

[20] Scott Mandelbrote, "The Uses of Natural Theology in Seventeenth-Century England," *Science in Context* 20 (2007): 457–58.

[21] John Gascoigne, "Anglican Latitudinarianism and Political Radicalism in the Late Eighteenth Century," *History* 71, no. 231 (1986): 23. The term "latitudinarian" must be used with caution: originally a pejorative term applied to those who were willing to change their allegiances during the civil war, it reflects a more moderate position than Gascoigne suggests. That said, in the 1770s, with the subscription debate creating new divisions within the church, those of a more moderate position were once again presented with a compromising and by no means straightforward choice between two opposed sides. For a useful corrective, see John Spurr, "'Latitudinarianism' and the Restoration Church," *Historical Journal* 31, no. 1 (1988): 61–82.

[22] Martin Fitzpatrick, "Latitudinarianism at the Parting of the Ways: A Suggestion," in *The Church of England c. 1689–c. 1833: From Toleration to Tractarianism*, ed. John Walsh, Colin Haydon, and Stephen Taylor (Cambridge: Cambridge University Press, 1993), 209–27. Parallel with the Feathers Tavern petition was Edward Pickard's 1772–74 petition that sought to modify the 1689 Toleration Act, which insisted that Dissenters' places of worship be registered, their preachers licensed, and certain oaths of allegiance accepted.

from around the country, the vast majority being Cambridge clergymen.[23] That Primatt was a signatory of this petition is therefore not all that remarkable. That he resigned his living after Parliament's rejection of the petition is more unusual, however, and suggests a more determined belief in the principle of religious freedom.[24] On closer inspection, it appears that far from a being a "retired" or "loyal cleric," Primatt was in fact identifying with and even espousing Rational Dissent. In 1773 Primatt received an honorary degree from Marischal College, Aberdeen, a recognition that had previously been awarded to the Scottish Dissenting minister and writer Rev. Dr. John Calder (1733–1815) and that seems to have been granted to Primatt on the recommendation of the Scottish poet and moral philosopher James Beattie.[25] In his letters to Calder between 1773 and 1774, Primatt reveals that he was an avid reader of Joseph Priestley's Dissenting mouthpiece, the *Theological Repository* (1769–71), and discusses with interest numerous other Rational Dissenters, such as Thomas Amory, Ebenezer Radcliffe, William Graham, Richard Price, and Theophilus Lindsey (1723–1808).[26] Primatt clearly valued Calder's friendship, confessing that he was otherwise "debarred from all rational discourse, through the narrow and bigoted notions of his [church] brethren."[27] For the same reason he regrets Lindsey's "resolution to quit the Church," reflecting that "it is absolutely necessary some of our friends should stay in it to help our common cause. . . . I fear, if all the friends of truth renounce the Church Communion, spiritual tyranny will raise again its Gorgon head, and the fires of Smithfield again be kindled by the flashes of lightning from the Vatican."[28] Lindsey was Blackburne's son-in-law and one of the most active campaigners against compulsory subscription, but unlike

---

[23] For a list of 197 of the circa 250 signatories to the 1771–72 Feathers Tavern petition, including a "Humphrey Primott," see V. M. H., "List of the Petitioning Clergy, 1772," *Monthly Repository* 13 (January 1818): 17.

[24] Helen Braithwaite, *Romanticism, Publishing and Dissent: Joseph Johnson and the Cause of Liberty* (Basingstoke: Palgrave Macmillan, 2003), 23, 26. The petition was voted down in Parliament, 217 to 71, in February 1772 and once again (without a division) in May 1774.

[25] Wm. S. Mitchell, "Humphry Primatt," *Notes and Queries* 194, no. 1 (January 8, 1949): 19. See James Beattie, *James Beattie's London Diary 1773*, ed. Ralph S. Walker (Aberdeen: Aberdeen University Press, 1946), 78, 134. For the growing links between Marischal College and leading Dissenters in the eighteenth century, see Paul B. Wood, *The Aberdeen Enlightenment: The Arts Curriculum in the Eighteenth Century* (Aberdeen: Aberdeen University Press, 1993), 50–55.

[26] Nichols, *Illustrations*, 5:839–44. The six letters cover the period from June 16, 1773, to March 16, 1774 (one slightly later letter is undated).

[27] Humphry Primatt to John Calder, November 11, 1773, in Nichols, *Illustrations*, 5:840.

[28] Humphry Primatt to John Calder, November 20, 1773, in Nichols, *Illustrations*, 5:842. One thing that Protestants, and even latitudinarians, had in common in the eighteenth century was an absolute aversion to the existential (and geopolitical, considering its predominance in the rest of Europe) threat of Catholicism.

most clergymen who acquiesced to the petition's defeat—perhaps compromising, like Blackburne, by refusing any further promotions—Lindsey
publicly declared his intent to resign his Yorkshire living in 1773.[29] The dismissal of the petition was likewise the final straw for Primatt, who confided
to Calder in no uncertain terms, "For my own part, I am heartily sick . . . and
shall be glad to get out of bondage, and fully purpose to do it."[30]

Primatt resigned from his remaining Higham living at the end of 1774.[31]
Although only a couple of his letters survive from this year, they reveal that
he was already in contact with Lindsey and incorporating himself increasingly into Dissenting networks. In 1774 Lindsey was planning to establish a
new chapel in London, an action that confirmed him as "one of the most controversial clergymen of the late eighteenth century" and led to the establishment of Unitarianism as a distinctive denomination in Britain.[32] Although
Lindsey's original intention had been "to bring about internal ecclesiastical
reform, not to assail the church from without," as George Ditchfield argues,
Essex Hall subsequently became "a focus for both theological and political
radicalism and [Lindsey] himself became a point of contact for relations between leading reformers, both anglican and dissenting."[33] Despite Primatt's
initial doubts about the scheme, records reveal that he was soon brought
into the fold.[34] In fact, Lindsey's table of the thirty original benefactors (for
the purchase of Essex House and the building of the chapel) began with
an entry for "Revd. Dr. Primatt," for a sum of fifty pounds.[35] The opening
of the chapel on Sunday, April 17, 1774, was a spectacle that drew over two
hundred Londoners, and numerous witnesses described the scene. One

[29] For an excellent explanation of the petition process and the various positions that petitioners
took following its failure in Parliament, see Braithwaite, *Romanticism, Publishing and Dissent*, 21–23.
[30] Humphry Primatt to John Calder, November 20, 1773, in Nichols, *Illustrations*, 5:841.
[31] Notice that Primatt had "resigned . . . from a Dissatisfaction at his having complied with the
Subscription required by Law to the 39 Articles, and a Disapprobation of certain Particulars in the
Doctrine of the and public Worship of the Church of England" was printed in the "Postscript" to the
St. James's Chronicle or the British Evening Post 2166 (December 29–31, 1774). As discussed previously, Primatt had already resigned both of his Norfolk livings in 1771.
[32] Ditchfield, introduction to *The Letters of Theophilus Lindsey*, 1:xvii. The chapel did not formally
announce itself as Unitarian, since Unitarianism's exclusion from the Toleration Act of 1689 meant it
was technically illegal, but Lindsey made no secret of his sympathies. For a good account of the emergence of Unitarianism, see John Seed, "The Role of Unitarianism in the Formation of Liberal Culture
1775–1851: A Social History" (PhD diss., University of Hull, 1981).
[33] Ditchfield, introduction to *The Letters of Theophilus Lindsey*, 1:xvii.
[34] As Primatt writes in early 1774, he had attempted "to dissuade [Lindsey] from his present
scheme of erecting a new Church, lest it should obstruct the Dissenter's cause." Humphry Primatt to
John Calder, March 16, 1774, in Nichols, *Illustrations*, 5:844.
[35] Theophilus Lindsey, letter to William Tayleur, May 20, 1777, in *Letters of Theophilus Lindsey*,
1:238–41. The table of benefactors also includes "Mr Cadell," Primatt's later publisher, who matched
his contribution.

contemporary, the barrister John Lee, wrote the following day that there were "about ten coaches at the door," and among the notable individuals in attendance whom he "knew and remember[ed] were Lord Despenser, Dr. Franklin, Dr. Priestley, Dr. Calder, . . . Dr. Hinckley, Dr. Chambers, Dr. Primatt, and two or three other clergymen."[36] Also in attendance—the historian John Seed notes—were the Dukes of Norfolk and Richmond, Sir Francis Dashwood, and several other barristers, as well as a government spy; as Seed argues, Lindsey's chapel epitomized a "gentlemanly form of religious dissent,"[37] drawing prominent Dissenters but also establishment figures, which no doubt helped to protect the chapel from state interference. Moving to London later that year, Primatt thus found himself in the midst of this Dissenting community, which presented significant opportunities for the "rational discourse" of which he had formerly been deprived.

Primatt's latitudinarian tendencies and his further immersion within the culture of dissent in the mid-1770s had a tangible impact on *Duty of Mercy*. As Spurr has argued, although the term "latitudinarian" tends to suggest that those to whom the term was applied held positive views "on reason, science, toleration, and moderation" distinct from other clergymen, in reality these concerns were much more commonplace.[38] Far from being "enabled" to express his opinions in the 1770s by a "new libertine attitude towards religion"[39]—as Wolloch puts it— Primatt should be considered as part of a much longer tradition of Protestant progressives who had been making theological and ethical statements about animals in an attempt "to direct the mainstream of the nation's religious life."[40] That being said, Primatt's engagement with leading Dissenters undoubtedly exposed him to a broader range of thinking on animals, as well as ideas about the importance of practical moral reasoning within religion. For example, in the *Book of Common Prayer Reformed according to the Plan of the Late Dr. Samuel Clarke* (1774), which was designed for use in the Essex Hall chapel, Lindsey channels into his morning prayer the opening of Clarke's celebrated sermon "The Great Duty of Universal Love" (1705):

---

[36] John Lee, Esq. to Mr. Cappe at York, April 18, 1774, qtd. in Thomas Belsham, ed., *Memoirs of the Late Reverend Theophilus Lindsey* (London: Williams and Norgate, 1873), 70n.

[37] John Seed, "Gentlemen Dissenters: The Social and Political Meanings of Rational Dissent in the 1770s and 1780s," *Historical Journal* 28, no. 2 (1985): 305.

[38] Spurr, "'Latitudinarianism' and the Restoration Church," 62.

[39] Wolloch, *Subjugated Animals*, 62.

[40] Spurr, "'Latitudinarianism' and the Restoration Church," 77.

Make us sincere in heart and uncorrupt before thee, and just and upright in all our dealings with our fellow-creatures; and dispose us to acts of kindness towards them, to share in their distresses and relieve them, and to rejoice in and embrace all opportunities of doing them good, especially of promoting their eternal happiness.[41]

As a latitudinarian and affiliate of the Cambridge Platonists, Clarke (1675–1729) was the preeminent clerical advocate of rational religion in England, which held that understanding of God could be perfected through the scientific study of nature as well as through humankind's own moral intuitions.[42] This development had huge implications for eighteenth-century philosophy and, not surprisingly, destabilized old customs and opened up new avenues for the consideration of animals qua animals, as well as consideration of human responsibilities toward them.[43] Therefore, while many have sought to claim Primatt as a "modern," perceiving his prioritization of deductive reasoning in *Duty of Mercy* as a revolutionary "secularization of ethics"—much as how Benjamin Franklin's famous editing of the opening of the Declaration of Independence has since been received—at the heart of this new rational emphasis was nevertheless the fundamental belief in God.[44] In short, it was believed that God had bestowed reason upon humans for good ends and for the discovery of religious truth.

While latitudinarianism thus shapes Primatt's desire to communicate with readers regardless of their "faiths or forms of worship" and "to prove, that Mercy to Brutes is as much a doctrine of divine revelation, as it is itself reasonable, amiable, useful, and just" (iv–viii), he also emphasizes a *social* universalism that is suggestive of his more radical influences. A comparable work of animal welfare thinking, the Reverend James Granger's sermon

<hr />

[41] Theophilus Lindsey, *The Book of Common Prayer Reformed according to the Plan of the Late Dr. Samuel Clarke Together with Psalter or Psalms of David and A Collection of Hymns for Public Worship* (London: J. Johnson, 1774), 125.

[42] Thomas C. Pfizenmaier, *The Trinitarian Theology of Dr. Samuel Clarke (1675–1729): Context, Sources, and Controversy* (Leiden: E. J. Brill, 1997), 29–42.

[43] Mandelbrote, "Uses of Natural Theology," 456.

[44] Carol Stewart, *The Eighteenth-Century Novel and the Secularization of Ethics* (Farnham: Ashgate, 2010), 150. For a typical discussion of Franklin's editing of the Declaration from an "assertion of religion . . . into an assertion of rationality," see Walter Isaacson, *Benjamin Franklin: An American Life* (New York: Simon & Schuster, 2003), 312. Much has been made of Franklin's alteration of the line "We hold these truths to be sacred and undeniable" to "We hold these truths to be self-evident" in the Declaration draft, when in either case an explicit religious argument is presented immediately following. Far from displaying an abandonment of God, it was the rather the force of reason *within* religious thinking that contributed to these "revolutionary" changes.

An Apology for the Brute Creation (1772), earlier argued that animals had an "equal right" to life and happiness and that causing animals unnecessary suffering thus was a "sin against the great law of humanity."[45] However, Granger added, more conservatively, that this admonition was "only applicable to the most stupid, ignorant, and uncivilized part of our countrymen. Those of higher rank and knowledge are far more humane and benevolent."[46] Absolving the educated classes of any culpability for animal harm, Granger is perfect fodder for the cynical view that the anticruelty movement was "reinforced by the solicitude for public order and labour discipline"[47] and hence "betrayed a pronounced class bias."[48]

By contrast, Primatt states that cruelty is "a subject in which men of all ranks are concerned" and explains that he writes principally for those "who have not had the advantage of a liberal education" (v). Given that the length and cost of *Duty of Mercy* would have precluded most lower-class readers, it is clear that Primatt immediately sought to reeducate middle- and upper-class audiences laboring under the darkness of *illiberal* prejudices. Accordingly, Primatt draws attention to the "foolish and detestable" (76) cruelty "of every class and denomination" (77): his examples include popular entertainments such as cockfighting and bullbaiting but also upper-class sports ("to chace [*sic*] a Stag, to hunt a Fox, or course a Hare") and culinary predilections ("to roast a Lobster, or to crimp a Fish") (75). He rejects the supposition, therefore, "that no diversion can be *cruel* that has the sanction of Nobility; and that no dish can be *unblessed* that is served up at a Great man's table, though *the kitchen is covered with blood, and filled with the cries of creatures expiring in tortures*" (26).[49] Although reviewers of *Duty of Mercy* praised Primatt's benevolence, they objected to this universalism, stating sanctimoniously that "a sixpenny sermon is more likely to be read by offenders against the dictates of

---

[45] James Granger, *An Apology for the Brute Creation, a Sermon Preached by James Granger, Vicar of Shiplake, Oxfordshire, in October 18, 1772* (London: T. Davies, 1772), 8.

[46] Granger, *An Apology for the Brute Creation*, 12.

[47] Robert Malcolmson, *Popular Recreations in English Society, 1700–1850* (Cambridge: Cambridge University Press, 1973), 138.

[48] Malcolmson, *Popular Recreations*, 152.

[49] Here Primatt italicizes quotations from Alexander Pope's (1688–1744) essay, [Against Barbarity to Animals], published in the *Guardian* 61 (May 21, 1713). This source is also quoted on pages 56 and 260 of *Duty of Mercy*. Pope influentially wrote: "I Cannot think it extravagant to imagine, that mankind are no less in proportion, accountable for the ill use of their dominion over creatures of the lower rank of beings, than for the exercise of tyranny over their own species. The more entirely the inferior creation is submitted to our power, the more answerable we should seem for our mismanagement of it; and the rather, as the very condition of nature renders these creatures incapable of receiving any recompence in another life for their ill treatment in this."

humanity."[50] Whether Primatt had channeled similar views into his sermons is unknown, but like other fellow Dissenters, Primatt did not shrink from condemning the practices of his own class.[51] Quite unique for the politically polarized late eighteenth century, Primatt held culpable all classes and faiths, and indeed humanity as a whole, for humans' viciousness toward animals.

Accessing the Margins of Animal Rights Thinking

While critics have contextualized Primatt among (and typically as the culmination of) a number of eighteenth-century clergymen, such as John Hildrop (1682–1756), Francis Hutcheson (1694–1746), Joseph Butler (1692–1752), Philip Doddridge (1702–1751), Robert Morris (1702–1754), John Wesley (1704–1791), and Richard Dean (1727–1788), Primatt's involvement in Essex Hall chapel offered him access to an even broader range of thinking on animals.[52] The practical benevolent ethos of the chapel aside, the various theologians it attracted offered Primatt unparalleled opportunities for developing his ideas about animals more specifically. One of a number of Dissenters Lindsey invited to preach at the chapel was Joseph Priestley, whom Primatt later drew upon in his discussion of the hopelessness of animal misery.[53] While the pulpit was a likely source for thinking on animals, equally significant would have been the congregation. Given its centrality, the chapel was visited by Anglicans and Dissenters from a plurality of backgrounds—in passing as well as on a more permanent basis. In the former category was the Calvinist Augustus Toplady (1740–1778), who attended a sermon at Essex

---

[50] "A Dissertation on the Duty of Mercy, and Sin of Cruelty, to Brute Animals," review of *Duty of Mercy*, by Humphry Primatt, *Monthly Review* 54 (May 1776), 415.

[51] An uncompromising notion of the greater moral responsibilities—and hence failings—of the powerful was not uncommon in gentlemanly radicalism. The Duke of Grafton, for example, one of the earliest members of the Essex Street chapel, in his portentous 1789 *Hints, &c,. Submitted to the Serious Attention of the Clergy, Nobility and Gentry, . . . by a Layman*, directed criticism at the ruling classes from an assumed lower-class perspective.

[52] See, for example, Simons, *Animal Rights*, 43; Aaron Garrett, "Francis Hutcheson and the Origin of Animal Rights," *Journal of the History of Philosophy* 45, no. 2 (2007): 260–65; and Margaret Puskar-Pasewicz, ed., *Cultural Encyclopedia of Vegetarianism* (Santa Barbara, CA: Greenwood, 2010), 230. The vegetarian architect Robert Morris, referred to as "an apostle of 'English reason,'" is one of the few nonclerical figures Primatt is placed alongside. Morris's work *A Reasonable Plea for the Animal Creation* (1746) is, in fact, one of the more compelling analogues for Primatt's *Duty of Mercy*. Carol J. Adams, "Robert Morris and a Lost 18th Century Vegetarian Book," *Organization & Environment* 18, no. 4 (2005): 459.

[53] Ditchfield, introduction to *The Letters of Theophilus Lindsey*, 1:lxiv. Primatt references Priestley's *Institutes of Natural and Revealed Religion* (1772–74), vol. 1, part 1, sec. 3, on page 67 of *Duty of Mercy*.

Hall on May 23, 1774.[54] He disliked Lindsey's sermon and never returned; nevertheless, Toplady had written and preached extensively against cruelty to animals.[55] Although no records can tell us about the entire constituency of the chapel, it undoubtedly would have formed a significant background to the development (and even emergence) of Primatt's outspoken animal protection views.

Given the lack of information about Primatt's reading, a consideration of his potential contacts in the 1770s seems to be the most plausible means of inferring (some of) his influences.[56] There is one individual in particular whose involvement in Essex Hall may help shed light on the development in moral thinking that Primatt's *Duty of Mercy* presented. Benjamin Franklin was one of the notable attendees at the chapel's opening, as described above.[57] Between 1757 and 1775, Franklin was lodging in London, on Craven Street near the Strand, and besides his duties as a colonial agent, he spent his time conducting experiments, writing, traveling, and meeting various contemporary thinkers. A political and religious antiauthoritarian, Franklin was friends with the Dissenters Richard Price and Joseph Priestley and had recently asked for advice as to where in central London he might find a church practicing "*rational* Christianity."[58] It is little surprise, therefore, that Franklin, like Primatt, was one of the earliest contributors to Essex Hall, and it is more than likely that he continued to attend services until his fateful return to America in March 1775—the chapel was, after all, only a five-minute walk from his lodgings.[59]

---

[54] Ditchfield, introduction to *The Letters of Theophilus Lindsey*, 1:lvii–lviii.

[55] Keith Thomas, *Man and the Natural World: Changing Attitudes in England, 1500–1800* (London: Penguin, 1984), 140, 173.

[56] Other than the works noted in his letters, the only records we have for Primatt's reading are the nine rare works in Latin, Hebrew, and Greek that he bequeathed to Marischal College, Aberdeen. The titles of these books can be seen at http://www.abdn.ac.uk/library/provenance/owners/906/. In *Duty of Mercy*, Primatt likewise lists very few contemporary sources: he quotes Alexander Pope and cites Joseph Priestley, as discussed previously, but the only other thinkers he references are the latitudinarian Arthur Ashley Sykes (1684–1756), quoting from his 1756 *Scripture Doctrine of the Redemption of Man by Jesus Christ* (at 132), and Anglican bishop Thomas Newton (1704–1782), recommending his 1754 *Dissertation on the Prophecies* (at 233).

[57] Franklin's own correspondence relating to his attendance at the Essex Hall opening is available in Benjamin Franklin, *The Papers of Benjamin Franklin*, ed. William B. Willcox et al., 43 vols. to date (New Haven, CT: Yale University Press, 1959–), 21:195–97.

[58] Benjamin Franklin, letter to Richard Price, September 28, 1772, in Franklin, *Papers*, 19:303–4.

[59] Alongside Lord Despencer's ten, Franklin contributed five guineas to the building of the chapel. See Franklin, *Papers*, 21:196 n. 7. As late as 1784, Franklin asked Priestley about the chapel's progress. See Benjamin Franklin, letter to Joseph Priestley, August 21, 1784, in Benjamin Franklin, *The Writings of Benjamin Franklin*, ed. Albert Henry Smyth, 10 vols. (New York: Macmillan, 1907), 9:266–67.

Whether Primatt met Franklin at Essex Hall or rather in some more in-formal social setting, the strongest suggestion of Primatt's encounter and moreover engagement with Franklin comes from a comparison of their works.[60] For brevity, I will limit my discussion to the resemblances between Primatt's *Duty of Mercy* and "the most ambitious metaphysical inquiry"[61] that Franklin had attempted, *A Dissertation on Liberty and Necessity, Pleasure and Pain* (1725). In this latter pamphlet, Franklin proceeds from the core beliefs that unite "People of almost every Sect and Opinion"—namely, God's om-nipotence and omnibenevolence—to deduce facts about nature of pain and pleasure, capacities that he argued all creatures possessed.[62] As he explains, being *"form'd and endu'd with Life,"* animals—like humans—must be able to *"receive a Capacity of the Sensation of* Uneasiness *or* Pain."[63] Franklin argued that pain, far from being a design flaw, is in fact essential for the perpetua-tion of life and for self-improvement: "We are first mov'd by *Pain,* and the whole succeeding Course of our Lives is but one continu'd Series of Action with a View to be freed from it."[64] In the midst of this providentialist argu-ment, Franklin also claims the essential equality between all created beings. He argues that *"If there is no such Thing as Free-Will in Creatures, there can be neither Merit or Demerit in Creatures. . . . And therefore every Creature must be equally esteem'd by the Creator."*[65] Franklin goes on to argue, moreover, that just as they are "equally esteem'd," animals "are, as in Justice they ought to be, equally us'd."[66] Although not the main thrust of his *Dissertation,* this tentative statement about the moral *equality* of humans and animals is im-portant; the idea that animals lacked free will but were nevertheless valued in the creation was common in seventeenth-century thought, but the combina-tion of this with the Aristotelian notion of animal sensitivity to pain (and an-imals' natural motivating desire to be freed from it) was more profound and

[60] Since 1765, Franklin's "Club of Honest Whigs" had met fortnightly at the London Coffee House to discuss religion, politics, science, and other topics, and its regulars included Calder, Price, Priestley, and some also think Lindsey. Although the entire roll call of this unusually inclusive club has "never been determined with reasonable accuracy," it would not be surprising if Primatt was invited at some point or accompanied one of his Dissenting friends as a guest. Verner W. Crane, "The Club of Honest Whigs: Friends of Science and Liberty," *William and Mary Quarterly* 23, no. 2 (1966): 210, 219–21.

[61] Douglas Anderson, *The Radical Enlightenments of Benjamin Franklin* (Baltimore: Johns Hopkins University Press, 1997), 33. See 33–53 for an extensive contextualization of Franklin's *Dissertation.*

[62] Benjamin Franklin, *A Dissertation on Liberty and Necessity, Pleasure and Pain* (London, 1725), 4–5.

[63] Franklin, *A Dissertation on Liberty,* 14.

[64] Franklin, *A Dissertation on Liberty,* 15.

[65] Franklin, *A Dissertation on Liberty,* 13.

[66] Franklin, *A Dissertation on Liberty,* 14.

underpins Franklin's quite decisive normative statement that humans had a moral duty of *care* toward animals—just as much as they had toward other human beings.[67]

Primatt employs the same observations as Franklin to arrive at a further and more forceful range of conclusions. He repeats the traditional view that creatures are endued with "different powers, appetites, perfections, and even comparative defects . . . necessary to answer the different purposes for which they were created, and to promote the common good of the whole" (2). In an unmistakable echo of Franklin's terminology, Primatt adds that since all beings are "neither more nor less than God made them, there is no more de-merit in a beast being a beast, than there is merit in a man being a man; that is, there is neither merit nor demerit in either of them" (13). While Primatt accepts that animals are mentally inferior to humans, he insists that this cannot be used (pace Descartes) to suggest that animals do not feel pain. Like Franklin, he states that pain is "necessary in itself"—"the spur to incite us to self-preservation"—but which "we nevertheless are naturally averse to," and this rule applies regardless of "Superiority of rank or station" (7). There being only differences in degree, not nature, between humans and animals, Primatt concludes that "Pain is pain, whether it be inflicted on man or on beast; and the creature that suffers it, whether man or beast, being sensible of the misery of it whilst it lasts, suffers *Evil*" (7–8). While Franklin notes how animals ought to be treated "in Justice,"[68] Primatt explicates the critical sub-text of Franklin's statement, protesting the actual *injustice* of humans' current treatment of animals. Although Primatt could have drawn these ideas from elsewhere, the terms he uses and the objections he makes suggest a conscious engagement with Franklin's work and thus Franklin himself.[69]

[67] Franklin's tentative theories therefore predate Francis Hutcheson's far better-known, more com-prehensive, and generally more influential argument for animal rights upon the basis of sentience in Hutcheson's posthumously published *System of Moral Philosophy* (1755), which he began composing in the 1730s. See Garrett, "Francis Hutcheson and the Origin of Animal Rights," 256.

[68] Franklin, *A Dissertation on Liberty*, 14.

[69] If Primatt did know of this work, it would have been through Franklin himself. Franklin recalled, "There were only a hundred Copies printed, of which I gave a few to Friends, and afterwards disliking the Piece, as conceiving it might have an ill Tendency, I burnt the rest, except one Copy." Benjamin Franklin, letter to Benjamin Vaughan, November 9, 1779, in Franklin, *Papers*, 31:58–60. A pirated edition was printed in Dublin in 1733, but copies appear to have been extremely rare. The only known surviving copies are in the Library of Congress and Yale University Library. At the time of writing, Franklin was in his second month as a printer's apprentice in London: his employer, Samuel Palmer, was impressed by his work but found the argument "abominable." See Hazel Wilkinson, "Benjamin Franklin's London Printing 1725–26," *Papers of the Bibliographical Society of America* 110, no. 2 (2016): 143–44.

If Primatt was in discussion with Franklin, it is also possible that he was apprised of one of Franklin's most formative influences—the seventeenth-century shepherd turned vegetarian divine Thomas Tryon (1634–1703). In his youth, Franklin had read Tryon's practical, spiritual, and ethical compendium *The Way to Health, Long Life, and Happiness* (1683) and had become an immediate convert: in addition to Franklin's becoming vegetarian, Tryon's unusual writing style, experimentalism, and interest in unseen forces seems to have rubbed off on the similarly self-made Franklin. It is commonly thought that "Master Tryon"—as Franklin referred to him in his unfinished autobiography, begun in 1771—was only a passing influence on the young Franklin.[70] Recently, however, Dana Medoro made an excellent case for the "long-term" influence of Tryon's writing on Franklin, describing that influence as "tenacious rather than temporary."[71] As Medoro argues, not only did Tryon's vegetarian philosophy shape Franklin's dietary regime well into his later years, but Tryon also remained a profound influence on Franklin's conceptions and even self-conception. As late as 1774, in fact, Franklin put out his own self-help guide called *The Way to Wealth*, which compiled various aphorisms from Franklin's long-running Tryonesque almanac *Poor Richard* into a sixteen-page speech.[72] Thanks to his autobiographical testimony, Franklin is now one of the more obvious examples of Tryon's lasting influence; however, his engagement with Tryon's ideas cannot have been altogether uncommon. The possible existence of a "Tryonist" sect aside, the most straightforward way in which Tryon's thinking persisted into the eighteenth century was through the endurance of his works—which, as Nigel Smith writes, "seem to have been the backbone of an eighteenth-century vegetarian canon."[73] His *Memoirs* were published posthumously in 1705 (and once again in America in 1761), alongside a handful of works he had written sometime

[70] Joyce E. Chaplin, ed., *Benjamin Franklin's Autobiography: An Authoritative Text, Contexts, Criticism* (New York: Norton, 2012), 20, 37.

[71] Dana Medoro, "Benjamin Franklin's Autobiography as an Eighteenth-Century Omnivore's Dilemma," *English Studies in Canada* 36, no. 4 (2010): 95.

[72] Benjamin Franklin, *The Way to Wealth, as Clearly Shewn in the Preface of an Old Pennsylvania Almanack, Intitled, Poor Richard Improved* (London, 1774). For an account of the vast popularity of this work, which apparently went through 145 editions, see Sophus A. Reinert, "*The Way to Wealth* around the World: Benjamin Franklin and the Globalization of American Capitalism," *American History Review* 120, no. 1 (2015): 61–97. Tryon had also published *The Way to Save Wealth* (1695) and *The Way to Get Wealth* (1703).

[73] Nigel Smith, "Enthusiasm and Enlightenment: Of Food, Filth, and Slavery," in *The Country and the City Revisited*, ed. Donna Landry, Gerald McLean, and Joseph P. Ward (Cambridge: Cambridge University Press, 1999), 107.

before his death.[74] More importantly, *The Way to Health* was printed in at least five editions before 1700, and it has been calculated that on average Tryon went to press once every four months.[75] Accordingly, Tryon left not only an important autobiographical memorial but also a substantial material legacy. It would not therefore have been terribly difficult for Primatt to access Tryon's work(s)—particularly, *The Way to Health*—whether via Franklin, through the secondhand book trade, or in libraries were he inclined (Hans Sloane, for example, was a collector of Tryon's works and donated more than fifteen of them to the British Museum in 1759).[76]

In some ways Tryon and Primatt were very different. Whereas Tryon was a resolute vegetarian who pulled no punches in describing the ferocity and also foolishness of flesh-eating, Primatt did not attack carnivorism directly. However, it is difficult to see how Primatt's anticruelty admonitions could be compatible with the slaughter of animals. Indeed, he speaks quite profoundly—as someone perhaps himself struggling with the implications of a carnivorous diet—of the guilt of humans' consumption of animal flesh. With clear rhetoric he expresses amazement at how "our hands are so imbrued in blood, that in spite of the shame of it, we cannot wash them clean" (50), before proceeding to address some of the rationalizations that were used to justify violence toward animals. Responding to the idea that "*Man has a permission to eat the flesh of some animals*," Primatt argues that this "cannot be done without . . . putting them to some degree of pain." Even were this acceptable, Primatt argues, such "permission" could not allow putting animals "to *unnecessary* pain, or *lingering* death" (52). The question he implicitly poses to his readers, therefore, is whether eating flesh was indeed necessary, a notion further placed in doubt given his later citation of the Edenic vegetarianism of Genesis 1:29 in his discussion of what God had originally

[74] Thomas Tryon, *Some Memoirs of the Life of Mr. Tho. Tryon* (London: T. Sowle, 1705; Philadelphia: W. Dunlap, 1761).

[75] Tristram Stuart, *The Bloodless Revolution: Radical Vegetarians and the Discovery of India* (London: HarperCollins, 2006), 62–63. Although not always carrying his name, further printings of Tryon's writing were soon to follow, such as *The Way to Health and Long Life: or, A Discourse of Temperance* (London: G. Conyers, 1726).

[76] *The Sloane Printed Books Catalogue*, s.v. "Tryon/Tryton," accessed March 29, 2017, http://www.bl.uk/catalogues/sloane. The availability of Tryon's works is further suggested by the fact that his name appears repeatedly in a new wave of vegetarian thinking in the early nineteenth century. Joseph Ritson quotes "old Tryon" at length in his Joseph Ritson *Essay on Abstinence from Animal Food, as a Moral Duty* (London: Richard Phillips, 1802), 192–95. "Sallads by Tryon" appears in George Nicholson's *On Food* (London: Poughnill, 1803), 33–34, and Sir John Sinclair lavishes praise on Tryon's works, which he provides a full bibliography of, in his *Code of Health and Longevity*, 4 vols. (Edinburgh: Constable and Company, 1807), 2:297–98.

"appointed unto Man his *proper* food, and declared *what should be meat for Him*" (116).

Few individuals could match the profundity of Tryon's vegetarian world-view and activism, and so it is perhaps an unhelpful comparison in this case. In other respects, however, there are numerous similarities between Tryon's and Primatt's animal theology—likely arising from their mutual emphasis on reasoning, natural observation, and a core belief in Christian fellowship and compassion. Such characteristics were of course quite common in pro-animal theological positions, but between Tryon and Primatt there are also some more unusual correspondences. The most notable similarity, I argue, is how they draw attention to the compound injustice of humankind's domination over animals by reference to acts of discriminatory violence between humans — and particularly, colonial slavery.

Although a connection between human slaughter and flesh-eating had been around since classical times, the antislavery framework through which both Tryon and Primatt make this parallel was timely and unique.[77] The depth of Tryon's thought on this issue, as a one-time witness and outspoken critic of slavery, is explained in my previous chapter in this collection. To summarize, from early on in his career, Tryon made various comparisons between humans' violent consumption of animals and humankind's exploitation of fellow humans: it was not reason, he argued, but mistaken "Custom" that made the "killing, handling, and feeding upon *Flesh* and *Blood*, without distinction, so easy and familiar unto Mankind: And the same is to be understood of men, *killing and Oppressing those of their own Kind*."[78] Extending this comparison to colonial slavery, Tryon observed how authority was maintained, psychologically as much as physically, over African slaves, and applied these insights to suggest the enslavement of *animals* to humans' carnivorous appetites. Making explicit Tryon's allusive rhetoric, Primatt condenses both antislavery and anticruelty views into one succinct frame, in a memorable statement of the comparative injustice of racism and speciesism:

It has pleased God, the Father of all races, to cover some men with white skins, and others with black skins: but as there is neither merit nor demerit

[77] Diane Kelsey McColley, *Poetry and Ecology in the Age of Milton and Marvell* (Aldershot: Ashgate, 2007), 172–74, 181.

[78] Thomas Tryon [Philotheos Physiologus, pseud.], *The Way to Health, Long Life, and Happiness* (London: Andrew Sowle, 1683), 378.

in complexion, the *white* man (notwithstanding the barbarity of custom and prejudice) can have no right, but virtue of his *colour*, to enslave and tyrannise over a *black* man; nor has a *fair* man any right to despise, abuse, and insult a *brown* man. Nor do I believe that a *tall* man, by virtue of his *stature*, has any legal right to trample a *dwarf* under his foot. For, whether a man is wise or foolish, white or black, fair or brown, tall or short, and I might add *rich* or *poor* (for it is no more a man's choice to be poor, than it is to be a fool, or a dwarf, or black, or tawney,) such he is by God's appoint-ment. . . . Now if amongst men the differences of their powers of the mind, and of their complexion, stature, and accidents of fortune, do not give to any one man a right to abuse or insult any other man on account of these differences; for the same reason, a man can have no natural right to abuse and torment a beast, merely because a beast has not the *mental* powers of a man. (11–12)[79]

Just as slavery is an evil falsely justified on the basis of "custom and prejudice," Primatt makes very clear that the same debunking should apply to humans' contempt for animals. Though Primatt's greater confidence in denouncing slavery can be attributed to a recent upsurge in protests against slavery in the early 1770s, particularly among Dissenting thinkers known to him person-ally, this provocative reference to colonial slavery to draw attention to the similar plight of animals was an approach first pioneered by Tryon.[80]

---

[79] Interestingly, this passage proceeds through precisely the same steps as Tryon's early antisla-very tract, with the addition of the explicit statement on the injustice of animal cruelty. Arguing in "The Negro's Complaint" against supremacist "pretensions"—the assumed physical and intellectual perfections by which Christians "claim[ed] a Right to make [Africans their] Slaves and Vassals"—Tryon has the slave pose three questions: (1) "As for the *blackness* of our Skins, we find no reason to be ashamed of it, 'tis the *Livery* which our great Lord and Maker hath thought fit we should wear; . . . Can we help it, if the Sun by too close and fervent Kisses, and the nature of the Climate and Soil where we were Born, hath tinctur'd us with a dark Complexion?"; (2) "Have not you [a] variety of Complexions amongst your selves; some very *White* and *Fair*, others *Brown*, many *swarthy*, and several *Cole-black*?"; and (3) "And would it be reasonable that each sort of these should quarrel with the other, and a man be made a *Slave* forever, meerly because his Beard is *Red*, or his Eyebrows *Black*?" Thomas Tryon [Philotheos Physiologus, pseud.], *Friendly Advice to the Gentlemen Planters of the East and West Indies* (London: Andrew Sowle, 1684), 114–16.

[80] Primatt's Dissenting circle held some of the most outspoken antislavery opinions at the time: in his *Essay on the Nature and Immutability of Truth* (Edinburgh: A. Kincaid & J. Bell, 1770), James Beattie launched a demolition of the racist arguments in Hume's *Treatise of Human Nature* (1739–40). In 1772, Granville Sharpe (a friend of Dr. Calder, in fact) won a case on behalf of James Somerset, a black slave whose owner sought to take him by force out of Britain. Known as the Mansfield Judgment, the ruling effectively made slavery illegal within Britain (although it did not, of course, alter the case overseas). Prompted by this, in April 1772, Franklin began corresponding with the Philadelphia abolitionist Anthony Benezet, which seems to have inspired a piece Franklin then wrote for the *London Chronicle* (June 18–20, 1772) in which he abjured, uncompromisingly, the "constant

Another similarity between Tryon and Primatt is the reformed vision of human–animal relations that they accordingly propose. Both thinkers move on from their conception of the vast degree of humans' abuse over creatures to articulate the necessity of animal rights, as a protective response to the anthropocentric prerogatives customarily claimed by humankind. Just as Tryon decries the vanity of imagining that the human "has Right, because he has Power to Oppress,"[81] Primatt reaches the same anti-Hobbesian conclusion that "the Power granted unto Men to *rule over* the Brutes, cannot be a Power to abuse or oppress them" (141). Although not uncommon in Christian thought, this reconceptualization of humankind's place in the creation—as a "dependent and *accountable*" creature with "a Duty [of mercy to other creatures], from which the Superiority of his station cannot exempt him" (33–34)—reaches a new pitch in Tryon's and Primatt's writing. Indeed, both present the fundamental logic of animal protectionism by making the argument that the rights of the weaker should *outweigh* the claims of the stronger. Given the evident disparity in the power between humans and innocent animals, and hence the "unparallel'd Barbarity"[82] enacted on animals without end, Tryon believed that animals in particular required "a natural Right of being exempted from our Power."[83] Primatt similarly perceived that humans' superiority rendered the "cruelty of Men to Brutes more heinous (in point of justice) than the cruelty of Men unto Men," (35) justifying this statement by explaining how animals were unable to defend themselves, plead their cause, or receive justice or restitution for injury. In response to this silence—or rather humankind's dismissal of the cries of animals—Tryon sought to give them "a Voice to cry against their Oppressions" in his imaginative monologues;[84] in development of this approach, Primatt explicates its rational basis as a form of advocacy, stating that "the less [animals] are able to vindicate themselves against the abuse of human power, the more they stand in need of superior Interposition on their behalf" (143).

butchery of the human species by this pestilent detectable traffic in the bodies and souls of men." See "The Sommersett Case and the Slave Trade," in Franklin, *Papers*, 19:187–88.

[81] [Thomas Tryon], *Averroeana: Being A Transcript of Several Letters from Averroes . . . Also Several Letters from Pythagoras to the King of India* (London: T. Sowle, 1695), 156.
[82] Thomas Tryon [Philotheos Physiologus, pseud.], *The Country-Man's Companion, or a New Method of Ordering Horses & Sheep* (London: Andrew Sowle, 1684), 151.
[83] Tryon, *Several Letters from Averroes*, 149.
[84] Tryon, *Country-Man's Companion*, A3r.

Conclusion: Primatt's Establishment Influence

It is possible that Primatt did not meet Franklin nor had any knowledge of Tryon. His arguments about the value of animal lives, their physiological and even psychological similarity to humans, and the ethical problem of their suffering could have been drawn from a range of classical and early modern thinkers—indeed not only Protestant theologians but also humanist philosophers such as Pierre Gassendi, Walter Charleton, John Evelyn, and Margaret Cavendish (who were themselves drawing on Erasmus, Agrippa, Vives, and also classical authors).[85] Primatt's ownership of sixteenth- and seventeenth-century works, in Hebrew, Greek, and Latin, indicates more than the necessary prerequisites for engaging with this learned tradition; his reference to his "literary pursuits" in late 1773 also suggests a sustained course of reading.[86] Nevertheless, the close connections between Primatt and Franklin, in terms of their discussions of pain, and the conceptual similarities between Primatt and Tryon, in terms of their comparisons of speciesism and racism, remain significant. Not only is it highly probable that Primatt met Franklin, given their vicinity in Dissenting circles in London, but it also is not unlikely that this meeting led to further discussion. Whether or not this led to an engagement with the work of Thomas Tryon is harder to determine. Regardless, it is significant how in each case a conception of the logic of animal rights was arrived at through a consideration of the oppressive effects of racism. Far more than animal protection being simply an extension of humanitarianism, therefore, it seems that the horrors of colonial slavery, long before they were outlawed in Britain, were provoking not only antislavery sentiments but also a questioning of anthropocentrism more specifically.

We must reject the view that Primatt was a singular Anglican thinker, who simply "retired" from holy orders in order to compose his thoughts in peace and quiet. New biographical evidence indicates that Primatt not only resigned from the church following the rejection of the Feathers Tavern petition, but he also befriended and sought the acquaintance of various Dissenting thinkers throughout the 1770s, and he even went on to support Theophilus Lindsey's radical project for a new, Unitarian chapel in London. With Primatt having moved to the city in 1774, Essex Hall and the Anglicans

---

[85] I thank Justin Begley author of Chapter 1 in his volume for suggestions on earlier authors Primatt could have read.

[86] Humphry Primatt to John Calder, November 11, 1773, in Nichols, *Illustrations*, 5:840.

and Dissenters alike congregating there formed an important background to the conception of *Duty of Mercy*. Whether from the pulpit or from the congregation, whether from the Dissenter Joseph Priestley or from the Calvinist August Toplady, Primatt would have encountered opinions from a wide range of perspectives. Thus surrounded by theologians, and by no means averse to "rational discussion," Primatt would not have found it difficult at all to sound out his ideas and moreover to gain recommendations for further study. These were opportunities he likely leaped at. Although in historical studies Primatt has been repeatedly referred to as a "revolutionary" ethicist—the progenitor of the modern animal welfare movement—his thinking is nevertheless highly *embedded* in a dynamic late eighteenth-century Dissenting context, and harkens back to older debates as much as it looks forward to new ones. While he certainly gained authority from his reputation as a "loyal cleric" of the established church, the strength of Primatt's thinking arrives rather from his engagement with the *peripheries* of Protestant thought and his ability to bring unorthodox views back into the center ground.

In connecting Primatt with a longer history of animal protection, this chapter also acts as a corrective to the view that Primatt's ideas would have been disapproved of one hundred or two hundred years earlier. More importantly, it defends Primatt from the more extreme teleology that his ideas were not even accepted in his own time. Peter Singer recently remarked that Primatt's "ideas about animals [were] so progressive that until the late twentieth century they found very few supporters."[87] Although *some* animal welfare arguments, such as James Granger's, received "almost universal disgust" from parishioners,[88] nowhere is such a negative reception recorded for Primatt. In fact, the *Monthly Review* praised his "learned and laboured deductions,"[89] while the *Critical Review* gave his book its "warmest approbation," praising its "considerable extent" and "excellent *design*."[90] *Duty of Mercy* not only drew public praise but also influenced numerous other thinkers in the 1780s and 1790s, who proclaimed it with enthusiasm.[91]

[87] Peter Singer, foreword to "Animals in the Eighteenth Century," special issue, *Journal for Eighteenth-Century Studies* 33, no. 4 (2010): 429.
[88] Granger, *An Apology for the Brute Creation*, postscript.
[89] "A Dissertation on the Duty of Mercy, and Sin of Cruelty, to Brute Animals," review of *Duty of Mercy*, by Humphry Primatt, *Monthly Review* 54 (May 1776), 415.
[90] "A Dissertation on the Duty of Mercy and Sin of Cruelty to brute Animals," review of *Duty of Mercy*, by Humphry Primatt, *Critical Review, or, Annals of Literature* 41 (February 1776): 143. A lengthy and laudatory review also appears in *The London Review of English and Foreign Literature* 3 (February 1776): 133–39.
[91] See, for example, "The Rights of the Brute Creation to Tenderness from Man, deduced from the twofold Consideration, amongst many others, particularly the Tenor of the sacred Writings in their

One such thinker was the Dorset clergyman John Toogood, whose popular abridgment of *Duty of Mercy* went into three editions before the end of the century and subsequently appeared in America also.[92] In a valuable example of reader response, the playwright and clergyman James Plumptre (1771–1832) described *Duty of Mercy* as "a rare book, upon a peculiar topic, by a kindly man, a Clergyman of the Establishment."[93] Inspired by Primatt, Plumptre went on to preach on the "Duties of Man to the Brute Creation" to the University of Cambridge in 1796 and published *Three Discourses on the Case of the Animal Creation and the Duties of Man to Them* in 1816.[94] In 1822, and then again in 1831 and 1834, *Duty of Mercy* was republished by Rev. Arthur Broome (1779–1837), the founder of the SPCA. Even if Primatt's work had begun as a somewhat specialist production, in less than fifty years it had been reprinted in a wide variety of forms and moreover had inspired a new generation of animal rights thinkers as well as the first animal welfare laws. By contrast, Primatt has been republished just once in the twentieth century, in a loving (though now out of print) edition by Richard Ryder.[95] Far from Singer's supposition, therefore, it would seem that it is modern-day audiences who have lost touch with the radically *reasonable* articulations of this rebellious eighteenth-century theologian.

Favour, of their being so susceptible of Pain and Pleasure as well as Man himself, tho' not susceptible of a just Compensation of any Evils Man may inflict on them. From the Rev. Dr. Primatt's most excellent Dissertation on the Duty of Mercy and Sin of Cruelty to Brute Animals," *Town and Country Magazine, or Universal Repository* 11 (August 1779): 414–16; "The Country Clergyman's Shrovetide Gift to his Parishioners. Taken chiefly from Dr. Primatt's Dissertation on the Duty of Mercy, and Sin of Cruelty to Brutes," review, *Monthly Review* 68 (January 1783): 90–91. A more provocative discussion referencing Primatt is [Old Mingo, pseud.], "Cruelty to Asses, and Horses, and Negroes," *Diary or Woodfall's Register* 236 (December 29, 1789).

   92 See also John Toogood, *The Country Clergyman's Shrovetide Gift to His Parishioners. Taken Chiefly from Dr. Primatt's Dissertation on the Duty of Mercy, and Sin of Cruelty to Brutes*, 3rd ed. (Sherborne: Goadby and Lerpiniere, 1792). The first and second editions arrived in the 1780s. A fourth edition was published in Boston, Massachusetts, in 1802. In fact, *Duty of Mercy* had already inspired the American sermons of the Presbyterian preacher Herman Daggett; see Norm Phelps, *The Longest Struggle: Animal Advocacy from Pythagoras to PETA* (New York: Lantern Books, 2007), 87–88. *Duty of Mercy* was also translated into German in 1778, as *Ueber Barmherzigkeit und Grausamkeit gegen die thierische Schöpfung* (Halle, 1778).
   93 Plumptre's copy of *Duty of Mercy*, with annotations, is preserved in the New York Public Library (ESTC T140541). The quotation is from Plumptre's inscription on the blank leaf preceding the title page.
   94 See Perkins, *Romanticism and Animal Rights*, 2. Perkins overlooks Primatt's influence on Plumptre.
   95 Richard D. Ryder, "Editor's Introduction," in *The Duty of Mercy and the Sin of Cruelty to Brute Animals*, by Humphry Primatt, ed. Richard D. Ryder (Fontwell, Sussex: Centaur, 1992), 13.

Bibliography

Adams, Carol J. "Robert Morris and a Lost 18th Century Vegetarian Book." *Organization & Environment* 18, no. 4 (2005): 458–66.

Anderson, Douglas. *The Radical Enlightenments of Benjamin Franklin*. Baltimore: Johns Hopkins University Press, 1997.

Beattie, James. *Essay on the Nature and Immutability of Truth*. Edinburgh: A. Kincaid & J. Bell, 1770.

Beattie, James. *James Beattie's London Diary 1773*. Edited by Ralph S. Walker. Aberdeen: Aberdeen University Press, 1946.

Belsham, Thomas, ed. *Memoirs of the Late Reverend Theophilus Lindsey*. London: Williams and Norgate, 1873.

Bentham, Jeremy. *Introduction to the Principles of Morals and Legislation*. London: T. Payne and Son, 1789.

Braithwaite, Helen. *Romanticism, Publishing and Dissent: Joseph Johnson and the Cause of Liberty*. Basingstoke: Palgrave Macmillan, 2003.

Carson, James P. "The Great Chain of Being as an Ecological Idea." In *Animals and Humans: Sensibility and Representation, 1650–1820*, edited by Katherine M. Quinsey, 99–118. Oxford: Oxford University Press, 2017.

Chambers, John. *A General History of the County of Norfolk*. 2 vols. Norwich: John Stacy, 1829.

Chaplin, Joyce E., ed. *Benjamin Franklin's Autobiography: An Authoritative Text, Contexts, Criticism*. New York: Norton, 2012.

Copsey, Tony. *Suffolk Writers from the Beginning until 1800: A Catalogue of Suffolk Authors with Some Account of Their Lives and a List of Their Writings*. Ipswich: Book Company, 2000.

"Country News." *London Chronicle*, February 25–27, 1777, 194–95.

"The Country Clergyman's Shrovetide Gift to his Parishioners. Taken chiefly from Dr. Primatt's Dissertation on the Duty of Mercy, and Sin of Cruelty to Brutes." Review. *Monthly Review* 68 (January 1783): 90–91.

Crane, Verner W. "The Club of Honest Whigs: Friends of Science and Liberty." *William and Mary Quarterly* 23, no. 2 (1966): 210–33.

"A Dissertation on the Duty of Mercy and Sin of Cruelty to Brute Animals." Review of *Duty of Mercy*, by Humphry Primatt. *London Review of English and Foreign Literature* 3 (February 1776): 133–39.

"A Dissertation on the Duty of Mercy, and Sin of Cruelty, to Brute Animals." Review of *Duty of Mercy*, by Humphry Primatt. *Monthly Review* 15 (May 1776): 415.

Ditchfield, G. M. Introduction to *The Letters of Theophilus Lindsey (1723–1808)*, by Theophilus Lindsey. Edited by G. M. Ditchfield. 2 vols. Woodbridge: Boydell Press, 2007.

Fairholme, Edward G., and Wellesley Pain. *A Century of Work for Animals*. London: J. Murray, 1924.

Fitzpatrick, Martin. "Latitudinarianism at the Parting of the Ways: A Suggestion." In *The Church of England c. 1689–c. 1833: From Toleration to Tractarianism*, edited by John Walsh, Colin Haydon, and Stephen Taylor, 209–27. Cambridge: Cambridge University Press, 1993.

Franklin, Benjamin. *A Dissertation on Liberty and Necessity, Pleasure and Pain*. London, 1725.

Franklin, Benjamin. *The Papers of Benjamin Franklin*. Edited by William B. Willcox et al. 43 vols. to date. New Haven, CT: Yale University Press, 1959–.

Franklin, Benjamin. *The Way to Wealth, as Clearly Shewn in the Preface of an Old Pennsylvania Almanack, Intitled, Poor Richard Improved*. London, 1774.

Franklin, Benjamin. *The Writings of Benjamin Franklin*. Edited by Albert Henry Smyth. 10 vols. New York: Macmillan, 1907.

Garrett, Aaron. *Animal Rights and Souls in the Eighteenth Century*. 6 vols. Bristol: Thoemmes Press, 2000.

Garrett, Aaron. "Animals and Ethics in the History of Modern Moral Philosophy." In *The Oxford Handbook of Animal Ethics*, edited by T. L. Beauchamp and R. G. Frey. Oxford: Oxford University Press, 2011.

Garrett, Aaron. "Francis Hutcheson and the Origin of Animal Rights." *Journal of the History of Philosophy* 45, no. 2 (2007).

Gascoigne, John. "Anglican Latitudinarianism and Political Radicalism in the Late Eighteenth Century." *History* 71, no. 231 (1986).

Granger, James. *An Apology for the Brute Creation, a Sermon Preached by James Granger, Vicar of Shiplake, Oxfordshire, in October 18, 1772*. London: T. Davies, 1772.

Isaacson, Walter. *Benjamin Franklin: An American Life*. New York: Simon & Schuster, 2003.

Lindsey, Theophilus. *The Book of Common Prayer Reformed according to the Plan of the Late Dr. Samuel Clarke Together with Psalter or Psalms of David and A Collection of Hymns for Public Worship*. London: J. Johnson, 1774.

Linzey, Andrew. *Animal Theology*. London: SCM Press, 1994.

Maehle, Andreas-Holger. "Cruelty and Kindness to the 'Brute Creation': Stability and Change in the Ethics of the Man–Animal Relationship, 1600–1850." In *Animals and Human Society: Changing Perspectives*, edited by Aubrey Manning and James Serpell. London: Routledge, 1994.

Malcolmson, Robert. *Popular Recreations in English Society, 1700–1850*. Cambridge: Cambridge University Press, 1973.

Mandelbrote, Scott. "The Uses of Natural Theology in Seventeenth-Century England." *Science in Context* 20 (2007).

McColley, Diane Kelsey. *Poetry and Ecology in the Age of Milton and Marvell*. Aldershot: Ashgate, 2007.

Medoro, Dana. "Benjamin Franklin's Autobiography as an Eighteenth-Century Omnivore's Dilemma." *English Studies in Canada* 36, no. 4 (2010).

Mitchell, Wm. S. "Humphry Primatt." *Notes and Queries* 194, no. 1 (January 8, 1949).

Morris, Jan. "On the Animal Revelation Front: 'The Duty of Mercy.'" Review of *Duty of Mercy*, by Humphry Primatt. *The Independent*, March 20, 1993. Accessed February 28, 2019. http://www.independent.co.uk/arts-entertainment/books/book-revi.ew-on-the-animal-revelation-front-the-duty-of-mercy-humphrey-primatt-centaur-press-899-1498795.html.

Nichols, John. *Illustrations of the Literary History of the Eighteenth Century: Consisting of Authentic Memoirs and Original Letters of Eminent Persons*, 6 vols. (London: Nichols, Son, and Bentley, 1822.

Nicholson, George. *On Food*. London: Poughnill, 1803.

[Old Mingo, pseud.] "Cruelty to Asses, and Horses, and Negroes." *Diary or Woodfall's Register* 236 (December 29, 1789).

Perkins, David. *Romanticism and Animal Rights*. Cambridge: Cambridge University Press, 2003.

Pfizenmaier, Thomas C. *The Trinitarian Theology of Dr. Samuel Clarke (1675–1729): Context, Sources, and Controversy*. Leiden: E. J. Brill, 1997.

Phelps, Norm. *The Longest Struggle: Animal Advocacy from Pythagoras to PETA*. New York: Lantern Books, 2007.

Porter, Roy S. "Philosophy and Politics of a Geologist: G. H. Toulmin (1754–1817)." *Journal of the History of Ideas* 39 (1978): 435–50.

Primatt, Humphry. *A Dissertation on the Duty of Mercy and the Sin of Cruelty to Brute Animals*. London: T. Cadell, 1776.

Puskar-Pasewicz, Margaret ed. *Cultural Encyclopedia of Vegetarianism*. Santa Barbara, CA: Greenwood, 2010.

Reinert, Sophus A. "*The Way to Wealth* around the World: Benjamin Franklin and the Globalization of American Capitalism." *American History Review* 120, no. 1 (2015): 61–97.

"The Rights of the Brute Creation to Tenderness from Man, deduced from the twofold Consideration, amongst many others, particularly the Tenor of the sacred Writings in their Favour, of their being so susceptible of Pain and Pleasure as well as Man himself, tho' not susceptible of a just Compensation of any Evils Man may inflict on them. From the Rev. Dr. Primatt's most excellent Dissertation on the Duty of Mercy and Sin of Cruelty to Brute Animals." *Town and Country Magazine, or Universal Repository* 11 (August 1779): 414–16.

Ritson, Joseph. *Essay on Abstinence from Animal Food, as a Moral Duty*. London: Richard Phillips, 1802.

Ryder, Richard D. *Animal Revolution: Changing Attitudes towards Speciesism*. Oxford: Berg, 2000. First published 1989.

Ryder, Richard D. "Editor's Introduction." In *The Duty of Mercy and the Sin of Cruelty to Brute Animals*, by Humphry Primatt, edited by Richard D. Ryder. Fontwell, Sussex: Centaur, 1992.

Ryder, Richard D. *The Political Animal: The Conquest of Speciesism*. London: McFarland, 1998.

Ryder, Richard D. "Primatt, Humphry (bap. 1735, d. 1776/7)." *Oxford Dictionary of National Biography*, January 2008. Accessed March 17, 2017. http://dx.doi.org/10.1093/ref:odnb/47020.

Seed, John "Gentlemen Dissenters: The Social and Political Meanings of Rational Dissent in the 1770s and 1780s." *Historical Journal* 28, no. 2 (1985).

Seed, John. "The Role of Unitarianism in the Formation of Liberal Culture 1775–1851: A Social History." PhD diss., University of Hull, 1981.

Simons, John. *Animal Rights and the Politics of Literary Representation*. Basingstoke: Palgrave Macmillan, 2002.

Sinclair, John. *Code of Health and Longevity*. 4 vols. Edinburgh: Constable and Company, 1807.

Singer, Peter. Foreword to "Animals in the Eighteenth Century," special issue, *Journal for Eighteenth-Century Studies* 33, no. 4 (2010).

Smith, Nigel. "Enthusiasm and Enlightenment: Of Food, Filth, and Slavery." In *The Country and the City Revisited*, edited by Donna Landry, Gerald McLean, and Joseph P. Ward. Cambridge: Cambridge University Press, 1999.

Stewart, Carol *The Eighteenth-Century Novel and the Secularization of Ethics*. Farnham: Ashgate, 2010.

Spurr, John. "'Latitudinarianism' and the Restoration Church." *Historical Journal* 31, no. 1 (1988): 61–82.

Stuart, Tristram. *The Bloodless Revolution: Radical Vegetarians and the Discovery of India.* London: HarperCollins, 2006.

Thomas, Keith. *Man and the Natural World: Changing Attitudes in England, 1500–1800.* London: Penguin, 1984.

Toogood, John. *The Country Clergyman's Shrovetide Gift to His Parishioners. Taken Chiefly from Dr. Primatt's Dissertation on the Duty of Mercy, and Sin of Cruelty to Brutes.* 3rd ed. Sherborne: Goadby and Lerpiniere, 1792.

[Tryon, Thomas]. *Averroeana: Being A Transcript of Several Letters from Averroes . . . Also Several Letters from Pythagoras to the King of India.* London: T. Sowle, 1695.

Tryon, Thomas [Philotheos Physiologus, pseud.]. *The Country-Man's Companion, or a New Method of Ordering Horses & Sheep.* London: Andrew Sowle, 1684.

Tryon, Thomas [Philotheos Physiologus, pseud.]. *Friendly Advice to the Gentlemen Planters of the East and West Indies.* London: Andrew Sowle, 1684.

Tryon, Thomas. *Some Memoirs of the Life of Mr. Tho. Tryon.* London: T. Sowle, 1705; Philadelphia: W. Dunlap, 1761.

Tryon, Thomas [Philotheos Physiologus, pseud.]. *The Way to Health, Long Life, and Happiness.* London: Andrew Sowle, 1683.

Tryon, Thomas. *The Way to Health and Long Life: or, A Discourse of Temperance.* London: G. Conyers, 1726.

"Tryon/Tryton." *The Sloane Printed Books Catalogue.* Accessed March 29, 2017, http://www.bl.uk/catalogues/sloane.

Turner, James. *Reckoning with the Beast: Animals, Pain, and Humility in the Victorian Mind.* Baltimore: Johns Hopkins University Press, 1980.

V. M. H. "List of the Petitioning Clergy, 1772." *Monthly Repository* 13 (January 1818).

Watson, Robert N. "Protestant Animals: Puritan Sects and English Animal-Protection Sentiment, 1550–1650." *English Literary History* 81, no. 4 (2014): 1111–48.

Wilkinson, Hazel. "Benjamin Franklin's London Printing 1725–26." *Papers of the Bibliographical Society of America* 110, no. 2 (2016).

Wolloch, Nathaniel. *Subjugated Animals: Animals and Anthropocentrism in Early Modern European Culture.* Amherst, NY: Humanity Books, 2006.

Wood, Paul B. *The Aberdeen Enlightenment: The Arts Curriculum in the Eighteenth Century.* Aberdeen: Aberdeen University Press, 1993.

6

William Bartram (1739–1823)

A Quaker-Inspired Animal Advocacy

Michael J. Gilmour

In a handwritten manuscript dating from the mid-1790s, perhaps the draft of an unfinished essay or letter, we find a religiously informed understanding of the dignity and worth of animals that is remarkable for its startling claims. The University of Georgia Press published this unsigned, unnamed document in 2010 under the title "The Dignity of Human Nature," and in it the American naturalist William Bartram challenges commonplace assumptions about the status of nonhuman species and humanity's moral responsibility toward them. Though he places humans at "the head, or first in the Animal Kingdome," attributing to them a unique wisdom, power, and prerogative, he also acknowledges their penchant for violence and ability "to subjugate, & even tyrannize over every other Animal."[1] This is a capability with dark potential. The human race has within its grasp the resources to eradicate all animal life and indeed would have done so by now had the "Supreme Creator & preserver"[2] not restrained them. Bartram further insists that humanity's superior intellect is no reason for hubris, nor is its greater strength proof it "is the most divine" among living things.[3]

These are not the speculations of a cloistered thinker far removed from nature but instead the musings of a well-traveled, well-studied, pious man who spent years exploring and studying the flora and fauna of eighteenth-century North America. What we find in this striking essay and throughout

---

[1] The manuscript appears in Bartram, *William Bartram: The Search for Nature's Design—Selected Art, Letters and Unpublished Writings*, ed. Thomas Hallock and Nancy E. Hoffman (Athens: University of Georgia Press, 2010), 348–58, with manuscript alterations and textual comments listed at 531–32. I cite here pp. 352–53. See, too, the introduction and commentary by Laurel Ode-Schneider that appears with the manuscript, "'The Dignity of Human Nature': William Bartram and the Great Chain of Being," 340–46.

[2] Bartram, *The Search for Nature's Design*, 353.

[3] Bartram, *The Search for Nature's Design*, 353.

Michael J. Gilmour, *William Bartram (1739–1823)* In: *Animal Theologians*. Edited by: Andrew Linzey and Clair Linzey, Oxford University Press. © Oxford University Press 2023. DOI: 10.1093/oso/9780197655542.003.0007

the diverse writings of William Bartram is a richly theological vision of the natural world, which for him is the "glorious apartment of the boundless palace of the sovereign Creator."[4] He is a useful though unlikely ally for those contemplating animal ethics in light of religious discourses, and though there is hardly sufficient space here for a thorough defense of this claim, I offer a few brief notes on the man and his writings as a first step.

William Bartram lived from 1739 to 1823 and is best known for a 1791 publication with the unwieldy title *Travels through North and South Carolina, Georgia, East and West Florida, the Cherokee Country, the Extensive Territories of the Muscogulges, or Creek Confederacy, and the Country of the Chactaws; Containing an Account of the Soil and Natural Productions of Those Regions, Together with Observations on the Manners of the Indians.* Mercifully, most refer to it simply as Bartram's *Travels*. This book rewards close reading because we find here a generous understanding of the Genesis language of dominion, one that informed the ways this eccentric flower hunter engaged other living things sharing the garden with him.

Travels is difficult to categorize. It is at once a travelogue documenting the author's journeys through parts of the North American Southeast between 1773 and 1777 and also a work of science. Bartram was a botanist who set out from his home near Philadelphia "at the request of [a patron in] London, to search ... [for] rare and useful productions of nature, chiefly in the vegetable kingdom" (1). In this book we find long lists of plant species replete with Linnaean taxonomies, as well as detailed examinations of insects and animals. But as scientific writing goes, it is a gripping tale as well. Bartram's close observations of the natural world often put life and limb at significant risk, including perilous encounters with criminals and alligators, not to mention the threats posed by illness and a hurricane. Bartram relates it all with an energetic prose every bit as entertaining as books by near contemporaries, such as Crèvecoeur's *Letters from an American Farmer* (1782)[5] or Charles Brockden Brown's *Wieland: or, The Transformation: An American Tale* (1798). *Travels* is also a study of indigenous cultures, a vehicle for philosophical and ethical musings coinciding with the birth of a new nation, and a witness to early

---

[4] William Bartram, *Bartram's Living Legacy: The "Travels" and the Nature of the South*, ed. Dorinda G. Dallmeyer (Macon, GA: Mercer University Press, 2010), xxix. There are various editions of Bartram's *Travels* available. In this chapter I use Dallmeyer's edition. Most subsequent page references to *Travels* appear in the text of the chapter, in parentheses.

[5] This book of fictional correspondence, loosely based on the writer's experiences, includes a description of William's father, John Bartram. The author J. St. John de Crèvecoeur was a friend of the Bartrams.

European settlements offering firsthand accounts of the role of slavery in the New World economy. And surprisingly for a work of science, *Travels* is beautifully poetic. Some of the English Romantic poets certainly thought so. The "incense-bearing trees" and "mighty fountains" of Coleridge's "Kubla Khan" hint at Bartram's writing, and so too does the "glorious world" of an idealized America depicted in Wordsworth's "Ruth."[6] Additionally, Thomas Carlyle, James Fenimore Cooper, and Henry David Thoreau were among Bartram's better-known readers.[7] He was also an artist, and since 1791, editions of his famous book invariably have included a selection of his drawings.

Most importantly for our purposes, Bartram observes the world through a theological lens.[8] He was a man of deep faith—a Quaker in background, though not in all respects a traditional one[9]—and his religiously informed consideration of animals, including birds, insects, reptiles, and fish, is not merely abstract. He traveled to remote parts of the continent in search of them; he touched and drew them, chased and was chased by them, and most interestingly of all, defended them, and he gave thanks to the Creator for their very existence. He was both a real-world animal advocate and a literary Adam, two descriptors I explain in turn.

Bartram the Advocate

For an illustration of Bartram's theologically motivated animal advocacy, consider his account of a "fishing and fowling" expedition on Sapelo Island, Georgia. He and some companions camped near a cool spring "amidst a

[6] Noted by the editor of a 1928 edition of Bartram's *Travels*. See Mark van Doren, "Editor's Note," in *Travels of William Bartram*, by William Bartram, ed. Mark Van Doren (New York: Dover, 1955), 5. Thomas Hallock and Nancy E. Hoffmann also remark on the "admired proto-Romantic author of *Travels*, who inspired Samuel Taylor Coleridge, William Wordsworth, Ralph Waldo Emerson, and an entire tradition of nature writing in America, [who] did not live a life of literary distinction but instead dutifully prepared lists and tables to support his brothers' apothecary and horticultural businesses." Hallock and Hoffman, introduction to Bartram, *The Search for Nature's Design*, 2.

[7] On this see, e.g., Matthew C. Smith, "Stone Blind," in Bartram, *Bartram's Living Legacy*, 511; Thomas P. Slaughter, *The Natures of John and William Bartram* (Philadelphia: University of Pennsylvania Press, 1996), xv–xvi.

[8] For further reflections on this topic, see my book *Eden's Other Residents: The Bible and Animals* (Eugene, OR: Cascade, 2014), 140–53.

[9] For helpful notes on the religious views of John and William Bartram and the ways they differed from one another and their contemporaries, see Larry R. Clarke, "The Quaker Background of William Bartram's View of Nature," *Journal of the History of Ideas* 46, no. 3 (1985): 435–48. For a rejoinder questioning some of Clarke's assertions, see Bruce Silver, "Clarke on the Quaker Background of William Bartram's Approach to Nature," *Journal of the History of Ideas* 47, no. 3 (1986): 507–10. Silver is less inclined than Clarke to attribute Bartram's view of nature to Quaker influences.

grove of the odoriferous Myrica," he says with lovely poetic flourish, and "the winding path to this salubrious fountain led through a grassy savannah" (168). He reports that several times during the night, he and members of the party visited the spring, oblivious to a lurking hazard underfoot, which came to light only the next morning when Bartram again walked along the path. This time he saw "a hideous serpent, the formidable rattle snake, in a high spiral coil, forming a circular mound half the height of [his] knees, within six inches of the narrow path" (169). Whereas the great snake remained calm, Bartram confesses, "My imagination and spirits were in a tumult, almost equally divided betwixt thanksgiving to the Supreme Creator and preserver, and the dignified nature of the generous though terrible creature, who had suffered us all to pass many times by him during the night, without injuring us in the least, although we must have touched him" (169).

Returning to report the find, Bartram was determined "to protect the life of the generous serpent." Those with him were "surprised and terrified at the sight of the animal, and in a moment acknowledged their escape from de-struction to be miraculous." Bartram writes happily, "All of us, except one person, agreed to let him lay undisturbed, and that person at length was prevailed upon to suffer him to escape" (169). This is a stranger story than it might first appear. His New World contemporaries were at war with snakes, and "whacking a rattler was something of a male rite of passage in colonial America—a moral obligation, a public service, and dangerous fun all in one."[10] That Bartram intervenes in the unnecessary killing of a snake on this and other occasions is both unexpected and illustrative of a distinctive way of thinking.

There are two things to notice in this brief scene. First, Bartram relates this particular tale to explain why he has a reputation for being, as he puts it, "an advocate or vindicator of the benevolent and peaceable disposition of animal creation in general, not only towards mankind, whom they seem to venerate, but also towards one another, except where hunger or the rational and nec-essary provocations of the sensual appetites interfere" (168). Animal advo-cacy seems oddly out of place in frontier writing, as does his insistence that even dangerous rattlesnakes have a "benevolent and peaceable disposition" (168). He speaks of the two themes at the same time, finding in this particular snake's restraint both a critique of human violence and a motivation to pro-tect animal life. The decision to kill or not kill a potentially lethal rattlesnake

---

[10] Slaughter, *Natures of John and William Bartram*, 132.

is a moral issue. As he notes in the unfinished essay mentioned previously, humans have greater power, yes, but they are prone to abuse it and so must stay their hand. This is true even when an animal is the aggressor, as we see in his account of an alligator approaching the camp of a different hunting party. Whereas some wanted to end the animal's life quickly with a rifle ball on that occasion, most "thought this would too soon deprive them of the diversion and pleasure of exercising their various inventions of torture" (159). Bartram certainly did not participate in this grisly behavior, which included thrusting fire-hardened javelins down the alligator's throat, and his use of the harsh term "torture" indicates that his companions' actions were at least gratuitous and distasteful, if not immoral.

A second thing to note about the rattlesnake story is its context. It occurs during a "fishing and fowling" expedition, and I suspect the inclusion of this narrative detail is more than incidental. Bartram tells us that animals show aggression only because of "hunger or the rational and necessary provocations of the sensual appetites" (168). Rattlesnakes bite only out of perceived necessity. Alligators attack only when hungry. Strange as it sounds, here within animal creation humans have an example of ethical behavior worthy of emulation. The hunting party in question had already been successful: "The diverting toils of the day were not fruitless, affording us opportunities of furnishing ourselves plentifully with a variety of game, fish and oysters for our supper" (168). They already had food enough. Killing the peaceful rattlesnake therefore would not have served any purpose, and so Bartram was anxious "to protect the life of the generous serpent" (169).

Turning to another story, we see Bartram attending to the subject of power relations between humans and animals in the negative. On this occasion he was in a boat with a hunter-guide and reports they saw eleven bears during the course of the day (xxxv). His companion decided to shoot one, but subtle narrative details preface the incident in ways that put this act of aggression in an unfavorable light. First, Bartram suggests that the killing of the bears was unnecessary: "in the evening my hunter, who was an excellent marksman, said that he would shoot one of them, for the sake of the skin and oil, for we had plenty and variety of provisions in our bark" (xxxv). Though bearskin and oil are certainly useful products, Bartram's phrasing indicates the absence of real need. They already had enough food. Second, they were in no danger. Not only were they in a boat observing bears on the shore, but also, he observes, the bears they saw "seemed no way surprized or affrighted at the sight of us" (xxxv). Like the generous serpent along the path, these bears posed no threat.

This preamble to the hunter's aggression makes Bartram's account of the violence all the more tragic.

> The hunter fired, and laid the largest [bear] dead on the spot, where she stood, when presently the other . . . approached the dead body, smelled, and pawed it, and appearing in agony, fell to weeping and looking upwards, then towards us, and cried out like a child. Whilst our boat approached very near, the hunter was loading his rifle in order to shoot the survivor, which was a young cub, and the slain supposed to be the dam; the continual cries of this afflicted child, bereft of its parent, affected me very sensibly, I was moved with compassion, and charging myself as if accessary to what now appeared to be a cruel murder, and endeavoured to prevail on the hunter to save its life, but to no effect! for by habit he had become insensible to compassion towards the brute creation, being now within a few yards of the harmless devoted victim, he fired, and laid it dead, upon the body of the dam. (xxxv–xxxvi)

The passage is highly anthropomorphic, with Bartram likening the weeping cub to a child, and the shooting of the dam to "cruel murder." There is also an undisguised emotional alignment of Bartram and the cub, with both of them grief-stricken after the first shot. In telling us he "was moved with compassion," Bartram indicates what he considers the appropriate response to such unrestrained violence, juxtaposing this with the attitude of the hunter, who "had become insensible to compassion towards the brute creation" (xxxv–xxxvi).

We find similar efforts to defend animals throughout *Travels*. In one story, Bartram recounts attempting to rescue a herd of deer without success: "I endeavoured to plead for their lives . . . unfortunately for their chief . . . the lucky old hunter fired and laid him prostrate upon the green turf" (128). On another occasion, those with him roused "a litter of young wolves," and after giving chase, they "soon caught one of them"; the wolf "being entangled in high grass, one of our people caught it by the hind legs and another beat out its brains with the but [*sic*] of his gun." The incident disturbed Bartram, who refers to this behavior as a "barbarous sport!" (253).

In these few anecdotes we see his disdain for human aggression against animals, which invites speculation on his motives. Why does he advocate for rattlesnakes, alligators, bears, and wolves?[11] Part of the answer lies in a worldview shaped by a particularly theological and biblical frame of reference. In *Travels*, the author-narrator operates with a very specific sense of *where* he is and *who* he is.

Bartram as Adam

Bartram insists we have "duties to each other, and all creatures and concerns that are submitted to our care and controul [*sic*]" (36). This remark recalls the subdue-and-have-dominion language of the book of Genesis and indicates Bartram's interpretation of the scripture's meaning. It also provides a clue how best to understand the William Bartram character within *Travels* who wanders through the wilderness from 1773 through 1777. He is a dominion-granted Adam in the Garden of Eden, charged by God to care for the Creator's good world. The author makes this orientation explicit in the opening pages of the book. Bartram travels from Philadelphia to the South by sea, and when he first arrives, he describes the lands before him as presenting "to the imagination, an idea of the first appearance of the earth to man at the creation" (2).[12] Bartram thus identifies with Adam and Eve and views the territories he is about to explore as a paradise—a remote colonial Garden of Eden. This literary device also presents a suggestive link with the Quaker mysticism that is part of his heritage. The Quakers generally held the natural world in higher esteem than other Protestants,[13] and George Fox himself, the founder of the movement, similarly aligned himself with Adam a hundred years earlier when celebrating an encounter with God mediated by nature.[14]

---

[11] As his participation in hunting expeditions makes clear, Bartram allows that killing animals in some circumstances is morally permissible. He writes often about hunting and his meals in *Travels*. For a fascinating examination of his diet during his time in the southeastern territories, see Kathryn E. Holland Braund, "William Bartram's Gustatory Tour," in *Fields of Vision: Essays on the "Travels" of William Bartram*, ed. Kathryn E. Holland Braund and Charlotte M. Porter (Tuscaloosa: University of Alabama Press, 2010), 33–53.

[12] Cf. Bartram, *Travels*, 32, where he refers to nature unmodified by human hands. For other Adamic language, see 121.

[13] See, e.g., Clarke, "The Quaker Background," 440: "The Quakers . . . had a more positive view of nature than previous Protestant thinkers, who, in fact, had had little interest in nature. Most early Protestants believed that man was so depraved that he could not benefit from the contemplation of nature."

[14] For instance:

The Lord's power brake forth more and more wonderfully. Now was I come up in spirit through the flaming sword into the paradise of God. All things were new, and all the creation gave another smell than before, beyond what words can utter. I knew nothing but

Bartram's incorporation of Genesis at the opening of *Travels* inevitably shapes everything that follows, and he seems to reinforce this Adam-in-Eden ethos in a number of ways. For instance, the wilderness he explores occasionally reveals an almost unnatural tranquility. On one such occasion, he describes a beautiful pool of water, so clear that predatory fish and reptiles cannot take advantage of the element of surprise as they do in murky waters. For Bartram, "this paradise of fish [seems] to exhibit a just representation of the peaceable and happy state of nature which existed before the fall" (105). Here he finds a trout passing by the nose of an alligator instead of a lion lying down with a lamb, but the echo of the Isaianic peaceful kingdom is unmistakable (Isa. 11:6–9).

At another time, he describes a beautiful scene as a "blessed unviolated spot of earth!"—a "blissful garden"—and when the moment comes for him to move on, he says he "at last broke away from the enchanting spot, and stepped on board [the] boat, hoisted sail and soon approached the coast of the main, at the cool eve of day" (98). Here he is not just Adam in Eden but arguably like the Lord God himself, "walking in the garden at the time of the evening breeze" (Gen. 3:8). He even names, in Adamic fashion, some of the natural wonders he encounters, including a bird and various species of plants, naming one among them in honor of family friend Benjamin Franklin.[15]

If indeed Bartram is Adam and southeastern North America is Eden, what are the implications of this symbolic use of the Bible? At the very least, Bartram's *Travels* offers a commentary on Genesis 1:28 and the meaning of humankind's "dominion" over other living things, and his views are progressive when compared with those of many of his contemporaries. We see this in a remark about horses. After a description of what he calls this "useful part of the creation," he adds that "if they are under our dominion," they "have consequently a right to our protection and favour" (224).

---

pureness, and innocency, and righteousness, being renewed up into the image of God by Christ Jesus, so that I say I was come up to the state of Adam which he was in before he fell. The creation was opened to me, and it was showed me how all things had their names given them according to their nature and virtue. And I was at a stand in my mind whether I should practice physic for the good of mankind, seeing the nature and virtues of the creatures were so opened to me by the Lord. But I was immediately taken up in spirit, to see another or more steadfast state than Adam's in innocency, even into a state in Christ Jesus, that should never fall. (George Fox, *The Journal*, ed. Nigel Smith [London: Penguin, 1998], 27–28)

[15] See, e.g., Bartram, *Travels*, 93, 297 n. 57. The Franklin plant is a "flowering shrub" resembling a gardenia that he says "we [including here is father] have honoured with the name of the illustrious Dr. Benjamin Franklin, Franklinia Alatamaha" (296 n. 56).

Reconstructing William Bartram's worldview is not unambiguous; he remains in many respects enigmatic. He was an idiosyncratic Quaker,[16] but this designation alone hardly accounts for his philosophical views. At times he appears pantheistic, almost equating God and the natural world, which is likely what many Romantic readers assumed.[17] Others recognize a resemblance between Bartram's *Travels* and the ideas of contemporary deists for whom God is a remote first principal who set the world in motion but no longer enters into or disrupts its processes.[18] Thus, some consider him typical of the intellectual fervor of the eighteenth-century American Enlightenment. For his part, historian Kerry S. Walters locates Bartram within the Neoplatonic tradition because physical reality for the botanist and artist is an emanation of divine being.[19] And again, further complicating all of this, we must beware of equating the "William Bartram" described in *Travels* with its author; *Travels* is a work of literature, and the explorer depicted within it is to some degree a construction, even though the travelogue relates actual events.

With these cautions in place, however, it remains that Bartram's piety owes much to his Quaker roots. We find this in his insistence on simplicity in living, his passivity, his high estimate of North American aboriginals, and his slowly evolving views on slavery that eventually culminated in calls for abolition later in life.[20] Bartram's high view of nature was also consistent with certain tendencies within contemporary Quaker thought. Hayley Rose Glaholt reminds us that Quaker attitudes toward the nonhuman were not

[16] For instance, it seems likely that William Bartram, like his father John, did not believe in the divinity of Christ. He refers often to God in *Travels* but never to the Son of God (Clarke, "Quaker Background," 446). His use of the term "divine monitor" (e.g., *Travels*, 36) also illustrates the diverse influences contributing to his thought. On the one hand, it recalls the Quaker doctrine of the "inner light" (Clarke, "Quaker Background," 446), but on the other, Bartram also uses it to distinguish intellectual reason (an ability to use language, symbols, etc.) from moral reason, the ability to distinguish good from evil. Ode-Schneider suggests that Bartram's use of the term in "The Dignity of Human Nature" derives from Plato (*The Republic* and *Euthyphro*), where it indicates the interior moral guide (Bartram, *The Search for Nature's Design*, 351n; cf. Ode-Schneider, "The Dignity of Human Nature," 340). On this term, see also Kerry S. Walters, "The Creator's Boundless Palace: William Bartram's Philosophy of Nature," *Transactions of the Charles S. Peirce Society* 25, no. 3 (1989): 314.

[17] Walters, "The Creator's Boundless Palace," 310.

[18] One commentator observes similarities between the writings of the deist Thomas Paine and Bartram and warns against overstating the distance between Bartram's Quakerism, which would allow that God does intervene in human affairs by performing miracles, and deism, which would not. If Bartram and the deists "disagreed about God's direct involvement in nature," writes Bruce Silver, "they disagreed about what God might do and not about what God can do. But it is wrong to exaggerate their disagreement" ("Clarke on the Quaker Background," 509). On the similarities between Paine and Bartram, see Silver, "Clarke on the Quaker Background," 508–9.

[19] Walters, "The Creator's Boundless Palace," 309–32.

[20] On the evolution of Bartram's attitudes toward slaves and slavery, see Slaughter, *Natures of John and William Bartram*, 204–7.

as uniformly positive as often assumed, noting as evidence Quaker domination of the whaling industry from the late seventeenth century through the early nineteenth.[21] In accounting for the Quakers' participation in such a brutal blood industry, Glaholt concludes that "the 'animal question' had not yet entered the moral consciousness of Friends . . . in any significant way," though she adds that "among a small group of influential Friends in America and England . . . a spark was ignited," listing among examples the New Jersey Quaker John Woolman (1720–1772), Anthony Benezet (1713–1784), and John Churchman (1705–1775). She does not mention William Bartram in this context, though he certainly serves as further evidence in support of her argument, which is that a high regard for animals "selectively characterized 18th-century American Quakerism."[22]

Bartram's adoption of an Adamic persona within an imagined, mythically cast New World presents a compelling way to imagine nonviolence within religious traditions rooted in the Jewish and Christian scriptures. It is interesting to note, in closing, that William Bartram's famous journey through the Edenic lands of the largely unsettled Southeast occurred while the colonies of the settled Northeast were at war. Bartram does not mention the Revolutionary War at all in *Travels*, a conspicuous omission that perhaps indicates a subtle critique of the ambition, warmongering, and militarism occurring back home.[23] His flower hunting and observations of animals made while wandering through the savannahs and forests of Georgia, the Carolinas, and Florida prove to be a spiritually enriching experience that within the symbolic world of *Travels* is a return to Garden innocence. And humans in that paradise are not only at peace with one another; they are also at peace with nonhuman species sharing the garden with them.

---

[21] Hayley Rose Glaholt, "Vivisection as War: The 'Moral Diseases' of Animal Experimentation and Slavery in British Victorian Quaker Pacifist Ethics," *Society & Animals* 20 (2012): 157.

[22] Glaholt, "Vivisection as War," 158.

[23] Though he is not nearly as romantic in his portrayal of nature as Rousseau, it is plausible to understand Bartram's retreat into the wilderness during a period of war as polemic. This is a long way from a Hobbesian notion that humanity in its natural state is wicked, whereas civilization is a rising above this corruption. That said, the natural world Bartram describes in *Travels* is certainly not a naively peaceful one: "His was a clear-eyed knowledge of the harshness of nature, an acceptance of the violence and pain that were as natural as the serenity of a summer's blue sky. All consumed all in William's wilderness, in a relentless warfare among animals and plants" (Slaughter, *Natures of John and William Bartram*, 197).

Bibliography

Bartram, William. *Bartram's Living Legacy: The* Travels *and the Nature of the South*. Edited by Dorinda G. Dallmeyer. Macon, GA: Mercer University Press, 2010.

Bartram, William. *William Bartram: The Search for Nature's Design—Selected Art, Letters and Unpublished Writings*. Edited by Thomas Hallock and Nancy E. Hoffman. Athens: University of Georgia Press, 2010.

Clarke, Larry R. "The Quaker Background of William Bartram's View of Nature." *Journal of the History of Ideas* 46, no. 3 (1985): 435–48.

Fox, George. *The Journal*. Edited by Nigel Smith. London: Penguin, 1998.

Gilmour, Michael J. *Eden's Other Residents: The Bible and Animals*. Eugene, OR: Cascade, 2014.

Glaholt, Hayley Rose. "Vivisection as War: The 'Moral Diseases' of Animal Experimentation and Slavery in British Victorian Quaker Pacifist Ethics." *Society & Animals* 20 (2012): 154–72.

Hallock, Thomas, and Nancy E. Hoffman. Introduction to *William Bartram: The Search for Nature's Design—Selected Art, Letters and Unpublished Writings*, by William Bartram, 1–15. Edited by Thomas Hallock and Nancy E. Hoffman. Athens: University of Georgia Press, 2010.

Holland Braund, Kathryn E. "William Bartram's Gustatory Tour." In *Fields of Vision: Essays on the "Travels" of William Bartram*, edited by Kathryn E. Holland Braund and Charlotte M. Porter, 33–53. Tuscaloosa: University of Alabama Press, 2010.

Ode-Schneider, Laurel. "'The Dignity of Human Nature': William Bartram and the Great Chain of Being." In *William Bartram: The Search for Nature's Design—Selected Art, Letters and Unpublished Writings*, by William Bartram, 340–46. Edited by Thomas Hallock and Nancy E. Hoffman. Athens: University of Georgia Press, 2010.

Silver, Bruce. "Clarke on the Quaker Background of William Bartram's Approach to Nature." *Journal of the History of Ideas* 47, no. 3 (1986): 507–10.

Slaughter, Thomas P. *The Natures of John and William Bartram*. Philadelphia: University of Pennsylvania Press, 1996.

Smith, Matthew C. "Stone Blind." In *Bartram's Living Legacy: The "Travels" and the Nature of the South*, by William Bartram, 491–511. Edited by Dorinda G. Dallmeyer. Macon, GA: Mercer University Press, 2010.

van Doren, Mark. "Editor's Note." In *Travels of William Bartram*, by William Bartram, 5–6. Edited by Mark van Doren. New York: Dover, 1955.

Walters, Kerry S. "The Creator's Boundless Palace: William Bartram's Philosophy of Nature." *Transactions of the Charles S. Peirce Society* 25, no. 3 (1989): 309–32.

7

Henry David Thoreau (1817–1862)

Capturing the *Anima* in Animals

Wesley T. Mott

"I saw deep in the eyes of the animals the human soul look out upon me." So reads a popular "Henry David Thoreau Animal Rights Quote Poster" for sale on the internet. An expanded version of the quotation is given at other animal rights websites: "I saw where it [the human soul] was born deep down under feathers and fur, or condemned for awhile to roam fourfooted among the brambles. I caught the clinging mute glance of the prisoner, and swore that I would be faithful." This startling recognition of human kinship with other species—echoing the American transcendentalist's well-known celebration of "the wild" in *Walden*—is expressed in pointedly religious terms. But the words are not Thoreau's.

The passage quoted here appears facing the title page of *Animals' Rights Considered in Relation to Social Progress* (1892) by Henry S. Salt, an English socialist and vegetarian and, ironically, an early important, sympathetic biographer of Thoreau.[1] Nor are the words by Salt, who gives his source only as *Towards Democracy*. The author of that volume of loosely related poems, presented in the manner of Walt Whitman's *Leaves of Grass*, was Edward Carpenter, Salt's socialist mentor and friend, an advocate of gay rights and vegetarianism.[2]

The impulse to recruit Thoreau to the animal rights cause is understandable. He has long been canonized as a champion of moral principle and civil disobedience and as a founder of the American conservation ethic. Misattribution of words to Thoreau, however—even for a good cause—raises

---

[1] Henry S. Salt, *Life of Henry David Thoreau*, enl. ed. (London: Walter Scott, 1896).

[2] Edward Carpenter, *Towards Democracy*, 2nd ed. (Manchester: John Heywood, 1885). The poster quotation is from "Have Faith," stanza 4, 2nd ed., 179. Salt credited Carpenter with introducing him to *Walden*. George Hendrick, *Henry Salt: Humanitarian Reformer and Man of Letters* (Urbana: University of Illinois Press, 1977), 26.

Wesley T. Mott, *Henry David Thoreau (1817–1862)* In: *Animal Theologians*. Edited by: Andrew Linzey and Clair Linzey, Oxford University Press. © Oxford University Press 2023. DOI: 10.1093/oso/9780197655542.003.0008

two critical questions: What do his life and works actually express about animal rights? And in the context of his supposed recognition of animal souls, were his views theologically grounded?

Thoreau's "attractions for the lower creatures" struck one of his first English admirers, A. H. Japp, who in 1878 likened the American to Saint Francis of Assisi.[3] Indeed, in 1862, while eulogizing his young friend, dead at forty-four from tuberculosis, Ralph Waldo Emerson charmingly described Thoreau's "intimacy with animals" and in so doing helped create an idealized image of Thoreau as a cross between Saint Francis and the Greek nature god Pan: "Snakes coiled round his leg; the fishes swam into his hand . . . he pulled the woodchuck out of its hole by the tail, and took the foxes under his protection from the hunters."[4] Emerson's Thoreau was, moreover, "a protestant à l'outrance [to the utmost] . . . he never went to church . . . he ate no flesh . . . and, though a naturalist, he used neither trap nor gun."[5] Though based on passages in Thoreau's own writings, Emerson's compelling depiction is inaccurate on two scores: (1) Thoreau often fished and occasionally used a gun; and (2) he sometimes ate flesh. In the late twentieth century, some scholars began asking harder questions about the depth, consistency, and sincerity of Thoreau's identification with sentient creatures. He lived, after all, in an agricultural community where hunting for sustenance and sport was ubiquitous, and many of his published and unpublished descriptions of hunters and hunting are cordial, even admiring. We might frame our consideration of Thoreau's ambivalence toward killing and eating animals by first addressing that *other* paradox implied by Emerson and ask, Did that ultra-protestant Thoreau—who indeed scorned formal religion—bring anything resembling a religious outlook to his encounters with what, in his masterpiece, *Walden; or, Life in the Woods* (1854), he called his "brute neighbors"?

Thoreau's mother was a member of First Parish Church in Concord, which by the early nineteenth century had evolved from orthodox Calvinism to Unitarianism. But Henry claimed no denominational affiliation. Asked as he lay dying, "'how he stood affected toward Christ,' he replied that 'a snowstorm was more to him than Christ.' When his Aunt Louisa asked him if he had made his peace with God, he answered, 'I did not know we had ever

---

[3] Quoted in Alan D. Hodder, *Thoreau's Ecstatic Witness* (New Haven: Yale University Press, 2001), 17. Japp (1839–1905) wrote under the pseudonym H. A. Page.

[4] Ralph Waldo Emerson, "Thoreau," in *The Collected Works of Ralph Waldo Emerson*, ed. Alfred R. Ferguson, Joseph Slater, Douglas Emory Wilson, Ronald A. Bosco, et al. (Cambridge, MA: Harvard University Press, 1971–2013), 10:424.

[5] Emerson, "Thoreau," 10:414–15.

quarrelled, Aunt.'"[6] Like many in his transcendentalist circle, Thoreau had a reputation for infidelity, which he wore as a badge of honor. In the "Sunday" chapter of his first book, *A Week on the Concord and Merrimack Rivers*, he needled orthodox readers: "Really, there is no infidelity, now-a-days, so great as that which prays, and keeps the Sabbath. . . . The church is a sort of hospital for men's souls, and as full of quackery as the hospital for their bodies."[7] Yet Thoreau was well versed in the Bible, which he invoked with devastating irony to skewer individual and institutional moral cowardice and resistance to reform. His influential essay known as "Civil Disobedience" echoes Jesus's condemnation of a Jerusalem "that killest the prophets, and stonest them which are sent unto thee" (Matt. 23:37, KJV): "Why," Thoreau asks, "does [government] always crucify Christ, and excommunicate Copernicus and Luther, and pronounce Washington and Franklin rebels?"[8] Though he mocked the hypocrisy of Christians, he held genuine Christian (and other religious) principles in high esteem: "It is remarkable, that notwithstanding the universal favor with which the New Testament is outwardly received, and even the bigotry with which it is defended, there is no hospitality shown to, there is no appreciation of, the order of truth with which it deals."[9] Indeed, *Walden* reveals Thoreau's informed admiration for the universal wisdom of the world's great religions, especially as found in the Judeo-Christian Bible and Asian sacred literature.

Understanding Thoreau's relation to religion is not much helped by the term *transcendentalism*, which is something of a misnomer. Transcendentalists were diverse (often idiosyncratic) and never united by formal tenets, but they broadly conceived of divinity (Emerson's "Over-Soul") *not* as transcendent but as immanent in the creation, infusing the material world and human experience with life itself. "My profession," Thoreau wrote in his journal in September 1851, "is to be always on the alert to find God in nature—to know his lurking places."[10] Alan D. Hodder has persuasively shown that Thoreau's entire life was indeed a religious quest—that he was receptive to,

---

[6] Walter Harding, *The Days of Henry Thoreau* (New York: Knopf, 1965), 24–25, 464.

[7] Henry D. Thoreau, *A Week on the Concord and Merrimack Rivers*, ed. Carl F. Hovde, William L. Howarth, and Elizabeth Hall Witherell (Princeton, NJ: Princeton University Press, 1980), 76.

[8] Henry D. Thoreau, "Resistance to Civil Government," in *Reform Papers*, ed. Wendell Glick (Princeton, NJ: Princeton University Press, 1973), 73.

[9] Thoreau, *Week*, 72. Abolitionists and advocates of Native American and women's rights used similar rhetoric to expose deep-seated social injustice.

[10] Henry D. Thoreau, *Journal*, in *The Writings of Henry D. Thoreau*, ed. Elizabeth Hall Witherell et al. (Princeton, NJ: Princeton University Press, 1981–), 4:55. This text is hereafter cited as *Journal* (Princeton).

actively sought, and wrote about ecstasy, moments when he experienced self-transcendence and a weird sense of doubleness. And when ecstasy ebbed, Thoreau poignantly recollected it in Wordsworthian tranquility.[11] Because the transcendentalists viewed nature and the human experience of it as organic and fluid, they resisted fixed codification of any doctrine, asserting that life consists in continually fresh insight, in surprise. David M. Robinson has extended Hodder's insight into Thoreau's religious outlook by stressing that as a naturalist, Thoreau thought the material a reflection of the spiritual and thus was stubbornly convinced that "facts" are "indicative of a more comprehensive idea or law."[12] According to Robinson, Thoreau's Walden experiment was a quest for "fundamental ethical laws and bedrock ontological realities,"[13] and in Thoreau's earthy, "compelling descriptions of his experience in the natural world," *facts* point to a larger interconnectedness in nature and to an "implicit advocacy of the preservation of the wild."[14] Thoreau thus stood outside the Christian tradition built on Aristotle, Augustine, and Aquinas that, as Andrew Linzey shows, disparaged "materiality and in particular . . . the worth of non-human animals."[15] Thoreau's derision of contemporary Christianity notwithstanding, his grasp of nature as divinely infused resembles the Christian understanding of how the incarnate God works, as described by Linzey: "Material substance, that is, flesh and blood, which is what humans share in particular with much of the animal kingdom, is the pivot of God's redeeming purposes."[16]

Thoreau's ecstatic life in nature took the form of fascination with tangible reality, identification, and classification, which he thought would *flower* into a comprehensive natural history of Concord. In 1847 he began sending countless specimens of wildlife (including a live fox) to Louis Agassiz, a recently installed professor of zoology and geology at Harvard. But Thoreau grew disaffected with Agassiz's methods and came to recoil from killing animals in the name of science. Asked in 1853 by the American Association for the Advancement of Science "to describe . . . that branch of science which specially interests me," he chafed in his journal: "The fact is I am a mystic—a transcendentalist—& a natural philosopher to boot."[17] Indeed, in *Walden*,

---

[11] Hodder, *Thoreau's Ecstatic Witness*.
[12] David M. Robinson, *Natural Life: Thoreau's Worldly Transcendentalism* (Ithaca, NY: Cornell University Press, 2004), 109.
[13] Robinson, *Natural Life*, 81.
[14] Robinson, *Natural Life*, 111.
[15] Andrew Linzey, *Christianity and the Rights of Animals* (New York: Crossroad, 1987), 37.
[16] Andrew Linzey, *Animal Theology* (Urbana: University of Illinois Press, 1994), 97–98.
[17] Thoreau, *Journal* (Princeton), 5:469.

he celebrated the vastness of "Nature": "We need to witness our own limits transgressed, and some life pasturing freely where we never wander."[18] This craving for a feeling of awe, for self-transcendence, links Thoreau to the Romantic movement, which in an increasingly secular world transferred religious concepts of sublimity to the realm of nature. And so the mystical edge to Thoreau's material transcendentalism is his most striking contribution to animal theology.

How to describe the material world and its creatures posed a challenge to Thoreau, who complained in *Walden* that we "live this mean life that we do because our vision does not penetrate the surface of things. We think that that *is* which *appears* to be."[19] In February 1860, just over two years before he died, he lamented the failure of modern science "to go beyond the shell; *i.e.*, it does not get to animated nature at all. A history of animated nature must itself be animated":

> I think that the most important requisite in describing an animal, is to be sure and give its character and spirit. . . . Surely the most important part of an animal is its *anima*, its vital spirit, on which is based its character. . . . Yet most scientific books which treat of animals leave this out altogether, and what they describe are as it were phenomena of dead matter. . . .
> If you have undertaken to write the biography of an animal, you will have to present to us the living creature, *i.e.*, a result which no man can understand, but only in his degree report the impression made on him.[20]

The very word *animal* derives from the Latin *anima*, sometimes translated as *soul* but rendered by the *Oxford English Dictionary* as "air, breath, life." For Thoreau, whose grasp of Latin and Greek was impressive, equating *anima* with "vital spirit" and not with the theologically charged "soul" recalls the biblical account of God's "breath[ing] into [man's] nostrils the *breath of life*; and man became a living soul."[21] In popular use, of course, the term "animal"

---

[18] Henry D. Thoreau, *Walden*, ed. J. Lyndon Shanley (Princeton, NJ: Princeton University Press, 1971), 318.

[19] Thoreau, *Walden*, 96.

[20] Henry D. Thoreau, *Journal*, in *The Writings of Henry David Thoreau*, ed. Bradford Torrey and Francis H. Allen (Boston: Houghton Mifflin, 1906), 13:154. This text is hereafter cited as *Journal* (Houghton Mifflin).

[21] Genesis 2:7 (KJV), emphasis added. In the Old Testament, Jerome H. Neyrey explains, the term *soul* (which apparently derives from Old English) carries "a wide range of meanings," including "life principle," "individual person," and "unity of a human person"; the Greek idea of a "dualism of soul and body" appears in the Wisdom of Solomon. This range of meanings appears also in the New

often implicitly refers to "subhuman" creatures or to coarse, physical aspects of humans. In his reflection on how to describe the essence of animals in words, Thoreau makes no such distinction between the "vital spirit[s]" of "brute" and human creatures.[22] He had learned from working for Agassiz that collecting, naming, and classifying living things risked becoming dead, dryasdust routine. "As soon as I begin to be aware of the life of any creature," he now declared, "I at once forget its name. . . . The name is convenient in communicating with others, but it is not to be remembered when I communicate with myself."[23]

Thoreau expressed his deeply moral literary theory after spending much of his brief lifetime capturing the "anima"—the ultimate mystery—of "living creature[s]." His descriptions are extensive and diverse—detailed, lively, amusing, complex, sometimes contradictory or even disturbing. Scores of animals—fish, an owl, mice, chickadees, squirrels, a phoebe, foxes, even dogs and cats—appear in *Walden*. Some serve as metaphors for the human condition, for as he punned, animals "are all beasts of burden, in a sense, made to carry some portion of our thoughts." A "striped snake," motionless at the bottom of the pond, suggests "the torpid state" of men who have yet to "rise to a higher and more ethereal life." The detailed, mock-heroic account of "war" between red and black ants satirizes warfare generally while tweaking local pride over Concord's role in the War of Independence. Thoreau's futile effort to paddle after an elusive loon, with her "demoniac laughter," is comical even as it hints at nature's refusal to give up its secrets.[24]

Walden, moreover, showcases the sort of delightful anecdotes of interspecies familiarity that tickled Emerson's fancy. Thoreau describes one interaction with a "wild native [mouse] (*Mus leucopus*)" who came "regularly at lunch time": "it ran up my clothes, and along my sleeve . . . and when at last I held still a piece of cheese between my thumb and finger, it came and nibbled it, sitting in my hand."[25] Once, a manic red squirrel "suddenly

---

Testament. See the entry "soul" by Neyrey in *Harper's Bible Dictionary*, ed. Paul J. Achtemeier (San Francisco: Harper & Row, 1985).

[22] In the *Harper's Bible Dictionary* entry "animals," Ilse U. Köhler-Rollefson suggests that in Genesis *animal* is synonymous with *mammal*, given that God created fowl and fish (including whales—which we now know are not fish but mammals!) on the fifth day (Gen. 1:20–23) and creatures of the land on the sixth day (Gen. 1:24–25).

[23] Thoreau, *Journal* (Houghton Mifflin), 13:155. For more on Thoreau's theory of describing animals, see Wesley T. Mott, ed., *Bonds of Affection: Thoreau on Dogs and Cats* (Amherst: University of Massachusetts Press, 2005), xxviii–xxxi.

[24] Thoreau, *Walden*, 225, 41, 228–32, 233–36.

[25] Thoreau, *Walden*, 225–26.

paus[ed] with a ludicrous expression and a gratuitous somerset, as if all the eyes in the universe were fixed on him."[26] Recalling another experience, he writes, "I once had a sparrow alight upon my shoulder for a moment while I was hoeing . . . and I felt that I was more distinguished by that circumstance than I should have been by any epaulet I could have worn."[27]

A grittier, philosophically bolder note appears in *Walden* where, in recurring images of digging, Thoreau declares his own earthy animality: "My instinct tells me that my head is an organ for burrowing, as some creatures use their snout and fore-paws." In the chapter "Higher Laws," he famously acknowledges and probes his dual nature: what he called "an instinct toward a higher, or, as it is named, spiritual life . . . and another toward a primitive rank and savage one." He opens with the disturbing declaration that once, returning from fishing, he "caught a glimpse of a woodchuck stealing across [his] path, and felt a strange thrill of savage delight, and was strongly tempted to seize and devour him raw." Notwithstanding his quick disclaimer—that he was "hungry" only for "that wildness which [the woodchuck] represented"— many readers of *Walden* seem to recall best that horrifying moment when Thoreau, they are convinced, describes eating a raw woodchuck! He admits to eating fish while at Walden but insists he has given up "fowling" because he now thinks "there is a finer way of studying ornithology than this." Moreover, he claims that the "repugnance to animal food is . . . an instinct" in one who seeks "to preserve his higher or poetic faculties." He refuses, however, to recommend abstaining from eating flesh as a rule because "sensuality" is inescapably part of being human. Nor can he bring himself to condemn hunting, which he has found to be good sport and an instructive part of growing up, a pursuit that links us to primordial instinct and mythic truths. He admits that "preying on other animals" is a "miserable" business. But he is content in the conviction that his own evolution is a microcosm of "the destiny of the human race, in its gradual improvement, to leave off eating animals."[28]

With respect to hunting and eating flesh, Thomas L. Altherr argues that Thoreau was "mired in a deep paradox" that he never fully resolved: he frequently described hunting as revolting and degrading yet never denounced it unequivocally or permanently.[29] The experience of killing and eating

---

26 Thoreau, *Walden*, 274.
27 Thoreau, *Walden*, 276.
28 Thoreau, *Walden*, 98, 210, 211–12, 214–15, 220, 216.
29 Thomas L. Altherr, "'Chaplain to the Hunters': Henry David Thoreau's Ambivalence toward Hunting," *American Literature* 56 (October 1984): 358.

animals haunted Thoreau. In fact, lengthy passages with the same trajectory as the *Walden* reverie about "animal food" appear in works that essentially bookend his creative life. In each, he recounts participating in or observing the killing of animals, laments his role, and seeks a higher understanding of human responsibility toward animals. The first of these accounts appears in *A Week on the Concord and Merrimack Rivers* (1849), which he largely wrote during his sojourn at Walden in 1845–47.[30] A tribute to his beloved late brother, John, who had shared that river journey in the summer of 1839, *A Week* is a work of mourning laced with reminders of mortality and an attempt to find purpose and redemption through memory and an imaginative encounter with the natural world. With subtle echoes of fishermen in the Gospels, Thoreau initially describes the brothers' fishing as "a sort of solemn sacrament and withdrawal from the world."[31] But a lengthy meditation ends in the anguished question "Who hears the fishes when they cry?"[32] Killing a pigeon also causes remorse: "it did not seem to be putting this bird to its right use, to pluck off its feathers, and extract its entrails, and broil its carcass on the coals; but we heroically persevered, nevertheless, waiting for further information."[33] The irony here is not flippant but self-effacing, embarrassed. The experience provokes disturbing new thoughts, introducing speaker and reader to "these incessant tragedies which Heaven allows."[34] With even greater shame and self-loathing, he confesses:

> The carcasses of some poor squirrels . . . the same that frisked so merrily in the morning, which we had skinned and embowelled for our dinner, we abandoned in disgust, with tardy humanity, as too wretched a resource for any but starving men. It was to perpetuate the practice of a barbarous era. . . . Their small red bodies, little bundles of red tissue, mere gobbets of venison, would not have "fattened fire." With a sudden impulse we threw them away, and washed our hands, and boiled some rice for our dinner.[35]

Thoreau immediately offers two unidentified passages of wisdom:

---

[30] Thoreau moved to the woods in part "to transact some private business with the fewest obstacles"—namely, to write what became *A Week*. Thoreau, *Walden*, 19–20.
[31] Thoreau, *Week*, 25.
[32] Thoreau, *Week*, 37.
[33] Thoreau, *Week*, 223.
[34] Thoreau, *Week*, 223.
[35] Thoreau, *Week*, 224.

"Behold the difference between the one who eateth flesh, and him to whom it belonged! The first hath a momentary enjoyment, whilst the latter is deprived of existence!"—"Who could commit so great a crime against a poor animal, who is fed only by the herbs which grow wild in the woods, and whose belly is burnt up with hunger?"[36]

The orphic power of these quotations (they are from the ancient Hindu *Hitopadésa*)[37] stirs deeper guilt: "We remembered a picture of mankind in the hunter age, chasing hares down the mountains, O me miserable! Yet sheep and oxen are but larger squirrels, whose hides are saved and meat is salted, whose souls perchance are not so large in proportion to their bodies."[38] Thoreau tries to understand his personal struggle with cruelty and barbarism in melioristic terms. That he continued to wrestle with carnivorousness, however, suggests that he found the struggle an eternal, tragic, human cycle.[39]

After *A Week* and *Walden*, Thoreau's third sustained published commentary on hunting appeared in his 1858 article "Chesuncook," recounting his second trip to the Maine woods, in September 1853. Here Thoreau dispassionately notes the hunting of bears, deer, a hedgehog, and beavers. Most startling, he describes eating "moose meat fried for supper," which reminds him of "tender beef" or veal. His reflection on this experience again turns remorseful. Killing the moose was a "tragedy" that "destroyed the pleasure of [his] adventure." "Explorers, and lumberers generally," he now sees, "are all hirelings. . . . Other white men and Indians who come here are for the most part hunters, whose object is to slay as many moose and other wild animals

[36] Thoreau, *Week*, 224.

[37] The Hindu quotations appear in Emerson's "Extracts from the Heetopades of Veeshnoo Sarma," *The Dial* 3 (July 1842): 83. Emerson had Charles Wilkins's translation of *Hitopadésa* (Bath: R. Cruttwell, 1787) in his library. See Robert Sattelmeyer, *Thoreau's Reading: A Study in Intellectual History with Bibliographical Catalogue* (Princeton, NJ: Princeton University Press, 1988), 202, item 704.

[38] Thoreau, *Week*, 224–25.

[39] Michelle C. Neely notes that Thoreau's "ethical reasoning from his observations does not always please." Neely, "Reading Thoreau's Animals," *Concord Saunterer: A Journal of Thoreau Studies*, n.s., 22 (2014): 126. She argues, however, that he "decenters the human . . . representing himself as one 'neighbor' among many—human and 'brute' alike" (130)—a technique that opens "the potential for a more open and ecological understanding of community" (132). In a brilliant essay on the historical contexts of Thoreau's writing about animals, Neely acknowledges his complex and paradoxical comments but stresses his "recognition of 'kindred mortality'" and a "shared capacity for suffering [that] forms the basis of the continuity and fluidity Thoreau recognizes between human and non-human animals." Neely, "Animals," in *Henry David Thoreau in Context*, ed. James S. Finley (New York: Cambridge University Press, 2017), 271.

as possible." Thoreau stays behind as the rest of his party continues hunting, and he meditates further on the evil of using nature solely as a commodity. "Can he who has discovered only some of the values of whalebone and whale oil be said to have discovered the true use of the whale? Can he who slays the elephant for his ivory be said to have 'seen the elephant'?"[40]

As in the passages in *A Week* and *Walden*, the Chesuncook moose narrative moves from a rather straightforward description of killing and/or eating flesh to palpable revulsion and guilt, followed by Thoreau's effort to redeem the experience by grasping a "higher law," which he pledges to pursue. In this sense, his hunting accounts serve as recurring autobiographical conversion narratives, recording lapses in his own spiritual practice that periodically must be redeemed afresh.

For all his conflicted statements about hunting, Thoreau was capable of what Andrew Linzey calls a "covenanted fellow-feeling and empathy towards animals."[41] Radiant—even numinous—moments of love, especially for cats, appear throughout Thoreau's journal. He can tenderly reflect, "What bond is it relates us to any animal we keep in the house but the bond of affection. In a degree we grow to love one another."[42] Thinking of cats, he can be startled by the mystery of interspecies empathy: "Wonderful, wonderful is our life and that of our companions! That there should be such a thing as a brute animal, not human! and that it should attain to a sort of society with our race!"[43]

Thoreau thought that domesticated animals and humans alike partake of the "wild," the source of life itself. Equally, he appreciated the anima of nondomesticated creatures. Two narratives must suffice to exemplify the ways he captured both the integrity of and his empathy for such animals.

Thoreau wrote the first such narrative—about foxes—in his journal in late January 1841, when he was twenty-three. In his eulogy for Thoreau, Emerson observed shrewdly that Thoreau "knew the country like a fox or a bird."[44] Fittingly, this journal entry begins with our narrator observing and following fox tracks in fresh snow. We "glance up these paths, closely imbowerd by bent trees, as through the side aisles of a cathedral." Indeed, the whole account is luminous, bathed in religious phrasing of "expectation" and grace, as though

---

[40] Thoreau, *The Maine Woods*, ed. Joseph J. Moldenhauer (Princeton, NJ: Princeton University Press, 1972), 117, 119–21. "Chesuncook" is the second chapter in the posthumously published *The Maine Woods* (1864).

[41] Linzey, *Christianity and the Rights of Animals*, 32.

[42] Thoreau, *Journal* (Princeton), 3:210. See also Thoreau selections in Mott, *Bonds of Affection*.

[43] Thoreau, *Journal* (Houghton Mifflin), 9:178.

[44] Emerson, "Thoreau," 423.

Thoreau is recounting a holy quest in nature. The speaker feels "on the trail of the spirit itself which resides in these woods, and expected soon to catch it in its lair." Even the patterns of snow on trees seem "predetermined"—"So one divine spirit *descends* alike on *all*, but bears a *peculiar fruit in each*" (emphases added).[45] In this sentence, Thoreau conveys the manifestation of the divine in nature by conflating New Testament accounts of the Spirit "descending" upon Jesus "like a dove" (cf. Matt. 3:16, Luke 3:22, John 1:32–33); the Holy Ghost "rushing [like a] mighty wind" upon "all" the Apostles on the day of Pentecost (Acts 2:1–4); and Paul's explanation for why Christ's followers receive "diversities of gifts, but the *same Spirit*" (1 Cor. 12:4; emphasis added).

The narrative proceeds with digressions and sudden revelations that mirror the intricate spacing and "graceful curvatures" of the tracks themselves. Will they reveal "the fluctuations of some mind"? Trying to analyze the tracks in order to think like a fox, Thoreau simply yields to awed fellowship with the unseen animal, exclaiming, "Here was one expression of the divine mind this morning." In this numinous moment, the creature who inspired this sense of wondrous unity requires no name. Thoreau's journal describes the experience of essentially *reading* the *fox's* record: "The pond was his journal, and last nights snow made a *tabula rasa* for him. I know which way a mind wended this morning." Basking in this sense of sublime connectedness, Thoreau digresses, pondering the surprise of "com[ing] out suddenly upon a high plain." Just as biblical revelation often occurs on mountaintops, Thoreau and the Romantics loved natural vistas; here was a "place where a decalogue might be let down or a saint translated." We are then brought back to earth, where "Fair Haven Pond is *scored* with the trails of foxes."[46]

After seven meandering and meditative paragraphs in which Thoreau infers qualities of foxes from their tracks, we are jolted to specificity, reality, and mutual animality: "Suddenly looking down the river I saw a fox some sixty rods off, making across to the hills on my left. . . . So yielding to the instinct of the chase, I tossed my head aloft, and bounded away, snuffing the air like a fox hound." Mock-heroically invoking "Diana and all the satyrs" to his cause, he tries to intercept the frightened fox even as he admires the animal's "remarkable presence of mind" and grace. As suddenly as the chase began, "[h]aving got near enough for a fair view," the narrator "gracefully yielded [the fox] the palm." Mirroring the narrator's gesture at the start of

45 Thoreau, *Journal* (Princeton), 1:239–40.
46 Thoreau, *Journal* (Princeton), 1:240–41.

the "chase," the fox "toss[es] his head aloft, when satisfied of his course," and then slides down a "declivity" "like a cat." The episode ends with Thoreau's tongue-in-cheek gloating about his victory over the fox: "So hoping this experience would prove a useful lesson to him—I returned to the village by the highway of the river." Clearly, however, the prey has outrun, outmaneuvered, and outfoxed the "hunter." Thoreau has captured a fleeting vision of beauty, even of the divine. Watching the fox slip away, he is content to be the object of the last laugh.[47]

Our second exemplary narrative reveals how even common, timid hares could make the daily routine at Walden transcendent. One hare lived under Thoreau's cabin floor "all winter," and Thoreau writes, "she startled me each morning by her hasty departure when I began to stir,—thump, thump, thump, striking her head against the floor timbers in her hurry." He takes "pity" on another hare he meets "[o]ne evening" near his door:

[The rabbit was] at first trembling with fear, yet unwilling to move; a poor wee thing, lean and bony, with ragged ears and sharp nose, scant tail and slender paws. It looked as if Nature no longer contained the breed of nobler bloods, but stood on her last toes. Its large eyes appeared young and unhealthy, almost dropsical. I took a step, and lo, away it scud with an elastic spring over the snow crust, straightening its body and its limbs into graceful length, and soon put the forest between me and itself,—the wild free venison, asserting its vigor and the dignity of Nature. Not without reason was its slenderness. Such then was its nature. (*Lepus*, *levipes*, light-foot, some think.)[48]

The narrative of this encounter begins with a sentimentalized anthropomorphism—pity for the seemingly forlorn, terrified, emaciated creature. Thoreau then lets us feel his own thrilled surprise at seeing the

[47] Thoreau, *Journal* (Princeton), 1:241–42. A more polished version of the fox passage appears in Thoreau's essay "Natural History of Massachusetts" (1842), in Thoreau, *Excursions*, ed. Joseph J. Moldenhauer (Princeton, NJ: Princeton University Press, 2007), 15–16. The American painter N. C. Wyeth brilliantly captures the encounter in *Fox in the Snow*, which served as the endpaper illustration for the popular selection of Thoreau journal entries portraying humans, *Men of Concord*, ed. Francis H. Allen (Boston: Houghton Mifflin, 1936). Wyeth's angle of vision is behind and closer to the fox, who is poised mid-stride on the crest of a hill in the upper-right corner of the painting, head cocked alertly to the left, keenly gazing down at Thoreau, who appears miniscule, slightly above center-left, gazing up the hill at the fox. The mutually regarding figures convey an electric moment of psychic contact even as the fox has the upper hand. See the exhibition catalog *N. C. Wyeth's Men of Concord* (Concord, MA: Concord Museum, 2016), 54–55.

[48] Thoreau, *Walden*, 280–81.

hare bound gracefully away—according to "its nature." The hare, Thoreau comes to see, is constructed precisely as she must be and is perfectly attuned to her environment, which Thoreau shares as a tactful neighbor. Lost in the wonder of beholding the hare's anima, he then seems to forget his own dictum that in becoming "aware of the life of any creature, I at once forget its name": reverting to the skilled naturalist's habit, he concludes his epiphany with a slightly tongue-in-cheek noting of the hare's genus. Even in this seeming lapse of imagination, he feels connected to the ancient naturalists who coined the scientific term *Lepus, levipes*—because the label *recognizes* an essential trait of hares. As with the more spontaneous journal account of the fox, the narrative of the hare is a record of natural grace, of Thoreau's recognition of and communion with nonhuman animals.

Thoreau never suggests that animal rights depend somehow on "brute" creatures having "souls" in the sense of an essence transcending the flesh. Andrew Linzey has argued that a more valid (and still theologically grounded) measure of our ethical obligation to animals is "the sense of moral community."[49] Ecstatically embracing the divine material here and now, Thoreau—contrary to the misattributed sentiments of that animal rights poster—spent little time worrying about the theological concept of souls, human or otherwise. Instead, he *engages* us in pursuing his conviction that "Our whole life is startlingly moral."[50] As a child, Emerson's son Edward idolized Thoreau as a guide to the wonders of nature and to human bonds with so-called "lower animals." Thoreau, Edward recalled in adulthood, "felt real respect for the personality and character of animals, [who] . . . rewarded his regard by some measure of friendly confidence . . . . For all life he had reverence, and just where the limits of conscious life began and ended he was too wise, and too hopeful, to say."[51] The anima of the animals Thoreau loved and described so faithfully still lives for us.

Dedication

This chapter is dedicated to the memory of my beloved friend Harry (?—February 7, 2020). A stray cat who came in from the cold in 2011, he was a

---

[49] Linzey, *Christianity and the Rights of Animals*, 32.
[50] Thoreau, *Walden*, 218.
[51] Edward Waldo Emerson, *Henry Thoreau as Remembered by a Young Friend* (Boston: Houghton Mifflin, 1917), 82–83.

big, gentle, engaging soul who liked sitting among guests. While I prepared the chapter, Harry usually was stretched beside, around, behind, or on my laptop. We truly shared what Thoreau called the "bond of affection" that "relates us" to domestic animals.

Bibliography

Altherr, Thomas L. "'Chaplain to the Hunters': Henry David Thoreau's Ambivalence toward Hunting." *American Literature* 56 (October 1984): 345–61.

Carpenter, Edward. *Towards Democracy*. 2nd ed. Manchester: John Heywood, 1885.

Emerson, Edward Waldo. *Henry Thoreau as Remembered by a Young Friend*. Boston: Houghton Mifflin, 1917.

Emerson, Ralph Waldo. "Thoreau." In *Uncollected Prose Writings: The Collected Works of Ralph Waldo Emerson*, vol. 10, edited by Ronald A. Bosco, Joel Myerson, and Glen M. Johnson, 413–31. Cambridge, MA: Harvard University Press, 2013.

Harding, Walter. *The Days of Henry Thoreau*. New York: Knopf, 1965.

Hendrick, George. *Henry Salt: Humanitarian Reformer and Man of Letters*. Urbana: University of Illinois Press, 1977.

Hodder, Alan D. *Thoreau's Ecstatic Witness*. New Haven: Yale University Press, 2001.

Linzey, Andrew. *Animal Theology*. Urbana: University of Illinois Press, 1994.

Linzey, Andrew. *Christianity and the Rights of Animals*. New York: Crossroad, 1987.

Mott, Wesley T., ed. *Bonds of Affection: Thoreau on Dogs and Cats*. Amherst: University of Massachusetts Press, 2005.

Neely, Michelle C. "Animals." In *Henry David Thoreau in Context*, edited by James S. Finley, 269–78. New York: Cambridge University Press, 2017.

Neely, Michelle C. "Reading Thoreau's Animals." *Concord Saunterer: A Journal of Thoreau Studies*, n.s., 22 (2014): 126–35.

Robinson, David M. *Natural Life: Thoreau's Worldly Transcendentalism*. Ithaca, NY: Cornell University Press, 2004.

Salt, Henry S. *Animals' Rights Considered in Relation to Social Progress*. London: George Bell & Sons, 1892.

Salt, Henry S. *Life of Henry David Thoreau*. Enl. ed. London: Walter Scott, 1896.

Sattelmeyer, Robert. *Thoreau's Reading: A Study in Intellectual History with Bibliographical Catalogue*. Princeton, NJ: Princeton University Press, 1988.

Thoreau, Henry D. *Excursions*. Edited by Joseph J. Moldenhauer. Princeton, NJ: Princeton University Press, 2007.

Thoreau, Henry D. *Journal*. Vols. 7–20 of *The Writings of Henry David Thoreau*. Edited by Bradford Torrey and Francis H. Allen. Boston: Houghton Mifflin, 1906.

Thoreau, Henry D. *Journal*. In *The Writings of Henry D. Thoreau*, edited by Elizabeth Hall Witherell et al. 8 vols. to date. Princeton, NJ: Princeton University Press, 1981–.

Thoreau, Henry D. *The Maine Woods*. Edited by Joseph J. Moldenhauer. Princeton, NJ: Princeton University Press, 1972.

Thoreau, Henry D. *Reform Papers*. Edited by Wendell Glick. Princeton, NJ: Princeton University Press, 1973.

Thoreau, Henry D. *Walden*. Edited by J. Lyndon Shanley. Princeton, NJ: Princeton University Press, 1971.

Thoreau, Henry D. *A Week on the Concord and Merrimack Rivers*. Edited by Carl F. Hovde, William L. Howarth, and Elizabeth Hall Witherell. Princeton, NJ: Princeton University Press, 1980.

PART II
SOCIAL SENSIBILITY

8

John Ruskin (1819–1900)

"Beholding Birds"—A Visual Case against Vivisection

Linda M. Johnson

In March 1872, John Ruskin instructed his student artists, in a drawing exercise on birds, to draw the true appearance of animals from their "wholeness" rather than their parts—the latter a reference to the anatomical dissection of animal corpses, a technical method of drawing instruction popular at Oxford. For Ruskin, to render a drawing through the meticulous detail of "dead" appendages would be to somehow fail in communicating an animal's true appearance. Ruskin's view on drawing nonhuman life was the subject of a series of ten lectures published as *The Eagle's Nest*, thirteen years before his resignation as Slade Professor of Art in response to an issue linked to anatomical study: vivisection. In regards to how humankind should treat animals he stated, "He is to know how they are spotted, wrinkled, furred, and feathered; and what the look of them is, in the eyes; and what grasp, or cling, or trot, or pat, in their paws and claws. He is to take every sort of view of them, in fact, except one, —the Butcher's view. He is never to think of them as bones and meat."[1]

Ruskin's "wholeness" approach was an organic one, understood as the living expression of an animal dependent on an intact physical body. His process was clear:

> The anatomy and chemistry of their bodies, I shall very rarely, and partially, as I told you, examine at all: but I shall take the greatest pains to get at the creature's habits of life; and know all its ingenuities, humours, delights, and

---

[1] John Ruskin, *The Eagle's Nest: Ten Lectures on the Relation of Natural Science to Art, Given before the University of Oxford in Lent Term, 1872* (New York: John Wiley & Sons, 1880), lecture 8, sec. 150, p. 146.

Linda M. Johnson, *John Ruskin (1819–1900)* In: *Animal Theologians*. Edited by: Andrew Linzey and Clair Linzey, Oxford University Press. © Oxford University Press 2023. DOI: 10.1093/oso/9780197655542.003.0009

intellectual powers. That is to say, what art it has, and what affection; and how these are prepared for in its external form.[2]

To "get at the creature's habits of life," an artist had to see differently. This was based on the dictum *fiat lux* ("let there be light")—Ruskin's belief that spiritual sight was an untapped potential to see something anew, a process I will refer to as "beholding."[3] Ruskin contended, "You do not see *with* the lens of the eye. You see *through* that, and by means of that, but you see with the soul of the eye."[4] It should be stressed that for Ruskin "spiritual sight" meant that there are no new things, only different ways of seeing something already present. Ruskin defined art as the great imitator of science and stated that the knowledge of constant things "is not the arrangement of new systems, nor the discovery of new facts, which constitutes a man of science; but the submission to an eternal system; and the proper grasp of facts already known."[5] "Beholding" inferred that his art would bear a revelation; it would be a catalyst that embodied an existent truth.[6] Moreover, Ruskin referred to spiritual sight as an active process, stating, "Even the power of the eye itself, as such, is *in* its animation."[7] For Ruskin, seeing was dependent not only on the physical science of light but also on some active power within the eye he called *fiat anima*: a dynamic generator that drove the seer to see the soul of creation with "the eyes of the heart" rather than through the mechanics of optics.[8] When a person beholds creation through spiritual eyes, Ruskin stated,

All Nature, with one voice—with one glory,—is set to teach you reverence for the life communicated to you from the Father of Spirits. The song of birds, and their plumage; the scent of flowers, their colour, their very existence, are in direct connection with the mystery of that communicated

---

[2] Ruskin, *Eagle's Nest*, lecture 9, sec. 181, pp. 175–76.

[3] Ruskin, *Eagle's Nest*, lecture 6, sec. 97, p. 103. While acknowledging that art was connected with the principles of optics in the sciences of light and form, Ruskin qualified "light" by citing examples of what *fiat lux* is not. Ruskin argues, "The study of the effect of light on nitrate of silver is chemistry, not optics; and what is light to us may indeed shine on a stone; but it is not light to the stone." Instead, optics, the science of seeing, is described by Ruskin "of that power, whatever it may be, which (by Plato's definition), 'through the eyes, manifests colour to us.'"

[4] Ruskin, *Eagle's Nest*, lecture 6, sec. 98, p. 103.

[5] Ruskin, *Eagle's Nest*, lecture 3, sec. 37, p. 42.

[6] John Shea, *The Art of Theological Reflection* (Chicago: ACTA Publications, 1997). The traditional spiritual perspective of beholding is called the "third eye," the inner vision, and perhaps most provocatively, the eye of the heart, the locus of the soul.

[7] Ruskin, *Eagle's Nest*, lecture 6, sec. 98, p. 103.

[8] Ruskin, *Eagle's Nest*, lecture 6, sec. 97, p. 103.

life: and all the strength, and all the arts of men, are measured by, and founded upon, their reverence for the passion, and their guardianship of the purity, of Love.[9]

According to Dinah Birch, Ruskin believed that the discipline best suited to the "right training of young artists was theology, not anatomy."[10] Theology, nature, and art were mirrors for the soul and mirrors for God, who was love, and each living thing revealed some aspect of God's presence. This was not so much pantheism as a pan*en*theism: holding that God both was greater than the whole of our universe and, as the Creator, interpenetrated all created things. Ruskin wrote that he believed love was the artist's motivation:

> Every painter ought to paint what he himself loves, not what others have loved; if his mind be pure and sweetly toned, what he loves will be lovely; if otherwise, no example can guide his selection, no precept govern his hand; and farther let it be distinctly observed, that all this mannered landscape is only right under the supposition of its being a background to some super-natural presence.[11]

Love for Ruskin was at the core of all beings, and the world became a communion of subjects more than a collection of objects. The image of the Great Chain of Being became the ontological basis for viewing everything sacred. He believed the chain had to be kept intact and that it linked "together the whole of creation, from its Maker to the lowest creature."[12] Anatomical dissection—and worse yet, vivisection—broke important links in the chain and thus stopped the flow of the divine soul. Drawing dissected parts such as "bones and meat" involved merely looking at soulless dead tissue rather than how God uniquely "animated" every living thing. Referring to animals in the chain, Ruskin affirmed that they were to be viewed in their wholeness: "In representing, nay, in thinking of, and caring for, these beasts, man

[9] Ruskin, *Eagle's Nest*, lecture 8, sec. 169, p. 166.

[10] Dinah Birch, "'That Ghastly Work': Ruskin, Animals and Anatomy," *Worldviews: Environment, Culture, Religion* 4, no. 2 (2000): 143.

[11] John Ruskin, *Modern Painters* (New York: John W. Lovell Company, 1885), part 3, sec. 2, chap. 5, subsec. 12, pp. 213–14. http://hdl.handle.net/2027/nyp.33433082218714.

[12] John Ruskin, *The Works of John Ruskin*, ed. E. T. Cook and Alexander Wedderburn, 39 vols. (London: G. Allen, 1903–12); quoted in Jed Mayer, "The Expression of the Emotions in Man and Laboratory Animals," *Victorian Studies* 50, no. 3 (2008): 412. See Psalm 101:4 and Romans 1:20 (KJV). The Great Chain of Being included the divine Creator, the angelic heavenly hosts, the humans, the animals, the world of plants and vegetation, and planet Earth itself with its minerals and waters.

has to think of them essentially with their skins on them, and with their souls in them."[13]

While literary scholars have stated that Ruskin's animal advocacy has taken a back seat to his impassioned essays on the environment, Birch argues, "The study of animal life brought together all his major intellectual occupations."[14] Critics state that Ruskin's resignation from Oxford was disingenuous, that his arguments were long term and political in nature, and that he was already suffering from mental depression. Jed Mayer suggests differently, stating that his reason for reacting against vivisection was animals' place in his vision for a just society. He believed that Ruskin found kinship in looking at animals, not in dissecting them, and through his loving observation of the nonhuman world, he discovered that "all the distinctions of species, both in plants and animals, appear to have similar connections with human character."[15] The hiring of physiologist Sir John Burden-Sanderson, along with the endowment of new laboratories allocated for vivisection, triggered Ruskin's final break with Oxford. Ruskin stated, "I cannot lecture next door to a shrieking cat, nor address myself to men who have been—there's no word for it."[16]

While there is no shortage of texts regarding Ruskin's theories on art and religious and sociopolitical matters, this chapter will address the intimate connection between Ruskin's writings and several drawings of birds to illustrate his process of "beholding." Indeed, if mining just a small sampling of Ruskin's tomes reveals volumes about the author himself, examination of his art reveals a similar introspective labor on his part and the most literal relationship between his art and the moral piety he felt toward nonhuman life. An excellent artist in his own right, Ruskin created vivid watercolors and finely executed drawings of birds that have been shown in numerous exhibitions and galleries. Ruskin's birds are a product of his spiritual seeing rather than

[13] Ruskin, *Eagle's Nest*, lecture 8, sec. 150, pp. 145–46.

[14] Birch, "That Ghastly Work," 138.

[15] Jed Mayer, "Ruskin, Vivisection, and Scientific Knowledge," *Nineteenth-Century Prose* 35, no. 1 (2008): 1–6. According to Mayer, Ruskin's criticisms of vivisection were timely and had much in common with the language used by leading antivivisectionists such as Frances Power Cobbe, whose objections were on moral and aesthetic grounds as well. Ruskin was a member of the Victoria Street Society, known today as NAVS.

[16] Letter to Joan Severn, March 22, 1885, quoted in Joann Abse, *John Ruskin: The Passionate Moralist* (New York: Alfred A. Knopf, 1981), 311. Abse states that one reason for Ruskin's irritability was that although the lab had been approved, a new room for the drawing school had not been, and the university had refused his recommendations of two paintings by J. M. W. Turner.

a mere record of anatomical parts or Linnaean taxonomy. Ruskin's love for ornithology is well known, and his paintings of birds capture an inner essence of dignity in contrast to mere textbook models of Darwinian biology. Critiqued as symbols of medieval Romantic sentimentalism, Ruskin's birds offer new evidence for his abhorrence of the demands of science. His birds embody their "true appearances" and their unique "habits of life" that can be understood only in terms of their "wholeness." Of the many birds Ruskin animated in word and image, I have chosen the imposing eagle, the little egret, the snipe, and the partridge to examine how, through his unique gestural applications of paint, color, directional lines, light, shadow, and texture, his drawings evoke the realities the birds express—in a word, what makes them *them*.

Driven by a deep religious faith, Ruskin exhorted his students to pursue both the arts and the sciences as disciplines to be undertaken with unselfish motivations in the service of humankind, stating: "You are to recognize, or know, beautiful and noble things—notable, notabilia, or nobilia; and then you are to give the best possible account of them you can, either for the sake of others, or for the sake of your own forgetful apathetic self, in the future."[17] Disappointed and dismayed by art drawn from purely anatomical study, Ruskin instructed his students to examine natural history books "from end to end," challenging them to find a drawing that could illuminate "the true appearance of things," fully believing they could not. Ruskin describes these textbook drawings as having "a total want of sympathy with the nobler qualities of any creature."[18] Drawing "the nobler qualities" became more important in Ruskin's later life, during the various crises of leadership at Oxford, and can be viewed as a visual testimony to his reverence for life and his pivotal role as an animal ethicist who advocated for the humane treatment of animals (as it was understood in the later decades of Victorian England). This chapter verifies a harmony between Ruskin's aesthetic complexity and ethical values toward nonhuman creation, symbiotic with theological orthodoxy. Ruskin's approach was modern in thought, and his strategy can be perceived as an early model of evoking an empathetic response to effect change.

[17] Ruskin, *Eagle's Nest*, lecture 8, sec. 39, p. 43.
[18] Ruskin, *Eagle's Nest*, lecture 8, sec. 158, p. 157.

Beholding Ruskin's Birds

Many of Ruskin's beliefs developed from childhood travels and the influence of his parents. Born in 1819, the only child of John James Ruskin, a wealthy wine merchant, and Margaret Ruskin, he was much influenced by his mother's strong Protestant beliefs and his father's literary interests. His parents encouraged his love of drawing and took him on numerous Continental holidays, which awoke his passionate interest in and sense of responsibility toward the natural landscape. Ruskin became the most influential art critic of the Victorian era, as well as an art patron, draftsman, watercolorist, prominent social thinker, and philanthropist.[19] Ruskin was additionally a geologist who understood the dynamism of the land, yet he was adamant that his students did not need to be geologists to draw landscapes. He challenged his students, in reference to drawing a stone, "Do you expect me to teach you, here, the relations between quartz and oxide of iron?"[20] Referring to animals, Ruskin was emphatic, stating, "Anatomy, then, . . . will not help us to draw the true appearances of things."[21] He adamantly affirms, "You do not, I have told you, need either chemistry, botany, geology, or anatomy, to enable you to understand art, or produce it."[22] Ruskin admitted that to see the true appearances of things, it would be helpful to know the elements of natural history. He states, "Thus we have first to know the poetry of it—*i.e.*, what it has been to man, or what man has made of it. Secondly, the actual facts of its existence. Thirdly, the physical causes of these facts, if we can discover them."[23] Ruskin argued, "Those appearances you are to test by the appliance of the scientific laws relating to aspect; and to learn, by accurate measurement, and the most fixed attention, to represent with absolute fidelity."[24]

According to Birch, this "fixed attention," relating appearances to aspects, led Ruskin to propose what he called a "science of aspects," a study of the surface of things.[25] The "surface," more properly understood, is a subject's unique features, attributes, or qualities, which are not superficial but deeply awe-inspiring, mysterious, and part of God's infinite plan, when seen through

[19] Abse, *John Ruskin*, 13–60.
[20] Ruskin, *Eagle's Nest*, lecture 8, sec. 160, p. 159.
[21] Ruskin, *Eagle's Nest*, lecture 8, sec. 158, p. 156.
[22] Ruskin, *Eagle's Nest*, lecture 8, sec. 161, p. 159.
[23] Ruskin, *Eagle's Nest*, lecture 9, sec. 180, p. 175.
[24] Ruskin, *Eagle's Nest*, lecture 7, sec. 148, p. 142.
[25] Birch, "That Ghastly Work," 136.

the process of a fixed attention or "beholding." In view of this interpretation, I approach Ruskin's images by way of the formal analysis practiced by art historian Jules D. Prown, whose modern methodology is not far removed from Ruskin's theories. Following the description and deduction of an artwork, Prown's third step involves as much creative imagining as possible to form an interpretive hypothesis within the boundaries of common sense, judgment, and research involving diverse allied disciplines.[26]

Eagle

For Ruskin, imagination is an act of receiving a transcendent knowledge that takes place *through* the artist, not *by* the artist. Thus, the organic nature of Ruskin's subjects, while chemically and anatomically bound, is to be freed (at least onto Ruskin's own canvas) by the process of beholding. Ruskin believed that having learned to represent these actual "appearances" or "aspects" faithfully, the artist would naturally experience "visionary appearances" not available to the mortal senses: "Having learned to represent actual appearances faithfully, if you have any human faculty of your own, visionary appearances will take place to you which will be nobler and more true than any actual or material appearances; and the realization of these is the function of every fine art, which is founded absolutely, therefore, in truth, and consists absolutely in imagination."[27] Using his own drawing of an eagle to make his case (Figure 8.1), he describes how a "fixed attention" to the eagle's unique aspects (not anatomical dissection) will change the rendering.

> But there is another quite essential point in an eagle's head, in comprehending which, again, the skull will not help us. The skull in the human creature fails in three essential points. It is eyeless, noseless, and lipless. It fails only in an eagle in the two points of eye and lip; for an eagle has no nose worth mentioning; his beak is only a prolongation of his jaws. But he has lips very much worth mentioning, and of which his skull gives no account . . . for he is distinct from other birds in having with his own eagle's

[26] Jules David Prown, *Art as Evidence: Writings on Art and Material Culture* (New Haven: Yale University Press, 2000), 69–91. Prown's methodology is a three-step format of interpretation—description, deduction, and speculation; the last utilizes critical theories such as psychoanalysis to examine portraits as a process of interpretative hypothesis.

[27] Ruskin, *Eagle's Nest*, Lecture 7, sec. 148, p. 143.

Figure 8.1 The Head of a common Golden Eagle from Life

eye, a dog's lips, or very nearly such; and entirely fleshy and ringent mouth, bluish pink, with a perpetual grin upon it.[28]

Ruskin admonished his students for thinking that the study of the "mechanical arrangement," as seen in "the circular bones of [an eagle's] eye-socket,"[29] would ever help them draw the true "aspects" of an eagle itself. Ruskin states:

> But don't suppose that drawing these a million of times over will ever help you in the least to draw an eagle itself. On the contrary, it would almost to a certainty hinder you from noticing the essential point in an eagle's head— the projection of the brow. All the main work of the eagle's eye is, as we saw, in looking down. To keep the sunshine above from teasing it, the eye is put under a triangular penthouse, which is precisely the most characteristic

---

[28] Ruskin, *Eagle's Nest*, Lecture 8, sec. 157, p. 155.
[29] Ruskin, *Eagle's Nest*, Lecture 8, sec. 156, p. 154.

thing in the bird's whole aspect. . . . But that projection is not accounted for in the skull;.and so little does the anatomist care about it, that you may hunt through the best modern works of ornithology: and you will find eagles drawn with all manner of dissections of skulls, claws, clavicles, sternums, and gizzards; but you won't find so much as one poor falcon drawn with a falcon's eye.[30]

Ruskin centers the head of the eagle approximate to the vertical and horizontal axes of the composition in order to direct the viewer to the focal point of the drawing—the eagle's eye. The rounded pupil, the central aperture of the eye's seeing, is cast in shadowy grays and golden hues and is held within an oval gilded iris, a stable ground to fix our gaze. This focal point is further intensified by sweeps of white paint heavily applied to the pruned feathers of the eagle's projected brow, converging into the corner of the eye with darker gray-blue tones, before the eye is finally enclosed in pink fleshy hues of bright light in a U-shaped pattern. Proximal to the eagle's eye is the application of bright white paint on the upturned fleshy lips referred to by Ruskin as the eagle's "perpetual grin." Ruskin animates the bird's long undulating lips, painting them slightly apart with red and blue streaks to depict a salivating orifice, suggestive of soft capillary tissue pulsating with blood. The eagle's sharp pointed beak, complete with nares (nostrils) at the base of the bill, is an ample weapon of predation, descending and terminating in the pointy arc of a craggy corkscrew; the blues and grays of the beak's hard, stonelike surface are in opposition to the soft, wispy black feathers that embellish the animal's face.[31] Without language, Ruskin provides a visual vocabulary of the eagle's nobility. The eagle is painted in a state of prepared readiness—his combed, slicked-back feathers, in various shades of brown and gold, swirling forward and backward in curved lines, as if windswept, an allusion to movement and flight. Ruskin employs two colors to represent the tension between the celestial and earthly realms: gold, used widely in ancient to Renaissance art to symbolize divinity and depict an otherworldliness, and brown, the predominant earth tone.[32]

---

[30] Ruskin, *Eagle's Nest*, Lecture 8, sec. 156, p. 154–155.

[31] Ruskin, *Eagle's Nest*, Lecture 8, secs. 157, 155. See Janine Rogers, *Eagle*, (London: Reaktion Books, 2015), 11–44.

[32] Hugh Honor and John Fleming, *The Visual Arts: A History* (London: Laurence King, 2009), 146–54, 395–402.

Ruskin's eagle is a *golden* eagle, alive and alert, his furrowed brow terminating in a V-shaped pattern to indicate an active concentration *before* the act of hunting. We behold the eagle's ingenuities, his delights, his intellectual powers, his "scientific aspects" emanating from Ruskin's pencil, embodied in his hooded brow and fleshy grin, an animated metaphor for an inherent beauty immediately recognizable as worthy of honor. Ruskin claims:

> The beauty of the animal form is in exact proportion to the amount of moral or intellectual virtue expressed by it; and whenever beauty exists at all, there is some kind of virtue to which it is owing, as the majesty of the lion's eye is owing not to its ferocity, but to its seriousness and seeming intellect, and of the lion's mouth to its strength and sensibility, and not its gnashing of teeth, nor wrinkling in its wrath; and farther be it noted, that of the intellectual or moral virtues, the moral are those which are attended with more beauty, so that the gentle eye of the gazelle is fairer to look upon than the more keen glance of men, if it be unkind.[33]

Like the beauty of the lion, the beauty of the eagle is directly related to the animal's moral and intellectual virtue. Ruskin states that humankind would do well to imitate the virtue of the eagle, who follows the wisdom of her Creator to take care of her own, "as the eagle stirreth up her nest, and fluttereth over her young," unlike those who neglect "this great nest of ours in London," as a result of human greed and indifference.[34] Art then becomes a responsibility, and for Ruskin it is "Wisdom" itself, not knowledge, that will teach his young artists to paint animals in their moral virtue. When we behold animals' "ingenuities, humors, and delights," Ruskin proclaims, "if she [Wisdom] cannot grant us to surpass the art of the swallow or the eagle, she may not require of us at least, to reach the level of their happiness."[35] Conversely, Ruskin states that no art can be found in the dry and vacuous images of popular textbook illustrations, and "neither White of Selborne, Bewick, Yarell nor Gould" can capture "the most interesting, power of the bird."[36] He states, "Now look through your natural history books from end to

---

[33] Ruskin, *Modern Painters*, Part III, sec. 1, chap. XII, subsec. 10, p. 97–98, http://hdl.handle.net/2027/nyp.33433082218714.

[34] Ruskin, *Eagle's Nest*, Lecture 3, sec. 63, p. 64.

[35] Ruskin, *Eagle's Nest*, Lecture 3, sec. 64, p. 65.

[36] John Ruskin, *Love's Meinie: Lectures on Greek and English Birds* (New York: J. Wiley, 1886), Lecture 2, sec. 48, p. 43, http://hdl.handle.net/2027/ucl.c026138429.

BRITISH BIRDS.   47

THE GOLDEN EAGLE.

(*Falco Chryfætos,* Linnæus.—*Le grand Aigle,* Buffon.)

THIS is the largest of the genus; it measures, from
the point of the bill to the extremity of the toes, upwards
of three feet; and in breadth, from wing to wing, above
eight; and weighs from sixteen to eighteen pounds.

Figure 8.2 Golden Eagle

end; see if you can find one drawing, with all their anatomy, which shows you
either the eagle's eye, his lips, or this essential use of his beak, so as to enable
you thoroughly to understand."[37]

Ruskin is referring to the innumerable bird illustrators in nineteenth-
century Britain. Two of the most influential, according to historian Jonathan
Smith, were Thomas Bewick and John Gould, whose images were frequently
copied by Ruskin as ornithological illustrations (Figure 8.2).[38] However,

---

[37] Ruskin, *Eagle's Nest*, Lecture 8, sec. 157, p. 156.
[38] Jonathan Smith, *Charles Darwin and Victorian Visual Culture* (New York: Cambridge University
Press, 2006), 99–114. I am indebted to Smith's comprehensive survey on the types, uses, and

Smith states, while Ruskin rated Gould's books highly, he warned his students not to view Gould's work as exemplary art.[39] Moreover, static profiles failed to capture any sense of "uniqueness," or a bird's *fiat anima:*

> I have in my hand thirteen plates of thirteen species of eagles; eagles all, or hawks all, or falcons all, whoever name you choose for the great race of the hook-headed birds of prey—some so like that you can't tell the one from the other, at the distance at which I show them to you, all absolutely alike in their eagle or falcon character, having, every one, the falx for its beak, and every one, flesh for its prey.[40]

The illustrators Ruskin criticizes provided rote examples of eagles to fill a popular curiosity for natural history, but missing is the uniqueness of each eagle's intellectual powers that can be beheld only in external form: the animal's eyes and lips. According to Ruskin, Thomas Bewick failed to behold his birds and did not take into consideration their living expression:

> You know I have always spoken of Bewick as pre-eminently a vulgar or boorish person, though of splendid honour and genius; his vulgarity shows in nothing so much as in the poverty of the details he has collected, with the best intentions, and the shrewdest sense, for English ornithology. His imagination is not cultivated enough to enable him to choose, or arrange.[41]

Snipe

Similar to the eagle's nobility, the intellectual virtue of Ruskin's lively snipe is in her ability to discern (Figure 8.3). She returns our gaze, beholding the viewer in a wary yet strong-willed glance, her cocked head turned slightly upward in an air of self-importance and readiness to flee. Ruskin compositionally orients her body with less attention to her camouflage and more to

---

production of illustrated textbooks on birds of Great Britain. Smith states that one reason Ruskin used these illustrations was that he "was pleased by the frequent 'mythological' references in Gould's text, the quotations from the Bible and English poets" (128). Smith elaborates on the relationship between Ruskin and Darwin. See also Ruskin, *Love's Meinie*, Lecture 1, sec. 10, p. 13.

[39] Smith, *Charles Darwin*, 126.
[40] Ruskin, *Love's Meinie*, Lecture 1, sec. 5, p. 8.
[41] Ruskin, *Love's Meinie*, Lecture 1, sec. 3, pp. 7–8.

Figure 8.3 A Snipe

her rounded belly, painted in cool blues, purples, and grays that draw our eyes to her most important attribute—her long slender bill, its tip darkened with mud. Her keen sight, unlike the eagle's, is found in this organ of heightened nerve sensitivity that enables her to distinguish her food while foraging. Apprising the viewer of her unique external aspects, Ruskin wants us to behold her crown of dampened feathers: her head appears to have been submerged underwater while she probed in a series of bobbing, "sewing machine" movements.[42] Unlike his image of the eagle, Ruskin paints her *after* the hunt to demonstrate her particular "ingenuities."

While external appearances are important to Ruskin's overall method of spiritually seeing, insight acquired from mythology and heraldry are alternate means of beholding, as their lessons embody deeper truths inherent in the creature. Ruskin states, "But, in the accounts of animals that I prepare for my schools at Oxford, the main point with me will be the mythology of them."[43] Historically, Ruskin affirms that humankind has imitated the most beautiful external aspects of an animal's features. Ruskin describes wings, manes, crests, and plumes of eagles, lions, and horses as the most coveted, stating, "The beginning of heraldry, and of all beautiful dress, is, however,

---

[42] Andrew N. Hoodless, Julie A. Ewald, and David Baines, "Habitat Use and Diet of Common Snipe *Gallinago gallinago* Breeding on Moorland in Northern England," *Bird Study* 54, no. 2 (2007). 188–89.

[43] Ruskin, *Eagle's Nest*, Lecture 9, sec. 181, p. 175.

simply in the wearing of the skins of slain animals."[44] Sadly, Ruskin laments, "But in all our books of human history we only care to tell what has happened to men, and how many of each other they have, in a manner eaten, when they are, what Homer calls people-eaters; and we scarcely understand, even to this day, how they [animals] are truly minded."[45] In any event, it was Ruskin's hope that when used properly, the splendor of costume heraldry would encourage new ways of beholding animals, despite the self-interest of humankind. Yet his optimism was precarious: "Nay, I am not sure that even this art of heraldry, which has for its main object the telling and proclamation of our chief minds and characters to each other . . . has always understood clearly what it had to tell."[46]

Little Egret

In a lecture on the little egret, Ruskin admonishes humankind in an antianthropocentric invective regarding the extinction of the little egret due to the mercantile sport of poaching for plumes (Figure 8.4). The hunting of egrets for headdresses, popular in Victorian London, dramatically altered the bird's migratory habits. This loss is painfully addressed by Ruskin, who describes the bird as "the most beautiful, I suppose, of all birds that visit, or at least, once visited, our English shores."[47] Describing the little egret as ethereal in nature, Ruskin focuses on her purity and innocence through various descriptions of achromatic color. The egret, he states, is "Perfectly delicate in form, snow-white in plumage, the feathers like frost-work of dead silver, exquisitely slender, separating in the wind like the streams of a fountain, the creature looks a living cloud rather than a bird."[48] White snow, silver frost, wind, water, and cloud vapor—material forms of chemical compounds of the purest white—connect the vanishing egret to the organic elements of earth in which she can no longer partake. Ruskin's poetic words are elegiac and prescient—lamenting a mystical creature who has passed by like a cloud, unreachable, untouchable in her materiality.

[44] Ruskin, *Eagle's Nest*, Lecture 10, sec. 223, p. 214.
[45] Ruskin, *Eagle's Nest*, Lecture 10, sec. 207, p. 201–202.
[46] Ruskin, *Eagle's Nest*, Lecture 10, sec. 207, p. 202.
[47] Ruskin, *Eagle's Nest*, Lecture 9, sec. 174, p. 170.
[48] Ruskin, *Eagle's Nest*, Lecture 9, sec. 174, p. 170.

Figure 8.4 The Little Egret

In this lecture featuring the egret, Ruskin depends on the mythological literature of both Aristotle and Plutarch to instruct his students. He stands in awe of the egret, likening the bird to its mythical ancestor, the clever and loving halcyon. He recounts, from the fable of the halcyon, the bird's genius and wisdom in her creative powers:

But we take no notice of the wisdom and art of other creatures in bringing up their young, as for instance, the halcyon, who as soon as she has conceived, makes her nest by gathering the thorns of the sea-needle fish; and, weaving these in and out, and joining them together at the ends, she finishes her nest; round in the plan of it, and long, in the proportion of a fisherman's net; and then she puts it where it will be beaten by the waves, until the rough surface is all fastened together and made close. And it becomes so hard that a blow with iron or stone will not easily divide it; but, what is more wonderful still, is that the opening of the nest is made so exactly to the size and measure of the halcyon that nothing larger can get into it, and nothing smaller! —so they say;—no, not even the sea itself, even the least drop of it.[49]

In an affront to popular bird illustrators as well as anatomists, Ruskin states:

The transformations believed in by the mythologists are at least spiritually true; you cannot too carefully trace or accurately consider them. But the transformations believed in by the anatomist are as yet proved true in no single instance, and in no substance, spiritual or material; and I cannot too often, or too earnestly, urge you not to waste your time in guessing what animals may once have been, while you remain in nearly total ignorance of what they are.[50]

Partridge

Beholding animal death in a haunting portrait of a dead partridge, Ruskin renders an element of drama, premeditated harm, and unprecedented empathy (Figure 8.5). His antihunting sentiments were in line with those held by British animal rights advocates, and he remained adamant that a moral spiritual sight was key. He stated, "We cannot live in the country without hunting animals, or shooting them, unless we learn how to look at them."[51] Ruskin groups sparrows with partridges and finds them equally important as, if not more important than, humans:

Yet it is fast becoming the only definition of aristocracy, that the principle business of its life is the killing of sparrows. Sparrows or pigeons, or partridges, what does it matter! That is indeed too often the sum of the life

[49] Ruskin, *Eagle's Nest*, Lecture 9, sec. 193, p. 185.
[50] Ruskin, *Love's Meinie*, Lecture 2, sec. 63, p 54.
[51] John Ruskin, *On Himself and Things in General* (Liverpool: Office of the Cope's Tobacco Plant, 1893), 56.

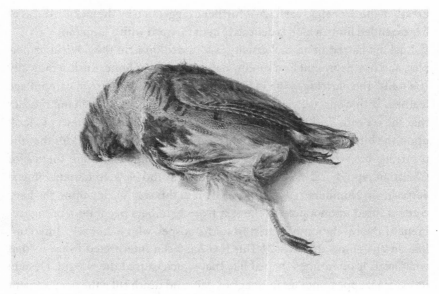

Figure 8.5 Study of the Plumage of a Partridge

of an English lord; much questionable now, if *indeed* of more value than that of many sparrows.[52]

The unique feature of Ruskin's partridge is her camouflage. He has painted her lying motionless, grounded in the neutral space of a vacant mushroom-colored background. Lush bits of feathery camouflage project in coppers, reds, browns, yellows, and grays, evoking a woodland landscape. Ruskin's textural application of paint creates a tactile softness on the partridge's shoulder and belly, making the bird appear far more weighty and tangible. The partridge's head is nestled into her chest, turned and curled inward so that her open eye can meet the gaze of the viewer, imbuing the image with a quality of tenderness. In this position, the bird appears to be alive again, but her short gray beak points to the smattering of brown paint on her central chest, the focal point of the composition, which highlights the partridge's true state: a corpse. Resembling a wound, her chest no longer possesses the

[52] Ruskin, *Love's Meinie*, Lecture 1, sec. 2, pp. 6–7. See Matthew 10:29 (KJV). Ruskin was dependent on scriptural precedent to demonstrate in his art the value of a sparrow's life.

breath of life. Her rigid carriage is further exaggerated by the awkwardness of her extended limb, which is delicately bent forward with a limp foot.

Ruskin's hatred of animal cruelty is founded on firm theological principles, and in what might be a subliminal expression of hope; Ruskin radically "beholds" the partridge's life in her death. He paints her brown camouflage feathers with a surface vibrancy that continues to flourish, belying the fact that she is dead. Ruskin's compositional technique forces the viewer to look upon the bird's wound; this act of beholding begets a new wisdom that the partridge has worth. Ruskin represents her *fiat anima* through the use of Christian typological exegesis, contrasting Old and New Testament biblical verses from Numbers 21:8 with John 3:14. In this way, gazing upon the fiery serpent lifted upon a pole in the text from Numbers becomes a prefigurement of the revelation of Christ in John's gospel, who is himself "lifted up" like an ensign on the cross.[53] This text has been interpreted to mean that what heals is oftentimes shaped like that which caused the wound. Despite its external appearance as an image of pain and death (like the fiery serpent in the book of Numbers), and the partridge's wound (like the cross in John's gospel), the partridge is the supreme "sign" that reveals hope for resurrection and merciful love. However sad and despondent Ruskin became about the institutional and bureaucratic communities of his time, he countered the finality of many different types of "deaths" through his steadfast belief in eternal life.

According to Birch, Ruskin believed that all the new sciences were ultimately concerned with death, and he wanted to align art and science in non-invasive practices.[54] The new disciplines prophesied species' extinction and cosmic catastrophes that were in conflict with Ruskin's typological Christian worldview. Birch argues that for Ruskin, the world seemed very unstable and "filled with a sense of ending."[55] Anxious about birds, Ruskin stated, "Nor much can be said for modern science in its observations of birds. It is vulgar in a far worse way, in its arrogance and materialism."[56]

---

[53] Numbers 21:8 (KJV), "And the Lord said unto Moses, make thee a fiery serpent, and set it upon a pole: and it shall come to pass, that every one that is bitten, when he looketh upon it, shall live," and Cf. John 3:14 (KJV). "And as Moses lifted up the serpent in the wilderness, even so must the Son of man be lifted up."

[54] Birch, "That Ghastly Work," 143.

[55] Birch, "That Ghastly Work," 138.

[56] Ruskin, *Love's Meinie*, Lecture 1, sec. 4, p. 8.

Conclusion

Ruskin's birds are expressions of his visionary imagination and products of what he felt was his "just thought." He stated:

> Your first purpose must be to seek what is to be praised; and disdain the rest: and in doing so, remember always that the most important part of the history of man is that of his imagination. . . . The real history of mankind is that of the slow advance of resolved deed following laboriously just thought; and all the greatest men live in their purpose and effort more than it is possible for them to live in reality. If you would praise them worthily, it is for what they conceived and felt; not merely for what they have done.[57]

This would have to be enough to assuage his grief regarding human indifference and cruelty toward animals.[58] Worth noting is Ruskin's biblical language entwined with moral chastisement as he demonstrated the *fiat anima* present in the beholding of nonhuman life. Ruskin's ministry was to relieve the "sluggishness in our hearts" that sees creation only from the vantage point of physical consciousness.[59] His techniques of line, color, and texture provide a sensory engagement with an animal's organic form without the invasive anatomical dissection of the animal's carcass. The body was to be honored in its wholeness, not in the "Butcher's view."

Ruskin's holistic view of birds demonstrates other ways of seeing, by evoking reverence without sentimentality. He insisted on the relationship of art to human life and offered an ideology based on noninvasive observation and stewardship. Throughout his life, he maintained that it was the eyes of the heart, the moral faculty in humankind, that would heal the world. He stated, "If ever he [man] is to know any of the secrets of his own or brutal existence, it will assuredly be through discipline of virtue, not through inquisitiveness of science."[60]

---

[57] Ruskin, *Eagle's Nest*, Lecture 10, sec. 214, p. 207.
[58] Mayer, "Ruskin, Vivisection, and Scientific Knowledge," 3. Vexing for Ruskin were the factions developing between the antivivisection organizations that broke off from the politically acceptable RSPCA. One side consisted of apologists who sought to gain the support of the scientific community, while others became extreme, sentimental, and fundamentalist, with neither group effecting the changes Ruskin hoped for, in terms of a "noninvasive science of aspects."
[59] Luke 24:25 (KJV).
[60] Ruskin, *Eagle's Nest*, Lecture 9, sec. 185, p. 178.

Bibliography

Abse, Joann. *John Ruskin: The Passionate Moralist*. New York: Alfred A. Knopf, 1981.

Birch, Dinah. "That Ghastly Work: Ruskin, Animals and Anatomy." *Worldviews: Environment, Culture, and Religion* 4, no. 2 (2000): 131–45.

Hoodless, Andrew N., Julie A. Ewald, and David Baines. "Habitat Use and Diet of Common Snipe (*Gallinago gallinago*) Breeding on Moorland in Northern England." *Bird Study* 54, no. 2 (2007): 182–91.

Honor, Hugh, and John Fleming. *The Visual Arts: A History*. London: Laurence King, 2009.

Mayer, Jed. "The Expression of the Emotions in Man and Laboratory Animals." *Victorian Studies* 50, no. 3 (Spring 2008): 412.

Mayer, Jed. "Ruskin, Vivisection, and Scientific Knowledge." *Nineteenth-Century Prose* 35, no. 1 (2008): 1–6.

Prown, Jules David. *Art as Evidence: Writings on Art and Material Culture*. New Haven: Yale University Press, 2000.

Rogers, Janine. *Eagle*. London: Reaktion Books, 2014.

Ruskin, John. *The Eagle's Nest: Ten Lectures on the Relation of Natural Science to Art, Given before the University of Oxford in Lent Term, 1872*. New York: John Wiley & Sons, 1880.

Ruskin, John. *Love's Meinie: Lectures on Greek and English Birds*. New York: J. Wiley, 1886.

Ruskin, John. *Modern Painters*. New York: John W. Lovell, 1885.

Ruskin, John. *On Himself and Things in General*. Liverpool: Office of the Cope's Tobacco Plant, 1893.

Ruskin, John. *The Works of John Ruskin*. Edited by E. T. Cook and Alexander Wedderburn. 39 vols. London: G. Allen, 1903–12.

Shea, John. *The Art of Theological Reflection*. Chicago: ACTA Publications, 1997.

Smith, Jonathan. *Charles Darwin and Victorian Visual Culture*. New York: Cambridge University Press, 2006.

9

Frances Power Cobbe (1822–1904)

Theology, Science, and the Antivivisection Movement

Chien-hui Li

Beginning in the 1870s, in response to the rise of experimental physiology in Britain, the first wave of protest against animal experimentation swept across Britain. In 1875, a Royal Commission on Vivisection was appointed. In 1876, with intensive lobbying from both the pro-vivisection men of science and the anticruelty movement, the world's first legislation regarding the licensing and inspecting of animal experiments was passed. This Cruelty to Animals Act, however, deeply disappointed the antivivisectionists, who believed it offered "protection to the vivisectors, and not to the animals."[1] A broad-based movement campaigning against animal experimentation that would last for well over three decades hence began. In accounting for the inception, the leadership, and more importantly, the underlying philosophy of the movement, one cannot bypass the work and religious thought of its most prominent leader in the nineteenth century—Frances Power Cobbe.[2]

Cobbe was born into a distinguished, wealthy, landed Anglo-Irish family in 1822. After her mother passed away, Cobbe, being the only daughter in the family, became housekeeper and companion to her father. When freed of familial duties upon her father's death in 1857, Cobbe first worked for a period in charitable schools for the poor and in a workhouse for girls in Bristol, then turned to writing as a means of supplementing her modest annuity. In the 1860s, she established herself as a successful journalist, writing

---

[1] *Hansard's*, July 15, 1879, 426.
[2] For recent scholarship on Cobbe, see Sandra J. Peacock, *The Theological and Ethical Writings of Frances Power Cobbe, 1822–1904* (Lewiston, NY: Edwin Mellen Press, 2002); Sally Mitchell, *Frances Power Cobbe: Victorian Feminist, Journalist, Reformer* (Charlottesville: University of Virginia Press, 2004); Lori Williamson, *Power and Protest: Frances Power Cobbe and Victorian Society* (London: Rivers Oram Press, 2005); Susan Hamilton, *Frances Power Cobbe and Victorian Feminism* (Basingstoke: Palgrave Macmillan, 2006); Diana Donald, *Women against Cruelty: Animal Protection in Nineteenth-Century Britain* (Manchester: Manchester University Press, 2020)

Chien-hui Li, *Frances Power Cobbe (1822–1904)* In: *Animal Theologians.* Edited by: Andrew Linzey and Clair Linzey, Oxford University Press. © Oxford University Press 2023. DOI: 10.1093/oso/9780197655542.003.0010

for both prestige journals and the popular press on social, religious, and ethical subjects. Her writings on issues such as marriage and celibacy, domestic violence, the education of women, and suffrage also led her to the forefront of the emerging feminist movement. At around the same time in the 1860s, the issue of animal experimentation came to her notice. The movement for the prevention of cruelty had been in existence since the 1820s; the idea of humaneness to animals was already to a certain extent familiar to the British public. In 1863, Cobbe penned her first article on animal ethics, "The Rights of Man and the Claims of Brutes,"[3] in protest against experiments carried out on animals in the veterinary schools at Alfort near Paris. In the same year, while acting as the Italian correspondent for the *Daily News* in Florence, she organized a petition to spare the animal victims in the laboratory of the Italian physiologist Moritz Schiff (1823–1896), generating further controversy in both Florence and Britain. This was a time when criticism of animal experiments was often directed at the practices in European countries where experimental physiology had developed earlier, but with the rise of British physiology in the 1870s, Cobbe quickly turned her attention to the British practice.

In 1874, after the Royal Society for the Prevention of Cruelty to Animals unsuccessfully attempted to prosecute vivisectors under the 1822 Martin's Act, most people realized the need for a new act for the protection of animals being used in scientific experiments. In 1875, drawing on her impressive social connections, Cobbe prepared a petition with six hundred signatures of noteworthy persons urging the RSPCA to press for the necessary law to ban painful experiments on animals. When the RSPCA failed to fulfill its expected role, Cobbe led the parliamentary campaign, with the help of Lord Henniker, against the influential lobby of the scientific and medical communities.[4] She also formed a society devoted exclusively to the issue of animal experimentation—the Victoria Street Society (VSS). For two decades, the VSS was the most influential antivivisection group in Britain, while Cobbe remained the movement's most prominent and outspoken leader. To account fully for the rationale and philosophy of the movement, we turn next

---

[3] First published in *Fraser's Magazine*, November 1863; afterward reprinted in Cobbe, *Studies New and Old of Ethical and Social Subjects* (Boston: William V. Spencer, 1866), 211–60.

[4] Lord Henniker's bill was eventually replaced by Playfair's bill, backed by the pro-vivisection party, with names such as Thomas Huxley, Charles Darwin, and Burdon Sanderson behind it. On the parliamentary struggles behind the Cruelty to Animals Act 1876, see Richard D. French, *Antivivisection and Medical Science in Victorian Society* (Princeton, NJ: Princeton University Press, 1975), 61–158.

to the religious thought of Cobbe and the controversies concerning religion and science in the Victorian age.

The Age of Doubt and the Way Out

The nineteenth century paradoxically was known as both an "age of faith" and an "age of doubt." The evangelical revival that swept the country first threw Britain into one of its most intense, self-consciously religious ages, yet beginning in the 1840s, the advance in sciences, the advent of higher criticism, and the moral earnestness that was itself a product of evangelicalism plunged many Christians into a crisis of faith that shattered their religion and moral foundation. Cobbe was deeply affected by both currents and underwent a crisis of faith that was fairly typical of the time.[5]

Cobbe had been brought up in a strict, evangelical household governed by patriarchal authority. She described herself as a "very religious child" and "*devout* beyond what was normal at [her] age."[6] She constantly felt an overpowering sense of the love of God and combined duty with devotion. Despite her early doubts, she underwent what the evangelicals called a "conversion" experience at the age of seventeen, and religion increasingly became the supreme interest of her life. Yet doubts crept in one after another: first, regarding the truthfulness of the Bible, then about the morality of the Old Testament history, the doctrine of atonement, and finally, about the divinity of Christ. Cobbe remained an agnostic for a short while and then became a deist. But like many Victorians who emerged from their crisis of faith not without faith, but with a transformation of faith, Cobbe gradually advanced toward theism.

In her metamorphosis, Cobbe was predominantly influenced by Theodore Parker, an American theologian whose writings she later edited (in fourteen volumes) and also Immanuel Kant, whose notion of a pure reason giving transcendental knowledge of necessary truths Cobbe developed and popularized in her first book, *An Essay on Intuitive Morals* (1855).[7] Through

---

[5] On the crisis of faith, see Richard J. Helmstadter and Bernard Lightman, eds., *Victorian Faith in Crisis: Essays on Continuity and Change in Nineteenth-Century Religious Belief* (Basingstoke: Macmillan, 1990).

[6] F. P. Cobbe, *Life of Frances Power Cobbe, by Herself* (London: Richard Bentley & Son, 1894), 1:82, 86. On Cobbe's religious upbringing and crisis of faith, see Cobbe, *Life*, 1:81–116.

[7] See F. P. Cobbe, ed., *The Collected Works of Theodore Parker*, 14 vols. (London: Trübner, 1863–71); F. P. Cobbe, *An Essay on Intuitive Morals: Being an Attempt to Popularise Ethical Science* (London: Longman, Brown, Green, and Longmans, 1855).

the ideas of Parker, Cobbe confirmed the "triune faith" that she had accessed earlier through prayer and intuitive reasoning—faith in the existence of a righteous God, faith in the divine authority of conscience, and faith in the immortality of the soul. In addition, she disposed of evangelical creeds such as original sin, atonement, and eternal damnation and became convinced of a brighter vision of life devoted to positive action for the betterment of the human condition on earth. Through reading Kant, Cobbe vindicated her belief in the power of intuitive reasoning for the attainment of divine truth and in the divine source and embodiment of the moral law. The basic premise from which Cobbe derived her religious and moral views was that humans were creatures with innate religious and moral sentiments as well as reasoning ability. This "fundamental and ineradicable" moral and religious nature of humans, Cobbe believed, impelled humanity "to find some One to whom to look up with absolute moral reverence."[8] Due to this innate nature, humans were able to follow their intuition and have direct recognition of God and understand God as a perfect moral being with infinite goodness and justice. With the recognition of the moral perfection of God came also the duty of humans to do good, since this was the sole rational basis upon which God could claim the absolute obedience and adoration of humans.[9] In obeying and loving God and striving to be in union with God, humans were at the same time striving after the highest moral ideals conceivable. Under this view, religion and morality shared not only the same motives but also the same end, which was the love of God and thus the infinite goodness that God embodied.[10]

Cobbe reemerged from her crisis of faith with no less religious and moral fervor than before and was thereafter committed not only to leading people out of the moral abyss in the age of doubt but also to advocating the theist faith, which she believed to be a purer and nobler religion for a better world to come. She moved in the circles of religious liberals, was acquainted with unorthodox theologians such Francis W. Newman, John Colenso, and

---

[8] F. P. Cobbe, *Hopes of the Human Race: Hereafter and Here* (London: Williams and Norgate, 1874), liv–lv.

[9] Being acutely aware of the moral imperfections of this world and the immensity of suffering of both humans and animals, Cobbe also believed immortality to be the "indispensable corollary" of the infinite goodness and justice of God, as a good and just God would not have intended the world to be unfulfilled. For Cobbe's view on immortality, see Cobbe, *Hopes of the Human Race.*

[10] For more on Cobbe's religious and moral views and her proposed system of practical ethics, see her *Religious Duty* (Boston: William V. Spencer, 1865); *An Essay on Intuitive Morals, Part II: Practice of Morals* (London: John Chapman, 1857); and *Broken Lights: An Inquiry into the Present Condition & Future Prospects* (London: Trübner, 1864).

Arthur P. Stanley, and occasionally attended the Unitarian Church of James Martineau. In the 1860s, as with the religious liberals of the period, Cobbe's chief mission was to free Christianity from its dogmatic creeds, a job that she described after the Broad Churchmen—the theologically more liberal section of the Anglican Church—as "liberating the kernel of Christianity from the husk."[11] She wrote fiercely opposing orthodox Christianity, urged for reforms in the Church of England, and advocated the power of reason and scientific thinking in bringing about the religion of the future—that is, theism. But if during the 1860s Cobbe was more concerned about liberating religion from Christian dogmatism and orthodoxies, from the mid-1870s onward, she was increasingly alarmed at the threats that science posed to religion and morality. Moreover, Cobbe's involvement in the antivivisection campaign from that time on should also be seen as part of her endeavor to strengthen the religious worldview in an increasingly skeptical age.

The Duty of Man and the Claims of Brutes

Before turning to the issue of animal experimentation and its relation to the larger question of religion and science, we should perhaps consider first Cobbe's general position on the animal question.

When approaching the issue of humans' obligation toward animals, Cobbe, as an activist writing for the general public, generally advanced two lines of argument: one from the pure standpoint of ethics, appealing to all thinking persons; the other from the religious perspective, appealing to those who could share in her broad theist faith. The first line of reasoning could be termed the "sentiency" argument, which entailed a particular conception of the different natures of humans and animals and hence of their different ends in life. In Cobbe's view, animals were neither moral nor religious, as opposed to humans, who were both; yet animals, like humans, were sentient beings capable of suffering pain and enjoying pleasure, and this alone was sufficient ground for people to refrain from inflicting pain and to bestow happiness on animals when it was within their power. Cobbe quoted Bishop Butler's (1692–1752) remark that from "the simple fact of a creature being *sentient, i.e.*, conscious of pain, arises our duty to spare it pain"; it "forms the

---

[11] Cobbe, *Life*, 1:90.

broad basis for all we have to build."[12] On this point Cobbe usually opted for the earlier authority of the intuitionist Butler over that of Jeremy Bentham (1748–1832), shunning the association with a purely utilitarian ethics. As an intuitionist who believed in an absolute and divine morality, Cobbe was against the utilitarian position that considered the pursuit of happiness to be the ultimate end of human lives and of human morality. For humans, who differed from animals in having a rational and moral nature, it was "virtue," not "happiness" that should constitute their moral end and obligation. Thus, while our concern for animals should be "solely with their happiness," for humans, "the wants of the soul must ever be placed in higher rank than those of the body."[13] Making her view clear, Cobbe wrote, "For the merely sentient being we desire to bestow happiness; for the being who is both moral and sentient we desire, first, to conduce to his virtue, and secondly, to produce his happiness. This is the great canon of social duty."[14] Proceeding from this distinction, Cobbe put the claims of humans over the claims of animals because, for her, the spirit was higher than the body, and moral interests took precedence over sentient interests. Under this view, humans were justified in using animals to promote their true (i.e., moral) interests even if that entailed compromising the happiness of animals. However, if the use of animals stemmed from, or was conducive to, humans' moral evils, such as wantonness, malignity, indolence, or parsimony, it could not be justified. Thus, while people could slay cattle for sustenance, they could not torture calves to produce white meat for their gluttony; while people could clear "every inhabited country of wild beasts and noxious reptiles," they could not kill harmless animals for the "mere gratification of destructive propensities."[15]

Cobbe based her religious argument on the same conception of the different natures and ends of humans and animals and arrived at essentially the same conclusion, with a similar tint of anthropocentrism. Cobbe drew on the concepts of creation, dominion, and divine benevolence, which have been commonly mobilized by the anticruelty movement since the 1820s. Humans and animals, being created by God, were "fellow-creatures"[16] in the first

[12] F. P. Cobbe, "The Right of Tormenting," in *The Modern Rack: Papers on Vivisection* (London: Swan Sonnenschein, 1889), 50. See also F. P. Cobbe, *The Moral Aspects of Vivisection* (London: Victorian Street Society for the Protection of Animals from Vivisection, 1884), 16; and F. P. Cobbe, "The Janus of Science," in *The Modern Rack*, 119.

[13] F. P. Cobbe, "The Rights of Man and the Claims of Brutes," in *Studies New and Old of Ethical and Social Subjects* (Boston: William V. Spencer, 1866), 225, 232.

[14] F. P. Cobbe, "Self-Development and Self-Abnegation," in *Studies New and Old*, 78.

[15] Cobbe, "The Rights of Man and the Claims of Brutes," 229.

[16] Cobbe, "The Rights of Man and the Claims of Brutes," 252.

place. Bound by their moral and religious nature to love God and to aspire after God's moral perfection, humans should not only love God's creatures as God loves them but also emulate God's divine sympathy in His dealings with them. Cruelty, being "the very converse and antagonism of Deity,"[17] was itself a sin that humans should avoid. Further, as lords of creation, humans also had a positive obligation to watch over the interests of animals, and for morally innocent animal creatures, pain had no higher meaning or countervailing good but was itself "the one supreme evil" of their existence.[18] It was therefore humans' duty to spare them their sufferings and facilitate their happiness as they were created to be. However, Cobbe's hierarchical view of creation that privileged the moral welfare of humans also led her to believe that the world was "made for Man," whose end was "Virtue and eternal union with god."[19] Some animals, Cobbe further believed, were "servants given us expressly by God, and fitted with powers and instincts precisely suiting them to meet our wants";[20] humans thus had the power to use them, though not abuse them.

Following both lines of argument, painful experimentation on animals was unjustifiable. Although Cobbe considered there to be an "absolute subordination between the claims of the animal and those of man," she still made clear that for humans, "the wants of the soul must ever be placed in higher rank than those of the body."[21] Cobbe quoted Harold Browne, bishop of Winchester, in saying, "It is true that Man is superior to the beast, but the part of Man which we recognize as such is his moral and spiritual nature. So far as his body and its pains are concerned, there is no particular reason for considering them more than the body and bodily pains of a brute."[22] The practice of sacrificing God's animal creatures for the bodily interests of humankind was therefore unjustifiable. Further, when done for the same purpose, causing pain to the weaker creatures put in humans' charge was also in direct contrast to the benevolence of God and the "very rudiments of virtue and all nobility of character," which were "Generosity, Self-sacrifice, the readiness to suffer."[23] Cobbe, in her campaign against vivisection, thus frequently denounced the practice as a moral evil that constituted not only "an *Offence*

---

[17] Cobbe, "The Rights of Man and the Claims of Brutes," 253.
[18] F. P. Cobbe, "Zoophily," in *The Peak in Darien* (Boston: Geo. H. Ellis, 1882), 133.
[19] Cobbe, "The Rights of Man and the Claims of Brutes," 252.
[20] Cobbe, "The Rights of Man and the Claims of Brutes," 252.
[21] Cobbe, "The Rights of Man and the Claims of Brutes," 226, 232.
[22] Cobbe, "Zoophily," 147.
[23] Cobbe, *The Moral Aspects of Vivisection*, 19.

in the forum of Morals" but also "a heinous Sin in the court of Religion."[24] Moreover, as an intuitive moralist who held moral laws to be independent of utility, Cobbe was normally disinclined to enter into discussions about the utility of vivisection, and she urged her fellow antivivisectionists to act likewise.[25] For Cobbe things could only be "Useful because they are Right and Right because they are Useful."[26] If the practice of torturing innocent animals went against the divine law of love and mercy, it could never be useful, because it was morally wrong.

The Spirit of Science and Its Moral Perils

As a theological writer and moralist driven by a greater concern for the moral and spiritual condition of humankind, Cobbe was apprehensive not only about vivisection but also about what the practice said regarding a society that allowed it to flourish. To Cobbe, the rapid growth of experimentation as a scientific method, physiology as a discipline, and science as a profession in the last quarter of the nineteenth century not only symbolized the victory of the new scientific spirit but also embodied all of its pernicious tendencies that could ultimately undermine religion and morality.

Cobbe was not against science per se but was opposed to a particular ideology that became increasingly dominant in the latter half of the nineteenth century—scientific naturalism. For over a century since the Enlightenment, scientific inquiries into the natural world had been underpinned by the natural theological tradition. With the aid of different theologies of nature, people considered investigating the natural world to be part of human endeavors to seek the laws and designs of the divine Creator. To study nature was to study God's work and to gain knowledge of God's divine scheme, and all designs in nature were shown to be evidence of God's power, wisdom, and goodness. Science, when properly guided by natural theology, was thought to be conducive to religious faith and a reverential spirit. However, from the mid-nineteenth century onward, with the aid of Dalton's atomic theory of matter, the law of the conservation of energy, and evolutionary

[24] F. P. Cobbe, "A Charity and a Controversy," address, Annual Meeting of the Victoria Street Society, London, June 20, 1889, 3; collected in *Animal Welfare & Anti-vivisection, 1870–1910*, vol. 1, *Frances Power Cobbe*, ed. Susan Hamilton (London: Routledge, 2004), 365–68.

[25] Cobbe, "A Charity and a Controversy," 4.

[26] F. P. Cobbe, Meeting at Stoke Bishop (London, 1883), quoted in French, *Antivivisection and Medical Science*, 301.

theories, scientific naturalism increasingly replaced natural theology as the guiding ideology of science.[27] More intellectuals came to believe that nature was completely explicable in naturalistic terms, such as matter, motion, and force, with no intervention from supernatural powers, and they actively sought to dispose of the metaphysical assumptions and teleology that had previously dominated scientific inquiries. In revolt against the religious worldview of the past, such intellectuals now sought to establish a cosmology that "separates Nature from God, subordinates Spirit to Matter, and sets up unchangeable law as supreme."[28]

The ambition of natural scientists is best illustrated by the Belfast Address of John Tyndall, delivered at a meeting of the British Society for the Advancement of Science in 1874: "All religious theories, schemes, and systems, which embrace notions of cosmogony, or which otherwise reach into its domain, must, in so far as they do this, submit to the control of science, and relinquish all thought of controlling it."[29] This noticeable intellectual trend was not a natural corollary of the advancement of science in the nineteenth century but was actively promoted by an aggressive coterie of leading scientists and intellectuals, such as Thomas Huxley, John Tyndall, William Clifford, E. Ray Lankester, Herbert Spencer, and G. H. Lewes. These men, who were known as natural scientists and who came mostly from the professional middle class, sought not only to break free from the control of theology in science but also to bring about a secular society led by scientific-oriented experts, free from the dominance of the clerical and aristocratic elites. In their public campaigns, they aligned themselves with the greater liberal party and associated science with causes such as intellectual freedom, material well-being, national efficiency, and the progress of civilization, in contrast with the narrow, vested interests of the religious and aristocratic

[27] For more on natural theology, see John Hedley Brooke, *Science and Religion: Some Historical Perspectives* (Cambridge: Cambridge University Press, 1991), chap. 6. For more on scientific naturalism, see Frank M. Turner, *Between Science and Religion: The Reaction to Scientific Naturalism in Late Victorian England* (New Haven: Yale University Press, 1974); Frank M. Turner, *Contesting Cultural Authority: Essays in Victorian Intellectual Life* (Cambridge: Cambridge University Press, 1993); Bernard Lightman, *Evolutionary Naturalism in Victorian Britain* (Farnham, UK: Ashgate, 2009); Gowan Dawson and Bernard Lightman, eds., *Victorian Scientific Naturalism: Community, Identity, Continuity* (Chicago: University of Chicago Press, 2014); Bernard Lightman and Michael S. Reidy, eds., *The Age of Scientific Naturalism* (London: Pickering & Chatto, 2014).

[28] James Ward, *Naturalism and Agnosticism: The Gifford Lectures Delivered before the University of Aberdeen in the Years 1896–1898* (London: Adam and Charles Black, 1903), 186.

[29] John Tyndall, *Fragments of Science* (New York: D. Appleton, 1896), 197.

establishment.[30] This aggressive campaign, which made the most headway in the 1860s and 1870s and continued throughout the late nineteenth century, invited criticism from diverse quarters, ranging from the religious orthodox community to the scientific community, the Oxford idealists, theosophists, psychical researchers, and antivivisectionists.[31] These various groups did not necessarily work with or agree with each other in their battle against scientific naturalism, but they shared dissatisfaction with the narrow confines of the scientific worldview in accommodating human feelings and aspirations and felt the need to preserve spiritual values in an increasingly secularized society. From within the antivivisection movement, it was Cobbe who saw most clearly the wider significance of the vivisection controversy and proffered a broad cultural critique concerning the general outlook of British society under the sway of scientific naturalism.

Subscribing to the natural theological tradition, Cobbe in the 1860s still considered physical science to be "in its highest sense a holy thing," in that it revealed the power, wisdom, and love of God, and regarded "the physical laws of life" as "the clearest expressions of our Creator's will concerning the ordering of our bodies."[32] She upheld scientific inquiries underpinned by natural theology and commended an older generation of scientists such as Johannes Kepler, Isaac Newton, John Herschel, and Charles Lyell against the newer school of physicists and physiologists who were influenced by scientific naturalism.[33] In the 1850s and 1860s, Cobbe was an enthusiastic advocate of science and regarded it as an instrument capable of leading people to God and morality while also combating supernaturalism and the worst forms of religious orthodoxy. However, as scientific naturalism gradually revealed its full force beginning in the 1870s, Cobbe began to form a darker view of science and became more pessimistic about the possibility of science aiding, or even being reconciled with, religion.[34] What she feared was exactly

[30] See Turner, *Contesting Cultural Authority*, 197–98, 201–28; Ruth Barton, "Huxley, Lubbock, and Half a Dozen Others: Professionals and Gentlemen in the Formation of the X Club, 1851–1864," *Isis* 89, no. 3 (1998): 410–44.

[31] See Bernard Lightman, "Science and Culture," in *The Cambridge Companion to Victorian Culture*, ed. Francis O'Gorman (Cambridge: Cambridge University Press, 2010), 12–60.

[32] Cobbe, "The Rights of Man and the Claims of Brutes," 231.

[33] F. P. Cobbe, *A Faithless World* (London: Williams and Norgate, 1885), 19. Though Cobbe welcomed science underpinned by natural theology, she disagreed with William Paley's utilitarian adaption of natural theology, and neither did she place the value of external evidence in the natural world over human's inner intuition in affirming the existence and attributes of God. See Cobbe, *Hopes of the Human Race*, xviii, xliii, lx–lxi; and F. P. Cobbe, "Decemnovenarianism," in *Studies New and Old*, 365.

[34] For more on this view, see French, *Antivivisection and Medical Science*, 365–72; Peacock, *The Theological and Ethical Writings of Frances Power Cobbe*, 231–69.

the predominance of a worldview in which God was separated from nature, spirit was subordinated to matter, and natural laws replaced moral laws as the supreme guidance for life.

For Cobbe, the "new" propagated by natural scientists such as Huxley, a nature that held no place for God, was in the first place a betrayal of the nobility and true purpose of science. She commented, "Science . . . is but a mere heap of facts, not a golden chain of truths, if we refuse to link it to the throne of God."[35] Cobbe believed that the fast-accumulating knowledge and dazzling achievement of science that directed people neither to God nor to a deeper meaning of life and moral goodness merely led people away from the true interests of life such as art, feelings, morality, and religion. Also, Cobbe was suspicious of the naturalistic explanation of life offered by the fast-advancing physiological science since the 1870s. The growing belief that the mind could be best explained in matter, such as the chemicals and physiological workings of the brain, especially alarmed her. She believed that in a world where the naturalistic explanation held sway, moral and spiritual values would wither; all things that once had been noble, such as thought, free will, consciousness, emotions, and feelings, would also be reduced to mere functions of matter and lose their true significance.[36] For example, the physiologist who had the material facts uppermost in his mind would tend to leave the spiritual meaning "more or less out of sight" and "view his mother's tears—not as expressions of her sorrow—but as solutions of muriates and carbonates of soda, and of phosphates of lime" and would reflect that they were "caused not by his heartlessness, but by cerebral pressure on her lachrymal glands."[37] Physiological science that reduced the mind—once belonging to the spiritual realm—to matter was therefore materializing not only itself but also the minds of its practitioners and society in general.

The attempt to employ natural law as guidance for human behavior, most evident in the discussions and intellectual development following the publication of Darwin's *Descent of Man* (1871), equally appalled Cobbe. While Cobbe saw nothing degrading in tracing humankind back to apes, she was alarmed by Darwin's naturalistic view of the origin of moral sense, which his view regarded as a product of animal species' chance adaptation to the social environment. This hereditary view of conscience that seemed able to justify

[35] F. P. Cobbe, "Magnanimous Atheism," in *The Peak in Darien*, 50.
[36] See F. P. Cobbe, *The Scientific Spirit of the Age* (Boston: Geo. H. Ellis, 1888), 12; Cobbe, "The New Morality," in *The Modern Rack*, 68.
[37] Cobbe, *The Scientific Spirit of the Age*, 12.

anything that had survival values for humans contributed, Cobbe felt, to the utilitarian morality, whose triumph would be all but the sounding of "the knell of the virtue of mankind."[38] As an intuitive moralist, she considered morality to be instilled by God in humankind and to be perceivable only through infallible intuition and not through any other means. "Spiritual truths are spiritually discerned, and moral truths are morally discerned," Cobbe often asserted, and "neither the one nor the other are to be got at through researches into things which are not spiritual and not moral."[39] Darwin's theory of hereditary conscience and the spate of scientists and politicians who drew upon it to direct human behavior and societal matters—including the pro-vivisectionists who employed the law of survival of the fittest to justify the use of animals in science—had therefore committed the naturalist fallacy, encroached upon "the precincts of traditional Theology," and set up a ruthless utilitarian morality in replacing the Christian ideal.[40]

Cobbe felt that all of these worrying tendencies of modern science would ultimately lead to an atheist or agnostic world directed by materialism and devoid of all the noble interests of life. Regarding animal experimentation as both a culprit and the worst symptom of the development of the "scientific spirit" of the age, she consequently regarded the antivivisection platform as the most suitable venue from which to voice her critique. Cobbe constantly warned that the world was in danger of losing higher things such as reverence, sympathy, art, and poetry due to the advancement of the scientific spirit.[41] She deplored also the "deification of mere knowledge" regardless of all moral restraint, witnessed daily in the modern laboratory.[42] The progress of the human race, Cobbe believed, was to be assessed not by material interests but by moral interests; it lay not in the "Progress of the Intellect," nor in the "conquest of fresh powers over the realms of nature," but in "the gradual dying out of [the human's] tiger passions, his cruelty and his selfishness, and the growth within him of the godlike faculty of love and self-sacrifice."[43] Toward the medical profession that rose to fame and institutional prominence through

---

[38] F. P. Cobbe, "Darwinism in Morals," in *Darwinism in Morals and Other Essays* (London: Williams and Newgate, 1872), 12; see also Cobbe, "The New Morality."

[39] Cobbe, "The New Morality," 68.

[40] Cobbe, "Darwinism in Morals," 5.

[41] For a dystopia envisioned by Cobbe under a pseudonym, see F. P. Cobbe [Merlin Nostradamus, pseud.], *The Age of Science: A Newspaper of the Twentieth Century* (London: Ward, Lock, and Tyler, 1877).

[42] F. P. Cobbe, "To Know, or Not to Know," in *The Scientific Spirit of the Age*, 160, 149. See also F. P. Cobbe, "The Education of the Emotions," in *The Scientific Spirit of the Age*, 48.

[43] F. P. Cobbe, "The Evolution of the Social Sentiments," in *Hopes of the Human Race*, 217–18.

the laboratory revolution, Cobbe also directed poignant criticism. The emerging medical science, in Cobbe's eyes, not only produced materialist knowledge that brutalized the minds of its practitioners, but also contributed to a culture that regarded bodily health as the "*summum bonum*" and saw everything that contributed to it as "*ipson fact*, morally lawful and right."[44] The focus of medical practice, which switched from the bedside to the laboratory; the change in gaze of the doctors, who saw no longer the patients but the disease; and the practice of subjecting the poor to experiments in hospitals, heard of from time to time in the late nineteenth century, were, to Cobbe, all signs of the once noble healing art losing ground to the materialistic, agnostic, and atheistic influence of the age of science. Furthermore, Darwinism especially, with all its moral implications, signaled a world in which science had usurped religion and set itself up as the new deity, with its own moral system and order of priests—physiologists. So Cobbe parodied the credo held by scientists: " 'Blessed are the merciless, for they shall obtain useful knowledge.' —*New Gospel of Science*, Chapter First."[45] She also repeatedly presented the struggle between antivivisectionists and pro-vivisectionists as that between the "opposite poles of the moral compass," one representing "the principles of which the Christian Beatitudes are the symbol" and the other standing for "the newer gospel of the Survival of the Fittest" that allowed the strong the right to trample on the weak and unfit.[46] For Cobbe the campaign against animal experimentation was therefore never just about the continuance or discontinuance of a particular scientific practice but was a battle that, if lost, would in effect signify the ultimate triumph of the "Age of Science" against the true moral interests of humankind. This explains Cobbe's unyielding stand on the total prohibition of animal experimentation from the passing of the 1876 act until the end of her life.[47]

Conclusion

French said of the nineteenth-century antivivisection movement, "It was not experiments on animals they were protesting, it was the shape of the century

---

[44] Cobbe, "Hygeiolatry," in *The Peak in Darien*, 78.

[45] Cobbe, "The New Morality," 65.

[46] F. P. Cobbe, "Vivisection: Four Replies," *Fortnightly Review*, no. 31 (1882): 88.

[47] For Cobbe's exposition of her abolitionist objective, see Cobbe, *Life*, 2:288–91; F. P. Cobbe, *The Fallacy of Restriction Applied to Vivisection* (London: Victoria Street Society, 1886).

to come."[48] This was particularly true of Cobbe, who exerted an enormous influence over the movement in the last quarter of the nineteenth century. Cobbe and the first generation of antivivisectionists stood at a historical point when science, with its accompanying ideology, most aggressively pressed forward; seeing into the morally bleak future of an age dominated by it, Cobbe led an equally aggressive campaign in return. Her fight against vivisection was therefore a vital and integral part of her lifelong battle against the growing influence of atheism, agnosticism, materialism, and utilitarianism, which she believed to be intimately connected with the ascendency of the "scientific spirit" in the last quarter of the nineteenth century.[49]

Toward the end of the nineteenth century, Cobbe was fighting an increasingly uphill battle, as science and medicine continued to rise in professional, institutional, and cultural prominence; the breakthroughs in microbiology and preventive medicine pioneered by scientific celebrities such as Louis Pasteur and Robert Koch further convinced the public of the utility of animal experiments. Due to her insistence on the policy of total prohibition, Cobbe also became gradually marginalized in the antivivisection society she had founded. In 1897, led by a younger generation of activists, the VSS was renamed the National Anti-Vivisection Society, and in the following year, its policy was switched from total abolition to restriction. Aged seventy-six, Cobbe again poured her energy into forming a new abolitionist society— the British Union for the Abolition of Vivisection. She died six years later, in 1902, without having had any success in introducing a new abolitionist bill or in achieving any changes to the 1876 act.

It perhaps would be easy to pass a negative verdict on the lifelong endeavors of Cobbe. However, the critical issues that she raised amid the radical transformation of Victorian society brought about by the "scientific spirits"—for example, issues concerning the ultimate ends of humankind, the purpose of civilization, and the respective roles that religion and science could play in the pursuit of these goals—were never issues that could be, or were intended to be, resolved once and for all. Whether we agree with the analysis and remedies offered by Cobbe, which bore much of the imprint of the Victorian mind, we continue to live with the legacies of the problems identified by Cobbe and many others of her time. In an age when science has become ever more powerful, scientism is ever more entrenched, and animal experiments

[48] French, *Antivivisection and Medical Science*, 412.
[49] See Cobbe, "Magnanimous Atheism," in *The Peak in Darien*, 11–74.

are routinely carried out on a scale unimaginable two centuries ago, Cobbe's ideas concerning religion, morality, and science and their connection with the issue of animal experimentation remain even more pertinent to us.

Bibliography

Barton, Ruth. "Huxley, Lubbock, and Half a Dozen Others: Professionals and Gentlemen in the Formation of the X Club, 1851–1864." *Isis* 89, no. 3 (1998): 410–44.

Brooke, John Hedley. *Science and Religion: Some Historical Perspectives.* Cambridge: Cambridge University Press, 1991.

Cobbe, Frances Power [pseud. Merlin Nostradamus]. *The Age of Science: A Newspaper of the Twentieth Century.* London: Ward, Lock, and Tyler, 1877.

Cobbe, Frances Power. *Broken Lights: An Inquiry into the Present Condition & Future Prospects.* London: Trübner, 1864.

Cobbe, Frances Power. "A Charity and a Controversy." Address at the Annual Meeting of the Victoria Street Society, London, June 20, 1889. Collected in *Animal Welfare & Antivivisection, 1870–1910,* vol. 1, *Frances Power Cobbe,* edited by Susan Hamilton, 365–68. London: Routledge, 2004.

Cobbe, Frances Power, ed. *The Collected Works of Theodore Parker.* 14 vols. London: Trübner, 1863–71.

Cobbe, Frances Power. "Darwinism in Morals." In *Darwinism in Morals and Other Essays,* 1–33. London: Williams and Newgate, 1872.

Cobbe, Frances Power. *Darwinism in Morals and Other Essays.* London: Williams and Newgate, 1872.

Cobbe, Frances Power. "Decemnovenarianism." In *Studies New and Old of Ethical and Social Subjects,* 359–96. Boston: William V. Spencer, 1866.

Cobbe, Frances Power. "The Education of the Emotions." In *The Scientific Spirit of the Age,* 37–67. Boston: Geo. H. Ellis, 1888.

Cobbe, Frances Power. *An Essay on Intuitive Morals: Being an Attempt to Popularise Ethical Science.* London: Longman, Brown, Green, and Longmans, 1855.

Cobbe, Frances Power. *An Essay on Intuitive Morals, Part II: Practice of Morals.* London: John Chapman, 1857.

Cobbe, Frances Power. "The Evolution of the Social Sentiments." In *Hopes of the Human Race: Hereafter and Here,* 149–218. London: Williams and Norgate, 1874.

Cobbe, Frances Power. *A Faithless World.* London: Williams and Norgate, 1885.

Cobbe, Frances Power. *The Fallacy of Restriction Applied to Vivisection.* London: Victoria Street Society for the Protection of Animals from Vivisection, 1886.

Cobbe, Frances Power. *Hopes of the Human Race: Hereafter and Here.* London: Williams and Norgate, 1874.

Cobbe, Frances Power. "Hygeiolatry." In *The Peak in Darien: An Octave of Essays,* 77–86. Boston: Geo. H. Ellis, 1882.

Cobbe, Frances Power. "The Janus of Science." In *The Modern Rack: Papers on Vivisection,* 109–46. London: Swan Sonnenschein, 1889.

Cobbe, Frances Power. *Life of Frances Power Cobbe, by Herself.* 2 vols. London: Richard Bentley & Son, 1894.

Cobbe, Frances Power. "Magnanimous Atheism." In *The Peak in Darien: An Octave of Essays*, 11–74. Boston: Geo. H. Ellis, 1882.

Cobbe, Frances Power. *The Modern Rack: Papers on Vivisection*. London: Swan Sonnenschein, 1889.

Cobbe, Frances Power. *The Moral Aspects of Vivisection*. London: Victorian Street Society for the Protection of Animals from Vivisection, 1884.

Cobbe, Frances Power. "The New Morality." In *The Modern Rack: Papers on Vivisection*, 65–69. London: Swan Sonnenschein, 1889.

Cobbe, Frances Power. *The Peak in Darien: An Octave of Essays*. Boston: Geo. H. Ellis, 1882.

Cobbe, Frances Power. *Religious Duty*. Boston: William V. Spencer, 1865.

Cobbe, Frances Power. "The Right of Tormenting." In *The Modern Rack: Papers on Vivisection*, 49–60. London: Swan Sonnenschein, 1889.

Cobbe, Frances Power. "The Rights of Man and the Claims of Brutes." In *Studies New and Old of Ethical and Social Subjects*, 211–60. Boston: William V. Spencer, 1866.

Cobbe, Frances Power. *The Scientific Spirit of the Age*. Boston: Geo. H. Ellis, 1888.

Cobbe, Frances Power. "Self-Development and Self-Abnegation." In *Studies New and Old of Ethical and Social Subjects*, 49–88. Boston: William V. Spencer, 1866.

Cobbe, Frances Power. *Studies New and Old of Ethical and Social Subjects*. Boston: William V. Spencer, 1866.

Cobbe, Frances Power. "To Know, or Not to Know." In *The Scientific Spirit of the Age*, 149–71. Boston: Geo. H. Ellis, 1888.

Cobbe, Frances Power. "Vivisection: Four Replies." *Fortnightly Review*, no. 31 (1882): 88–104.

Cobbe, Frances Power. "Zoophily." In *The Peak in Darien: An Octave of Essays*, 125–47. Boston: Geo. H. Ellis, 1882.

Dawson, Gowan, and Bernard Lightman, eds. *Victorian Scientific Naturalism: Community, Identity, Continuity*. Chicago: University of Chicago Press, 2014.

Donald, Diana. *Women against Cruelty: Animal Protection in Nineteenth-Century Britain*. Manchester: Manchester University Press, 2020.

French, Richard D. *Antivivisection and Medical Science in Victorian Society*. Princeton, NJ: Princeton University Press, 1975.

Hamilton, Susan, ed. *Animal Welfare & Anti-vivisection, 1870–1910*. Vol. 1, *Frances Power Cobbe*. London: Routledge, 2004.

Hamilton, Susan. *Frances Power Cobbe and Victorian Feminism*. Basingstoke: Palgrave Macmillan, 2006.

Helmstadter, Richard J., and Bernard Lightman, eds. *Victorian Faith in Crisis: Essays on Continuity and Change in Nineteenth-Century Religious Belief*. Basingstoke: Macmillan, 1990.

Lightman, Bernard. *Evolutionary Naturalism in Victorian Britain*. Farnham, UK: Ashgate, 2009.

Lightman, Bernard. "Science and Culture." In *The Cambridge Companion to Victorian Culture*, edited by Francis O'Gorman, 12–42. Cambridge: Cambridge University Press, 2010.

Lightman, Bernard, and Michael S. Reidy, eds. *The Age of Scientific Naturalism*. London: Pickering & Chatto, 2014.

Mitchell, Sally. *Frances Power Cobbe: Victorian Feminist, Journalist, Reformer*. Charlottesville: University of Virginia Press, 2004.

Peacock, Sandra J. *The Theological and Ethical Writings of Frances Power Cobbe, 1822–1904*. Lewiston, NY: Edwin Mellen Press, 2002.

Turner, Frank M. *Between Science and Religion: The Reaction to Scientific Naturalism in Late Victorian England*. New Haven: Yale University Press, 1974.

Turner, Frank M. *Contesting Cultural Authority: Essays in Victorian Intellectual Life*. Cambridge: Cambridge University Press, 1993.

Tyndall, John. *Fragments of Science*. New York: D. Appleton, 1896.

Ward, James. *Naturalism and Agnosticism: The Gifford Lectures Delivered before the University of Aberdeen in the Years 1896–1898*. London: Adam and Charles Black, 1903.

Williamson, Lori. *Power and Protest: Frances Power Cobbe and Victorian Society*. London: Rivers Oram Press, 2005.

10

Frank Buckland (1826–1880) and Henry Parry Liddon (1829–1890)

Vivisection in Oxford

Serenhedd James

How very horrible it is to read the accounts which sometimes meet us of cruelties exercised on brute animals. Does it not sometimes make us shudder to hear tell of them, or to read them in some chance publication which we take up? At one time it is the wanton deed of barbarous owners who ill-treat their cattle, or beasts of burden; and at another, it is the cold-blooded and calculating act of men of science, who make experiments on brute animals, perhaps from a sort of curiosity.

—John Henry Newman[1]

In *Why Animal Suffering Matters*, Andrew Linzey notes the significance of John Henry Newman's Good Friday sermon of 1842, in which the then vicar of the University Church at Oxford exhorted his congregation to ponder the suffering of Christ on Calvary by meditating on the cruelty meted out to animals by uncaring—or at least unnecessarily callous—humans.[2] "Think then, my brethren," he continued, "of your feelings at cruelty practised upon brute animals, and you will gain one sort of feeling which the history of Christ's Cross and Passion ought to excite within you."[3]

---

[1] John Henry Newman, "The Crucifixion," in *Parochial and Plain Sermons* (London: Rivingtons, 1868), 136.

[2] Andrew Linzey, *Why Animal Suffering Matters: Philosophy, Theology, and Practical Ethics* (Oxford: Oxford University Press, 2009).

[3] Newman, "The Crucifixion," 138.

Serenhedd James, *Frank Buckland (1826–1880) and Henry Parry Liddon (1829–1890)* In: *Animal Theologians*. Edited by: Andrew Linzey and Clair Linzey, Oxford University Press. © Oxford University Press 2023. DOI: 10.1093/oso/9780197655542.003.0011

Linzey develops his thoughts on the possibility of viewing animal pain through the lens of the Passion in *Animal Gospel*,[4] but in *Animal Suffering* he uses Newman's sermon as a way of regarding the issues "from a specifically theological perspective." Theological perspective on the relationship between humans and animals is not new, of course, but many modern writers in the field of animal ethics have considered historic biblical scholarship, coupled with the Thomist tradition—as later developed by the animal-machine model of rational Cartesianism in the seventeenth century—to be responsible for the development of a school of Christian thought that Linzey describes as "largely negative in relation to animals."[5] It is probably fair to say, for example, that most of the post-Descartes animal-centered pastimes enumerated by Edward Brooke-Hitching in *Fox Tossing, Octopus Wrestling and Other Forgotten Sports*[6] held appeal in part because of the Port Royalists' theory that the agonized screams of dying animals were little more than "the noise of breaking machinery."[7] As Linzey notes, however, "Christian theology comprises more than the Aristotelian-Thomist tradition."[8] To that end, we must place John Henry Newman in context.

Newman, one of the most significant and controversial theologians of the nineteenth century, was for many years at the forefront of what has become known as the Oxford Movement. From the late 1820s its university-based members sought to recall the Church of England to its identity as part of the Catholic (but not Roman Catholic) Church and as a continuation of the primitive church as evinced in the writings of the early church fathers.[9] Because of the evolving way in which theology was being taught at Oxford under the Regius Professorship of Charles Lloyd in the 1820s, it is important to regard Newman's own theological position as having been thoroughly infused with patristic thought. His personal scholarship focused on Athanasius's refutation of the Arian heresy in the fourth century, and in 1846 he became a Roman Catholic. His Good Friday sermon of 1842 represents not just a general Christian perspective on animal suffering but a specifically Oxford Movement perspective of the 1840s—although, as we

---

[4] Andrew Linzey, *Animal Gospel* (Westminster: John Knox Press, 2004), 73ff.
[5] Linzey, *Animal Suffering*, 37.
[6] Edward Brooke-Hitching, *Fox Tossing, Octopus Wrestling and Other Forgotten Sports* (New York: Simon & Schuster, 2015).
[7] See A. Richard Kingston, "Theodicy and Animal Welfare," *Theology* 70 (November 1967): 482–88.
[8] Linzey, *Animal Suffering*, 37.
[9] See George Herring, *What Was the Oxford Movement?* (London: Continuum, 2002).

shall see, Oxford Movement perspectives did not remain static as the century progressed.

Newman's departure from both the Church of England and Oxford shook, but did not destroy, the movement that he had led. His former disciples galvanized themselves as the years passed to deal with various perceived assaults on what they regarded, in the middle of the nineteenth century, as the historic and classic Christian position on a number of issues. These threats included the ongoing developments of "higher criticism"—the liberal school of biblical exegesis that emerged from the late eighteenth-century German theological tradition (whose influence in the Church of England led to the 1860 publication of the controversial volume *Essays and Reviews* and the eventual excommunication of the controversial John Colenso, bishop of Natal, in 1863)—and the obvious difficulties presented to the generally received understanding of the Genesis creation narratives by the work of Charles Darwin and the publication in 1859 of his seminal *Origin of Species*. The infamous exchange between Samuel Wilberforce and Thomas Huxley at the British Association meeting in June 1860 itself belongs to the history of the Oxford Movement, because many clergy who sought to uphold the movement's principles found "Soapy Sam" to be among their doughtiest episcopal supporters.[10]

In the 1840s the members of the Oxford Movement inclined toward conservatism in theology and exegesis—which is what leads Linzey to see Newman's regard for animal welfare as particularly noteworthy. Fifty years later, a new generation of clergy influenced by the movement's principles had found a way of embracing developments in both biblical criticism and scientific research. *Lux Mundi*, a series of essays published in 1889 and edited by Charles Gore, engaged with the idea that both schools could be complementary to divine revelation, rather than antagonistic. Although it caused a good deal of anger in many quarters, *Lux Mundi* nevertheless paved the way for a more liberal engagement with both scripture and science—one that does not seem at all controversial to modern sensibilities. For the purposes of this discussion, however, we must return in the first instance to the general conservatism of the 1840s, and look to Christ Church in particular.

Christ Church became an obvious focus of the Oxford Movement in the 1840s because of the presence within its walls of Edward Bouverie Pusey,

[10] David Newsome, "The Churchmanship of Samuel Wilberforce," *Studies in Church History* 3 (1966): 28.

Regius Professor of Hebrew and de facto leader of the movement after Newman's secession to Rome. Pusey's prodigious scholarly output, ascetic lifestyle, and engaging preaching made him an attractive figure to many; his influence was enormous, but he was no stranger to controversy—he was banned from preaching at the university for a period in the 1840s, after a sermon on the Real Presence was deemed by the vice-chancellor to have offended Oxford's ecclesiological sensibilities. Despite the varying degrees of public opprobrium meted out to the members of the Oxford Movement, generations of young men left the college persuaded of the movement's claims on the life of the Church of England. They inevitably carried those ideals into their public lives in church and state, even though, as Michael Chandler has observed, Pusey's unfashionable religious positions caused his friendship to be "considered by many to be detrimental to the career prospects of a young man."[11] That said, William Ewart Gladstone was among his neophytes.

Of the young men who matriculated at Christ Church in the mid-1840s, two names in particular should detain us: those of Henry Parry Liddon and Francis Trevelyan Buckland. Liddon came immediately under Pusey's spell—and later also received spiritual direction from John Keble—and may be safely identified as a firm adherent to Oxford Movement principles. He took holy orders in 1852 and in 1870 became Dean Ireland Professor of the Exegesis of Holy Scripture and a canon of St Paul's, where his renowned preaching drew large crowds. As he never married, he retained his studentship of Christ Church, to which he had been elected in 1847—with its corresponding membership of the college's governing body—until his death in 1890. By then he was one of the best-known churchmen in England and an Oxford Movement grandee.

Buckland, the eccentric son of eccentric parents, would later become one of the leading naturalists of his age. He is the subject of Richard Girling's recent book *The Man Who Ate the Zoo*[12] and was the progeny of the influential naturalists William and Mary Buckland. William Buckland was dean of Westminster, but he previously had been a canon of Christ Church. Frank Buckland, therefore, had spent most of his childhood in the college, and his return in 1844—having failed to win a scholarship to Corpus Christi—was something of a homecoming. Ten years earlier, he had ridden a large turtle in

[11] Michael Chandler, *The Life and Work of Henry Parry Liddon* (Leominster: Gracewing, 2000), 4.
[12] Richard Girling, *The Man Who Ate the Zoo: Frank Buckland, Forgotten Hero of Natural History* (London: Penguin, 2016).

Mercury (the deep pond in the middle of Tom Quad)—an animal destined to become the soup course at the dinner to celebrate the Duke of Wellington's installation as chancellor of the university[13]—and almost certainly it was his strong family links with Christ Church that caused the college authorities to tolerate, up to a point, the benign chaos that he soon visited on his alma mater.

Through a biography of Liddon and Buckland's contemporary Richard Meux Benson, written by Mildred Woodgate in 1953, we catch a glimpse of the life of these young men at Christ Church in the mid-1840s. Woodgate wrote *Father Benson of Cowley* as a hagiography of the man who had become, in the course of a long life, the founder of the Society of St John the Evangelist and one of the Church of England's best-regarded authorities on the spiritual life. She was keen to note that there had been plenty of frivolity in Benson's student life, despite his later deeply ascetic nature. In the evenings the students dined in Hall—now one of the most famous dining rooms in the world, thanks to its use as a model for the Hogwarts dining hall in the *Harry Potter* films—and through her presentation of Benson's circle Woodgate pointed to the parties, the long walks in the surrounding countryside, and Buckland's various interesting visitors. The other element of an Oxford undergraduate's daily schedule in those days was, of course, the routine of compulsory prayer. At Christ Church there was a daily service at eight o'clock in the morning, before college breakfast; and on Sundays students attended the choral services at the cathedral, wearing their surplices.[14]

In this pious routine Benson and Liddon immersed themselves thoroughly. How enthusiastically Buckland engaged with the routine is unclear, although certainly in later life he was himself an Oxford Movement adherent, being a regular worshiper at St Mary Magdalene, Munster Square.[15] According to Bompas, Liddon considered that "it was impossible to talk to him and not be sure that God, life, death and judgment were to him solid and constantly present realities,"[16] while Richard Girling has drawn out some of the tensions between Buckland's theological conservatism—what would now be called creationism—and his scientific studies.[17] Benson was closely linked to his curious neighbor, whose exact contemporary he was and whose rooms were opposite his own. Liddon, two years behind them and with rooms on

[13] Timothy Collins, "From Anatomy to Zoophagy: A Biographical Note on Frank Buckland," *Journal of the Galway Archeological and Historical Society* 55 (2003): 94.

[14] Mildred Woodgate, *Father Benson of Cowley* (London: Geoffrey Bles, 1953), 28–30.

[15] Girling, *Buckland*, 261.

[16] George C. Bompas, *Life of Frank Buckland* (London: Smith & Elder, 1885), 47–48.

[17] Girling, *Buckland*, 284ff.

the other side of college, was also caught up in Buckland's orbit: he recalled that Buckland was his first visitor after his arrival.[18]

Buckland did not return to Christ Church alone. He soon established in and around his rooms in Fell's Buildings (roughly where the Meadow Buildings now stand) a hair-raising menagerie of creatures of varying sizes and temperaments.

> Various pets would be strewn about the floor and lying on chairs or tables—
> marmots, guinea pigs, several snakes, a monkey, a chameleon, while in the
> courtyard outside were an eagle, a jackal, a pariah dog and even a bear. "In
> our day," writes Benson, "the little courtyard was large enough to contain
> various animals, who acknowledged the supremacy of man in the form of
> Christ Church students with more or less unwillingness—a bear, a jackal,
> an eagle. One inmate of the establishment was confined to the house as
> dangerous—a viper! 'Benson, put on your gloves and bring the tongs! The
> viper has got loose!' The bones of the departed, including one of the human
> race, were under the sofa where the present generation of mortality met for
> wine-parties."[19]

A sketch of Buckland's cluttered sitting room is preserved among his effects at the Royal College of Surgeons. Called "The Wizard's Cave," it bears out much the same scene as that described in Woodgate's book, although the grinning human skeleton is propped up in the corner, rather than mixed up with the others under the sofa.[20]

George Bompas's *Life of Frank Buckland* was published in 1885, five years after its subject's early death and in the year of *Vivisection in Oxford*—a petition presented to Convocation, the university's instrument of self-government, in an unsuccessful attempt to secure a guarantee that no teaching or research in the new physiological laboratory would be carried out on conscious animals. Bompas's work included memories from Buckland's contemporaries which flesh out the extent to which his menagerie was a college-wide phenomenon. Richard St John Tyrwhitt—who by then felt that evolution was compatible with Christianity[21]—noted that often "various sounds intermittently broke

[18] Girling, *Buckland*, 41.

[19] Woodgate, *Father Benson*, 27.

[20] *Commonplace Book*, Buckland Papers, Royal College of Surgeons (RCS), MS0035/1. My thanks to Sophie Gibbs at the RCS for her help with this.

[21] Geoffrey Cantor and Sally Shuttleworth, eds., *Science Serialized: Representations of the Sciences in Nineteenth-Century Periodicals* (Cambridge, MA: MIT Press, 2004), 224.

the spell of academic silence . . . a bear would utter his voice, or it might be a monkey; or one or both animals might obtain temporary freedom and wander about college, causing effervescence; in short, tranquillity was far from slumberous in the more retired parts of 'the House.' "[22]

"Once," wrote Woodgate, "the viper escaped and found its way into Benson's bedroom, whence it was pursued and caught by a number of undergraduates, of whom Liddon was one."[23] Liddon's own memory of the incident differed only slightly from Benson's, in that he identified the escapee as "Frank's adder."

> It had escaped into Mr Benson's rooms, and was pursued into the bed-room by a group of undergraduates, who had however different objects in view. Frank certainly had the well-being of the adder chiefly at heart; the rest of us, I fear, were governed by the lower motive of escaping being bitten anyhow—if, consistently with the adder's safety, well—if not, still of escaping.[24]

Walter Spencer-Stanhope, meanwhile, recalled sitting on the sofa and keeping his feet up to avoid being nipped by the jackal underneath, who turned out to be making a meal of a few hapless guinea pigs.[25]

The adder, the bear, and the monkey were not exceptions. Buckland seems to have treated the small quad outside his rooms as an exercise ground for his animals, and they frequently wandered off in search of their own adventures. The marmot once had to be extracted from the chapter house so that the cathedral canons could meet unmolested. One morning the eagle took to pecking at the undergraduates on their way to prayers and had to be "rolled up in one of the students' gowns and carried off ignominiously,"[26] and on another occasion the bird made an appearance in the cathedral at Sunday matins: "two or three men left their places to deal with it; Dean Gaisford looked unspeakable things."[27]

Two of Buckland's creatures require distinct attention. The first is perhaps the most famous of all—his tame bear, Tiglath Pileser—and the second is the less originally named jackal, Jacky. Tiglath Pileser was named after the

[22] Bompas, *Buckland*, 49.
[23] Woodgate, *Father Benson*, 28.
[24] Quoted in Bompas, *Buckland*, 46-47.
[25] Bompas, *Buckland*, 47.
[26] Bompas, *Buckland*, 39.
[27] Bompas, *Buckland*, 43.

ancient king of Assyria, whose name was on the lips of the poor undergraduate reading the first lesson at Evensong one afternoon when he had to
abandon the lectern, pursued by a bear.[28] Tig, as he was called, was thoroughly anthropomorphized: "He was provided with a cap and gown, and in
this costume was taken to wine parties, or went boating with his master, to
the wonderment of the children in Christ Church Meadow . . . [He] took part
in the proceedings of the British Association at Oxford in 1847, attending
in cap and gown the garden party at the Botanic Gardens."[29] He also rode
with Buckland and went for walks with anyone who would let him suck their
fingers. But eventually the dean, Thomas Gaisford (who had himself known
Buckland as a child), decided that a bear in college was too much, and so
Tig had to go. He was sent to Islip, not far from Oxford—a parish that was
at that time held in plurality by the deans of Westminster and so was effectively Buckland's parents' country home—where he joined a number of other
members of the menagerie whose various indiscretions had necessitated
their removal from college. He died a few years later—but not before his various near-human exploits had passed into local legend and caused him to be
exiled to the zoological gardens in the Regent's Park—and was stuffed and
placed in the deanery at Westminster.[30]

Jacky, when he was not munching his way through the rodents, was kept
tied up outside Fell's Buildings. It should be noted that while Buckland was
deeply interested in animals, he was interested in a scientific sense. Apart
from his willingness to anthropomorphize Tig, he does not appear to have
indulged in great sentimentality toward his charges, nor was he averse to
trapping animals for the sole purpose of dissection. Jacky seems to have
displayed signs of zoochosis: Liddon recalled that "under some odd and
painful irritation, he used to go round and round, eating off his tail," and
that Buckland "expressed great sympathy with him, modified by strong
curiosity—he wondered how far Jacky would eat up into his back!"[31]

To animal ethicists, both Tig and Jacky—perhaps even the whole arkful—
may present a moral quandary. By the standards of his own time, Buckland
seems to have been an enlightened and diligent animal owner to a great extent, but he was first and foremost a scientist, and to that end his animals
were subjects of study first and companions second. There remains, certainly,

[28] William Tuckwell, *Reminiscences of Oxford* (London: Dutton, 1908), 106.
[29] Bompas, *Buckland*, 47.
[30] Girling, *Buckland*, 51.
[31] Quoted in Bompas, *Buckland*, 47.

a distinct tension between his innate fascination with animal anatomy and Newman's criticism of those who carried out experiments on animals "from a sort of curiosity," although Girling notes that Buckland confined his dissection work to dead animals only.[32] To those around him, however, his creatures were objects of diversion, interest, and even affection.

Before moving on to the debate on vivisection at Oxford, we must introduce an eminent character who hovers—at present, uncertainly—around the Liddon–Buckland connection and whom we might reasonably co-opt as at least a friend of the Oxford Movement through his friendship with Liddon: Charles Lutwidge Dodgson, better known to millions as the stammering, lovesick author Lewis Carroll. Dodgson, as we shall call him, came up to Christ Church in early 1851. Buckland had left three years earlier, but is it possible that Dodgson could have been totally unaware of such a colorful character, given his prominence in the recent history of the college and in society generally? Dodgson and Liddon were on intimate terms, and Morton N. Cohen demonstrates that they were in regular contact with one another until Liddon's death in 1890.[33] Cohen does not mention Buckland, however, nor do Dodgson's modern biographers Edward Wakeling, Derek Hudson, and Michael Bakewell. Certainly, Dodgson possessed a copy of Buckland's four-volume *Curiosities of Natural History* (although it is not clear when he acquired it), but none of Buckland's other publications appear in the lists from the sale of Dodgson's library after his death.[34] Neither is Buckland mentioned in Roger Lancelyn Green's edition of Dodgson's surviving diaries.[35] But could Liddon have resisted telling his friend about Buckland's fantastic bestiary in the course of their shared conversations at High Table or resisted recounting the comic tales of the adventures of his animals within Christ Church's ancient walls?

Derek Hudson pertinently observed that in Dodgson's time animals in college were a familiar sight at Christ Church, but most students kept dogs; this waned under Henry Liddell and was entirely obsolete by the time Hudson published his *Lewis Carroll* in 1954.[36] When the old Fell's Buildings, where Dodgson himself had his rooms for a while,[37] were demolished not long after

[32] Girling, *Buckland*, 318.
[33] Morton N. Cohen, *Lewis Carroll* (London: Macmillan, 1995), 273–75.
[34] Jeffrey Stern, *Lewis Carroll, Bibliophile* (Stonewood, WV: White Stone Publishing for the Lewis Carroll Society, 1997), 15–48.
[35] Roger Lancelyn Green, *The Diaries of Lewis Carroll* (London: Cassell, 1953).
[36] Derek Hudson, *Lewis Carroll* (London: Constable, 1954), 61–63.
[37] Hudson, *Lewis Carroll*, 82.

Dodgson's election to the studentship, did Liddon really keep stony silence on their exotic former inhabitants? For now we can only speculate on whether the memory of Frank Buckland's menagerie at Christ Church influenced the anthropomorphic creatures of *Alice's Adventures in Wonderland* and *Through the Looking-Glass* or the later animal antics of *Sylvie & Bruno*. We might also reasonably ask whether it influenced Dodgson's writing on vivisection in the 1870s and 1880s—as collated by Götz Kluge[38]—and particularly his robust paper *Some Popular Fallacies about Vivisection*, circulated privately in Oxford in 1875.[39]

Speculation aside, what is certain is that in the early 1880s both Liddon and Dodgson were of one mind on the matter of animal experimentation at Oxford, and they were not alone. Many members of the university were unconvinced by the reassurance that a Decree of Convocation, the university's chamber of self-governance, in 1885—ostensibly to provide funds for the Department of Physiology and the new post of lecturer on human anatomy—would not in the end involve "no experiments upon the living animal involving pain."[40] *Vivisection in Oxford* appealed to the members of Convocation, assuring them that its signatories objected not to the teaching of physiology in the university, "but to the establishment of a centre of *Vivisection in Oxford*." Principally, its objection was that during the previous votes to establish the physiological laboratory in 1883 and 1884, no safeguards had been provided for the ongoing prevention of the use of conscious animals for medical research.

> The present Professor has given certain promises which ought to satisfy the demands of the opponents of Vivisection, and that the restrictions of the present Act (39 & 40 Vict.) furnish sufficient safeguards.[41] But, whatever promises the present Professor has given, it is perfectly certain that no promises of his will bind his successors.
>
> It is true that the Act provides (§3)

---

[38] Götz Kluge, "Lace-Making: An Infringement of Right" (2015), www.academia.edu/9962213/Lace-Making_An_Infringement_of_Right.

[39] Charles Lutwidge Dodgson, *Some Popular Fallacies about Vivisection* (Oxford, June 1875).

[40] *The Physiological Laboratory and Oxford Medical Teaching*, Pusey House, Liddon Papers, box 2, folder 5, document 1a.

[41] This refers to the Act to Amend the Law relating to Cruelty to Animals of 1876, which amended the Cruelty to Animals Act of 1849 and was superseded by the Animals (Scientific Procedures) Act of 1986.

(3) "That the animal must during the whole of the experiment be under the influence of some anaesthetic of sufficient power to prevent its feeling pain." **But the Professor may hold a certificate which will exempt him from this restriction.**

(4) "That the animal must, if the pain is likely to continue after the effect of the anaesthetic has ceased, or if any serious injury has been inflicted on the animal, be killed before it recovers from the influence of the anaesthetic which has been administered." **But by holding a certificate the Professor may be exempt from this also.**

(5) "That the experiment shall not be performed as an illustration of lectures in medical schools, hospitals, college or elsewhere." **But future Professors may hold certificates allowing them to use these experiments for purposes of demonstration.**

"An amendment," it concluded, "might very easily have met the case and prevented opposition to the grant: but amendments to decrees cannot in any circumstances be proposed, and Hebdomadal Council has refused already to make any compromise. There is therefore no other course but to meet the proposed grant with a simple *non-placet*."[42]

The signatories were distinguished, and like Liddon, a number of them were Oxford Movement panjandrums. Chief among them were Edward King, Regius Professor of moral theology (and soon-to-be-consecrated bishop of Lincoln); William Bright, Regius Professor of ecclesiastical history; Thomas Chamberlain, vicar of St Thomas the Martyr, Oxford, and a leading Ritualist; and Dodgson. Samuel Wilberforce's successor as bishop of Oxford, John Fielder Mackarness—also a supportive friend of Oxford Movement clergy—signed in his own right as a fellow of Exeter.

Liddon had resigned his chair in 1882 and did not sign the original document, but he clearly followed developments closely. He discussed *Vivisection in Oxford* in detail with Dodgson, and some of their correspondence on the matter—as well as annotated copies of relevant papers—survives among his papers in the archives at Pusey House. On March 8, 1885, two days before the meeting of Convocation, Liddon was persuaded to speak against the motion to provide funds for the Department of Physiology by William Bright; Edward Augustus Freeman, Regius Professor of modern history; and Edward Moore, principal of St Edmund Hall. He noted in his diary, "Bright,

---

[42] *Vivisection in Oxford*, Pusey House, Liddon Papers, box 2, folder 5, document 3.

Freeman, and Moore called on me to beg me to lead the opposition."[43] Two days later, on the morning of the March 10 meeting, Dodgson sent Liddon a note to remind him that "it is above all things essential to be *audible*" and that on a previous occasion people had had to strain to hear him.[44]

The Oxford Movement vote, however, was divided. Among those who signed a statement rejecting the concerns of *Vivisection in Oxford* before the discussion in Convocation were Edward Talbot, Aubrey Moore, Robert Ottley, and Walter Lock. All four were intimately linked with the movement, and Talbot and Lock were respectively warden and subwarden of Keble College. Liddon had been instrumental in the foundation of the college in memory of his mentor, and he noted with sadness that "the whole Keble vote (alas!)" was in favor of the motion.[45] The three speakers against—Freeman, Mackarness, and Liddon himself—failed to carry the day.

Four years later, Talbot, Moore, Ottley, and Lock would all contribute to *Lux Mundi*. By this time, the Oxford Movement had moved on to its third-generation phase, in which Young Turks such as those whose votes had so disappointed Liddon were taking the lead and engaging with the theological liberalism that their predecessors had rejected. For second-generation men, those who had been formed by the movement's founders, there was a distinct tension in this state of affairs. Richard Meux Benson was the longest-lived of all of the second-generation Oxford Movement adherents—he died in 1915, well into his nineties—and Mildred Woodgate described him as having been in the mid-1880s "a staunch conservative . . . cut off from the young and rapidly changing world around him."[46] To some extent, this too was Liddon's experience—and by extension Dodgson also shared in it.

Liddon's theological conservatism was founded—to return to where we began—in the Aristotelian-Thomist tradition perceived from a position of Catholic Anglicanism. He and his supporters nevertheless eschewed the traditional notion of humans' dominion over animals; they called instead for the implementation of safeguards to prevent unnecessary cruelty from being carried out in the name of the university's burgeoning engagement with science. He was voted down by (among many others) those who sought ways of applying theology to the challenges presented by Darwin's theory of evolution

[43] Liddon Diaries, March 8, 1885, Pusey House.
[44] Charles Dodgson to Henry Parry Liddon, March 10, 1885, Pusey House, Liddon Papers, box 2, folder 5 document 5.
[45] Liddon Diaries, March 10, 1885, Pusey House.
[46] Woodgate, *Father Benson*, 151.

and other scientific developments. By the time of the Oxford debate on viv-isection, Liddon was something of a relic in the movement in which he had been regarded as a hero for so long.[47] Nevertheless, it could be argued that his ill-fated stand of 1885 at least contributed to a way of Christian thinking about animal experimentation that reached a particular Oxford Movement apogee with C. S. Lewis—another author whose most abiding works involve anthropomorphic animals—and Lewis's "Vivisection" of 1947.[48]

Perhaps a clue to Liddon's motives lies in the vignettes of his shared life with Buckland at Christ Church in the 1840s, described by William Tuckwell, George Bompas, and, most recently, Richard Girling. Liddon's description of a spring breakfast that coincided with the reappearance of the marmots after their hibernation in the cellar is delightful: "There was great excitement; the creatures ran about the table, as entitled to the honours of the day; though there were other beasts and reptiles in the room too, which in later life would have made breakfasting difficult."[49] Liddon's friendship with Buckland ensured that he had an introduction to the *regnum animalia* unique to those in a particular circle at Oxford in the 1840s; their contemporary St John Tyrwhitt thought that to outsiders a man of Buckland's interests and talents "was considered simply off his head for caring about nature."[50]

Dodgson presumably had a similar, if secondary, introduction through the recollections of Liddon and the collective memory of the college community at Christ Church in the 1850s. It cannot be a coincidence that out of the same *convivium* that held Buckland's legendary creatures in the 1840s emerged in the 1860s and 1870s the most enduring tales in English of animals with ad-vanced anthropomorphic characteristics, including a rabbit who not only wore a watch but also could tell the time, a caterpillar who smoked, oysters who were self-aware enough to be terrified of being eaten, and an eccentric or perhaps zoochotic hare. Robert Douglas-Fairhurst makes a similar obser-vation in *The Story of Alice*, but he mistakenly conflates William and Frank Buckland and identifies Dodgson's muse as having been the former.[51]

In the absence of solid archival evidence, any conclusions can only be speculative. But it does not seem too much of a stretch of the

[47] Chandler, *Life and Work of Henry Parry Liddon*, 219.
[48] Lewis's "Vivisection" was written for the New England Anti-Vivisection Society. It later appeared (posthumously) in Lewis, *God in the Dock*, ed. Walter Hooper (Grand Rapids, MI: Eerdmans, 1970).
[49] Bompas, *Buckland*, 42.
[50] Bompas, *Buckland*, 48.
[51] Robert Douglas-Fairhurst, *The Story of Alice: Lewis Carroll and the Secret History of Wonderland* (Cambridge, MA: Harvard University Press, 2015), 61–62.

imagination to contend that Dodgson likely was influenced to some extent by Frank Buckland's menagerie when he created the animal characters whose interactions with Alice have now been translated into nearly two hundred languages and continue to delight children across the world.

As for Henry Parry Liddon, perhaps he had two things in mind when he rose in Convocation to speak against vivisection at Oxford on March 10, 1885: Dodgson's admonition to speak up and the long-dead Jacky. "Of the bear I have a much less distinct recollection," he had observed a few years earlier, "but the jackal was, I might almost say, a personal friend."[52]

Bibliography

Bompas, George C. *Life of Frank Buckland*. London: Smith & Elder, 1885.
Brooke-Hitching, Edward. *Fox Tossing, Octopus Wrestling and Other Forgotten Sports*. New York: Simon & Schuster, 2015.
Buckland Papers. Royal College of Surgeons, London.
Cantor, Geoffrey, and Sally Shuttleworth, eds. *Science Serialized: Representations of the Sciences in Nineteenth-Century Periodicals*. Cambridge, MA: MIT Press, 2004.
Carroll, Lewis. *Alice's Adventures in Wonderland*. London: Macmillan, 1865.
Carroll, Lewis. *Sylvie and Bruno*. London: Macmillan, 1889.
Carroll, Lewis. *Through the Looking-Glass, and What Alice Found There*. London: Macmillan, 1871.
Chandler, Michael. *The Life and Work of Henry Parry Liddon*. Leominster: Gracewing, 2000.
Cohen, Morton N. *Lewis Carroll*. London: Macmillan, 1995.
Collins, Timothy. "From Anatomy to Zoophagy: A Biographical Note on Frank Buckland." *Journal of the Galway Archeological and Historical Society* 55 (2003): 91–109.
Dodgson, Charles Lutwidge. *Some Popular Fallacies about Vivisection*. Oxford, June 1875.
Douglas-Fairhurst, Robert. *The Story of Alice: Lewis Carroll and the Secret History of Wonderland*. Cambridge, MA: Harvard University Press, 2015.
Girling, Richard. *The Man Who Ate the Zoo: Frank Buckland, Forgotten Hero of Natural History*. London: Penguin, 2016.
Green, Roger Lancelyn. *The Diaries of Lewis Carroll*. London: Cassell, 1953.
Herring, George. *What Was the Oxford Movement?* London: Continuum, 2002.
Hudson, Derek. *Lewis Carroll*. London: Constable, 1954.
Kingston, A. Richard. "Theodicy and Animal Welfare." *Theology* 70 (November 1967): 482–88.
Kluge, Götz. "Lace-Making: An Infringement of Right." 2015. http://www.academia.edu/ 9962213/Lace-Making_An_Infringement_of_Right.
Lewis, C. S. "Vivisection." In *God in the Dock*, by C. S. Lewis, edited by Walter Hooper. Grand Rapids, MI: Eerdmans, 1970.
Liddon Papers. Pusey House, Oxford.

---

[52] Bompas, *Buckland*, 43.

Linzey, Andrew. *Animal Gospel*. Westminster: John Knox Press, 2004.

Linzey, Andrew. *Why Animal Suffering Matters: Philosophy, Theology, and Practical Ethics.* Oxford: Oxford University Press, 2009.

Newman, John Henry. "The Crucifixion." In *Parochial and Plain Sermons*, vii, 136–45. London: Rivingtons, 1868.

Newsome, David. "The Churchmanship of Samuel Wilberforce." *Studies in Church History* 3 (1966).

Stern, Jeffrey. *Lewis Carroll, Bibliophile*. Stonewood, WV: White Stone Publishing for the Lewis Carroll Society, 1997.

Tuckwell, William. *Reminiscences of Oxford*. London: Dutton, 1908.

Woodgate, Mildred. *Father Benson of Cowley*. London: Geoffrey Bles, 1953.

11

Leo Tolstoy (1828–1910)

Literature and the Lives of Animals

Alice Crary

In his 1892 essay "The First Step," written when he was in his sixties, Leo Tolstoy offers a vivid account of a couple of visits to a slaughterhouse.[1] On his first visit, he reports, he arrived too late to witness any actual killing and had to content himself with a description of the slaughtering process provided by one of the butchers. He didn't properly understand what the butcher had told him, and he formed "a wrong, but very horrible, idea of the way that animals are slaughtered."[2] Although at that point he "fancied that, as is often the case, the reality would . . . produce on [him] a weaker impression than the imagination . . . in this [he] was mistaken."[3] On his second visit, it became clear to him that slaughter is much more terrible than he had believed. He writes:

> Through the door opposite the one at which I was standing, a big, red, well-fed ox was led in. Two men were dragging it, and hardly had it entered when I saw a butcher raise a knife above its neck and stab it. The ox, as if all four legs had suddenly given way, fell heavily upon its belly, immediately turned over on one side, and began to work its legs and all its hindquarters. Another butcher at once threw himself upon the ox from the side opposite to the twitching legs, caught its horns and twisted its head down to the ground, while another butcher cut its throat with a knife. From beneath the head there flowed a stream of blackish-red blood, which a besmeared boy caught in a tin basin. All the time this was going on the ox kept incessantly twitching its head as if trying to get up, and waved its four legs in the air. The basin was quickly filling, but the ox still lived, and, its stomach heaving

[1] Leo Tolstoy, "The First Step," introduction to Howard Williams, *The Ethics of Diet: An Anthology of Vegetarian Thought* (Guildford: White Crow Books, 2009), 11–46.

[2] Tolstoy, "The First Step," 40.

[3] Tolstoy, "The First Step," 40.

Alice Crary, *Leo Tolstoy (1828–1910)* In: *Animal Theologians*. Edited by: Andrew Linzey and Clair Linzey, Oxford University Press. © Oxford University Press 2023. DOI: 10.1093/oso/9780197655542.003.0012

heavily, both hind and fore legs worked so violently that the butchers held aloof. When one basin was full, the boy carried it away on his head to the albumen factory, while another boy placed a fresh basin, which also soon began to fill up. But still the ox heaved its body and worked its hind legs.

When the blood ceased to flow the butcher raised the animal's head and began to skin it. The ox continued to writhe. The head, stripped of its skin, showed red with white veins, and kept the position given it by the butcher; on both sides hung the skin. Still the animal did not cease to writhe. Then another butcher caught hold of one of the legs, broke it, and cut it off. In the remaining legs and the stomach the convulsions still continued. The other legs were cut off and thrown aside, together with those of other oxen belonging to the same owner. Then the carcass was dragged to hoist and hung up, and the convulsions were over.[4]

After this characterization of what he observed at the abattoir, Tolstoy mentions that he stayed for the killing of more oxen and that the only significant difference he noticed was that sometimes the butcher "did not strike at once so as to cause the animal's fall"[5] and that the act of butchering was therefore yet more protracted and horrible.

Tolstoy's aim in these passages is to get his contemporaries to register something about the brutality of slaughter that they may be missing even if they know what we might call the basic *facts* about how it happens—taking "facts" as states of affairs that are available without any emotionally demanding effort of mind. Tolstoy was in possession of "the fundamental facts of slaughter," thus understood, once he had spoken to the butcher on his first visit to the slaughterhouse. However, he emphasizes that he needed something further to grasp significant aspects of what slaughter is like.[6] He then attempts to share with readers the additional insight he takes to be relevant by offering, not a neutral or clinical account, but rather an expressive account focused on the horror of what is done to an individual animal. This leads him to a tale of the torment of one "big, red, well-fed ox," who was conscious, breathing heavily, and kicking "so violently that the butchers held aloof," while being forcibly and methodically bled to death, and who not only had

---

[4] Tolstoy, "The First Step," 41–42.

[5] Tolstoy, "The First Step," 42.

[6] See also Tolstoy, "The First Step," 38 and 41, where Tolstoy discusses butchers and cattle dealers who, despite being in possession of all relevant facts about how animals are killed in abattoirs, fail to register what he regards as the awfulness of slaughter, having the attitude that what is done to animals doesn't raise any questions of right and wrong.

the skin torn off his head—so that it "showed red with white veins"—but was also partly dismembered while still in his last mortal convulsions.

When Tolstoy offers his charged account of the killing of an ox, he isn't urging the adoption of a merely noncognitive attitude toward an antecedent set of facts or, alternately, recommending that we gild such a set of facts in a certain evaluative color. He takes himself to be making a direct contribution to our grasp of what he calls the "reality" of slaughter.[7] While his slaughterhouse narrative is designed to elicit certain attitudes, he is assuming that the attitudes in question are internal to the kind of undistorted, world-directed understanding of what is done to oxen in slaughterhouses that we require in ethics; he is concerned with a morally loaded kind of understanding encompassing more than plain facts. And when elsewhere in his fictional as well as nonfictional writings he is concerned not with oxen in slaughterhouses but with animals of other varieties in other settings, he often operates with similar assumptions about how we arrive at the sort of unclouded empirical images of animal life that are relevant to ethics and about how such images will be morally charged.[8] He invites us to see that animals have moral characteristics that are in a straightforward sense open to view and that determining how they should be treated is at bottom a matter of clearly discerning their worldly lives.

This feature of Tolstoy's thought is worth underlining not only because, as I argue here, it is sound and important but also because it is regrettably absent from dominant trends of thought in animal ethics.

Animal ethics is a discipline that has grown up, within philosophy departments and other university programs within the Anglophone world and, increasingly, also beyond it, over the last fifty years. Its central ambition is establishing that animals are objects of moral concern. The compelling project is to decisively respond to modern intellectual traditions that deny that animals matter and, along the way, to develop resources for challenging society-wide practices, such as factory farms, in which animals are treated as disposable things.

Animal ethicists typically undertake this project in a manner informed by some very general, and widely held, philosophical assumptions about what it is to get the world in view. They assume that the world only comes into focus from a morally neutral, aperspectival stance. It seems to follow from

[7] See the passage from Tolstoy, "The First Step," 40, cited above.
[8] For a selection of fictional and nonfictional examples from Tolstoy, see below.

this assumption that we're obliged to winnow from our understanding of the world anything that needs to be understood in terms of attitudes, and this suggests that we're confronted with something like the purging of values from the world. The resulting outlook, which is the source of culturally entrenched notions of a fact/value divide, is typically taken to be so self-evident that it doesn't appear to call for defense. Apart from critical asides about what Kantian moral philosopher Christine Korsgaard refers to as "an outdated teleological conception of the world,"[9] there is, within animal ethics, rarely even a hint that we might need to show that the wholesale moral evacuation of the world is an apt starting point for work in ethics.

The idea of such an evacuation seems to oblige animal ethicists to regard the plain worldly fact that a creature is an animal of some kind as morally indifferent. That is the point of departure of various different approaches to animal ethics. The most influential approaches start with the idea that merely being an animal of some kind doesn't matter and suggest that we can understand the moral worth of animals by seeing that they have a "moral status" grounded in their individual capacities. Advocates of these endeavors differ over, among other things, which individual capacities are morally significant; whether the capacities in question come in degrees, representing a continuum of grades of moral standing; or, alternately, whether possession of the relevant capacities is an all-or-nothing affair, representing discreet levels of moral standing.[10] A number of serious moral objections have been raised about the resulting theories, some alleging that they outrageously oblige us to look upon some human beings with significant cognitive disabilities as morally less worthy, others alleging that they saddle us with prejudices about humans' and animals' moral worth that prevent us from responding justly to particular individuals. Despite the existence of these and other moral criticisms, so much of the literature on animals and ethics is devoted to trying to fine-tune these accounts of "moral status" that preoccupation with them is sometimes taken to be constitutive of the field.

But some animal ethicists who also work with aperspectival images of thought about the world ask us to regard the very idea of individual capacities-indexed "moral status" as an expression of moral theorizing gone astray. That is the stance favored by Korsgaard, who explicitly embraces not only the

---

[9] Christine Korsgaard, *Fellow Creatures: Our Obligation to the Other Animals* (Oxford: Oxford University Press, 2018), 12; see also 11, 145 and 168.

[10] For an overview of this family of theories, see Shelly Kagan, *How to Count Animals: More or Less* (Oxford: Oxford University Press, 2019).

aperspectival image but the familiar fact/value distinction that comes with it, in telling a revised Kantian story about animals' moral standing. Rather than trying to "form a bridge" between "natural facts" about animals' psychological capacities and "normative facts" about how their bearers should be treated, Korsgaard bases her view of the value of animate life forms on claims about "necessary presuppositions of rational activity."[11] She argues that in acting we can't help but place value on our own animal natures, thereby conferring value on animals in general.[12] This strategy diverges sharply from the strategies of the theorists who look to creatures' individual capacities to gauge their moral standing. Still, it resembles these strategies in its intolerance of the prospect that the moral worth of human beings and animals is, in an entirely plain sense, open to view.

This intolerance would seem justifiable if there were compelling arguments for the aperspectival picture of world-directed thought that speaks for it. It is hard to find even the suggestion of a defense of this account within animal ethics. But there is a body of work in analytic philosophy, running back to the middle of the twentieth century, containing lines of reasoning in the account's favor, and it might seem plausible to see this material as licensing the animal ethicists' methods. Central to the lines of thought is the idea that we approach an undistorted view of the world by progressively abstracting from all our subjective responses, those that are perceptual as well as those that are affective. This is what seems to support a call for point-of-viewless thought about the world. And if we say that the world is entirely composed of things that can be adequately conceived apart from any reference to our sensory responses or attitudes,[13] we seem compelled to conclude that it is devoid of value in a manner that excludes the possibility that the detection of value could be a matter of sensitive discernment.

Yet a survey of the arguments in favor of this familiar vision of our predicament as thinkers reveals that they are more vulnerable to criticism than the vision's enormous influence might have led us to assume. These arguments tend to amount at bottom to strategies of one of the following two kinds. They

---

[11] Korsgaard, *Fellow Creatures*, 133.

[12] Korsgaard, *Fellow Creatures*, chap. 8, esp. 168; see also Christine Korsgaard, "Fellow Creatures: Kantian Ethics and Our Duties to Animals." vol. 24 of *Tanner Lectures on Human Values*, 77–110 (Salt Lake City: University of Utah Press, 2004), https://dash.harvard.edu/bitstream/handle/1/3198692/korsgaard_FellowCreatures.pdf?sequence=2.

[13] See Thomas Nagel, "Subjective and Objective," in *Mortal Questions*, 196–213 (Cambridge: Cambridge University Press, 1979); see also Bernard Williams, *Descartes: The Project of Pure Enquiry* (New York: Penguin, 1978) and *Ethics and the Limits of Philosophy* (Cambridge, MA: Harvard University Press, 1985), esp. chap. 8.

are typically either little more than appeals to an image of the relationship between mind and world, traceable to early modern European thought, on which this relationship is viewed as if from "sideways on,"[14] or local attacks on any suggestion of departure from this image. The result is that it appears that the massive reception of the belief that all world-guided thought is regulatively aperspectival is not accounted for by the considerations adduced in its favor.[15] This suggests that we ought to leave room for finding that we may need to develop our sensibilities to get worldly phenomena, such as the lives of humans and animals, in view in ethics. It suggests, further, that we would be remiss not to take an interest in the kinds of difficulties presented by moral thought, when conceived in this manner.

These observations return us to the distinctive interest of Tolstoy's writings on animals. His treatments are valuable not only because, as we have begun to see, they are a rich source of illustrations of undistorted, world-directed thought about animals that essentially draws on attitudes. They are also valuable because they contain helpful second-order reflections on how, in light of the illustrations, we should conceive challenges of bringing animal life into view in ethics.

When, in "The First Step," Tolstoy enters into such reflections, he does so in the context of addressing the religious question of how to start on the path to an upright Christian life. He claims that "self-control [is] the first step in every righteous life,"[16] and, in elaborating this claim, he broaches the topic of diet and—as in his account of the killing of a red ox—evokes the terribleness of slaughter. His ambition is to show that abstention from the flesh of animals is part of proper self-control and to distance himself from any hint of a Christianity that is not of "fasting and privation—but of beefsteaks."[17] He is attacking the idea that it is possible to lead a good and Christian life without the kind of work on ourselves that is reflected in how we respond and act. He rejects "the doctrine that personal effort is not necessary for the attainment of spiritual perfection by man,"[18] and, in a gesture that echoes throughout his religious writings, he insists we attain virtue not by espousing

---

[14] For the inset quotation, see John McDowell, *Mind and World* (Cambridge, MA: Harvard University Press, 1996).

[15] See Alice Crary, "Objectivity," in *Wittgenstein: Basic Concepts*, ed. James Conant and Sebastian Sunday Greves (Cambridge: Cambridge University Press, 2019) and "Objectivity's Politics," forthcoming.

[16] Tolstoy, "The First Step," 33.

[17] Tolstoy, "The First Step," 37–38.

[18] Tolstoy, "The First Step," 16.

proper doctrines but by changing the way we live, say, by turning our backs on the conventional, self-indulgent life characteristic of the Russian upper classes of his time.[19]

We misunderstand Tolstoy if we represent the type of exercise of self-control that he recommends in "The First Step" and elsewhere to be inessential to the growth of understanding. A recurring theme of Tolstoy's religious writings is that appropriate practical exertion is internal to the grasp of moral and spiritual truth. At one point in *A Confession* (1879) he declares that "if I do not do what is asked of me I will never understand what is asked of me,"[20] and again in *The Gospel in Brief* (1881) he writes that "he who shall do good shall know the truth."[21] These sorts of remarks shed light on the passages in "The First Step" in which Tolstoy calls on us to abstain from eating animals. He is promoting a practice that he believes contributes internally to understanding. At issue are ways of acting that cultivate capacities of feeling that, as he sees it, are necessary for bringing important aspects of animal life into focus. He is horrified by slaughter not only because it involves "the suffering and death of the animals" but also because, in falling into complicity with it, we unnecessarily suppress in ourselves capacities "of sympathy and pity toward living creatures" that by his lights are internal to a clear-sighted view of animals.[22] It is because he believes that he may need to reawaken our feelings if he is to bring within our reach a just and accurate vision of animal life that, when he turns to slaughter, he presents narratives that play on our feelings.

On Tolstoy's distinctive view, our ability to follow a sound stretch of moral thought essentially presupposes the possession of particular attitudes or resources of emotional responsiveness. So, in any given situation, a willingness to rework or re-enliven our attitudes may accordingly be a necessary prerequisite of understanding. It is possible to formulate this view, as I just did, without using any specifically religious concepts. This view of the nature and demands of moral thought is, as noted earlier, very poorly represented in contemporary, secular animal ethics. Perhaps this is an expression of the tendency, within the academy, to conceive of ethics as a professional pursuit that places no special demands on its practitioners for good behavior. Without

---

[19] See Tolstoy, "The First Step," sections 3–5. For passages elsewhere in which Tolstoy sounds these themes, see *The Gospel in Brief*, trans. Isabel Hapgood (Lincoln: University of Nebraska Press, 1997), where he discusses how true life is that of the spirit and not of the flesh, chaps. 2, 3, 6, and 7; and *A Confession and Other Religious Writings*, trans. Jane Kentish (London: Penguin, 1987), esp. 29–31.

[20] Tolstoy, *A Confession and Other Religious Writings*, 61.

[21] Tolstoy, *The Gospel in Brief*, 134. See also closely related passages at 130–31, 132, 140, and 141.

[22] Both inset quotations are from Tolstoy, "The First Step," 39.

speculating further about reasons for its foreignness to academic ethics, the view of moral thought under consideration in any case admits a formulation in nonreligious terms—there is nothing to prevent secular thinkers from embracing it.

Tolstoy's engagement with the view that moral understanding has an essentially affective and practical component is not confined to his religious and other nonfictional writings. This view is also at play in his fictional oeuvre. His stories and novels are filled with characters whose cognitive and existential situations in different ways reflect the view that moral understanding is inseparable from personal effort. There are many individuals of at least ordinary intelligence who make no attempt at good works and who lack the kind of self-understanding that is pertinent to ethics (e.g., Ivan Ilych of "The Death of Ivan Ilych" [1886]); there are also scholars whose extensive learning, unaccompanied by practical struggle, leaves them without any particular moral insight (e.g., Levin of *Anna Karenina* [1877]); and there are peasants whose practical involvements endow them with an insight into what matters in life that is entirely compatible with their ignorance of books (e.g., Platon of *War and Peace* [1869]).

In addition to being reflected in his descriptions of a wide range of characters, Tolstoy's concern with the view that practical attitudes contribute internally to moral understanding is also frequently formally exemplified in his literary writings. Tolstoy often crafts his narratives with an eye to directing readers' feelings in ways that make available the sort of understanding from which his practically and emotionally more limited characters are cut off. His story "The Death of Ivan Ilych" provides a good case of this type of formal endeavor. The story is about a bureaucrat, Ivan, who, having contracted the illness that will ultimately end his life, is unable to grasp what is happening to him because he sees no need to make a practical effort, focusing instead on the collection of plain facts about health and disease. The portrait we are given of Ivan in this way reflects Tolstoy's interest in the idea that moral understanding is inseparable from practical stance. Tolstoy also works with this idea in shaping his story's narrative structure. He uses literary devices to prompt practical responses and attitudes that, by the lights of the story's themes, are internally related to the kind of moral understanding that eludes Ivan. Readers are positioned to disparage the conventional arrangements of Ivan's life, to regard with irritation and impatience the interventions of Ivan's friends and family members who resemble him in being unable to make sense of his predicament, and to experience a kind of relieved satisfaction at the ministrations of the peasant who cares for Ivan in his last days simply and without fuss. By orchestrating a complex of different emotional responses intended to position readers to understand what is happening to Ivan better than Ivan does, Tolstoy's story exhibits a formal preoccupation with the view that moral understanding is tied to practical attitudes.[23]

When, in his literary works, Tolstoy explores this view formally, he is most often attempting to shed light on aspects of the human world. But there are passages in a number of novels and stories in which he uses narrative devices to engage us in ways that aim to illuminate animal life, and in which he urges us to undertake the sort of moral thought about animals that he is concerned with in "The First Step." This includes works written well before the 1890s when he became an outspoken advocate of vegetarianism. There is a scene in *War and Peace* about a wolf-hunting excursion that, despite focusing largely on the strategies and states of mind of the hunters, brings us a couple of times into the wolf's experience and perspectives, and that in this way might plausibly construed as making an internal contribution to our ability to understand the terrible significance of what's being done to the wolf.[24] There is also a scene in *Anna Karenina* that, after recounting how Vronsky shifts in his saddle during a jump in a steeple chase and how he causes his mare Frou-Frou to fall and break her back, describes the horse's heaving and struggling in an expressive manner that internally informs our ability to fathom the great tragedy of her accident.

For a more involved literary work dealing with animal life, we can turn to "Strider," a story Tolstoy completed in 1886. This story tells the tale of the life of the eponymous Strider, a horse who was abused by his various human owners and suffered a dramatically accelerated physical decline.[25] The story's central human character is an aristocrat named Sepurkhovskoy, the person singly most responsible for Strider's ill-treatment and subsequent deterioration. Sepurkhovskoy is a vain and indolent man who has never tried to get

---

[23] For a more detailed discussion of the formal strategy of "The Death of Ivan Ilych," see Crary, *Beyond Moral Judgment*, 154–157. Although in the book just cited I defend this formal project of Tolstoy's, I should note that it is possible to acknowledge that Tolstoy is, in "The Death of Ivan Ilych," formally concerned with the view that moral understanding is tied to practical attitudes while challenging—on either a priori or a posteriori grounds—the idea that his efforts to shape our attitudes are capable of contributing internally to moral understanding. I discuss relevant issues below in reference to "The First Step."

[24] Leo Tolstoy, *War and Peace*, trans. Richard Pevear and Larissa Volokhonsky (New York: Vintage Classics, 2008), 499–500.

[25] Leo Tolstoy, "Strider: The Story of a Horse," in *Leo Tolstoy: Collected Shorter Fiction, and Other Religious Writings*, trans. Louise Maude, Aylmer Maude, and Nigel J. Cooper (London: Everyman Publishers, 2001), 1:583–626.

on the path to virtue, and who lacks the insight to comprehend the wrong he did to Strider. In sketching Sepurkhovskoy's character, Tolstoy descriptively takes up the idea that practical attitudes are necessary for moral understanding, and "Strider" is written not only to explore this idea descriptively but also to exemplify it formally.

Early on we are given a rich, evocative account of the herd in which the aged Strider now lives, an account that equips us to see glory in wild play and mischievous antics of the herd's healthy young members. A bit later we are told the story of Strider's life, and we are shown that, when in his prime, with the "long and sweeping strides" to which he owes his name, he could outrun any horse in the region, he himself partook of this glory.[26] Later we learn that Sepurkhovskoy, in pursuit of his mistress, ran Strider relentlessly on a day on which the horse had already raced, exposing him to a serious illness from which he never fully recovered. Having at this point already been invited to imagine the greatness of equine physical self-expression, and the extent of what an individual horse stands to lose, we are in a position to understand much better than Sepurkhovskoy does the magnitude of the injury that he does to Strider. That is what it means to say that this story of Tolstoy's exhibits a formal concern with the idea that doing justice to the worldly lives of animals in ethics essentially presupposes the possession of particular attitudes.[27]

In grappling formally with this idea, "Strider" presents us with an example of the very kind of moral thought about animals that Tolstoy discusses and seeks to elicit within the polemical context of "The First Step." Tolstoy's account of the slaughter of a "well-fed red ox" represents but one of his attempts, in "The First Step," to shape our attitudes in ways that contribute internally to a better understanding of what slaughter is like. Tolstoy also describes the chillingly clumsy killing of a pig who briefly escaped a small group of men trying to butcher her, running out slashed and blood-smeared into a small yard;[28] he describes the butchering of a black bull that he witnessed in the same slaughterhouse in which he watched the slaughter both of the red ox

---

[26] The inset quotation is from Tolstoy, "Strider," 596.

[27] For a more detailed discussion of the formal strategy of "Strider," see Crary, *Inside Ethics*, 213–24. Although in the passage to which I just referred I defend this formal project of Tolstoy's, I want here to add a qualification like the one I placed in a note after my earlier remarks on "The Death of Ivan Ilych." A critic might consistently recognize that Tolstoy is, in "Strider," formally preoccupied with the idea that moral understanding is inseparable from practical stance while also rejecting—on either a priori or a posteriori grounds—the idea that his efforts to shape our attitudes can directly inform moral understanding. As I mentioned in an earlier note, I discuss relevant issues below in reference to a passage of "The First Step."

[28] Tolstoy, "The First Step," 39.

and of other oxen;[29] and he describes how, when he ventured into a part of the slaughterhouse dedicated to the butchering of small animals, he beheld the killing of a young ram. This last testimonial depends for its power and interest on his success in evoking, on the one hand, the casualness of the attitudes of the men who kill the ram and, on the other, the terror of their innocent victim.

Tolstoy initially focuses on giving us an impression of the men's casualness, reporting that when he entered the small animal compartment of the slaughterhouse:

> The work was already finished; in the long room, impregnated with the smell of blood, were only two butchers. One was blowing into the leg of a dead lamb and patting the swollen stomach with his hand; the other, a young fellow in an apron besmeared with blood, was smoking a cigarette.[30]

Tolstoy mentions that an ex-soldier entered the compartment after him carrying "a young yearling ram, black with a white mark on its neck, and its legs tied." And Tolstoy gestures at what he depicts as the soldier's offhand manner, noting that the soldier placed the animal on one of the tables "as if upon a bed" and that he then struck up a conversation with the butchers about their work hours.[31] After thus trying to capture the relaxed human atmosphere of the room, Tolstoy turns to the plight of the bound creature. He writes:

> The live ram was lying as quietly as the dead inflated one, except that it was briskly wagging its short little tail and its sides were heaving more quickly than usual.[32]

This tender image of the vulnerability of the frightened creature is followed by a flat-footed description of how one of the butchers, "still continuing the conversation," stepped up to the ram and "grasped with his left hand the head of the ram and cut its throat."[33] Tolstoy tells us that "the ram quivered, and the little tail ceased to waive" while the butcher, waiting for the blood to flow, began to relight his cigarette."[34] Tolstoy is here endeavoring to get us

[29] Tolstoy, "The First Step," 42.
[30] Tolstoy, "The First Step," 43.
[31] Tolstoy, "The First Step."
[32] Tolstoy, "The First Step."
[33] Tolstoy, "The First Step."
[34] Tolstoy, "The First Step."

to register the contrast between, on the one hand, the nonchalance of the butchers and, on the other, the mortal seriousness of what they are doing to a small helpless creature. It is in this manner, by directing our responses in specific, calculated ways, that he hopes to get us to recognize, as the butchers do not, the reality of the injury that they are inflicting on the ram.

A critic might well acknowledge that Tolstoy is here, as elsewhere in "The First Step," trying to shape our attitudes in ways that directly contribute to an undistorted understanding of slaughter while also denying that he is successful. Such a critic could be motivated by the philosophical view that attitudes cannot internally inform an accurate, world-directed take on things, but, as we saw, there is good reason to suspect that this kind of objection can be answered. But a critic might also allow for the possibility that attitudes can internally inform an accurate, world-directed take on things and maintain that the portions of Tolstoy's prose in question here fail to mobilize attitudes in ways that realize this possibility. A critic of this persuasion might charge, for instance, that in inviting us to look tenderly upon a yearling lamb Tolstoy is giving us a portrait of what's happening to the creature that is distorted by sentimentality. To engage this critic we need to be willing to step back from the tender vantage point that Tolstoy's words cultivate and ask whether it has a tendency to block our view of what's going on, or whether instead the person who fails to see the aspects of the ram's predicament that it makes accessible, such as his innocence and vulnerability, would be missing something. We might reasonably proceed by bringing out how analogous perceptions of innocence and vulnerability inform our understanding of human children and companion animals and how it's not clear that we can make sense of our relationships with human beings and animals without the illumination that these perceptions furnish.

Tolstoy's larger goal in "The First Step" is to convince readers of the wrongness of killing and eating animals. His efforts remain relevant today. Since the 1890s there has been a revolution in how animals are raised and killed for food in many parts of the world. Within the United States, Europe and, to an increasing extent, also other parts of the world, animals destined for slaughter are overwhelmingly "processed" with industrial methods. They are brought up in confined feeding operations (CAFOs), genetically engineered for the size and growth rates of their edible tissues, and slaughtered on assembly lines. The plain facts of what gets done to animals in "factory farms" have been featured in enough newspapers, documentary films, books, and blogs that any person who takes an interest ought to be familiar with them.

But there is a respect in which it can be difficult for even sincerely thoughtful people to recognize the sheer awfulness of what is going on. This has to do partly with the fact that access to CAFOs and industrial slaughterhouses is tightly controlled. In a number of states within the United States, there are now antiwhistleblower laws that make it a criminal offense to obtain access to industrial farms under false pretenses or to videotape or photograph what goes on in them without the owner's permission.[35] These obstacles to documenting the treatment of animals in industrial food production make it difficult for members of the public to arrive at an understanding of industrial slaughter, of the sort requisite in ethics, that goes beyond plain facts. Not that simply exposing atrocities committed in slaughterhouses will lead to meaningful social change. Campaigns for greater visibility may depend for their political power on reactions of horror and disgust that are functions of things having previously been hidden from view—and so may be sustained by the very strategies of disguise they aim to combat.[36] This does not mean that we don't still require the efforts of activists who are willing, often at great risk to themselves, to report on what is happening in slaughterhouses.[37] But it suggests that we also require the interventions of literary authors and other artists who are capable of presenting what we know in engaging ways that directly contribute to an understanding of the forms of cruelty and callousness, the horrors, that are in question.[38] Contemporary literary authors and artists

[35] Mark Bittman coined the term "ag-gag" for this class of laws (see "Who Protects the Animals?," *New York Times*, April 26, 2011). To appreciate the politically chilling effect of ag-gag legislation it's necessary to bear in mind that activists have repeatedly used undercover videotapes to expose shocking and sometimes illegal abuses in CAFOs and industrial slaughterhouses and that in many cases new bills have been introduced in response to the backlash inspired by such revelations, as efforts to keep further abuses from coming to light. For a comprehensive discussion of the political issues, see Will Potter, *Green Is the New Red: An Insider's Account of a Social Movement under Siege* (San Francisco: City Light Books, 2011).

[36] See Timothy Pachirat, *Every Twelve Seconds: Industrialized Slaughter and the Politics of Sight* (New Haven, CT: Yale University Press, 2009), 252.

[37] Activists associated with People for the Ethical Treatment of Animals have done much of the undercover work to which we owe our filmic record of abuses in industrial farms. For a range of nonfilmic testimonials, we are indebted to activists affiliated, e.g., with different farm sanctuary movements (see, e.g., Gene Bauer, *Farm Sanctuary: Changing Hearts and Minds about Animals and Food* [New York: Simon & Schuster, 2008]) as well as to many unaffiliated activists (see, e.g., Pachirat, *Every Twelve Seconds*).

[38] Any reasonable list of notable contemporary literary authors who thus take us beyond the "plain facts" of industrial slaughter would need to include J. M. Coetzee (see esp. *The Lives of Animals* [Princeton, NJ: Princeton University Press, 1999]) and Jonathan Safran Foer (see *Eating Animals* [New York: Little, Brown, 2009]). The set of other artists who likewise take us beyond the "plain facts" of slaughter includes, e.g., the painter Sue Coe (see *Dead Meat* [New York: Four Walls Eight Windows, 1995]) and the photographer Isa Leshko (see *Isa Leshko Photography*, isaleshko.com [accessed September 16, 2017]).

whose productions fit this description are doing for our time the kind of decisive moral work that Tolstoy did for his.

There is a yet more straightforward sense in which Tolstoy's writings on animals remain pertinent. There are increasingly urgent criticisms of factory farms not only because of their utterly indifferent treatment of animals but because they are major sources of greenhouse gases and other environmental hazards, because they pose serious public health risks, and because they have been the sites of systematic human rights abuses.[39] One expression of this critical trend is a movement among affluent and educated people toward joining "meat collectives" or small private clubs in which groups of individuals learn to butcher animals on a small scale in local shops.[40] Within the relatively quiet settings of these shops (and other abattoirs that likewise resemble their preindustrial ancestors), it may be easier to overlook the momentousness of what is being done to the animals whose death and dismemberment is the primary business at hand. Tolstoy's work is immediately to the point here. In his accounts of the slaughter-practices of his time, he imparts a lesson that is pertinent to this "new carnivore movement" and, indeed, also to familiar efforts to promote smaller farms that eschew standard industrial abattoirs and rely instead on "mobile slaughter units." However casual the human context of slaughter, it is still the case that a living creature is being snuffed out, deprived of every possible good.

It would be misleading to suggest that Tolstoy's reflections on animals are relevant only to the question of killing animals and eating them for food. His reflections have a value that extends beyond their bearing on this issue. Unlike most contemporary work on animals and ethics, they call for and illustrate the use of expressive techniques to internally inform the kind of worldly understanding of animals that we are after in ethics. Tolstoy invites his readers to pursue lines of thought about animals that presuppose the possession of particular modes of emotional responsiveness. Thinking of this emotionally demanding sort is of decisive importance for getting an undistorted view of what is done to animals not only in CAFOs, industrial abattoirs, and other slaughterhouses but also in, among other places, laboratories, zoos, and areas of land and in the seas in which animals are hunted. There is also good reason to think that we need to foreground such perspectival thought if we are to build bridges between animal ethics and critical theories that are concerned

---

[39] Each of these additional topics deserves a kind of serious attention that I cannot give here.

[40] See, e.g., Kurt Soller, "Head to Hoof: Inside the New Carnivore Movement," *Newsweek*, January 27, 2009.

with larger social mechanisms, within advanced capitalist societies, that reliably reproduce not only horrific treatment of animals but also the oppression of vulnerable groups of human beings. It is characteristic of these critical theories, including various different strands of ecological Marxism and ecofeminism, to insist that only engaged thought can supply the kind of understanding of unjust social structures they seek to impart. If we recognize that doing justice to the worldly lives of animals in a manner that can inform meaningful political action as well as just ethical responses requires an openness to the practical exercise of revisiting and reworking our modes of appreciation, we are still—today—Tolstoy's heirs.

Acknowledgment

A version of this chapter's reflections on Tolstoy and animals was published as part of the essay "Seeing Animal Suffering," in, *Cora Diamond on Ethics*, ed. Maria Balaska (London: Palgrave Macmillan, 2021). I am grateful for Springer Nature for allowing the reuse of this material.

Bibliography

Bauer, Gene. *Farm Sanctuary: Changing Hearts and Minds about Animals and Food*. New York: Simon & Schuster, 2008.
Bittman, Mark. "Who Protects the Animals?" *New York Times*, April 26, 2011.
Carruthers, Peter. *The Animals Issue: Moral Theory in Practice*. Cambridge: Cambridge University Press, 1992.
Coe, Sue. *Dead Meat*. New York: Four Walls Eight Windows, 1995.
Coetzee, J. M. *The Lives of Animals*. Princeton, NJ: Princeton University Press, 1999.
Crary, Alice. *Beyond Moral Judgment*. Cambridge, MA: Harvard University Press, 2007.
Crary, Alice. *Inside Ethics: On the Demands of Moral Thought*. Cambridge, MA: Harvard University Press, 2015.
Crary, Alice. "Objectivity." In *Wittgenstein: Basic Concepts*, edited by James Conant and Sebastian Sunday Greves. Cambridge: Cambridge University Press, 2019.
Crary, Alice. "Objectivity's Politics." Forthcoming.
Crary, Alice. "Seeing Animal Suffering." In *Cora Diamond on Ethics*, edited by Maria Balaska. London: Palgrave Macmillan, 2021.
Diamond, Cora. "Eating Meat and Eating People [1975–76]." In *The Realistic Spirit: Wittgenstein, Philosophy and the Mind*, 319–34. Cambridge, MA: MIT Press, 1991.
Foer, Jonathan Safran. *Eating Animals*. New York: Little, Brown, 2009.
Kagan, Shelly. *How to Count Animals: More or Less*. Oxford: Oxford University Press, 2019.

Korsgaard, Christine. "Fellow Creatures: Kantian Ethics and Our Duties to Animals." Vol. 24 of *Tanner Lectures on Human Values*, 77–110. Salt Lake City: University of Utah Press, 2004. https://dash.harvard.edu/bitstream/handle/1/3198692/korsgaard_Fell owCreatures.pdf?sequence=2.

Korsgaard, Christine. *Self-Constitution: Agency, Identity, and Integrity*. Oxford: Oxford University Press, 2009.

Korsgaard, Christine. *The Sources of Normativity*. Cambridge: Cambridge University Press, 1996.

Leahy, Michael. *Against Liberation: Putting Animals in Perspective*. Rev. ed. London: Routledge, 1994.

Leshko, Isa. Isa Leshko Photography. isaleshko.com. Accessed September 16, 2017.

McDowell, John. *Mind and World*. Cambridge, MA: Harvard University Press, 1996.

Nagel, Thomas. "Subjective and Objective." In *Mortal Questions*, 196–213. Cambridge: Cambridge University Press, 1979.

Pachirat, Timothy. *Every Twelve Seconds: Industrialized Slaughter and the Politics of Sight*. New Haven: Yale University Press, 2009.

Potter, Will. *Green is the New Red: An Insider's Account of a Social Movement under Siege*. San Francisco: City Light Books, 2011.

Singer, Peter. Foreword to *The Death of the Animal: A Dialogue*, edited by Paolo Cavalieri, ix–xii. New York: Columbia University Press, 2009.

Singer, Peter. *How Are We to Live? Ethics in an Age of Self-Interest*. Amherst, NY: Prometheus Books, 1995.

Singer, Peter. "Reasoning toward Utilitarianism." In *Hare and His Critics: Essays on Moral Thinking*, edited by Douglas Seanor and N. Fotion, 147–60. Oxford: Clarendon Press, 1988.

Singer, Peter. "Reply to Michael Huemer." In *Peter Singer under Fire: The Moral Iconoclast Faces His Critics*, edited by Jeffrey A. Schaler, 380–94. Chicago: Open Court, 2009.

Singer, Peter, and Anton Leist. "Introduction: Coetzee and Philosophy." In *Coetzee and Ethics*, edited by Anton Leist and Peter Singer, 1–18. New York: Columbia University Press, 2010.

Soller, Kurt. "Head to Hoof: Inside the New Carnivore Movement." *Newsweek.com*. Last modified January 27, 2009. http://www.newsweek.com/head-hoof-inside-new-carniv ore-movement-77899.

Tolstoy, Leo. *A Confession and Other Religious Writings*. Translated by Jane Kentish. London: Penguin, 1987.

Tolstoy, Leo. "The First Step." Introduction to *The Ethics of Diet: An Anthology of Vegetarian Thought*, by Howard Williams, 11–46. Guildford: White Crow Books, 2009.

Tolstoy, Leo. *The Gospel in Brief*. Translated by Isabel Hapgood. Lincoln: University of Nebraska Press, 1997.

Tolstoy, Leo. "Strider: The Story of a Horse." In *Leo Tolstoy: Collected Shorter Fiction*, translated by Louise Maude, Aylmer Maude, and Nigel J. Cooper, 1:583–626. London: Everyman Publishers, 2001.

Tolstoy, Leo. *War and Peace*. Translated by Richard Pevear and Larissa Volokhonsky. New York: Vintage Classics, 2008.

Williams, Bernard. *Descartes: The Project of Pure Enquiry*. New York: Penguin, 1978.

Williams, Bernard. *Ethics and the Limits of Philosophy*. Cambridge, MA: Harvard University Press, 1985.

12

Elizabeth Stuart Phelps (1844–1911)

Writer and Reformer

Robyn Hederman

In 1901, the writer and activist Elizabeth Stuart Phelps spoke before the Massachusetts Committee on Probate and Chancery in support of a bill regulating vivisection. In 1902 and 1903, she again addressed the Massachusetts State Legislature on animal experimentation, describing vivisection as "the infliction of avoidable torture by the powerful upon the weak, by human intellect and the human hand upon the helpless body and the dumb soul."[1]

Phelps's extensive writings (approximately fifty-six books) tackled religion, heaven, antivivisection, temperance, women's rights, marriage, class, and labor reform. In her autobiography *Chapters from a Life* (1896), Phelps asserted that "moral character is to human life what air is to the natural world;—it is elemental."[2] She claimed that "the province of the artist is to portray life as it is; and life *is* moral responsibility," where "an artist can no more fling off the moral sense from his work than he can oust it from his private life."[3]

In her later years, Phelps focused on the plight of lab animals. Although Phelps's antivivisection writings touched on the social issues of feminism, marriage, and poverty, she was devoted to the antivivisection cause, and her spiritual and religious beliefs greatly influenced her work. In *Elizabeth Stuart Phelps*, Mary Angela Bennett claims that "religion, which played a large part in her devotion to anti-vivisection, was never far from Ms. Phelps's thoughts."[4] Bennett states that although Phelps found the topic repulsive,

---

[1] Quoted in Carol Farley Kessler, *Elizabeth Stuart Phelps* (Boston: Twayne, 1982), 111–12; Kessler cites "Address," March 16, 1903, 8.
[2] Elizabeth Stuart Phelps, *Chapters from a Life* (Boston: Houghton, Mifflin, 1897), 261.
[3] Phelps, *Chapters from a Life*, 263.
[4] Mary Angela Bennett, *Elizabeth Stuart Phelps* (Philadelphia: University of Pennsylvania Press, 1939), 115.

Robyn Hederman, *Elizabeth Stuart Phelps (1844–1911)* In: *Animal Theologians*. Edited by: Andrew Linzey and Clair Linzey, Oxford University Press. © Oxford University Press 2023. DOI: 10.1093/oso/9780197655542.003.0013

once "her convictions deepened she threw herself unreservedly into the cause."[5] According to Bennett, Phelps's belief that the practice of vivisection deadened the "humane instincts of the race" became the basis for the novel *Trixy*.[6]

Religious Writings

Elizabeth Stuart Phelps, born Mary Gray, was raised in a strict, religious household in Andover, Massachusetts. Her father, Austin Phelps, graduated from Andover Theological Seminary, a stronghold of orthodox Calvinism. He became a minister, following in the steps of Mary's maternal and paternal grandfathers. In 1848, Austin Phelps became the chair of rhetoric at Andover Seminary.[7] He kept this chair until his retirement and wrote several influential books. Mary Gray's mother, Elizabeth Stuart Phelps, authored several books, as well as a series of Sunday school stories. Her last book, *Sunnyside* (1851), sold one hundred thousand copies in its first year.[8] Mary was eight years old when her mother died. From that time, she took her mother's name as her own. Phelps wrote that her mother "lived before women had careers and public sympathy in them. Her nature was drawn against the grain of her times and of her circumstances; and where our feet find easy walking, hers were hedged."[9]

In *The Gates Ajar* (1868), Phelps questioned the orthodox vision of the celestial kingdom. She asserted that Jesus Christ would not have "pictured [people's] blessed endless years with him in such bleak colors. They are not the hues of his Bible."[10] Instead, Phelps depicted heaven as a place where one can attend concerts and play the piano. In "Defenders of the Faith," historian Barbara Welter points out that Phelps presented many of her beliefs in fictional form.[11] Welter asserts that "her personal creed softened to a general religion she called 'Christlove.'"[12]

---

[5] Bennett, *Elizabeth Stuart Phelps*, 114.
[6] Bennett, *Elizabeth Stuart Phelps*, 114.
[7] Kessler, *Elizabeth Stuart Phelps*, 11.
[8] Kessler, *Elizabeth Stuart Phelps*, 14.
[9] Phelps, *Chapters from a Life*, 12–13.
[10] Elizabeth Stuart Phelps, *The Gates Ajar* (Cambridge, MA: Belknap Press of Harvard University Press, 1964; first published 1868), 99.
[11] Barbara Welter, "The Defenders of the Faith: Women Novelists of Religious Controversy in the Nineteenth Century," in *Dimity Convictions: The American Woman in the Nineteenth Century* (Athens: Ohio University Press, 1976), 112–13.
[12] Welter, "Defenders of the Faith," 112.

In *Chapters from a Life*, Phelps claimed that *The Gates Ajar* came naturally to her: "The angel said unto me 'Write!' and I wrote."[13] The novel was published in the aftermath of the US Civil War when the country was "dark with sorrowing women."[14] Phelps spoke to "the helpless, outnumbering, unconsulted women; they whom war had trampled down, without a choice or protest . . . [those who] loved much, and, loving, had lost all."[15]

In *The Gates Ajar*, the central character, Mary Cabot grieves the loss of her brother killed in the war. Mary finds no solace from her deacon, who instructs her that she must submit to "afflictions from God."[16] Mary is comforted by the arrival of her aunt, Winifred Forsythe. Winifred informs Mary that she will see her brother again when he leads her "into the light and warmth" of her new home.[17] In her study of Phelps, Ronna Coffey Privett claims that Winifred's view of the celestial kingdom is "more corporal than the traditional reading of heaven."[18] Trees, gardens, cottages, and pianos inhabit Winifred's heaven. It is "a place where individuals can be their own best selves, where a woman can stand up to a man on an intellectual and spiritual level."[19]

The Gates Ajar received mixed reviews. Religious newspapers denounced Phelps's "notions of the life to come, as if she had been an evil spirit let loose upon accepted theology for the destruction of the world."[20] Although religious critics denounced *The Gates Ajar*, contemporary women, stirred by the tale, sent letters to Phelps seeking comfort and hope. By 1897, circulation of the book had reached eighty-one thousand in the United States.[21] Phelps returned to the subject of the afterlife in *Beyond the Gates* (1883), *The Gates Between* (1887), and *Within the Gates* (1901). James D. Hart claims that these novels helped to establish Phelps as "America's foremost authority on the home life of heaven."[22]

---

[13] Phelps, *Chapters from a Life*, 95.
[14] Phelps, *Chapters from a Life*, 96.
[15] Phelps, *Chapters from a Life*, 98.
[16] Phelps, *The Gates Ajar*, 14.
[17] Phelps, *The Gates Ajar*, 38.
[18] Ronna Coffey Privett, *A Comprehensive Study of American Writer Elizabeth Phelps, 1841–1911: Art for Truth's Sake* (Lewiston, NY: Edwin Mellen Press, 2003), 34.
[19] Privett, *A Comprehensive Study*, 42.
[20] Phelps, *Chapters from a Life*, 118. For a contemporary review of *The Gates Ajar*, see "A. Dean, *"The Gates Ajar": Critically Examined* (London: Hatchards, Piccadilly, 1871), accessed January 31, 2019, https://archive.org/details/gatesajarbyesph01phelgoog/page/n6.
[21] Kessler, *Elizabeth Stuart Phelps*, 30.
[22] James D. Hart, *The Popular Book: A History of America's Literary Taste* (Westport, CT: Greenwood Press, 1976), 121.

In her review of *A Singular Life* (1895), Privett contends that this novel represents "the natural progression" of Phelps's beliefs since the release of *The Gates Ajar*.[23] The main character, Emanuel Bayard, is Phelps's "dearest hero."[24] Minister Bayard, a Christlike figure, rebels against the teachings of his orthodox church and favors the Social Gospel movement of the late nineteenth century. Bayard received seminary training on predestination and election, yet he ponders why he never received a lesson on the "Christian socialism of our day."[25]

Phelps's other religious works include *The Story of Jesus Christ* (1897) and *The Struggle for Immortality* (1889). *The Struggle for Immortality* is a collection of essays examining a variety of religious issues. Phelps defined *The Story of Jesus Christ* as a narrative.[26] According to Mary Bennett, the story emphasizes "the humanity of Jesus."[27] In 1898, Phelps connected her completion of *The Story of Jesus Christ* to the beginning of her antivivisection work:

> A year ago a few students of the biography of Jesus Christ, coming to the end of their happy and ennobling work, wished to signalize its completion by some act that would embody the spirit of the Great Life in which they had absorbed. It was determined to select the unnecessary torment of animals in the name of science as a department of mercy in which a group of Christian people might find one of the "duties nearest"; and it was hoped by April last to organize an attack on the barbarities of vivisection which would be felt in every laboratory in the land.[28]

Antivivisection Work

In her later novels and short stories, Phelps focused on antivivisection and animal cruelty. At a 1902 address before a committee of the Massachusetts legislature, Phelps indicated that her interest in vivisection dated back to 1896.[29] She investigated the medical profession's use of animals and wrote

---

[23] Privett, *A Comprehensive Study*, 50.
[24] Phelps, *Chapters from a Life*, 273.
[25] Elizabeth Stuart Phelps, *A Singular Life* (Boston: Houghton, Mifflin, 1898), 153.
[26] Elizabeth Stuart Phelps, *The Story of Jesus Christ: An Interpretation* (Boston: Houghton, Mifflin, 1897), note.
[27] Bennett, *Elizabeth Stuart Phelps*, 116.
[28] Bennett, *Elizabeth Stuart Phelps*, 113–14, citing "Russia as a Missionary," *Independent*, December 8, 1898.
[29] Bennett, *Elizabeth Stuart Phelps*, 114.

articles, pamphlets, and novels revealing the cruelties of vivisection. Phelps's antivivisection pamphlets included *A Plea for the Helpless* (1901), *Vivisection Denounced* (1902), and *Vivisection and Legislation in Massachusetts* (1902).[30]

Phelps further addressed animal cruelty in her children's books. In the story "The Great Woodchuck Society," published in 1872, Phelps instructed boys that killing woodchucks was not as fun as going to picnics and other events.[31] Phelps also contemplated animal immortality. In *The Gates Ajar*, Aunt Winifred recounts the story of a boy who is mourning the death of his guinea pig. The boy asks his mother whether animals have souls, and he is despondent when she tells him no. The boy cries, "Don't little CLEAN— *white—guinea-pigs* have souls?" Winifred tells Mary, "I never should have had the heart to say no to that; especially as we have no positive proof to the contrary."[32] In Phelps's novel *Beyond the Gates* (1883), animals exist in the celestial community. A "fine dog" is sunning himself on the steps of a "small and quiet house" and cordially meets the central character as she approaches.[33] Horses walk along the streets, and birds sing, "*Te Deum laudamus—laudamus.*"[34]

Despite Phelps's early interest in preventing animal cruelty, some of her biographers have minimized Phelps's zeal to eliminate animal experimentation. In *Elizabeth Stuart Phelps*, Carol Farley Kessler describes Phelps's "antivivisection concern" as an "indirect expression of her feminist interests" where the "link to feminism was symbolic."[35] Kessler points out that in the novel *Though Life Us Do Part* (1908), Phelps linked the fate of women in marriage with the vivisection of animals. Phelps described the world as being "full of women" who "endure the lives that men inflict."[36] Phelps wrote, "A man may vivisect a woman nerve by nerve, anguish by anguish, as truly as if he put the scalpel to the tissue. And nobody knows it. She never cries out."[37]

---

[30] Lori Duin Kelly, *The Life and Works of Elizabeth Stuart Phelps, Victorian Feminist Writer* (Troy, NY: Whitston, 1983), 19.

[31] Bennett, *Elizabeth Stuart Phelps*, 40, citing *Our Young Folks*, June 1872, reprinted in *Trotty's Wedding Tour*.

[32] Phelps, *The Gates Ajar*, 124.

[33] Elizabeth Stuart Phelps, *Beyond the Gates* (Floyd, VA: Black Curtain Press, 2014; first published 1883), 70.

[34] Phelps, *Beyond the Gates*, 29.

[35] Kessler, *Elizabeth Stuart Phelps*, 111.

[36] Elizabeth Stuart Phelps, *Though Life Us Do Part* (Boston: Houghton Mifflin, 1908), 165. In 1888, Phelps married Herbert Dickinson Ward. Herbert was a journalist and was seventeen years younger than Phelps. Ward supported her antivivisection work; she dedicated *Trixy* to her husband and called him a "collaborator."

[37] Phelps, *Though Life Us Do Part*, 56.

Similarly, in her extensive study of Phelps's literary work, Ronna Coffey Privett asserts the "mute cries" of the "intelligent, loving dogs" in the novel *Trixy* (1904), often resemble "voiceless" women "who depend upon their 'masters' to save them from their inhumane situations."[38]

Phelps's antivivisection writings do draw parallels between animal experimentation, women's legal status, and nineteenth-century marriage. But, as Alyssa Chen Walker notes in her article, Phelps's antivivisection work was more than "metaphorical or analogic," because Phelps's commitment to the cause was "ardent, enduring, and multifaceted."[39] Instead, Phelps and her contemporaries saw a direct connection between animal experimentation and the medical treatment of women.[40] Phelps believed that vivisection defiled physicians who either witnessed or practiced such procedures. In her article "Elizabeth Stuart Phelps, *Trixy*, and the Vivisection Question," Lori Duin Kelly claims that Phelps proposed that continued exposure to vivisection desensitized physicians, and "contributed to making them bad doctors."[41] According to Kelly, although the novel *Trixy* (1904) is a "standard polemic against vivisection," it further ponders a woman's fear of receiving medical treatment "from a cold and indifferent laboratory trained clinician."[42]

This sentiment was shared by Dr. Elizabeth Blackwell, a contemporary of Phelps, and the first woman to receive a medical degree from an American medical school. Blackwell described animal experimentation as both

---

[38] Privett, *A Comprehensive Study*, 246.

[39] Alyssa Chen Walker, "Bringing the Laboratory Dog Home: Elizabeth Stuart Phelps and the Antivivisection Narrative," *Humanimalia: A Journal of Human/Animal Interface Studies* 4, no. 2 (Spring 2013): 101–126, 106.

[40] See, Craig Beuttinger, "Women and Antivivisection in Late Nineteenth-Century America," *Journal of Social History* 30, no. 4 (1997): 857–70; Susan Hamilton, "Gender and the Literature of the Victorian Vivisection Controversy," *Victorian Review* 17, no. 2 (Winter 1991): 21–34; Hilda Kean, "The 'Smooth Cool Men of Science': The Feminist and Socialist Response to Vivisection," *History Workshop Journal* 40 (1995): 16–38; Mart Ann Elston, "Women and Anti-vivisection in Victorian England," 1870–1900," in *Vivisection in Historical Perspective*, ed. Nicolaas A. Rupke (London: Croom Helm, 1987), 259–94. See also Coral Lansbury, *The Old Brown Dog: Women, Workers, and Vivisection in Edwardian England* (Madison: University of Wisconsin Press, 1985).

[41] Lori Duin Kelly, "Elizabeth Stuart Phelps, *Trixy*, and the Vivisection Question," *Legacy* 27, no. 1 (2010): 62.

[42] Kelly, "Elizabeth Stuart Phelps, *Trixy*, and the Vivisection Question," 62; see also Ann Douglas Wood, "'The Fashionable Diseases': Women's Complainants and Their Treatment in Nineteenth-Century America," in *Women and Health in America: Historical Readings*, ed. Judith Walzer Leavitt (Madison: University of Wisconsin Press, 1984), 222–38; Coral Lansbury, "Gynaecology, Pornography, and the Antivivisection Movement," *Victorian Studies* 28, no. 3 (1985): 413–37. For a full discussion of the medical profession's attitude toward women in the nineteenth century, see Cynthia E. Russett, *Sexual Science: The Victorian Construction of Womanhood* (Cambridge, MA: Harvard University Press, 1989).

"ethically unjustifiable and intellectually fallacious."[43] In her 1891 address to the Alumni Association of the Women's Medical College of the New York Infirmary, Blackwell challenged the view that vivisection was necessary to educate medical students. She cautioned that it was an "exercise of curiosity," which inevitably tended to "blunt the moral sense" of the physician.[44] Blackwell warned that "audacious human surgery," including an increase in "ovariotomy, and its extension to the insane," resulted from "unrestrained experiment on the lower animals."[45]

Phelps continued to proclaim that vivisection chilled the nobler instincts of those who participated in the practice. She approached her activism from a "religious standpoint."[46] According to Bennet, Phelps's conviction resulted from her love of animals and from "her feeling of revulsion of the thought that any good might come out of experimentation with animals."[47]

Novels and Short Stories

Phelps's short story "Loveliness: A Story," about the theft of a pet by vivisectors, appeared in the *Atlantic Monthly* in 1889. Loveliness, a silver Yorkshire, is stolen from a sickly child, Adah. Adah is "transparent of coloring" and bears "in her delicate face the pathetic patience which only sick children, of all human creatures, ever show."[48] Adah "weakened visibly" when she learns that Loveliness is missing.[49] She "scarcely walked at all" and "wasted to a little wraith."[50]

Adah's father, a professor, searches the city's dog-trafficking industry after he uncovers "the authenticated records of the torments imposed upon dumb animals in the name of science."[51] The professor detects that Loveliness is being held at the University of St. George—his very own college.[52] The

[43] Elizabeth Blackwell, "Scientific Method in Biology," in *Essays in Medical Sociology*, vol. 2 (London: Elliot Stack, 62 Paternoster Row, E.C., 1898), 2:136, accessed February 8, 2019, https://archive.org/details/39002006316807.med.yale.edu.

[44] Elizabeth Blackwell, "Erroneous Method in Medical Education," in *Essays in Medical Sociology*, vol. 2 (London: Ernest Bell, 1902), 2:43, accessed February 17, 2019, https://archive.org/details/39002006316807.med.yale.edu.

[45] Blackwell, "Scientific Method in Biology," 119, 120.

[46] Bennett, *Elizabeth Stuart Phelps*, 114.

[47] Bennett, *Elizabeth Stuart Phelps*, 114.

[48] Elizabeth Stuart Phelps, *Loveliness: A Story* (Boston: Houghton, Mifflin, 1899), 5, Kindle.

[49] Phelps, *Loveliness*, 15.

[50] Phelps, *Loveliness*, 15.

[51] Phelps, *Loveliness*, 17.

[52] Phelps, *Loveliness*, 20.

professor finds the Yorkshire "stretched, bound, gagged, gasping, doomed to a doom which the readers of this page would forbid this pen to describe."[53] As the operator is set to make the first incision, without the benefit of anesthesia and amid the laughter of the students, the dog kisses "his vivisector's hand."[54] The professor rescues the Yorkshire and brings the dog home. Loveliness and Adah are reunited, and "peals of laughter and ecstatic barks" echo through the "happy house."[55]

In her novel *Trixy* (1904), Phelps again focused on the abduction of a beloved pet— Trixy—this time from Dan Badger, a crippled boy cared for by the philanthropist, Miriam Lauriet. Miriam's dog, Caro, has also been missing for the past two years. Lauriet has two romantic suitors— the lawyer Phillip Surbridge and Olin Steele, a professor of physiology at Galen Medical School. Surbridge later learns that both Caro and Trixy had been stolen and sold to the Galen Medical School for experimentation.

Early in his career, the physiologist Steele is repulsed by vivisection. "A sick faintness surged upon him," and "every fibre of his body and soul protested" because "the medical student had a soul and it was young and sensitive."[56] But as Steele adapts to experimenting on sentient beings, he ponders "what dark election" he has made of his soul after ten years of carving "the living animal in the interests of physiology."[57]

For the past year, Steele has been conducting experiments on the brain of his "most valuable subject," a black cocker spaniel.[58] His research subject is Caro. The missing dog's once "large hazel eyes" are now "mysteriously dulled."[59] During the last two years, "misery was his life, and torment his pastime."[60]

Trixy escapes her cage at Galen Medical School and finds Caro, whose head is "bound with a bandage of cloth."[61] Trixy coaxes Caro to escape with her through an opened door—allowing the injured dog to leave first. Caro escapes and makes it home to Lauriet, but Trixy is recaptured. "Hers was the saving mission, and it had, as all salvation, whether higher or lower beings,

---

[53] Phelps, *Loveliness*, 25.
[54] Phelps, *Loveliness*, 25.
[55] Phelps, *Loveliness*, 28.
[56] Elizabeth Stuart Phelps, *Trixy* (Boston: Houghton, Mifflin, 1904), 11, accessed February 4, 2019, https://archive.org/details/trixywardphelps00phelrich.
[57] Phelps, *Trixy*, 54.
[58] Phelps, *Trixy*, 197.
[59] Phelps, *Trixy*, 99.
[60] Phelps, *Trixy*, 167.
[61] Phelps, *Trixy*, 165.

must have, its element of potential sacrifice."[62] Steele's colleague, the vivisector Charles Bernard, attempts to fasten Trixy to a dog-board, while Trixy struggles and cries like a "human baby."[63] Nevertheless, Bernard completes the task "without any sign of emotion."[64] Before Bernard begins the vivisection, Surbridge barges into the lab and rescues Trixy.

Steele continues to search for "his lost material."[65] When he visits Lauriet, he observes Caro's "marred head" and recognizes "his own work."[66] Steele blurts out, "Why that's my dog! Where did you get it? I've been all the morning hunting for it."[67] Lauriet responds, "The dog is mine. This is Caro. I lost him two years ago."[68]

Surbridge reveals to Lauriet that Caro and Trixy had been imprisoned at Galen Medical School. He tells Lauriet that Caro was "a special case," who had been reserved by Steele "for a series of experiments upon the brain."[69] Surbridge gives her Caro's silver collar, which he found at Galen.

Lauriet confronts Steele, and he accuses her of taking a "very feminine view of the circumstances."[70] Steele cries, "You set the animal above the human race" and asks, "What is one dog—what are ten thousand dogs compared with the life of one baby?" Lauriet rebukes Steele. "You have tormented many dogs. . . . Have you ever saved the life of one baby?"[71]

Charles Bernard is charged with receiving stolen property. He is adjudged guilty, and the judge imposes "the heaviest fine" allowed by law.[72] Steele becomes infected by an inoculation he administered to a guinea pig. Barry, Steele's faithful Saint Bernard, is his sole comforter as Steele's past vivisection subjects haunt his sickbed.

Steele is subjected to the medical care of the coldhearted vivisector Charles Bernard. After examining Steele, Bernard remarks, "It's a beautiful case, isn't it?"[73] Bernard leaves the sickroom to visit a hospital where a "curious

[62] Phelps, Trixy, 174.

[63] Phelps, Trixy, 184.

[64] Phelps, Trixy, 184. According to Lorin Duin Kelly in "Elizabeth Stuart Phelps, Trixy, and the Vivisection Question," Charles Bernard is modeled after the French vivisector Claude Bernard. See also Claude Bernard, An Introduction to the Study of Experimental Medicine, trans. Henry Copley Greene (New York: Dover, 1957).

[65] Phelps, Trixy, 191.

[66] Phelps, Trixy, 193.

[67] Phelps, Trixy, 193.

[68] Phelps, Trixy, 193.

[69] Phelps, Trixy, 197.

[70] Phelps, Trixy, 218.

[71] Phelps, Trixy, 218–19.

[72] Phelps, Trixy, 257.

[73] Phelps, Trixy, 266.

operation" is taking place "upon the brain of an underwitted house-maid."[74] He resolves that "no experiment is absolutely satisfactory unless it has been tried on a human being."[75]

Lauriet writes a letter to Steele declaring she cannot marry him, and she cannot see "how any true woman can take a vivisector's hand."[76] She asserts that cruelty may be "the unpardonable sin; it is a sin against the Spirit of Mercy."[77] "Shrieks out of his laboratory" torment Steele.[78] Steele's soul confronts him. It "arose and looked upon him" with "unappeasable regret."[79] Steele ponders these "curious old words": "What shall it profit if a man gain professional glory . . . and lose his own soul—for how long?"[80]

Phelps avoided explicit descriptions of vivisection, describing *Trixy* as a "story" and not a "polemic."[81] Although *Trixy* "verges towards one of the great tragedies of the day," being an "artist" and not an "apostle," Phelps closed the pages to "scenes too painful for admission."[82] Phelps claimed that although a novel "cannot be a homily," it "may be an illumination."[83]

Phelps claimed that *Trixy* "approaches regions whose very existence is unknown to the majority of readers" and "doubted by many intelligent and kind-hearted people."[84] Phelps informed her readers, "I am familiar with the map of those dark sections of life and know whereof I write."[85] Phelps described the basement of Galen Research Facility as "that inferno" where "the circles of misery gave out the inarticulate expression of a doom worse because neither understood, elected, nor deserved."[86] It is a "den of anguish" where "most of the victims endured with the silence and patience by which the suffering animal shames the human race."[87]

---

[74] Phelps, *Trixy*, 271.
[75] Phelps, *Trixy*, 271.
[76] Phelps, *Trixy*, 274.
[77] Phelps, *Trixy*, 274.
[78] Phelps, *Trixy*, 277.
[79] Phelps, *Trixy*, 275–76.
[80] Phelps, *Trixy*, 276.
[81] Phelps, *Trixy*, note, vii.
[82] Phelps, *Trixy*.
[83] Phelps, *Trixy*, note, vii.
[84] Phelps, *Trixy*, note, vii–viii.
[85] Phelps, *Trixy*, note, viii.
[86] Phelps, *Trixy*, 160.
[87] Phelps, *Trixy*, 160. See Andreas-Holger Maehle and Ulrich Trohler, "Animal Experimentation from Antiquity to the End of the Eighteenth Century: Attitudes and Arguments," in *Vivisection in Historical Perspective*, ed. Nicolaas A. Rupke (London: Croom Helm, 1987), 15–16. This article claims that Galen Research Facility is most likely named after Galen of Pergamon from the second century AD. Galen, the physician to Emperor Marcus Aurelius, stressed the value of vivisection in his treatise *De Anatomicis Administrationibus*.

Those four walls, packed with suffering, kept their secrets well. Into this tragic place no curious reporter was admitted; from it the omnipotence of the press was excluded; into this pit no sister of mercy stepped; to these wounded no hospital nurse brought the ministrations of her gentle art; into this lair no preacher entered, and, leaving it, challenged Christian civilization with its existence; into this hell no Christ descended.[88]

A vivisecting physician and a stolen pet again appear in *Though Life Us Do Part* (1908). In this novel, the protagonist Cara Sterling, described as "the very blossom and promise of essential womanhood," is romantically pursued by the village doctor Chanceford Dane and the vivisectionist Dr. Thomas Frost.[89] Cara is the guardian of Clyde, a collie who is a victim of animal experimentation by Dr. Frost. Clyde has a scar "high on the forehead," which "was noticeable, but did not disfigure him."[90] At the sound of Dr. Frost's voice, the dog's expression transforms from sinister to "one of inexplicable terror."[91] Clyde attempts to bite Dr. Frost on his right wrist— "the hand that had torn a hundred veins and nerves from living dogs bound and helpless, but conscious of their torments"— but he is stopped by Cara.[92]

Cara's cousin, Reverend Sterling Hart, tries to prevent Dr. Frost from courting his cousin. Three months ago, Clyde had been missing for a week, and Reverend Hart rescued the dog from Dr. Frost's laboratory. Hart now threatens to expose the doctor to Cara unless Frost promises to stop pursuing Cara. Dr. Frost insists he did not know that Clyde belonged to Cara, claiming, "I did not recognize the dog; they are so changed by the conditions—the shaving, and—the general discomfort."[93] But Reverend Hart rebukes Dr. Frost. "Before you made your first incision, he was trying to kiss your hand." Hart laments that "the worst of it was that poor Clyde thought he had found a friend."[94]

Dr. Frost heeds Reverend Sterling's demand, and Cara ultimately marries Chanceford Dane. According to Mary Angela Bennett, this novel involves "Christianity, and compassion towards human beings and animals."[95] This

[88] Phelps, *Trixy*, 161.
[89] Phelps, *Though Life Us Do Part*, 15.
[90] Phelps, *Though Life Us Do Part*, 13.
[91] Phelps, *Though Life Us Do Part*, 20.
[92] Phelps, *Through Life Us Do Part*, 25.
[93] Phelps, *Though Life Us Do Part*, 54.
[94] Phelps, *Though Life Us Do Part*, 54.
[95] Bennett, *Elizabeth Stuart Phelps*, 126.

novel, however, also involves retribution. Clyde, "raging with memory of the unforgiven," pounces upon Dr. Frost.[96] Clyde fastens his teeth "upon the vivisector's cruel, valuable right hand, and crushed it, crunching."[97] But Clyde does not feel remorse. "He spurned the floor with a lofty pride. He had the air of a noble avenger, who had righted the wrongs of a race."[98]

Phelps's short story "Tammyshanty" (1909) was first published in *Home Woman's Companion*. An Irish terrier, a "pauper dog," rescues newsboy Peter Roosevelt Tammany, nicknamed "Jacket," from drowning in the lake. This story celebrates the love of "a friendless boy for a homeless dog," where the "outcast animal" and the "desolate child" become inseparable.[99] Phelps wrote that "the gamin acquired that splendid fortune which may be the supreme ennobler of a human creature—he had experienced a great passion."[100]

An unnamed "philanthropist" gives Jacket two dollars to license his dog. The man is old and "an officer in some society that occupied itself with the reduction of human cruelty."[101] A man with "cold" and "repulsive" eyes offers Jacket money for the dog he has come to call Tammyshanty.[102] Angry, Jacket refuses. Nevertheless, Tammyshanty disappears, and Jacket concludes his dog was stolen by a private vivisector. The philanthropist, a reporter, a policeman, and two newsboys, Freckles and Blinders, investigate the whereabouts of Tammyshanty. They uncover that he is imprisoned in a "gloomy house, destitute of family ties, of the sense of home, [and] of the consciousness of human love."[103] The police cannot obtain a search warrant without further evidence, but Freckles and Blinders state, "We're law-abidin' citizens, Cop, but we're er goin' to hev dat dog."[104] The vivisector tries to escape, leading his subjects out of the house. As the vivisector "tiptoed out," "dogs on leashes . . . and fastened to a rope dragged at the heels of their tormentor."[105] A thousand newsboys—colleagues of Jacket— occupy the street. They surround the vivisector while Jacket rescues Tammyshanty. The mob liberates the rest of the captive dogs and some with a "dogless home" adopt the "poor

---

[96] Phelps, *Though Life Us Do Part*, 262.
[97] Phelps, *Though Life Us Do Part*, 262.
[98] Phelps, *Though Life Us Do Part*, 266–267.
[99] Elizabeth Stuart Phelps, "Tammyshanty," in *The Oath of Allegiance and Other Stories* (London: Houghton, Mifflin Company, 1909), 214, accessed February 17, 2019, http://archive.org/details/oathallegiance00phelrich/page/214.
[100] Phelps, "Tammyshanty," 215.
[101] Phelps, "Tammyshanty," 216.
[102] Phelps, "Tammyshanty," 218.
[103] Phelps, "Tammyshanty," 226.
[104] Phelps, "Tammyshanty," 230.
[105] Phelps, "Tammyshanty," 232.

creatures."[106] In the "old philanthropist's third-story back room," Jacket and Tammyshanty discuss their trauma:

> "Say your prayers, amen," said the boy.
> "Amen," replied the dog.
> "An' we ain't no relations, nuther," suggested the boy.
>   Beneath the bandages on his wounded head a spark
>   in the eye of the Irish dog fired as if he said:—
> "Doncher be too sure of that!"[107]

Conclusion

Elizabeth Stuart Phelps believed "it to be the province of the literary artist to tell the truth about the world he lives in," and "in so far as he fails to be an accurate truth-teller, he fails to be an artist."[108] She further stated that the "literary artist portrays life as it is, or has been, as it might be, or as it should be."[109] The extent of the numerous social problems examined by Phelps in her articles, short stories, and novels is beyond the scope of this chapter. Phelps represented the nineteenth-century social activist's view of the commonalities among social evils.

In her later life, Phelps focused on exposing the evil of vivisection. Phelps's dedication to ending animal experimentation is evident in her essays, her short stories, and her novels. Further, she was a social activist who continued to lobby against vivisection until her death in 1911. She addressed legislative committees on behalf of proposed bills to regulate animal experimentation. She also wrote letters to influential proponents of vivisection, for example, Dr. William W. Keen, seeking support for bills restricting the practice— unfortunately, Dr. Keen rejected her appeals.[110]

In her 1896 autobiography *Chapters from a Life*, Phelps professed her life "creed":

---

[106] Phelps, "Tammyshanty," 236.
[107] Phelps, "Tammyshanty," 237, 238.
[108] Phelps, *Chapters from a Life*, 259.
[109] Phelps, *Chapters from a Life*, 259.
[110] Kelly, "Elizabeth Stuart Phelps," 61. See William W. Keen, "Our Recent Debts to Vivisection," *Popular Science Monthly* 27 (1885): 1–15; Keen, "The Early Days of Anti-vivisection," *Science*, n.s., 65, no. 1672 (January 1927): 35–36.

I believe that the urgent protest against vivisection which marks our immediate day, and the whole plea for lessening the miseries of animals as endured at the hands of men, constitute the "next" great moral question, which is to be put to the intelligent conscience, and that only the educated conscience can properly reply to it.[111]

Bibliography

Bennett, Mary Angela. *Elizabeth Stuart Phelps*. Philadelphia: University of Pennsylvania Press, 1939.

Bernard, Claude. *An Introduction to the Study of Experimental Medicine*. Translated by Henry Copley Greene. New York: Dover, 1957.

Beuttinger, Craig. "Women and Antivivisection in Late Nineteenth-Century America." *Journal of Social History* 30, no. 4 (1997): 857–70.

Blackwell, Elizabeth. "Erroneous Method in Medical Education." In Blackwell, *Essays in Medical Sociology*, 2:33–45. London: Ernest Bell, 1902. https://archive.org/details/390 02006316807.med.yale.edu.

Blackwell, Elizabeth. "Scientific Method in Biology." In Blackwell, *Essays in Medical Sociology*, 2:87–150. London: Ernest Bell, 1902. https://archive.org/details/3900200 6316807.med.yale.edu.

Dean, A. *"The Gates Ajar": Critically Examined*. London: Hatchards, Piccadilly, 1871. https://archive.org/details/gatesajarbyesph01phelgoog.

Elston, Mary Ann. "Women and Anti-vivisection in Victorian England, 1870–1900." In *Vivisection in Historical Perspective*, edited by Nicolaas A. Rupke, 259–94. London: Croom Helm, 1987.

Hamilton, Susan. "Gender and the Literature of the Victorian Vivisection Controversy." *Victorian Review* 17, no. 2 (Winter 1991): 21–34.

Hart, James D. *The Popular Book: A History of America's Literary Taste*. Westport, CT: Greenwood Press, 1976.

Kean, Hilda. "The 'Smooth Cool Men of Science': The Feminist and Socialist Response to Vivisection." *History Workshop Journal* 40 (1995): 16–38.

Keen, William W. "The Early Days of Anti-vivisection." *Science*, n.s., 65, no. 1672 (January 1927): 35–36.

Keen, William W. "Our Recent Debts to Vivisection." *Popular Science Monthly* 27 (1885): 1–15.

Kelly, Lori Duin. "Elizabeth Stuart Phelps, *Trixy*, and the Vivisection Question." *Legacy* 27, no. 1 (2010): 61–82.

Kelly, Lori Duin. *The Life and Works of Elizabeth Stuart Phelps, Victorian Feminist Writer*. Troy, NY: Whitston, 1983.

Kessler, Carol Farley. *Elizabeth Stuart Phelps*. Boston: Twayne, 1982.

---

[111] Phelps, *Chapters from a Life*, 251.

Lansbury, Coral. "Gynaecology, Pornography, and the Antivivisection Movement." *Victorian Studies* 28, no. 3 (1985): 413–37.

Lansbury, Coral. *The Old Brown Dog: Women, Workers, and Vivisection in Edwardian England*. Madison: University of Wisconsin Press, 1985.

Maehle, Andreas-Holger, and Ulrich Trohler. "Animal Experimentation from Antiquity to the End of the Eighteenth Century: Attitudes and Arguments." In *Vivisection in Historical Perspective*, edited by Nicolaas A. Rupke, 14–47. London: Croom Helm, 1987.

Phelps, Elizabeth Stuart. *Beyond the Gates*. Floyd, VA: Black Curtain Press, 2014. First published 1883.

Phelps, Elizabeth Stuart. *Chapters from a Life*. Boston: Houghton, Mifflin, 1897.

Phelps, Elizabeth Stuart. *The Gates Ajar*. Cambridge, MA: Belknap Press of Harvard University Press, 1964. First published 1868.

Phelps, Elizabeth Stuart. *Loveliness: A Story*. Boston: Houghton, Mifflin, 1899.

Phelps, Elizabeth Stuart. *A Singular Life*. Boston: Houghton, Mifflin, 1898.

Phelps, Elizabeth Stuart. *The Story of Jesus Christ: An Interpretation*. Boston: Houghton, Mifflin, 1897.

Phelps, Elizabeth Stuart. "Tammyshanty." In Phelps, *The Oath of Allegiance and Other Stories*. London: Houghton, Mifflin, 1909. Accessed February 17, 2019. http://archive.org/details/oathallegiance00phelrich.

Phelps, Elizabeth Stuart. *Though Life Us Do Part*. Boston: Houghton, Mifflin, 1908.

Phelps, Elizabeth Stuart. *Trixy*. Boston: Houghton, Mifflin, 1904. Accessed February 4, 2019. https://archive.org/details/trixywardphelps00phelrich.

Privett, Ronna Coffey. *A Comprehensive Study of the American Writer Elizabeth Phelps, 1841–1911: Art for Truth's Sake*. Lewiston, NY: Edwin Mellen Press, 2003.

Russett, Cynthia E. *Sexual Science: The Victorian Construction of Womanhood*. Cambridge, MA: Harvard University Press, 1989.

Walker, Alyssa Chen. "Bringing the Laboratory Dog Home: Elizabeth Stuart Phelps and the Antivivisection Narrative." *Humanimalia: A Journal of Animal/Animal Interface Studies* 4, no. 2 (Spring 2013): 101–29.

Welter, Barbara. "The Defenders of the Faith: Women Novelists of Religious Controversy in the Nineteenth Century." In *Dimity Convictions: The American Woman in the Nineteenth Century*, 111–20. Athens: Ohio University Press, 1976.

Wood, Ann Douglas. "'The Fashionable Diseases': Women's Complaints and Their Treatment in Nineteenth-Century America." In *Women and Health in America: Historical Readings*, edited by Judith Walzer Leavitt, 222–38. Madison: University of Wisconsin Press, 1984.

13

Muḥammad ʿAbduh (1849–1905)

The Transvaal Fatwa and the Fate of Animals

Nuri Friedlander

Are There Muslim Animal Theologians?

What does it mean for someone to be a Muslim animal theologian? Would such a person view nonhuman animals as inherently equal to humans, or would that person highlight animals' subjectivity even while situating them within a theology that views them as inferior to humans? Do questions regarding animals have to be front and center in their work, or could those questions show up in discussions of issues not directly related to the lives and experiences of nonhuman animals? Is the Muslim animal theologian an exceptional figure, or has a concern for animals been incorporated into Islamic theology in such a way as to make all Muslim theologians animal theologians in some respect? This chapter attempts to answer some of these questions through the study of the legal and theological opinions of Muḥammad ʿAbduh (d. 1905), the grand mufti of Egypt at the beginning of the twentieth century. His most relevant works for this discussion are select passages from his theological treatise *The Theology of Unity*[1] and a fatwa that he issued to Muslims in South Africa. The fatwa, commonly referred to as the Transvaal fatwa, concerns how animals were killed by non-Muslims and raised questions regarding the nature of animal slaughter in Islam. Though apparently straightforward, the fatwa generated robust debate at the time it was issued, and it continues to resonate with Muslims today as they explore

---

[1] There are multiple editions of *The Theology of Unity*. All translations in this chapter are made by the author from the Muḥammad ʿImārah edition: Muḥammad ʿAbduh, *Risālat Al-Tawḥīd*, ed. Muḥammad ʿImārah (Beirut: Dār al-Shurūq, 1994). The entire work was translated by Musaʿad and Cragg: Muḥammad ʿAbduh, *The Theology of Unity*, trans. Isḥāq Musaʿad and Kenneth Cragg (London: George Allen & Unwin, 1966).

Nuri Friedlander, *Muḥammad ʿAbduh (1849–1905)* In: *Animal Theologians*. Edited by: Andrew Linzey and Clair Linzey,
Oxford University Press. © Oxford University Press 2023. DOI: 10.1093/oso/9780197655542.003.0014

how Islamic law and theology can respond to challenges raised by modern methods of animal slaughter. *The Theology of Unity*, while lacking the direct applicability of a fatwa, includes a deep consideration of animal experiences that helps reveal the complexity of Islamic theology when it comes to animals.

Some might argue that Muḥammad ʿAbduh should not be counted as an animal theologian. Does he object to the practice of animal slaughter? He does not. In fact, he affirms its permissibility and even allows for practices that other jurists have found problematic. So why include him here? For one thing, we would be hard-pressed to identify Muslim theologians who do ideologically object to killing animals for food. The practice is explicitly permitted in the Qurʾan[2] and in traditions of the Prophet Muḥammad (hadith),[3] the two main sources of Islamic law and theology, which makes it nearly impossible for a Muslim theologian to argue that it is wrong or immoral in absolute terms. In light of this, I think we would be doing Muslim theologians a disservice if we demanded of them something akin to a contemporary animal rights discourse. Many Muslim theologians, however, do express nuanced views of non-human animals that take animals' experiences into consideration while still endorsing a hierarchy that places humans above them.[4] ʿAbduh's fatwa and the debates surrounding it exemplify the kinds of discussions regarding animals that Muslims engage in and reveal some of the possibilities and limitations of Islamic animal theologies.

Questions related to the lives and deaths of animals are ubiquitous in Islamic intellectual history. The Qurʾan is replete with references to animals as signs of the divine,[5] as subjects engaged in the worship of God[6] who have

[2] "Forbidden for you are carrion, blood, pig flesh, that which is killed for other than God, animals that die by strangulation, being beaten, falling from a height, a sheep killed by another sheep's horn, and animals eaten by other animals of prey, except those that you have slaughtered" (5:3).

[3] There are numerous traditions of the Prophet Muḥammad that either refer to practices of hunting and slaughter or describe him eating meat from slaughtered animals.

[4] For a discussion of the ways in which animals can be both objects within a hierarchical schema and theological subjects in the context of animal theologies within Abrahamic traditions, see Kimberley C. Patton, "'He Who Sits in the Heavens Laughs': Recovering Animal Theology in the Abrahamic Traditions," *Harvard Theological Review* 93, no. 4 (2000): 401–34. On theocentric rather than anthropocentric readings of the Qurʾan, see Sarra Tlili, *Animals in the Qurʾan* (New York: Cambridge University Press, 2012).

[5] "There are signs for the believers in the heavens and on earth. In your creation and in the animals that are spread upon the earth there are signs for people of certainty" (45:3–4); "Do you not consider how the camel was created?" (88:17).

[6] "Have you not seen that everyone in the heavens and on the earth, and the birds spreading their wings, glorifies God? Each know their prayer and their glorification, and God is All Knowing of what they do" (24:41); "The seven heavens and the earth, and all within them, praise Him. There is nothing except that it glorifies Him with praise, but you do not understand their glorification. He is

their own communities,[7] as creatures who benefit humans as protectors and companions,[8] and as sources of food[9] and labor.[10] Traditions of the Prophet Muḥammad also include many references to animals that exhibit consideration of animals' experiences,[11] admonish others for harming them,[12] and allow animals to be killed for food while requiring that the killing be done in a way that reduces the animals' suffering.[13] Muslim theologians have discussed the implications of animal experiences of pain and suffering for an understanding of God as just,[14] and saints, sages, and mystics have related stories where animals feature as companions to ascetics and as recipients of human compassion and mercy.[15] Every comprehensive work of Islamic

---

Forbearing, Forgiving" (17:44); "Have you not seen that everyone in the heavens and on earth prostrate to God: the sun, the moon, and the stars, the trees, and the animals" (22:18).

[7] "There is not an animal on earth or a bird flying on its wings except they are communities like you" (6:38).

[8] "You think they are awake but they slumber. We turn them right and left and their dog spreads his legs at the entrance" (18:18).

[9] "There are lessons for you in livestock. We provide drink for you from their bellies, between filth and blood is pure milk good for the drinker" (16:66); "There are lessons for you in livestock. We give you to drink from what is in their bellies and in them you have many benefits, and of them you eat" (23:21); "It is God who has made livestock for you that you may ride them and eat from them" (40:79).

[10] "They bear your loads for you to countries you would not have reached without great hardship" (16:8).

[11] The Messenger of God said, "Once a man was walking down a road and he became very thirsty. He found a well and went down into it and drank. He left and came upon a dog who was panting and eating dust out of thirst. The man said, 'This dog has reached the same state of thirst as I had,' so he descended into the well, filled his shoe with water, then held it in his mouth. He gave the dog water to drink. The dog thanked God for him, so God forgave the man." His companions said, "Messenger of God, are we rewarded for [how we treat] animals?" He replied, "For everything that has a moist liver there is a reward." Muḥammad b. Ismāʿīl al-Bukhārī, Ṣaḥīḥ al-Bukhārī: kitāb al-adab, bāb raḥmat al-nās wa al-bahāʾim.

[12] It is related that the Prophet came upon a camel in someone's garden. When the camel saw the Prophet, the animal moaned and wept. The Prophet went to the camel and rubbed his head, and the camel quieted down. The Prophet said, "Who is the master of this camel? Whose camel is this?" A young man from the Anṣār came and said, "It is mine, Messenger of God." He said, "Do you not fear God in regards to this animal that God has put into your possession? It has complained to me that you leave it hungry and exhaust it." Abū Dāwūd al-Sijistānī, Al-Sunan: kitāb al-jihād, bāb mā yuʾmar bihi min al-qiyām ʿalā al-dawābb wa al-bahāʾim.

[13] It is related that the Prophet said regarding slaughtering well, "Sharpen your knife and put the animal at ease." Muslim b. al-Ḥajjāj, Ṣaḥīḥ Muslim: kitāb al-ṣayd wa al-dhabāʾiḥ wa mā yuʾkal min al-ḥayawān, bāb al-amr b-iḥsān al-dhabḥ wa al-qatl wa taḥdīd al-shafrah.

[14] On theological debates regarding animal pain and suffering, see Margaretha T. Heemskerk, Suffering in the Muʿtazilite Theology: ʿAbd Al-Jabbār's Teaching on Pain and Divine Justice (Leiden: Brill, 2000).

[15] For example, "Al-Fudayl said: 'He who has shown every [possible] virtue, yet has mistreated his chicken, should not be considered to be among the virtuous.'" Abu al-Qasim al-Qushayri, Al-Qushayri's Epistle on Sufism, trans. Alexander D. Knysh (Reading, UK: Garnet, 2007), 253. Ibn Ata' Allah al-Iskandari relates an encounter that Abū al-Hasan al-Shādhilī had: "Once while traveling, I spent the night atop a hill. As I slept, some lions came and walked in circles around me, then remained with me until morning. Never have I experienced intimate companionship as I did that

jurisprudence includes chapters on hunting, slaughtering, and sacrificing animals, as well as detailed discussions of animals as property owned by humans. In many respects these discussions are fairly uncontroversial in that Muslim jurists tend to broadly agree in their descriptions of practices that define and mediate human–animal relationships. There are, however, important disagreements between jurists, and ʿAbduh's Transvaal fatwa is just one example of the impact those differences have on the lives—and deaths—of nonhuman animals.

Animal Slaughter in Islamic Law

In recent years halal meat has become a subject of contention in some European Union countries and in the United States. Much of the conflict revolves around the treatment of animals during the process of halal slaughter, particularly the resistance among its advocates to implement preslaughter stunning. Increasingly, preslaughter stunning has been seen as necessary for animal slaughter to meet basic ethical standards, so halal slaughter—which, like kosher slaughter, often does not involve preslaughter stunning—has been targeted by a number of animal rights groups as inhumane. For example, when Denmark banned halal and kosher slaughter in 2015, the Danish minister for agriculture and food stated, "Animal rights come before religion."[16] While his prioritization of animal welfare is laudable, the implication of his statement—that religion is at odds with animal rights—risks alienating many potential allies to the animal rights cause and demonizing communities that are, in many cases, already marginalized. As this current volume shows, however, there are robust religious traditions of thinking deeply about animals and attempting to develop theologies that consider their subjective experiences. Even theologies that permit humans to kill animals for food often take animals' suffering seriously and incorporate practices that seek to minimize their suffering. The irony of the Danish minister's statement is that many Muslims believe that Islamic rituals of animal slaughter are

night. When I arose the following morning, it occurred to me that I had experienced something of the station of intimacy with God." Aḥmad ibn Muḥammad Ibn ʿAṭa.

[16] Adam Withnall, "Denmark Bans Kosher and Halal Slaughter as Minister Says 'Animal Rights Come Before Religion," *The Independent*, February 18, 2014, accessed May 25, 2017, http://www.

intended to be humane, and they emphasize the importance of treating animals well even when slaughtering them.

More detailed works on Islamic law may devote upward of fifty pages to discussions of animal slaughter and hunting. Islamic law has generally categorized human actions in one of five ways: obligatory, forbidden, recommended/laudable, discouraged/reprehensible, and permissible. All of the Sunni schools of law consider animal slaughter permissible, but there is a difference of opinion among the schools regarding some of the associated practices. Muslim jurists address who can carry out slaughter, what tools should be used, and how it should be done. As for who can carry out slaughter, jurists appear to agree that the person must be either a Muslim or a member of the People of the Book (*ahl al-kitāb*).[17] Slaughter must be performed with a tool that cuts with a sharp edge. Although this tool is typically a metal blade, one could also use stone or another substance as long as it is sharp and can hold an edge. The practice involves cutting the animal's throat to sever a combination of the trachea, esophagus, and carotid arteries.[18] It is important that the animal be alive when his or her throat is cut so that the heart can pump out blood.[19] According to some of the schools, the person performing the slaughter must also invoke the name of God when making the cut. There are additionally a number of actions that are recommended or discouraged. Recommended actions include turning animals to face the direction of Mecca while they are being slaughtered and letting animals drink water beforehand. Discouraged actions include sharpening a knife in front of the animal, slaughtering an animal in front of other animals, slaughtering an animal with a dull blade, cutting through to the spine, and other actions that would cause an increase in the animal's pain or distress. Through these legal and moral guidelines, Muslim jurists advocate for animals by condemning practices that entail suffering beyond what is necessary to the slaughter process, while still upholding that some pain and suffering is acceptable.

independent.co.uk/news/world/europe/denmark-bans-halal-and-kosher-slaughter-as-minister-says-animal-rights-come-before-religion-9135580.html.

[17] Typically understood to refer to Jews or Christians.
[18] The Sunni legal schools differ regarding which and how many of the vessels have to be severed.
[19] One of the stated purposes of slaughter is to purify animals by removing their blood. Additionally, when an animal is rendered unconscious, it can be a challenge to discern the signs that indicate that an animal is still alive, such as voluntary movement.

Muḥammad ʿAbduh and His Legacy

Muḥammad ʿAbduh was born in 1849 and grew up in a village in the Egyptian Nile Delta.[20] He memorized the Qurʾan as a child and was sent to study Islamic sciences in Tanta when he was thirteen years old. He made his way to Cairo when he was seventeen and enrolled in al-Azhar University, from which he obtained the prestigious ʿalamiya degree in 1877, which authorized him to teach religious sciences. It was during his time as a student at al-Azhar that he formed a relationship with the Persian intellectual Jamāl al-Dīn al-Afghānī, who had significant influence on ʿAbduh's thought and approach.[21] ʿAbduh taught in both al-Azhar and the newly formed teacher's college Dar al-ʿUlūm University. Through Afghānī, ʿAbduh became active in opposition politics. Because of some of these activities, ʿAbduh was banished from Cairo, but he was able to return a year later, in 1880, when he became editor in chief of the official Egyptian journal al-Waqaʾiʿ al-Masrīya. Subsequently, due to his involvement in the ʿUrābī uprising, the British temporarily exiled ʿAbduh from Egypt in 1882. During his exile, ʿAbduh spent time in Damascus and Beirut before joining Afghānī in Paris, where they published the periodical al-ʿUrwat al-Wuthqā. After some time, ʿAbduh split with Afghānī and relocated to Beirut, where he taught at the Sultaniyya school until his exile came to an end and he moved back to Cairo in 1888. ʿAbduh's career oscillated between journalism, education, and religious leadership, and he formed ties with representatives of the British in Cairo. In 1899 he was appointed to the position of grand mufti of Egypt by the Khedive Ismaʿīl, and he held this position until his death in 1905.

After ʿAbduh's death, his student Rashīd Riḍā published a biography of him as well as a new edition of *The Theology of Unity* and a collection of ʿAbduh's commentaries on the Qurʾan, to which Riḍā added his own material. For Riḍā, ʿAbduh served as a link to Afghānī and was an important figure in the burgeoning Salafi movement that Riḍā promoted. Orientalist scholarship also latched onto ʿAbduh as a Muslim modernist reformer, and

---

[20] Much has been written about ʿAbduh's life and thought. Interested readers can refer to Mark Sedgwick's recent biography for more details. Mark J. Sedgwick, *Muhammad Abduh* (Oxford: Oneworld, 2010).

[21] On the relationship between Muḥammad ʿAbduh and Jamāl al-Dīn al-Afghānī, see Elie Kedourie, *Afghani and ʿAbduh: An Essay on Religious Unbelief and Political Activism in Modern Islam* (New York: Humanities Press, 1966); and Itzchak Weismann, "The Sociology of Islamic Modernism: Muḥammad ʿAbduh, the National Public Sphere and the Colonial State," *Maghreb Review: Majallat al-Maghrib* 32, no. 1 (2007): 104–21.

he was hailed as one of the most important Muslim scholars of the early twentieth century.[22] While some of these descriptions may be exaggerated,[23] the fact remains that 'Abduh's legacy has been highly influential in the development of Muslim reformist thought. The Transvaal fatwa is an example of how his ideas have continued to be relevant as Muslims grapple with addressing contemporary industrialized forms of animal slaughter.

The Role of the Grand Mufti

A fatwa is a nonbinding legal opinion issued by a qualified jurist, referred to as a mufti, in response to a question that someone has posed. Fatwas can address all topics covered by Islamic jurisprudence, ranging from the correct performance of religious rituals to the ways in which inheritance should be distributed or procedures of the courts. While all Muslim jurists who have attained a certain level of scholarship may issue fatwas, at different points in history, the role of muftis has been institutionalized and incorporated into the state apparatus in various ways, with muftis often serving as official consultants affiliated with the courts.[24] In Egypt, the institutionalization of the position of grand mufti (*Mufti al-Diyār al-Misrīyah*) grew out of shifts in the organization of religious authority in the nineteenth and early twentieth centuries. As the Ḥanafī school[25] of law became the official school of law applied in Egyptian courts during the nineteenth century, the position of the Ḥanafī mufti gained in importance. In 1880 a law was passed stipulating that the president of the Cairo Court had to consult the Ḥanafī mufti in "complicated situations."[26] There were also muftis who served courts at lower levels,

---

[22] Itzchak Weismann, "The Sociology of Islamic Modernism," 1–2.

[23] Itzchak Weismann argues that this depiction of 'Abduh is the combined product of his student Rashīd Riḍā's attempt to establish a connection with Afghānī and the uncritical reproduction of these narratives in Western scholarly writings which further portrayed 'Abduh as the pivotal figure in Islamic reform, (Itzchak Weismann, "The Sociology of Islamic Modernism," 4–6).

[24] On muftis and fatwas, see Muhammad Khalid Masud, Brinkley Morris Messick, and David Stephan Powers, *Islamic Legal Interpretation: Muftis and Their Fatwas*, (Cambridge, MA: Harvard University Press, 1996); Jakob Skovgaard-Petersen, *Defining Islam for the Egyptian State: Muftis and Fatwas of the Dār Al-Iftā* (Leiden: Brill, 1997); Kevin Reinhart, "Transcendence and Social Practice: Muftis and Qadis as Religious Interpreters," *Annales Islamologiques* 27 (1993): 5–28; Brinkley Messick, "The Mufti, the Text and the World: Legal Interpretation in Yemen," *Man* 21, no. 1 (1986): 102–19; Rudolph Peters, "Muhammad Al-'Abbasi Al-Mahdi Grand Mufti of Egypt, and His Al-Fatawa Al-Mahdiyya," *Islamic Law & Society* 1 (1994): 66.

[25] There are four main schools of Sunni Islamic law: Ḥanafī, Mālikī, Shāfiʿī, and Hanbalī. On the development of Islamic law, see Wael B. Hallaq, *An Introduction to Islamic Law* (Cambridge: Cambridge University Press, 2009).

[26] Skovgaard-Petersen, *Defining Islam*, 102.

and while their rulings were binding on the courts, they consulted the Ḥanafī mufti if they were unsure of the proper ruling in a case.[27] With the establishment of the office of the grand mufti of Egypt in 1895, many of the duties and responsibilities—as well as the authority—of the Ḥanafī mufti were transferred to this newly created position. In fact, Muḥammad al-ʿAbbāsī al-Mahdī (d. 1897), the last mufti of the Ḥanafī school, was appointed grand mufti, although toward the end of his life, the duties of the office were carried out by his successor, Hasūnā al-Nawāwī (d. 1924).[28] Al-Nawāwī stayed in the position of grand mufti until 1899, when he was dismissed and Muḥammad ʿAbduh was appointed in his stead.[29]

Although ʿAbduh was part of a venerable tradition of Muslim scholars issuing legal opinions, he was only the third individual to hold this particular role in the Egyptian state and thus was able to have significant influence on how it developed. Whereas the Ḥanafī mufti would issue fatwas solely according to the Ḥanafī school,[30] over time the grand mufti relied more and more on rulings from other schools in order to arrive at the most appropriate answer to a given question. This was certainly the case with ʿAbduh. Although he often cited the Ḥanafī school, particularly in his numerous fatwas on pious endowments (awqāf),[31] he also had recourse to rulings in other schools. At the time this was a break from what was generally expected from the mufti, but it soon became the new norm as the position of the mufti expanded and evolved. In this sense, ʿAbduh's influence can still be felt at Dār al-Iftāʾ today, even if the muftis there have not always agreed with all of his opinions.[32] Another way in which ʿAbduh was distinct from his predecessor in the position of grand mufti was that he did not just answer questions presented by the government or even by Egyptians.[33] Partly due to his visibility through the journal al-Manār, ʿAbduh became well known as a scholar outside of Egypt. One effect of printing fatwas in international journals was that the mufti was no longer just responding to the specific questioner but

---

[27] Skovgaard-Petersen, Defining Islam, 102. Over time this role diminished such that the muftis' opinions were seen as recommendations rather than binding or enforceable rules.

[28] Skovgaard-Petersen, Defining Islam, 113.

[29] Skovgaard-Petersen, Defining Islam, 119.

[30] Skovgaard-Petersen, Defining Islam, 110.

[31] Skovgaard-Petersen, Defining Islam, 126.

[32] Dār al-Iftāʾ al-Misriyya is the Egyptian state institution that is run by the grand mufti and is responsible for issuing religious legal opinions, determining the beginning of Islamic lunar months, and reviewing sentences of capital punishment. For more on the history and role of the institution see Skovgaard-Petersen, Defining Islam.

[33] While both of his predecessors had received questions from abroad, they were relatively few in number. Skovgaard-Petersen, Defining Islam, 126.

had to consider that his fatwa would be read and commented on by a broader audience.[34] In this way, fatwas became an important vehicle through which Muslim scholars could authoritatively engage with and generate discussions regarding issues of contemporary global concern.

The Context of the Transvaal Fatwa

The Transvaal fatwa was a response to a set of three questions that 'Abduh received from Muslims in South Africa. As mentioned previously, the new means of disseminating fatwas meant that a mufti could assume that they would be read outside the narrow context in which they were issued. As a result, it is likely that 'Abduh considered the broader implications of his fatwa when composing it. Although the three questions were relevant for Muslims in Egypt and elsewhere, they emerged from the specific context of the Transvaal at the time. Unlike other areas of South Africa, where there was some level of religious uniformity among Muslims, the Transvaal region had become home to a Muslim minority with significant internal diversity. Some Muslims in the Transvaal adhered to the Ḥanafī school, and others adhered to the Shāfi'ī school, and this diversity was a significant contributing factor to the questions that were sent to 'Abduh.[35] The three questions were as follows:

> First: There are individuals in the Transvaal who wear western style hats in order to achieve their goals and gain personal benefits. Is this permissible?
> Second: The way they slaughter animals is contrary to the *shari'ah* because they strike cattle with an ax and then slaughter them without invoking God's name, and they slaughter sheep without invoking God's name. Is this permissible?
> Third: Shāfi'īs pray behind Ḥanafīs without saying, "Bismillāh al-Rahmān al-Rahīm," and they pray behind them during the two 'Eids. It is known that there is a difference between the Shafi'is and the Ḥanafīs with regards to the obligation to say, "Bismillāh al-Rahmān al-Rahīm"

---

[34] Skovgaard-Petersen, *Defining Islam*, 99.
[35] For more on this context of the fatwa, see John Voll, "Abduh and the Transvaal Fatwa: The Neglected Question," in *Islam and the Question of Minorities*, ed. Tamara Sonn. (Atlanta, GA: Scholars Press, 1996).

and the *takbīrāt*[36] of the ʿEids, so is it permissible for them to pray behind each other?[37]

Significantly, the three questions all raise issues related to Muslims living as minorities among non-Muslims.

ʿAbduh's Response

As for the slaughtered animals, my opinion is that Muslims in those areas should adopt the explicit text (*naṣ*) of God's book where it states, "And the food of those who have been given the book is permissible for you" (5:5). They should rely on what the respected imam Abū Bakr al-ʿArabī al-Mālikī said, which is that the essential point is that the slaughtered animals be eaten by the people of the book, their priests and lay people, and be considered food for all of them.[38] When their norm is to end an animal's life by any means, and the leaders of their religion eat it after the slaughter, then it becomes allowed for Muslims to eat it since it would be called food of the people of the book. Christians were, during the time of the Prophet (upon him be blessings and peace), as they are today, particularly as the Christians of the Transvaal are of the most zealous in regards to their religion and holding to their scriptures. Whatever then is slaughtered is considered food of the people of the book as long as the slaughter was performed according to their norms which are accepted by the leaders of their religion. The verse, "This day, that which is pure has been permitted you, and the food of the people who have been given the book is permitted for you,"[39] following the verse that forbids carrion and that which is slaughtered to other than God, prevents one from imagining that the food of the people of the book is impermissible because they believe in the divinity of Jesus. They were all like this during the time of the Prophet (upon him be blessings and peace) except those of them who converted to Islam. The term "People of the Book" is absolute (*muṭlaq*) and it cannot be interpreted as referring to this small

---

[36] This refers to the number times one says "Allāhu Akbar" in the ʿEid prayer, which varies depending on the school of law a person follows.

[37] *Al-Fatāwā Al-Islāmīyah Min Dār Al-Iftāʾ Al-Miṣrīyah* (Cairo: Jumhūrīyat Miṣr al-ʿArabīyah, Wizārat al- Awqāf, al-Majlis al-Aʿlá lil-Shuʾūn al-Islāmīyah, 1980), 4:1298.

[38] Abū Bakr Ibn al-ʿArabī (d. 1148) was an Andalusian jurist of the Mālikī school who is also well known as a judge and a commentator on the Qurʾan.

[39] Qurʾan 5:5.

minority. Thus, the verse is explicit in permitting their food without qualification whenever they believe it to be permissible in their religion, in order
to prevent difficulty in living with them and dealing with them.[40]

'Abduh's responses to the first and third questions are quite brief. He has
no problem with Muslims wearing Western-style hats for any reason, and he
dismisses the possibility that doing so could take someone out of the religion
of Islam. 'Abduh's answer for the third question is quite forceful. Not only
does he affirm the permissibility of Shāfi'īs and Ḥanafīs praying behind each
other, but he also indicates that were one to object to this, it would destroy
the unity of Islam. It is important to note that 'Abduh and other like-minded
modernist reformers highly valued the principle of a unified global Muslim
community.[41] In this light, the image of Muslims who adhere to different
schools of law refusing to pray behind each other is symbolic of the frac-
turing of the Muslim community. Today 'Abduh's answers to the questions
about Western-style hats and prayer behind an adherent of another school of
law are generally uncontroversial. Anxieties about eating meat slaughtered
by non-Muslims, however, have not subsided, and the similarity between
the contemporary practice of stunning animals before slaughter and what is
described in the question makes 'Abduh's fatwa a useful resource for contemporary Muslims attempting to navigate these issues.

While 'Abduh makes it clear that his fatwa is in response to the specific
context of the petitioner, it is also apparent that he is supporting certain general principles in the answers that he provides. In stating that Muslims may
wear Western-style hats, 'Abduh is asserting that what one wears does not
determine one's religious identity, but he is also making a statement about
Muslims adopting Western styles and habits, which he does not consider
antithetical to Muslim identity. In answering the question regarding Shāfi'īs
praying behind Ḥanafīs, 'Abduh is commenting on the importance of
Muslims standing together and resisting ways in which they may be divided.
Similarly, we may ask what principles and values are at play in 'Abduh's answer to the question regarding animal slaughter. The following sections will
attempt to answer this question by examining the text of the fatwa as well as
issues raised by 'Abduh's critics and supporters.

---

[40] The fatwa can be found in *Al-Fatāwā Al-Islāmīyah Min Dār Al-Iftā' Al-Miṣrīyah*
(Cairo: Jumhūrīyat Miṣr al-'Arabīyah, Wizārat al- Awqāf, al-Majlis al-A'lá lil-Shu'ūn al-Islāmīyah,
1980), 4:1298–99. Also see Charles Adams's translation of the entire fatwa in Charles C. Adams,
"Muḥammad 'Abduh and the Transvaal Fatwā," in *The Macdonald Presentation Volume: A Tribute to
Duncan Black Macdonald* (Princeton: Princeton University Press, 1933), 16–18.

[41] Adams, "Muḥammad 'Abduh and the Transvaal Fatwā," 23.

Analysis of the Fatwa

Much of what has been written about this fatwa has focused on the impact the controversy surrounding it had on 'Abduh's career, the political allegiances and grievances that led to the controversy, the legal reasoning that 'Abduh employed in the fatwa, and the reformist principles that it embodies.[42] Absent from these discussions—and it must be said, from the fatwa itself— is an explicit concern for what the fatwa means for animal lives. In this regard we may turn to the final line of the fatwa, where 'Abduh states that the reason the Qur'an allows Muslims to consume animals slaughtered by the People of the Book is "to prevent difficulty in living with them and dealing with them." This is, of course, 'Abduh's own interpretation of the verse, and it reveals that his chief goal is to make it easier for Muslims to live alongside non-Muslims. While this could apply equally to situations in which Muslims are the majority and situations in which they are a minority, there seems to be more at stake for Muslims when they are living as religious minorities in predominantly Christian regions such as the Transvaal.[43] In fact, all three questions presented to 'Abduh concern situations in which Muslims are living as minorities and struggling to maintain their religious identities and practices. In light of this, one may wonder whether 'Abduh's answer would have addressed other aspects of the issue if the question regarding animal slaughter had been presented alongside other questions focused on animals instead of Muslim minority life. Perhaps that fatwa would have paid more attention to the experiences of the animals rather than prioritizing Muslim coexistence with Christians. As it stands, the absence of a discussion of slaughter practices in 'Abduh's fatwa is striking. As Charles Adams notes, because the fatwa does not attend to the details of the slaughter process, it effectively "declares that they are not essential to the decision."[44] Thus, 'Abduh does not explicitly address what appears to be the central concern of the questioner: whether striking cattle on the head before slaughtering them and

---

[42] See Adams, "Muḥammad 'Abduh and the Transvaal Fatwā;" Indira Falk Gesink, *Islamic Reform and Conservatism: Al-Azhar and the Evolution of Modern Sunni Islam* (London: Tauris Academic Studies, 2010); and Skovgaard-Petersen, *Defining Islam*.

[43] In describing this aspect of the fatwa, Charles Adams states, "'Abduh, however, has attempted to make his reply as simple as possible, avoiding casuistical details, in order to meet the situation in the Transvaal, where the Muslim minority cannot afford to be isolated by unnecessary restrictions form their Christian neighbors nor separated from one another." "Muḥammad 'Abduh and the Transvaal Fatwā," 23–24.

[44] Adams, "Muḥammad 'Abduh and the Transvaal Fatwā," 25.

omitting the invocation of God's name at the time of slaughter are permissible actions.

As mentioned previously, classical manuals of Islamic law described slaughter practices in great detail. The question of invoking God's name at the time of slaughter is the less challenging aspect of the fatwa because there is an extensive tradition of scholarly disagreement on this issue. Striking an animal on the head before slaughter, however, could mean that the animal falls into the category of al-mawqūdhah,[45] which is described as forbidden in the Qur'an and books of Islamic law.[46] Instead of addressing these issues, however, 'Abduh focuses on the religious affiliation of the person carrying out the slaughter, and the result is that concern for animal experiences of slaughter gets sidelined. In 'Abduh's view, the characteristics of the person performing the slaughter are more important than the process the person uses. Rashīd Riḍā, publisher of the al-Manār journal, made some of this explicit in his defense of 'OAbduh. Regarding the question of whether Christians have to slaughter animals in accordance with Islamic teachings, Riḍā states, "The slaughter of the People of the Book is permissible according to the majority of Muslims even if it is not performed according to the Islamic method, actually even if it contravenes the Islamic method."[47] Unlike 'Abduh, Riḍā engages in extended discussions of various practices related to animal slaughter, identifying which of them are permissible and which are impermissible. In the end, however, he concludes, "These rulings are particular to Muslims. As for People of the Book, they are not required to follow them."[48]

In the very next issue of al-Manār, however, a different view is presented. Here it is argued that the practice described in the fatwa is permissible in itself and not merely because it is performed by a non-Muslim. The evidence provided for this position is the use of the term "slaughter" (dhabh) in the question submitted to 'Abduh, which indicates that the animal was still alive after being struck by the ax. If an animal is alive when slaughtered, then, according to Riḍā, the animal does not fall into the category of an animal killed by a blow (al-mawqūdhah). This means that the slaughtered animal would be permissible according to a consensus of Muslim jurists.[49] But stating that Muslims could consume the meat of animals slaughtered in this way does not

---

[45] An animal who is killed by being struck or beaten instead of having his or her throat cut.
[46] Qur'an 5:4.
[47] Muhammad Rashīd Riḍā, "al-Fatāwā al-Thalāth," Al-Manār 6, no. 20 (January 4, 1904): 774.
[48] Riḍā, "al-Fatāwā al-Thalāth,"" 777.
[49] Muhammad Rashīd Riḍā, "Masalat Dhabā'iḥ Ahl al-Kitāb," Al-Manār 6, no. 21 (January 19, 1904): 812–13.

address the question of whether it is morally acceptable to strike animals on the head with an ax before slaughtering them since this could cause animals unnecessary pain. Might Muslims have a responsibility to avoid eating meat from animals slaughtered in this way, not because the act is impermissible in itself, but because of the negative impact it might have on animals at the end of their lives? Unfortunately, neither ʿAbduh nor Riḍā provides us with an answer to this question.

ʿAbduh's critics approached the issue differently than his supporters. For them the actual process of slaughter was more important than the religious affiliation of the person carrying it out. Like ʿAbduh, however, their concern did not seem to be for animal suffering; rather, their concern was the preservation of the ritual practice. While they agreed that Muslims could eat animals slaughtered by Christians or Jews, they also held that the process had to follow the same guidelines laid out in works of Islamic jurisprudence. Thus, they argued that animals slaughtered by Christians were permissible only if they were slaughtered in accordance with the rules of Islamic law. According to these critics, the process described in the fatwa contravenes Islamic law and is therefore impermissible.[50] This is not to say that animal suffering cannot have a role in such debates. If one holds that the stipulations of Islamic law are intended not only to render meat permissible for human consumption through a ritualized practice, but also to ensure that animals are treated well at the time of slaughter, then it would make sense to hold to those practices regardless of who is performing the slaughter. Doing so would ensure that Islamic ethical standards are maintained and that all animals consumed by Muslims have the same experience of slaughter. Indeed, some of ʿAbduh's critics asserted that the practice described in the fatwa was cruel and tortuous for the animals,[51] but the majority of the critiques seemed to focus on ʿAbduh's departure from the Ḥanafi school, his apparent betrayal of tradition, and his claims to independent legal judgment (*ijtihād*).[52] As we consider the implications of ʿAbduh's fatwa for contemporary practices, we may attempt to recenter the concern for animals' experiences of pain and suffering that features in many of the Islamic scriptural sources on animal slaughter.

[50] Skovgaard-Petersen, *Defining Islam*, 128.
[51] Gesink, *Islamic Reform and Conservatism*, 192.
[52] Gesink, *Islamic Reform and Conservatism*, 192–94; Skovgaard-Petersen, *Defining Islam*, 130.

Echoes of the Fatwa

'Abduh was not the only prominent Muslim jurist to issue a fatwa of this nature. In the second half of the twentieth century, Yūsuf al-Qaraḍāwī wrote a nearly identical opinion in his book *al-Halāl wa al-Ḥarām*, although due to various social and economic shifts he was addressing questions related to slaughtering animals by electrocution and importing meat from non-Muslim countries. Similarly to 'Abduh, al-Qaraḍāwī based his fatwa on the ruling of Abū Bakr Ibn al-'Arabī, and he determined that animals slaughtered by Jews or Christians are permissible for consumption regardless of the process of slaughter, as long as Jews or Christians consider it permissible for themselves.[53] It should be noted that al-Qaraḍāwī's fatwa has received a fair amount of criticism[54] and that the questions it raised regarding halal slaughter continue to be debated by contemporary Muslims.[55] This fatwa has significant implications for nonhuman animals. On the one hand it opens the door for permitting preslaughter stunning as part of the process of halal slaughter. This is the way that Febe Armanios and Boğaç Ergene frame the issue in their book *Halal Food: A History*. After discussing the question of preslaughter stunning, they cite al-Qaraḍāwī's fatwa as allowing it, and they refer to 'Abduh's fatwa in a footnote ascribing the same position to him.[56] This could be seen as a boon by certain animal rights activists who advocate for preslaughter stunning as a way to minimize animal pain at the time of slaughter. On the other hand, one could also argue that it opens the door for Muslims to wholeheartedly take part in the consumption of factory-farmed animals without concern for some of the constraints that Islamic ethics might place on the practice. This could contribute significantly to the continued suffering of the millions of animals who are raised and slaughtered in inhumane conditions throughout the world.

---

[53] Yūsuf al-Qaraḍāwī, *al-Halāl wa al-Ḥarām fī al-Islām* (Cairo: Dār al-'Itiṣām, 1974), 66-67.

[54] This includes a book-length refutation by 'Abd al-Ḥayy al-Ghumārī titled *The Ruling of Meat Imported from Christian Europe* (*Ḥukm Al-Laḥm Al-Mustawrad Min Ūrubah Al-Naṣrānīyah*).

[55] For example, see this discussion between two prominent Muslim religious educators in the U.S. (Digital Mimbar, "Chai-Chat by Yasir Qadhi and Yaser Birjas," April 11, 2011, Video, 50:10, https://www.youtube.com/watch?v=kiMlT6NYbXI), as well as this lecture by a Canadian Muslim educator (Seekers Guidance: The Global Seminary, "Is It Permissible to East Non-Zabiha Meat in North America?" March 21, 2017, Video, 12:40, https://www.youtube.com/watch?v=HP3IPEfbmJY).

[56] Febe Armanios and Boağaç Ergene, *Halal Food: A History* (Oxford: Oxford University Press, 2018), 75-76.

MUHAMMAD ʿABDUH (1849–1905) 251

The Theology of Unity

While the bulk of this chapter is devoted to a study of ʿAbduh's legal opinions in the Transvaal fatwa, he also mentions animals in his more explicitly theological work *The Theology of Unity*. The Transvaal fatwa is a response to specific questions, but *The Theology of Unity* contains clues to how ʿAbduh generally understood animals and their relationship to human beings beyond this one legal opinion. *The Theology of Unity* is based on a series of lectures that ʿAbduh delivered when he was employed at the Sultaniyya school in Beirut in 1885.[57] The first edition was published in Cairo in 1897, and it was followed by a posthumous edition edited by Rashīd Riḍā in 1907.[58] This short treatise covers topics that one might expect to find in a work of Islamic theology, such as the nature of God and prophecy, as well as issues that were of particular interest to ʿAbduh, such as ideas of human progress and the global nature of the Muslim community.

While *The Theology of Unity* does not have a section devoted to animals, ʿAbduh refers to them in a number of places. This allows us to draw some conclusions about how he broadly thought both of animals and of humans. In discussing good and evil, ʿAbduh makes reference to aesthetics in order to establish that humans distinguish between what is beautiful and what is ugly, just as they distinguish between what is good and what is evil.[59] ʿAbduh acknowledges that "tastes may differ," but he also asserts that "things are either beautiful or ugly."[60] Although some may want to debate this point, what is significant for this chapter is that ʿAbduh ascribes the ability to distinguish beauty from ugliness to both human beings and "certain animals."[61] This should not lead us to think that ʿAbduh views humans and animals as equals. He asserts a distinction between humans and animals in terms of free will and intellect: "One of the things that sets humans apart from all other animals is that they possess reason and choice, which are the basis of their actions."[62] That being said, he allows that animals have the capacity to make some moral determinations.

---

[57] ʿAbduh, *Risālat Al-Tawḥīd*, 13.
[58] Sedgwick, *Muhammad Abduh*, 63–64.
[59] The language used by Muslim theologians to discuss ethics is a language of aesthetic value. *Al-Ḥusn* means both beautiful and good, while *al-qabīh* means both ugly and evil.
[60] ʿAbduh, *Risālat Al-Tawḥīd*, 67.
[61] ʿAbduh, *Risālat Al-Tawḥīd*, 67.
[62] ʿAbduh, *Risālat Al-Tawḥīd*, 65.

'Abduh defines good and evil in two ways. The first is in terms of immediate experiences of pain and pleasure. Regarding this, 'Abduh states, "There is little difference between humans distinguishing between good and evil, when understood in these terms, and animals that are higher on the chain of existence doing so. The only difference is in the strength of feeling and the determination of the degree to which something is beautiful or ugly."[63] While 'Abduh is certainly not the only Muslim theologian to express good and evil in terms of pleasure and pain, his explicit inclusion of animals and their capacity to make moral determinations, albeit of a limited sort, is noteworthy. 'Abduh considers nonhuman animals to be at a disadvantage, however, when it comes to actions whose moral determination rests on whether they bring about benefit or harm. Here 'Abduh states, "Humans are unique in being able to distinguish between good and evil in these terms if we consider it in all of its aspects. Other animals rarely share in this unless it is in its most base aspects. This is a peculiarity of the intellect and the secret of divine wisdom in granting reason."[64] 'Abduh makes the distinction between humans and nonhuman animals clearer when he states, "God has gifted, or imposed upon, human beings three faculties that distinguish them from animals: memory, imagination, and reason."[65] 'Abduh affirms, however, that human beings are in need of prophets and divine revelation, for there are some actions that reason alone cannot evaluate. This is particularly the case when it comes to devotional rituals found in Islam, Judaism, and Christianity. It is God who informs humans that these actions will bring about their felicity, not reason alone.[66] In light of this, the question of whether animal slaughter is categorized as a ritual is important since it determines the extent to which the practice can be modified based on rational investigation alone.

I will share one last example of how 'Abduh discusses nonhuman animals in *The Theology of Unity*. 'Abduh cites a story about ant behavior as part of his argument that certain forms of knowledge are inherently known through reason without recourse to revelation. He relates that someone was observing a group of ants and saw that they were building a house. An ant approached them who appeared to be in charge of directing their actions. This ant saw that the other ants had built the ceiling too low, so he ordered them to dismantle it and start over, building the ceiling higher. 'Abduh sees

---

[63] 'Abduh, *Risālat Al-Tawḥīd*, 69.
[64] 'Abduh, *Risālat Al-Tawḥīd*, 69.
[65] 'Abduh, *Risālat Al-Tawḥīd*, 73.
[66] 'Abduh, *Risālat Al-Tawḥīd*, 86.

this as an example of the ability to distinguish between harm and benefit, which disproves the point of those who argue that there is no such thing as good and evil. "This is differentiation between harm and benefit," he writes of the ants, "so whoever claims that there is absolutely no good or evil in regards to actions has negated their intellect and has made themselves more foolish than ants."[67] While this story seems to go against ʿAbduh's previous statement about "animals of a higher order," as well as his arguments that only humans possess rational faculties, it does show a certain sensitivity to animal experiences, and it seems to ascribe a certain kind of sentience to an animal many would consider to be one of the lowest among them.[68]

Conclusion

Although ʿAbduh's reflections on animals in his theological work *The Theology of Unity* reveal a deep consideration of animals as possessing meaningful subjective experiences, those considerations are largely absent from the Transvaal fatwa. Given ʿAbduh's acknowledgment of nonhuman animals' capacity for experiencing pain and knowing it as evil, we might expect to find him placing more emphasis on their subjective experience of the slaughter process. As we have seen, however, the focus of ʿAbduh's fatwa seems to be on the people carrying out the slaughter rather than on the animal being slaughtered. What is it that prevents him from integrating his attention to animal experiences into his legal opinion? Why does the fatwa lack a discussion of whether certain slaughter practices, such as striking cattle on the head, are more or less harmful to animals? Had he engaged in this kind of inquiry, would his response have been different? It may be that in the particular context of this fatwa, the experiences of the minority Muslim community in the Transvaal were more critical for ʿAbduh than the suffering of the animals being slaughtered. Or perhaps his theology of animals presented in *The Theology of Unity* was merely theoretical and never intended for practical application.

---

[67] ʿAbduh, *Risālat Al-Tawḥīd*, 72.

[68] This is not as surprising as it may at first seem. Ants show up in Islamic scripture more than once. The twenty-seventh chapter of the Qurʾan is even named "The Ants" because of a story it contains about the Prophet Sulaymān passing by a community of ants with his army made up of humans, jinn, and birds (Qurʾan 27:17–19).

Though 'Abduh does not appear to explicitly engage in an Islamic animal theology in the framing of the Transvaal fatwa, the ways in which the fatwa has resonated in debates regarding the treatment of animals and the place of ritual in animal slaughter make it one of the most important twentieth-century contributions to Islamic debates on the ethical treatment of animals. At the heart of the controversy surrounding 'Abduh's fatwa is the question of whether it is permissible to eat meat slaughtered by Christians if they have engaged in practices that appear to violate Islamic guidelines. For many Muslims reading 'Abduh's fatwa, the practice of striking cattle on the head with an ax before slaughter appeared to be an example of cruelty, and since it is possible that such a blow might kill the animal, it could invalidate the slaughter. Muslims who objected to this fatwa may have done so to preserve the ritual from being corrupted by the addition of foreign actions or the omission of requirements. But striking an animal on the head also might have appeared to involve an unnecessary element of brutality that betrayed the Islamic principle of treating animals well when slaughtering them. Examining the fatwa and the debates that followed it in this light shows that when Muslims advocate for ritual slaughter that does not involve preslaughter stunning, it may actually be an expression of concern for animal suffering. This concern for animal pain, however, should not prevent us from acknowledging that most Muslim theologians and jurists subscribe to a hierarchical view of the world that places humans above animals and allows for animals to suffer if it benefits humans. Cases such as 'Abduh's, with all of their contradictions, help us identify the challenges of Islamic animal theology and reveal the importance of allowing space to consider it alongside other animal theologies. At the same time, we may hope that theoretical concerns for animals may be transformed into policies and practices that reduce animal suffering in the world.

Bibliography

'Abduh, Muḥammad. *Risālat Al-Tawḥīd*. Edited by Muḥammad 'Imārah. Beirut: Dār al-Shurūq, 1994.

'Abduh, Muḥammad. *The Theology of Unity*. Translated by Isḥāq Musa'ad and Kenneth Cragg. London: George Allen & Unwin, 1966.

Adams, Charles C. "Muḥammad 'Abduh and the Transvaal Fatwā." In *The Macdonald Presentation Volume: A Tribute to Duncan Black Macdonald*, 13–29. Princeton, NJ: Princeton University Press, 1933.

Armanios, Febe, and Boğaç A. Ergene. *Halal Food: A History*. Oxford: Oxford University Press, 2018.

Bukhārī, Muḥammad b. Ismāʿīl al-. *Ṣaḥīḥ al-Bukhārī*. Cited according to chapter, subchapter system.

Digital Mimbar. "Chai-Chat by Yasir Qadhi and Yaser Birjas." April 11, 2011. Video, 50:10. https://www.youtube.com/watch?v=kiMlT6NYbXI.

Al-Fatāwā Al-Islāmīyah Min Dār Al-Iftāʾ Al-Miṣrīyah. Cairo: Jumhūrīyat Miṣr al-ʿArabīyah, Wizārat al-Awqāf, al-Majlis al-Aʿlá lil-Shuʾūn al-Islāmīyah, 1980.

Gesink, Indira Falk. *Islamic Reform and Conservatism: Al-Azhar and the Evolution of Modern Sunni Islam*. London: Tauris Academic Studies, 2010.

Ghumārī, ʿAbd al-Ḥayy al-. *Ḥukm Al-Laḥm Al-Mustawrad Min Ūrubah Al-Naṣrānīyah*. Tanja: al-Maṭbaʿah al-Maghribīyah wa al-Dawlīyah, n.d.

Hallaq, Wael B. *An Introduction to Islamic Law*. Cambridge: Cambridge University Press, 2009.

Heemskerk, Margaretha T. *Suffering in the Muʿtazilite Theology: ʿAbd Al-Jabbārʾs Teaching on Pain and Divine Justice*. Leiden: Brill, 2000.

Ibn ʿAṭāʾ Allāh, Aḥmad ibn Muḥammad. *The Subtle Blessings in the Saintly Lives of Abū Al-ʿAbbās Al-Mursī and His Master Abū Al-Ḥasan Al-Shādhilī, the Founders of the Shādhilī Order*. Translated by Nancy N. Roberts. Louisville, KY: Fons Vitae, 2005.

Kedourie, Elie. *Afghani and ʿAbduh: An Essay on Religious Unbelief and Political Activism in Modern Islam*. New York: Humanities Press, 1966.

Masud, Muhammad Khalid, Brinkley Morris Messick, and David Stephan Powers. *Islamic Legal Interpretation: Muftis and Their Fatwas*. Cambridge, MA: Harvard University Press, 1996.

Messick, Brinkley. "The Mufti, the Text and the World: Legal Interpretation in Yemen." *Man* 21, no. 1 (1986): 102–19.

Muslim b. al-Hajjāj. *Ṣaḥīḥ Muslim*. Cited according to chapter, subchapter system.

Patton, Kimberley C. "'He Who Sits in the Heavens Laughs': Recovering Animal Theology in the Abrahamic Traditions." *Harvard Theological Review* 93, no. 4 (2000): 401–34.

Peters, Rudolph. "Muhammad Al-ʿAbbasi Al-Mahdi, Grand Mufti of Egypt, and His Al-Fatawa Al-Mahdiyya." *Islamic Law and Society* 1 (1994): 66.

Qaraḍāwī, Yūsuf al-. *Al-Ḥalāl Wa-Al-Ḥarām Fī Al-Islām*. Cairo: Dār Al-Iʿtiṣām, 1974.

Qushayri, Abu al-Qasim al-. *Al-Qushayriʾs Epistle on Sufism*. Translated by Alexander D. Knysh. Reading, UK: Garnet, 2007.

Reinhart, Kevin. "Transcendence and Social Practice: Muftis and Qadis as Religious Interpreters." *Annales Islamologiques* 27 (1993): 5–28.

Riḍā, Muḥammad Rashīd. "Bāb al-Fiqh wa Aḥkām al-Dīn," *Al-Manār* 6, no. 20 (January 4, 1904): 771–88.

Riḍā, Muḥammad Rashīd. "Masalat Dhabāʾiḥ Ahl al-Kitāb," *Al-Manār* 6, no. 21 (January 19, 1904): 812–31.

Seekers Guidance: The Global Seminary. "Is It Permissible to East Non-Zabiha Meat in North America?" March 21, 2017. Video, 12:40. https://www.youtube.com/watch?v=HP3IPEfbmJY.

Sedgwick, Mark J. *Muhammad Abduh*. Oxford: Oneworld, 2010.

Sijistānī, Abū Dāwūd al-. *Al-Sunan*. Cited according to chapter, subchapter system.

Skovgaard-Petersen, Jakob. *Defining Islam for the Egyptian State: Muftis and Fatwas of the Dār Al-Iftā*. Leiden: Brill, 1997.

Tlili, Sarra. *Animals in the Qurʾan*. New York: Cambridge University Press, 2012.

Voll, John. "Abduh and the Transvaal Fatwa: The Neglected Question." In *Islam and the Question of Minorities*, edited by Tamara Sonn, 27–39. Atlanta, GA: Scholars Press, 1996.

Weismann, Itzchak. "The Sociology of Islamic Modernism: Muhammad 'Abduh, the National Public Sphere and the Colonial State." *Maghreb Review: Majallat al-Maghrib* 32, no. 1 (2007): 104–21.

Withnall, Adam. "Denmark Bans Kosher and Halal Slaughter as Minister Says 'Animal Rights Come before Religion.'" *The Independent*, February 18, 2014. Accessed May 25, 2017. http://www.independent.co.uk/news/world/europe/denmark-bans-halal-and-kosher-slaughter-as-minister-says-animal-rights-come-before-religion-9135 580.html.

14

Josiah Oldfield (1863–1953)

Vegetarianism and the Order of the Golden Age in Nineteenth-Century Britain

A. W. H. Bates

Josiah Oldfield was variously a lawyer, doctor, and director of hospitals and vegetarian colonies in the home counties. Though it is chiefly as a pioneering vegetarian that he is now remembered, his contributions to humanitarian and animal welfare causes were considerable, and he made a sustained effort to reform Christian attitudes toward animals and the natural environment. A Shropshire grocer's son, Oldfield went to Oxford in 1882 to read theology, a relatively new subject for an undergraduate degree and less prestigious than more established courses. His decision was probably determined by financial constraints, since theology students were not typically attached to a college but lived in lodgings, a cheaper option for those of modest means. Nevertheless, Oldfield still needed to work as a road-mender for two hours a day before breakfast in order to pay his fees. His capacity for hard work would last a lifetime, though the demands of physical labor, along with a raft of extracurricular activities—including campaigning against capital punishment and cruelty to animals—may have been responsible for this obviously talented young man taking what was then considered only a second-class degree.[1]

His decision to join the Vegetarian Society, which had a branch in Oxford, was an extension of his humanitarian activities: adopting vegetarianism, Oldfield believed, would help reduce poverty and conflict—the former because the poor could be fed more cheaply on a vegetable diet and the latter because the risk of war would lessen as people's economic circumstances improved and as abstinence from meat rendered them less aggressive. The

---

[1] For details of Oldfield's biography, see Rosemary Dellar, *Josiah Oldfield: Eminent Fruitarian* (Rainham, UK: Rainmore Books, 2008).

A. W. H. Bates, *Josiah Oldfield (1863–1953)* In: *Animal Theologians*. Edited by: Andrew Linzey and Clair Linzey, Oxford University Press. © Oxford University Press 2023. DOI: 10.1093/oso/9780197655542.003.0015

undergraduate Oldfield's vegetarianism was thus no simple dietary preference but a controversial social commitment, linked with pacifism, left-wing
politics, and social improvement. The Vegetarian Society was something of
a magnet for political and religious reformers, attracting former members of
the Concordium—a socialist utopian community that had closed in 1848—
and Cowherdites, followers of the Bible Christian Church, for whom vegetarianism was a religious obligation. Of course, some members, such as Oldfield,
were also motivated by an aversion to cruelty; he would be appalled by the
scenes he later witnessed while investigating English slaughterhouses, which
he vividly described in a pamphlet titled *The Evils of Butchery*, published by
the Humanitarian League in 1895.

Given that most of his fellow theologians were destined for a career in the
church, it is reasonable to ask why Oldfield did not follow this path. Perhaps
he was already planning to be more actively involved in campaigning work
than would have been feasible for someone with the responsibility for curing
souls, or maybe he recognized a tendency to heterodoxy in his religious views
and lifestyle that would prove problematic were he to take holy orders. After
graduating, he remained at Oxford to read for a degree in civil law, which set
him up for a professional career in which he could practice independently
and which also helped with his campaigning work. He was called to the bar
in 1892, a year after his friend and fellow vegetarian Mohandas Gandhi, but
he practiced law on the Oxford circuit only sporadically, as in the same year
he registered at St Bartholomew's Hospital as a student of medicine.

In 1896, Oldfield assumed oversight of a small vegetarian hospital, the
Oriolet, at Loughton in Essex. This was the personal project of the Vegetarian
Society's president, the wealthy shipbuilder Arnold Hills, who made his
patients promises:

> No surgical experiments on patients!
> No flesh food.
> Plenty of fresh air, sunshine, fruit, and the singing of birds.[2]

It was the perfect proving ground for Oldfield's ideas about the benefits of a
vegetable diet, although the medical profession was skeptical about the objectivity of the experiment, given that most of the patients were vegetarians
who chose the Oriolet because they were sympathetic to the hospital's aims.[3]

---

[2] "A Vegetarian Hospital," *Herald of the Golden Age* 1 (1896): 150.
[3] "A Medical Sack Race," *British Medical Journal* 2 (1897): 1115–16.

In order to take on a more active role, Oldfield, who initially ran the hospital as "warden," studied at St Bartholomew's Hospital, qualified as a doctor in 1897, and became the Oriolet's medical officer.

Before long, he took advantage of his medical status to start an independent hospital of his own, opening Britain's—and quite possibly the world's—first antivivisection hospital, the Hospital of St Francis, in 1898 in a converted townhouse in a poor district of South London. At the time, antivivisection was enjoying considerable public support, and he initially found it easier to attract patrons and donors than patients, though for a hospital with only eleven beds, it was soon busy enough: in the five years before it closed, it treated over four hundred inpatients and a hundred thousand outpatients, mostly local people who had no other access to free treatment.[4]

The hospital's critics dismissed it as Oldfield's personal anticruelty protest rather than an institution run for the benefit of patients, and some objected to what they saw as ideological medicine—the profession's leaders expected doctors to provide what was best for patients rather than promoting their own personal fads and fancies. The force of this criticism depended, however, on how patients' interests were judged, a question that exposed a deep ideological difference between Oldfield and the medical hierarchy over whether medicine had become overreliant on scientific experimentation to the detriment of care and compassion. For Oldfield, it was not enough simply to provide the latest treatments: patients must be able to trust doctors to treat them humanely, which required doctors to foreswear all cruelty. The animal protection movement had long assumed that cruelty to animals led to cruelty to humans and that doctors who carried out vivisection would treat their patients in the same cold, rational way, as subjects for experimentation.[5] Oldfield's contention was not that the rise in laboratory medicine had failed to produce results, but that acquiescence to cruel experiments betrayed a fundamental lack of compassion among the new generation of experimentalist physicians, a lack that they had carried with them from the laboratory into the clinic. In some of the poorest districts of London, patients were afraid to go into the free hospitals because they thought the doctors there intended to

[4] Flyer for Lady Margaret Hospital, reprinted in *South London Press*, August 29, 1904, London Metropolitan Archives A/FWA/C/D330/1.

[5] Hilda Kean, "The 'Smooth Cool Men of Science': The Feminist and Socialist Response to Vivisection," *History Workshop Journal* 40 (1995): 16–38.

use them as experimental subjects, whereas in Oldfield's hospital, the staff were pledged not to perform experiments of any kind.[6]

Oldfield's high ideal of the true scientist who respects all life is a central theme in his writings, particularly in his work for the Order of the Golden Age. The order, a Christian vegetarian society, was founded in 1882 with four grades of membership: the first for those who sympathized with its aims and the next three for progressive abstainers from meat, fish, and alcohol.[7] In 1904, when his friend Sidney Beard restructured the order, Oldfield became its secretary.[8] Under Beard's leadership, the Order set itself the ambitious goal of bringing about the biblical "peaceable kingdom"—a new age of peace and prosperity that would be hastened by the adoption of a healthy and beneficent vegetarian lifestyle.

Oldfield served as editor of the order's journal, the *Herald of the Golden Age*, the first issue of which (with an ambitious print run of ten thousand copies) explained the order's objects to the public by using the phrase "Thy Will be done on Earth" (familiar to all Christians from the Lord's Prayer) to introduce the lesser-known concept of the messianic kingdom, an era of global peace prophesied in the book of Isaiah.[9] This earthly paradise, the "Golden Age" of the order's title, would be achieved when humans lived "in perfect harmony with God's Physical and Spiritual Laws" and followed a rule of "love, benevolence and mercy," which required, among other things, the adoption of a vegetarian diet (which Genesis 1 indicated was the original state of sinless humanity).[10] Because vegetarianism and the prevention of cruelty to animals were necessary steps toward building God's kingdom on earth, they were, according to Oldfield, the proper Christian choices. Butchery, by contrast, was a selfish, regressive option, because meat-eating was unnecessary in a developed society.[11]

The Order of the Golden Age was only one of many fin de siècle societies combining religion or spirituality with self- and social improvement. Its utopian outlook, which it shared with other antimaterialist movements such as

---

[6] "Hospital of St. Francis," London Metropolitan Archives A/FWA/C/D330/1. On the link between vivisection and experiments on the poor, see Mark Thornhill, *Experiments on Hospital Patients* (London: Hatchards, 1889).

[7] "A New Guild," *Dundee Courier*, July 27, 1882, 3. Oldfield ate neither meat nor fish but enjoyed alcohol in moderation.

[8] *The Order of the Golden Age: Its Aims, Its Objects and Its Rules* (n.p., 1904), 1.

[9] Isa. 2:4 and 11:6–9.

[10] "Is It Only a Dream?," editorial, *Herald of the Golden Age* 1 (1896): 1.

[11] Josiah Oldfield, "Concerning Butchery and Vivisection," *Herald of the Golden Age* 10 (1905): 59–60.

theosophy and homeopathy, can be seen as part of a nostalgic turn toward a more natural and holistic lifestyle, in response to growing concerns that "progress" in its many forms, from mass production to laboratory medicine, was leading humankind into an unnatural and demoralizing state.[12] It was hoped that a deeper understanding of science and philosophy would bring home the importance of restoring the natural balance. In his short monograph *The Claims of Common Life*, Oldfield extolled what he termed "those heights of scientia and gnosis, which are the crowning stamp of the true scientist"[13]—a person whose discoveries gave him or her greater reverence for life and an appreciation of the "brotherhood" of all living things. If these insights were more widely shared, claimed Oldfield, people would achieve such respect for life that cruelty to animals would become "impossible."[14] Since he anticipated that this deeper understanding was close at hand, he saw no need to pursue animal rights: once people valued all life, appeals not to violate the "rights" of animals or humans would become redundant.[15]

The supposed ethical superiority of this "true," holistic science over the so-called science of materialism is reminiscent of Saint Paul's advice to shun "oppositions of science, falsely so called: which some professing have erred concerning the faith."[16] For Oldfield, all knowledge could be tested against an ethical standard (specifically, a Christian ethical standard). In claiming, "That which is true in the light of science can never be opposed to the ethical law, and that which is contrary to ethics can never be aught else than a scientific blunder," his point was not that scientific findings ought to be made to conform to doctrinal preconceptions, but that *scientia*, or knowledge, could not properly be so called unless it was conducive to moral and spiritual development. Because, he wrote, "the world [is] governed by cosmic law instead of chaotic chance, we shall know that science and ethics can never be in antagonism."[17]

Because the cosmic law was laid down by the Creator, it followed that it could not be fully comprehended from studying the material world in isolation. Science and religion were complementary, and reliance on either

---

[12] On the history of the fin de siècle's "thousand movements," see Alex Owen, *The Place of Enchantment: British Occultism and the Culture of the Modern* (Chicago: University of Chicago Press, 2004).

[13] Josiah Oldfield, *The Claims of Common Life, or the Scientific Relations of Humans and Nonhumans* (London: Ideal Publishing Union, n.d.), 72.

[14] Oldfield, *Claims of Common Life*, 70–71.

[15] Oldfield, *Claims of Common Life*, 43.

[16] Tim. 6:20–21.

[17] Oldfield, *Claims of Common Life*, 6.

alone was insufficient. Indeed, Oldfield blamed many of the early twentieth century's problems on the two being inadequately integrated, the pendulum having merely swung in the opposite direction, with dogmatic science having replaced dogmatic religion.[18] The import of statements such as "the truest scientist is the one who comprehends most clearly the whole working of the laws of the universe, and who consciously puts himself and his work into harmony with the umbra and the adumbration of the cosmic forces" was that complex systems cannot always be explained in purely materialistic terms.[19] There were certainly some life scientists, including notably Alfred Russel Wallace, who thought it necessary to look beyond the material for explanations of phenomena such as the development of intelligence, and according to Oldfield, it was this willingness to accept that "some other power" was at work that characterized exponents of what he rather immodestly called "higher science" and that made them "always reverent in the presence of the mystery of life."[20]

The Order of the Golden Age encouraged its members to approach nature with a sense of awe, eschewing a reductive, materialistic worldview and cultivating a respect for all life that would lead them from the "butchery of the past" to live as "friend[s] of all creation."[21] This latter phrase, which Oldfield got from an admiring correspondent, implies a harmony with the world that is reminiscent of nineteenth-century transcendentalism. Though Oldfield did not claim to be a transcendentalist himself (and seems never to have used the word in print), he was evidently in agreement with the movement's ethos. His was a "nature religion," in which God revealed Himself through the living creation: everyday encounters with a bird building her nest or an animal caring for her young revealed to Oldfield "the glimmer of the holy sunlight peeping through the chinks of Heaven's door," letting him "know that there is a heaven to which all creation is tending."[22] The dynamic process implied by use of the word "tending" was significant: Oldfield thought that carnivorism among animals was as "transient" as it was for humankind, for

---

[18] Oldfield, *Claims of Common Life*, 10.

[19] Oldfield, *Claims of Common Life*, 41.

[20] Oldfield, *Claims of Common Life*, 70; Charles Gross, "Alfred Russell [sic] Wallace and the Evolution of the Human Mind," *Neuroscientist* 16 (2010): 496–507.

[21] Josiah Oldfield, "A Changing World," *Vegetarian World Forum* 6 (1952), accessed December 17, 2016, http://www.ordergoldenage.co.uk/assets/documents/JOachangingworld.pdf.

[22] Josiah Oldfield, "Is There a Heaven?," *Herald of the Golden Age* 12 (1908): 9–10. There are parallels with the "cosmological Catholicism" of Pierre Teilhard de Chardin, of which Oldfield does not seem to have been aware.

whom "refusal to eat of the bodies of the dead" was a step toward a future state when "human conscience would be awakened."[23]

After World War I, during which Oldfield—a pacifist, of course— commanded a medical unit, achieved the rank of lieutenant-colonel, and was decorated for bravery, he scaled down his medical activities, and his main center of practice, a vegetarian convalescent home in Kent known as the Lady Margaret Hospital, became Margaret Lodge Colony, a community where paying guests and children from London's East End slums could enjoy simple living and a meat-free diet. This utopian colony was both a foretaste of the Golden Age and a harking back to the prelapsarian state: nudity and sunbaths were encouraged, and vegetarians "walked with God" as Adam and Eve had in the Garden of Eden.[24] For Oldfield, giving up meat in order to re- store this purer, more natural state was an act of discipline and self-sacrifice, a deliberate decision to "cultivate the angel side"[25] and seek the realm of the spirit rather than be weighed down by indulgence in fleshly appetites. With a self-confidence not uncommon among social reformers of the time, he prophesied that such colonies were the heralds of a vegetarian revolution, at least among the educated, and that vegetarianism would prevail in time, ex- cept among "the lower classes and . . . the unimaginative-minded."[26] He was confident that vegetarianism was healthy—he lived to be ninety years old and attributed his own longevity to it—but vegetarianism's supposed benefits to society were what he valued most: by lessening the suffering of their fellow creatures through reducing animal slaughter, vegetarians were helping hu- manity along a "higher pathway."

According to Oldfield, the dominion over animals granted to humankind in Genesis 1 was intended to be exercised with mercy. He used the parable of the unmerciful servant (Matt. 18:21–35), in which a forgiven debtor has another servant imprisoned for failing to repay a smaller debt, to show that Christians should express their gratitude for God's mercy by being mer- ciful in turn to those, including animals, who are weaker than themselves. Likewise, while he did not dispute that "God has given man the right to take away the life of an animal," he maintained that it was a right to be used spar- ingly and with due regard for one's moral character.[27] Killing vermin, for

[23] Josiah Oldfield, "The Mystery of Ministry," *Herald of the Golden Age* 16 (1913): 145–46.
[24] Josiah Oldfield, "Humaneness Put to the Test," *Herald of the Golden Age* 11 (1909): 130–31.
[25] Editorial, "Cultivate the Angel Side," *Universal Republic* 21 (1906): 621.
[26] Josiah Oldfield, quoted in *Good Health* 42 (1907): 157.
[27] Josiah Oldfield, "But Who Slew All These?," *Herald of the Golden Age* 6 (1901): 16–17.

example, was permissible out of necessity but ought not to be enjoyed as a sport, and any killing at all was best avoided by those committed to the advancement of the Golden Age.[28]

Part of the rationale behind Oldfield's call for Christians to be gentle in their treatment of animals was his understanding of animal suffering as a reflection of, or even contributory to, the sufferings of Christ. He wrote, for example, of the "*via dolorosa*" of cattle on their way to slaughter,[29] and by calling the killing of animals for meat "this tremendous sacrifice," he linked it not only to Christ's sacrifice but also to the animal sacrifices offered in the temple, suggesting that because the commemoration of Christ's sacrifice had, for Christians, superseded blood offerings, it had thus been made on behalf of animals as well as humans.[30] The institution of the Eucharist not only spared animals from being ritually killed but also shifted the focus of human devotion from a sacrifice of flesh to one of the spirit, by which "the demands of the spirit were made plain to the very materialist, and the feast of the *agape* was substituted for the sorrows of the blood stained altar."[31] The commemorative offering of bread and wine at the Eucharist was thus an epoch-making change in the course of human religious development—a permanent, "mystic reminder for all after days that bloodshedding and cruelty are fleeting and are transient but that Mercy and Self-Sacrifice are permanent and are eternal."[32] Oldfield claimed that the inherent impermanence of the blood sacrifice was foreshadowed in the Old Testament, for example, in Psalms 50 and 51, where the Lord asks, "Thinkest thou that I will eat bulls' flesh: and drink the blood of goats?" and states that He "delighteth not in burnt offering."[33]

Oldfield argued that "it is not an answer to the claims of the humanitarian prophet to say that animals were *sent* for man's use, or were *created* for his pleasure," because such treatment of them was a transient phase that those seeking spiritual maturity must leave behind: " 'Glory to God in the Highest'

[28] Josiah Oldfield, "The Lust of Bloodshed," *Herald of the Golden Age* 6 (1901): 76–77. Here Oldfield obviously opposes utilitarianism, which obliges those who must kill animals to take pleasure in doing so, or at least does not discourage it.

[29] Josiah Oldfield, *A Groaning Creation* (London: Ideal Publishing Union, n.d.), 43. On linguistic parallels between religious sacrifice and vivisection, see Lloyd G. Stevenson, "Religious Elements in the Background of the British Anti-vivisection Movement," *Yale Journal of Biology and Medicine* 29 (1956): 125–57.

[30] An idea later taken up by, among others, Ethel Douglas Hume, in *Christianity and Animal Sacrifice* (London: LPAVS, n.d.).

[31] Josiah Oldfield, "The Imitation of the Divine," *Herald of the Golden Age* 2 (1897): 14–15.

[32] Oldfield, "The Imitation of the Divine."

[33] Pss. 50:13, 51:16; cf. Isa. 1:11.

can only be given when the Divine lesson of God's compassion to men is imitated by men to their dependents."[34] Christians were called to follow the example of the "Good Shepherd" in their treatment of animals, not some "godly butcher"—provided, that is, they accepted Oldfield's assertion that the saving work of Christ embraced the whole of animal creation:

> Every bleeding lamb can lay its poor little hoof upon the Bible page and can lift its gentle eyes to the butcher's face and claim its heritage from the Master's words. Christ's words belong as much to the dying lamb as to the butchering man ... to Him the lesson from the lamb was one of mercy and compassion.[35]

Ending slaughter and, by doing so, initiating the reign of peace were goals that would take time and effort to achieve. An important aspect of Oldfield's theology was the idea of the "groaning creation," a phrase he used in the title of a book on animal ethics published early in his career. The term was meant to signify the process of development necessary to bring about the messianic kingdom, a spiritual gestation that was hampered by, among other things, humans' attachment to cruelty and meat-eating and their overly mechanistic view of animals as "mere machines."[36]

The image of a groaning creation was, of course, taken from Saint Paul's letter to the Romans, where he likened the sufferings of the present time to labor pains preceding the coming of the kingdom: "we know that the whole creation groaneth and travaileth in pain together until now."[37] In the same chapter, Paul wrote of the need to struggle against the flesh in order to free the spirit, because "the carnal mind is enmity against God."[38] The flesh/spirit dichotomy was crucial to Oldfield, who wrote that "the battle of all time has been a contest between the material and the spiritual"; he viewed his insight as a young man that "God is a Spirit" as a personal "Mount Everest of revelation" that defined his future philosophy.[39]

In Romans, the term "flesh" can be interpreted as standing for both materialistic thinking and physical indulgence. Oldfield took it somewhat more literally, as an indication that the consumption of flesh meat was itself a

---

[34] Oldfield, "The Imitation of the Divine."
[35] Josiah Oldfield, "Thoughts Are Things," *Herald of the Golden Age* 6 (1901): 26–27.
[36] Oldfield, *Groaning Creation*, 3, 9.
[37] Rom. 8:22.
[38] Josiah Oldfield, "The Field of Ardath," *Herald of the Golden Age* 9 (1904): 19–20.
[39] Oldfield, "The Field of Ardath."

hindrance to spiritual development.[40] A favorite text of his was the some-what obscure 2 Esdras 9:24: "Go into a field of flowers, where no house is builded, and eat only the flowers of the field; taste no flesh, drink no wine, but eat flowers only; And pray unto the Highest continually, then will I come and talk with thee." It was to this fruitarian field of abstinence that Oldfield called his readers, with the promise of wisdom to be gained there: "who would approach nearer to the gate, and who would learn the mysteries of the beyond . . . come unto the field of Ardath and eat no food of slaughtered things."[41]

In describing the pleasures of the messianic kingdom, Oldfield was at his most eloquent:

> When the battle is over and the victory of Christ is won, the dog shall lick the vivisector's hand, for he shall no more torture, and the lamb shall frolic round the blouse of a butcher, for he shall no more torture, and the bird shall rest upon the sportsman's shoulder, for neither shall he torture any more. The sorrow and the sighing of creation shall be done away with, and the love which flows from higher God to lower man, and from higher man to lower animals, shall find its power to bring in the age of Peace and the age of Gold.[42]

The accomplishment of the peaceable kingdom, inaugurated by the death and resurrection of Christ, would occur in the fullness of time through inspired human action; in the interim, while human and animal suffering continued, Christians had the promise of recompense in the life to come.[43] Indeed, the sheer quantity of suffering in the world was such that without the prospect of some future good, the claim that "GOD IS LOVE" would be, wrote Oldfield, "a gaunt lie, a staring skeleton of hypocrisy."[44] Only the confidence that "there will be a future life for every one of us, or that both a past and future connect this little span of life, and unite it into the perfection of a great whole,"[45] made it possible for Christians to declare that the world was under the control of a loving God. Oldfield felt strongly that the promise of life to come must include animals as well as humans. During a visit to a "vivisection

---

[40] Oldfield, "Imitation of the Divine."
[41] Oldfield, "The Field of Ardath."
[42] Oldfield, "Field of Ardath."
[43] Josiah Oldfield, "Are Animals Immortal?," *Herald of the Golden Age* 3 (1898): 134–35.
[44] Oldfield, "Are Animals Immortal?"
[45] Oldfield, "Are Animals Immortal?"

prison," he was deeply moved by the cries of the suffering creatures, which seemed to "tell [him] more forcibly than words can speak, that they, too, have a future of recompense."[46] Since it was inconceivable to him that a compassionate God would allow these caged dogs and cats to know nothing other than brief lives of torment in a laboratory, he was convinced they were destined for a better existence.

Oldfield's obviously heartfelt sympathy for suffering animals may seem to have led him astray into sentimentality and wishful thinking on this point, but his conception of the state awaiting animals was far from any sort of Christian heaven where their immortal souls would enjoy a state of eternal bliss. What Oldfield envisaged was more akin to the Eastern concept of rebirth, with which he was familiar from his travels in India, where he had become convinced that by "understanding the continuity of all life, we shall be able to understand something more of the universal Love of God, a love not restricted to a few creatures called men, but widely extended to all His creation."[47] What survived of animals would be a continuing, common life force rather than distinct, individual souls: Oldfield called it the "banyan tree solution—the stretching out into the infinite and getting into touch again with the great fountain mother from which we get our power to live in the flesh."[48]

Oldfield had as much experience as any Westerner with what were then often known collectively as "Eastern religions." He had spent some time in India, according to his own account, living in "a Yogi's cave,"[49] and on his return to England, he acknowledged that in some areas of particular concern to him, Hinduism seemed to have a moral advantage over Christianity: "No Christian priest," he lamented, "prays a prayer for the groaning creation daily done to death in pain and misery."[50] He thought that one reason Christian missions to India tended to fail was that meat-eating missionaries in a predominantly vegetarian country were seen as self-indulgent. Their failure to give up meat suggested that instead of being focused on spiritual matters, they were bound in "stomach servitude" to the world of the flesh.

Notwithstanding his openness to Hindu influences and his doctrinal unorthodoxy, Oldfield remained a practicing Christian throughout his life.

---

[46] Oldfield, "Are Animals Immortal?"

[47] Josiah Oldfield, "Conditional Immortality," *Herald of the Golden Age* 6 (1901): 100–101.

[48] Oldfield, "Conditional Immortality."

[49] "Obituary," *Vegetarian News*, Spring 1953, accessed December 19, 2016, http://www.ordergoldenage.co.uk/page39.html.

[50] Josiah Oldfield, "Caste and Aestheticism," *Herald of the Golden Age* 7 (1902): 3–4.

He had a private chapel constructed in each of his vegetarian colonies and presided over worship there, though the liturgies were predictably unconventional. His practice of addressing God as "Mother of Heaven," because motherhood was as much a representation of the divine essence as fatherhood, would have been a step too far for even the most liberal Anglicans of the day, and the prayer for animals that he wrote for morning office—"that we may bring no pain into their realm, nor wantonly break the golden bowls of life, but may help every gentle creature to live in gracious fulfilment of its own life's mystery"—reads like something from an eco-Christian liturgy for the twenty-first century.[51] Quite apart from these liturgical novelties, his lifestyle—he lived with a woman other than his wife and allegedly fathered several illegitimate children[52]—still would have precluded his holding any office in the Church of England, whose leaders he did not, in any case, count among the more spiritually enlightened thinkers of the age.[53] Dressed on special occasions in the gown and bands proper to his degree as an Oxford doctor of law and known in Margaret Lodge Colony by the Trollopian-sounding title of "Mr. Warden," Oldfield might have been taken for a clergyman, but he remained free to do God's work as he saw it, unfettered by any obligations to doctrinal and social conformity.

In his later years, he entertained ideas of the afterlife—a return to the world soul, a spiritual existence on a higher level, passage "from the human to the angelic through the mystery of death!"[54]—that were not expressly Christian and perhaps were not far from panentheism, which may be a fair description of his mature position. He certainly rejected the doctrine of the physical resurrection, which he thought a logical impossibility because each particle of matter in a living body must pass through countless creatures over the course of the ages, though doubts on this matter were probably not uncommon even among practicing Christians. His own conception of what awaited the faithful after death was, however, quite unorthodox and little different from what he had proposed for animals:

All life is in a constant state of change. Every life is destined to become higher, cleaner and purer. Every life, therefore, passes through many schools

---

[51] Josiah Oldfield, *Myrrh and Amaranth: Two Lectures* (London: Samson Low, Marston, 1905), 32–33.

[52] Dellar, *Josiah Oldfield*, 298.

[53] Josiah Oldfield, "Christian Leaders and Humane Teaching," *Herald of the Golden Age* 6 (1901): 61–62.

[54] Josiah Oldfield, *The Mystery of Death* (London: Rider, 1951), 121.

of training, teaching and purifying. Between each stage there is a period of rest and assimilation. During each such period of rest the "memory" of the "past" is blotted out. . . . Translated into a time sequence, this would mean that each one of us has already had many periods of consciousness which we call "lives."[55]

Though he believed that progress in future lives was dependent on our actions in this one, he did not think that reward or punishment would be brought about through the law of karma. Rather, he attributed such outcomes to the will of the Creator. "I am satisfied," he wrote toward the end of his life, "that the Universe is in the careful control of God."[56] He remained a member of the Church of England until his death and was buried according to its rites.

The key to Oldfield's philosophy might be found in the title of a piece he wrote for the *Herald* in 1889: "thoughts are things."[57] This transcendental affirmation underpinned much of his work, especially that for the Order of the Golden Age: "Immaterial things—thoughts—come first, and then later, material things follow."[58] In other words, in order to improve human and animal lives, one must begin by changing people's way of thinking. In time, as their outlook becomes more holistic and less uncaring and materialistic, both their own sufferings and those of the creatures dependent on them will diminish. By accepting the primacy of the spiritual, we can be freed from the limitations of our baser appetites: "Who then shall dare to limit the scope, or to limit the power of this great thought force, which has been set free in the world, and upon which The Order of the Golden Age has been built?"[59]

Oldfield's aim as a Christian was "mystic kinship of [his] soul with that of the Divine man."[60] His personal faith was worked out through private thought, observation of nature, and emotional sensitivity, and to his position that "thoughts are things" might be added the characteristically new age view that emotions are evidence. He *knew* that meat-eating was

---

[55] Oldfield, *Mystery of Death*, 74–75, 121, 156.
[56] Oldfield, *Mystery of Death*, 171.
[57] Presumably a deliberate allusion to the book by the well-known humorist Prentice Mulford, *Thoughts Are Things* (London: Bell, 1911; first published 1889), which set out the ideas of the transcendentalist New Thought movement.
[58] Oldfield, "Thoughts Are Things," 26–27.
[59] Oldfield, "Thoughts Are Things."
[60] Oldfield, "Thoughts Are Things."

wrong from the strong reaction he experienced when confronted by animal slaughter, and he knew that animals must be part of God's saving plan
because their sufferings in the laboratory could not be in vain; scriptural
study only confirmed intellectually what his feelings told him. Like many
social reformers of the time, he was unashamedly elitist—he liked to refer
to vegetarianism as "aristophagy"—and he thought it incumbent on the
most forward-thinking individuals, among whom he numbered himself,
to lead others toward the messianic kingdom: "we are more truly in harmony with Nature if we copy her efforts towards beauty and harmony, and
peace, and gentleness, and compassion." This utopian optimism was balanced by an acknowledgment that nature, as well as humanity, was yet to be
perfected, and Oldfield exhorted his readers (or followers) to look forward
to what nature would become, not backward at her failings. Implicit in his
view of the natural world as a groaning creation was an understanding that
Christ had redeemed not only humankind but also the animal kingdom
and perhaps the whole of creation, that this redemption was a process
yet to be completed, and that it would be completed only through human
cooperation.[61]

Oldfield never set out to expound a theology of nature but rather sought to
point out how he thought people needed to change in order to bring in a new
and better age: "I am not setting up as a teacher of Theology. It is fitter for me
to learn than to teach, but I am venturing, as a humble student of science, to
point to the great forces that are at work around us and to show whither they
are bearing us."[62] A new age was in prospect, and Christians were called to be
active participants in God's plan to establish the peaceable kingdom on earth,
by working for animal welfare. Nature was not the backdrop to salvation
but was integrally bound up with it, though as yet only an enlightened few
realized "that Nature's laws have an esoteric as well as an exoteric interpretation."[63] Those who understood this could look "through Nature to Nature's
God," and it is perhaps not unreasonable to suggest that in Oldfield's religious
life, he came to see nature as the primary scripture.[64]

[61] Josiah Oldfield, "Facing Backwards," Herald of the Golden Age 6 (1901): 86–87.
[62] Oldfield, "Facing Backwards."
[63] Josiah Oldfield, "From Dust to God," Herald of the Golden Age 10 (1905): 36–38.
[64] William Forsyth, A Sermon Preached at Danville (Peacham, VT: Farley and Goss, 1798), 13. On
nature as the primary scripture in modern theology, see Michael Dowd, Earthspirit: A Handbook for
Nurturing an Ecological Christianity (New London, CT: Twenty-Third, 1991).

Bibliography

Dellar, Rosemary. *Josiah Oldfield: Eminent Fruitarian.* Rainham, UK: Rainmore Books, 2008.

Douglas Hume, Ethel. *Christianity and Animal Sacrifice.* London: LPAVS, n.d.

Dowd, Michael. *Earthspirit: A Handbook for Nurturing an Ecological Christianity.* New London, CT: Twenty-Third, 1991.

Flyer for Lady Margaret Hospital. Reprinted in *South London Press,* August 29, 1904. London Metropolitan Archives A/FWA/C/D330/1.

Forsyth, William. *A Sermon Preached at Danville.* Peacham, VT: Farley and Goss, 1798.

Gross, Charles. "Alfred Russell [*sic*] Wallace and the Evolution of the Human Mind." *Neuroscientist* 16 (2010): 496–507.

"Hospital of St. Francis." London Metropolitan Archives A/FWA/C/D330/1.

"Is It Only a Dream?" Editorial. *Herald of the Golden Age* 1 (1896): 1.

Kean, Hilda. "The 'Smooth Cool Men of Science': The Feminist and Socialist Response to Vivisection." *History Workshop Journal* 40 (1995): 16–38.

"A Medical Sack Race." *British Medical Journal* 2 (1897): 1115–16.

Mulford, Prentice. *Thoughts Are Things.* London: Bell, 1911. First published 1889.

"A New Guild." *Dundee Courier,* July 27, 1882, 3.

"Obituary." *Vegetarian News,* Spring 1953. Accessed December 19, 2016. http://www.ordergoldenage.co.uk/page39.html.

Oldfield, Josiah. "Are Animals Immortal?" *Herald of the Golden Age* 3 (1898): 134–35.

Oldfield, Josiah. "But Who Slew All These?" *Herald of the Golden Age* 6 (1901): 16–17.

Oldfield, Josiah. "Caste and Aestheticism." *Herald of the Golden Age* 7 (1902): 3–4.

Oldfield, Josiah. "A Changing World." *Vegetarian World Forum* 6 (1952). Accessed December 17, 2016. http://www.ordergoldenage.co.uk/assets/documents/JOachangingworld.pdf.

Oldfield, Josiah. "Christian Leaders and Humane Teaching." *Herald of the Golden Age* 6 (1901): 61–62.

Oldfield, Josiah. *The Claims of Common Life, or the Scientific Relations of Humans and Non-humans.* London: Ideal Publishing Union, n.d.

Oldfield, Josiah. "Concerning Butchery and Vivisection." *Herald of the Golden Age* 10 (1905): 59–60.

Oldfield, Josiah. "Conditional Immortality." *Herald of the Golden Age* 6 (1901): 100–101.

Oldfield, Josiah. "Facing Backwards." *Herald of the Golden Age* 6 (1901): 86–87.

Oldfield, Josiah. "The Field of Ardath." *Herald of the Golden Age* 9 (1904): 19–20.

Oldfield, Josiah. "From Dust to God." *Herald of the Golden Age* 10 (1905): 36–38.

Oldfield, Josiah. *A Groaning Creation.* London: Ideal Publishing Union, n.d.

Oldfield, Josiah. "Humaneness Put to the Test." *Herald of the Golden Age* 11 (1909): 130–31.

Oldfield, Josiah. "The Imitation of the Divine." *Herald of the Golden Age* 2 (1897): 14–15.

Oldfield, Josiah. "Is There a Heaven?" *Herald of the Golden Age* 12 (1908): 9–10.

Oldfield, Josiah. "The Lust of Bloodshed." *Herald of the Golden Age* 6 (1901): 76–77.

Oldfield, Josiah. *Myrrh and Amaranth: Two Lectures.* London: Samson Low, Marston, 1905.

Oldfield, Josiah. *The Mystery of Death.* London: Rider, 1951.

Oldfield, Josiah. "The Mystery of Ministry." *Herald of the Golden Age* 16 (1913): 145–46.

Oldfield, Josiah. "Thoughts Are Things." *Herald of the Golden Age* 6 (1901): 26–27.

The Order of the Golden Age: Its Aims, Its Objects and Its Rules. n.p., 1904.

Owen, Alex. *The Place of Enchantment: British Occultism and the Culture of the Modern*. Chicago: University of Chicago Press, 2004.

Stevenson, Lloyd G. "Religious Elements in the Background of the British Anti-vivisection Movement." *Yale Journal of Biology and Medicine* 29 (1956): 125–57.

Thornhill, Mark. *Experiments on Hospital Patients*. London: Hatchards, 1889.

"A Vegetarian Hospital." *Herald of the Golden Age* 1 (1896): 150.

15

Abraham Isaac Kook (1865–1935)

Biblical Ethics as the Basis of Rav Kook's *A Vision of Vegetarianism and Peace*

Idan Breier

This chapter examines the biblical sources Rav Kook adduces in his *A Vision of Vegetarianism and Peace*—texts from diverse volumes written at various periods that reflect disparate perspectives but together constitute the sacred canon of his thought. In addition to discussing the use Rav Kook makes of these biblical sources in support of his arguments, I shall also explore the way they have been understood in classical and modern exegesis, also adducing ancient Near Eastern literature.

Between 1903 and 1904, Harav Abraham Isaac Hacohen Kook published two essays, out of which one of his disciples and colleague, David Cohen (known as the "ascetic rabbi"), extracted sections in order to produce a Hebrew-language collection of the Rav's thought in 1961. Published as *A Vision of Vegetarianism and Peace*, this was translated with additional notes by Jonathan Rubenstein as part of his rabbinical thesis.[1] Most of the sources included in Cohen's collection were written before Kook settled in Palestine. Philosophical rather than halakhic in nature, *A Vision of Vegetarianism and Peace* is the first systematic Jewish treatise on human–animal relations.[2]

---

[1] Unless otherwise stated, all quotations from Rav Kook's writings refer to Avraham Yitzhak Hacohen Kook, *A Vision of Vegetarianism and Peace*, ed. David Cohen (1961), trans. with additional notes by Jonathan Rubenstein in an unpublished rabbinic thesis: http://www.jewishveg.com/AVision ofVegetarianismandPeace.pdf. Biblical quotations are taken from the NSRV.

[2] Michael Yechiel Barilan, "*The Vision of Vegetarianism and Peace*: Rabbi Kook on the Ethical Treatment of Animals," *History of Human Science* 17, no. 4 (2004): 71–73.

Idan Breier, *Abraham Isaac Kook (1865–1935)* In: *Animal Theologians*. Edited by: Andrew Linzey and Clair Linzey, Oxford University Press. © Oxford University Press 2023. DOI: 10.1093/oso/9780197655542.003.0016

Rav Kook and His View of Human–Animal Relations

Rav Abraham Isaac Hacohen Kook was born in 1865 in the Baltic strip of the Russian Empire into a family that combined halakhic erudition with the Lithuanian *musar* movement that stressed human moral conduct founded on ethical discipline. In his youth, he learned primarily at his father's feet, entering a yeshiva at the age of thirteen.[3] Although he received no formal general education, he taught himself the philosophy and science of his day, developing a great interest in both subjects.[4] Living in an age of revolution, when Christian theologians were also producing original work in response to the new schools of thought, he engaged in creative thought, foreseeing the emergence of nationalism, socialism, secularization, and Zionism.[5]

Believing in the progress of the human race, he was fundamentally optimistic with regard to the future of humankind (the prevalent view at the end of the nineteenth century and beginning of the twentieth century in Europe) and also attached great importance to ethics and biblical justice.[6] He perceived humanity to be on the brink of the messianic age and called for individual improvement that would result in collective betterment, considering it vital to apply the standard of divine ethics to the technologically advancing world.[7] In his writings, he made extensive use of Jewish sources—the Hebrew Bible, Mishna, and Talmud, the Kabbalah, and rationalistic

---

[3] Avinoam Rosnak, *Rabbi A. I. Kook* [in Hebrew] (Jerusalem: Zalman Shazar Centre, 2006), 11–12.

[4] Eliezer Schweid, *A History of Modern Religious Philosophy* [in Hebrew] (Tel Aviv: Am Oved, 2006), 4:82.

[5] Yehuda Mirsky, *Rav Kook: Mystic in a Time of Revolution* (New Haven: Yale University Press, 2014), 2; Benjamin Ish-Shalom, *Rav Avraham Itzhak Hacohen Kook: Between Rationalism and Mysticism*, trans. Ora Wiskind-Elper (New York: SUNY Press, 1993), 9.

[6] Carmy, "On Optimism and Freedom," in *Essays on the Thought and Philosophy of Rabbi Kook*, ed. Ezra Gellman (Teaneck, NJ: Fairleigh Dickenson University Press / Cornwall Books, 1991), 114–20; Barilan, "The Vision of Vegetarianism and Peace," 90; Michael Biddiss, "Intellectual and Cultural Revolution, 1890–1914," in *Themes in Modern European History, 1890–1945*, ed. Paul Hayes (London: Routledge, 1997), 83–84.

[7] Lawrence A. Englander, "On Repentance," in *Essays on the Thought and Philosophy of Rabbi Kook*, ed. Ezra Gellman (Teaneck, NJ: Fairleigh Dickenson University Press / Cornwall Books, 1991), 125–28; Barilan, "The Vision of Vegetarianism and Peace," 88; Batya Gallant, "On Spirituality and Law," in Gellman, *Essays on the Thought and Philosophy of Rabbi Kook*, 140; David S. Shapiro, "On World Perspective," in Gellman, *Essays on the Thought and Philosophy of Rabbi Kook*, 196; Tamar Ross, "Immorality, Law, and Human Perception in the Writings of Rav Kook," in *Rabbi Abraham Isaac Kook and Jewish Spirituality*, ed. Lawrence J. Kaplan and David Shatz (New York: New York University Press, 1995), 245–46; Mirsky, *Rav Kook*, 28–29; Alan T. Levenson, *Modern Jewish Thinkers: An Introduction* (Northvale, NJ: Jason Aronson, 2000), 230.

Jewish philosophy.[8] His thought is thus characterized by an antithetical dialectic.[9] Ish-Shalom observes:

> The writings of Rabbi Abraham Isaak Hacohen Kook are a unique phenomenon in the history of Jewish thought. Even for the scholarly and experienced reader, they often seem impenetrable and strange both in content and form. In these two areas ... Rav Kook does not tread the paths broken by his predecessors in Jewish cogitation, whether philosophical, kabbalistic, or Hassidic; his unmethodical style appears figurative and obscure, or lacking an explicit framework of intellectual coordinates. He does not use known philosophical terms or even classical kabbalistic symbolism with any consistency or method, although he was intimately familiar with both realms.[10]

Calls to act compassionately toward the animal kingdom occur only sporadically in Jewish sacred works down the ages.[11] Early-modern European thinkers—from the sixteenth century onward—related to animals in the framework of the Christian ethical system.[12] The British scholars who addressed the issue in the seventeenth and eighteenth centuries founded their arguments on the biblical text, some also being influenced by Indian vegetarian concepts and Greek philosophy.[13] While the latter also cited health reasons, some expressly called for the suffering of animals to be minimized as far as possible.[14]

---

[8] Ish-Shalom, *Kook*, 131–32, 185; Mirsky, *Rav Kook*, 4.

[9] Rosnak, *Kook*, 49, 280; Marvin Fox, "Rav Kook: Neither Philosopher nor Kabbalist," in *Rabbi Abraham Isaac Kook and Jewish Spirituality*, ed. Lawrence J. Kaplan and David Shatz (New York: New York University Press, 1995), 78–87.

[10] Ish-Shalom, *Kook*, ix.

[11] Ronald H. Isaacs, *Animals in Jewish Thought and Tradition* (Northvale, NJ: Jason Aronson, 2000), 57–87; Richard H. Schwartz, *Judaism and Vegetarianism* (New York: Lantern, 2001), 15–32; Zeʾev Levy and Nadav Levy, *Ethics, Emotions and Animals: On the Moral Status of Animals* [in Hebrew] (Tel Aviv: Sifriyat Poalim, 2002), 57–68; Yael Shemesh, "Compassion for Animals in Midrashic Literature and Traditional Biblical Exegesis" [in Hebrew], *Studies in Bible and Exegesis* 8 (2008): 677–99.

[12] Andrew Linzey, *Animal Theology* (Urbana: University of Illinois Press), 20; Tom Regan, "The Rights of Humans and Other Animals," *Ethics & Behavior* 7, no. 2 (1997): 107.

[13] Tristram Stuart, *The Bloodless Revolution: A Cultural History of Vegetarianism from 1600 to Modern Times* (London: Norton, 2007), 13, 19, 32–33, 40–41, 80–81, 97–108.

[14] Daniel A. Dombrowski, *Vegetarianism: The Philosophy behind the Ethical Diet* (Wellingborough, UK: Thorsons, 1984), 19–89.

Rav Kook's Attitude toward Humankind's Primordial State

A Vision of Vegetarianism and Peace is based on the premise that humanity has yet to become perfect in the area of human–animal relations. This vocation is one of the highest ethical callings of human beings, who are required to act in such a way as to reveal the moral aspect imprinted within human nature (Sec. 1, p. 1).[15]

According to Rav Kook, in the natural and original human state depicted in Genesis, God's decree "Let us make humankind in our image, according to our likeness; and let them have dominion over the fish of the sea, and over the fowl of the air, and over the cattle, and over all the wild animals of the earth, and over every creeping thing that creeps upon the earth" (Gen. 1: 26) does not license killing animals for consumption (Sec. 2, 27, pp. 2, 29). Elsewhere, he stresses that human beings must improve the physical and spiritual state of animals and that it is forbidden to exploit or abuse them.[16] In Lights of Holiness, he asserts that despite the superiority of the human over the animal soul, both are hewed from the same life source.[17]

This approach differs from that prevalent in the classical world, which emphasized the disparity between the two realms.[18] In this respect, Rav Kook is closer to the modern scientific view that reads Genesis as demanding that human beings treat animals humanely rather than exploiting their intellectual advantage over the animal world.[19] The idea that human beings must defend weak animals is found as early as the eighth to seventh century BCE; an Assyrian cylinder seal from this time depicts a man fighting a lion to save a lamb.[20]

---

[15] All page citations refer to the pages of the essay.

[16] Avraham Yitzhak Hacohen Kook, Otzrot Harav Kook [The Treasures of Rav Kook] (Rishon le-Tzion, Israel: Yeshivat Hesder Rishon le-Tzion, 2002), 2:507.

[17] Avraham Yitzhak Hacohen Kook, Orot ha-qodesh [Lights of Holiness] (Jerusalem: Shlomo Gilat, 2014), 2:359. For the value of human versus animal life, see Raymond G. Frey, "Animals," in The Oxford Handbook of Practical Ethics, ed. H. Lafollette (Oxford: Oxford University Press, 2005), 176–79.

[18] Stephan R. L. Clark, "Animals," in The Oxford Handbook of Practical Ethics, ed. H. Lafollette (Oxford: Oxford University Press, 2005), 37.

[19] Gerhard von Rad, Genesis: A Commentary (London: SCM, 1964), 58; Claus Westermann, Genesis 1–11: A Commentary, trans. John S. Scullion (London: SPCK), 159–60; Andrew Linzey, Why Animal Suffering Matters: Philosophy, Theology, and Practical Ethics (Oxford: Oxford University Press, 2009), 14–15, 28–29, 37–42; Michael Yechiel Barilan, Human Dignity, Human Rights, and Responsibility: The New Language of Global Bioethics and Biolaw (Cambridge: MIT Press, 2012), 35, 38.

[20] Moshe Weinfeld, Bereishit [Genesis], Olam Hatanach (Tel Aviv: Davidson-Itai, 1993), 23.

. On a number of occasions, Rav Kook maintains that the compassionate attitude human beings are required to demonstrate toward animals is a duty imposed on them by God.[21] He thus discusses the implications of God's creation of the animal kingdom and what responsibility He has placed on human beings in regard to this realm.[22] He adduces biblical proof texts to demonstrate that cruel treatment of animals directly contravenes the divine attributes, given that God exhibits mercy to all His creatures—"The Lord is good to all, and his compassion is over all that he has made" (Ps. 145:9)—and founded the world upon His loving-kindness: "I declare that your steadfast love is established forever; your faithfulness is as firm as the heavens" (Ps. 89:2).[23] The fact that human beings are expected to treat animals humanely (Sec. 2, pp. 2–3) is evident from the primordial world, wherein human beings refrained from eating meat:

> God said, "See, I have given you every plant yielding seed that is upon the face of all the earth, and every tree with seed in its fruit; you shall have them for food. And to every beast of the earth, and to every bird of the air, and to everything that creeps on the earth, everything that has the breath of life, I have given every green plant for food." And it was so. (Gen. 1:29–30)

Not only is this primordial state, in which killing for eating is forbidden, humanity's natural state in the wake of its moral decline (Sec. 2, pp. 2–3), but even within the animal kingdom itself, preying on others is an "uncivilized" habit.[24]

The biblical passage in Genesis emphasizes that it is God who gives vegetation and flora as food to all creatures on the earth. This idea differs from Mesopotamian mythology, according to which human beings were created in order to supply the gods' needs rather than the reverse.[25] In justifying humanity's existence, the gods' demand, "Let him establish lavish food

---

[21] Avraham Yitzhak Hacohen Kook, *Shemona qvatzim* [*The Eight Folios from Unpublished Notes*]; cf. Kook, *Ein ayah: Berakhot* (Jerusalem: Mossad Harav Kook, 1995), 159–60, http://www.daat.ac.il/daat/vl/einayabracot/einayabracot01.pdf.

[22] Linzey, *Animal Theology*, 12, 28.

[23] Gershon Brin, *Tehilim* [*Psalms*] *II:80–89*, Olam Hatanach (Tel Aviv: Davidson-Itai, 1995), 77, 80–89; Arthur Weiser, *The Psalms: A Commentary* (London: SCM, 1971), 827; Leslie C. Allen, *Psalms 101–150* (Waco, TX: Word, 1983), 298; Hans Joachim Kraus, *Psalms 1–59: A Commentary*, trans. Hilton C. Oswald (Minneapolis: Augsburg, 1989), 548

[24] See Kook, *Ein ayah: Berakhot*, 286; von Rad, *Genesis*, 59.

[25] Thorkild Jacobsen, *The Harps That Once . . . : Sumerian Poetry in Translation* (New Haven: Yale University Press, 1987), 155, line 24; Gordon J. Wenham, *Genesis 1–15* (Waco, TX: Word, 1987), 33.

offerings for his fathers, let him provide for their maintenance and be care-
taker of their sanctuaries."[26] In this system, the gods become dependent on
human beings![27] Ancient Near Eastern kings also boasted of feeding the gods
with their generous sacrifices.[28] This view differs essentially from the biblical
theological principle outlined here.

At the same time, some of the mythologies of the lands of the Bible also reflect the idea of a primordial state in which killing for eating is prohibited.[29]
Thus, for example, the ancient Egyptian hymn to Amun-Re states that the
ancients—both humans and animals—subsisted on vegetation: "He who
made herbage for the cattle, and the fruit tree for mankind."[30] The Sumerian
myth of Enki and Ninhursag similarly asserts that even before humanity was
created, no animal preyed on another: "The lion slew not, the wolf was not
carrying off lambs."[31]

Rav Kook thus clearly regarded the primordial state as corresponding to
the account of the world's creation in Genesis, with God in His mercy providing food from the plants and trees and with no live creatures hunting or
killing one another.

On the "Fall" of Humanity and the Temporary License to Eat Meat

Having presented the "Eden" that prevailed immediately following the creation, Rav Kook proceeds to discuss humanity's ethical decline and how this
state is to be addressed. In Rav Kook's view, God originally created human
beings as ethical creatures. This position appears to be based on Qohelet
(Ecclesiastes), in which the sage asserts that human beings, originally moral
and upright, were brought low by their thoughts: "See, this alone I found,
that God made human beings straightforward, but they have devised many

---

[26] Wilfred G. Lambert, "Mesopotamian Creation Stories," in *Imagining Creation*, ed. Markham
Geller and Mineke Schipper (Leiden: Brill, 2007), 54, https://brill.com/view/book/edcoll/978904
7422976/Bej.9789004157651.i-424_003.xml.

[27] Benjamin R. Foster, *The Epic of Gilgamesh* (London: Norton, 2001), 90; Andrew R. George,
The Babylonian Gilgamesh Epic: Introduction, Critical Edition and Cuneiform Texts (Oxford: Oxford
University Press, 2003), 1:518.

[28] Martha T. Roth, *Law Collections from Mesopotamia and Asia Minor* (Atlanta: Scholars Press,
1997), 15, 80.

[29] Westermann, *Genesis*, 162–64.

[30] James B. Pritchard, *Ancient Near Eastern Texts relating to the Old Testament* (Princeton,
NJ: Princeton University Press, 1969), 366.

[31] Jacobsen, *Harps*, 186, lines 15–17.

ABRAHAM ISAAC KOOK (1865–1935) 279

schemes" (Qoh. 7:29).[32] Rav Kook argues that human beings' earthly existence has caused them to forget their pristine nature; being confronted by
multiple situations in which they can sin, they must attempt to withstand the
temptation to do so. God tells Cain following the first murder in human history, "If you do well, will you not be accepted? And if you do not do well, sin is
lurking at the door; its desire is for you, but you must master it" (Gen. 4:7).[33]

For human beings to be guided away from sinking into sin, the ideals to
which they should aspire must be revealed to them gradually.[34] As we shall
see, this idea is central to Rav Kook's thought, with only this process allowing
humans to reach mental and ethical perfection. When they achieve this, a
new era will be ushered in, characterized by the knowledge of God, with
both humanity and the earth renewed (cf. Isa. 54:12–13).[35] Continuing,
Rav Kook cites an additional eschatological vision, according to which after
the forefathers transgressed and were punished by the destruction of the
First Temple, their offspring would observe God's commandments (cf. Jer.
31:32).[36]

According to Rav Kook, as of now, however, human beings are still far from
this perfect state, as demonstrated, *inter alia*, by their desire for meat (Deut.
12:20).[37] This weakness is the reason the Pentateuch temporarily permits this
act—under certain conditions.[38] The Torah license follows a similar "accommodation" after Noah and his sons' departure from the ark:

God blessed Noah and his sons, and said to them, "Be fruitful and multiply,
and fill the earth. The fear and the dread of you shall rest on every animal

[32] See Haggai Londin, "The Composition *A Vision of Vegetarianism and Peace*" [in Hebrew], in
*R. A. I. Kook, A Vision of Vegetarianism and Peace: Human-Animal Relations in Our Days in the
Eschaton*, edited by Haggai Londin (Eli: Machon Binat Hatorah, 2009), 47; Coon-Leong Seow,
Ecclesiastes: A New Translation with Introduction and Commentary (New York: Doubleday, 1997),
106; Roland E. Murphy, *Ecclesiastes* (Dallas: Word, 1992), 77; Antoon Schoors, *Ecclesiastes*, Historical
Commentary on the Old Testament (Leuven: Peeters, 2013), 587.
[33] See von Rad, *Genesis*, 101; Westermann, *Genesis*, 300.
[34] Kook, "Vision," Sec. 3, pp. 3–4. Cf. Andrew Linzey, "The Bible and Killing for Food," in *The
Animal Ethics Reader*, 2nd ed., ed. Susan J. Armstrong and Richard G. Botzler (London: Routledge,
2008), 289.
[35] Claus Westermann, *Isaiah 40–66: A Commentary* (London: SCM, 1966), 277–78; Shalom M.
Paul, *Isaiah 40–66: A Commentary* [in Hebrew], Mikra Leyisra'el (Jerusalem: Magnes; Tel Aviv: Am
Oved, 2008), 389–90; John Goldingay and David Payne, *Isaiah 40–55* (Edinburgh: T&T Clark,
2006), 2:356.
[36] Robert P. Carroll, *Jeremiah: A Commentary* (Philadelphia: Westminster, 1986), 611–12; Gerald
L. Keown, Pamela J. Scalise, and Thomas G. Smothers, *Jeremiah 26–52* (Dallas: Word, 1995), 131;
William McKane, *Jeremiah* (Edinburgh: T&T Clark, 1986, 1996), 2:827; Jack R. Lundbom, *Jeremiah
21–36: A New Translation with Notes and Commentary* (New York: Doubleday, 2004), 465–66.
[37] Schwartz, *Judaism and Vegetarianism*, 4.
[38] Kook, *Berakhot*, 253.

of the earth, and on every bird of the air, on everything that creeps on the ground, and on all the fish of the sea; into your hand are they delivered. Every moving thing that lives shall be food for you; and just as I gave you the green plants, I give you everything. Only, you shall not eat flesh with its life, that is, its blood." (Gen. 9:1–4)[39]

Modern commentators note that this limitation may have been intended to remind human beings that life is in God's hands.[40] Although the moral decline appears to have begun as early as Adam and Eve, in the wake of the eating from the tree of knowledge, Rav Kook highlights the deterioration by citing the fact that "the inclination of the human heart is evil from youth" (Gen. 8:21) (Sec. 14, p. 15).[41]

According to Rav Kook, this moral decline led to the relationship human beings now have with the animal kingdom and with one another as nations. In order to demonstrate the "banality of evil," he cites a verse from Job that illustrates the human proclivity toward sin, which has become a normal activity on a par with drinking: "How much less [God puts His trust in] one who is abominable and corrupt, one who drinks iniquity like water!" (Job 15:16).[42] Eliphaz's words to Job here may be based on a proverb prevalent during that period that reflects the pessimism of Babylonian theodicy: "And goddess Mani, the queen who fashioned them, gave twisted speech to the human race."[43]

According to Rav Kook, as long as human bloodshed continues to exist, humans require great ethical and mental resources to treat the animal kingdom properly and completely refrain from killing its members. These faculties being limited, they must be channeled first and foremost into improving interpersonal relations:

[39] For the principle of condescension or accommodation (*synkatabasis*)—i.e., God's adjustment of Himself and His standards to the human level—see Francois Dreyfus, "Divine Condescension as a Hermeneutical Principle of the Old Testament in Jewish and Christian Tradition," *Immanuel* 19 (1984–85): 74–86; Stephen Benin, *The Footprints of God: Divine Accommodation in Jewish and Christian Thought* (Albany: SUNY Press, 1993).

[40] Von Rad, *Genesis*, 126; Wenham, *Genesis*, 192–93; Linzey, "Bible," 288.

[41] Weinfeld, *Genesis*, 63. For a similar attitude within Christianity, see Richard Sorabji, *Animal Minds and Human Morals: The Origins of the Western Debate* (Ithaca, NY: Cornell University Press, 1993), 198.

[42] Marvin H. Pope, *Job: Introduction, Translation, and Notes* (New York: Doubleday, 1973), 116; Norman C. Habel, *The Book of Job: A Commentary* (Philadelphia: Westminster, 1985), 256–57; David J. A. Clines, *Job 1–20* (Dallas: Word, 1989), 353.

[43] Pritchard, *Ancient Near Eastern Texts*, 604; Jacob Klein and Shin Shifra, *In Those Distant Days: Anthology of Mesopotamian Literature in Hebrew* [in Hebrew] (Tel Aviv: Am Oved, 1996), 575.

There is no doubt that if the prohibition of the killing of animals was made known as a religious and moral pronouncement issuing from the untainted sensibility of divine justice, whose nature it is to radiate out to all creatures and to instill the recognition that the holiness of God's gifts suffices all living beings, and all humanity—[if this prohibition were in force] while at the same time the general moral condition were still impaired, and the spirit of impurity had not yet passed from the world, there is no doubt that this circumstance would result in many impediments [to spiritual progress]. (Sec. 6, p. 7 [brackets in original])[44]

When human relations are perfected, human relations with the animal world will immediately be affected (Sec. 27, pp. 29–30). In the future, animals as well as human beings will become more moral and ethical, ceasing to hunt and prey on one another—as in the picture Isaiah paints of the eschaton: "And the cow and the bear shall graze, their young shall lie down together; and the lion shall eat straw like the ox" (Isa. 11:7). Some commentators argue that animals will thus return to their "primordial" state.[45] Others, however, view this ideal as an allegory of interpersonal and international relations.[46] Not among the latter, Rav Kook cites Isaiah 30:24 to highlight the fact that the food consumed by animals in the future will be more "refined" (Sec. 6, p. 7; Sec. 32, p. 33).[47] After the period of temporary license to eat meat under specific conditions will come a higher era in which the true knowledge of God will fill the earth. In practical terms, this will entail acting justly and compassionately: "Thus says the Lord: Do not let the wise boast in their wisdom, do not let the mighty boast in their might, do not let the wealthy boast in their wealth" (Jer. 9:23). These are the values God wishes to see implemented on earth, manifesting the good He so desires to see in it.[48]

[44] For limited human moral capacities, see Elazar Weinryb, *Problems in Moral Philosophy* [in Hebrew] (Raanana: Open University Press, 2008), 1:20.

[45] Otto Kaiser, *Isaiah 1–12: A Commentary* (Philadelphia; Westminster, 1983), 260; John D. W. Watts, *Isaiah 1–33* (Waco, TX: Word, 1985), 173; Joseph Blenkinsopp, *Isaiah 1–39: A New Translation with Introduction and Commentary* (New York: Doubleday, 2000), 265; Brevard S. Childs, *Isaiah* (Louisville: Westminster John Knox, 2001), 104.

[46] Hans Wildberger, *Isaiah 1–12: A Continental Commentary*, trans. T. H. Trapp (Minneapolis: Fortress, 1991), 480–81.

[47] See Hans Wildberger, *Isaiah 28–39: A Continental Commentary*, trans. T. H. Trapp (Minneapolis: Fortress, 2002), 179; William A. M. Beuken, *Isaiah 28–39*, Historical Commentary on the Old Testament (Leuven: Peeters, 2000), 137.

[48] McKane, *Jeremiah*, 1:213; Leslie C. Allen, *Jeremiah: A Commentary* (Louisville: Westminster John Knox, 2008), 120–21.

In Rav Kook's thought, the eating from the tree of knowledge set human beings on the path toward a mental and moral decline (which was also paralleled in the animal world), leading God to condescend to their weakness and permit them to eat meat. This age will eventually end, however, when human beings attain an ideal existence that restores their primordial state (Sec. 6, p. 6).

How Will This Intermediate Stage Pass?

Rav Kook devotes extensive space to the temporary license to eat meat, propounding that it is a matter of necessity. As God's will, this should not astonish us, because God knows how human history will unfold and guides its paths (Sec. 7, pp. 7–8). In support of this claim, Rav Kook offers as evidence numerous verses from Isaiah, such as "Who has performed and done this, calling the generations from the beginning? I, the Lord, am first, and will be with the last" (Isa. 41:4).[49]

Noting that modern culture has developed too rapidly—his primary reference here apparently being to science and technology—he argues that some fields require a moderate and precisely balanced form of advance. Human ethical progress is one of the areas that must evolve very cautiously and with great love, as Hosea observes: "I drew them with cords of a man, with bands of love; and I was to them as they that take off the yoke from their jaws, and I laid meat before them" (Hos. 11:4 [NASB]). This proof text relates to human relations with the animal kingdom—with the farmer's compassion, patience, and affection for his beasts of labor (which recall the parent–child relationship) serving as a metaphor for God's relations with His creatures.[50]

At the same time, human beings are expected to preserve their ethical and mental superiority over animals, ensuring that they do not become "beasts," by cultivating true self-love, sensuality, and advancement via meeting the demands of the body (Sec. 8, pp. 8–9; Sec. 10, p. 10). They must therefore transcend the level of the masses and develop mentally, enhancing their understanding of divine wisdom (Sec. 9, pp. 9–10). Here, too, Rav Kook cites

---

[49] See Joseph Blenkinsopp, *Isaiah 40–55: A New Translation with Introduction and Commentary* (New York: Doubleday, 2000), 197; Childs, *Isaiah*, 318; Paul, *Isaiah*, 117.

[50] Francis I. Andersen and David N. Freedman, *Hosea: A New Translation with Notes and Commentary* (New York: Doubleday, 1980), 580; Douglas Stuart, *Hosea–Jonah* (Dallas: Word, 1987), 175; Andrew A. Macintosh, *Hosea: A Critical and Exegetical Commentary* (Edinburgh: T&T Clark, 1997), 445.

a metaphorical example in support of his argument: "Do not be like a horse or mule, without understanding, whose temper must be curbed with bit and bridle, else it will not stay near you" (Ps. 32:9). Herein, God cautions human beings that, unlike animals, they are required to comprehend their master's will and rise above the masses who are unable to reach this level.[51]

The intermediate stage of controlled injustice thus helps human beings progress toward the perfect ethical standard. In its original form, creation held out the possibility of an ideal ethical life and perfect standing of the test of judgment (Sec. 10, p. 10). Here, Rav Kook quotes the very first verse of the Bible: "In the beginning when God created the heavens and the earth" (Gen. 1:1). Although modern commentators posit that this presents God as the Creator of the world, Rav Kook understands it as also alluding to another important issue—namely, the attribute of judgment.[52] According to the midrash and *Zohar*, the name "Elohim" in Hebrew refers to the attribute of judgment according to which God determined to create the world. In the end, God also used the attribute of mercy because the world could not sustain the attribute of judgment.[53] According to Rav Kook, however, the world will be able to contain this attribute in the future (Sec. 10, p. 10).

With respect to the way in which creation progresses toward perfection, Rav Kook writes: "And existence is created through such a quality as this, which never ceases to ascend, because it is an endless action."[54] When perfection has been achieved, the rule of the mind will have arrived, in which pure and perfect ethics will prevail. At this point, human beings will have no desire to eat meat (Sec. 12, p. 12).[55] The proof text Rav Kook cites here is Hosea 2:20: "And in that day will I make a covenant for them with the beasts of the field, and with the fowls of the heavens, and with the creeping things of the ground; and I will break the bow and the sword and warfare out of the earth, and will make them to lie down safely." This picture of the eschaton envisions a future covenant between God, human beings, and animals—similar to that made after the Flood (Gen. 8:8, 11). Recalling the story of creation (Gen.

---

[51] Cf. Weiser, *Psalms*, 286; Peter C. Craigie, *Psalms 1–50* (Waco, TX: Word, 1983), 268. For the low mental level of the masses, see Maimonides, *Guide for the Perplexed*, trans. Michael Friedländer (New York: Cosimo, 2007), 1.4, 17, 28, 33.

[52] See Ephraim A. Speiser, *Genesis: Introduction, Translation, and Notes* (New York: Doubleday, 1964), 8; von Rad, *Genesis*, 47; Westermann, *Genesis 1–11*, 97; Wenham, *Genesis*, 5.

[53] Cf. Genesis Rabbah 12:15; *Zohar* 2, 22b; 3, 302b.

[54] Kook, *Lights of Holiness*, 2.531.

[55] For the link between perfection of mind and ethics, see Weinryb, *Problems in Moral Philosophy*, 1:70.

1:25, 2:19), this idea appears to relate to a return to the primordial state in which no creature is afraid.[56]

According to Rav Kook, the Torah seeks to bring life by illuminating the mind and by inculcating pure divine ethics (Sec. 12, p. 12). In *Lights of Holiness* (3.19), he states that the mind and morality are intertwined, and all ethical darkness is thus a mental darkness—wherever wickedness exists, there also is folly. In the future, when human beings' minds are illuminated, morality will thus be pure and polished like precious stones. Here, Rav Kook adduces the description of Jerusalem in Isaiah 54:12–14 (Sec. 13, p. 13) as built out of such jewels, a passage that indicates that the change that will occur in the eschaton will be behavioral as well as physical.[57]

In order to illustrate the coming of the age of wisdom and morality, he also cites a verse from Canticles (Song of Songs), in which the perfect beloved (representing ethics) asks the beloved maiden (the people of Israel) to open the door for him (Cant. 5:2) (Sec. 14, p. 16).[58] He supports the argument that perfect morality will be achieved by appealing to Isaiah 35:5: "Then the eyes of the blind shall be opened, and the ears of the deaf shall be unstopped"— which also makes use of a metaphor to point to the age of wisdom.[59] In light of the importance of the idea, he also cites Ezekiel's statement that human hearts of stone (a symbol of obtuseness) will be replaced by hearts of flesh (representing compassion) (Ezek. 11:19) (Sec. 17, p. 20).[60] In the future state, human beings will not harm animals because God's compassion will rule over all things: "The Lord is good to all, and his compassion is over all he has made" (Ps. 145:9).[61]

The intermediate stage in which human beings are allowed to eat meat under certain conditions is thus a necessary step along the way to achieving the future world, in which a pure mind and pure ethics will rule.

---

[56] Andersen and Freedman, *Hosea*, 280; Stuart, *Hosea–Jonah*, 58; Ze'ev Weismann, *Trei asar [Twelve Minor Prophets]*, Olam Hatanach (Tel Aviv: Davidson-Itai, 1994), 1:36.

[57] Westermann, *Isaiah 40–66*, 277–78; Paul, *Isaiah*, 2:388–89.

[58] Michael Fuchs and Jacob Klein, *Shir hashirim [Canticles]*, Olam Hatanach (Tel Aviv: Davidson-Itai, 1993), 49; Duane Garrett, *Song of Songs* (Nashville: Thomas Nelson, 2004), 206; J. Cheryl Exum, *Song of Songs: A Commentary* (Louisville: Westminster John Knox, 2005), 192–93.

[59] Blenkinsopp, *Isaiah 1–39*, 457; Kaiser, *Isaiah*, 364.

[60] Gershon Brin, *Yehezkel [Ezekiel]*, Olam Hatanach (Tel Aviv: Davidson-Itai, 1993), 57.

[61] Weiser, *Psalms*, 827; Allen, *Psalms*, 298; Andrew Linzey and Dan Cohn-Sherbok, *After Noah: Animals and the Liberation of Theology* (London: Cassel, 1997), 23.

The Link between the Dietary Laws, Animal Suffering, and Israel's Role

Rav Kook then proceeds to examine the significance of dietary laws in rela-tion to the treatment of animals. He believes that in the flawed reality in which we now live, strict observance of the dietary laws—regarding the method of slaughtering animals and the eating of meat—enables human beings to grad-ually progress toward the eschaton. He notes here that eating carnivores is forbidden lest we come to resemble them (Sec. 13, pp. 13–14). Even when permitted animals are slaughtered, the act must be sanctified (Deut. 12:21)—that is, they must be killed humanely, with their feelings taken into consid-eration and their suffering minimized (Sec. 14, pp. 15–16).[62] In other words, we must not perceive them—as many do today—merely as a consumer product.[63] Indeed, modern research points to the fact that while they have no sophisticated verbal language like human beings in which to express them, animals nonetheless do have feelings.[64] Experts thus maintain that human beings have an ethical duty to treat animals well, because it is immoral to confine ethics to human beings.[65]

Here, Rav Kook cites several biblical verses that demonstrate the human responsibility for treating animals humanely:

> When an ox or a sheep or a goat is born, it shall remain seven days with its mother, and from the eighth day on it shall be acceptable as the Lord's of-fering by fire unto the Lord. But you shall not slaughter, from the herd or the flock, an animal with its young on the same day. (Lev. 22:27–28) (Sec. 14)

[62] For the human lack of understanding of animals' feelings, see Steven M. Wise, "Animal Rights, One Step at a Time," in *Animal Rights: Current Debates and New Directions*, ed. Cass R. Sunstein and Martha C. Nussbaum (Oxford: Oxford University Press, 2004), 19–50; James Rachels, "The Basic Argument for Vegetarianism," in *The Animal Ethics Reader*, ed. Susan J. Armstrong and Richard G. Botzler (London: Routledge, 2008), 260–67.

[63] Peter Singer, *Practical Ethics*, 2nd ed. (Cambridge: Cambridge University Press, 1993), 63, 133; Margo DeMello, *Animals and Society: An Introduction to Human-Animal Studies* (New York: Columbia University Press, 2012), 130, 133; Nik Taylor, *Humans, Animals, and Society: An Introduction to Human-Animal Studies* (New York: Lantern, 2013), 54.

[64] Jeffrey Moussaieff Masson and Susan McCarthy, *When Elephants Weep: The Emotional Lives of Animals* (New York: Delacorte, 1995), 4–16; Marc Bekoff, *The Emotional Lives of Animals: A Leading Scientist Explores Animal Joy, Sorrow, and Empathy—and Why They Matter* (Novato, CA: New World Library, 2007), 5–82; Carl Safina, *Beyond Words: What Animals Think and Feel* (New York: Henry Holt, 2015), 34, 54.

[65] Lori Gruen, *Ethics and Animals: An Introduction* (Cambridge: Cambridge University Press, 2011), 75; Tony Milligan, *Animal Ethics: The Basics* (London: Routledge, 2015), 100–101, 118.

If you come on a bird's nest in any tree or on the ground, with fledglings or
eggs, with the mother sitting on the fledglings or on the eggs, you shall not
take the mother with the young. Let the mother go, taking only the young
for yourself, in order that it may go well with you and you may live long.
(Deut. 22:6–7) (Sec. 14)[66]

The importance of the biblical ordinance in Leviticus is evident in light of
modern practice, industrial farming and factory farms removing the young
from their mothers at a very early age.[67] Current scholars also note that animal young need to stay with their mothers in the same way as human babies
do.[68] With respect to the precept in Deuteronomy, while some scholars argue
that it derives from consideration of animal feelings, others maintain that it is
designed to preserve the biological species.[69]

According to Rav Kook, the temporary license the Torah gives for eating
meat is for nutritional reasons alone, not to satisfy voracity. This is the rationale behind the prohibition against eating *helev*—a part of the animals'
fat (Lev. 7:23). In relation to the blood of the animals slaughtered, he notes
that the express ordinance pertaining to leaving the blood of a domesticated
animal is meant to make human beings feel disgust over the act of killing
the animal, thus prompting them to act morally (Deut. 12:21–24). With regard to birds or other animals abandoned in the field, their blood must be
covered over first and foremost due to shame (Lev. 17:13–14) (Secs. 16–17,
pp. 18–20).

Rav Kook also discusses the exploitation of animal "property"—milk,
wool, and so on. Here, he stresses that the fat is meant for newborn babies,
and it is thus forbidden to steal it (Secs. 19–21, pp. 21–24).[70] This is the reason
the Torah prohibits the cruel act of cooking a kid in his or her mother's milk

[66] Gerhard von Rad, *Deuteronomy: A Commentary*, 2nd ed., OTL (London: SCM, 1973), 141; John
E. Hartley, *Leviticus* (Dallas: Word, 1992), 362; Jacob Milgrom, *Leviticus 17–22: A New Translation
with Introduction and Commentary* (New York: Doubleday, 2000), 183–84; Milgrom, *Leviticus: A
Book of Ritual and Ethics*, Continental Commentaries (Minneapolis: Fortress, 2004), 273; Linzey and
Cohn-Sherbok, *After Noah*, 23–24.
[67] Rachels, "Basic Argument," 877.
[68] Isabel Gay and A. Bradshaw, "Not by Bread Alone: Symbolic Loss, Trauma, and Recovering
Elephant Communities," *Society and Animals* 12, no. 2 (2004): 151.
[69] See von Rad, *Deuteronomy* (London: SCM, 1973), 141; Richard D. Nelson, *Deuteronomy: A
Commentary*, OTL (Louisville: Westminster John Knox, 2002), 268.
[70] Cf. also Kook, *Otzrot*, 2:97. For this phenomenon in factory farming, see David DeGrazia,
"Meat-Eating," in *The Animal Ethics Reader*, ed. Susan J. Armstrong and Richard G. Botzler
(London: Routledge, 2008), 220.

(Exod. 23:19; Deut. 14:21).[71] Some attach a different significance to this ordinance, however.[72]

Rav Kook also relates to the dietary restriction against eating carcasses—that is, the flesh of animals who have died without human intervention—and animals killed by other animals, asserting that these prohibitions are based on the idea of compassion. Rather than partaking of the same barbarity as animals and enjoying or exploiting their weakness (Exod. 22:30; Deut. 14:21), human beings must have mercy on them in their suffering (Sec. 26, pp. 28–29).

By observing the Torah's dietary commandments in relation to animals, the people of Israel can raise themselves to a higher ethical and moral level, thereby fulfilling their calling to be a holy people set apart for God (Deut. 14:2–3).[73] Israel's exemplary ethical behavior will prompt other nations to value the ordinances instituted by God and adopt them:

> You must observe them diligently, for this will show your wisdom and discernment to the peoples, who, when they hear all these statutes, will say, "Surely this great nation is a wise and discerning people!" For what other great nation has a god so near to it as the Lord our God is whenever we call to him? And what other great nation has statutes and ordinances as just as this entire law that I am setting before you today? (Deut. 4:6–8) (Sec. 28, pp. 30–31)[74]

In order to illustrate this idea more clearly, Rav Kook presents Isaiah's eschatological picture of Israel's redemption in terms of a torch lighting the way (Isa. 62:1) (Sec. 25, pp. 27–28).[75] He nonetheless reiterates that due to the present state of humanity, human beings must progress gradually rather than attempting to make a great leap—whereby they would never gain moral perfection. In this spirit, he offers the words of Qohelet: "Do not be too righteous, and not act too wise; why should you destroy yourself?" (Qoh. 7:16). In other words, human beings must avoid the pride that comes from feeling

---

[71] Brevard S. Childs, *Exodus: A Commentary* (London: SCM, 1974), 486; Cornelis Houtman, *Exodus*, Historical Commentary on the Old Testament (Leuven: Peeters, 2000), 3:272.

[72] Duane L. Christensen, *Deuteronomy 1:1–21:9* (Nashville: Thomas Nelson, 2001), 293; Nelson, *Deuteronomy*, 181.

[73] Nelson, *Deuteronomy*, 178.

[74] Moshe Weinfeld, *Deuteronomy 1–11: A New Translation with Introduction and Commentary* (New York: Doubleday, 1991), 65.

[75] Joseph Blenkinsopp, *Isaiah 56–66: A New Translation with Introduction and Commentary* (New York: Doubleday, 2003), 235; Paul, *Isaiah*, 2:501.

that they are already perfect, which makes them stop fearing God and become hypocritical.[76] They must first correct their ethical failings in regard to their own interpersonal relations. Here, Rav Kook appeals to biblical verses that call for social justice based on observance of the commandments (Deut. 15:4).[77] To illustrate this idea, he adduces another metaphor, this time Isaiah's portrayal of the redeemed returning to Zion as God's flock, whom God guides with infinite mercy and compassion: "They shall not hunger or thirst, neither scorching wind nor sun shall strike them down, for he who has pity on them will lead them, and by springs of water will guide them" (Isa. 49:10).

At the end of days, Israel and the entire world will return to their original state (Sec. 29, p. 31), the nations living in harmony and peace: "They shall beat their swords into plowshares, and their spears into pruning hooks" (Isa. 2:4). At this point in time, human beings shall rise to ethical heights and walk solely in accordance with God's will (Sec. 30, p. 32). Here, too, Rav Kook makes use of a faunal biblical metaphor, in which God is likened to a lion: "They shall go after the Lord, who roars like a lion; when he roars, his children shall come trembling from the west" (Hos. 11:10).[78] When the proper time arrives for the advent of the mental-ethical world, human beings will be able to draw on many more resources to help raise the animal kingdom physically and spiritually (Sec. 31, pp. 32–33).

Conclusion

In this chapter, I have presented the biblical bases upon which Rav Kook's arguments in *A Vision of Vegetarianism and Peace* rest. This work, compiled from Rav Kook's writings by his disciple R. David Cohen, is widely regarded as a broad, innovative philosophical contribution that understands creation as the original ideal state, where God provided food for human beings and animals from trees and plants. Following Adam and Eve's sin, the ensuing moral decline, and the Flood, God allowed human beings to eat meat under certain conditions. Rav Kook grounds his view on verses from Genesis and Psalms that refer to God's mercy, using these to argue that human beings were created upright but then began to sin, with transgression eventually

---

[76] James L. Crenshaw, *Ecclesiastes: A Commentary* (Philadelphia: Westminster, 1987), 141; Fuchs and Klein, *Shir hashirim*, 192–93; Seow, *Ecclesiastes*, 273.

[77] See Christensen, *Deuteronomy*, 313; Nelson, *Deuteronomy*, 195.

[78] James L. Mays, *Hosea: A Commentary* (London: SCM, 1969), 158; Macintosh, *Hosea*, 466.

becoming second nature to them. In a human society in which bloodshed is so prevalent, a complete interdiction against killing animals is impossible. This can be achieved only in the future, when the earth is filled with the knowledge of God and when justice and mercy govern the human and animal worlds. In this area, Rav Kook bases his view on verses from the prophets that have an eschatological tinge. Progress from our present state toward the ideal must be gradual and guided by God, as indicated by verses containing metaphors that liken God to a farmer who takes care of the livestock who depend on him. Rav Kook stresses the Jewish dietary laws and other commandments relating to animals, asserting that they are intended to prevent animal suffering and educate human beings to be considerate of the animal kingdom and animals' feelings. Israel's exemplary conduct in this regard will form the model for the nations of the world to imitate, with all humanity eventually being restored to the ethical and mental level it possessed before the "original sin," when the blood of neither humans nor animals was shed.

Bibliography

Allen, Leslie C. *Jeremiah: A Commentary*. Louisville: Westminster John Knox, 2008.

Allen, Leslie C. *Psalms 101–150*. Waco, TX: Word, 1983.

Andersen, Francis I., and David N. Freedman. *Hosea: A New Translation with Notes and Commentary*. New York: Doubleday, 1980.

Barilan, Michael Yechiel. *Human Dignity, Human Rights, and Responsibility: The New Language of Global Bioethics and Biolaw*. Cambridge, MA: MIT Press, 2012.

Barilan, Michael Yechiel. "The Vision of Vegetarianism and Peace: Rabbi Kook on the Ethical Treatment of Animals." *History of Human Science* 17, no. 4 (2004): 69–101.

Bekoff, Marc. *The Emotional Lives of Animals: A Leading Scientist Explores Animal Joy, Sorrow, and Empathy—and Why They Matter*. Novato, CA: New World Library, 2007.

Benin, Stephen. *The Footprints of God: Divine Accommodation in Jewish and Christian Thought*. Albany: SUNY Press, 1993.

Beuken, William A. M. *Isaiah 28–39*. Historical Commentary on the Old Testament. Leuven: Peeters, 2000.

Biddiss, Michael. "Intellectual and Cultural Revolution, 1890–1914." In *Themes in Modern European History, 1890–1945*, edited by Paul Hayes, 83–105. London: Routledge, 1997.

Blenkinsopp, Joseph. *Isaiah 1–39: A New Translation with Introduction and Commentary*. New York: Doubleday, 2000.

Blenkinsopp, Joseph. *Isaiah 40–55: A New Translation with Introduction and Commentary*. New York: Doubleday, 2000.

Blenkinsopp, Joseph. *Isaiah 56–66: A New Translation with Introduction and Commentary*. New York: Doubleday, 2003.

Brin, Gershon. *Tehilim [Psalms] II:80–89*. Olam Hatanach. Tel Aviv: Davidson-Itai, 1995.

Brin, Gershon. *Yehezkel [Ezekiel]*. Olam Hatanach. Tel Aviv: Davidson-Itai, 1993.

Carmy, Shalom. "On Optimism and Freedom." In *Essays on the Thought and Philosophy of Rabbi Kook*, edited by Ezra Gellman, 114–20. Teaneck, NJ: Fairleigh Dickenson University Press / Cornwall Books, 1991.

Carroll, Robert P. *Jeremiah: A Commentary*. Philadelphia: Westminster, 1986.

Childs, Brevard S. *Exodus: A Commentary*. London: SCM, 1974.

Childs, Brevard S. *Isaiah*. Louisville: Westminster John Knox, 2001.

Christensen, Duane L. *Deuteronomy 1:1–21:9*. Nashville: Thomas Nelson, 2001.

Clark, Stephan R. L. "Animals in Classical and Late Antique Philosophy." In *The Oxford Handbook of Animal Ethics*, edited by Tom L. Beauchamp and R. G. Frey, 35–60. Oxford: Oxford University Press, 2011.

Clines, David J. A. *Job 1–20*. Dallas: Word, 1989.

Craigie, Peter C. *Psalms 1–50*. Waco, TX: Word, 1983.

Crenshaw, James L. *Ecclesiastes: A Commentary*. Philadelphia: Westminster, 1987.

DeGrazia, David. "Meat-Eating." In *The Animal Ethics Reader*, edited by Susan J. Armstrong and Richard G. Botzler, 219–24. London: Routledge, 2008.

DeMello, Margo. *Animals and Society: An Introduction to Human-Animal Studies*. New York: Columbia University Press, 2012.

Dombrowski, Daniel A. *Vegetarianism: The Philosophy behind the Ethical Diet*. Wellingborough, UK: Thorsons, 1984.

Dreyfus, Francois. "Divine Condescension as a Hermeneutical Principle of the Old Testament in Jewish and Christian Tradition." *Immanuel* 19 (1984–85): 74–86.

Englander, Lawrence A. "On Repentance." In *Essays on the Thought and Philosophy of Rabbi Kook*, edited by Ezra Gellman, 121–32. Teaneck, NJ: Fairleigh Dickenson University Press / Cornwall Books, 1991.

Exum, J. Cheryl. *Song of Songs: A Commentary*. Louisville: Westminster John Knox Press, 2005.

Foster, Benjamin R. *The Epic of Gilgamesh*. London: Norton, 2001.

Fox, Marvin. "Rav Kook: Neither Philosopher nor Kabbalist." In *Rabbi Abraham Isaac Kook and Jewish Spirituality*, edited by Lawrence J. Kaplan and David Shatz, 78–87. New York: New York University Press, 1995.

Frey, Raymond G. "Animals." In *The Oxford Handbook of Practical Ethics*, edited by H. Lafollette, 161–87. Oxford: Oxford University Press, 2005.

Fuchs, Michael, and Jacob Klein. *Shir hashirim* [*Canticles*]. Olam Hatanach. Tel Aviv: Davidson-Itai, 1993.

Gallant, Batya. "On Spirituality and Law." In *Essays on the Thought and Philosophy of Rabbi Kook*, edited by Ezra Gellman, 133–44. Teaneck, NJ: Fairleigh Dickenson University Press / Cornwall Books, 1991.

Garrett, Duane. *Song of Songs*. Nashville: Thomas Nelson, 2004.

Gay, Isabel, and A. Bradshaw. "Not by Bread Alone: Symbolic Loss, Trauma, and Recovering Elephant Communities." *Society and Animals* 12, no. 2 (2004): 143–58.

George, Andrew R. *The Babylonian Gilgamesh Epic: Introduction, Critical Edition and Cuneiform Texts*. Vol. 1. Oxford: Oxford University Press, 2003.

Goldingay, John, and David Payne. *Isaiah 40–55*. Edinburgh: T&T Clark, 2006.

Gruen, Lori. *Ethics and Animals: An Introduction*. Cambridge: Cambridge University Press, 2011.

Habel, Norman C. *The Book of Job: A Commentary*. Philadelphia: Westminster, 1985.

Hartley, John E. *Leviticus*. Dallas: Word, 1992.

Houtman, Cornelis. *Exodus*. Vol. 3. Historical Commentary on the Old Testament. Leuven: Peeters, 2000.

Isaacs, Ronald H. *Animals in Jewish Thought and Tradition*. Northvale, NJ: Jason Aronson, 2000.

Ish-Shalom, Benjamin. *Rav Avraham Itzhak Hacohen Kook: Between Rationalism and Mysticism*. Translated by Ora Wiskind-Elper. New York: SUNY Press, 1993.

Jacobsen, Thorkild. *The Harps That Once . . . : Sumerian Poetry in Translation*. New Haven: Yale University Press, 1987.

Kaiser, Otto. *Isaiah 1–12: A Commentary*. Philadelphia: Westminster, 1983.

Keown, Gerald L., Pamela J. Scalise, and Thomas G. Smothers. *Jeremiah 26–52*. Dallas: Word, 1995.

Klein, Jacob, and Shin Shifra. *In Those Distant Days: Anthology of Mesopotamian Literature in Hebrew* [in Hebrew]. Tel Aviv: Am Oved, 1996.

Kook, Avraham Yitzhak Hacohen. *Ein ayah: Berakhot*. Jerusalem: Mossad Harav Kook, 1995. http://www.daat.ac.il/daat/vl/einayabracot/einayabracot01.pdf.

Kook, Avraham Yitzhak Hacohen. *Orot ha-qodesh* [*Lights of Holiness*]. Jerusalem: Shlomo Gilat, 2014. For an abbreviated English text, see *The Lights of Penitence: The Moral Principles, Lights of Holiness, Essays, Letters, and Poems*. Translated by Ben Zion Bokser. New York: Paulist Press, 1978, 189–252.

Kook, Avraham Yitzhak Hacohen. *Otzrot Harav Kook* [*The Treasures of Rav Kook*]. Rishon le-Tzion: Yeshivat Hesder Rishon le-Tzion, 2002.

Kook, Avraham Yitzhak Hacohen. *Shmona qvatzim* [*Eight Folios from the Unpublished Notes*]. Jerusalem: n.p., 1999. For an English translation of some of the text, see http://www.orvishua.org.il/en/?location=torah_insights.

Kook, Avraham Yitzhak Hacohen. *A Vision of Vegetarianism and Peace: The Torah's Point of View*. Edited by David Cohen. Jerusalem: Nezer David, 1983. http://www.jewishveg.com/AVisionofVegetarianismandPeace.pdf.

Kraus, Hans Joachim. *Psalms 1–59: A Commentary*. Translated by Hilton C. Oswald. Minneapolis: Augsburg, 1989.

Lambert, Wilfred G. "Mesopotamian Creation Stories." In *Imagining Creation*, ed. Markham Geller and Mineke Schipper, 15–59. Leiden: Brill, 2007. https://brill.com/view/book/edcoll/9789047422976/Bej.9789004157651.i-424_003.xml.

Levenson, Alan T. *Modern Jewish Thinkers: An Introduction*. Northvale, NJ: Jason Aronson, 2000.

Levy, Ze'ev, and Nadav Levy. *Ethics, Emotions and Animals: On the Moral Status of Animals* [in Hebrew]. Tel Aviv: Sifriyat Poalim, 2002.

Linzey, Andrew. *Animal Theology*. Urbana: University of Illinois Press, 1995.

Linzey, Andrew. "The Bible and Killing for Food." In *The Animal Ethics Reader*, 2nd ed., edited by Susan J. Armstrong and Richard G. Botzler, 286–93. London: Routledge, 2008.

Linzey, Andrew. *Why Animal Suffering Matters: Philosophy, Theology, and Practical Ethics*. Oxford: Oxford University Press, 2009.

Linzey, Andrew, and Dan Cohn-Sherbok. *After Noah: Animals and the Liberation of Theology*. London: Cassel, 1997.

Londin, Haggai. "The Composition *A Vision of Vegetarianism and Peace*" [in Hebrew]. In *R. A. I. Kook, A Vision of Vegetarianism and Peace: Human-Animal Relations in Our Days in the Eschaton*, 19–20. Edited by Haggai Londin. Eli: Machon Binat Hatorah, 2009.

Lundbom, Jack R. *Jeremiah 21–36: A New Translation with Notes and Commentary.* New York: Doubleday, 2004.

Macintosh, Andrew A. *Hosea: A Critical and Exegetical Commentary.* Edinburgh: T&T Clark, 1997.

Maimonides, Moses. *Guide for the Perplexed.* Translated Michael Friedländer. New York: Cosimo, 2007.

Mays, James L. *Hosea: A Commentary.* London: SCM, 1969.

McKane, William. *Jeremiah.* 2 vols. Edinburgh: T&T Clark, 1986.

Milgrom, Jacob. *Leviticus: A Book of Ritual and Ethics.* Continental Commentaries. Minneapolis: Fortress Press, 2004.

Milgrom, Jacob. *Leviticus 17–22: A New Translation with Introduction and Commentary.* New York: Doubleday, 2000.

Milligan, Tony. *Animal Ethics: The Basics.* London: Routledge, 2015.

Mirsky, Yehuda. *Rav Kook: Mystic in a Time of Revolution.* New Haven: Yale University Press, 2014.

Moussaieff Masson, Jeffrey, and Susan McCarthy. *When Elephants Weep: The Emotional Lives of Animals.* New York: Delacorte, 1995.

Murphy, Roland E. *Ecclesiastes.* Dallas: Word, 1992.

Nelson, Richard D. *Deuteronomy: A Commentary.* OTL. Louisville: Westminster John Knox, 2002.

Parpola, Simo, and Kazuko Watanabe, eds. *Neo-Assyrian Treaties and Loyalty Oaths.* State Archives of Assyria 2. Helsinki: Helsinki University Press, 1988. http://oracc.museum.upenn.edu/saao/corpus.

Paul, Shalom M. *Isaiah 40–66: A Commentary* [in Hebrew]. Mikra Leyisra'el. Jerusalem: Magnes; Tel Aviv: Am Oved, 2008.

Pope, Marvin H. *Job: Introduction, Translation, and Notes.* New York: Doubleday, 1973.

Pritchard, James B. *Ancient Near Eastern Texts relating to the Old Testament.* Princeton, NJ: Princeton University Press, 1969.

Rachels, James. "The Basic Argument for Vegetarianism." In *The Animal Ethics Reader*, edited by Susan J. Armstrong and Richard G. Botzler, 260–67. London: Routledge, 2008.

Rad, Gerhard von. *Deuteronomy: A Commentary.* 2nd ed. OTL. London: SCM, 1973.

Rad, Gerhard von. *Genesis: A Commentary.* London: SCM, 1964.

Regan, Tom. "The Rights of Humans and Other Animals." *Ethics & Behavior* 7, no. 2 (1997): 103–11.

Rosnak, Avinoam. *Rabbi A. I. Kook* [in Hebrew]. Jerusalem: Zalman Shazar Centre, 2006.

Ross, Tamar. "Immorality, Law, and Human Perception in the Writings of Rav Kook." In *Rabbi Abraham Isaac Kook and Jewish Spirituality*, edited by Lawrence J. Kaplan and David Shatz, 237–53. New York: New York University Press, 1995.

Roth, Martha T. *Law Collections from Mesopotamia and Asia Minor.* Atlanta: Scholars Press, 1997.

Safina, Carl. *Beyond Words: What Animals Think and Feel.* New York: Henry Holt, 2015.

Schoors, Antoon. *Ecclesiastes.* Historical Commentary on the Old Testament. Leuven: Peeters, 2013.

Schwartz, Richard H. *Judaism and Vegetarianism.* New York: Lantern, 2001.

Schweid, Eliezer. *A History of Modern Religious Philosophy* [in Hebrew]. Tel Aviv: Am Oved, 2006.

Seow, Coon-Leong. *Ecclesiastes: A New Translation with Introduction and Commentary.* New York: Doubleday, 1997.

Shapiro, David S. "On World Perspective." In *Essays on the Thought and Philosophy of Rabbi Kook*, edited by Ezra Gellman, 187–210. Teaneck, NJ: Fairleigh Dickenson University Press / Cornwall Books, 1991.

Shemesh, Yael. "Compassion for Animals in Midrashic Literature and Traditional Biblical Exegesis" [in Hebrew]. *Studies in Bible and Exegesis* 8 (2008): 677–99.

Singer, Peter. *Practical Ethics*. 2nd ed. Cambridge: Cambridge University Press, 1993.

Sorabji, Richard. *Animal Minds and Human Morals: The Origins of the Western Debate*. Ithaca, NY: Cornell University Press, 1993.

Speiser, Ephraim A. *Genesis: Introduction, Translation, and Notes*. New York: Doubleday, 1964.

Stuart, Douglas. *Hosea–Jonah*. Dallas: Word, 1987.

Stuart, Tristram. *The Bloodless Revolution: A Cultural History of Vegetarianism from 1600 to Modern Times*. London: Norton, 2007.

Taylor, Nik. *Humans, Animals, and Society: An Introduction to Human-Animal Studies*. New York: Lantern, 2013.

Watts, John D. W. *Isaiah 1–33*. Waco, TX: Word, 1985.

Weinfeld, Moshe. *Bereishit [Genesis]*. Olam Hatanach. Tel Aviv: Davidson-Itai, 1993.

Weinfeld, Moshe. *Deuteronomy 1–11: A New Translation with Introduction and Commentary*. New York: Doubleday, 1991.

Weinryb, Elazar. *Problems in Moral Philosophy* [in Hebrew]. Raanana: Open University Press, 2008.

Weiser, Arthur. *The Psalms: A Commentary*. London: SCM, 1971.

Weismann, Ze'ev. *Trei asar [Twelve Minor Prophets]*. Olam Hatanach. Tel Aviv: Davidson-Itai, 1994.

Wenham, Gordon J. *Genesis 1–15*. Waco, TX: Word, 1987.

Westermann, Claus. *Genesis 1–11: A Commentary*. Translated by John S. Scullion. London: SPCK, 1984.

Westermann, Claus. *Isaiah 40–66: A Commentary*. London: SCM, 1966.

Wildberger, Hans. *Isaiah 1–12: A Continental Commentary*. Translated by T. H. Trapp. Minneapolis: Fortress, 1991.

Wildberger, Hans. *Isaiah 28–39: A Continental Commentary*. Translated by T. H. Trapp. Minneapolis: Fortress, 2002.

Wise, Steven M. "Animal Rights, One Step at a Time." In *Animal Rights: Current Debates and New Directions*, edited by Cass R. Sunstein and Martha C. Nussbaum, 19–50. Oxford: Oxford University Press, 2004.

16

Mohandas K. Gandhi (1869–1948)

In the Service of All That Lives

Kenneth R. Valpey (Krishna Kshetra Swami)

God demands nothing less than complete self-surrender as the price
for the only real freedom that is worth having. And when a man
thus loses himself, he immediately finds himself in the service of all
that lives. It becomes his delight and his recreation. He is a new man
never weary of spending himself in the service of God's creation.

—Gandhi[1]

Mohandas Karamchand Gandhi became known as Mahatma—"great
soul"—soon after being so designated by Rabindranath Tagore in 1915.
"Mahatma" is a Sanskrit term (*mahātmā*) that appears in the Bhagavad-Gita,
the important scripture of ancient Brahmanical tradition, where it describes
the adept practitioner of devotional spirituality known as *bhakti-yoga*. In this
work, the greatness of such a soul is attributed to his or her inclusiveness, as a
soul that embraces all souls—in whatever form of creature they may live—in
a higher vision of divine relationality. Widespread recognition of Gandhi as
a person who held, or at least effectively pursued, such a vision has endured
well past his lifetime.

And yet with such an exalted reputation, some admirers during his lifetime were occasionally surprised, dismayed, and even angered by some of his
actions and statements that to them appeared counter to what they understood a mahatma to be.[2] Such was the case when, in 1928, Gandhi wrote to an

---

[1] Mohandas Karamchand Gandhi, *Young India*, December 20, 1928, in *The Collected Works of
Mahatma Gandhi* (New Delhi: Publications Division, Ministry of Information and Broadcasting,
Government of India, 1969), 43:417.

[2] In 1926 Gandhi wrote, "They once regarded me as a mahatma, they were glad that my influence
on the people was according to their liking. Now I am an *alpatma* (a little soul) in their opinion; my

Kenneth R. Valpey (Krishna Kshetra Swami), *Mohandas K. Gandhi (1869–1948)* In: *Animal Theologians.*
Edited by: Andrew Linzey and Clair Linzey, Oxford University Press. © Oxford University Press 2023.
DOI: 10.1093/oso/9780197655542.003.0017

acquaintance near his hermitage, "I have a calf here that is suffering terrible pain. It has broken a leg. Now it has developed sores all over the body. The veterinary surgeon has given up all hope. I have therefore decided to have it shot. Please send one of your guards with a gun if possible."[3] Later I will discuss Gandhi's reasoning in this particular decision. Here it suffices to note the apparent tension between Gandhi's self-avowed absolute nonviolence and his practical application of the principle; further, I suggest that the particular sort of virtue ethics Gandhi demonstrated in the course of his own life was integral to his animal ethics. This is a virtue ethics that calls on humans to strive tirelessly to become "great souls" even as it reminds one to be ever aware of one's human failings.

Significantly, for Gandhi this tension and pursuit of nonviolence was borne particularly in the care and protection of cattle. Indeed, cattle care and protection—a practice considered typical of persons who identify as Hindu—may be located centrally in Gandhi's animal theology. I will explore this idea in this chapter, which, more broadly, will attempt to map Gandhi's thought and practice with respect to animals into his overall vision of human flourishing and how this flourishing was to be pursued. To this end, I will draw from Larry Shinn's presentation of the "inner logic" of Gandhi's ecological thinking, consisting of four principles that—I would point out in passing—are foundational to successful classical yoga practice.[4] These principles—namely, *satya*, or truth; *ahiṁsā*, or nonviolence; *tapas*, or austerity; and *svarāj*, or self-governance—form an essential matrix of ideals into which Gandhi invested ethical valuation.

Further, this fourfold foundation of Gandhi's thought positions us to view the contours of what Nancy Martin identifies as a threefold process of ethical decision-making in Gandhi's thought and life.[5] With these tools we may comprehend such an action as the calf-killing incident. More broadly, we can

influence on the people they now regard as unwholesome and they are pained by the discovery; and as they cannot control themselves, they turn the feeling of pain into anger." "Is This Humanity? III," October 24, 1926, in *Collected Works*, 36:426.

[3] Gandhi, letter to Amalal Sarabhai, August 21, 1928, in *Collected Works*, 42:396.

[4] Classical yoga, as presented in Patañjali's *Yoga Sūtras*, lists *ahiṁsā*, *satya*, and *tapas* among five principles of self-restraint (*yama*) and five principles of engagement (*niyama*), which in turn are preliminary prescriptions of self-cultivation, the first two of eight limbs (*aṣṭāṅga*) of yoga discipline. Although *svarāj*, self-governance, is not indicated explicitly within this yoga system's categories of *yama* and *niyama*, it may be taken either as *yama* and *niyama* as a whole, or more broadly, as a key principle behind the entire system of yoga, by which freedom (*kaivalya*) is attained.

[5] Nancy Martin, "Ethics," in *Brill's Encyclopedia of Hinduism*, ed. Knut A. Jacobsen, Helena Basu, Angelika Malinar, and Vasudha Narayanan (Leiden: Brill, 2009), 4:688.

begin to appreciate the breadth and depth of animal care in Gandhi's thought as having implications for the whole range of his vision, a vision for not just human flourishing but world flourishing—a vision of souls realizing their greatness in all their potential of approaching God.

Gandhi's Eco-logic in Four Features

As Shinn shows, there is an interlocking matrix of four principles constituting Gandhi's thought and methodology for fostering human well-being, whereby each principle is nurtured and realized by cultivation of the other three. Among the four, Gandhi considered truth to be the "sovereign," inclusive principle, which he famously equated with God: "But I worship God as Truth only. I have not found him, but I am seeking after him."[6] Truth is understood as a "qualitative and integral dimension of the natural order," a "vital force" that demands a commitment to spiritual practice and moral action to be realized.[7] Such practice and action are summed up in Gandhi's neologism *satyagraha*, which he defined as "the force that is born of Truth and Love or non-violence."[8] To practice *satyagraha* consequently requires a high level of courage. If one is not prepared to "lay down one's life for the sake of truth," one must expect to have to "submit to oppression like the animals."[9]

As we shall see later more fully, Gandhi's distinction between humans and animals was important for him. In particular, the dividing line is the human imperative and capacity to practice nonviolence.[10] "Man as animal is violent but as spirit is non-violent. The moment a man wakens to the spirit within

[6] Gandhi, introduction to *An Autobiography*, in *The Selected Works of Mahatma Gandhi*, ed. Shriman Narayan (Ahmedabad, India: Navajivan, 1968), 1: xxi.

[7] Larry D. Shinn, "The Inner Logic of Gandhian Ecology," in *Hinduism and Ecology: The Intersection of Earth, Sky, and Water*, ed. Christopher Key Chapple (Cambridge, MA: Harvard University Press, 2000), 217–18.

[8] Gandhi, *Selected Works*, 3:151; Gandhi, *Satyagraha in South Africa*, trans. Valji Govindji Desai (Madras: S. Ganesan, 1928), 109–10. Satyagraha (Sanskrit: *satyāgraha*), often translated as "truth force," calls attention to the power of practices rooted in nonviolence to effect transformations. In the context of animal theology, for Gandhi it was the willful, strict observance of a vegetarian or vegan diet that he considered basic to an understanding of proper human–nonhuman relationships.

[9] Gandhi, speech at Kheda, April 6, 1918, in *Collected Works*, 16:395.

[10] Also, importantly, the human/nonhuman distinction relates to the capacity to attain ultimate freedom. "In an animal body, the soul cannot attain to the highest knowledge and cultivate devotion to God. Without these, there can be no freedom for the soul and, so long as the soul has not attained freedom, there cannot be any true happiness and no ending to our real suffering." Gandhi, *Indian Opinion*, August 16, 1913, in *Collected Works*, 11:165.

he cannot remain violent."[11] Violence is, for Gandhi, the "law of the brute," whereas nonviolence is the "law of our species," a higher law, for which "the dignity of man requires obedience to a higher law—to the strength of the spirit."[12] And to the extent one becomes nonviolent, to that extent human beings "become Godlike."[13]

For a person to awaken and sustain a spirit of nonviolence, there must be "self-purification" and "self-rule." Regarding self-purification or "purity of heart," Gandhi insisted on its necessity as the basis for a sense of communion with all living beings, which in turn is required to practice comprehensive nonviolence. In his autobiographical work *The Story of My Experiments with Truth*, Gandhi locates all these connections in God realization:

> Identification with everything that lives is impossible without self-purification; without self-purification the observance of the law of Ahimsa must remain an empty dream; God cannot be realized by one who is not pure of heart. Self-purification therefore must mean purification in all the walks of life. A purification being highly infectious, purification of oneself necessarily leads to the purification of one's surroundings.[14]

By "self-purification," Gandhi generally meant practices of self-denial, especially restriction of diet—to a vegetarian or preferably vegan (though he did not use this latter term) diet—and the observance of fasting in certain contexts. Gandhi considered such purposeful self-control essential to effecting any significant sociopolitical reforms or changes for a better world ("purification of one's surroundings"), and this is the reasoning behind his comment that "all the tendencies present in the outer world are to be found in the world of our body. If we could change ourselves, the tendencies in the world would also change."[15]

[11] Gandhi, quoted in Vithalbhai K. Jhaveri and D. G. Tendulkar, eds., *Mahatma in Eight Volumes*, vol. 5 (Bombay: Jhaveri and Tendulkar, 1952), 392–393.

[12] Gandhi, *Young India*, November 8, 1920, in *Collected Works*, 21:134, quoted in Shinn, "Inner Logic," 219–20.

[13] Gandhi, *Harijan*, December 11, 1938, in *Collected Works*, 74:130, quoted in Shinn, "Inner Logic," 222.

[14] Gandhi, *An Autobiography: The Story of My Experiments with Truth*, trans. Mahadev H. Desai (London: Phoenix Press, 1949), 753, quoted in Shinn, "Inner Logic," 222.

[15] Gandhi, *Collected Works*, 13:241. Apparently, it was this statement that later commentators paraphrased into what would become a slogan attributed to Gandhi: "Be the change you wish to see in the world."

Working hand in hand with self-purification is self-rule (*svarāj*), a concept that includes several levels of understanding, from individual self-rule (in the sense of self-control) to community and village self-rule (in economic and political senses) and up to self-rule of the nation of India (in terms of political and economic independence from Britain). For Gandhi, although "independence" was a highly valued principle, a corollary to self-rule, it presupposed an apparently opposite conception—namely, an assumption of "the continuity and interdependence between humans and the natural world."[16] As we will discuss further on, this interdependent connection is, in Gandhi's view, best realized in the (relatively independent) village. The village is, in this sense, a small but complete universe,[17] where humans interact with and protect domesticated animals, most especially cattle. The basis of self-rule on the village level is conduct of life by simple, minimally technological means. For example, Gandhi is famous for advocating the hand-spinning of cotton by the masses, a practice he greatly valued as a symbol of interrelated principles. To realize these principles of human well-being, he envisioned an agrarian-based economy that would, in particular, give great importance to the maintenance of cattle who were never to be slaughtered.

Humans, Cows, and Other Animals

Gandhi felt that to foster human well-being on the basis of the aforementioned four principles, humans must recognize their place in the cosmic order and act accordingly. Of special concern for Gandhi was how humans are to act in relation to animals; interacting with them rightly means comprehending human "identity with all that lives." The practical means for realizing such identity—which "takes the human beyond his species"—is possible specifically through the culture of cattle care and protection. "Cow protection . . . is one of the most wonderful phenomena in all human evolution; for it takes the human being beyond his species. The cow to me means the entire sub-human world. Man through the cow is enjoined to realise his identity with all that lives."[18] With his special regard here for the cow (a

---

[16] Shinn, "Inner Logic," 223.
[17] Shinn, "Inner Logic," 224.
[18] C. F. Andrews, *Mahatma Gandhi's Ideas, Including Selections from His Writings* (New York: Macmillan, 1930), 38; Gandhi, "Hinduism," *Young India*, June 10, 1921, in *Collected Works*, 24:373.

term that Gandhi, like many Indians, uses largely in a gender-neutral sense for both female and male cattle), Gandhi expressly identifies himself as a Hindu, as one who follows Hindu scriptural laws forbidding cow slaughter and enjoining identification with other living beings. For Gandhi, commitment to cattle protection is a defining characteristic of Hindu identity. This is further suggested by his equation of the cow with the natural "sub-human world" as a whole, pointing to the ancient Brahmanical (and later Hindu) notion that all living beings are nonmaterial souls or selves (*ātman*), ontologically equal and, in some sense, identical.[19] From this perspective, for Gandhi the cow in particular is "a plea for justice on behalf of the animal world"[20]— indeed, "a poem of pity."[21]

Thus, acting justly in relation to the animal world begins with cow protection, and Gandhi explicitly links cow protection, in turn, to abstinence, or "self-denial." Self-denial, as we have seen, brings about self-purification, a prerogative of human beings that can propel them toward their "highest station"—the spiritually elevated and noble position that, following Hindu scriptural reasoning, properly distinguishes human from nonhuman animals.[22] In a letter to a Muslim acquaintance, Gandhi urges the importance of cow protection and yet grants leeway for consumption of other animals:[23]

I have no right to slaughter all animal life because I find it necessary to slaughter some animal life. Therefore if I can live well on goats, fish and fowl (surely enough in all conscience) it is sin for me to destroy cows for my sustenance. And it was some such argument that decided the rishis [sages] of old in regarding the cow as sacred, especially when they found that the cow

---

[19] As Nicholas Gier discusses in detail, Gandhi's philosophical position in relation to classical Indian Vedanta is ambiguous. Gier offers the term "organic holism" as his way of characterizing Gandhi's thought, whereby Gandhi rejects the monistic illusionism of Shankara's Vedanta while nonetheless subscribing to a nondualism that leans toward pantheism and insists on the reality of the world and of individual souls. Nicholas F. Gier, *The Virtue of Nonviolence: From Gautama to Gandhi* (Albany: State University of New York Press, 2004), 39–46.

[20] Glyn Richards, *Philosophy of Gandhi: A Study of His Basic Ideas* (Richmond, UK: Curzon Press, 1991), 65.

[21] Gandhi, "Hinduism," 24:373.

[22] Several texts regarded by Hindus as sacred underscore a notion that although all forms of living beings carry an atemporal atman—spirit, soul, or self—the human form is set apart as uniquely equipped for pursuing and achieving spiritual elevation to approach the supreme being. A nonhuman animal, in contrast, must endure a succession of lives until the atman within receives a human body by which the being may then consciously pursue spiritual perfection.

[23] Gandhi argued strongly that it was self-defeating for Hindus to attack Muslims for their practice of cattle slaughter; rather, it was in the Hindus' interest to support the Khilafat movement (1919–22, the beginnings of the movement for a separate Pakistan).

was the greatest economic asset in national life. And I see nothing wrong, immoral or sinful in offering worship to an animal so serviceable as the cow so long as my worship does not put her on a level with her Creator.[24]

Because cows were given special recognition by India's ancient sages due to their economic value, the importance of cattle is to be understood in nonreligious, nonsectarian terms. While representing the nonhuman animal world as a whole, bovine animals are thought to be worthy of particular care and protection because of their special relationship to humans by virtue of their essential contributions to human well-being—their rendering of milk, fuel (from their manure), traction, medicine (from their urine), and after natural death, leather.

Moreover, as indicated before, this relationship between cattle and humans is best fostered in the village, where the specifically economic value of cattle can and must be recognized and cherished: "Our worker will have to keep a careful eye on the cattle wealth of his village. If we cannot use this wealth properly India is doomed to disaster and we also shall perish. For these animals will then, as in the West, become an economic burden to us and we shall have no option before us save killing them."[25]

Proper treatment of cattle was a major concern for Gandhi, such that he aimed sharp critique at fellow Hindus for their neglect and mistreatment of them. Not only were Hindus blameworthy for improper cattle treatment (including the overmilking of cows, the overworking and beating of bulls or oxen, and negligence in feeding aged cattle); they were more blameworthy than Muslims who slaughtered cattle because Hindus should know better. Even worse, Hindus were habitually selling aging cattle for slaughter— typically to the British administrators in India, whom Gandhi regarded as worse than Muslims because they (the British) indulged in far more cattle slaughter than Muslims.[26]

---

[24] Gandhi, letter to Asaf Ali, January 25, 1920, in *Collected Works*, 19:349.

[25] Gandhi, *Collected Works*, 85:16, discussion with Srikrishnadas Jaju, October 8, 1944.

[26] Cow worshipers typically show no concern that the cows they venerate will eventually be slaughtered. Florence Burgat, "Non-violence toward Animals in the Thinking of Gandhi: The Problem of Animal Husbandry," *Journal of Agricultural and Environmental Ethics* 14 (2004): 227. In a letter dated August 22, 1921, Gandhi wrote, "How can we say anything whatever to others so long as we have not rid ourselves of sin? Do we [Hindus] not kill cows with our own hands? How do we treat the progeny of the cow? What crushing burdens do we not lay on bullocks! To say nothing of bullocks, do we give enough feed to the cow? How much milk do we leave for the calf? And who sells the cow [to the butcher]? What can we say of the Hindus who do this for the sake of a few rupees? What do we do about it?" "To the People of Bihar," in *Collected Works*, 24:121.

Gandhi was acutely aware that the practical implementation of his vision for cattle protection demanded specific measures to counter the economic forces underlying their neglect and mistreatment. Since for him comprehensive cattle protection included their maintenance until their natural death, he saw it as imperative that cattle shelters (*goshalas*) be established in such a way that they include both economically viable dairies and tanneries for processing into leather the skins of cattle after their natural deaths. But such an implementation would require the institution of policies and funding on a national level—in apparent contradiction to Gandhi's notion of relatively independent villages.[27]

Acknowledging Human Imperfection and Pursuing Divine Perfection

Gandhi famously titled his autobiography *An Autobiography: The Story of My Experiments with Truth*.[28] Gandhi's sense of personal experimentation highlights both the tentativeness of his efforts to effectively act on his convictions and his acute sense of personal shortcomings in the attainment of his ideals. As we have seen, truth holds a foundational position in Gandhi's approach to animal ethics, and truth can be realized only in conjunction with the practice of *ahiṁsā*, the cultivation of self-purification, and the pursuit of self-rule.

To better understand how Gandhi applied these principles to his animal ethics in specific circumstances, I draw on Nancy Martin's identification of a three-part approach to his practice of ethics in general.[29] First is *motive*: for Gandhi, actions must be based on more than even enlightened self-interest. They must grow from an understanding of "man's aim in life," which is "from day to day to come nearer his own Maker," an orientation facilitated by consciously limiting one's own material ambition.[30] For Gandhi, inspiration to

---

[27] Burgat, "Non-violence toward Animals," 224.

[28] Gandhi published this work in his journal *Navajivan* in installments, between 1925 and 1929. The work has a strongly confessional mood, especially with regard to his "experimenting" with meat-eating in England and his preoccupations with sex. His decisions to restrict his diet (at one point, restricting himself to five vegetarian items per day; at another time, refraining from eating dairy products) and to permanently abstain from sex figure prominently in his self-understanding as a seeker of truth.

[29] Martin, "Ethics," 4:689, quoting M. V. Nadkarni, *Ethics for Our Times: Essays in Gandhian Perspective* (Delhi: Oxford University Press, 2011), 9.

[30] Gandhi, speech at Trivandrum, on or before October 10, 1927, in Collected Works, 40:229.

reform motivation came from his regular reading of the Bhagavad-Gita, in which Krishna exhorts Arjuna to raise himself to where he views all beings as nonmaterial souls: "The wise see the same (Atman) / In a brahman endowed with wisdom and cultivation, / in a cow, in an elephant, / and even in a dog or an outcaste."[31] Such vision becomes possible, according to this text, when one relinquishes the mistaken identification with one's temporal body and its supposed possessions. This, the Bhagavad-Gita insists, is essential for any substantial progress along the path of yoga or in linking with God.

Gandhi's second ethical consideration is *means*, which must be pure and nonviolent. In this spirit, as one example, he exhorted cowherds to treat their cattle gently: "You should treat them [cattle] so kindly and handle them so gently that they will understand a word or a gesture from you without the use of any stick at all."[32] Referring back to the suffering calf whom he ordered killed, Gandhi wrote that he *felt* it was a duty for the animal to be killed, and "there was certainly no violence in killing it."[33] In another letter some weeks later, Gandhi elaborated on his decision in four points. Essentially, he insists that the act of killing was one of nonviolence and that to propose that only God has the right to take life may be, in such a case of abject suffering, tantamount to violence. Significantly, Gandhi concludes, "I thought that dharma lay in killing it."[34] Dharma—an important and difficult-to-translate Sanskrit term—is here invoked by Gandhi in the sense of "the right thing to do in a particular circumstance, in accord with cosmic order and the pursuit of higher principles."[35] More generally, Gandhi insisted on honesty in acknowledging the limits of individual power to control and protect other beings. He recognizes that "the preservation of life (one's own and that of

---

[31] Bhagavad-Gita 5.18; Winthrop Sargeant, trans., *The Bhagavad Gītā* (Albany: State University of New York Press, 2009), 260. Gandhi's insistence on the equality of all beings leads him to deplore the Hindu and more broadly Indian practice of "untouchability"—the identification of particular groups of persons as essentially subhuman. Apparently addressing Buddhists on one occasion, Gandhi said, "I have no hesitation in saying without fear of contradiction that if you believe in untouchability, you deny totally the teaching of the Buddha. He who regarded the lowest animal life as dear as his own would never tolerate this cursed distinction between man and man and regard a single human being as an untouchable." Gandhi, speech at a public meeting, Bardula, November 19, 1927, in *Collected Works*, 40:400. And yet Gandhi was not an absolute egalitarian. He considered the traditional Hindu social typology of four varnas as a mandate to recognize differences in innate working propensities, each person equally valued for his or her particular contribution of service to the social body.

[32] Gandhi, *Harijan*, September 15, 1940, in *Collected Works*, 79:172.

[33] Gandhi, letter to Jethalal Joshi, August 26, 1928, in *Collected Works*, 42:409.

[34] Gandhi, letter to Bhaishri Bhogilal, September 22, 1928, in *Collected Works*, 43:43.

[35] Gandhi elaborates further on this issue with regard to monkeys who destroy crops; in this case, what is harmful to an entire community calls for protective measures, with violence applied only as a last resort. See Burgat, "Non-violence toward Animals," 225n5.

people and animals under one's responsibility) inevitably leads to violence but it should be limited to strict necessity."[36]

Finally—and of course, closely related to the previous two components—Gandhi is concerned with *consequences* of actions, such that they must contribute to the welfare of all beings. Yet here we come to the point of tension that Gandhi felt between his ideal of absolute nonviolence and the natural human imperative for self-preservation.

> I must rid myself of all venomous thoughts. I shall not do so if in my impatient ignorance and in my desire to prolong the existence of the body I seek to kill the so-called venomous beasts and reptiles. If in not seeking to defend myself against such noxious animals I die, I should die to rise again a better and a fuller man. With that faith in me how should I seek to kill a fellow-being in a snake? But this is philosophy. Let me pray and let my readers join in the prayer to God that He may give me the strength to live up to that philosophy.[37]

In Gandhi's desire to live up to his philosophy is the acknowledgment of his personal shortcomings. Gandhi therefore would not insist that others practice what he himself was unable to do.[38] Yet he also set one absolute limit on his tolerance of human violence against animals—namely, in the matter of vivisection and other forms of experimentation on animals: "I abhor vivisection with my whole soul. I detest the unpardonable slaughter of innocent life in the name of science and humanity so-called, and all the scientist discoveries stained with innocent blood I count as of no consequence."[39]

---

[36] Burgat, "Non-violence toward Animals," 225. In connection with recognizing the limits of individuals' or small groups' ability to organize and sustain cattle protection as he envisioned it, it is interesting to note that despite promoting his ideal of village-based economies, he regarded success in cattle care to be possible only through implementation of a national-level policy of cattle support and protection.

[37] Gandhi, *Young India*, September 14, 1927, in *Collected Works*, 38:283.

[38] In a conversation with his niece Mirabehn in 1943, Gandhi commented, "If I were faced with the option of killing a tiger or a snake, or otherwise being killed by it, I would rather be killed by it than take its life. But that is a personal position, not to be put forward for adoption for others. If I had the fearless power to tame these dangerous creatures by the force of my love and my will, and could show others how to do likewise, then I should have the right to advise other people to follow my example." Gandhi, "Talk with Mirabehn," November 8, 1943, in *Collected Works*, 77:207–8, quoted in Burgat, "Non-violence toward Animals," 226.

[39] Gandhi, *Young India*, December 12, 1925, in *Collected Works*, 33:312. We should note that Gandhi had the same abhorrence for ritual animal sacrifice, even if sanctioned in Hindu sacred texts. See my article for a discussion on animal experimentation in relation to traditional Hindu sacrificial practices. Kenneth R. Valpey [Krishna Kshetra Swami], "Igniting Hanuman's Tail: Hindu and Indian Secular Views on Animal Experimentation," *Journal of Animal Ethics* 6, no. 2 (Fall 2016): 213–22.

Gandhi rejects in this instance any utilitarian notion of justified animal experimentation, regarding all supposed justifications of the practice as hypocritical and, by implication, completely misguided in their failure to comprehend humanity's higher purpose.

Conclusion: Pursuing Divine–Human–Nonhuman Harmony in the Ashram

I will conclude this sketch of Gandhi's animal theology and ethics by pointing out his eagerness to establish hermitages, or ashrams (Sanskrit: *āśrama*), as the laboratories for practicing his "experiments with truth." Ashram culture is an ancient tradition in India, and in our consideration of Gandhi's ashram development, it is relevant that ancient and classical Sanskrit literature typically celebrates the hermitage as the idyllic locale transcending the contrast of town and village (signifying human culture) and forest (signifying absence of culture, the wild). Significantly, ascetics who retreated to the forest to practice their spiritual disciplines established hermitages that became educational centers as well as sanctuaries for some animals.[40] Gandhi's hope was that his ashrams could function as incubators for the practice and realization of his vision of *sarvodaya*, "upliftment of all," by establishing "a strict regimen of vegetarian food, manual labor, social service, celibacy, and sleep."[41] In his Satyagraha Ashram (established in 1915 in Kochrab and then in Sabarmati, Gujarat), although the work emphasis was on the production of hand-spun and handwoven cotton products (*khadi*), there were also cattle.

In contrast to the traditional ashrams of ascetics, which were essentially inwardly oriented, Gandhi regarded his ashram project as thoroughly outward in its orientation, aiming to educate its members to fan out into neighboring and eventually far-flung villages as guides for village renewal. Such was the ideal, yet Satyagraha Ashram was destined to face manifold problems, including improper dealings with money and illicit departures from celibacy vows on the part of some members. The point to note here is that Gandhi regarded all shortcomings of the ashramites as arising out of his own

---

[40] That protection of forest animals in such hermitages was considered expected is suggested in, for example, the opening scene of Kalidāsa's famous classical Sanskrit drama *Abhijñānaśākuntala*. As King Dushyanta lays chase to a deer in the forest, he is commanded to desist by a resident of a forest ashram, who claims that the deer belongs to the ashram.

[41] Mark Thompson, *Gandhi and His Ashrams* (Mumbai: Popular Prakashan, 1993), 107.

shortcomings, for which he, on occasion, felt that he must observe penance (in the form of fasting). Despite the troubles, Gandhi would never abandon the pursuit of his ideal—namely, the development of an egalitarian, village-based society in harmony with nature and in communion with God.[42]

At this point, one may well wonder whether Gandhi's animal ethics requires a person to first become qualified as a mahatma. Gandhi seems to demand hardly reachable qualifications for a person to act perfectly—especially in perfect nonviolence—in relation to animals. Indeed, it is fair to say that Gandhi's approach leans strongly in this direction. We must remember his conviction, which is common to Indic religious traditions generally, that humans have a calling that is unique among creatures—namely, to realize their highest being, which enables them to approach God and to put an end to the cycle of misery (Sanskrit: *saṁsāra*) that forces living beings into repeated rebirths into animal and even plant species, destined to struggle for existence as predator and prey.

Yet to pursue this human calling is, Gandhi would insist, not to withdraw from the world (a typical notion of classical asceticism) but rather to engage fully with the world in such a way that other humans may be positively influenced to strive toward the higher purpose. To be a mahatma, then, is to show others how to become a mahatma, and the substance of such showing is giving an example of living *for* all beings—and hence being prepared to sacrifice oneself, even one's life, for all beings. Becoming a mahatma would seem to be Gandhi's understanding of the whole purpose of "Hindu dharma"—right action for Hindus—which is, however, truly right only if it brings one beyond all temporal designations of oneself (including the designation "Hindu"), to encompass a universal, inclusive vision. In this universal vision, all living beings are cared for, even ants, whose holes, Gandhi wrote, "should be filled with flour" (as food) because "we owe kindness to the animals."[43]

To engage fully with the world is to engage with all of God's creation, and to be a "great soul" is to help other human beings to appreciate the greatness of God's creation. Hence, becoming a mahatma is accessible to all, simply by our beginning to appreciate this greatness of the creation. Then our natural response will be to cherish and respect all creatures and indeed to love all creatures—the positive sense in which Gandhi conceived the term *ahiṁsā*. It is not enough to be nonviolent, or rather, as long as one limits the concept

[42] Thompson, *Gandhi and His Ashrams*, 134–39.
[43] Gandhi, *Mahadevbhaini Diary*, 7:101–6, in *Collected Works*, 30:122.

of *ahiṁsā* to its negative sense of "not harming," one will surely remain prone to acting violently, by force of habit. The higher vision (returning to this chapter's epigraph) that the mahatma strives for and tries to share is that one finds oneself "immediately ... in the service of all that lives." And for Gandhi, as we have seen, the most important and in many respects most accessible way for humans to engage in service to the animal world is by serving—caring for and protecting—the animals who most comprehensively serve humans: namely, cattle. Bovine animals, the prototypical domesticated species, link humans to the animal world and to nature as a whole, and when they are properly cared for, Gandhi would claim, they link human beings individually and collectively to God.

Bibliography

Andrews, C. F. *Mahatma Gandhi's Ideas, Including Selections from His Writings.* New York: Macmillan, 1930.

Burgat, Florence. "Non-violence toward Animals in the Thinking of Gandhi: The Problem of Animal Husbandry." *Journal of Agricultural and Environmental Ethics* 14 (2004): 223–48.

Gandhi, Mohandas Karamchand. *An Autobiography: The Story of My Experiments with Truth.* Translated by Mahadev H. Desai. London: Phoenix Press, 1949.

Gandhi, Mohandas Karamchand. *The Collected Works of Mahatma Gandhi.* 98 vols. New Delhi: Publications Division, Ministry of Information and Broadcasting, Government of India, 1999.

Gandhi, Mohandas Karamchand. *The Essential Gandhi: An Anthology.* Edited by Louis Fischer. New York: Random House, 1962.

Gandhi, Mohandas Karamchand. *Gandhiji on Villages.* Selected and compiled with an introduction by Divya Joshi. Mumbai: Gandhi Book Centre, 2002.

Gandhi, Mohandas Karamchand. *Satyagraha in South Africa.* Translated by Valji Govindji Desai. Madras: S. Ganesan, 1928.

Gandhi, Mohandas Karamchand. *The Selected Works of Mahatma Gandhi.* 6 vols. Edited by Shriman Narayan. Ahmedabad, India: Navajivan, 1968.

Gandhi, Mohandas Karamchand. *Truth Is God: Gleanings from the Writings of Mahatma Gandhi Bearing on God, God-Realization, and the Godly Way.* Compiled by R. K. Prabhu. Ahmedabad, India: Navajivan, 1969.

Gier, Nicholas F. *The Virtue of Nonviolence: From Gautama to Gandhi.* Albany: State University of New York Press, 2004.

Jhaveri, Vithalbhai K., and D. G. Tendulkar, eds. *Mahatma in Eight Volumes.* Vol. 5. Bombay: Jhaveri and Tendulkar, 1952.

Martin, Nancy M. "Ethics." In *Brill's Encyclopedia of Hinduism,* edited by Knut A. Jacobsen, Helena Basu, Angelika Malinar, and Vasudha Narayanan, 4:677–91. Leiden: Brill, 2009.

Nadkarni, M. V. *Ethics for Our Times: Essays in Gandhian Perspective.* Delhi: Oxford University Press, 2011.

Richards, Glyn. *The Philosophy of Gandhi: A Study of His Basic Ideas.* Richmond, UK: Curzon Press, 1991.

Sargeant, Winthrop, trans. *The Bhagavad Gītā.* Albany: State University of New York Press, 2009.

Shinn, Larry D. "The Inner Logic of Gandhian Ecology." In *Hinduism and Ecology: The Intersection of Earth, Sky, and Water,* edited by Christopher Key Chapple, 213–39. Cambridge, MA: Harvard University Press, 2000.

Thompson, Mark. *Gandhi and His Ashrams.* Mumbai: Popular Prakashan, 1993.

Valpey, Kenneth R. [Krishna Kshetra Swami]. "Igniting Hanuman's Tail: Hindu and Indian Secular Views on Animal Experimentation." *Journal of Animal Ethics* 6, no. 2 (Fall 2016): 213–22.

PART III
DEEPER PROBING

17

Albert Schweitzer (1875–1965)

The Life of Reverence

Carl Tobias Frayne

If you desire peace in the world, do not pray that everyone share your beliefs. Pray instead that all may be reverent.

—Paul Woodruff[1]

Only such thinking as establishes the sway of the mental attitude of reverence for life can bring to mankind perpetual peace.

—Albert Schweitzer[2]

Introduction

Albert Schweitzer's philosophy of civilization is primarily concerned with the moral and spiritual betterment of the individual and of society.[3] The notion of "reverence for life" (*Ehrfurcht vor dem Leben*) is at the heart of this endeavor. Often regarded as a vague and shallow concept that ultimately fails to provide practical guidance, reverence for life is more complex than it first appears. Schweitzer's ethics is in fact broader in scope than most systematic moral theories because it encompasses dimensions of the moral life that such theories tend to overlook. Reverence for life is "a necessary widening and refining of ordinary ethics."[4]

Schweitzer was a visionary. In addition to his groundbreaking theological work, he pioneered the animal rights and modern environmental

---

[1] Paul Woodruff, *Reverence: Renewing a Forgotten Virtue* (Oxford: Oxford University Press, 2001).
[2] A. Schweitzer, *The Philosophy of Civilization*, trans. C. T. Campion (New York: Prometheus Books, 1987).
[3] A. Schweitzer, *Civilization and Ethics*, trans. C. T. Campion (London: Unwin Books, 1961), 95.
[4] Schweitzer, *Civilization and Ethics*, 218.

Carl Tobias Frayne, *Albert Schweitzer (1875–1965)* In: *Animal Theologians*. Edited by: Andrew Linzey and Clair Linzey, Oxford University Press. © Oxford University Press 2023. DOI: 10.1093/oso/9780197655542.003.0018

movements by developing a biocentric ethics. Thereby, he challenged the anthropocentric human–animal dichotomy that had historically prevailed in
Western philosophical thought since its dawn in ancient Greece. Yet at the
same time, his philosophy is, in important ways, closer to the ancients' conception of *philosophia*—that is, the view of philosophy as a total way of life,
as opposed to a merely intellectual pursuit. Anticipating the revival of what
is now commonly known as virtue ethics, Schweitzer put forth an ethics of
excellence that he strove to embody in his own life.[5]

How can reverence for life help us flourish morally and spiritually? What
are its implications for the animal cause? This chapter will develop some of
the central tenets of Schweitzer's ethics and argue that reverence for life is
best understood as a way of life centered upon a number of core virtues that
engage all aspects of one's existence. First, I shall show that Schweitzer's understanding of the role of philosophy bears a strong resemblance to ancient
philosophy and contemporary virtue ethics. Second, I shall turn to the question of animals' moral status and look at Schweitzer's rejection of hierarchies
of moral worth. Finally, I shall examine Schweitzer's notion of ethical mysticism and emphasize the roles of wonder, aesthetic contemplation, and the
sublime in the moral life. My hope is that seen in this light, reverence for life
can foster new edifying insights as regards the genuine ethical life and our relations to the more-than-human world.

The Ethics of Reverence for Life

The Role of Ethics

The ethics of a humane and flourishing society must address the complexity
of human persons and include their actual experience of the world, including
their character, psychology, emotions, and so on. Schweitzer recognizes that
human beings are not purely rationalistic calculators whose lives fit neatly
into fixed models of behavior. Ethics should not be reduced exclusively to an
externally imposed set of principles. Nor should it be restricted to choosing

---

[5] Henry Clark, *The Philosophy of Albert Schweitzer* (London: Methuen, 1964); Mike W. Martin,
"Rethinking Reverence for Life," in *Reverence for Life: The Ethics of Albert Schweitzer for the
Twenty-First Century*, ed. Marvin Meyer and Kurt Bergel (New York: Syracuse University Press,
2002); Mike W. Martin, *Albert Schweitzer's Reverence for Life: Ethical Idealism and Self-Realization*
(London: Ashgate, 2007).

between certain courses of actions at one moment in time. Such narrow conceptions of the moral life are bound to be found wanting, if not plainly alienating and dehumanizing.[6] They lure people into taking "refuge in arguments, thinking that they are doing philosophy, and that this is the way to become excellent people."[7] As David Goodin argues, for Schweitzer the solution to the crisis of civilization is "not in a better rulebook but in making better people."[8] A person cannot be said to lead a fully ethical life by donating 10 percent of her income to charity every month or becoming an expert on some abstruse metaethical theory and yet not strive to cultivate a virtuous character and examine her conscience day after day. Seeking to go beyond the confines of academic discourse, Schweitzer intends reverence for life to be a realistic and practical "living ethics."

Reverence as a Way of Life

The phrase "reverence for life" encapsulates much more than it literally conveys. The German term translated as "reverence," *Ehrfurcht*, is somewhat misleading because it connotes a passive attitude.[9] Schweitzer recognized this problem and suggested the Latin word *reveratio* to clarify what he meant. *Reveratio* is not simply a sentiment but a drive or an activity. Hence, reverence for life is not only a passive state of mind or outlook; it is also an active attitude. As Ara Barsam succinctly explains, "Ehrfurcht . . . indicates that Schweitzer's reverence for life is [concerned with] . . . 'a mental attitude' and a 'new temper of mind,' which includes the development of emotions, dispositions and attitudes that influence actions."[10] Schweitzer asserts that we naturally strive to be moral because of an inner necessity, a kind of moral conscience that is part of our being.[11] Reverence for life is an outlook as well as an attitude that any reflective person will achieve who seriously considers "the fundamental questions about the relations of man to the universe,

---

[6] Schweitzer, *Civilization and Ethics*, 208.

[7] Aristotle, *Nicomachean Ethics*, trans. Terence Irwin (Indianapolis: Hackett, 1999), 1105b13–5.

[8] David K. Goodin, *The New Rationalism: Albert Schweitzer's Philosophy of Reverence for Life* (Montreal: McGill University Press, 2013), 185.

[9] E. Spranger, "Différence entre *respect de la vie* et *Ehrfurcht*," *Cahiers Albert Schweitzer*, no. 37 (1977–78).

[10] Ara Paul Barsam, *Reverence for Life: Albert Schweitzer's Great Contribution to Ethical Thought* (Oxford: Oxford University Press, 2008), 30.

[11] Albert Schweitzer, *The Decay and Restoration of Civilization*, trans. C. T. Campion (New York: Prometheus Books, 1987), 29–32.

about the meaning of life, and about the nature of goodness."[12] This is why Schweitzer describes it as a "necessity of thought" that constitutes the "elementary and inward" foundation of ethics.[13]

Yet reverence for life is more than a springboard that gets ethics started; it pervades and sustains one's entire moral life. In this sense, Schweitzer's philosophy of reverence for life is similar to the conception of philosophy as a total way of life (βίος), which was the view held by most ancient philosophers. The French scholar Pierre Hadot emphasizes this neglected aspect of philosophy as it was practiced in antiquity.[14] According to Hadot, ancient philosophy was a transformative "art of living" that engaged all aspects of one's being.[15] Likewise, for Schweitzer, reverence for life "penetrates unceasingly and in all directions a man's observations, reflection, and resolutions."[16] As we shall see, Schweitzer also shares with Hadot and the ancients the yearning to be spiritually united with the world.[17] In sum, reverence for life is not so much a moral principle as an existential *way of being*. It is therefore not a stretch to see Schweitzer embarking on the pursuit of wisdom through living a life of reverence.

Virtue and Self-Fulfillment

A person pursuing an ethics of reverence for life seeks self-fulfillment and self-perfection through leading a life of virtue. "Ethics," Schweitzer writes, "is the activity of man directed to secure the inner perfection of his own personality."[18] We should strive to reach our full potential by cultivating the virtues constitutive of an excellent character. Following Henry Clark, who first noted the similarities between reverence for life and virtue ethics,[19] Mike Martin describes reverence for life as "a character-centred or virtue-oriented ethical theory that focuses on what it means to be a good person."[20] Schweitzer

[12] Albert Schweitzer, *Out of My Life and Thought*, trans. C. T. Campion (London: George Allen & Unwin, 1933), 260, 199.

[13] Schweitzer, *Decay and Restoration*, 74–75.

[14] Pierre Hadot, *Philosophy as a Way of Life*, ed. Arnold Davidson, trans. Michael Chase (Oxford: Blackwell, 1995); Pierre Hadot, *What Is Ancient Philosophy?*, trans. Michael Chase (Cambridge, MA: Harvard University Press, 2002).

[15] Hadot, *Philosophy as a Way of Life*, 83.

[16] Schweitzer, *Philosophy of Civilization*, 316.

[17] Schweitzer, *Out of My Life*, 261.

[18] Schweitzer, *Decay and Restoration*, 94.

[19] Clark, *Philosophy of Albert Schweitzer*.

[20] Martin, *Schweitzer's Reverence for Life*, 19.

explicitly presents it as a combination of multiple virtues: "Just as white light unites the colour spectrum, reverence for life unifies specific virtues; and just as white light refracts into colours, reverence for life refracts into specific virtues and their accompanying ideals."[21] Martin and Clark identify a number of virtues that are central to Schweitzer's ethics, including compassion, love, respect, honesty, forbearance, mercy, gratitude, forgiveness, peace-loving, and humility.[22] One is to embody, cultivate, and exhibit these virtues in all areas of one's life.

It is crucial to bear in mind that these virtues have to be directed toward all life forms, no matter how seemingly insignificant.[23] Schweitzer's ethics is biocentric, not anthropocentric. He speaks of reverence for *life*, not for human beings. In the words of Charles Hartshorne, "the morally good individual is one who wills to optimize the harmony and intensity of living for all those lives he or she is in a position to affect."[24] In short, reverence for life can be seen as bringing together various virtues and other kinds of excellences that shape one's entire outlook on life and transform one's way of being and living in the world. Let us now examine how reverence for life addresses the question of animals' moral status.

Moral Status

The Capability Approach

The traditional approach at the center of the contemporary debate on animal rights seeks to identify what kinds of beings are worthy of moral consideration on the basis of their possession of certain morally relevant capabilities.[25] This approach is too narrow and only calls into question *some* of our anthropocentric biases. First of all, it fails to account for the complexity of circumstances and situations in which we often find ourselves when confronted with moral choices. Second, the ambiguous notion of morally

---

[21] Albert Schweitzer, *The Teaching of Reverence for Life*, trans. Richard and Clara Winston (New York: Holt, Rinehart and Winston, 1965), 41.
[22] Martin, *Schweitzer's Reverence for Life*, 17–31; Clark, *Philosophy of Albert Schweitzer*, 38–53.
[23] Schweitzer, *Out of My Life*, 271.
[24] Charles Hartshorne, *Wisdom as Moderation: A Philosophy of the Middle Way* (New York: State University of New York Press, 1987), 124.
[25] Paola Cavalieri, *The Animal Question*, trans. Catherine Woollard (Oxford: Oxford University Press, 2001).

relevant capability needs to be defined. Are linguistic abilities significant? To what extent is self-awareness important? Whereas some philosophers, such as Tom Regan and Peter Singer, claim that only some species (often mammals and birds) have moral worth,[26] others, such as Michael Leahy, hold that we do not have any moral obligations toward animals.[27] These questions have been addressed by various thinkers, and I do not wish to discuss them here. The important point is that what constitutes a morally relevant capability is a subject of much debate and controversy. More importantly, the traditional approach does not tell us how we ought to treat beings deemed to lack moral status. May I, for instance, use birds as shooting targets because they are not moral agents, or may I pluck the wings from butterflies because they lack nerve cells?

While philosophers disagree as to what constitutes a morally relevant capability, most agree on the significance of suffering—or, more generally, sentience as the capacity to experience pleasure and pain. However, viewing sentience as the sole determinant of moral status is a myopic perspective; it reduces nonsentient beings to mere objects devoid of moral worth. As Schweitzer puts it, "following such a distinction there comes next the view that there can be life that is worthless, injury to which or destruction of which does not matter."[28] Proponents of the capability approach end up dismissing forms of life with whom we cannot identify as unworthy of moral consideration. Singer illustrates this position unequivocally: "If a being is not capable of suffering, or of experiencing enjoyment or happiness, there is nothing to be taken into account [morally]."[29] He asserts that "a stone does not have interests because it cannot suffer."[30] According to this account of moral value, animals thought not to possess pain receptors such as butterflies are viewed as no more valuable than inanimate objects such as stones. As a matter of fact, this view implies that billions of nonsentient living beings have no intrinsic moral worth and hence cannot be considered proper moral subjects.

We now can see that overemphasizing the importance of animals' capacities is a severely limited approach. In fact, Singer, Regan, and others ultimately adhere to what David DeGrazia calls "the sliding-scale model," according to which humans are at the top of both a hypothetical phylogenetic

[26] Tom Regan, *The Case for Animal Rights*, rev. ed. (Berkley: University of California Press, 2004); Peter Singer, *Animal Liberation: A New Ethics for Our Treatment of Animals* (London: Cape, 1975).
[27] Michael P. T. Leahy, *Against Liberation: Putting Animals in Perspective* (London: Routledge, 1991).
[28] Schweitzer, *Out of My Life*, 271.
[29] Singer, *Animal Liberation*, 8–9.
[30] Singer, *Animal Liberation*, 8–9.

and a moral scale.[31] Simply put, in this model, humans are the most cognitively complex and have the highest moral status. The more capabilities an animal shares with humans, the more morally valuable that animal is. It becomes clear that humans (or rather, humans' capabilities) are still the measure of all things. Thus, this approach remains fundamentally speciesist and anthropocentric.

The Rejection of Moral Status

Schweitzer refused to rank the value of different species and types of life, for he believed such rankings would inevitably be "subjective" or "arbitrary."[32] He states, "The ethics of reverence for life makes no distinction between higher and lower, more precious and less precious lives."[33] Sentience should not be the boundary of our moral concern: "the ethical person does not ask how far this or that life deserves one's sympathy as being valuable, nor, beyond that, whether and to what degree it is capable of feeling."[34] Criticizing sentientism, Andrew Linzey concisely argues that "the issue is how to recognize the value and moral relevance of sentiency as *a* criterion, while avoiding falling into the error of previous generations who have isolated one characteristic or ability—for example, reason, language, or friendship—and used it as *a barrier to wider moral sensibility*."[35] The ethics of reverence for life does not rely on the acknowledgment of animals' possession of some humanlike capability. Rather, it attempts to fully divest ethics of its anthropocentric biases by urging us to think about nature in nonhierarchical ways. Schweitzer's ethics finds an echo in various contemporary environmentalists, such as Paul Taylor.[36] Taylor calls for a radical "biocentric egalitarianism" that "regards all living things as possessing inherent moral worth."[37] Several scholars have put forth distinct visions of a biocentric ethics in recent decades,[38] but they

[31] David DeGrazia, *Animal Rights: A Very Short Introduction* (Oxford: Oxford University Press, 2002), 36.

[32] Schweitzer, *Teaching of Reverence*, 47.

[33] Schweitzer, *Out of My Life*, 270–71.

[34] Schweitzer, *Civilization and Ethics*, 214.

[35] Andrew Linzey, *Why Animal Suffering Matters* (Oxford: Oxford University Press, 2009), 512; emphasis added.

[36] Paul W. Taylor, *Respect for Nature: A Theory of Environmental Ethics*, 25th anniv. ed. (Princeton, NJ: Princeton University Press, 2011).

[37] P. W. Taylor, "The Ethics of Respect for Nature," *Environmental Ethics* 3 (1981): 217.

[38] For example, see Paul W. Taylor, *Respect for Nature: A Theory of Environmental Ethics* (Princeton, NJ: Princeton University Press, 1986); Aldo Leopold, *A Sand County Almanac, and Sketches Here*

all share the wish to move away from anthropocentrism and strive to adopt a broader "human-in-nature" perspective.[39]

Again, Schweitzer's approach shares a number of similarities with contemporary virtue ethicists. As Rosalind Hursthouse tells us, virtue ethicists need not attempt to define moral status, for many of them find the concept superfluous and dangerously divisive.[40] Virtue ethics offers a "pluralistic, context sensitive, and open ended" approach; it rejects "the idea that there is just one monolithic set of principles concerning just one form of value that can be fruitfully used to address the great variety of moral issues we encounter when we extend our moral concern beyond ourselves."[41] Although knowledge of a being's faculties and ability to suffer should certainly be taken into account, this knowledge per se is not a prerequisite for a person to exhibit the virtues of reverence for life. Intentionally trampling on insects is cruel, no matter how developed their central nervous system; saving an injured puppy is compassionate, regardless of the animal's level of self-awareness.

To reiterate, for the point cannot be too strongly stressed, certain capabilities such as sentience are incontestably important factors that should *inform* the virtuous/reverent person's judgment, but they do not *determine* how the virtuous person should act in every situation. Since no two situations are identical, the virtuous/reverent person will need practical wisdom (*phronesis*) in order to deliberate on how to act in a given situation. As Schweitzer puts it, "reverence for all being[s] must attend to each specific situation."[42] There is thus a multiplicity of ways in which one can behave virtuously toward living beings. One of the virtuous attitudes that reverence for life demands is humility.

and There (Oxford: Oxford University Press, 1987); Nicholas Agar, *Recent Defences of Biocentrism* (New York: Colombia University Press, 2001).

[39] Robert L. Chapman, "The Goat-Stag and the Sphinx: The Place of the Virtues in Environmental Ethics," *Environmental Values* 11 (2002): 136.

[40] Rosalind Hursthouse, "Applying Virtue Ethics to Our Treatment of the Other Animals," in *The Practice of Virtue, Classical and Contemporary Readings in Virtue Ethics*, ed. Jennifer Welchman (Indianapolis: Hackett, 2006); "Virtue Ethics and the Treatment of Animals," in *The Oxford Handbook of Animal Ethics*, ed. T. L. Beauchamp and R. G. Frey (Oxford: Oxford University Press, 2011); "Normative Virtue Ethics," in *Ethical Theory: An Anthology*, 2nd ed., ed. Russell Shafer-Landau (Oxford: Wiley-Blackwell, 2013).

[41] Hursthouse, "Virtue Ethics and the Treatment of Animals," 124.

[42] Albert Schweitzer, "The Ethics of Reverence for Life," in *Reverence for Life: The Ethics of Albert Schweitzer for the Twenty-First Century*, ed. Marvin Meyer and Kurt Bergel (New York: Syracuse University Press, 2002), 11.

Humility

To be humble means to acknowledge and accept our limitations. That is, we should recognize that we are not fallen angels but just another thread within the web of life. "If you ask the poets of reverence," writes Paul Woodruff, " 'What must I believe in order to be reverent?' they will fall silent. But ask them, 'What must I not believe?' Then they have an answer: any belief that trespasses on divine ground is the enemy of reverence. Do not believe that you are supreme in any way; do not believe that you alone know the mind of God."[43] Just as awareness of our finitude brings our experience of being alive into sharp focus, awareness of our dependence on other life forms makes us conscious of our vulnerable nature. What would happen to us if there were no more trees and plankton to produce oxygen or no more bats and bees to pollinate our crops? Most of us do not realize how utterly reliant on other life forms we are.

The humble person places herself not above nature but as part of it— alongside other living beings. Humility may, in this sense, be conceived as an antianthropocentric virtue. Warning us against ethnocentrism, Claude Lévi-Strauss contended that "respect for one's fellow men cannot be based on certain special dignities that humanity claims for itself as such, because then one fraction of humanity will . . . decide that it embodies those dignities in some pre-eminent manner. We should rather assert at the outset a sort of *a priori* humility . . . *Humility in the face of life*, because life represents the rarest and most astonishing creation observable in the universe."[44] If we replaced the terms "fellow men" and "humanity" with "fellow creatures" and "living beings," this passage could equally be about anthropocentrism and speciesism. Humility begins from the simple acknowledgment that we are not almighty masters of the universe but mere animals dependent on other animals and that it would be a mark of pride and arrogance to place ourselves above all other living beings.

In summation, drawing a sharp line between beings who have moral status and those who do not is a myopic and divisive approach. It leads to unconstructive dichotomies, such as Singer's distinction between sentient beings with interests and nonsentient beings bereft of moral worth.

---

[43] Woodruff, *Reverence*, 132.
[44] Quoted in Ronald W. Hepburn, *Wonder and Other Essays* (Edinburgh: Edinburgh University Press, 1984), 146; emphasis added.

Schweitzer rejects the notion of moral status that rests on the two questions at the heart of the animal rights debate—namely, (1) "What capabilities count as morally relevant?" and (2) "Which animals possess these capabilities?" Though he recognizes the importance of suffering, he refuses to make it the sole criterion of moral consideration. We should adopt a position of epistemic modesty and practice the virtue of humility. In addition, ethics must be complemented by an inward and precognitive compulsion to affirm life. This is one of the central aims of Schweitzer's ethical mysticism, to which we now turn.

Ethical Mysticism

For Schweitzer, the rational and the mystical are complementary: "reason and heart must work together if a true morality is to be established."[45] Indeed, they are both necessary conditions for the life of reverence. The moral life is ultimately artificial or superficial if it is reduced to a set of rational principles bereft of spiritual truths.[46] We cannot live a genuine moral life if we are guided only by systematic moral philosophy, for it is "too narrow and shallow for spiritual development."[47] What ethics, along with philosophy as a whole, need is to begin with an experience of the universe that is grounded in rationality yet at the same time transcends it: "The ethical mysticism of reverence for life is rationalism thought to a conclusion."[48] "Our great mistake," says Schweitzer, "is thinking that without mysticism we can reach an ethical world- and life-view, which shall satisfy [rational] thought."[49]

It is worth noting that contrary to the English language, which has come to view the rational and the mystical as antipodal notions, the German language has only one word, *Geistig*, for "intellectual" and "spiritual." We can now better understand why Schweitzer tells us that "the true heart is rational, and the true reason is sensitive."[50] Thus, Schweitzer's ethical mysticism is not a wholly irrational experience rooted in some kind of fideism. Nonetheless,

---

[45] Albert Schweitzer, *A Place for Revelation: Sermons on Reverence for Life*, trans. David Larrimore Holland (New York: Macmillan, 1988), 7.

[46] Albert Schweitzer, "First Sermon on Reverence for Life," in *Reverence for Life: The Ethics of Albert Schweitzer for the Twenty-First Century*, ed. Marvin Meyer and Kurt Bergel (New York: Syracuse University Press, 2002), 68.

[47] Schweitzer, *Teaching of Reverence*, 132.

[48] Schweitzer, *Out of My Life*, 151.

[49] Schweitzer, *Philosophy of Civilization*, 303.

[50] Schweitzer, *A Place for Revelation*, 13.

it does rely on our being attuned to certain precognitive intuitions and sensibilities, so that we may respond to the inward compulsion "to show to all [beings'] will-to-live the same reverence" that we show to our own.[51] Above all, it is a necessary condition for a complete ethics—a fully realized life of reverence—and a philosophy that provides a cure for the "spiritual decadence" of humanity.[52]

Wonder

According to Schweitzer, the only way to find meaning in life is to raise our "natural relation to the world to a spiritual one."[53] I suggest that Schweitzer's ethical mysticism should be seen as stemming from an *aesthetico-moral* response to the mystery of life, which is characterized by the convergence of the experience of wonder *at* the grandeur of life and wonder *about* how to react to it.[54] Wonder is not restricted to aesthetic or intellectual contemplation, for existence is neither meant to be solely a subject of intellectual analysis nor meant to be solely a subject of aesthetic appreciation. The scientific mind and the poetic mind meet in wonder. Einstein, a close friend of Schweitzer, wrote that "The most beautiful thing we can experience is the mysterious. It is the source of all true art and science. He to whom this emotion is a stranger, whoever does not know it and can no longer wonder, no longer marvel, is as good as dead, and his eyes are dimmed."[55]

Art and religion may speak the language of awe and wonder better than philosophy, but the "love of wisdom," like science, desperately needs these essential aspects of reverence for life. Wonder nourishes the philosophical mind and impels philosophical inquiry, as Plato and countless other philosophers have maintained.[56] The impetus to philosophize is the same as the impetus to be ethical, since ethics, as Wittgenstein remarks, ultimately springs up from "an impulse to speak about the meaning of life and

---

[51] Schweitzer, *Civilization and Ethics*, 214; Schweitzer, *Out of My Life*, 264.
[52] Schweitzer, *Out of My Life*, 254.
[53] Schweitzer, cited in Roy Pascal, *Design and Truth in Autobiography* (London: Routledge, 2016), 104.
[54] Schweitzer, *Civilization and Ethics*, 213.
[55] Quoted in Stanislaw M. Ulam, *Adventures of a Mathematician* (New York: Charles Scribner's Sons, 1976), 76.
[56] Plato, *Theaetetus* 155c–d, *The Dialogues of Plato*, trans. Benjamin Jowett (Oxford: Oxford University Press, 1892).

the experience of wonder at its magnitude."[57] "How much would already be accomplished toward the improvement of our present circumstances in Western civilization," ponders Schweitzer, "if only we would all give up three minutes of every evening to gazing up into the infinite world of the starry heavens and meditating on it."[58] This strongly echoes Kant, who famously wrote, "Two things fill the mind with every increasing awe and admiration, the oftener and more steadily I reflect upon them; the starry heavens above me, and the moral law within me."[59] We must first awaken to the miracle of life and be "roused to ever greater astonishment" at its mystery in order to see its value and internalize a sense of duty toward it.[60] In this sense, wonder can be conceived as the *precognitive requisite of the cognitive*. Hence, the restoration of wonder can be an important steppingstone toward establishing a fully realized ethics of reverence for life.

The problem is that wonder tends to ebb and fade away as one progressively grows accustomed to its objects. This is why one needs to constantly renew one's mode of perception. We should, in Coleridge's words, seek "to combine the child's sense of wonder and novelty with the appearances which every day for perhaps forty years had rendered familiar."[61] More worryingly, wonder may be morally ambivalent. The relationship between wonder and the protection and preservation of life is not that clear-cut. In fact, there very well may be a fine line between awe and alienation. Indeed, wonder may give rise to attitudes inconsistent with reverence for life, such as the desire to manipulate nature for human ends. For example, Descartes, who identified wonder as "the first of all the passions," regarded science as a way of rendering humans "the masters and possessors of nature."[62] By contrast, in his celebrated essay on wonder, Ronald Hepburn argues that a person who stands in awe of nature cannot imagine modifying or utilizing it for his or her own ends but rather seeks to cherish and sustain it. He states, "There is . . . a close affinity between the attitude of wonder itself—non-exploitative,

---

[57] Quoted in Aaron Gross and Anne Vallely, eds., *Animals and the Human Imagination* (New York: Columbia University Press, 2012), 261.

[58] Schweitzer, *Decay and Restoration*, 102–3.

[59] Note that this quote is inscribed on Kant's tombstone. Immanuel Kant, *Critique of Practical Reason* 5:161.33–6, trans. Paul Guyer and Allen W. Wood (Cambridge: Cambridge University Press 1992).

[60] Schweitzer, *Civilization and Ethics*, 234.

[61] Samuel Taylor Coleridge, *Biographia Literaria*, vol. 7 of *The Collected Works of Samuel Taylor Coleridge*, ed. James Engell and Walter Jackson Bate (Princeton, NJ: Princeton University Press, 1983), 80–81.

[62] René Descartes, *The Passions of the Soul*, trans. Stephen H. Voss (Indianapolis: Hackett, 1989), 52.

non-utilitarian—and attitudes that seek to respect other-being."[63] Hepburn also cites humility, respect, compassion, and other attitudes as moral correlates of wonder.[64] Thus, it is clear that wonder can also be congruent with the virtues fostered by reverence for life.

I suggest that one way to steer the experience of wonder in the right direction is to cultivate a reverent outlook through a number of contemplative practices. This will prevent wonder from falling into an alienating or transient passion and turn it into a virtuous habit. The contemplative practices to which I am referring are similar to what Hadot calls "spiritual exercises"—that is, regular meditative exercises whose aim is the "transformation of our vision of the world and . . . a metamorphosis of our personality."[65] Aesthetic contemplation can be seen as a form of spiritual exercise. Viewed in this light, it can be part of the remedy for our spiritual decline and our moral blindness toward nonhuman living beings.

Aesthetic Contemplation

The spiritual exercise of aesthetic contemplation enables one to better appreciate the value of life, for appreciation of the beauty of life is concurrent with the compulsion to cherish and treasure life. As Iris Murdoch rightly argues, "the appreciation of beauty in art or nature is not only the easiest available spiritual exercise; it is also a completely adequate entry into the good life."[66] Just as the physicist feels moved to capture the beauty of the world through elegant theories and the poet through graceful rhymes, so too should the ethical person feel moved to protect, preserve, and contribute to the beauty of the world through virtuous living.

Reason alone cannot give us any meaningful sense of being at home in the world because we are not pure intellects but are also social, spiritual, and aesthetic beings. Through our growing more attuned to the beauty of the world, our conscience awakens to the interconnectedness of all things. As Roger Caillois asserts, "the feeling man has of beauty merely reflects his condition as a living being and integral part of the universe."[67] Accordingly, the

[63] Hepburn, *Wonder and Other Essays*, 36.
[64] Hepburn, *Wonder and Other Essays*, 36.
[65] Hadot, *Philosophy as a Way of Life*, 82.
[66] Iris Murdoch, *The Sovereignty of the Good* (London: Routledge and Kegan Paul, 1970), 64.
[67] Roger Caillois, *Esthétique généralisée* (Paris: Gallimard, 1988), 154.

experience of the beautiful may overcome feelings of alienation and restore a sense of belonging, thereby answering Schweitzer's longing to bring himself "into a spiritual relation with the world, and become one with it."[68]

Finally, contemplation of the beauty of the world invites us to become self-conscious participants in life by attending to and relishing in nature as it is, rather than regarding it as something instrumental (something to be transformed or humanized) or as something alien (something to be tamed or subdued). Wordsworth famously describes this ennobling experience in his *Lines Written a Few Miles above Tintern Abbey*:

> To look on nature, not as in the hour
> Of thoughtless youth; but hearing oftentimes
> The still, sad music of humanity,
> Not harsh nor grating, though of ample power
> To chasten and subdue. And I have felt
> A presence that disturbs me with the joy
> Of elevated thoughts; a sense sublime,
> Of something far more deeply infused.[69]

In short, developing one's aesthetic sensitivity can have a morally uplifting effect; the value of life is revealed through aesthetic contemplation when one lets oneself be astonished by the beauty of life.

Gratitude

One may argue that contemplation of the beauty of nature is a naive sentimentalist outlook that ignores the reality of pain, destruction, and waste inherent to the evolutionary process. Nature, we are told, is red in tooth and claw—a constant war of all against all—and we are but powerless spectators of a cosmic drama watching the tragedy of life with no prospect of ever escaping our fate. What meaning is there in beauty except an illusion of benevolent teleology?

---

[68] Schweitzer, *Out of My Life*, 261; Schweitzer, "First Sermon," 68.
[69] William Wordsworth, "Lines Written a Few Miles above Tintern Abbey, on Revisiting the Banks of the Wye during a Tour, 13 July 1789," in *Selected Poems*, ed. Stephen Gill (London: Penguin Books, 2004), 63.

Appreciation of the beauty of nature is not an act of self-delusion that views life as guided by providence. Schweitzer accepted the Darwinian picture of evolution; he was well aware of the sheer amount of unnecessary suffering in the world, to which he was exposed on a daily basis as a medical doctor: "Our existence makes its way at the cost of another; one destroys the other."[70] Although Schweitzer acknowledges this undisputable fact of life, he urges us not to be disheartened or conquered by despair but to confront reality with resilience, hope, and most importantly, the determination to affirm life. This act of affirmation should come from a precognitive inward compulsion; it requires that one put one's trust in life. We should see the world aright yet at the same time see it through reverent eyes—that is, from a perspective that views life as a blessing, not a predicament. In other words, reverence for life demands that we regard life as a gift. The natural response to having been given a gift is to feel grateful, and to feel grateful is to give thanks for acts of benevolence that we have not necessarily done anything to deserve. To put it crudely, gratitude repudiates attitudes that take life for granted.

Gratitude is more than an ephemeral feeling; it should shape one's outlook on and attitude toward life as a whole. As a virtue, gratitude is a central characteristic of reverence for life; it prompts charitable actions by calling forth the virtue of generosity. Indeed, gratitude arouses in us a sense of responsibility. Gifts, as anthropologist Marcel Mauss tells us, are never free; they invite the receiver to reciprocate.[71] The recipient of the gift of life thus bears the responsibility to protect and sustain life.

Given that we can survive only at the cost of other lives, Schweitzer argues that we are constantly "guilty" for the lives we take.[72] The German words used by Schweitzer and rendered as "guilt" are *Schuld* and *schuldig*. The translation to English is misleading and led Martin to conclude that Schweitzer's ethics was ultimately "guilt mongering."[73] In fact, as Goodin points out, in the contexts in which they appear, the German terms *Schuld* and *schuldig* do not connote guilt so much as a *debt* that we owe life; we have a "life-debt that must be repaid through ethical service."[74] Schweitzer does not want us to feel guilty—in the sense of feeling bad for having done something wrong—but seeks to instill a sense of "reverential obligation . . . in the moral fabric of the

[70] Schweitzer, *Civilization and Ethics*, 216.
[71] Marcel Mauss, *The Gift*, trans. W. D. Halls (London: Routledge, 2002).
[72] Schweitzer, *Philosophy of Civilization*, 317–18.
[73] Martin, "Rethinking Reverence for Life," 166.
[74] Goodin, *The New Rationalism*, 91–92.

person."[75] We are called to feel grateful and exhibit the virtue of reciprocal generosity. Having devoted the better part of his life to helping the sick in Africa, Schweitzer is a living illustration of the kind of generosity that reverence for life requires.[76]

In a nutshell, despite all the hardships and afflictions that life brings, we should embrace it as a gift to which the only appropriate response is gratitude. Gratitude induces a sense of responsibility toward other living beings and instills in us the virtue of generosity. In this sense, gratitude can be conceived as the moral memory of humanity.

The Sublime

Schweitzer's ethical mysticism is also partly inspired by the notion of the sublime, in particular as it is described by Schopenhauer.[77] The experience of the sublime is overwhelming. In contrast with the beautiful, which is characterized by pleasure, the sublime is tempered with feelings of pain, hostility, and even terror. As noted previously, appreciation of beauty in nature may belie the reality of the human condition. Conversely, the sublime reminds us that we shall never be able to completely merge with nature—to fully understand animals' perspectives and gain access to their experience of the world.[78] Whereas the beautiful makes one feel at home in the world, the sublime revives feelings of estrangement; it restores the fundamentally uncanny (*Unheimliche*) and tragic character of the world.

We find a similar duality to that of the beautiful and the sublime in the very concept of reverence for life. *Ehrfurcht* (reverence) is composed of the word *Ehre*, which signifies homage, honor, or consideration, and the word *Furcht*, which means fear, dread, or apprehension.[79] This is reminiscent of Rudolf Otto's account of the numinous as a mystery that is both fascinating (*fascinans*) and at the same time terrifying (*tremendum*).[80] For Schweitzer, life has this dual character; it is the source of both joys and sorrows and ultimately resists rational understanding: "The mystery of life is always too

[75] Goodin, *The New Rationalism*, 91–92.
[76] Schweitzer, *Out of My Life*, 82; Schweitzer, *Philosophy of Civilization*, 322.
[77] Arthur Schopenhauer, *The World as Will and Representation*, 2 vols., trans. E. F. J. Payne (New York: Dover, 1958).
[78] Peter Heymans, *Animality in British Romanticism* (New York: Routledge, 2012), 34.
[79] Spranger, "Différence entre *respect de la vie* et *Ehrfurcht*."
[80] Rudolf Otto, *The Idea of the Holy*, trans. John W. Harvey (Oxford: Oxford University Press, 1923).

profound for us . . . its value is beyond our capacity to estimate."[81] Therefore, the sublime can be seen as an exercise in cultivating a sincere and realistic outlook on the world.

In addition to shedding light on the nature of the human condition, the spiritual exercise of the sublime can play an important role in reverence for life by taking us through a journey of self-transcendence and life-affirmation. Both Schopenhauer and Schweitzer agree that the sublime is characterized by aesthetic disinterestedness. However, whereas for Schopenhauer, aesthetic detachment ultimately aims to annihilate the will, Schweitzer seeks to redirect its object. The Schweitzerian sublime does not negate the will but rather transforms it; it establishes the transition from the selfish will to the selfless will.[82] In other words, it is not passive "will-lessness" so much as active goodwill.

It is important to note that aesthetic detachment need not be life-denying. In quite the reverse, Schweitzer vehemently rejects Schopenhauer's pessimism, which he attributes to Eastern thought: "in no way does reverence for life allow the individual to give up interest in the world."[83] The transfiguration of the self through the sublime is not the attainment of some kind of apathetic, otherworldly bliss. Rather, it is the *reaffirmation* of this world seen from a renewed and purified perspective—a perspective brought about by a conversion from egoistic self-love to all-encompassing neighbor-love, or to phrase it in a more Darwinian manner, from the instinct of self-preservation to the drive to preserve nature as a whole. As Schweitzer declares, "ethical is more than unegoistic. Only the reverence felt by my will to live for every other will to live is ethical."[84] The sublime shatters obstacles to wider moral sensibility. In that sense, the experience of sublimity should be seen as establishing the conditions for sharing a genuinely moral connection with others. The sublime enables us to "experience in ourselves something of the truth of the saying: 'He that loseth his life shall find it.'"[85] As Rousseau puts it, genuine empathy arises from our "transporting ourselves outside of ourselves and identifying with the suffering animal, by leaving, as it were, our

---

[81] Schweitzer, *Teaching of Reverence*, 131.

[82] Schopenhauer, *The World as Will and Representation*, 330–55; Schweitzer, *Teaching of Reverence*, 151; *Civilization and Ethics, 224.*

[83] Schweitzer, *Civilization and Ethics*, 150, 232.

[84] Albert Schweitzer, *Albert Schweitzer's Ethical Vision: A Source Book*, ed. Predrag Cicovacki (Oxford: Oxford University Press, 2009), 149.

[85] Schweitzer, *Civilization and Ethics*, 226.

own being to take on its being."[86] Similarly, Coleridge writes: "Strange & generous Self, that can only be such a Self, by a complete divesting of all that men call self."[87] In other words, one distances oneself from life in order to better affirm it. As a result, the experience of sublimity may render the individual's will and self more compassionate.

Compassion is a cardinal virtue in Schweitzer's ethics of reverence for life. The virtue of compassion may be described as the long-term commitment to feel empathy toward other living beings and the enduring disposition to act accordingly.[88] Compassion often connotes a passive attitude; "it denotes . . . only interest in the suffering will-to-live."[89] To clarify the role of compassion, it is helpful to consider one of its correlated virtues: love, in particular Christian love (*caritas/agape*). Christian love is a virtue with which Schweitzer, as a Lutheran theologian and pastor, was well acquainted. In fact, he once claimed that "the ethics of reverence for life is nothing but Jesus' great commandment to love."[90] It is worth stressing that love is not a matter of mere feeling or passion, as common parlance sometimes suggests. Rather, Christian love is volitional; it is primarily characterized by an attitude of beneficence or goodwill. This is why the opposite of Christian love is not hate but mere "indifference, simply not caring."[91] Compassion in reverence for life encompasses both the passive and active dimensions of love. The compassionate person cares for all life.

To summarize, Schweitzer's ethical mysticism is characterized by a spiritual awakening that serves as a gateway to the genuine moral life. For Schweitzer, being truly ethical demands an existential commitment to a life-affirming world- and life-view. The spiritual exercise of aesthetic contemplation of the beautiful and the sublime can contribute to this goal. Aesthetic detachment should be understood as a transformative experience aimed at transcending our egoistic inclinations. This will result in a renewed and

[86] Jean-Jacques Rousseau, *Emile, or On Education*, trans. Barbara Foxley (London: Everyman's Library, 1974), 184.

[87] Samuel Taylor Coleridge, *Shorter Works and Fragments*, vol. 11, bk. 1, of *The Collected Works of Samuel Taylor Coleridge*, ed. H. J. and J. R. de J. Jackson (Princeton, NJ: Princeton University Press, 1995), 215.

[88] Schweitzer, *Philosophy of Civilization*, 311.

[89] Schweitzer, *Civilization and Ethics*, 215.

[90] Albert Schweitzer, *Letters, 1905–1965*, ed. Hans Walter Bähr, trans. Joachim Neugroschel (New York: Free Press, 1992), 123; Schweitzer, *Out of My Life*, 270.

[91] Joseph F. Fletcher, *Situation Ethics: The New Morality* (Louisville, KY: Westminster John Knox Press, 1966), 104–5.

purified outlook on life imbued with a sense of deep compassion for all living beings.

Conclusion

The concept of reverence for life is holophrastic. It is simultaneously an individualistic ethics of character and excellence and an outlook, a mindset, and a mystical necessity of thought. What is clear is that it cannot be reduced to a set of inflexible principles that uphold the inviolability of life in all situations. Going beyond the mainstream systematic moral theories of his day, Schweitzer sought to "produce a deepening of ethical insight."[92] To this end, he put forth a simple but not unsophisticated ethics grounded in all aspects of human experience. In this respect, his philosophy is more akin to the ancients' concern with human flourishing and their vision of philosophy as a way of life. In many ways, Schweitzer also remained faithful to the Christianity of his younger years; treading in the footsteps of Jesus of Nazareth, he takes us on a path of profound simplicity and sincerity, as well as hope and charity.[93]

This chapter has not delved into the depths of Schweitzer's philosophy, such as his metaphysical understanding of the will-to-live or the influence of Eastern schools of thought on his views.[94] Instead, I have endeavored to examine and build upon the practical life- and worldview for which he wished to be remembered and whose primary aim is to help us become genuinely ethical persons. I have explored where the notion of reverence for life might take us by developing two core features of Schweitzer's philosophy of civilization: (1) virtue and (2) mysticism. I have described the former as essentially a self-centered ethics of self-realization and the latter as mainly an other-centered aesthetico-spiritual outlook and transformative experience. These should be seen as two complementary aspects of Schweitzer's spiritual and moral enterprise insofar as they reconcile the heart with the mind by intertwining reflective virtuous character with mystical sublime character. The union of these two constitutes the fully realized life of reverence.

---

[92] Schweitzer, *Civilization and Ethics*, 217.
[93] Schweitzer, *Out of My Life*, 274; Schweitzer, *Civilization and Ethics*, 242.
[94] See, respectively, Goodin, *The New Rationalism*; and Barsam, *Reverence for Life*.

Reverence makes us kneel down in gratitude and bow our heads in humility, but it also compels us to stand firm in the determination and commitment to affirm and preserve life with the aid of all the virtues and excellences that we can muster. Reverence for life can help us reevaluate our ways of conceiving of, relating to, and interacting with our fellow creatures as well as nature as a whole—for when we see the world through reverent eyes, we cannot but be dazzled by the inestimable and awesome beauty of the mystery of life.

Bibliography

Agar, Nicholas. *Recent Defences of Biocentrism.* New York: Colombia University Press, 2001.

Aristotle. *Nicomachean Ethics.* 2nd ed. Translated by Terence Irwin. Indianapolis: Hackett, 1999.

Barsam, Ara Paul. *Reverence for Life: Albert Schweitzer's Great Contribution to Ethical Thought.* Oxford: Oxford University Press, 2008.

Caillois, Roger. *Esthétique généralisée.* Paris: Gallimard, 1988.

Cavalieri, Paola. *The Animal Question.* Translated by Catherine Woollard. Oxford: Oxford University Press, 2001.

Chapman, Robert L. "The Goat-Stag and the Sphinx: The Place of the Virtues in Environmental Ethics." *Environmental Values* 11 (2002): 112–44.

Clark, Henry. *The Philosophy of Albert Schweitzer.* London: Methuen, 1964.

Coleridge, Samuel Taylor. *Biographia Literaria.* Vol. 7 of *The Collected Works of Samuel Taylor Coleridge,* edited by James Engell and Walter Jackson Bate. Princeton, NJ: Princeton University Press, 1983.

Coleridge, Samuel Taylor. *Shorter Works and Fragments.* Vol. 11 of *The Collected Works of Samuel Taylor Coleridge,* edited by H. J. and J. R. de J. Jackson. Princeton, NJ: Princeton University Press, 1995.

DeGrazia, David. *Animal Rights: A Very Short Introduction.* Oxford: Oxford University Press, 2002.

Descartes, René. *The Passions of the Soul.* Translated by Stephen H. Voss. Indianapolis: Hackett, 1989.

Fletcher, Joseph F. *Situation Ethics: The New Morality.* Louisville, KY: Westminster John Knox Press, 1966.

Goodin, David K. *The New Rationalism: Albert Schweitzer's Philosophy of Reverence for Life.* Montreal: McGill University Press, 2013.

Gross, Aaron, and Anne Vallely, eds. *Animals and the Human Imagination.* New York: Columbia University Press, 2012.

Hadot, Pierre. *Philosophy as a Way of Life.* Edited by Arnold Davidson. Translated by Michael Chase. Oxford: Blackwell, 1995.

Hadot, Pierre. *What Is Ancient Philosophy?* Translated by Michael Chase. Cambridge, MA: Harvard University Press, 2002.

Hartshorne, Charles. *Wisdom as Moderation: A Philosophy of the Middle Way.* New York: State University of New York Press, 1987.

Hepburn, Ronald W. *Wonder and Other Essays.* Edinburgh: Edinburgh University Press, 1984.

Heymans, Peter. *Animality in British Romanticism.* New York: Routledge, 2012.

Hursthouse, Rosalind. "Applying Virtue Ethics to Our Treatment of the Other Animals." In *The Practice of Virtue: Classical and Contemporary Readings in Virtue Ethics*, edited by Jennifer Welchman. Indianapolis: Hackett, 2006.

Hursthouse, Rosalind. "Normative Virtue Ethics." In *Ethical Theory: An Anthology*, 2nd ed., edited by Russell Shafer-Landau. Oxford: Wiley-Blackwell, 2013.

Hursthouse, Rosalind. "Virtue Ethics and the Treatment of Animals." In *The Oxford Handbook of Animal Ethics*, edited by Tom L. Beauchamp and R. G. Frey. Oxford: Oxford University Press, 2011.

Leahy, Michael P. T. *Against Liberation: Putting Animals in Perspective.* London: Routledge, 1991.

Leopold, Aldo. *A Sand County Almanac, and Sketches Here and There.* Oxford: Oxford University Press, 1987.

Linzey, Andrew. *Why Animal Suffering Matters.* Oxford: Oxford University Press, 2009.

Martin, Mike W. *Albert Schweitzer's Reverence for Life: Ethical Idealism and Self-Realization.* London: Ashgate, 2007.

Martin, Mike W. "Rethinking Reverence for Life." In *Reverence for Life: The Ethics of Albert Schweitzer for the Twenty-First Century*, edited by Marvin Meyer and Kurt Bergel. New York: Syracuse University Press, 2002.

Mauss, Marcel. *The Gift.* Translated by W. D. Halls. London: Routledge, 2002.

Murdoch, Iris. *The Sovereignty of the Good.* London: Routledge and Kegan Paul, 1970.

Otto, Rudolf. *The Idea of the Holy.* Translated by John W. Harvey (Oxford: Oxford University Press, 1923.

Pascal, Roy. *Design and Truth in Autobiography.* London: Routledge, 2016.

Plato. *Theaetetus.* In *The Dialogues of Plato*, translated by Benjamin Jowett. Oxford: Oxford University Press, 1892.

Regan, Tom. *The Case for Animal Rights.* Rev. ed. Berkley: University of California Press, 2004.

Rousseau, Jean-Jacques. *Emile, or On Education.* Translated by Barbara Foxley. London: Everyman's Library, 1974.

Schopenhauer, Arthur. *The World as Will and Representation.* 2 vols. Translated by E. F. J. Payne. New York: Dover, 1958.

Schweitzer, Albert. *Albert Schweitzer's Ethical Vision: A Source Book.* Edited by Predrag Cicovacki. Oxford: Oxford University Press, 2009.

Schweitzer, Albert. *Civilization and Ethics.* Translated by C. T. Campion. London: Unwin Books, 1961.

Schweitzer, Albert. *The Decay and Restoration of Civilization.* Translated by C. T. Campion. New York: Prometheus Books, 1987.

Schweitzer, Albert. "The Ethics of Reverence for Life." In *Reverence for Life: The Ethics of Albert Schweitzer for the Twenty-First Century*, edited by Marvin Meyer and Kurt Bergel. New York: Syracuse University Press, 2002.

Schweitzer, Albert. "First Sermon on Reverence for Life." In *Reverence for Life: The Ethics of Albert Schweitzer for the Twenty-First Century*, edited by Marvin Meyer and Kurt Bergel. New York: Syracuse University Press, 2002.

Schweitzer, Albert. *Letters, 1905–1965.* Edited by Hans Walter Bahr. Translated by Joachim Neugroschel. New York: Free Press, 1992.

Schweitzer, Albert. *Out of My Life and Thought.* Translated by C. T. Campion. London: George Allen & Unwin, 1933.

Schweitzer, Albert. *A Place for Revelation: Sermons on Reverence for Life.* Translated by David Larrimore Holland. New York: Macmillan, 1988.

Schweitzer, Albert. *The Philosophy of Civilization.* Translated by C. T. Campion. New York: Prometheus Books, 1987.

Schweitzer, Albert. *Reverence for Life: The Words of Albert Schweitzer.* Edited by Harold E. Robles. New York: HarperCollins, 1993.

Schweitzer, Albert. *The Teaching of Reverence for Life.* Translated by Richard Winston and Clara Winston. New York: Holt, Rinehart and Winston, 1965.

Singer, Peter. *Animal Liberation: A New Ethics for Our Treatment of Animals.* London: Cape, 1975.

Spranger, E. "Différence entre *respect de la vie* et *Ehrfurcht.*" *Cahiers Albert Schweitzer* 37 (Winter 1977–78).

Taylor, Paul W. "The Ethics of Respect for Nature." *Environmental Ethics* 3 (1981): 197–218.

Taylor, Paul W. *Respect for Nature: A Theory of Environmental Ethics.* 25th anniv. ed. Princeton, NJ: Princeton University Press, 2011.

Ulam, Stanislaw M. *Adventures of a Mathematician.* New York: Charles Scribner's Sons, 1976.

Woodruff, Paul. *Reverence: Renewing a Forgotten Virtue.* Oxford: Oxford University Press, 2001.

Wordsworth, William. *Selected Poems.* Edited by Stephen Gill. London: Penguin Books, 2004.

18

Martin Buber (1878–1965)

Encountering Animals, a Prelude to the Animal Question

Ryan Brand

Alles wirkliche Leben ist Begegnung.

—Martin Buber[1]

Do animals have a companion in Martin Buber?[2] Do his writings unfurl the possibility of ethical comportment with other animals? Or might

[1] Martin Buber, *Ich und Du* (Leipzig: Insel-Verlag, 1923). My use of "encountering" in the title is a
play on the difference between Ronald Gregor Smith's and Walter Kaufmann's translations of Buber's
phrase quoted here: "all real living is meeting" versus "all actual life is encounter," respectively (I
combine Smith's emphasis on the gerund and Kaufman's specific diction). See Martin Buber, *I and
Thou*, trans. Ronald Gregor Smith (New York: Scribner's, 1958); and Martin Buber, *I and Thou*, trans.
Walter Kaufmann (New York: Scribner's, 1970). Moreover, the phrase "encountering animals" plays
on its own grammatical ambiguity. Looking forward to the end of this chapter, not only do *we* (as the
subject) encounter animals, but other animals too, it can be read, encounter us (as subjects themselves)—but also, of course, more than us (as we too may encounter a plurality of beings). This later
presupposition would have been difficult for Buber to accept, at least in part, given how he defined
human nature. However, as I will argue, aspects of Buber's life and work do not prohibit widening
his own direction; indeed, they open possibilities for support of such a thesis, and this is partly why
I refer in the title to a "prelude." This chapter focuses on aspects that provide the space for addressing
the question of the animal in Buber's work. Detailed discussion of Buber on human nature, however, is outside the scope of this chapter. See Martin Buber, *Between Man and Man*, trans. Ronald
Gregor Smith (London: Routledge, 2002; first published 1947), or any of his many articulations
of Hebrew humanism and the distinctions therein between the human and the animal—for example, Martin Buber, *A Believing Humanism: My Testament, 1902–1965*, trans. Maurice Friedman
(New York: Simon and Schuster, 1967), 119–20.

[2] By "companion" I do not merely mean friendship or another synonym, but the significance
due Donna Haraway's notion of "companion species" as "less a category than a pointer to an ongoing 'becoming with,' to be a much richer web to inhabit" (Donna Haraway, *When Species Meet*
[Minneapolis: University of Minnesota Press, 2008], 16), which for me seems to foreshadow Buber's
own emphasis on the significance of reciprocity. For Haraway, "partners do not precede their relating;
all that is, is the fruit of becoming with: those are the mantras of companion species" (17). She notes
that the etymology of "companion" derives from the Latin *cum pains*, "with bread," its verb form
meaning "to consort, to keep company" (17). "To knot companion and species together in encounter,
in regard and respect, is to enter the world of becoming with, where *who and what are* is precisely

Ryan Brand, *Martin Buber (1878–1965)* In: *Animal Theologians*. Edited by: Andrew Linzey and Clair Linzey,
Oxford University Press. © Oxford University Press 2023. DOI: 10.1093/oso/9780197655542.003.0019

the ostensible opening afforded by his various reflections on animals remain chained by his own humanist presuppositions and the modern confinement of human exceptionalism? On the one hand, his initial inclusion of animals in his 1923 magnum opus *Ich und Du* (*I and Thou*), a book that Buber himself deemed his most important,[3] might answer the question of Buber as a companion for other animals.[4] However, on the other hand, in 1958 Buber suggested a revision of *I and Thou*, using different terminology for how one comes to be a subject of encounter and positing a qualitative difference between humans and other animals. This revision effectively caged the latter, limiting how they are included within Buber's formation of the intersubjective I–You relation.[5] Though he does not entirely efface animals from the possibility of encounter, Buber reflects the inured humanism of his time, affirming, in his words, "a primal abyss,"[6] an ontological divide between humans and other animals, and privileging the human as special—transcending animality. For Buber what is distinctive about the human is the

---

what is at stake. . . . I am not posthumanist; I am who I become with companion species, who and which make a mess out of categories in the making of kin and kind" (19). Echoes of Buber here in Haraway, albeit not named, unite the two through time in a kind of strange kinship. In arguing for the nature of the I–Thou, Maurice Friedman writes, "What is essential is not what goes on in the mind of the partners but what happens between them." Maurice Friedman, "Martin Buber and Mikhail Bakhtin: The Dialogue of Voices and the Word That Is Spoken," in *Dialogue as a Means of Collective Communication*, ed. Bela H. Banathy and Patrick M. Jenlink (New York: Springer, 2004), 29.

[3] Kaufmann notes that Buber understood *I and Thou* as his most important book and his contribution to philosophy. Walter Kaufmann, "Buber's Failure and Triumphs," in *Martin Buber: A Centenary Volume*, ed. Haim Gordon and Jochanan Bloch (Jersey City: Ktav, 1984), 8.

[4] The word "thou" is the Anglo-Saxon informal pronoun; however, given its association with the KJV Bible, it has colloquially taken formal status, which belies its earlier use, not in formal address but in the intimacy due a personal relationship. In this chapter I will use "Thou" when citing the title specifically, but "you" (highlighting the informal pronoun) when speaking directly about the relation of encounter itself. As a book, *I and Thou* emerged from Buber's lectures in the Freie Jüdische Lehrhaus, originally titled "Religion as Presence." Bernhard Casper, "Franz Rosenzweig's Criticism of Buber's *I and Thou*," in *Martin Buber: A Centenary Volume*, ed. Haim Gordon and Jochanan Bloc (Jersey City: Ktav, 1984), 142.

[5] Friedman explains,

> Early in 1957, Buber began preparation for a new German and English edition of *I and Thou*. Buber asked me to draw up for him a list of the questions that I felt most often occurred to people concerning *I and Thou*, and to address these questions he wrote what he originally conceived of as a preface but later changed to a postscript, or afterword. Although Buber was not willing to give up the I–Thou relationship with nature, he recognized that it was confusing to the reader and even said to me that if he were to write *I and Thou* again, he would try to find some different vocabulary to make the distinction. (Maurice Friedman, *Encounter on the Narrow Ridge: A Life of Martin Buber* [New York: Paragon House, 1993], 378)

For the aforementioned "afterword," see Buber, *I and Thou*, trans. Ronald Gregor Smith, 123–37.

[6] Buber, *Between Man and Man*, 91. "It is not radicality that characterizes man as separated by a primal abyss from all that is merely animal, but it is his potentiality. . . . Man is the crystallized potentiality of existence" (91).

potentiality for fullness of an I–You encounter. The essence of being human is the capacity for being in relation.[7] Buber's own writing was an attempt to recover a form of humanism—specifically, "the relation of man to all existing beings"[8]—and position it in relation to Jewish thought;[9] however, I argue that his rich reflections on encountering animals manifest the space to read Buber against his own humanist (re)capitulations.

This chapter confronts aspects of his contact with other animals that call into question his own hierarchical divide. His inclusion of and respect for other animals were well ahead of his time. Maurice Friedman, Buber's biographer, suggests it was Buber's personal intimacy with other animals that made it impossible for him to cull them entirely from his philosophy of dialogue, even in the face of dogged, collegial discontent (e.g., Bergmann, Levinas, Fackenheim, Rotenstreich).[10] Animals, for Buber, are more than a

---

[7] The step into relation for Buber is voluntary. The relational ontology of Haraway posits our becoming as never not in relation (for Haraway it is not a form of voluntarism).

[8] Buber, A Believing Humanism, 119.

[9] Buber uses the term "humanism" to identify his own position, distinguishing between European humanism and Hebrew humanism. The former is a focus on the inner life of humanity alone; the latter, for Buber, includes both the life of individuals *and* the life of the community. Hebrew humanism includes, he writes, "all of life's reality." Martin Buber, *Israel and the World: Essays in a Time of Crisis* (Syracuse: Syracuse University Press, 1997), 241. See Matthew Calarco, "The Retrieval of Humanism in Buber and Levinas," in *Levinas and Buber: Dialogue and Difference*, ed. Peter Atterton, Matthew Calarco, and Maurice Friedman (Pittsburgh: Duquesne University Press, 2004), 250–61.

[10] In a letter to Buber dated December 1, 1947, Hugo Bergmann writes: "I noticed two difficulties.... One is the mutuality of the I–Thou relationship when the partner is an animal, a plant, or a stone. In my lecture, I emphasized that you did not mean empathy, which is a one-sided relationship, but true mutuality. I must confess, however, that things are not quite clear to me when the dialogue involves an inanimate partner." Martin Buber, *The Letters of Martin Buber: Life of Dialogue*, ed. Nahum N. Glatzer and Paul Mendes-Flohr, trans. Richard Winston, Clara Winston, and Harry Zohn (New York: Schocken Books, 1991), 525. Peter Atterton writes, apropos of Emmanuel Levinas, "Levinas is one critic for whom the possibility of Thou-saying (*Du-Sagen*) to nonhuman beings constitutes a retreat from the fundamental insight of *I and Thou*.... To speak of an I–Thou with anything other than the human undermines what for Levinas is 'Buber's fundamental contribution to the theory of knowledge,'" replacing its potential ethical significance with formalism so supposed. Peter Atterton, "Face-to-Face with the Other Animal?," in *Levinas and Buber: Dialogue and Difference*, ed. Peter Atterton, Matthew Calarco, and Maurice Friedman (Pittsburgh: Duquesne University Press, 2004), 262. Levinas repeats this critique in *Totality and Infinity*, even though Buber continued to address this criticism in his many replies to his interlocutors. Emmanuel Levinas, *Totality and Infinity*, trans. Alphonso Lingis (Pittsburgh: Duquesne University Press, 1969; first published 1961), 68. Apropos of Fackenheim and Rotenstreich, Buber addresses their concerns on the inclusion of nature (and God) as "the problem of mutuality" in his "Replies to My Critics," in *The Philosophy of Martin Buber*, ed. Paul Arthur Schilpp and Maurice Friedman (Chicago: Open Court, 1967), 124–31. There he reproduces at length large sections of the 1958 "postscript" from *I and Thou*. Elsewhere Buber writes, "Only in our time has the insight into the relationship between I and Thou as an all-embracing one begun to become clear" (*A Believing Humanism*, 129). However, this expansion is what would lead both Rosenzweig and Levinas to reject the I–Thou, though Levinas would still find room for it in terms of erotic relation. Richard A. Cohen, *Elevations: The Height of the Good in Rosenzweig and Levinas* (Chicago: University of Chicago Press, 1994), 93. "Levinas agrees [with Rosenzweig] that Buber's account of the I–Thou is indeed distorted, and that it is distorted because it is too general, thereby claiming to account for more than it actually does account for." Cohen, *Elevations*, 26.

series of pulleys, levers, and strings; they transcend Cartesian instrumentality. However, given his own humanism, their status as subjects of encounter remains a live question unsettled by his corpus.[11] Buber continues the humanist legacy of his forebears but attends to other animals in ways that temper the epistemological privilege of human reason. My chapter unearths this tension between Buber's anticipation or empathy for the question of the animal and his metaphysical humanism.[12] His reflections on animals in his philosophy of dialogue, in the I–You relation, and in his analysis of mutuality (*Mutualität*) maintain the hegemony of humanism and yet say more than they intend to say. It is not only for the birds to read Buber as a prelude to contemporary formations of the animal question. Indeed, one may read Buber as the dawn chorus for the coming deconstruction of a univocal, universal notion of "the Animal" in the general singular, which effaces significant differences between different animals.[13] I show how Buber's animals, corralled by the humanist legacy, bite back, vying for a seat at the proverbial table.

The significance of Buber for doing animal ethics emerges in conversation between his person and his writing. My chapter is a prolegomenon for folding Buber into the conversation on religion, animals, and ethics, addressing a tension in Buber's texts that we cannot ignore if we are to call on Buber as a potential source (and kindred spirit) for critical animal studies.[14]

---

[11] The mechanical language to describe other animals remains largely from the infamous Cartesian legacy.

[12] My use of the term "humanism" follows contemporary philosophical positions that have been called "posthumanist," which, in short, deconstruct modern notions of "the human." My hope (beyond the scope of this chapter) is to position Buber for the study of contact in our more-than-human world, which is to say a world constituted by "natureculture entanglements" (Haraway's term). This means not bifurcated places but related spaces, opposing well-worn modernist oppositions, *always already* embodied through material practices, enmeshed in various relatings. In broad terms, a "posthumanist" orientation does not efface "the human" as a generative category but deconstructs that which historically has been the more common interpretation of this term—specifically, the "human" as autonomous or sovereign, the locus of what gets to count as knowledge and truth and for whom alone meaning matters (as opposed to other creatures defined by a constitutive lack for meaningful engagement). Buber too rejects human reason as the essence of humanity, yet he separates the human from other life, including animal life, on account that animals do not inhabit the fullness of the world, remaining captive to an environment or realm. See Maurice Friedman, *Martin Buber: The Life of Dialogue* (London: Routledge, 2002), 92.

[13] The contemporary philosopher David Wood highlights the problem with this notion of the general singular. He says, "There are no animals 'as such,' rather only the extraordinary variety that in the animal alphabet would begin with ants, apes, arachnids, antelopes, aardvarks, anchovies, alligators, Americans, Australians . . ." David Wood, *The Step Back: Ethics and Politics after Deconstruction* (New York: State University of New York Press, 2006), 29.

[14] Reading Buber for doing animal ethics is only the beginning. His work on animals may also unfurl possibilities for engaging the question of religion and how Buber understood religiosity, including the potentiality of shaping categories for mapping animals themselves as religious subjects, specifically in mutual religious becoming.

Ultimately, attending to Buber's animal encounters augments his relational ethics, framing him as a resource for communities to better understand not only the variety of ways animals comport themselves within the world but also our own comportment in animal worlds, which we are always already becoming-with.

The I–You Relation and the Other-Than-Human

The I–You relation is Buber's most popular contribution to modern thought. In *I and Thou* he posits an account of two fundamental forms of being human, represented in two word pairs, I–You and I–It. The former is the world of personal encounter—akin to that colloquial moment in which time stands still when one is face-to-face with a lover; the latter, the objective world of experience.[15] Encounters happen as lived participation. The I does not experience You as another object in the world but lives You through relation. Defining the human, the two modes of being—the interpersonal I–You and the instrumental I–It relation—compose, Buber notes, "the double structure of human existence itself."[16] Our dual nature as humans, for Buber, delineates us from other animals. Though Buber includes other animals as potential partners of encounter, the defining element of any I–You relation is the human in relation.[17]

The I–You relation is fundamentally different from relations of instrumentality or pragmatic utility. It names the shared space between two interlocutors, mutually joined yet still, and importantly, distinct. The

[15] Interestingly, the metaphor of a single lover extended to lovers plural does not work in this context. For better or for worse, Buber's I–Thou relation is deeply isolating. Concerning other animals, it may prove difficult to think of the I–Thou relation given the phenomenal worlds of other animals for whom being-in-the-world means embodied collectivity. Which animals Buber actually mentions (e.g., cats and horses) is perhaps here most significant because they are animals who may live in isolation. Here the potential limitations of the I–Thou relation for doing animal ethics (with some animals) are more obvious.
[16] Martin Buber, "Religion and Philosophy," in *Eclipse of God: Studies in the Relation between Religion and Philosophy*, trans. Maurice Friedman (Atlantic Highlands, NJ: International Humanities Press, 1988; first published 1952), 44.
[17] In his introduction to Buber's *Knowledge of Man*, Friedman writes, "Buber defines man as the creature capable of entering into living relation with the world of things." Maurice Friedman, "Introductory Essay," in *The Knowledge of Man: Selected Essays*, by Martin Buber, trans. Maurice Friedman and Ronald Gregor Smith (New York: Harper & Row, 1965; first published 1952), 16. Friedman further nuances Buber's humanism: "Buber concludes 'What is Man?' with the statement that the uniqueness of man is to be found not in the individual, nor in the collective, but in the meeting of 'I and Thou'" (16). However, I argue, imparting to other animals the human capacity to initiate an encounter does not undermine Buber's philosophical anthropology.

embodiment of the human in terms of the I–You and I–It relations—the meeting of another within encounter and the coordination of things as experienced, respectively—is, for Buber, "part of the basic truth of the human world."[18] His ontology precludes him from thinking of animals as subjects of encounter as he does humans. Buber remains skeptical of conferring on animals volitional capacities: "The question may be asked at this point whether we have any right to speak of a 'reply' or 'address' that comes from outside the sphere to which in our consideration of the orders of being we ascribe spontaneity and consciousness as if they were like a reply or address in the human world in which we live."[19] In this sense Buber remained true to his own self-titled philosophical anthropology—the apex of which was the interhuman (*Zwishenmenschlichen*) mutual relation.[20] The question of mutuality (*Mutualität*) in relation to nature (the other-than-human) is the tension between Buber's sensitivity toward other beings and the primacy he gives to our human being.[21] This tension was the greatest roadblock to the reception of Buber's philosophy.[22]

His inclusion of other beings begins in one of his earliest publications, an essay on Jakob Böhme,[23] which notes kinship with both a tree and the eyes of animals. Buber returns to these themes in *Extase und Bekenntnis* (1909)[24]

---

[18] Buber, *I and Thou*, trans. Walter Kaufmann, 81.

[19] Buber, afterword to *I and Thou*, trans. Walter Kaufmann, 169–83. In what sense does Buber allow the possibility for an animal to address me as a human or respond to my advance creatively, rather than simply react mechanically? Here, in the afterword, Buber cages his cats from *I and Thou*—who, being moved by his breath, are now for him understood as more metaphorical than actual.

[20] In his 1938 inaugural lecture delivered at the Hebrew University, "What Is Man?," Buber identifies himself as a "philosophical anthropologist" (*der Philosoph der Anthropologie treibt*). See Martin Buber, *Das Problem des Menschen* (Heidelberg: Schneider, 1948), 95, and *Between Man and Man*, trans. Ronald Gregor Smith (London: Kegan Paul, 1947), 164. His most popular works, *I and Thou*, *Between Man and Man*, and *The Knowledge of Man*, aim to articulate the elements of being human. In a deep sense Buber is an ideal humanist.

[21] The question of reciprocity is Levinas's main objection. Animals, as part of nature, are "things" for Levinas, incapable of reciprocity, not subjects of his ethical imperative. For the place of animals in Levinas see his interview with Tamra Wright, Peter Hughes, and Alison Ainley, "The Paradox of Morality: An Interview with Emmanuel Levinas," trans. A. Benjamin and T. Wright, in *The Provocation of Levinas: Rethinking the Other*, ed. Robert Bernasconi and David Wood (London: Routledge, 1988), 168–180.

[22] Friedman notes, "In the discussion that followed the delivery of 'Religion and Philosophy' at Columbia University [1951], Buber said that he had been often criticized for the I–Thou relationship with nature than for any other part of his philosophy. But when he looked at the great tree outside his window, he could not deny the reality of the meeting with it." Friedman, *Encounter on the Narrow Ridge*, 341–42. Peter Atterton, a contemporary reader of Buber, agrees: "It is perhaps no exaggeration to say that the inclusion (*Umfassung*) . . . of nature within the I–Thou relation has been the biggest obstacle to the reception of Buber's thought." Atterton, "Face-to-Face," 262.

[23] Martin Buber, "Ueber Jakob Böhme," *Wiener Rundschau* 5, no. 12 (1901): 251–53.

[24] Martin Buber, "Exstase und Bekenntnis," in *Ekstatische Konfessionen* (Jena: Eugen Diederichs Verlag, 1909).

and *Daniel* (1913),[25] but the themes are most fully developed in *I and Thou*, which Buber himself identified as his mature thought.[26] His inclusion of other animals would not end there, however; as Friedman writes, "Buber's experience of inclusion in relation to nature is perhaps the most consistent thread in his entire philosophy."[27] Among the animals Buber mentions, cats reign supreme. In a passage as famous as it is unprecedented, Buber ruminates on the arresting allure of a cat's gaze, of which he says, "No other event has made me so deeply aware of the evanescent actuality in all relationships to other beings, the sublime melancholy of our lot."[28]

For Buber cats were not just good to think with but were also good companions with whom he lived.[29] Friedman cites a 1921 letter from Paula, Buber's spouse, to a friend, E. E. Rappeport, with a mention of their cats: "Do you still remember the little cat whose matted hair you cut off? He is still with us and I hope to have him for a long time. He has become my favorite. At every meal he sits on my knees and lays his forepaws on the table. He lives among us like an imp. He loves Martin most respectfully, me most tenderly, Eva he trusts boundlessly, but with Raffi [Buber's son] he has, with reason, some anxiety."[30] Moreover, Friedman continues, "along with books, his study was never lacking cats, which entered freely through the open window and lay on the sofa in his study. Buber spoke to the cats as if they were human beings, and they minded him in the same way. If he said to a familiar cat, 'Ja,

---

[25] Martin Buber, *Daniel: Dialogues on Realization*, trans. Maurice Friedman (New York: McGraw-Hill, 1965); first published as Martin Buber, *Daniel: Gespräche von der Verwirklichung* (Leipzig: Insel, 1913).

[26] Of these occurrences that mention trees and cats, Friedman says that "the emotional content of the experience as described in these two works is almost identical!" Friedman, *Life of Dialogue*, 56.

[27] Friedman, *Encounter on the Narrow Ridge*, 67.

[28] Buber, *I and Thou*, trans. Walter Kaufmann, 144–45:

> The eyes of an animal have the capacity of a great language. . . . I sometimes look into the eyes of a house cat. The domesticated animal has not by any means received the gift of the truly "eloquent" glance from us, as a human conceit suggests sometimes; what it has from us is only the ability—purchased with the loss of its elementary naturalness—to turn this gaze upon us brutes. . . . Undeniably, this cat began its glance by asking me with a glance that was ignited by the breath of my glance: "Can it be that you mean me? Do you actually want that I should not merely do tricks for you? Do I concern you? Am I there for you? Am I there? What is that coming from you? What is that around me? What is it about me? What is that?!" . . . There the glance of the animal, the language of anxiety, had risen hugely—and set almost at once.

[29] "Now it is not merely the horse on his father's farm that is uncanny but the household cat (Martin and Paula were great lovers of cats and always had a number in house)." Friedman, *Encounter on the Narrow Ridge*, 130. In 1948, seventeen years before his death, Buber, Friedman notes, had nine cats, though the number sadly dropped to only three by 1960. Friedman, *Encounter on the Narrow Ridge*, 280, 437.

[30] Friedman, *Encounter on the Narrow Ridge*, 116.

what are you doing? Lie down in the corner and don't disturb me,' the cat obeyed."[31] If only the relationship with his critics had been as easy.

The pervading philosophical metaphysical humanism (or human exceptionalism) of Buber's day became more pronounced in his work as he struggled to assuage the fears of his colleagues concerning the inclusion of other animals in the I–You relation. The ideology of humanism that was in play (and that today largely remains intact across the humanities) posits a privileged position of the human through an ontological divide, not in Darwinian terms of degree but in kind: a divide between the human and the animal. In the afterword of *I and Thou*, Buber posits a qualitative difference between humans and other animals, encaging the latter and limiting their possibilities within the intersubjective encounter. This difference manifests in the hierarchy within the three metaphors he uses to distinguish a nuanced I–You relation (or event of encounter) between beings—"over-threshold" (*Überschwelle*), "threshold" (*Schwelle*), and "pre-threshold" (*Vorschwelle*), which define the collective spaces of humans, animals, and plants, respectively. Interestingly, this hierarchy shares a similar structure to Martin Heidegger's distinction between humans as *Dasein* (being-in-the-world), animals as poor in world, and plants as worldless.[32] What, then, might we infer from this nuanced language for Buber's animals in the I–You relation? What does this say about other animals for Buber and their place in the world? Does the animal here become a liminal figure, not yet human but more than mere utility?

The significance of this hierarchy for Buber is more than merely grammatical. In addition to the preposition *über* to define the human over against the animal, he gives this metaphor biblical significance, invoking the Latin *superliminare* to define the "over-threshold," against the others; Kaufman, Buber's translator, explains that this parallels use of the term in the Vulgate to describe the image of the bloodstained lintel of Exodus 12:22.[33] Interestingly, the sign of what is proper to the human is thus made possible by the death of a lamb. This is but one of many cases in Western history where animals function to help develop the special status of the human—a status Buber's contemporaries desired to reserve for humans alone.[34]

---

[31] Friedman, *Encounter on the Narrow Ridge*, 242.
[32] Martin Heidegger, *The Fundamental Concepts of Metaphysics: World, Finitude, Solitude*, trans. William McNeill and Nicholas Walker (Bloomington: Indiana University Press, 2006; first published 1929–30), 177, 193.
[33] Buber, *I and Thou*, trans. Walter Kaufmann, 173.
[34] Kelly Oliver terms this phenomenon "animal pedagogy." Oliver, *Animal Lessons: How They Teach Us to Be Human* (New York: Columbia University Press, 2009), 11.

The (In)Famous Inclusion (*Umfassung*) of Animals in the I–Thou Relation: Tension and Admiration from Buber's Readers

Many readers of Buber were critical of his inclusion of animals in the I–You relation.[35] Malcolm Diamond found it ethically suspect, inviting relativism; if the mutuality of the I–You relation were to include nature, Diamond says, "the exploiting of children in a sweatshop would be no more reprehensible than the exploiting of a forest."[36] Buber's answer, similar to his response to Levinas, points to the afterword to *I and Thou*, which Buber says explores gradations of "the capacity for mutuality."[37] Elsewhere, however, Levinas makes clear the problem of mutuality apropos of including other animals in the I–You relation: "Does this imply a vacillation in Buber's thought? Dating from the publication of *Ich und Du*, Buber admitted that things too can enter into the I–Thou relation, yet it frequently seems that the relation between humans—as soon as the Thou has a human face—has privileged status and even conditions all other relations." Levinas then quotes Buber: "everything else lives in its light."[38]

---

[35] Attending *specifically* (in terms of both species and specificity) to other animals in the responses to Buber (namely, in the responses of his critics) is difficult since the criticisms of Buber's inclusion of other animals in the I–Thou relation did not individuate animals, as Buber himself did (e.g., cats, a horse), but caged them within a larger coterie of beings as other-than-human, including stones and trees (i.e., nature). Animals were never merely one of many objects in nature for Buber (even if they ended up, for him, outside the human capacity for complete reciprocity within the I–Thou relation). Contrary to his critics, he would never reduce other animals to the status of objects petrified for eternity to the objective I–It relation.

[36] Diamond interrogates Buber directly on the inclusion of nature in the I–You relation in a series of correspondence with Buber collected and edited by Maurice Friedman, "Interrogations of Martin Buber," in *Philosophical Interrogations: Interrogations of Martin Buber, John Wild, Jean Wahl, Brand Blanshard, Paul Weiss, Charles Hartshorne, Paul Tillich*, ed. Sidney C. Rome and Beatrice K. Rome (New York: Harper & Row, 1964), 36–37:

> Therefore, it would seem that all beings are of equal worth as Thou's, and that within the framework of the philosophy of I and Thou there would be no basis of evaluation between different I–Thou meetings of different Thou's. If this is the case, the exploiting of children in a sweatshop would be no more reprehensible than the exploiting of a forest. Is this a fair picture of the consequences which follow from the emphasis upon the quality of man's relation with all beings in lieu of traditional moral concern with the nature of objects to which man relates, as well as with the quality of the relation? If so, is there any basis with the philosophy of I and Thou for affirming the humanistic distinctions with value a child above a tree?

[37] Letter from Buber to Diamond, ed. Maurice Friedman, in Rome and Rome, *Philosophical Interrogations*, 37.

[38] Emmanuel Levinas, *Proper Names*, trans. Michael B. Smith (London: Athlone Press, 1996; first published 1976), 20.

Similarly, a year before the publication of *I and Thou*, Franz Rosenzweig penned this correspondence, without subtlety: "How glad you would be to incorporate Buddha into your paradise, that Eden of yours over which I–Thou stands written. How gladly you would let in the domestic cat."[39] In short, Buber's critics shared the suspicion that the I–You relation must be revised or reoriented in the light of a deeper understanding of the nature and dynamics of intersubjectivity. Furthermore, according to Friedman, apropos of Levinas on Buber, "having no inkling of what Buber called 'the bestowing side of things' [*das Schenkende in die Dinge*] that comes to meet us when we bend over it with fervor, Levinas thought that Buber's concepts of the I–Thou relation with animals and plants originated in his artistic nature. If this were so, it would weaken the seriousness of Buber's approach to ethics"—indeed, an animal ethics.[40] For Levinas, the ethical face was a human face, and Buber's animals were ultimately metaphorical in nature.[41] Insofar as animals exist as part of nature for Levinas, he situates other animals outside the concern of ethics: "we may inquire first whether the I–Thou relation can be extended beyond the ethical realm to include nature."[42] However, Buber's influence and insistence on the status of animals may indeed have led Levinas to soften his own position: in 1954 he described the animal as "faceless,"[43] and in 1957, he said that "a being in its brutish dumbness, is not yet in touch with itself,"[44] but his position had evolved by the time of an interview in 1986: "One cannot entirely refuse the face of an animal. It is via the face that one understands, for example, a dog. . . . The phenomenon of the face is not in its purest form in the dog. . . . But it also has a face."[45] (Notice Levinas's use of "it"—the dog is still an object.) However, Levinas equivocates when pressed on the negation of being killable as not also present in the face of an animal (i.e., when certain lives become utterly discardable, outside ethical consideration—ethics here

---

[39] Franz Rosenzweig to Martin Buber, September 22, 1922, in Martin Buber, *Letters of Martin Buber*, 287.

[40] Friedman, *Life of Dialogue*, 347.

[41] In his section "Some Objections," responding to Buber, Levinas writes, "If we criticize Buber for extending the I–Thou relation to things, then, it is not because he is an animist with respect to our relations with the physical world, but because he is too much the artist in his relations with man" (Levinas, *Proper Names*, 148).

[42] Interrogation of Buber by Levinas, ed. Maurice Friedman, in Rome and Rome, *Philosophical Interrogations*, 25. In his response to Levinas, Buber writes, "I find, by the way, that our relationship to the domestic animals with whom we live, and even that to the plants in our garden, is properly included as the lowest floor of the ethical building." Rome and Rome, *Philosophical Investigations*, 28.

[43] Emmanuel Levinas, *Collected Philosophical Papers*, trans. Alphonso Lingis (Dordrecht: Martinus Nijhoff, 1987), 19.

[44] Levinas, *Collected Philosophical Papers*, 55.

[45] Levinas, "The Paradox of Morality," 169.

meaning the means of attending to the knotted kinships that emerge when species meet, which, following Haraway, must stay with the trouble or tension that to live is to kill,[46] the unavoidably messy situation of killing well): "I cannot say at what moment you have the right to be called 'face.' The human face is completely different and only afterwards do we discover the face of an animal. I don't know if a snake has a face. I can't answer that question."[47]

Many contemporary renderings, however, are more positive and generative in terms doing ethics and living better with our more-than-human world. In his last tome, *Religion in Human Evolution*, Robert Bellah draws on Buber in his reading of the world-renowned Dutch primatologist Frans de Waal,[48] to highlight de Waal's sensitivity to intersubjectivity in scientific inquiry. Significant for Bellah is the way Buber's I–You relation names a specific kind of relation, which, first, does not reduce the "I" position to a disinterested observer and, second, includes room for our relation to other animals (though still not relations between animals).

In a less productive adaptation of Buber, animal rights proponent Tom Regan draws on his work: "The bonds that unite these children and animals are the bonds of a special kind of friendship, a friendship that expresses itself in respect and loyalty. The relationship between the child and the animal (to use the helpful language of Martin Buber) is that of 'I–Thou,' not 'I–It.' Animals known, as well as animals imagined, are unique somebodies, not generic somethings."[49] This reading, in fact, neuters Buber's sophisticated I–You relation, which for Regan functions here as a shorthand for a more general relation between subjects. A closer reading of Buber's *I and Thou* on the dual nature of the human, including both the I–Thou and I–It relations, would not allow for Regan's simplification.[50]

[46] Haraway, *When Species Meet*, 296.
[47] Levinas, "The Paradox of Morality," 271. For more on Levinas and the question of animal faces, see Atterton, "Face-to-Face," 269–75.
[48] Robert Bellah, *Religion in Human Evolution: From Paleolithic to Axial Age* (Cambridge, MA: Belknap Press of Harvard University Press, 2011), 82.
[49] Tom Regan, *Empty Cages: Facing the Challenge of Animal Rights* (Lanham, MD: Rowman and Littlefield, 2005), 22.
[50] Though Regan does not directly cite this passage, Buber uses the encounter with a dog to explain his notion of meeting and the difference between realization and relation:

The experience from which I have proceeded and ever again proceeds simply this, that one meets another. Another, that does not mean, for example, a "dog," an "English sheep dog," one that is to be described thus-and-thus, but this particular animal, which a child once, about to run by him, looked in the eyes and remained standing, they both remained standing while the child laid his hand on the head of the dog and called him by name that he just invented or found. When later at home he sought to make clear to himself what had been special about the animal, he managed without concepts; he only needed them

Though both Bellah and Regan highlight Buber's sensitivity toward other animals, neither contends with the tension of this sensitivity juxtaposed with his humanism. Buber's aforementioned critics notice this tension but dismiss any focus on other-than-human worlds as insignificant. For his critics the possibility of mutual (or intersubjective) relations with other animals was not without suspicion. For them the idea of an animal as a subject of experience remained metaphorical opposite humanity's ontological subjectivity. Still, again, Buber would not cull other animals entirely from the I–You relation: "Some men have deep down in their being a potential partnership with animals."[51] Here examples for Buber might have been individuals similar to the contemporary notion of an "animal whisperer"—specifically, his father and the spiritually inclined masters of Hasidism.

Arguably the greatest influence on Buber's sensitivity to other animals was his father, Carl Buber, who displayed deep concern for the many animals with whom he worked. Friedman notes, "When [Carl] stood in the midst of his splendid herd of horses, he greeted one animal after the other, not merely in a friendly fashion but each one individually."[52] Buber himself says of his father, recollected to Friedman, "The wholly unsentimental and wholly unromantic man was concerned about genuine human contact with nature, as active and responsible contact."[53] Moreover, speaking to Aubrey Hode, Buber recalls his father approaching other animals "almost as if they were people."[54] Carl Buber was no doubt inspiration for Buber's notion of mutuality shared between nature and humanity.[55]

Buber also found animal whisperers in individuals and places generally not known for work in animal advocacy and welfare. In the same way I propose we read Buber to learn of his relationship with other animals, extending from his work into other aspects of his life, he cites stories about the biblical character Jacob: "One reads how Jacob lovingly gave water to and cared for the lamb; and here one may reach from the work of the poet into his own life

when he had to relate the occurrence to his best friend. (Buber quoted by Friedman, in Rome and Rome, *Philosophical Interrogations*, 47)

[51] Buber, *I and Thou*, trans. Walter Kaufmann, 172.
[52] Friedman, *Encounter on the Narrow Ridge*, 9.
[53] Friedman, *Encounter on the Narrow Ridge*, 9–10.
[54] Aubrey Hodes, *Martin Buber: An Intimate Portrait* (New York: Viking Press, 1971), 45.
[55] Friedman notes, "In his own person, Carl Buber anticipated one of the most fundamental aspects of his son's later thoughts: that the man who practices immediacy does so in relation to nature just as much as to his fellow man—the 'I–Thou' relation to nature is a corollary of the interhuman." Maurice Friedman, *Martin Buber's Life and Work: The Early Years, 1878–1923* (New York: E. P. Dutton, 1981), 12.

that followed later and think of what we learn of his relationship to an animal from his 'Song to the Dog Ardon.'"[56] In the same Jewish vein, Hasidism,
an eighteenth-century Jewish sect in Eastern Europe (that was scorned by
Levinas as mystical), had a profound effect on Buber and others regarding
the question of the animal.[57] However, there has not been significant work on
the potential relation of Buber's Hasidic narratives to his own sensitivity and
continued inclusion of animals in his I–You relation. Within the narratives
there are many examples that merit consideration—specifically, Rabbi Israel
ben Eliezer, Rabbi Wolf, Rabbi David, Rabbi Moshe Leib, and Rabbi Susya.

Rabbi Israel ben Eliezer (ca. 1700–1760), called the Baal-Shem, a title
meaning "Master of God's Name," had the power to perform miracles,
founded Hasidism,[58] and "taught the Maggid (among other things) how to
understand the language of birds and trees, and—so the rabbi of Polnoye tells
his son-in-law—it was his 'holy custom' to converse with animals."[59] Another
animal whisperer was Rabbi Zev Wolf of Zbarah (d. ca. 1802). Buber writes
that Wolf lavished love even on animals and held that humanity ought to
love all life.[60] Potentially drawing on the "holy custom" of the Baal-Shem,
Buber writes, "When Rabbi Wolf drove out in a carriage, he never permitted
the whip to be used on the horses. 'You do not even have to shout at them,'
[Wolf] instructed the coachman. 'You just have to know how to talk to
them.'"[61] Rabbi David of Lelov (d. 1813), "one of the most lovable figures
in Hasidism," writes Buber, "was wise and at the same time childlike, open
to all creatures. . . . He was particularly fond of horses and went into vehe-
ment explanations of how senseless it is to beat them."[62] In another story

[56] Buber, *A Believing Humanism*, 67–68. That this work was compiled just a few months before his
death (Friedman, *Encounters on the Narrow Ridge*, 21) makes it a deeply sobering place from which
to begin thinking about his life.

[57] For more on the juxtaposition of Buber the Hasid and Levinas, an opponent of Hasidism
(against its focus on mysticism and myth), see Friedman, *Life of Dialogue*, 337, and Emmanuel
Levinas, *Outside the Subject*, trans. Michael B. Smith (Stanford, CA: Stanford University Press), 2.
Interestingly, for reasons left to another discussion, Buber's presentation of a universal Hasidism was
not well received, which was "illustrated all too clearly in June 1975," Friedman writes, "when the
young men of the Hasidic Bratslaver Seminary in the Mea She'arim in Jerusalem spoke of Buber's
death with the Yiddish phrase that one uses for the death of an animal!" (Friedman, *Encounter on the
Narrow Ridge*, 298).

[58] Martin Buber, *The Legend of the Baal-Shem*, trans. Maurice Friedman (Princeton, NJ: Princeton
University Press, 1995; first published 1955), 9–10.

[59] Martin Buber, *Tales of the Hasidism*, trans. Olga Marx (New York: Schocken, 1991; first published
1947), 14.

[60] Buber, *Tales of the Hasidism*, 22.

[61] Buber, *Tales of the Hasidim*, 160.

[62] Buber, *Tales of the Hasidism*, 25. In a story in which he feeds a horse, perhaps reminiscent
of Buber's own experience, "Rabbi David . . . hold[s] out his cap full of barley to the horse, which

reminiscent of the Baal-Shem's holy custom of animal communication, Buber writes, "One Friday afternoon Rabbi David was on a journey, when suddenly the horse stopped and refused to go on. The driver beat the horse, but the zaddik objected. 'Rabbi,' cried the driver, 'the sun will soon be setting and the sabbath is almost here.' 'You are quite right,' answered Rabbi David, 'but what you have to do is to make the animal understand you. Otherwise, it will some day summon you to court in Heaven, and that will not be to your honor.' "[63] Other significant examples include Rabbi Moshe Leib, who upon his regular visits to the market found thirsty calves and provided them with water—"as if," Buber notes, "that had been his job all his life."[64] Also, Rabbi Susya "could not see a cage, 'and the wretchedness of the bird and its anxiety to fly in the air of the world and to be a free wanderer in accordance with its nature,' without opening it."[65] The proliferation of not only kindness to other animals but also a real sense of communion and understanding, the "holy custom" of Hasidism's founding figure, resonates deeply through Buber's Hasidic narratives.

Buber's Horse

Buber's autobiographical reflection on a distant but seemingly ubiquitous childhood memory with a horse stars in a collection of "Autobiographical Fragments" that are, for Buber, "moments that have exercised a decisive influence on the nature and direction of [his] thinking."[66] For my purposes, the fragment that follows functions as an example of the tension between his sensitivity to other animals and his metaphysical humanism.[67] Some

their driver in his hurry to get to the House of Prayer had left behind unfed." Buber, *Tales of the Hasidism*, 187.

[63] Buber, *Tales of the Hasidism*, 187.
[64] Buber, *Tales of the Hasidism*, 425.
[65] Buber, *The Legend of the Baal-Shem*, 46.
[66] Buber, "Autobiographical Fragments," in Buber, *The Philosophy of Martin Buber*, 3. Given its multiple (re)presentations and citations, this fragment holds a special place for Buber within his corpus, which makes reading it apart from its original context and connection to his notion of reflection even less a stretch.
[67] Contrast the subsequently quoted text from Buber with (1) Levinas, for whom our relation to (never *with*) other animals is not direct or immediate, and (2) Robert Scruton. Levinas writes, "In stroking an animal already the hide hardens in the skin." *Collected Philosophical Papers*, 118–19. According to Scruton,

> the relation of a mare to her foal is not an example of the "I–Thou" (*Ich–Du*) relation
> so poignantly explored by Martin Buber. The mare does not cherish her foal's life,

commentators have referred to this particular episodic fragment between Buber and the "dapple-grey horse [*Apfel-schimmel*]" as an I–You encounter.[68] However, Buber himself reflects on this moment not as a dialogical encounter, an I–You relation, but as its opposite—that is, a moment of objectification or monologue, not dialogue. This text says more than Buber intends, but his own reflections remain mired in human exceptionalism. Ultimately, the horse lacks the capacity to enter into relation,[69] a capacity that defines the human, which is, for Buber, "the only sort of entity that can encounter other beings as irreducible to the self and self-knowing."[70] At length the passage reads as follows:

> When I was eleven years of age, spending the summer on my grandparents' estate, I used, as often as I could do it unobserved, to steal into the stable and gently stroke the neck of my darling, a broad dapple-grey horse [*Apfel-schimmel*]. It was not a casual delight but a great, certainly friendly, but also deeply stirring happening. If I am to explain it now, beginning from the still very fresh memory of my hand, I must say that what I experienced in touch with the animal was the Other, the immense otherness of the Other [*ungeheure Anderheit des Anderen*], which, however, did not remain strange like the otherness of the ox and the ram, but rather let me draw near and touch [*Berührung*] it. When I stroked the mighty mane, sometimes marvelously smoothcombed, at other times just as astonishingly wild, and felt the life beneath my hand, it was as though the element of vitality [*Vitalität*] itself bordered on my skin, something that was not I, was certainly not akin

personality or identity; does not stand vigil over its moral and psychological development; does not feel its pains and joys as her own; does not, when it is weaned, retain her burning attachment; does not, in later life, seek its constant affection. All such attitudes require a consciousness of self and other and of the relation between them, which is inherently absent from the mental repertoire of the non-human animals. (*Animal Rights and Wrongs* [London: Demos, 1998], 30)

68 Steven Kepnes, *The Text as Thou: Martin Buber's Dialogical Hermeneutics and Narrative Theology* (Bloomington: Indiana University Press, 1992), 85–86. Kepnes notes the uniqueness of this event, in that it reverses the narrative structure of Buber's other accounts: grounding the I–You event and ending with its dissolution in the relation of the I–It, whereas the others begin with an I–It and end in the I–You relation. The moment of objectification occurs as Buber himself, "the child," shifts the narrative from the first person to the third person (86). Though I do not find this a compelling read, Kepnes is right to highlight an implicit respect for otherness, which is, in Buber's own words, "something that is absolutely not himself [*sic*] and at the same time something with which he nevertheless communicates" (*Between Man and Man*, 23). Kepnes sees the difference between the horse as an "other" and *it* as an "object."
69 Calarco, "The Retrieval of Humanism in Buber and Levinas," 255.
70 Buber, *A Believing Humanism*, 255.

to me, palpably the other, not just another, really the Other itself; and yet it
let me approach, confide itself to me, placed itself elementally in the relation of *Thou* and *Thou* with me. The horse [*Schimmel*], even when I had not
begun by pouring oats for him into the manger, very gently raised his massive head, ears flicking, then snorted quietly, as a conspirator gives a signal
meant to be recognized [*vernehmbar*] only by his fellow-conspirator; and
I was approved [*bestätigt*]. But once—I do not know what came over the
child, at any rate it was childlike enough—it struck me about the stroking,
what fun it gave me, and suddenly I became conscious of my hand. The
game went on as before, but something had changed, it was no longer the
same thing. And the next day, after giving him a rich feed, when I stroked
my friend's head he did not raise his head. A few years later, when I thought
back to the incident, I no longer supposed that the animal had noticed my
defection [*Abfall*]. But at the time I considered myself judged.[71]

Unfortunately, this marvelous account became for Buber, as Friedman puts
it, "a concrete example of 'reflexion,' the basic movement of the 'life of monologue.'"[72] What had indications of a dialogical relationship turned out to
be unidirectional. The monological, for Buber, models the I–It relation, and
the I–You, the dialogical. As Martina Urban puts it, "dialogue is primarily
a decisive act of the will to be open to the address of the other. Dialogue is
thus first and foremost a performative act."[73] The monological is not just a
turning away from the other, but a turning away that turns back on oneself
(*Rückbiegung*), a closing off of the other as object or analyzable content of
experience. In the I–You relation interlocutors are not objectified but share
a common center (*Mittel*), the in-between (*Zwischen*) of a mutual relation.[74]

Here this deeply moving reflection about his horse highlights most clearly
the tension between, on the one hand, Buber's anticipation of the animal
question (i.e., inclusion and individuality) and, on the other, his metaphysical
humanism (the animal defined by reaction). The former bespeaks his vivid
sensitivity to other animal worlds; the latter, Buber's resignation of this event
to another world—as Friedman puts it, "a concrete example of 'reflexion,'

[71] Buber, *Between Man and Man*, 26–27.
[72] Maurice Friedman, *Martin Buber's Life and Work* (Detroit: Wayne State University Press, 1988), 14.
[73] Martina Urban, "Deconstruction Anticipated: Koigen and Buber on a Self-Corrective Religion," *Shofar: An Interdisciplinary Journal of Jewish Studies* 27, no. 4 (2009): 125.
[74] If allowed the capacity to address the other, animals would no longer be captive to reacting, prisoners of a Cartesian legacy.

the basic movement of the 'life of monologue.' "[75] However, intentions aside, Buber's own language elsewhere parallels this event enough to warrant further consideration and to challenge his own suppositions about that day. Buber's horse passage, I contend, arguably anticipates what he says in "Right and Wrong," with respect to what it means to know (*kennen*):

> The original meaning of the Hebrew verb "to recognize, to know" [*erkennen, kennen*] in distinction from Western languages, belongs not to the sphere of reflection but to that of contact. The decisive event [*Vorgang*] for "knowing" in biblical Hebrew is not that one looks at an object, but that one comes into touch [*Berührung*] with it. The basic difference is developed in the realm of a relation of the soul to other beings, where the fact of mutuality [*Gegenseitigkeit*] changes everything. At the centre [*Mittelpunkt*] is not a perceiving of one another, but the contact of being, intercourse.[76]

This passage from "Right and Wrong" shares with Buber's equine encounter the visible dependence on the same German signifiers—specifically, the sense of knowing through touch (*Berührung*).[77] Also similar is his interpretation of Genesis: Adam knew Eve, his wife, meaning he became intimate with her. Moreover, in the original context of Buber's passage about the horse, in the very sentence preceding the story, Buber highlights the notion of a mutual center (*Mittel*) as the possibility of communion: "but nothing needs to mediate between me and one of my companions in the companionship of creation, whenever we come near one another, because we are bound up in relation to the same centre [*Mittel*]."[78] If read in this light, Buber's horse fragment is but one example of animals having a companion in the work of Buber.[79] His own concessions notwithstanding, the specificity of his

[75] Friedman, *Martin Buber's Life and Work*, 14.
[76] Martin Buber, *Right and Wrong: An Interpretation of Some Psalms*, trans. Ronald Gregor Smith (London: SCM Press, 1953), 58. In the German edition the term for "mutuality" is emphasized with italics. See Martin Buber, *Recht und Unrecht: Deutung Einiger Psalmen* (Klosterberg: Verlag Benno Schwabe, 1952), 69.
[77] Levinas's reading of *I and Thou* agrees: "The I in its relation with the Thou is further related to itself by means of the Thou, i.e., it is related to the Thou as to someone who in turn relates itself to the I, as though it had come into delicate contact with himself [sic] through the skin of the Thou" (Levinas, *Proper Names*, 142). Levinas here summons a keen point on *Berührung*: "Buber's Meeting has suggested a relation that cannot be cast in the molds of consciousness to which one is tempted to reduce all presence for us" (Levinas, *Outside the Subject*, 19).
[78] Buber, *Between Man and Man*, 25. Might we not also suggest that included in this "nothing" is species difference? Or given that individuality remains in the I–You relation, might this launch an ethics of difference *sans* difference?
[79] This is so even if his own humanist leanings led him to dismiss the possibility that this horse had the capacity for a response.

encounter with this particular horse is significant in its recognition of individuality. In defining *this* horse, Buber makes subtle a significant rupture within the category "the animal" or at least posits the possibility of distinguishing between different animals as he does with the ox and ram. I understand this difference (both in species and in person) as the difference between the I–You encounter with his horse and the I–It relations with other, at least less familiar animals. Beyond how this passage denotes a unique specificity with his horse that is altogether different—at least at that specific moment—from his relation to the ox and ram, this point about difference is especially instructive and suggests an affinity between Buber's thought and future philosophies of difference and their recent deconstruction that calls into question the category of "the animal" in the general singular. Ultimately, I believe that this horse passage and its context within the larger corpus of Buber's work on the I–You relation belies any primacy due to dialogue as *logos* or speech and signifies more of a speaking with one's being, privileging affect and embodiment and opening the door for the possibility of (re) framing Buber and his own reflections for contemporary animal studies and advocacy.[80]

Conclusion

The (in)famous inclusion of the I–You relation with nature, though radical for its time, maintained, at least on the surface, a metaphysical humanism or human exceptionalism, built on the ontological divide between humans and other animals—principally, a divide between the free and reflective human and the animal captivated by instincts. Even though Buber initially describes his encounter with his horse in terms of the horse extending an invitation (the same language he uses to speak about an encounter with the eternal You), he ultimately understands this extension of response-ability to the horse as a figure of speech. When Buber denies the possibility of response, his horse can only react to his invitation, the possibility of judgment dismissed. For Buber, to speak here of response is, in short, to speak a

---

[80] However, it should remain clear that what I read as an implicit I–You relation with his horse, Buber opposes, denying the event with his horse as an encounter. He conceptualizes the memory as an example of reflection, the utility of an I–It interaction, not an I–You relation. The possibility of anything like judgment from his horse is void for Buber, because the horse lacks the capacity for judgment and reflection on any potential meeting.

fable; however, if we remain faithful to Buber's shift from conceptualization within the I-You relation, highlighting notions of touch, affect, embodiment, and sociability, we may indeed reason in terms of the body language or the kinesis-ability of a horse.[81] The burgeoning work of contemporary animal philosophy reminds us that other animals know us in ways we cannot even know ourselves. Perhaps by pushing the boundaries of the primacy of the *logos*, we might learn to humbly listen to our fellow creatures speak through their own being, instead of growing deaf to anyone who does not speak in human language.[82] Indeed, to do so would mean becoming sensitive to our limitations and to other ways of comporting wisdom and knowledge that exceed, at least initially, human understanding. Encountering animals means more than us encountering them; it means that they too encounter us, but not only us—indeed, they too (in both senses) are encountering animals.

Bibliography

Atterton, Peter. "Face-to-Face with the Other Animal?" In *Levinas and Buber: Dialogue and Difference*, edited by Peter Atterton, Matthew Calarco, and Maurice Friedman, 262–81. Pittsburgh: Duquesne University Press, 2004.

Baker, Carole. "A Practice-Led Study of Human–Horse Communication." Paper presented at the "Living with Animals Conference," Eastern Kentucky University, March 21–23, 2013.

Bellah, Robert. *Religion in Human Evolution: From Paleolithic to Axial Age*. Cambridge, MA: Belknap Press of Harvard University Press, 2011.

Buber, Martin. *A Believing Humanism: My Testament, 1902–1965*. Translated by Maurice Friedman. New York: Simon and Schuster, 1967.

Buber, Martin. *Between Man and Man*. Translated by Ronald Gregor Smith. London: Routledge, 2004. First published 1947.

[81] This sense is what allows a horse used for racing, for example, to sense and know the desire of the jockey (through the jockey's muscle reflexes) before the jockey's own mind registers and computes the muscular datum or memory. See Vicki Hearne, *Adam's Task: Calling Animals by Name* (New York: Skyhorse, 2007), 123. Also, Carole Baker writes, in the abstract of her paper "A Practice-Led Study of Human–Horse Communication," that "positioning the horse as an active agent, capable of creativity and intentionality, forces us to reconsider our definition of agency; and to base it less on rational thought, language, and free will and more on affect, embodiment, and sociality" (paper presented at the "Living with Animals Conference," Eastern Kentucky University, March 21–23, 2013).

[82] Levinas here summons a keen point apropos of touch (*Berührung*) and knowing: "Buber's Meeting has suggested a relation that cannot be cast in the molds of consciousness to which one is tempted to reduce all presence for us. . . . But if these molds, these forms of consciousness, determined all presence, nothing else would be able to enter our world" (Levinas, *Outside the Subject*, 19). Furthermore, he says of Buber, "It is not truth that is the ultimate meaning of that relation [I-You], but sociality, which is irreducible to knowledge and truth" (*Outside the Subject*, 23).

Buber, Martin. *Daniel: Dialogues on Realization.* Translated by Maurice Friedman. New York: McGraw-Hill, 1965.

Buber, Martin. *Daniel: Gespräche von der Verwirklichung.* Leipzig: Insel, 1913.

Buber, Martin. *Das Problem des Menschen.* Heidelberg: Schneider, 1948.

Buber, Martin. "Exstase und Bekenntis." In *Ekstatische Konfessionen*, by Martin Buber, xi–xxvi. Jena, Eugen Diederichs Verlag, 1909.

Buber, Martin. *I and Thou.* Translated by Ronald Gregor Smith. New York: Scribner's, 1958. First published 1923.

Buber, Martin. *I and Thou.* Translated by Walter Kaufmann. New York: Scribner's, 1970. First published 1923.

Buber, Martin. *Ich und Du.* Leipzig: Insel-Verlag, 1923.

Buber, Martin. *Israel and the World: Essays in a Time of Crisis.* Syracuse: Syracuse University Press, 1997.

Buber, Martin. *The Knowledge of Man: Selected Essays.* Translated by Maurice Friedman and Ronald Gregor Smith. New York: Harper & Row, 1965. First published 1952.

Buber, Martin. *The Legend of the Baal-Shem.* Translated by Maurice Friedman. Princeton, NJ: Princeton University Press, 1995. First published 1955.

Buber, Martin. *The Letters of Martin Buber: Life of Dialogue.* Edited by Nahum N. Glatzer and Paul Mendes-Flohr. Translated by Richard Winston, Clara Winston, and Harry Zohn. New York: Schocken Books, 1991.

Buber, Martin. *The Philosophy of Martin Buber.* Edited by Paul Arthur Schilpp and Maurice Friedman. Chicago: Open Court, 1967.

Buber, Martin. *Recht und Unrecht: Deutung Einiger Psalmen.* Klosterberg: Verlag Benno Schwabe, 1952.

Buber, Martin. "Religion and Philosophy." In *Eclipse of God: Studies in the Relation between Religion and Philosophy*, by Martin Buber, translated by Maurice Friedman, 20–38. Atlantic Highlands, NJ: International Humanities Press, 1988. First published 1952.

Buber, Martin. *Right and Wrong: An Interpretation of Some Psalms.* Translated by Ronald Gregor Smith. London: SCM Press, 1953.

Buber, Martin. *Tales of the Hasidism.* Translated by Olga Marx. New York: Schocken, 1991. First published 1947.

Buber, Martin. "Ueber Jakob Böhme." *Wiener Rundschau* 5, no. 12 (1901): 251–53.

Calarco, Matthew. "The Retrieval of Humanism in Buber and Levinas." In *Levinas and Buber: Dialogue and Difference*, edited by Peter Atterton, Matthew Calarco, and Maurice Friedman, 250–61. Pittsburgh: Duquesne University Press, 2004.

Casper, Bernhard. "Franz Rosenzweig's Criticism of Buber's *I and Thou*." In *Martin Buber: A Centenary Volume*, edited by Haim Gordon and Jochanan Bloc 139–59. Jersey City: Ktav, 1984.

Cohen, Richard A. *Elevations: The Height of the Good in Rosenzweig and Levinas.* Chicago: University of Chicago Press, 1994.

Friedman, Maurice. *Encounter on the Narrow Ridge: A Life of Martin Buber.* New York: Paragon House, 1993.

Friedman, Maurice. "Interrogation of Martin Buber." In *Philosophical Interrogations: Interrogations of Martin Buber, John Wild, Jean Wahl, Brand Blanshard, Paul Weiss, Charles Hartshorne, Paul Tillich*, edited by Sydney C. Rome and Beatrice K. Rome, 13–118. New York: Holt, Rinehart and Winton, 1964.

Friedman, Maurice. "Introductory Essay." In *The Knowledge of Man: Selected Essays*, by Martin Buber, translated by Maurice Friedman and Ronald Gregor Smith, 11–58. New York: Harper & Row, 1965. First published 1952.

Friedman, Maurice. *Martin Buber: The Life of Dialogue*. London: Routledge, 2002.

Friedman, Maurice. "Martin Buber and Mikhail Bakhtin: The Dialogue of Voices and the Word That Is Spoken." In *Dialogue as a Means of Collective Communication*, edited by Bela H. Banathy and Patrick M. Jenlink, 29–39. New York: Springer, 2004.

Friedman, Maurice. *Martin Buber's Life and Work*. Detroit: Wayne State University Press, 1988.

Friedman, Maurice. *Martin Buber's Life and Work: The Early Years, 1878–1923*. New York: E. P. Dutton, 1981.

Gordon, Haim, and Jochanan Bloch, eds. *Martin Buber: A Centenary Volume*. Jersey City: Ktav, 1984.

Haraway, Donna. *When Species Meet*. Minneapolis: University of Minnesota Press, 2008.

Hearne, Vicki. *Adam's Task: Calling Animals by Name*. New York: Skyhorse, 2007.

Heidegger, Martin. *The Fundamental Concepts of Metaphysics: World, Finitude, Solitude*. Translated by William McNeill and Nicholas Walker. Bloomington: Indiana University Press, 2006. First published 1929–30.

Hodes, Aubrey. *Martin Buber: An Intimate Portrait*. New York: Viking Press, 1971.

Kaufmann, Walter. "Buber's Failures and Triumphs." In *Martin Buber: A Centenary Volume*, edited by Haim Gordon and Jochanan Bloch, 3–18. Jersey City: Ktav, 1984.

Kepnes, Steven. *The Text as Thou: Martin Buber's Dialogical Hermeneutics and Narrative Theology*. Bloomington: Indiana University Press, 1992.

Levinas, Emmanuel. *Collected Philosophical Papers*. Translated by Alphonso Lingis. Dordrecht: Martinus Nijhoff, 1987.

Levinas, Emmanuel. *Outside the Subject*. Translated by Michael B. Smith. Stanford, CA: Stanford University Press, 1994.

Levinas, Emmanuel. "The Paradox of Morality: An Interview with Emmanuel Levinas." By Tamra Wright, Peter Hughes, and Alison Ainley. Translated by Andrew Benjamin and Tamra Wright. In *The Provocation of Levinas: Rethinking the Other*, edited by Robert Bernasconi and David Wood, 168–80. London: Routledge, 1988.

Levinas, Emmanuel. *Proper Names*. Translated by Michael B. Smith. London: Athlone Press, 1996. First published 1976.

Levinas, Emmanuel. *Totality and Infinity*. Translated by Alphonso Lingis. Pittsburgh: Duquesne University Press, 1969. First published 1961.

Oliver, Kelly. *Animal Lessons: How They Teach Us to Be Human*. New York: Columbia University Press, 2009.

Regan, Tom. *Empty Cages: Facing the Challenge of Animal Rights*. Lanham, MD: Rowman and Littlefield, 2005.

Scruton, Robert. *Animal Rights and Wrongs*. London: Demos, 1998.

Urban, Martina. "Deconstruction Anticipated: Koigen and Buber on a Self-Corrective Religion." *Shofar: An Interdisciplinary Journal of Jewish Studies* 27, no. 4 (2009): 107–35.

Wood, David. *The Step Back: Ethics and Politics after Deconstruction*. New York: State University of New York Press, 2006.

19

Paul Tillich (1886–1965)

The Method of Correlation and the Possibility of an Animal Ethic

Abbey Smith

Paul Tillich was one of the most prolific theologians of the twentieth century. Although his shorter, single-topic books were what captured the imagination of the general public, his three-volume *Systematic Theology*, written between 1951 and 1963, received the greatest academic attention and has gone on to be influential around the globe to this day. It provides a unique approach to systematic theology, combining traditional theology with philosophy, deep psychology, sociology, biology, and even anthropology to arrive at an existential system quite unlike anything that had previously been written.

Much can be gleaned from examining the impact of some of *Systematic Theology*'s key concepts on the theological status of nonhuman animals. Among these ideas is Tillich's construct of "the multidimensional unity of life," which has inspired many eco-theologians in the late twentieth and early twenty-first centuries.[1]

In Tillich's estimation, humans can make sense of the huge diversity of beings they encounter only by grouping them together using "uniting principles."[2] The most universal way of grouping is a hierarchy of levels, where beings are placed in an order based on their species and relative attributes. Through use of such an order, all beings can be neatly assigned their place.

Tillich's system rejects the notion of a hierarchical order, however, because there is no room for movement between the levels, which results in their complete separation from each other.[3] The level metaphor means that

---

[1] See for example, Jeremy D. Yunt, *The Ecotheology of Paul Tillich: The Spiritual Roots of Environmental Ethics* (n.p.: CreateSpace Independent Publishing Platform, 2009).

[2] Paul Tillich, *Systematic Theology* (Chicago: University of Chicago Press, 1963), 3:13.

[3] For a fuller discussion of Tillich's concept level's and its inadequacies, see chapter 3, "Paul Tillich's Systematic Theology," in Abbey-Anne Smith, *Animals in Tillich's Philosophical Theology* (Basingstoke, UK: Palgrave Macmillan, 2017), 67–69.

Abbey Smith, *Paul Tillich (1886–1965)* In: *Animal Theologians.* Edited by: Andrew Linzey and Clair Linzey, Oxford University Press. © Oxford University Press 2023. DOI: 10.1093/oso/9780197655542.003.0020

beings occupying different levels are not able to have any sort of positive in-
terrelation, and Tillich argues that the relation of the levels remains that of
"interference, either by control or revolt."[4] Therefore, he wishes to replace
the metaphor of levels with that of dimensions, along with concepts such
as realm and grade.[5] This change would be to no avail, however, if it simply
amounted to the replacement of one metaphor with another; what really
matters is the changed vision of reality that the replacement expresses.

The metaphor of dimensions, like that of levels, is a spatial one. However,
unlike "levels," the term "dimensions" provides a description of the various
realms of beings in a way that precludes either control or revolt in the interaction between them. Tillich argues that if we view such life processes
in graphical form, dimensions all meet at a central point and overlap each
other without conflict or dominance. The peaceful interaction between the
dimensions provides an image of life processes in which "the unity of life is
seen above its conflicts."[6]

That is not to say that conflicts between different life processes do not exist,
because clearly they still do (e.g., most humans still eat other animals, and
herbivores still eat vegetation), but rather than these conflicts arising out of
control or revolt between the levels, they can be seen as merely an inherent
part of the ambiguity of all life processes. From this understanding of the relation between the different dimensions, Tillich believes that the ambiguities
and conflicts implicit in all life processes might be overcome without the
need for any dimension to engulf any other. This view then would appear to
be extremely promising from the perspective of animal theology.

Unfortunately, when Tillich's underlying motivation for advancing this
concept is examined, it is clear that his motivation was based on purely
humanocentric considerations. Although his theory relates to essential life
rather than life as we experience it, it is difficult to imagine how changing one
metaphor for another without fundamentally changing the accompanying
mindset could have any real impact on existential life. The use of the dimension metaphor rather than that of levels does nothing to change the reality
that the interaction between different subsections of our world remains that
of "interference, either by control or revolt."[7] In numerous instances, conflicts

[4] Tillich, *Systematic Theology*, 3:13.
[5] The difference between "level" and "grade" is little more than semantic. In practice, the terms describe precisely the same structure.
[6] Tillich, *Systematic Theology*, 3:16.
[7] Tillich, *Systematic Theology*, 3:13.

occur between the various dimensions, often brought about by human interference and control. At no point does Tillich's multidimensional unity of life compel us to lead our lives differently—or even indicate that we should give greater consideration to any of the inhabitants of other realms—so one might ask, "Why then does he wish to replace a hierarchy of levels with metaphors that according to him are nonhierarchical?" To answer this question, it is necessary to examine the specific considerations that led him to make such a replacement. Tillich gives four exclusively humanocentric reasons.

First, he points to the problems of this structure when attempting to explain the relation between the organic and inorganic levels of nature.[8] When there can be no dependence between the organic and inorganic levels, questions are raised as to whether biological, organic processes can be apprehended solely by viewing the world through the eyes of mathematical physics—or in fact any other means of human perception. Second, Tillich highlights the problems that a hierarchical view of the world causes when considering the relation between the organic and spiritual levels of life. This problem is most clearly evident in the relation between the body (organic) and the mind (spiritual).[9] Third, problems emerge from the inadequacies of a hierarchical way of viewing the world, when the relation of religion to culture is examined. Finally, the notion of independent levels of being poses serious questions for theological thought also. If God and humanity appear on different and wholly independent levels within a hierarchical order, Tillich is dubious as to whether there can be any meaningful description at all regarding the relation of God and humans.[10]

It is now clear that the preceding, purely humanocentric reasons are what motivated Tillich to drop the metaphor of level, in favor of dimensions, realms, and grades. This is not adequate from the point of view of the status of animals within his theology. By failing to account for the problems of interaction between the Creator and creation under the conditions of existence, not only does Tillich fail to represent a theological account of animals, but he also neglects to account for the Creator's own interests in relation to

---

[8] Tillich, *Systematic Theology*, 3:13–14.

[9] Also see Paul Tillich, *The Spiritual Situation in Our Technological Society*, ed. J. Mark Thomas (Macon, GA: Mercer University Press, 1992), 115–16.

[10] It is interesting to note that here Tillich talks exclusively of a relationship between God and humans. At no point does he make any reference to God and nonhuman animals or to God and the whole of the created order. If being on different levels of an independent hierarchy is problematic for the relation of God to humans, it is especially so in the case of the relation of God to the rest of creation.

animals. If Tillich is correct that theonomy, or a God-centered account of the world, is the goal of theology, then in his own terms, Tillich's account is wanting. Based on his entirely humanocentric motives for devising his multidimensional unity of life, it is hard to imagine that Tillich considered the difficulties and theological deficiencies inherent in the hierarchical metaphor (and the worldview it represents) from the perspective of the status of the Creator or animals.

In Tillich's estimation, although all dimensions are potentially present in each other, it is only in humans that all dimensions are actually present. For instance, only humans have actualized the historical realm. This does not mean that the inorganic and organic dimensions are not vital, because without the actualization of the inorganic dimension, no other dimension could have met the conditions required to actualize themselves either.[11] Thus, Tillich views the importance of the inorganic and organic dimensions in purely instrumental or utilitarian terms, because although they may not be as advanced as the historical dimension, for instance, the historical dimension could not exist without them. However, the key theological question should be not what animals are to humans, but what they mean to God the Creator. Tillich fails to address this question entirely.

This naturally leads the animal theologian to ask if there is anything in Tillich's *Systematic Theology* that could help to provide the basis of a Tillichian animal ethic, and the answer is affirmative. The method and structure of the system itself provide hope for an animal theology. The structure of his system comprises five separate parts, each dealing with a question that arises out of the ambiguities of human existence. Each question is then correlated to a Christian symbol that functions as an answer.

In the introduction to Tillich's book *The Irrelevance and Relevance of the Christian Message*, editor Durwood Foster asserts that Tillich "relentlessly insisted that authentic theology . . . must speak to the burning issues of human life."[12] In order to achieve this aim, Tillich utilized what he described as the "method of correlation,"[13] which brought together the foundational truths of the faith with the situation in which people were to receive this message.

---

[11] Tillich, *Systematic Theology*, 3:16. As Tillich points out, "only the inorganic dimension is actualized in the atom, but all the other dimensions are potentially present. Symbolically speaking, one could say that when God created the potentiality of the atom within himself, he created the potentiality of man, and when he created the potentiality of man, he created the potentiality of the atom—and all other dimensions between them."

[12] Durwood Foster, introduction to *The Irrelevance and Relevance of the Christian Message*, by Paul Tillich, ed. Durwood Foster (Cleveland, OH: Pilgrim Press, 1996), x.

[13] Tillich, *Systematic Theology*, 1:9.

The concept of correlation is of vital importance if one is to ask ethical questions regarding the interaction between humans and nonhuman animals. Since Tillich's death, a wealth of insight into the sophistication and complexity of nonhuman animal life has come to light, insight that simply was not available to him in his lifetime. By applying such information to the abstract framework of Tillich's system, this discussion will show that his system can indeed help to provide the basis of a theological account of animals.

His systematic theology remains dynamic because although the "giving" side of the correlation is fundamentally unchanging, the "receiving" side is perpetually in a state of development, as is human social existence, out of which the questions are asked. Tillich believes that the human experience of transcendence is to be found in the unique tensions of contemporary life and that the tensions experienced will alter from person to person, depending on the individual posing the question. In this respect, his system falls within the tradition of mediating theology—that is, theological thinking that begins with the premise that the Christian faith and modern thought, including moral and ethical dilemmas, share common ground and can be fundamentally united.

He posits that religion as a discipline in isolation, however, does not possess all of the "tools" required to forge this unity. Instead, he asserts that religion is related to other disciplines such as philosophy, depth psychology, politics, and culture in much the same way that form is related to content. Tillich suggests that "reality itself makes demands and the method must follow; reality offers itself in different ways and our cognitive intellect must receive it in different ways."[14]

Because the human pole of the correlation is constantly in a state of flux, adjusting itself according to the flow of social and cultural existence, the giving side of the correlation too has to allow for an interpretation of the faith that remains true to its foundation while maintaining its relevance as a living religion. Thus, Foster asserts that "the theological task is never finished but is always posed again somewhat differently by the incessant dynamism of history."[15]

Questions derived from everyday life, then, can be viewed as "the expression of an 'existential situation' and not the acceptance of an objective

[14] Paul Tillich, "The Problem of Theological Method," *Journal of Religion* 26 (January 1, 1947): 16.
[15] Foster, discussing Tillich's understanding of his method of correlation in the introduction to *The Irrelevance and Relevance*, xi.

assertion."[16] In Tillich's method of correlation, although the questions implied in our finite existence are largely relativistic because they emerge from the particularity of a definite social and cultural setting, Christian theology's responses to these questions are universal, because they are derived from the kerygma, or foundational message of Christian theology, which is of course unchanging.

Although the method of correlation receives much greater emphasis in Tillich's system than more widely used methods such as dogmatics, he nonetheless does not dispense with these tools altogether. Instead, he still regards the kerygma derived from a process of revelation to be at the heart of Christian theology. Thus, the core of the Christian message for Tillich is unrelated to a given time or situation, and this acknowledgment of the universality of the kerygma prevents his system from lapsing into relativism.

By combining apologetics with kerygmatic theology in his method of correlation, Tillich is able to accommodate both the changing and unchanging sides of the correlation. The consequence of such a method, in his opinion, is that a "much richer development of theological ethics"[17] is indeed possible.

It may not seem obvious from reading his *Systematic Theology*, but in some of his other writings, Tillich displays great sensitivity toward the nonhuman creation. This attitude is clear in his sermon "Nature Also Mourns for a Lost Good," where he recognizes the universal element of estrangement and longing for redemption among the whole of creation.[18] This more approachable side to his writing has been noted by Pauck and Pauck: "It is an irony that Tillich expressed himself more convincingly in his sermons than anywhere else, including even his *Systematic Theology*."[19] This may well, at least in part, be the result of the level of abstraction he employs throughout his system. This abstract nature, however, should not be interpreted as indicating a lack of interest in animals and creation. Indeed, Tillich is one of the few mainstream theologians who perceived the tragic element of nature and its longing for salvation. On this understanding, there can be no dichotomy between guilty humans and innocent nature, no schism between human and

---

[16] Tillich, "The Problem of Theological Method," 24.

[17] Tillich, *Systematic Theology*, 3:31.

[18] Paul Tillich, "Nature Also Mourns for a Lost Good," in Paul Tillich, *The Shaking of the Foundations: Sermons Applicable to the Personal and Social Problems of Our Religious Life* (New York: Charles Scribner's Sons, 1948), 76–86.

[19] Wilhelm Pauck and Marion Pauck, *Paul Tillich: His Life and Thought*, vol. 1, *Life* (New York: Harper & Row, 1976), 232.

animal salvation. The message is clear: we are firmly located within creation, not set apart from it.

Although at no point does Tillich specifically develop an ethical stance on animals in particular or creation in general, a faithful interpretation of his systematic theology nevertheless can provide much positive material and help to inform our attitude toward the rest of creation. His symbol of "the Fall" and especially his principle of "universal salvation"[20] can certainly help to provide the basis for a more ethical and evenhanded way of dealing with the other species with whom we share our planet.

In order to illustrate just how important and informative the method of correlation is in relation to both the theological and ethical status of animals in Tillich's system, at this juncture we are able to "update" his system (as Tillich himself wished), thanks to his method of correlation, using a tiny fraction of the information gleaned from cognitive ethology in the decades since his death.

In the last thirty years or so, a new field of science has opened up and shed a great deal of light on the cognitive, behavioral, psychological, and social lives of animals. Along with this new information has come a new understanding of the intricate complexity of animal life and how nonhuman animals are significantly more advanced both cognitively and psychologically than was thought to be the case at the time Tillich was writing.

Cognitive ethology, or the scientific endeavor of gaining information about all aspects of animals' mental, psychological, and social lives, has been evident in one form or another for around a century, although until the 1970s, most of the emphasis was placed purely on behavioral studies, rather than on trying to understand the mental and emotional states underlying animals' behavior. In 1976, Donald Griffin first started specifically researching the issue of animal consciousness, an area of study that, although still in its infancy, has proved greatly influential in informing our views regarding the complex and diverse lives of many different animal species. For Griffin, a being can be thought of as experiencing a simple level of consciousness if the being "subjectively thinks about objects and events."[21] Although questions and speculations about animal mentality are not a new idea, until recently the scientific and philosophical world thought of animals as predominantly

---

[20] Tillich, *Systematic Theology*, 2:29. For a discussion of these ideas see, Smith, *Animals in Tillich's Philosophical Theology*, 54–58.

[21] Donald R. Griffin, "Progress toward a Cognitive Ethology," in *Cognitive Ethology: The Minds of Other Animals*, ed. Carolyn A. Ristau (Hillsdale, NJ: Lawrence Erlbaum, 1991), 5.

devoid of conscious thought. The field of cognitive ethology has proved this to be far from the case.

Griffin points out that it would seem reasonable to believe that non-human animals experience conscious thought because the basic structure and functioning of neurons and synapses show marked similarities in all animals with an organized nervous system. In addition, as research into animal cognition continues, it is becoming clear that a huge variety of cognitive processes occur in animal brains, and on this basis it also is becoming "more and more difficult to cling to the conviction that none of this cognition [in animal brains] is ever accompanied by conscious thoughts."[22]

Stephen Walker argues that based on the evidence collected over the last thirty years or so, both from laboratory experiments and from observing animals in their natural environments, as cognitive ethologists primarily do, it seems apparent that many animals are capable of versatile adaptability in their cognitive processes and behaviors. Walker argues that it is almost inconceivable that animals could combine such complex cognitive processes without conscious thought.[23]

In Griffin's opinion, the most promising reason to infer animal consciousness lies in the data concerning animal communication, in which "animals sometimes appear to convey to others at least some of their thoughts."[24] The work of ethologists such as Carolyn Ristau certainly backs up the idea that animals are able to convey a wide variety of information, including simple thoughts, via a combination of vocalization and body language.[25]

In addition, ethologists have documented instances where animals have attempted to deceive others by giving "false" signals with the goal of personal gain. For example, while studying a troop of vervet monkeys, Cheney and Seyfarth found that there were particular individuals who "cried wolf" in order to keep a food source for themselves, rather than share it with the rest of their troop. It was also noted that the rest of the troop soon realized they were being misled, and the troop learned to ignore signals that they deemed to be from unreliable troop members.[26] In addition to many non-human animals' displays of consciousness, sophisticated communication

[22] Donald R. Griffin, *Animal Minds* (Chicago: University of Chicago Press, 1992), 3.
[23] Stephen Walker, *Animal Thought* (London: Routledge and Kegan Paul, 1983).
[24] Griffin, *Animal Minds*, 27.
[25] See Carolyn A. Ristau, ed., *Cognitive Ethology: The Mind of Other Animals* (Hillsdale, NJ: Lawrence Erlbaum Associates, 1991).
[26] D. L. Cheney and R. M. Seyfarth, "Assessment of Meaning and the Detection of Unreliable Signals by Vervet Monkeys," *Animal Behaviour* 36, no. 2 (1988): 477–86.

skills, and even the ability to deliberately deceive, ethologists such as David Williams have identified evidence of experiential, associative, and even insight learning, which was previously attributed only to humans.[27]

When we add the new information that cognitive ethology provides to our existential questions regarding nonhuman animals and apply it to Tillich's system, it is immediately obvious that many of Tillich's assumptions regarding nonhuman animals are totally incorrect. With the updated information, key Tillichian assertions are found to be inadequate in relation to nonhuman animals and to not represent the actuality of creaturely existence. The first of these is the assumption made regarding the dimension and realm that nonhuman animals should occupy within Tillich's multidimensional unity of life model.[28] He asserts that animals occupy the organic dimension and reside within the animal "realm" (or subset) within it. Although it is claimed that his system is nonhierarchical, in practice there is no difference between his "grades of being" and the original pyramidal hierarchy of being from which he wished to move away.

When we integrate the new information (as Tillich himself would wish us to do), it is clear that nonhuman animals need to be classified in a dimension that is characterized by a higher level of "actualization" than the one he believed they should occupy. Of course, Tillich is not at fault for making incorrect assumptions since he was acting on the best information available to him during his lifetime. The method of correlation provides a way of ensuring that the Christian message can be updated, allowing the foundational truths of Christianity to remain as relevant for people today as they were in the lives of the first-century people of Palestine.

The changing of dimension and realm for nonhuman animals has a variety of positive consequences both for the theological and ethical status of animals and for the coherency and consistency of Tillich's *Systematic Theology* as a whole. In the case of nonhuman animals, we have enough information regarding how advanced various species are to be confident that at least all mammals and most birds (and possibly many other classifications of creatures) comfortably qualify for inclusion in the dimension of the spirit within the "personal communal realm"[29] and possibly

---

[27] See David A. O. Williams, *The Intelligence of Animals and Other Papers: A Theory of Learning* (London: SPCK, 1992).
[28] For a fuller discussion of Tillich's concept of the interrelatedness of the whole of creation, see chapter 6, "The Multidimensional Unity of Life," in Smith, *Animals in Tillich's Philosophical Theology*, 125–40.
[29] Tillich, *Systematic Theology*, 3:21.

even within the historical dimension along with humans. This represents a jump of one to two dimensions and two to three realms.[30] The significance of this change is potentially substantial in terms of theological status. If nonhuman animals are much more sophisticated in terms of their ability to interact and communicate with each other than was thought during Tillich's lifetime, then it is difficult to see how their exclusion from the "Spiritual Presence" would be justified. The symbol "Spiritual Presence" for Tillich represents the inner-historical telos of history, and it also represents the medium through which revelation is received.[31] If nonhuman animals were to have access to the Spiritual Presence, it would follow that as "Final Revelation,"[32] they also would have direct access to the Christ. Theologically speaking, this is of huge significance and would indicate that God has a direct relationship with many other groups of creatures within creation and not simply the human species. This does not mean that humans can no longer be thought of as having a special relationship with God. On the contrary, as the creatures created in God's image, humans still have the unique ability (and it could even be argued a duty)[33] to take on the priestly responsibility of caring for the whole of creation in a way that no other species is capable of doing.

Because Christ is both the transhistorical telos of history and the center of history, it would seem that Tillich's previous assumptions (at least as far as mammals are concerned) that only humans have access to this dimension, based on humans' cognitive ability, must be overruled too. This exclusivist attitude must give way to the theologically important insight that in light of the complexity evident in other animals, they also have access to the Christ alongside humans.

From the perspective of the coherency of Tillich's system as a whole, it might be assumed that asking ethical and theological questions about animals would be damaging or at the very least would have nothing important to contribute. However, this is absolutely not the case. Without the animal question, Tillich's system contains a substantial inconsistency regarding the relationship of the Creator to the whole of creation. This is so because it

---

[30] For a discussion of these ideas see, Smith, *Animals in Tillich's Philosophical Theology*, 193–97.

[31] Tillich, *Systematic Theology*, 3:298–99.

[32] Tillich, *Systematic Theology*, 3:80.

[33] See Andrew Linzey, *Animal Theology* (Chicago: University of Illinois Press, 1994), especially chap. 3, "Humans as the Servant Species."

would appear that although God the Creator created everything on the earth and saw all of it, in its essential state, to be good, there is no direct access for any part of the creation other than humans to the Logos as sustainer or to Christ as redeemer. Clearly, this is not a satisfactory conclusion from the point of view of Tillich producing a theonomous system—that is, a system from the point of view of the Creator—or even a consistent one since non-human animals do not have access to "the Christ" but nonetheless seem to be directly included in universal salvation regardless of this. If we allow for nonhuman animals' access to the dimension of the spirit and, by implication, to the dimension of history, the inconsistencies in Tillich's system in relation to the separation of the Spirit and Son from the Father are removed. And this can play a substantial part in resolving the inconsistencies present in his system's Christology. Tillich's method of correlation then is not just the means by which the whole of creation can be theologically accounted for; it is also the means by which his system is able to overcome many of its own internal inconsistencies.

Bibliography

Cheney, D. L., and R. M. Seyfarth. "Assessment of Meaning and the Detection of Unreliable Signals by Vervet Monkeys." *Animal Behaviour* 36, no. 2 (1988): 477–86.

Foster, Durwood. Introduction to *The Irrelevance and Relevance of the Christian Message*, by Paul Tillich, ed. Durwood Foster. Cleveland, OH: Pilgrim Press, 1996.

Griffin, Donald R. *Animal Minds*. Chicago: University of Chicago Press, 1992.

Griffin, Donald R. "Progress toward a Cognitive Ethology." In *Cognitive Ethology: The Minds of Other Animals*, edited by Carolyn A. Ristau, 3–17. Hillsdale, NJ: Lawrence Erlbaum, 1991.

Linzey, Andrew. *Animal Theology*. Chicago: University of Illinois Press, 1994.

Pauck, Wilhelm, and Marion Pauck. *Paul Tillich: His Life and Thought*. Vol. 1, *Life*. New York: Harper & Row, 1976.

Ristau, Carolyn A., ed. *Cognitive Ethology: The Minds of Other Animals*. Hillsdale, NJ: Lawrence Erlbaum, 1991.

Smith, Abbey-Anne. *Animals in Tillich's Philosophical Theology*. Basingstoke, UK: Palgrave Macmillan, 2017.

Tillich, Paul. "The Problem of Theological Method." *Journal of Religion* 26 (January 1, 1947): 16–26.

Tillich, Paul. *The Shaking of the Foundations: Sermons Applicable to the Personal and Social Problems of Our Religious Life*. New York: Charles Scribner's Sons, 1948.

Tillich, Paul. *The Spiritual Situation in Our Technological Society*. Edited by J. Mark Thomas. Macon, GA: Mercer University Press, 1992.

Tillich, Paul. *Systematic Theology*. 3 vols. Chicago: University of Chicago Press, 1951–63.

Walker, Stephen. *Animal Thought*. London: Routledge and Kegan Paul, 1983.

Williams, David A. O. *The Intelligence of Animals and Other Papers: A Theory of Learning*. London: SPCK, 1992.

Yunt, Jeremy D. *The Ecotheology of Paul Tillich: The Spiritual Roots of Environmental Ethics*. N.p.: CreateSpace Independent Publishing Platform, 2009.

20

Charles Hartshorne (1897–2000)

Animals in Process Thought

Daniel A. Dombrowski

Introduction

Although Charles Hartshorne was not a theologian but a philosopher, throughout his long career he concentrated on questions regarding both the concept of God and the existence of God.[1] In the middle decades of the twentieth century, he was almost alone among philosophers in doing so. He is known chiefly as a neoclassical or process theist and is considered by many thinkers to have been the greatest metaphysician of the twentieth century.

Hartshorne's theism, which is thoroughly at home with an evolutionary worldview, is also noteworthy because of what it says about nonhuman animals (hereafter "animals"). Three claims in particular are quite remarkable: (1) Hartshorne (along with another great process theist, Alfred North Whitehead) thinks not only that animals are moral patients but also that they should be seen as *persons*, contra the anthropocentric view of traditional theists, which denies personhood status to subhuman beings. (2) Birds in particular, through their song, enable us to understand and appreciate the aesthetic factors that pervade the cosmos, from subatomic particles to God. And (3) Hartshorne quite explicitly refers to "the divine animal" in his rediscovery and retrieval of Plato's "world soul," where God is seen as the soul or mind who animates not this or that particular body, but the cosmos as a whole. By contrast, the judicious character of the traditional doctrine of analogy when talking about God is abandoned by many or most theists when

---

[1] See, e.g., Charles Hartshorne, *The Divine Relativity* (New Haven: Yale University Press, 1948); *Philosophers Speak of God* (Chicago: University of Chicago Press, 1953); *Anselm's Discovery: A Reexamination of the Ontological Proof for God's Existence* (LaSalle, IL: Open Court, 1965); *Creative Synthesis and Philosophic Method* (LaSalle, IL: Open Court, 1970); *Existence and Actuality* (Chicago: University of Chicago Press, 1984); and *The Philosophy of Charles Hartshorne*, ed. Lewis Hahn (LaSalle, IL: Open Court, 1991).

Daniel A. Dombrowski, *Charles Hartshorne (1897–2000)* In: *Animal Theologians*. Edited by: Andrew Linzey and Clair Linzey, Oxford University Press. © Oxford University Press 2023. DOI: 10.1093/oso/9780197655542.003.0021

the topic is divine embodiment. God is usually claimed to be pure spirit and in no way sullied by corporeality.

Commonality with Animals

This section of my chapter, along with the next section, constitutes an approach to animals that emphasizes unity-in-difference. The fact that human beings themselves *are* animals provides the basis for the present section. In response to the question "What do human beings have in common with other animals?" Hartshorne's primary answer is multicellular bodies, especially complex central nervous systems.[2] Along with the higher animals (i.e., those with central nervous systems—in contrast, say, to paramecia), human beings have bodies that are cases of social organization and cooperation. Higher animals, in general, are organized societies of individuals. Unlike plants, they are also individuals as wholes. Lacking a central nervous system, lower animals and plants have parts that are, for the most part, on their own. Relying on Whitehead, Hartshorne suggests that without a central nervous system, a tree is something of a democracy.[3]

Human and animal individuality at the supercellular level is not merely physiological but psychological as well. That is, two sorts of sentiency should be distinguished: proto-sentiency at the microscopic level of cells (and, in Hartshorne's panpsychism, at the level of molecules, atoms, and subatomic particles), which occurs in plants (and rocks) as well as in human beings and animals, which we will call S1; and sentiency per se, which consists in those experiences that enable a human being or an animal as a whole to feel pain or, at times, to remember or anticipate pain (i.e., to suffer), which we will call S2.[4]

What human beings have in common with higher animals is S2; this sentiency criterion distinguishes humans and higher animals from other existents. But those beings capable of S2 are but recent branches on a tree of life that is millions of years old. Countless steps led to the development of a central nervous system and its fruition: the brain. These steps we share with

[2] Charles Hartshorne, "Foundations for a Humane Ethics: What Human Beings Have in Common with Other Higher Animals," in *On the Fifth Day: Animal Rights and Human Ethics*, ed. Richard Knowles Morris (Washington, DC: Acropolis Press, 1978), 154.

[3] Charles Hartshorne, *Omnipotence and Other Theological Mistakes* (Albany: State University of New York Press, 1984), 79, 106.

[4] Hartshorne, "Foundations for a Humane Ethics," 155–56.

higher animals. To assume that all of this development over so many years was mere preparation for human beings is to exchange a sublime and coherent vision of the universe for a childishly arbitrary one.[5] Arbitrariness is one of the hallmarks of anthropocentric speciesism.

From the seventeenth century to the nineteenth, scientists tended to see the world as a machine whose parts (including animals) were submachines.[6] Hartshorne's concept of the universe as organic was meant to counteract this view. Human beings and animals are alike in providing evidence against (Cartesian) mechanism. Our task is to try to know, or at least to imagine, how it feels to be a sentient subject of feeling other than one's own present self.[7] This is often difficult even with respect to one's own past selves—say, one's time as an infant. Chimpanzees and cows make the project simpler, strange as that sounds. There is no need to even try for clouds or oceans; although S1 may be found in their microconstituents, clouds and bodies of water are not sentient as wholes because they lack a central nervous system that makes S2 possible:

> Although we do not know that there is such a thing as a mere machine, we do know that there are animals, creatures whose actions are at least altogether *as if* they were influenced by feelings, desires, hopes, fears, likes and dislikes, memories and expectations. We know, too, that in animals the principle of spontaneous motion, what Plato called the "self-motion" of soul, is normally apparent.[8]

The fact that pain (as when one stubs one's toe), as well as pleasure (as in sex), is localized counts as evidence in favor of S1, along with the clear evidence of S2 in both human beings and higher animals.

Perhaps most noteworthy about human beings and animals are the implications of temporal asymmetry for their lives. These beings are causally affected by what has happened to them in the past, but their futures are at least partially open. Once one views temporal relations as asymmetrical, there is a tendency to view both human beings and higher animals as *persons*, with "personhood" referring to a mental life that is temporally conditioned in the

---

[5] Charles Hartshorne, "The Rights of the Subhuman World," *Environmental Ethics* 1 (1979): 51.

[6] Hartshorne, "The Rights of the Subhuman World," 53.

[7] Hartshorne, *Insights and Oversights of Great Thinkers* (Albany: State University of New York Press, 1983), 347.

[8] Hartshorne, "The Rights of the Subhuman World," 53.

sense that there is continuity among the occasions or events in a series.[9] That is, a person is one whose experiences are temporally ordered in the same psychological line of inheritance. Personal order among the occasions or events in a temporal sequence is characterized both by an *internal relatedness* among the occasions or events that are serially ordered (in contrast to nonpersons, which are not internally related to previous events in a sequence, as in a rock at a later stage of its existence not being internally affected by what happened to it in an earlier stage) and by a sequence that *sustains a character*. Once one views persons as those who have a mental life that is temporally conditioned, that features an internal relatedness among the members of a series (later events are internally related to previous ones in the sequence, but not vice versa), and that exhibits a temporal sequence that sustains a character, there are no conceptual barriers to seeing higher animals as persons.[10]

The language regarding "sustaining a character" is meant to sidestep questions regarding consciousness and self-consciousness, questions that deal with the highest levels of mentality. By partial contrast, personhood concerns which lines of inheritance from the past and anticipations of the future make an internal difference to the being in question. A person is one who can feel intensely his or her inheritance from the past without being shackled by it, and there is a degree of spontaneity in the attempt to live well, perhaps even to live better, in the future. For this reason not all living things are persons, in that many of them lack the endurance and intensity of feeling and central direction reserved for those whose lives are personally ordered. Worms and jellyfish, for example, have very little of these characteristics in their ultraminimal life-threads. But other animals do exhibit them and to a high degree in the temporal character of their lives as they both inherit from the past and are thrown toward a future that is at least partially indeterminate. The affective tone of their lives is not inconsiderable. The lives of mentally challenged human beings should convince us that one can have a life that is personally ordered without achieving the highest levels of rationality.

Consider the example of a dog who is kicked by a particular human being on a Tuesday and who is later confronted by the same human on Wednesday. The dog starts to growl even before being kicked again by the human. The

[9] See Daniel Dombrowski, "Are Nonhuman Animals Persons? A Process Theistic Response," *Journal of Animal Ethics* 5 (2015): 135–43.

[10] See Alfred North Whitehead, *Process and Reality*, ed. David Ray Griffin and Donald Sherburne (New York: Free Press, 1978), 34–35, 90, 105, 107, 109, 119, 350. Also see Whitehead's *Adventures of Ideas* (New York: Free Press, 1967), 186–88, 205–15.

fact that it makes sense in everyday English to say that the dog *has reason* to growl speaks in favor of a certain mental life in the dog, who clearly remembers what happened on Tuesday and who is thus internally affected by the kicking event. Further, the dog exhibits a reaction to the human being that is in character both for dogs in general and for this dog in particular, whom we will call Tuffy, in that other dogs might either flee at one extreme or bite the kicker at the other. It can be said that Tuffy's character exhibits (Aristotelian) moderation.

Or consider a normally compliant cow whom we will call Daisy who, upon being brought to the abattoir, becomes restless and tries to turn around in her chute and run in the other direction. Granted, the future is not here yet and hence cannot be known in any detail, but it nonetheless makes sense for the cow to be skittish or, if she actually smells the blood of her conspecifics, to be filled with terror regarding what might happen in the future. Although she is typically mellow, it is obviously not unreasonable for her to resist going into the slaughterhouse in light of the fact that she has already internalized the importance of certain screams and smells and sights that have come from other cows in the past; the appearance of these in the present is enough to make her apprehensive regarding the immediate future. It is consistent with characteristic serenity to be agitated in an *in extremis* predicament.

For human beings and animals, intensity of feeling accompanies efforts to survive. Crystals survive, but the S1 feelings in them are not intense. And S2 feelings are altogether absent in crystals; hence, we call such entities "inorganic." There is thus no incompatibility between a doctrine of hierarchy of value on the one hand and noting human commonality with higher animals regarding personhood on the other. Both human beings and animals are living (S2) societies of momentary occasions of (S1) experience. The S2 experiences in their lives are serially ordered with a single line of inheritance. Further, they have a persistence of psychological traits and a dominant or presiding trait called mind.

Partial Transcendence of Animality

It is nonetheless appropriate for highly rational human beings to call attention to their superiority to other animals, at least so long as they remain cognizant of the fact that they themselves *are* animals and that there is a unity-in-difference in any such claims to partial transcendence of animality.

Dogs think doggishly. For all we know, however, dogs do not know this. Human beings are just as much prisoners of their own nature as dogs, but some human beings know this. "To know a mental limit as such is to be, in some sense and degree, beyond the limit."[11] In this way highly rational human beings can partially transcend their animality. The key question is: To what degree can such transcendence occur?

All animals die, although it seems that only human beings know this (although it must be acknowledged that even elephants have funeral rituals). The distinction between nascently rational animals and highly rational human beings does not lie in their being finite and our being infinite. Actually, in Hartshorne's view, to believe that human beings are infinite would hubristically make us into gods. Rather, the distinction lies in the fact that although animals can communicate and can perhaps even use language, only highly rational human beings have *logos* in the sense that only we can talk about talking and only we have the word "word."[12] Nor is our distinctiveness tied to our egocentricity, considering that animals are like us in perceiving themselves as "here" and everything else as "there." Rather, apparently only we have a relatively firm grasp on *abstract* objects; animals cannot speak in abstractions or about universal or necessary truth. But our superiority in this regard, which is real enough, is not absolute. For example, presumably all animals have something like the generalization "edible stuff" in mind, even if they do not have enough facility with abstract symbols to take courses in physiology.

It is crucial to emphasize that our partial transcendence of animality is not sufficient to support the case for an anthropocentric universe. We do know that higher animals have S2 feelings, both because we ourselves have such feelings and because such animals' internal bodily structure and behavior are similar to ours. So in very *abstract* terms language can formulate the alternatives regarding the differences among animals, human beings, angels (if there are such), and God. In this knowledge our animality is partially left behind. *Concrete* knowledge of all of the details regarding animal feelings, however, would require omniscience.[13]

Although all animals resolve indeterminacies, human beings turn future determinables into determinate actualities to a greater degree than animals.

[11] Charles Hartshorne, "Can Man Transcend His Animality?," *Monist* 55 (1971): 208.
[12] See Hartshorne's "Foundations for a Humane Ethics," 161.
[13] Charles Hartshorne, *Creativity in American Philosophy* (Albany: State University of New York Press, 1984), 142, 234. Also see Hartshorne, "Can Man Transcend His Animality?," 215.

Nonetheless, higher animals at least act as if they take for granted that the future is partly settled and foreseeable and partly in the process of being decided. A companion animal knows that he or she will eat and hence does not need to viciously prowl around to find food, yet the animal whimpers when hungry, out of ignorance regarding exactly when he or she will be fed. Once again, in Hartshorne's view we should think of our relations with animals in terms of a unity-in-difference.

Implications for Ethics

It speaks in favor of Hartshorne's neoclassical or process theism that he can with equanimity refer to Tuffy or Daisy (unfortunately, farmed animals seldom receive personalized names) as persons. By contrast, in the classical theistic view, Tuffy and Daisy would not be persons because the threshold for personhood status is species-dependent: only those beings made in the image of God are persons, and only human beings are made in the image of God. If one asks why only human beings are made in the image of God, classical theists typically fall back on certain functional criteria that (supposedly) only human beings exhibit: rationality, free will, moral agency, or autonomy. But in Hartshorne's view the possession of sense perception and the nascent mentality that sense perception involves, as illustrated above by Tuffy and Daisy, are sufficient to think of animals not only as moral patients but also as persons.

Hartshorne accepts two standard arguments in the animal rights literature. The first is called the argument from sentiency, which, in abbreviated form, goes something like this:

1. Any being who can experience pain or can suffer has, at the very least, the right not to be forced to experience pain or suffer or be killed unnecessarily.
2. It is not necessary that we inflict pain, suffering, or death on S2 sentient animals in order to eat because a vegetarian diet can be very healthy.
3. Therefore, to inflict unnecessary pain, suffering, or death on a S2 sentient animal in order to eat is morally reprehensible or cruel.

As the vegetarian commonplace (derived from Bentham) has it, the question is not "Can animals reason?" but rather "Can they suffer?" Higher animals raised for the table can suffer, whereas plants and lower animals such as amoebas, for all that we can tell, cannot.

Some might suspect that an escape from this argument can be found in "sneaking up" on the animal so as to kill him or her painlessly. There are many ways to respond to this objection, one of which is through the argument from marginal cases. It does seem peculiar that some think that pain is a "hurt" but that unnecessary killing is not. The key feature of the argument from marginal cases is that any proposed criterion for moral patiency status that is possessed by *all* human beings will not be possessed *only* by human beings. All humans, but not only humans, are capable of experiencing pain. Although only humans are capable of advanced rationality (this point is granted for the sake of argument), not all humans exhibit rationality—for example, those who are mentally deficient or in advanced dementia (i.e., the marginal cases of humanity, whose marginal status is created when rationality is unwisely proposed as a criterion for moral patiency status).

Classical theistic statements of a human being's privileged status cannot be philosophically justified. But to say that we can legitimately eat animals because human beings are rational or autonomous or religious believers or language users and so on is to make a claim that does not in fact apply to all human beings. These "marginal cases" include infants, the mentally feeble, and others. If we "lower" our standard for moral patiency to that of S2 sentiency, so as to understandably protect these people, we must also protect many animals, including those whom we eat, in order to be consistent.

If an animal has characteristics a, b, and c but lacks rationality (or autonomy, etc.), and if a human being has characteristics a, b, and c but lacks rationality (or autonomy, etc.), then we have just as much reason to believe that the animal has rights as the human. These rights would include the right not to be forced to experience pain or suffering or be killed unnecessarily.

The greatest impediment to acceptance of these two arguments, Hartshorne implies, is the absolutization of self-interest in Western ethics.[14] But in the long run we will not be here—only the everlasting whole of things (including God) will be—and a consideration of this fact tends to whittle away at our concentration on self-interest. Animals are immune to the sort of hubris often found in human beings because, through inherited arrangements, they are unwitting, humble servants of a cosmic cause. By thinking that ethical concern is a pie of a fixed size, however, such that if a

---

[14] Hartshorne, *Creative Synthesis and Philosophic Method*, 55–56.

slice is given to animals, there is less for us, anthropocentrists misunderstand the expandability of *agape* and compassion, Hartshorne thinks.[15]

Although individual human beings who are highly rational may be of more value than other beings (in part because they can have the idea of "idea"), this does not mean that they are infinitely more valuable or that they should be allowed to cause avoidable harm. There is actually a *burden* placed on our shoulders due to both our advanced rationality and our ability to love and to delight in the lives of others, which is arguably what puts us in the image of God. Another impediment to ethical relations with animals is our tendency to value human beings individually, whereas a hermit thrush is seen as significant chiefly as a specimen of his or her species. We should keep in mind, however, that it is not Platonic birdhood or cowness that suffer, but individual S2 members of species. Killing them unnecessarily does not constitute murder, in Hartshorne's view, but comes close to that.[16]

Hartshorne admits that if it were necessary to kill a single bird in order to save a human life in some hypothetical situation, then perhaps the bird should be killed. Each of us is of more value than many sparrows (see Matt. 10:28–32). But how *many* more? Hartshorne himself hypothetically suggested that he would have seriously considered giving up the remainder of his life if it would have saved a threatened bird species for millennia.[17]

Hartshorne is clear that mortality as such is not an evil, and hence we ought not to romantically hope to eliminate it in either the human or the animal case. It is premature, painful, or ugly modes of dying, rather than dying *simpliciter*, that are tragic. This provides the basis for an immanent critique of any version of theism, whether neoclassical process theism or classical theism, that would permit the killing of S2 animals in their prime for the table or for some other unnecessary purpose.

Birdsong

In addition to his work as a philosopher, Hartshorne was an ornithologist whose book on birdsong, *Born to Sing*, positively influenced some of the most

---

[15] Hartshorne, "Foundations for a Humane Ethics," 167, 169–70.

[16] Hartshorne, "The Rights of the Subhuman World," 51, 56.

[17] Hartshorne, "The Rights of the Subhuman World," 51, 57; "Foundations for a Humane Ethics," 171; *Omnipotence and Other Theological Mistakes*, 46; *Insights and Oversights of Great Thinkers*, 224; and "The Environmental Results of Technology," in *Philosophy and Environmental Crisis*, ed. William Blackstone (Athens: University of Georgia Press, 1974), 71–72.

important scientists in the field. He is thus the first person since Aristotle to do significant work in both philosophy and ornithology.

Scientific accounts of birdsong are typically mechanistic and explain the phenomenon in question in terms of two functions: birds sing either to attract a mate or to defend territory. Hartshorne asks a basic question: why do birds often sing outside of mating season or when territory is not threatened?[18] Hartshorne's parsimonious response to this question is that they *like* to sing. That is, even if birds are not sufficiently rational to be *moral* agents (though their sentiency nonetheless ensures that they should be seen as moral patients), their ability to have aesthetic feelings counts in favor of the claim that they are *aesthetic* agents. Hartshorne's great discovery in this regard is what he calls the "monotony threshold." Despite what inattentive listeners might think, bird singers do not keep singing the same song over and over. Rather, bird singers who have a large repertoire of songs tend to mix them up, and singers who have a small repertoire of songs tend to vary the length of the intervals between the few songs that they can sing. Birdsong exhibits an avoidance of the aesthetic disvalues of both monotony and chaos.[19]

It is not the purpose of the present discussion to explore the topics for which Hartshorne is most famous (i.e., his neoclassical or process *concept* of God and his modal version of the ontological argument for the *existence* of God),[20] but it is appropriate to note at this point that in his view, the prime aesthetic value, beauty, is like a medieval "transcendental" in that it refers to reality at all levels, both divine and nondivine (including animals). Specifically, beauty is, at the very least, a mean between the extremes of mere unity, absolute order, and hopeless predictability on the one hand and mere diversity, absolute disorder, and hopeless unpredictability on the other.[21] In a word, both God and birdsong are beautiful.

---

[18] Charles Hartshorne, *Born to Sing: An Interpretation and World Survey of Bird Song* (Bloomington: Indiana University Press, 1973). Also see Daniel Dombrowski, *Divine Beauty: The Aesthetics of Charles Hartshorne* (Nashville, TN: Vanderbilt University Press, 2004), chap. 4. One noted ornithologist influenced by Hartshorne is Alexander Skutch, "Bird Song and Philosophy," in *The Philosophy of Charles Hartshorne*, ed. Lewis Hahn (LaSalle, IL: Open Court, 1991).

[19] Hartshorne, *Born to Sing*.

[20] See Daniel Dombrowski, *Hartshorne and the Metaphysics of Animal Rights* (Albany: State University of New York Press, 1988); *Analytic Theism, Hartshorne, and the Concept of God* (Albany: State University of New York Press, 1996); "Charles Hartshorne," *Stanford Encyclopedia of Philosophy*, 2001, http://plato.stanford.edu; *A Platonic Philosophy of Religion: A Process Perspective* (Albany: State University of New York Press, 2005); and *Rethinking the Ontological Argument: A Neoclassical Theistic Response* (New York: Cambridge University Press, 2006).

[21] Dombrowski, *Divine Beauty*, chap. 2.

The Divine Animal

As a result of classical theism, we are accustomed to thinking in monopolar terms about God, who is seen as pure being rather than becoming, strictly permanent rather than changing, and so on. However, Hartshorne's theism is dipolar in that God is both permanent being and preeminent becoming. There is no contradiction here in that his claim is that God *always changes* (both words are needed), an everlastingness that contrasts with our ability to change for only a relatively short amount of time.[22] Classical theists also tend to be monopolar with respect to the spirit/body contrast. God is strictly immaterial, it is alleged, and is in no way embodied. Here again Hartshorne is a dipolar theist in that he thinks that God, as that than which no greater can be conceived, would have to exhibit both excellent spirituality and mentality on the one hand and excellent embodiment on the other.

Hartshorne tries to revitalize the ancient Greek concept of God as the "world soul," which was defended by all of the great ancient philosophers except for Aristotle and the atomists, according to Plutarch.[23] Plato, for example, discusses the world soul in at least five of his later dialogues,[24] discussions that were not lost on Origen, who tried to keep the concept of the world soul alive in Christianity.[25] The key idea here is that the cosmos is not an impersonal concatenation of unrelated parts. Rather, the universe is to be conceived in organic terms in that God is the besouled character of the world, the one who animates not this or that body, but the body of the entire world. One way to articulate this cosmic hylomorphism is to say that God is the soul for the body of the world, but another way is to say that the body of the world is the divine animal. There is no need to feel ashamed of our own animality, nor is there anything derogatory about linking divinity and animality so long as the divine animal is seen as having a living existence that is everlasting rather than finite in duration.

The concepts of the world soul and the divine animal are not merely parts of an idle theory in Hartshorne; rather, he notes that many people *feel*, as an element of everyday experience, that they are parts of a mighty whole, that God is omnipresent, and that, as Gerard Manley Hopkins put the point in

---

[22] Hartshorne, *The Divine Relativity*; also *Philosophers Speak of God*.
[23] See Plutarch, "Whether the World Be an Animal," in *Plutarch's Morals*, ed. William Goodwin (Boston: Little, Brown, 1870), 3:133.
[24] *Timaeus, Statesman, Philebus, Laws,* and *Epinomis*.
[25] See Dombrowski, *A Platonic Philosophy of Religion*, 29–32.

his famous poem "God's Grandeur," the world is filled with the grandeur of God. This is in contrast to the cosmic dualism often found in classical theism, wherein religiosity (counterintuitively) consists in pole-vaulting out of this natural world into an otherworldly supernatural one. Hartshorne's theistic naturalism can be illustrated in terms of the following four-term analogy, where, as we have seen, S1 refers to microscopic sentiency, S2 refers to sentiency per se as it is found in animals with central nervous systems (including human beings), and S3 refers to divine sentiency:

S1: S2 :: S2: S3

It would be correct to conclude from this analogy that S2 beings such as ourselves and higher animals are like cells in the divine life, in whom we live and move and have our being in Pauline fashion.

Conclusion

From a Hartshornian point of view, there is something hubristic about the anthropocentrism that characterizes the classical theistic concepts of God and human nature that have been prevalent in the Abrahamic religions. That is, classical theists in Judaism, Christianity, and Islam tend to say, or at least imply, that human beings have more in common with God than they do with fellow animals who happen to be nonhuman. However, because we, along with other animals, are both temporally and spatially fragmentary, in contrast to divine everlastingness and divine cosmic omnipresence, it makes more sense for theists to defend theocentrism than anthropocentrism.

Bibliography

Dombrowski, Daniel. *Analytic Theism, Hartshorne, and the Concept of God.* Albany: State University of New York Press, 1996.

Dombrowski, Daniel. "Are Nonhuman Animals Persons? A Process Theistic Response." *Journal of Animal Ethics* 5 (2015): 135–43.

Dombrowski, Daniel. "Charles Hartshorne." In *Stanford Encyclopedia of Philosophy*, edited by Edward N. Zalta. Fall 2022 ed. https://plato.stanford.edu/archives/fall2022/entries/hartshorne/.

Dombrowski, Daniel. *Divine Beauty: The Aesthetics of Charles Hartshorne.* Nashville, TN: Vanderbilt University Press, 2004.

Dombrowski, Daniel. *Hartshorne and the Metaphysics of Animal Rights*. Albany: State University of New York Press, 1988.

Dombrowski, Daniel. *A Platonic Philosophy of Religion: A Process Perspective*. Albany: State University of New York Press, 2005.

Dombrowski, Daniel. *Rethinking the Ontological Argument: A Neoclassical Theistic Response*. Cambridge: Cambridge University Press, 2006.

Hartshorne, Charles. *Anselm's Discovery: A Re-examination of the Ontological Proof for God's Existence*. LaSalle, IL: Open Court, 1965.

Hartshorne, Charles. *Born to Sing: An Interpretation and World Survey of Bird Song*. Bloomington: Indiana University Press, 1973.

Hartshorne, Charles. "Can Man Transcend His Animality?" *Monist* 55 (1971): 208–17.

Hartshorne, Charles. *Creative Synthesis and Philosophic Method*. LaSalle, IL: Open Court, 1970.

Hartshorne, Charles. *Creativity in American Philosophy*. Albany: State University of New York Press, 1984.

Hartshorne, Charles. *The Divine Relativity*. New Haven: Yale University Press, 1948.

Hartshorne, Charles. "The Environmental Results of Technology." In *Philosophy and Environmental Crisis*, edited by William Blackstone, 69–78. Athens: University of Georgia Press, 1974.

Hartshorne, Charles. *Existence and Actuality*. Chicago: University of Chicago Press, 1984.

Hartshorne, Charles. "Foundations for a Humane Ethics: What Human Beings Have in Common with Other Higher Animals." In *On the Fifth Day: Animal Rights and Human Ethics*, edited by Richard Knowles Morris, 154–72. Washington, DC: Acropolis Press, 1978.

Hartshorne, Charles. *Insights and Oversights of Great Thinkers*. Albany: State University of New York Press, 1983.

Hartshorne, Charles. *Omnipotence and Other Theological Mistakes*. Albany: State University of New York Press, 1984.

Hartshorne, Charles. *Philosophers Speak of God*. Chicago: University of Chicago Press, 1953.

Hartshorne, Charles. *The Philosophy of Charles Hartshorne*. Edited by Lewis Hahn. LaSalle, IL: Open Court, 1991.

Hartshorne, Charles. "The Rights of the Subhuman World." *Environmental Ethics* 1 (1979): 49–60.

Plutarch. "Whether the World Be an Animal." In *Plutarch's Morals*, edited by William Goodwin, 3:133. Boston: Little, Brown, 1870.

Skutch, Alexander. "Bird Song and Philosophy." In *The Philosophy of Charles Hartshorne*, edited by Lewis Hahn, 65–76. LaSalle, IL: Open Court, 1991.

Whitehead, Alfred North. *Adventures of Ideas*. New York: Free Press, 1967.

Whitehead, Alfred North. *Process and Reality*. Edited by David Ray Griffin and Donald Sherburne. New York: Free Press, 1978.

21

C. S. Lewis (1898–1963)

Rethinking Dominion

Michael J. Gilmour

Ingrid Newkirk, cofounder of People for the Ethical Treatment of Animals (PETA), describes the poet, novelist, and literary critic C. S. Lewis as "a kind man" whose writings elevate the status of animals and "blur the species barrier."[1] If Newkirk seems an unlikely commentator on Lewis's work, it is because so few give any attention to his views on animals and animal ethics. This is unfortunate because there is much to explore in this area even if he left no systematic, comprehensive statement of his ideas. As far back as his now-published juvenilia and his preconversion poetry, as well as in his adult and children's fiction, his theological and philosophical studies, and the extant, voluminous correspondence spanning most his life, we find him delighting in animals, both real and imagined.[2] That he thought often about humanity's moral obligations toward them is also apparent. Given his continued popularity more than a generation after his death, his theological views about nonhumans warrant the attention of those approaching animal ethics from a Christian perspective.

By necessity, any attempt to summarize ideas scattered across his voluminous output is piecemeal. At the same time, we find throughout said output an enchantment with nonhuman animals, a keen sense of a moral obligation to protect them, and an unambiguous loathing of all manner of cruelties.

---

[1] Ingrid Newkirk, "Would the Modern-Day C. S. Lewis Be a PETA Protester?," in *Revisiting Narnia: Fantasy, Myth and Religion in C. S. Lewis' Chronicles*, ed. Shanna Caughey (Dallas, TX: Benbella, 2005), 171, 166. She finds much to criticize in Lewis too, noting that he was a traditionalist reflecting cultural and religious contexts in such a way that "he felt it proper and right to view animals, women and, most likely, the poor as subspecies to be treated with magnanimity, within bounds" (167–68).

[2] For the juvenilia, see C. S. Lewis, *Boxen: The Imaginary World of the Young C. S. Lewis*, ed. Walter Hooper (London: Collins, 1985). For a touching illustration of Lewis's preconversion sympathies toward animal life, see his poem "The Ass," published under the name Clive Hamilton in *Spirits in Bondage: A Cycle of Lyrics* (London: William Heinemann, 1919), 75–77.

Michael J. Gilmour, *C. S. Lewis (1898–1963)* In: *Animal Theologians*. Edited by: Andrew Linzey and Clair Linzey, Oxford University Press. © Oxford University Press 2023. DOI: 10.1093/oso/9780197655542.003.0022

These attitudes are so persistent in Lewis that it almost does not matter where one jumps in with respect to the animal question. The primary aim here is a modest one: to simply capture something of the kindness Newkirk observes and something also of that ability to "blur the species barrier." And though hardly a treatment doing justice to the Lewis canon as a whole on this matter, this chapter also seeks to demonstrate that his place among the Christian tradition's more important voices on theological animal ethics is well deserved. To these ends, I focus on just one short poem. It is a minor text and rarely read but is broadly representative of the general tenor of Lewis's work.

John Donne, Genesis, and Lewis's Animal Poetry

C. S. Lewis first published "The Shortest Way Home" in the May 10, 1934, issue of the *Oxford Magazine* and later revised it under the title "'Man Is a Lumpe Where All Beasts Kneaded Be.'"[3] Lewis took the latter title from one of John Donne's "Letters to Several Personages" ("To Sir Edward Herbert at Juliers"), published in 1651. Here Donne grounds his meditation in biblical myth from the outset; his opening line, "Man is a lump where all beasts kneaded be,"[4] takes us back to Genesis, where we read of God forming Adam from the "dust of the ground" (2:7) and also forming "out of the ground . . . every beast of the field, and every fowl of the air" (2:19). Promising though this shared origin story is for the prospect of peace between the species, disharmony soon follows, and Donne attributes this and the animal suffering that results to both human action and human inaction.

Humanity has great potential, Donne maintains. Wisdom makes humankind "an ark, where all [species] agree," but when humans play the part of the "fool," violence and misery follow for other creatures, and "these beasts do live at jar" (lines 2–3). Humankind is, he continues, both the herd of swine and the devils leading them over the cliff (cf. Matt. 8:32; Mark 5:13; Luke 8:33) and thus is capable of adding "weight to heaven's heaviest curse" on

[3] He used the pen name Nat Whilk (Anglo-Saxon for "I know not whom") for the first release of "The Shortest Way Home," *Oxford Magazine* 52 (May 10, 1934): 665. The revised poem was published under the title "'Man Is a Lumpe Where All Beasts Kneaded Be,'" in *The Collected Poems of C. S. Lewis*, ed. Walter Hooper (London: HarperCollins, 1994), 82.

[4] See John Donne, *John Donne's Poetry*, 2nd ed., ed. Arthur L. Clements, Norton Critical Editions (New York: Norton, 1992), 94–95. I follow the spelling given in this edition when referring to Donne. Lewis uses the archaic spelling "Lumpe" in his poem. In keeping with that stylistic preference for the archaic, I use the Authorized Version of the Bible throughout.

animal life (line 18). Donne attributes this capacity to play the fool and increase the suffering of other life to "the poisonous tincture of original sin" (line 20). Consequently, those granted dominion miss an opportunity to play a more constructive role in the rest of creation, which is "to rectify / Nature to what she was" (lines 33–34).[5]

Picking up Donne's theme in "'Man Is a Lumpe Where All Beasts Kneaded Be,'" Lewis also considers humanity's failure to live up to its responsibilities toward nature but differs by striking a more optimistic note. Lewis introduces an eschatological vision that dares hope for an ultimate correction to corrupted human–animal relations.

This is one of his earliest postconversion writings[6] and it presents readers with an unambiguously high view of nonhuman creation. At the same time, it rejects an understanding of dominion as despotism. As a result, these twenty lines offer one of the more concise theological statements from Lewis's pen revealing his views on the place of animals vis-à-vis humanity's God-given dominion over the earth.

The poem divides into two main sections, with ellipses marking the shift between the two at the midpoint, in the third of five stanzas. At this structurally and attitudinally crucial transition, we read the words of a narrator who is suddenly chastened by conscience and undergoing a dramatic shift in his thinking about animals and human rule over them.

Dominion as Domination

Lewis's narrator begins with a demeanor characteristic of most who assume the biblical language of dominion (Gen. 1:26) gives permission to dominate

---

[5] Donne seems to anticipate Lewis's thinking about paradisal humanity's priestly potential. Lewis speculates that paradisal man "at his first coming into the world, had . . . a redemptive function to perform." C. S. Lewis, *The Problem of Pain*, in *The Complete C. S. Lewis Signature Classics* (1940; New York: HarperOne, 2002), 632. By this he means an undoing of a satanic mischief in material creation that occurred before humanity's arrival, resulting in the corruption of animals, something evident in predation. See also *The Problem of Pain*, 594. This idea is not without its critics. For an evaluation, see Andrew Linzey, "C. S. Lewis's Theology of Animals," *Anglican Theological Review* 80, no. 1 (1998): 64–65, 69–71; and Christopher Southgate, *The Groaning Creation: God, Evolution, and the Problem of Evil* (Louisville, KY: Westminster John Knox Press, 2008), 11, 28–35.

[6] Alister McGrath's recent review of the evidence argues that Lewis came to a belief in God in March to June 1930 and then accepted the divinity of Christ on September 28, 1931. McGrath, *C. S. Lewis: A Life* (Carol Stream, IL: Tyndale, 2013), 146. The first date is a year later than that given by Lewis himself in *Surprised by Joy*, his 1955 memoir. Either way, the poem in question is an early postconversion musing on a biblical concept.

nature. The speaker brooks no resistance, telling the tiger never to lay his ear against the skull and snarl and shouting down the bruin and "the whole pack" of animal life. He even rejects the panther's purrs, suspecting mere flattery in the sound. The image of the purring panther is particularly disturbing because, as discussed later, purring is emblematic of moments of peace and spiritual well-being in Lewis's writing. By rejecting the panther's overture, the narrator-as-representative-human mars the Edenic ideal of co-existence between the species found in the second creation narrative, particularly in the picture of animals approaching Adam in a nonthreatening way: "the LORD God formed every beast of the field, and every fowl of the air, and brought them unto Adam to see what he would call them" (Gen. 2:19). Eventually, all nonhuman creatures submit to the dominion holder in Lewis's poem, becoming "meek" before the human lords of creation. But why do the tiger, bruin, grimalkin, panther, and snake back down? Why does "the whole pack" of nonhuman creation bow before the dominion-granted man of the poem? We discover it is not out of love or respect for this overlord but rather because of a threat: "Down, the whole pack! or else . . ." (ellipsis original; emphasis added). Fear alone motivates the animals' compliance, in a subtle echo of Genesis 9:2: "And the fear of you and the dread of you shall be upon every beast of the earth, and upon every fowl of the air, upon all that moveth upon the earth, and upon all the fishes of the sea; into your hand are they delivered."

The aforementioned pause, occurring here at the middle point of the poem, also gets us to the crucial center of Lewis's views about animals because at this precise moment, his narrator has a change of heart.

A Troubled Conscience

In the context of Lewis's writing, demonstrations of power without love and affection are evil, particularly with reference to humanity's rule over the rest of creation.[7] At the same time, he upholds treading lightly on the rest of creation as a Christian virtue. His correspondence with an American woman in 1956 illustrates this kindhearted vision of dominion. She confesses to him feeling "like a murderer" because she had her cat Fanda euthanized, but in

---

[7] Lewis develops this theme most clearly in the novels of the Ransom trilogy (1938–45), particularly in the behaviors of the nefarious National Institute for Co-ordinated Experiments.

Lewis's comforting response he commends her for her compassionate exercise of dominion:

> No person, animal, flower, or even pebble, has ever been loved too much—
> i.e. more than every one of God's works deserve. But you need not feel "like
> a murderer." Rather rejoice that God's law allows you to extend to Fanda
> that last mercy which (no doubt, quite rightly) we are forbidden to extend
> to suffering humans.[8]

This unequal power between human and nonhuman is potentially an extension of God's grace and mercy. It is also potentially an evil and thus a sobering responsibility, as Lewis makes clear in *The Problem of Pain*: "Man was appointed by God to have dominion over the beasts, and everything a man does to an animal is either a lawful exercise, or a sacrilegious abuse, of an authority by Divine right."[9] His letter to the grieving woman illustrates that care for animals' well-being is theologically consequential: "I will never laugh at anyone for grieving over a loved beast," he tells her. "I think God wants us to love Him *more*, not to love creatures (even animals) *less*. We love everything *in one way* too much (i.e., at the expense of our love for Him) but in another way we love everything too little."[10]

At the midpoint of "'Man Is a Lumpe Where All Beasts Kneaded Be,'" the narrator looks at the animal world he just shouted into submission and finds himself chastened in conscience: "so; now you are meek. / But then, alas, your eyes. Poor cowering brutes." This is a revelatory moment, and at this conjunction ("But"), there is a dramatic about-face. The speaker differs from so many others because he actually looks—he actually sees animals and their plight ("your eyes")—and the result is nothing less than an epiphany. The animals' suffering "bites at [his] heart-roots," he admits, and the revelation he undergoes is so profound that he steps back from his presumptuous domination of animals. He accepts that he has a role to play among them but humbly confesses he does not understand what that requires as well as he ought: "I'll come back when I've grown shepherd." The despot becomes a would-be caregiver.

---

[8] From a letter dated August 8, 1956, in *The Collected Letters of C. S. Lewis*, vol. 3, *Narnia, Cambridge, and Joy 1950–1963*, ed. Walter Hooper (New York: HarperSanFrancisco, 2007), 781–82.

[9] Lewis, *The Problem of Pain*, 634.

[10] Lewis, *Collected Letters*, 782.

This humility is noteworthy because it touches on a recurring concern in Lewis's animal writing. His reflections on animal suffering in *The Problem of Pain* are cautious and tentative, and he remains wary of overreaching claims. He acknowledges that firm conclusions on some matters are simply out of reach:

> We must never allow the problem of animal suffering to become the centre of the problem of pain; not because it is unimportant—whatever furnishes plausible grounds for questioning the goodness of God is very important indeed—but because it is outside the range of our knowledge. God has given us data which enable us, in some degree, to understand our own suffering: He has given us no such data about beasts. We know neither why they were made nor what they are, and everything we say about them is speculative.[11]

Echoing these remarks in a 1962 letter, he acknowledges, "The animal creation is a strange mystery. We can make some attempt to understand human suffering: but the sufferings of animals from the beginning of the world till now (inflicted not only by us but by one another)—what is one to think?"[12] There is a paradox here. "God brings us into such intimate relations with creatures of whose real purpose and destiny we remain forever ignorant," he notes. "We know to some degree what angels and men are *for*. But what is a flea for, or a wild dog?"[13] Herein lies a caution against presumption. Since we do not know what animals are *for*, it is reckless to claim them as our own, to disregard their well-being. Said differently, inflicting pain on God's creatures for any reason—including scientific experimentation—is a serious matter.[14] If we do not fully understand God's purposes in creating animal life, how much more ought we to proceed with caution. The poem's narrator is likewise wary of hubris, both willing to exercise a gentle dominion but conscious of his inadequacy ("I'll come back when I've grown shepherd").

---

[11] Lewis, *The Problem of Pain*, 628–29.
[12] From a letter dated October 26, 1962, in Lewis, *Collected Letters*, 1376.
[13] Lewis, *Collected Letters*, 1377.
[14] I mention experimentation because vivisection was particularly abhorrent to Lewis. He published a short essay on the issue in 1947: Lewis, "Vivisection," in *God in the Dock: Essays on Theology and Ethics*, ed. Walter Hooper (Grand Rapids, MI: Eerdmans, 1970), 224–28. He also treats it in his fiction. The villains of the Ransom trilogy mentioned in a previous note experiment on living animals. On this, see Michael J. Gilmour, "C. S. Lewis and Animal Experimentation," *Perspectives on Science and Christian Faith* 67, no. 4 (2015): 254–62.

The End Is the Beginning

By the poem's end, the speaker has moved beyond the myopic grasping at power ostensibly warranted by Genesis 1:26 and toward a grander, more inclusive theological vision. Shamed by conscience and emotionally awakened to animal suffering ("alas, your eyes. Poor cowering brutes, / Your boundless pain . . . / bites at my heart-roots"), the poet rereads the prophets and finds there a theological basis for animal compassion. Specifically, they remind him that all creatures are beneficiaries of an eschatological restoration. Aware now that his earlier exercise of dominion was unsatisfactory, he begins the transition: "I'll come back when I've grown shepherd." The narrator is a tyrant no more, and it appears Isaiah's vision of the peaceable kingdom in particular occupies his thoughts. The poem includes various images echoing Isaiah 11, among them a child who leads the animals, a pasture for the leopard, and a stall for the wolf. According to the prophet,

> The wolf also shall dwell with the lamb, and the leopard shall lie down with the kid; and the calf and the young lion and the fatling together; and a little child shall lead them. And the cow and the bear shall feed; their young ones shall lie down together: and the lion shall eat straw like the ox. And the sucking child shall play on the hole of the asp, and the weaned child shall put his hand on the cockatrice' den. They shall not hurt nor destroy in all my holy mountain: for the earth shall be full of the knowledge of the Lord, as the waters cover the sea. (Isa. 11:6–9)

Peaceful coexistence between all creatures replaces the ironfisted despotism of the first half of the poem.

This is not the end of it, however. In a few lines, Lewis's poem moves rapidly from the Genesis creation stories (via Donne's poem), through Isaiah's vision of peace, and on toward a theme in Christian eschatology that is most obvious in the writings of Saint Paul. "I'll come back when I've grown shepherd," the poet promises the animals, ready to resume a benevolent and proper kind of dominion over the earth, "but not before I've come where I am bound / And made the end and the beginning meet." Lewis here recalls themes found in Romans 8:18–23:

> For I reckon that the sufferings of this present time are not worthy to be compared with the glory which shall be revealed in us. For the earnest

expectation of the creature waiteth for the manifestation of the sons of God. For the creature was made subject to vanity, not willingly, but by reason of him who hath subjected the same in hope, because the creature itself also shall be delivered from the bondage of corruption into the glorious liberty of the children of God. For we know that the whole creation groaneth and travaileth in pain together until now. And not only they, but ourselves also, which have the firstfruits of the Spirit, even we ourselves groan within ourselves, waiting for the adoption, to wit, the redemption of our body.

Having received the injunction to rule justly, humanity is unable to fulfill its task (cf. Donne's mention of the "poisonous tincture of original sin"). Our actions are imperfect, but there is an end goal. Paul anticipates the day when redeemed humanity will assume its godlike rule, returning in effect to the Garden of Eden, where the various lumps, humans and other animals, lived in harmony. A faint trace of that original harmony seems to reside in the purring panther—approaching meekly, without malice or violent intent—who was rejected earlier in the poem. Humans, not animals, broke the peaceful cohabitation known in Eden. According to Saint Paul, a hoped-for restoration promises an end to creation's subsequent groaning.

And what more of that purring panther? Within Lewis's fiction, a purring cat is a positive image. With the forces of evil routed at the end of *Prince Caspian*, the delighted creatures of Narnia crowd around Aslan: "the Talking Beasts surged round the Lion, with purrs and grunts and squeaks and whinnies of delight, fawning on him with their tails, rubbing against him, touching him reverently with their noses and going to and fro under his body and between his legs."[15] Aslan himself purrs, or at least the children think so, in *The Lion, the Witch and the Wardrobe*: "Aslan [spoke] . . . in a low voice; so low as to be almost a purr, if it is not disrespectful to think of a lion purring."[16] Aslan's purrs suggest moments of contentment, safety, and peace in *The Voyage of the "Dawn Treader"*: "What stood in the doorway was Aslan himself, The Lion, the highest of all High Kings. And he was solid and real and warm and he let her kiss him and bury herself in his shining mane. And from the low, earthquake-like sound that came from inside him, Lucy even dared

---

[15] C. S. Lewis, *Prince Caspian: The Return to Narnia* (New York: HarperCollins, 1994; first published 1951), 205.

[16] C. S. Lewis, *The Lion, the Witch and the Wardrobe* (New York: HarperCollins, 1994; first published 1950), 130.

to think that he was purring."[17] In these moments, Lewis associates purring with harmony between Creator and creation. Does the purring panther of Lewis's poem function the same way? If so, it reminds us again of humanity's culpability because that particular cat approaches the Adam-narrator in the garden, as it were (see Gen. 2:19), but that Adam turns the great cat away.

As the poem opens, the Adam-narrator is both Donne's fool and a devil running swine over a cliff. But this remarkably optimistic verse rejects the dark vision of an inescapable, permanent condition, as though cruelty were some immutable law. An eschatological transformation is in the offing— one that sees the chastened, newly humbled dominion-bearer embarking on a new way of cohabiting with animals, one in which Adam welcomes the panther's kindly purr.

Bibliography

Donne, John. *John Donne's Poetry*. 2nd ed. Edited by Arthur L. Clements. Norton Critical Editions. New York: Norton, 1992.

Gilmour, Michael J. "C. S. Lewis and Animal Experimentation." *Perspectives on Science and Christian Faith* 67, no. 4 (2015): 254–62.

Lewis, C. S. *Boxen: The Imaginary World of the Young C. S. Lewis*. Edited by Walter Hooper. London: Collins, 1985.

Lewis, C. S. *The Collected Letters of C. S. Lewis*. Vol. 3, *Narnia, Cambridge, and Joy, 1950–1963*, edited by Walter Hooper. New York: HarperSanFrancisco, 2007.

Lewis, C. S. *The Lion, the Witch and the Wardrobe*. New York: HarperCollins, 1994. First published 1950.

Lewis, C. S. "'Man Is a Lumpe Where All Beasts Kneaded Be.'" In *The Collected Poems of C. S. Lewis*, edited by Walter Hooper, 82. London: HarperCollins, 1994.

Lewis, C. S. *Prince Caspian: The Return to Narnia*. New York: HarperCollins, 1994. First published 1951.

Lewis, C. S. *The Problem of Pain*. In *The Complete C. S. Lewis Signature Classics*. New York: HarperOne, 2002. First published 1940.

Lewis, C. S [Nat Whilk, pseud.]. "The Shortest Way Home." *Oxford Magazine* 52 (May 10, 1934): 665.

Lewis, C. S. [Clive Hamilton, pseud.]. *Spirits in Bondage: A Cycle of Lyrics*. London: William Heinemann, 1919.

Lewis, C. S. "Vivisection." In *God in the Dock: Essays on Theology and Ethics*, edited by Walter Hooper, 224–28. Grand Rapids, MI: Eerdmans, 1970.

Lewis, C. S. *The Voyage of the "Dawn Treader."* New York: HarperCollins, 1994. First published 1952.

---

[17] C. S. Lewis, *The Voyage of the "Dawn Treader"* (New York: HarperCollins, 1994; first published 1952), 158.

Linzey, Andrew. "C. S. Lewis's Theology of Animals." *Anglican Theological Review* 80, no. 1 (1998): 60–81.

McGrath, Alister. *C. S. Lewis: A Life*. Carol Stream, IL: Tyndale, 2013.

Newkirk, Ingrid. "Would the Modern-Day C. S. Lewis Be a PETA Protester?" In *Revisiting Narnia: Fantasy, Myth and Religion in C. S. Lewis' Chronicles*, edited by Shanna Caughey, 165–71. Dallas, TX: Benbella, 2005.

Southgate, Christopher. *The Groaning Creation: God, Evolution, and the Problem of Evil.* Louisville, KY: Westminster John Knox Press, 2008.

22

Isaac Bashevis Singer (1904–1991)

"Myriads of Cows and Fowls . . . Ready to Take Revenge"

Beruriah Wiegand

The acclaimed Yiddish writer and Nobel Prize laureate Isaac Bashevis Singer (or Bashevis, as he was known to his Yiddish readers) was well known for his vegetarianism.[1] In one of his numerous interviews he stated, "Not only does anguish unite the Jewish and the non-Jewish, but the man and the animal. It does not express it in words, but when an animal screams it is the same scream as that of a human being. The animal also asks God, why have you forsaken us?"[2]

Bashevis's horror at animal slaughter finds its most forceful expression in the short story "Der shoykhet" where the main character, Yoyne Meyer, is forced against his will to become the ritual slaughterer of the shtetl of Kolomir.[3] But the killing of every animal causes him pain, and he starts questioning God for having created a universe that is full of animal suffering.

> In im aleyn, Yoyne Meyern, hobn geshturemt di kashes. Tsvor, tsu bashafn
> di velt hot der Eyn-Sof (di umendlekhkeyt) gemuzt aynshrenken zayn likht.

---

[1] Throughout this chapter, I will refer to Isaac Bashevis Singer as Bashevis, which was the name he himself employed to sign the Yiddish originals of most of his novels and short stories and the name under which he was known to his Yiddish readers and scholars of Yiddish literature.

[2] Grace Farrell, "Seeing and Blindness: A Conversation with Isaac Bashevis Singer," in *Isaac Bashevis Singer: Conversations*, ed. Grace Farrell (Jackson: University Press of Mississippi, 1992), 133. This interview was first published in the periodical *Novel: A Forum on Fiction* 9, no. 2 (Winter 1976).

[3] I. B. Singer [Yitskhok Bashevis], "Der shoykhet," in *Mayses fun hintern oyvn* (Tel Aviv: Y. L. Perets, 1982), 27–42; I. B. Singer, "The Slaughterer," trans. Mirra Ginsburg, in *Collected Stories* (New York: Library of America, 2004), 1:546–57. The story was first published in English translation in the *New Yorker* (November 25, 1967). The name of the main character is Yoyne Meyer according to the standard YIVO Yiddish transliteration, but it is given as "Yoineh Meir" in Mirra Ginsburg's English translation. I will present his name as "Yoyne Meyer" in my own text and in my quotations from the Yiddish original. But it will appear as "Yoineh Meir" in direct quotations from the existing English translation.

Beruriah Wiegand, *Isaac Bashevis Singer (1904–1991)* In: *Animal Theologians*. Edited by: Andrew Linzey and Clair Linzey, Oxford University Press. © Oxford University Press 2023. DOI: 10.1093/oso/9780197655542.003.0023

S'kon nit zayn keyn bkhire on payn. Ober vi bald di baley-khayim hobn nisht keyn bkhire, far vos kumt zey tsu laydn?

Yoyne Meyer hot tsugezen a fartsiterter vi di katsovim hakn di beheymes mit hek un m'shindt di feln nokh eyder zey hobn oysgehoykht dem letstn otem. Bay di hiner hobn di vayber un moydn geflikt di federn eyder zey zenen oysgegangen.[4]

And Yoineh Meir's own mind raged with questions. Verily, in order to create the world, the Infinite One had to shrink His light; there could be no free choice without pain. But since the beasts were not endowed with free choice, why should they have to suffer? Yoineh Meir watched, trembling, as the butchers chopped the cows with their axes and skinned them before they had heaved their last breath. The women plucked the feathers from the chickens while they were still alive.[5]

The term *Eyn-Sof* (the Infinite One), which Bashevis employs here, was coined by the early Kabbalists of Provence and Spain to refer to the unknowable aspect of God. The idea that "the Infinite One had to shrink His light" in order to create the world is an allusion to the concept of *zimzum* in Lurianic Kabbalah. The term *zimzum* means contraction, concealment, or self-limitation. According to the teachings of Rabbi Isaac Luria (1534–1572), in the beginning there was only the *Eyn-Sof*, the infinite God, and there was no space devoid of God for the creation of a world. Thus, God had to contract Himself and withdraw within Himself to leave room "for the creative processes to come into play."[6]

It has been suggested that *zimzum* is the "secret signature" in Bashevis's books.[7] In an interview with Irving Howe, Bashevis speaks about the influence of Kabbalah on his work and explains the Lurianic concept of *zimzum*, although he does not employ this term here: "The Cabala teaches us that to be able to create, God in a way had to dim His light, to extinguish part of His being to create a vacuum, and because of this, He could create. If He didn't dim His light, His radiance would have filled the cosmos to such a degree that creation would be impossible."[8] Continuing his explanation of the

---

[4] Singer, "Der shoykhet," 30.
[5] Singer, "The Slaughterer," 1:548.
[6] Gershom Scholem, *Kabbalah* (New York: Meridian, 1978), 129.
[7] Clive Sinclair, *The Brothers Singer* (London: Allison & Busby, 1983), 45.
[8] Isaac Bashevis Singer and Irving Howe, "Yiddish Tradition vs. Jewish Tradition: A Dialogue," in *Isaac Bashevis Singer: Conversations*, ed. Grace Farrell (Jackson: University Press of Mississippi, 1992), 127. This interview was first published in June–July 1973 in the periodical *Midstream*.

Lurianic doctrine of creation, Bashevis states, "To be able to create He had to have Satan, because if Satan wouldn't have been there, everything would be divinity, everything would be great and radiant," "and there would be no place for individuality, for free choice."[9] This teleological interpretation of the Lurianic concept of *zimzum*, brought forward by Bashevis, goes back to the writings of Moshe Ḥayim Luzzatto, who believed that in the act of *zimzum*, the Creator overcame "His innate law of goodness in creation," so that God's creatures would not be made perfect. Instead they should be given the opportunity to perfect themselves and to choose between good and evil.[10]

This, of course, applies to human beings but not to animals, who are not endowed with free will, which is exactly why, in Bashevis's short story, the unwilling ritual slaughterer Yoyne Meyer questions God's justice in allowing animals to suffer for no reason. He keeps repeating to himself the words of the *rebe* (Hasidic leader) of Trisk that one must not be more compassionate than God and that if one slaughters an animal with a kosher knife and with intention, one redeems the soul that dwells within the animal.[11] But becoming a ritual slaughterer plunges Yoyne Meyer more and more into melancholy. He develops a repugnance for everything connected to the body, which he sees as a prison. He even feels disgusted by his wife, Reytse Doshe, and her corpulent sisters, by his daughters, and by his whole household, which is overflowing with meat.

> Yoyne Meyer hot gevolt antloyfn fun dem gashmiyes, ober dos gashmiyes iz im nokhgelofn. A reyekh fun shekht-yatke iz arayn Yoyne Meyern in di noslekher, geblibn dortn shtekn.[12]

> Yoineh Meir wanted to escape from the material world, but the material world pursued him. The smell of the slaughterhouse would not leave his nostrils.[13]

He tries to escape into the world of the Torah but finds that the Torah itself is full of earthly matters, including animal sacrifices. It is only in the Kabbalah that he can find descriptions of the higher spheres, devoid of any slaughtering and pain. Yoyne Meyer's suffering becomes even more acute in

---

[9] Singer and Howe, "Yiddish Tradition vs. Jewish Tradition," 127–28. See also Grace Farrell, "Seeing and Blindness: A Conversation with Isaac Bashevis Singer," in *Isaac Bashevis Singer: Conversations*, ed. Grace Farrell (Jackson: University Press of Mississippi, 1992), 139.

[10] Scholem, *Kabbalah*, 135.

[11] Singer, "Der shoykhet," 27–29; Singer, "The Slaughterer," 1:546–47.

[12] Singer, "Der shoykhet," 31.

[13] Singer, "The Slaughterer," 1:548.

the month of Elul, when many animals are slaughtered for the New Year. The day before Yom Kippur, there is the ritual of *shlogn kapores*, of swinging a chicken around one's head and asking Gòd for atonement. More animals are slaughtered for the festival of Sukkot (Feast of Booths). "Each holiday brings its own slaughter. Millions of fowl and cattle now alive were doomed to be killed."[14] Yoyne Meyer starts having nightmares: "Cows assumed human shape, with beards and side locks, and skullcaps over their horns. . . . In one of his nightmares, he heard a human voice come from a slaughtered goat. The goat, with his throat split, jumped on Yoineh Meir and tried to butt him, cursing in Hebrew and Aramaic, spitting and foaming at him. Yoineh Meir awakened in a sweat."[15] Going out into the yard in the middle of the night, he starts reflecting on the world of nature and of animals, and an unfamiliar love wells up in him "for all that crawls and flies, breeds and swarms."[16]

Der mentsh kon nisht un tor nisht hobn mer rakhmones fun dem Har fun der velt, ober er, Yoyne Meyer, vert fartsart fun derbaremdikeyt. Vi ken men betn af a lebedik yor, a gut kvitl bes m'roybt tsu bay andere dem ruekh khayim?

S'iz ayngefaln Yoyne Meyern, az afile Meshiekh ken nisht oysleyzn di velt, vi lang s'geshet umrekht di baley-khayim. Al-pi yoysher voltn ale gedarft ufshteyn tkhies-hameysim: Yedes kalb, yeder fish, yeder muk, yedes babele. Afile in a vorm in der erd tliet a nitses Eloykim (a getlekher funk). Ven me shekht a bashefenish, shekht men Got.[17]

The rabbi may be right. Man cannot and must not have more compassion than the Master of the universe. Yet he, Yoineh Meir, was sick with pity. How could one pray for life for the coming year, or for a favorable writ in Heaven, when one was robbing others of the breath of life?

Yoineh Meir thought that the Messiah Himself could not redeem the world as long as injustice was done to beasts. By rights, everything should rise from the dead: every calf, fish, gnat, butterfly. Even in the worm that crawls in the earth there grows a divine spark. When you slaughter a creature, you slaughter God.[18]

---

14 Singer, "The Slaughterer," 1:551.
15 Singer, "The Slaughterer," 1:551–52.
16 Singer, "The Slaughterer," 1:553.
17 Singer, "Der shoykhet," 37.
18 Singer, "The Slaughterer," 1:553.

The idea of a *nitses Eloykim*, or "divine spark," found in every creature on earth goes back to another Lurianic concept. According to Lurianic Kabbalah, after the divine act of *ẓimẓum*, God filled the space vacated by His withdrawal with divine light, which formed the ten *Sfirot* (the ten emanations of God). The lights of the *Sfirot* were given vessels made of thicker light. But some of the vessels could not contain the divine light and broke. The broken shards were hurled down, and from them the *Klipot*, the "dark forces of the *sitra ahra*," were formed.[19] Sparks of divine light were scattered throughout the universe and can even be found among the *Klipot*. These sparks are often referred to as *nitsoytses dikedushe*, or "sparks of holiness." Bashevis frequently employs allusive images of sparks of light, which appear throughout his works as glimpses of redemptive good in contexts of darkness or evil.

Here in this story, the context of evil is the injustice done to animals when they are slaughtered cruelly even though they all carry a divine spark within them, which leads Yoyne Meyer to say that when "you slaughter a creature, you slaughter God." These are strong words that Bashevis puts into the mouth of his ritual slaughterer. With such sentiments it is not surprising that Yoyne Meyer eventually loses his mind. After another nightmare about animal slaughter—this time about a *dibek* (dybbuk) speaking from the body of a slaughtered animal—he throws away his knives, his *talis* (prayer shawl), and his *tfilin* (phylacteries) and runs away, crying out to God:

> Foter in himl, bist a shoykhet! . . . Bist a shoykhet un a malekh-hamoves! Di gantse velt iz eyn shekht-hoyz.[20]

> Father in Heaven, Thou art a slaughterer! . . . Thou art a slaughterer and the Angel of Death! The whole world is a slaughterhouse![21]

While running, Yoyne Meyer hears shouts and screams and the stamping of feet, and he sees a terrifying vision: the river has turned into blood; the intestines, livers, and kidneys of animals hang from the branches of trees; and myriad cows and fowl encircle him, ready to take revenge for every cut inflicted on them.[22] Two days later, Yoyne Meyer's body is found in the river. He has drowned. The rabbi rules that he behaved like a madman and thus this

---

[19] Scholem, *Kabbalah*, 138.
[20] Singer, "Der shoykhet," 40.
[21] Singer, "The Slaughterer," 1:555.
[22] Singer, "The Slaughterer," 1:556.

was not a suicide. So he is given a proper burial. But since this is the holiday season, and the shtetl of Kolomir is in danger of remaining without meat, the community hastily dispatches messengers to bring a new slaughterer.[23]

In this story, Bashevis is particularly critical of animal slaughter and of the traditional life of a small Jewish shtetl community that is so dependent on having its supply of meat for every season and festival and that does not care about the suffering inflicted on animals. Moreover, this traditional Jewish community does not recognize the inner conflicts of a young, sensitive scholar who is forced to become a ritual slaughterer against his will. Through the unwilling ritual slaughterer turned madman, Bashevis is even able to question God's justice in having created a world where animals are suffering, despite the fact that, unlike human beings, they are not endowed with free will and have no need to perfect themselves or choose between good and evil.

Of course, "Der shoykhet" ("The Slaughterer") is not the only work by Bashevis that reveals a special sensitivity toward animals. Animals feature particularly prominently in his novel *Der knekht* (*The Slave*), a seventeenth-century love story between a Jewish slave and the daughter of his Polish master.[24] Having survived the Chmielnicki massacres of 1648 and having been sold into slavery, the novel's main character, Yankev (Jacob), is given the task to watch over his master's cows together with his faithful dog Bilom (Balaam), which was very unusual for a Jew at the time, as dogs were traditionally considered to be unclean.

Refusing his master Jan Bzik's nonkosher meat, Yankev becomes a vegetarian. Living in a barn in the mountains with his dog and his master's cows, he picks mushrooms and berries for himself and eats whatever the earth produces. In addition to this, Jan Bzik's daughter Wanda brings him food every evening— barley kasha, honey, fruit from the orchard, and cucumbers from the garden, as well as bread and the occasional rare gift of an egg—all without the knowledge of her parents and sister, thus effectively assisting Yankev in keeping kosher.[25]

The opening paragraphs of the novel set the scene for the life of the Jewish slave in the mountains, surrounded by nature and far away from any Jewish community:

[23] Singer, "The Slaughterer," 1:557.
[24] I. B. Singer [Yitskhok Bashevis], *Der knekht* (Tel Aviv: Y. L. Perets, 1980); I. B. Singer, *The Slave*, trans. I. B. Singer and Cecil Hemley (London: Penguin, 1996). This novel was first serialized in the Yiddish *Forverts* (Forward) in New York in 1960–61. The English translation was first published in New York by Farrar, Straus & Cudahy in 1962. It was only published in book form in the Yiddish original in Tel Aviv by Y. L. Perets in 1967.
[25] Singer, *Der knekht*, 13–14, 19.

Der tog hot zikh ongehoybn mit an eyntsikn geshrey fun a foygl: yeder fartog der eygener foygl, der eygener vilder geshrey.[26]

The day began with a single scream of a bird: each morning the same bird, the same wild scream.[27]

Then we see Yankev waking up in his barn in the mountains, which he shares at night with four cows. He sleeps on a bed made of straw and hay, covering himself with an old, coarse linen sheet. Sometimes the nights are so cold that he gets up and warms his hands and feet against the warm bodies of the cows. He begins his day by washing his hands and saying the blessing *moyde ani* (I thank thee), closely watched by one of the cows:

Zi hot umgekert dem bahorntn kop un geton a kuk af hintervaylekhts, vi naygerik tsu zen vi azoy der mentsh hoybt on dem frimorgn. Di groyse oygn, ful mit shvartsapl, hobn opgeshlogn dem purpur fun zun-ufgang.
   —Gut morgn, Kviatula!—hot Yankev tsu ir geredt.—Zikh gut
                                              oysgeshlofn, ha?[28]

She turned her horned head and gave a glance backward, as if curious to see how a human being starts his morning. Her large eyes, almost all pupil, reflected the purple of the sunrise.
   "Good morning, Kwiatula!" Yankev said to her. "Did you sleep well, ha?"

Far away from his community, Yankev develops a close relationship with the animals around him, addressing the cows by name and chatting to them in Yiddish, so as not to forget his language. He learns to live in harmony with the animals in his care, as well as with the world of nature at large.

In fact, more than any other of Bashevis's novels, *Der knekht* is full of descriptions of animals and nature. There is also a constant tension between the main character's special relationship with nature, where he sees God's hand at work, and his experiences of suffering, exile, and human cruelty, which make him question God's goodness. When Yankev—in his situation of *farvoglenish* (homelessness, exile) in the mountains—witnesses the sky,

---

[26] Singer, *Der knekht*, 9.
[27] All translations of passages from *Der knekht* are mine except where the existing English translation is quoted in a footnote for comparison.
[28] Singer, *Der knekht*, 9.

the mountains, the valleys, and the wooded slopes disappearing in the fog, he understands the meaning of *hester-ponim* (the hiding of God's face) and *tsimtsem* (*ẓimẓum*) for the first time in his life. Before the fog everything was full of light; now everything is dark. Distances have shrunk and that which was once tangible has lost its substance.[29]

It is no coincidence that Yankev's insight concerning the hiding of God's face and *ẓimẓum* occurs during one of his contemplations of nature, because according to the Kabbalists, no "religious knowledge of God" can be gained except through the contemplation of the relationship of God to His creation.[30]

Yankev experiences God in two extreme forms. On the one hand, he experiences God as concealed and withdrawn, having hidden His face from His chosen people. On the other hand, he can detect God's hand everywhere in nature—for example, in the fiery clouds that he sees one morning at the very beginning of the novel.[31] In this paragraph early on in the novel, Bashevis already presents these two extreme experiences of God. They are reflected in the images of God's face, which is hidden or concealed, and God's hand, which is manifest in the beauty of nature and alludes to God's revelation in His creation.

The creature featuring most prominently in the novel, with whom Yankev develops a special relationship, is his dog Bilom. At the beginning he is still uncomfortable with keeping a dog, which is traditionally very un-Jewish, but this soon changes:

Yankev hot gemuzt haltn a hunt. Di hint hobn bashitst di beheymes un oykh di pastukher fun vilde bestyes. In onheyb hot Yankev nit gern gehat dem shvartsn keylev mit di sharfe tseyn un mit der shpitsiker morde. Er hot nisht gelitn nisht zayn biln un nisht zayn lekn. Zaynen den nisht di reshoim geglikhn tsu hint? Yankev hot gedenkt vos di gemore zogt vegn hint un vi azoy der ARI un andere mekubolim farglaykhn di hint tsu di klipes. Ober mit der tsayt hot Yankev ongehoybn zikh tsugevoynen tsu dem keylev. Er hot im afile gegebn a nomen: Bilom.[32]

Yankev had to keep a dog. The dogs protected the cattle, as well as the herdsmen, from wild animals. In the beginning, Yankev did not like the black dog with his sharp teeth and pointed muzzle. He could bear neither

[29] Singer, *Der knekht*, 60. In the English translation, *hester-ponim* is rendered as "God's hidden face" and *tsimtsem* as "the shrinking of His light." Singer, *The Slave*, 52.
[30] Scholem, *Kabbalah*, 88.
[31] Singer, *Der knekht*, 12.
[32] Singer, *Der knekht*, 15–16.

his barking nor his licking. Were the wicked not likened to dogs? Yankev remembered what the Talmud said about dogs and that the ARI [Rabbi Isaac Luria] and other Kabbalists had compared dogs to the *Klipot*. But eventually Yankev started to get used to the dog and even gave him a name: Bilom.

There is a whole article entitled "Bilom in Bashevis's *Der knekht* (The Slave): *A khaye hot oykh a neshome* (An Animal Also Has a Soul)" by Leonard Prager, in which Prager tries to answer the question of why Bashevis named Yankev's dog Bilom and what Bilom's symbolic roles in the novel are.[33] Bilom is, of course, the Yiddish name of the Gentile prophet in the book of Numbers, known as Bil'am in Hebrew and Balaam in English, who is summoned by the Moabite king Balak to curse the people of Israel, but who ends up blessing them instead. Bilom's status in Jewish tradition is paradoxical. On the one hand, he is God's obedient servant (Num. 22:1–21, 31–41; 23:1–24; 24); on the other, he is characterized as a "blind seer" (Num. 22:22–30) and is called a *rashah* (a wicked man) in rabbinic tradition.[34] This parallels the paradoxical attitude toward dogs, who are vilified by various Jewish sources but one of whom becomes the Jewish slave Yankev's faithful helper in Bashevis's novel, closely linked with his Gentile love Wanda, representing "instinctual freedom" but also being the "bearer of consciousness," in possession of a "soul."[35]

In one instance early in the novel, Wanda comes up to Yankev's mountain hut, and the dog approaches to greet her:

Der hunt vos iz geshtanen nebn Yankevn, iz ir akegngelofn, gedreyt mit dem ek, geshprungen af ir mit beyde fodershte lapes. Zi hot zikh tsu im tsugeboygn un er hot gelekt ir ponem.

—Bilom, genug!— hot zi bafoyln gutmutik. Tsu Yankevn hot zi zikh ongerufn:

—Er iz tsugelozener vi du.

—A hunt hot nisht keyn flikhtn.

—A khaye hot oykh a neshome.[36]

[33] Leonard Prager, "Bilom in Bashevis's *Der knekht* (The Slave): *A khaye hot oykh a neshome* (An Animal Also Has a Soul)," in *The Hidden Isaac Bashevis Singer*, ed. Seth Wolitz (Austin: University of Texas Press, 2001), 79–92.
[34] See, for example, b Ta'anit 20a.
[35] Prager, "Bilom in Bashevis's *Der knekht*," 85.
[36] Singer, *Der knekht*, 22–23.

The dog who had been standing next to Yankev ran up to her, wagged his tail, and jumped on her with his front paws. She bent down to him, and he licked her face.

"Bilom, enough!" she ordered him gently. Then she said to Yankev:

"He's more affectionate than you."

"A dog doesn't have any obligations."

"An animal also has a soul."

As a traditional Jew, Yankev is restricted by his religious obligations and knows it is forbidden for him to succumb to his longing for a Gentile woman. But Wanda is much more instinctual and open about her feelings for Yankev and much more in harmony with the world of nature around them. She is convinced that Yankev should follow his heart and his natural desires, just as animals do, and that animals also have souls. While Yankev preserves his Jewish way of life as much as he can and also instructs Wanda in the tenets of Judaism, and she eventually converts, she also manages to convince him both that animals have souls and that he should succumb to nature and to his longing for her, and Yankev and Wanda finally consummate their love.

Bashevis's novel *Der knekht* has been called a "mythic narrative with a hierogamy or sacred marriage at its core."[37] The love story between Yankev and Wanda is at the center of the novel, and at two points it is explicitly associated with images from the biblical love song Shir Hashirim (the Song of Songs),[38] which is also full of images of nature and animals. According to Jewish tradition, the love described in the Song of Songs is understood allegorically as referring to the love between God and the *Kneset Yisrael* (community of Israel). The Kabbalists identified the community of Israel with the *Shekhinah* (God's indwelling presence in the world, who accompanied the Jews into exile according to rabbinic literature). So the interpretation of the Song of Songs as referring to the community of Israel and its union with God was "transferred to the *Shekhinah*" and her union with the *Sfirah* (God's emanation) of *Tiferet* (beauty).[39] Thus all of the associations of Yankev and Wanda's love with images from the Song of Songs can also be understood

[37] Bonnie Lyons, "Sexual Love in I. B. Singer's Work," *Isaac Bashevis Singer: A Reconsideration*, ed. Daniel Walden (Albany: State University of New York Press, 1981), 69.

[38] Singer, *Der knekht*, 37, 69.

[39] Gershom Scholem, *On the Kabbalah and Its Symbolism*, trans. Ralph Manheim (New York: Schocken, 1996; first published 1965), 106.

as allusions to the *Zivuga kadisha*, or "sacred marriage," between the *Sfirot* (God's emanations) of *Tiferet* (beauty) and *Malkhut* (kingdom), which is none other than the *Shekhinah*.

There is one passage in the novel where Yankev reflects on the power of *tshuvah* (repentance), which can turn transgressions into good deeds and God's justice into loving-kindness: "Amol iz afile an aveyre a gefes far tikumim" (Sometimes even a transgression is a vessel for cosmic restorations).[40] Yankev knows that he has sinned in his longing for a Gentile woman. But the Polish Wanda has subsequently become the Jewish Sore bas Avrom, who is about to give birth to a Jewish child. This means that the union between Yankev and Wanda, which began in transgression, has been transformed through Wanda's conversion to Judaism and through the couple's marriage into "a gefes far tikumim" (a vessel for cosmic restorations).[41] Their act of procreation, leading to the birth of a Jewish child, reflects the "sacred union" in the realm of the *Sfirot*. In Lurianic Kabbalah, this "sacred union" forms part of the process of reunification of the *Shekhinah* with the rest of the Godhead. This is the process of *Tikun*, or cosmic restoration of the world to its intended state of harmony.

And who is instrumental in bringing all of this about? It is, of course, Bilom, the dog, who makes Yankev understand that animals also have souls and that the seemingly insurmountable differences between human and animal, as well as between Jew and Gentile, can sometimes be overcome![42]

I have purposefully chosen two extreme examples of Bashevis's treatment of animals in his works. His short story "Der shoykhet" ("The Slaughterer") presents a negative image of a small Jewish community in a typical Eastern European shtetl, where animal slaughter is very much part of people's daily life, where there is little sensitivity to the suffering of animals, and where any sensitive soul who might question this ultimately has no other choice than to become mad. Bashevis's novel *Der knekht* (*The Slave*), on the other hand, entails a positive vision of a Jewish life in harmony with the world of nature and animals. Here we find a Jewish individual far away from any traditional community, who does everything in his power to live his life according to the tenets of Jewish law, but who leads a life that is very unusual for a Jew

[40] Singer, *Der knekht*, 189–90.
[41] Singer, *Der knekht*, 190.
[42] There is an interesting treatment of this idea in Prager, "Bilom in Bashevis's *Der knekht*," especially 86–87, 90–91; and Leonard Prager, "Nature and the Language of Nature in Yitskhok Bashevis-Zinger's *Der knekht*," in *Isaac Bashevis Singer: His Work and His World*, ed. Hugh Denman (Leiden: Brill, 2002), 209–26, especially 214, 218, 225–26.

(especially at this period of time). He becomes a vegetarian. He lives among animals, and he succumbs to his love for a Gentile woman, who converts to Judaism and finally gives birth to a Jewish child. This is an unusual vision of harmony in Bashevis's works, in which all the deeply engrained boundaries between Jew and Gentile and between human and animal can be overcome. Yankev's relationship with the world of nature in this novel parallels Bashevis's own personal vegetarianism and criticism of animal abuse, which is evident throughout his works.

Bibliography

Farrell, Grace. "Seeing and Blindness: A Conversation with Isaac Bashevis Singer." In *Isaac Bashevis Singer: Conversations*, edited by Grace Farrell, 132–47. Jackson: University Press of Mississippi, 1992.

Lyons, Bonnie. "Sexual Love in I. B. Singer's Work." In *Isaac Bashevis Singer: A Reconsideration*, edited by Daniel Walden, 61–74. Albany: State University of New York Press, 1981.

Prager, Leonard. "Bilom in Bashevis's *Der knekht* (The Slave): *A khaye hot oykh a neshome* (An Animal Also Has a Soul)." In *The Hidden Isaac Bashevis Singer*, edited by Seth Wolitz, 79–92. Austin: University of Texas Press, 2001.

Prager, Leonard. "Nature and the Language of Nature in Yitskhok Bashevis-Zinger's *Der knekht*." In *Isaac Bashevis Singer: His Work and His World*, edited by Hugh Denman, 209–26. Leiden: Brill, 2002.

Scholem, Gershom. *Kabbalah*. New York: Meridian, 1978.

Scholem, Gershom. *On the Kabbalah and Its Symbolism*. Translated by Ralph Manheim. New York: Schocken, 1996. First published 1965.

Sinclair, Clive. *The Brothers Singer*. London: Allison & Busby, 1983.

Singer, Isaac Bashevis [Yitskhok Bashevis]. *Der knekht*. Tel Aviv: Y. L. Perets, 1980.

Singer, Isaac Bashevis [Yitskhok Bashevis]. "Der shoykhet." In Singer, *Mayses fun hintern oyvn*, 27–42. Tel Aviv: Y. L. Perets, 1982.

Singer, Isaac Bashevis. "The Slaughterer." Translated by Mirra Ginsburg. In *Collected Stories*, vol. 1: *Gimpel the Fool* to *The Letter Writer*, edited by Ilan Stavans, 546–57. New York: Library of America, 2004.

Singer, Isaac Bashevis. *The Slave*. Translated by Isaac Bashevis Singer and Cecil Hemley. London: Penguin, 1996.

Singer, Isaac Bashevis, and Irving Howe. "Yiddish Tradition vs. Jewish Tradition: A Dialogue." In *Isaac Bashevis Singer: Conversations*, edited by Grace Farrell, 124–31. Jackson: University Press of Mississippi, 1992.

23

Jürgen Moltmann (1926–)

Creation and Sabbath Theology

Ryan Patrick McLaughlin

One can hardly overstate the influence of Jürgen Moltmann on the land-scape of contemporary theology.[1] With his masterful and creative *Theology of Hope*,[2] first published in the 1960s, he burst onto the international theological scene. His subsequent works have not disappointed his readers in their ingenuity. They have impacted an ecumenical audience and have been paramount in the development of political theologies.

Although Moltmann's earlier works neither fully ignore nor emphasize cosmology, over the course of his prolific writing career he has made concern for the cosmos a central piece of his theology.[3] In the wake of Moltmann's cosmology, numerous other thinkers have engaged his eco-theological thought. However, there has been very little engagement with Moltmann in the particular field of animal theology. I find this dearth lamentable, given that Moltmann offers quite a gift to animal theology in terms of a theological framework.

As a remedy, I here aim to delineate the foundations of Moltmann's theology that hold potential for animal theology. It is my contention that although his ethics requires significant development with regard to concrete application, his theology nonetheless provides the grounds to challenge practices such as hunting and to affirm the propriety of practices such as

---

[1] For a much fuller exploration of Moltmann's theology of the nonhuman creation, see Ryan Patrick McLaughlin, *Preservation and Protest: Theological Foundations for an Eco-eschatological Ethics* (Minneapolis: Fortress Press, 2014), especially chaps. 7–9.

[2] Jürgen Moltmann, *Theology of Hope: On the Ground and Implications of Christian Eschatology*, trans. James W. Leitch (London: SCM Press, 2002).

[3] See especially Jürgen Moltmann, *God in Creation: A New Theology of Creation and the Spirit of God*, trans. Margaret Kohl (Minneapolis: Fortress Press, 1993); Jürgen Moltmann, *The Way of Jesus Christ: Christology in Messianic Dimensions*, trans. Margaret Kohl (Minneapolis: Fortress Press, 1993); and Jürgen Moltmann, *Sun of Righteousness, Arise! God's Future for Humanity and the Earth*, trans. Margaret Kohl (Minneapolis: Fortress Press, 2010).

Ryan Patrick McLaughlin, *Jürgen Moltmann (1926–)* In: *Animal Theologians*. Edited by: Andrew Linzey and Clair Linzey, Oxford University Press. © Oxford University Press 2023. DOI: 10.1093/oso/9780197655542.003.0024

vegetarianism as a proleptic witness (i.e., a real anticipation within history) to the eschatological future of the cosmos.

Moltmann's Theological Framework

In order to establish Moltmann's contribution, I must first wade through his rather broad and exploratory theology. I will limit myself to only those dimensions that contribute directly to his potential contribution to animal theology. Furthermore, I must truncate these dimensions—some of which are quite complicated.

Theology Proper

Moltmann seeks to dislodge what he refers to as the "radical monotheism" of Western Christianity.[4] Such views envision God as a monad completely isolated from relation (even trinitarian relation). Furthermore, they do not do justice to the self-disclosure of God in the history of the world.[5] Moltmann maintains that this emphasis on God's oneness has embedded ecologically harmful forms of anthropocentrism in Western Christian thought.[6]

In response to these monistic views, Moltmann seeks "to start with the special Christian tradition of the history of Jesus the Son, and from that to develop a historical doctrine of the Trinity."[7] Within this framework, he establishes his social doctrine of the Trinity, in which God's eternal existence is always and already a trinitarian existence of mutual love. Drawing on the imagery of perichoresis (i.e., the mutual penetration of each person of the Trinity into the other) developed by John Damascene, Moltmann maintains that God's oneness is constituted by the intimacy of the persons with and in one another. "God is a community of Father, Son, and Spirit, whose unity is

---

[4] Jürgen Moltmann, *The Crucified God: The Cross of Christ as the Foundation and Criticism of Christian Theology*, trans. R. A. Wilson (Minneapolis: Fortress Press, 1993), 215; see also Jürgen Moltmann, *The Trinity and the Kingdom: The Doctrine of God*, trans. Margaret Kohl (Minneapolis: Fortress Press, 1993), 10–20.

[5] See Jürgen Moltmann, *History and the Triune God: Contributions to Trinitarian Theology*, trans. John Bowden (New York: Crossroad, 1992).

[6] Jürgen Moltmann, *God for a Secular Society: The Public Relevance of Theology*, trans. Margaret Kohl (Minneapolis: Fortress Press, 1999), 94–101.

[7] Moltmann, *Trinity and the Kingdom*, 19.

constituted by mutual indwelling and reciprocal interpenetration."[8] In other words, the perichoretic union of the divine community of persons is what vouchsafes the claim that God is one.

For Moltmann, the Trinity is not only a social Trinity; it is also an open Trinity. The divine community does not have closed gates. Rather, "the trinitarian relationship of the Father, the Son, and the Holy Spirit is so wide that the whole creation can find space, time and freedom in it."[9] The Trinity seeks to incorporate the cosmos into its own perichoretic love. In part, it is this other-seeking love of God that leads Moltmann to dismantle the notion of divine impassibility.[10] The cross, which is a concrete manifestation of divine love, calls for "the revolution needed in the concept of God,"[11] in which the Trinity revealed therein replaces the immutable deity of a "theism" derivative of Hellenistic thought. When the love of God spills over onto creation, it requires a God who is willing to suffer the creation's existence to whatever end. "It is one divine passion which leads to the pain of the Father, the death of the Son and the sighing of the Spirit: the passion of love for lost creatures."[12]

In sum, the Trinity is a community of love that seeks perichoretic union with that which is other than divine. But what exactly is this "other" with which the Trinity seeks communion? To answer this question, I turn to Moltmann's cosmology.

Cosmology

Moltmann distinguishes between three phases of creation: *creatio originalis* ("original creation"), *creatio continua* ("ongoing creation"), and *creatio nova* (new creation).[13]

Creatio originalis is itself preceded by a divine decree and act. Moltmann adapts the traditional notion of *creatio ex nihilo* ("creation out of nothing") by addressing what the presence of "nothing" means. Drawing on the kabbalistic notion of *zimzum* (divine contraction), Moltmann maintains that the "nothing" within which the created order takes shape is necessarily preceded by God's decision to withdraw the divine presence in order to create space

---

[8] Moltmann, *Trinity and the Kingdom*, 174–75.
[9] Moltmann, *Trinity and the Kingdom*, 109.
[10] See especially Moltmann, *The Crucified God*.
[11] Moltmann, *The Crucified God*, 4.
[12] Moltmann, *History and the Triune God*, xvi.
[13] Moltmann, *God in Creation*, 208.

for the cosmos.[14] *Creatio originalis*, then, is the filling of the "nothing" with something. In self-withdrawal, God cedes the cosmos its own space and time, which is to say an existence of integrity not obliterated by divine presence. This kenotic act of *creatio ex nihilo* is simultaneously *creatio ex amore Dei* ("creation out of God's love"),[15] for "God loves the world with the very same love that he himself is in eternity."[16] The divine kenosis of creation is further-more significant in that it suggests that in the very act of creation, God must be passible, willing to suffer the cosmos its own space and time.

Creatio continua has two components. First, the created order has a dy-namic self-development within the space and time God has ceded to it.[17] That is, creation has its own integrity by which it moves within its space and develops within its time. It has randomness and unpredictability. It also has self-organizing principles. Thus, for Moltmann, creation's integrity includes the evolutionary development of life into increasingly complex forms. Second, God remains involved in the created order. Moltmann's pneuma-tology maintains that while giving creation its own space to develop, God is nonetheless present as the affirmation of life in all living things.[18] So God is both transcendent (i.e., distant and distinct from creation), a condition nec-essary for the created order's integrity, and immanent (i.e., near and with cre-ation), a condition necessary for the created order's life and well-being.

For Moltmann, the entire ongoing created order constitutes a commu-nity. Just as there can be no Father isolated from the Son, so also there can be no humanity isolated from the nonhuman world.[19] This affirmation of the cosmic community correlates to an affirmation of the intrinsic value of the nonhuman creation. The community as a whole has its own integrity in which human beings participate. Furthermore, all individual members of the community, including every single nonhuman animal, have a right to a life for their own sakes.[20] This vision shatters modern expressions of anthro-pocentrism, which Moltmann consistently claims is detrimental to cosmic well-being.[21]

---

[14] Moltmann, *God in Creation*, 86–89.

[15] Moltmann, *God in Creation*, 75–76.

[16] Moltmann, *Trinity and the Kingdom*, 57.

[17] Moltmann, *God in Creation*, 198–200.

[18] Jürgen Moltmann, *The Spirit of Life: A Universal Affirmation*, trans. Margaret Kohl (Minneapolis: Fortress Press, 1992), 35.

[19] Moltmann, *God in Creation*, 185–90.

[20] Moltmann, *God for a Secular Society*, 131.

[21] Jürgen Moltmann, *The Coming of God: Christian Eschatology*, trans. Margaret Kohl (Minneapolis: Fortress Press, 1996), 92–93; Moltmann, *God for a Secular Society*, 94–101.

Creatio continua, for Moltmann, points toward *creatio nova*. Indeed, there can be no new creation without the present creation. Thus, Moltmann writes, "*nulla salus sine terra*—there is no salvation without an earth."[22] For Moltmann, *creatio originalis* is destined to become *creatio nova* through the path of *creatio continua*. New creation means the transfiguration—which Moltmann defines as "a glorifying and a transformation"[23]—of the cosmos, entailing most importantly its perichoretic participation in God's own triune life. Transfiguration is thus the telos that the open Trinity is seeking with and for the cosmos.

Transfiguration entails an overturning of creation's transience. What the world will become is other than what the world is—even though it will be the same world that becomes it. This point is evident in the stark contrast Moltmann develops between the notions of "nature" and "creation."[24] The former is much of what one can currently observe in *creatio continua*. It is "the state of creation which is no longer creation's original condition, and is not yet its final one."[25] Nature is "full of beauties and full of catastrophes."[26]

"Creation" refers to the temporal *and* eternal scope of the cosmos, including its eschatological redemption. Moltmann's cosmology therefore defines God not according to nature (i.e., the way things are) but rather according to creation (the eschatological end of nature). God's love is ultimately incompatible with nature's catastrophes. It is for this reason that Moltmann rejects the cosmologies of creation spiritualists such as Pierre Teilhard de Chardin who accept evolution, including the suffering and death on which it depends, as a beautiful and grace-filled reality.[27] For Moltmann, these "forces of nature" cannot be redemptive. Indeed, they "are themselves in need of redemption."[28] In short, evolution can exhaust neither the divine aim for creation nor the means of realizing that aim; it has too many victims. Hence, in Moltmann's view, eschatology is the only "true natural theology."[29]

In sum, both *creatio originalis* and *creatio continua* are possible only because of divine kenosis. However, in its transience *creatio continua* does not

[22] Moltmann, *The Coming of God*, 274.
[23] Moltmann, *Trinity and the Kingdom*, 123.
[24] Moltmann, *God in Creation*, 37–40.
[25] Moltmann, *The Coming of God*, 91.
[26] Moltmann, *Sun of Righteousness*, 68.
[27] See Moltmann, *The Way of Jesus Christ*, 293–97; Moltmann, *Sun of Righteousness*, 209. Also see Richard Bauckham, *The Theology of Jürgen Moltmann* (Edinburgh: T&T Clark, 1995), 194.
[28] Moltmann, *God for a Secular Society*, 68.
[29] Moltmann, *God in Creation*, 60.

reflect God's eschatological desire. But then one must ask: whence comes this transience?

The Fall and Evil

Moltmann defines evil as "the perversion of good, the annihilation of what exists, the negation of the affirmation of life."[30] His struggle with evil tends to center on the problem of transience, particularly death. On the one hand, Moltmann wants to state unequivocally that neither suffering nor death pertains to the eschatological future of creation: "The living God and death are irreconcilable antitheses."[31] On the other hand, he wants to take seriously the findings of science, which suggest that neither suffering nor death can have originated with human disobedience.[32] He asks, "Did the dinosaurs become extinct because of the sin of the human beings who did not yet exist?"[33] In short, death cannot be the consequence of sin. It pertains to the transient stage of the creation—*creatio continua*. Death and also suffering are "characteristics of a frail, temporal creation which will be overcome through the new creation of all things for eternal life."[34]

At any rate, Moltmann does not want to accept that suffering and death are part of God's good creation.[35] He commonly refers to the current state of the cosmos (i.e., "nature") as disrupted.[36] He thus accepts some form of cosmic fallenness.

Concerning the origin of this fallenness, Moltmann is somewhat unclear. In his later works, he seems to suggest that the forces of annihilation result from the integrity of the space and time that God allots to the created order. Nature is transient because God "has conferred on creation its own scope for freedom and generation."[37] The space provided to creation entails its freedom, agency, and self-organization. But this space also necessitates the possibility of disruption, even before the arrival of humans. Thus, Moltmann maintains, "we even have to talk about the 'sin' of the whole creation, which

[30] Moltmann, *God in Creation*, 168.
[31] Moltmann, *Sun of Righteousness*, 81.
[32] See John Polkinghorne, "Jürgen Moltmann's Engagement with the Natural Sciences," in *God's Life in Trinity*, ed. Miroslav Volf and Michael Welker (Minneapolis: Fortress Press, 2006), 61–70.
[33] Moltmann, *The Coming of God*, 83.
[34] Moltmann, *The Coming of God*, 78.
[35] Moltmann, *Sun of Righteousness*, 81.
[36] Moltmann, *The Way of Jesus Christ*, 281; Moltmann, *History and the Triune God*, 71–72.
[37] Moltmann, *Sun of Righteousness*, 205.

has isolated itself from the foundation of its existence and the wellspring of its life, and has fallen victim to universal death."[38]

The "Fall" therefore may be interpreted as the straying of *the nonhuman creation*—both randomly and, much later, willfully—from the path toward eschatological consummation. It takes the form of a straying from the path toward the telos of the dynamic cosmos rather than an event that shatters protological harmony.[39] Hence, eschatological redemption entails both "surmounting the consequences of the Fall" and "the consummation of creation-in-the-beginning."[40] Regardless, the corruption related to this straying is systemic, affecting the entire cosmos, which now wanders in isolation from its true destiny. Human sin, then, can be interpreted not as the cause of this cosmic isolation but rather as the embracing and, in this embrace, the intensifying of it.

In sum, the current state of *creatio continua* is fallen inasmuch as the cosmos is wandering in isolation off the path toward eschatological consummation. In this isolation, death becomes a horrific reality. Suffering becomes an end itself, justified rather than lamented. The open Trinity desires to overcome this cosmic transience. But how so? Here, I must turn to Moltmann's Christology.

Christology

Christology is a cornerstone of Moltmann's theology.[41] Even his emphasis on eschatology is fundamentally derivative of Christology,[42] for in the incarnation, the Son becomes the concrete divine assumption of the world's corrupted condition. The cross constitutes the gathering of all the contradictions of the world into the history of the Trinity.[43] In it, Christ suffers the wounds of all the suffering. He dies the death of all the dying.

Yet the cross is not the end of Christ's life. For Moltmann, the cross is a dialectic event with the resurrection.[44] The cross reveals the present state

---

[38] Moltmann, *The Way of Jesus Christ*, 283.

[39] See Moltmann, *The Coming of God*, 261–67; Richard Bauckham, "Eschatology in *The Coming of God*," in *God Will Be All in All: The Eschatology of Jürgen Moltmann*, ed. Richard Bauckham (Minneapolis: Fortress Press, 2001), 17.

[40] Moltmann, *Sun of Righteousness*, 67.

[41] Bauckham, *The Theology of Jürgen Moltmann*, 4–5.

[42] Moltmann, *Theology of Hope*.

[43] Moltmann, *The Crucified God*, 246.

[44] Moltmann, *The Crucified God*, 178–87; Moltmann, *Theology of Hope*, 210–15; Bauckham, *The Theology of Jürgen Moltmann*, 32–33.

of creation; the resurrection reveals the fulfilled promise of its eschatological hope.[45] When the Son takes on the transience of the entire cosmos in
the incarnation, he also overcomes it for the entire cosmos in the resurrection. Hence, "the transfiguration of Christ's dead body is the beginning
of the transfiguration of all mortal life."[46] Christ is thus the eschatological
turning point in history, where the power of death fails in its encounter with
the divine affirmation of life.[47] Without the incarnation, including the assumption of the creation's contradictions in the cross and the healing of those
contradictions in the resurrection, Christianity is without promise and therefore without hope. Therefore, Moltmann claims that "Christianity stands or
falls with the reality of the raising of Jesus from the dead."[48]

For Moltmann, Christ's death and resurrection are maximally inclusive.[49]
There exists an ethical corollary to this inclusiveness:

> If Christ has died not merely for the reconciliation of human beings, but for
> the reconciliation of all other creatures too, then every created being enjoys
> infinite value in God's sight, and has its own right to live; this is not true of
> human beings alone. If according to the Christian view the uninfringeable
> dignity of human beings is based on the fact that "Christ died for them,"
> then this must also be said of the dignity of all other living things. And it is
> this that provides the foundation for an all-embracing reverence for life.[50]

In the incarnation, Christ becomes the ultimate victim of evolution—or
"nature"—and thereby gathers all nature, including death, into the triune
life.[51] Likewise, his resurrection gathers up all of evolution's victims.
Thus, Moltmann's maximally inclusive eschatology derives from his
Christology: "Unless *the whole* cosmos is reconciled, Christ cannot be the
Christ of God and cannot be the foundation of all things."[52]

In sum, in the incarnation Christ takes on the contradictions of the world,
even death. His resurrection, which is extended to all those caught in the
transience of *creatio continua*, is the overcoming of those contradictions. But

---

[45] Moltmann, *Theology of Hope*.
[46] Moltmann, *The Way of Jesus Christ*, 251.
[47] Jürgen Moltmann, *Ethics of Hope*, trans. Margaret Kohl (Minneapolis: Fortress Press, 2012), 55–56.
[48] Moltmann, *Theology of Hope*, 152.
[49] Moltmann, *The Coming of God*, 92–93.
[50] Moltmann, *The Way of Jesus Christ*, 256.
[51] Moltmann, *The Way of Jesus Christ*, 296.
[52] Moltmann, *The Way of Jesus Christ*, 306.

how do creatures still in transience experience this overcoming within history? This question leads to Moltmann's pneumatology.

Pneumatology

Moltmann's pneumatology has three significant dimensions for animal theology. First, the Spirit, as the breath of God, is the principle of life present in all living things. To establish this position, Moltmann draws on the linguistic connections in the Hebrew *ruach*, which translates as breath, wind, and/or spirit. That is, the "breath" (*ruach*) of all creatures is the "Spirit" (*ruach*) living in them, constituting their principle of life.[53]

Second, the Spirit is also present and active in *creatio continua*, preserving the cosmos as its ongoing principle of life.[54] "Everything that is," writes Moltmann, "exists and lives in the unceasing inflow of the energies of and potentialities of the cosmic Spirit."[55] Creation perseveres because of God's immanence. Furthermore, it is as the immanent Spirit that God suffers the fate of the created order—"*God's empathy*, his feeling identification with what he loves."[56] The Spirit is within all the breathy sighs of longing for redemption.

Third, the Spirit has a redemptive and transfigurative role.[57] The Spirit is a "sacrament of the kingdom."[58] In the redemption that pours out from the life of Christ, the Spirit becomes the principle of *new* life—eternal life—for the entire created order. The Spirit's presence is the burgeoning reality of the new creation already within history—the "advance pledge of foretaste of the coming kingdom of glory."[59] Thus, while God preserves the cosmos through immanent indwelling, in the Spirit God is more than a preservationist.

In sum, the Spirit is not only the divine immanence in *creatio continua*; it is also the presence of *creatio nova*. The Spirit renders present the eschatological future. Therefore, to better appreciate the effect of the Spirit within history, I must explore in greater detail Moltmann's eschatology.

---

[53] Moltmann, *The Spirit of Life*, 40–43.
[54] Moltmann, *History and the Triune God*, 75–77.
[55] Moltmann, *God in Creation*, 9.
[56] Moltmann, *The Spirit of Life*, 51.
[57] Moltmann, *God in Creation*, 12.
[58] Jürgen Moltmann, *The Church in the Power of the Spirit: A Contribution to Messianic Ecclesiology*, trans. Margaret Kohl (Minneapolis: Fortress Press, 1993), 199–206.
[59] Moltmann, *The Spirit of Life*, 74.

Eschatology

Moltmann's eschatology takes the form of panentheism. That is, in the eschatological consummation, all things will come to exist "in God."[60] As the persons of the Trinity interpenetrate each other in a perichoretic union, so also will the Trinity and creation interpenetrate one another, and the world will exist with and within the divine community. So the world becomes "*God's eternal home country.*"[61] Conversely, God becomes "*the eternal home of everything* he has created."[62]

This panentheism not only includes the world and animals in general but also *every single instantiation of life that has ever lived.* Moltmann emphasizes that *all flesh* will experience resurrection and redemption.[63] He is explicit that the word "all" includes every individual nonhuman animal.[64] Because Christ dies the death of all the victims of evolutionary emergence, his resurrection is the hope for a new future for all of those victims. Redemption thus "runs counter to evolution. . . . It is the divine tempest of the new creation, which sweeps out of God's future over history's fields of the dead, waking and gathering every last created being."[65] If redemption were not so—if the sufferings and death of any victim were left unredeemed *for that victim*—the eschaton would be an affront to justice.[66] "If we were to surrender hope for as much as one single creature, for us God would not be God."[67] For Moltmann, everything must be set right for every creature through resurrection; "otherwise God would not be God."[68]

Moltmann does not relegate this eschatological hope to the future. Moltmann offers the related notions of *adventus* and *novum* to develop this claim.[69] *Novum* is that which is genuinely new. It cannot burgeon

[60] See Moltmann, *The Coming of God.*

[61] Jürgen Moltmann, *In the End—the Beginning: A Life of Hope*, trans. Margaret Kohl (Minneapolis: Fortress Press, 2004), 158.

[62] Moltmann, *In the End*, 157.

[63] Moltmann, *The Coming of God*, 69–70.

[64] Moltmann, *The Way of Jesus Christ*, 335.

[65] Moltmann, *The Way of Jesus Christ*, 303.

[66] Moltmann, *Ethics of Hope*, 114.

[67] Moltmann, *The Coming of God*, 132.

[68] Moltmann, *Sun of Righteousness*, 141.

[69] This discussion derives mainly from Moltmann, *The Coming of God*, 25–29. It furthermore draws heavily on his understanding of time. For a good summary of this understanding, see Richard Bauckham, "Time and Eternity," in *God Will Be All in All: The Eschatology of Jürgen Moltmann*, ed. Richard Bauckham (Minneapolis: Fortress Press, 2001), especially 158–73.

out of "nature" as nature exists. It facilitates "eschatological surprise"[70] within history from outside of it. But *novum* does not obliterate history; it transfigures it.

Novum results from *adventus*, which Moltmann juxtaposes to *futurum*. *Futurum* is that which develops out of and within the flow of historical time. *Adventus*, on the other hand, is "*God's* future . . . the future of time itself."[71] God's eschatological future accosts history and in doing so opens a space for the "old" to be transformed into the genuinely "new"—*novum*.

Because newness (*novum*) is possible in the eschatological advent (*adventus*), there can be genuine proleptic experiences of the eschaton in history. However, these experiences are only anticipations that "correspond to the future of the coming God."[72] The fullness of the eschatological future is not a matter of human effort in history. Moltmann's hope for genuine newness and its *anticipations* even within the ebb and flow of historical time permits him to avoid, on the one hand, a mere preservation of the world as it is and, on the other, efforts to complete the kingdom progressively within history.

This position furthermore allows Moltmann to view the new creation as genuinely new without advocating the obliteration of the present creation. In other words, *creation is nature transfigured*. Christ provides this hope. The resurrected Christ does not evolve naturally from the crucified Jesus. Nature leaves victims in their tombs. Even so, the resurrected Christ *is* the crucified Jesus, but transfigured.[73] The new is not bound to the causal chain of the old. Neither is the old obliterated with newness. Such is the image of God's coming to the created order, a coming that will result in creation's transfiguration, not its replacement.

For Moltmann, humanity—especially the church—has a unique role in witnessing to this eschatological future. If this anticipatory life of hope is the true calling of the Christian, then it is also the true calling of the church: "The church in the power of the Holy Spirit is not yet the kingdom of God, but it is its anticipation in history."[74] In the words of Bauckham, the church is "the agent of eschatological unrest."[75]

[70] David Beck, *The Holy Spirit and the Renewal of All Things: Pneumatology in Paul and Jürgen Moltmann* (Eugene, OR: Pickwick, 2007), 126.

[71] Jürgen Moltmann, "The Liberation of the Future and Its Anticipations in History," in *God Will Be All in All: The Eschatology of Jürgen Moltmann*, ed. Richard Bauckham (Minneapolis: Fortress Press, 2001), 265.

[72] Moltmann, "Liberation of the Future," 289.

[73] Moltmann, *Theology of Hope*, 206–7.

[74] Moltmann, *Church in the Power of the Spirit*, 196.

[75] Bauckham, *The Theology of Jürgen Moltmann*, 102.

Because the church is not yet—nor can it be—*the* kingdom, its anticipatory role takes the form of the church suffering the contradictions of the world as an exilic community. In these contradictions, the church endures the afflictions of the entire created order in love. This solidarity with all creation drives the church to act as a herald of the eschatological future.[76] In this manner, "the *pro-missio* of the kingdom is the ground of the *missio* of love to the world."[77] Such is the church's essentially "eschatological orientation."[78]

Part of this witnessing entails contradicting the world by alleviating the suffering of creatures. "Those who hope in Christ can no longer put up with reality as it is, but begin to suffer under it, to contradict it."[79] The church is the locus of humanity's protest against nature's transience. In the Spirit, members of the church are led "into solidarity with all other created things. They suffer *with* nature under the power of transience, and they hope *for* nature, waiting for the manifestation of liberation."[80]

In sum, eschatology entails the hope for resurrection, which includes the end of transience. This hope extends to all individual creatures. This hope neither burgeons out of history nor is unrelated to it. The hope for new creation is present in the *adventus* of the eschatological future, which permits possibilities for genuine *novum* within history. The church, in its protest against nature's transience, is the locus of witness for this new creation.

Moltmann's Potential Contribution to Animal Theology and Ethics

Moltmann provides a powerful framework within which to construct an animal theology. He rejects anthropocentrism by claiming that the entire created order is the object of God's redemptive concern. Every single individual animal is part of the cosmic community. God desires each of them for their own sake. They share a destiny *with humanity*: a perichoretic participation in the Trinity. As evolution's ultimate victim, Christ died the death of all evolution's victims in order to draw every single one of them into the life of God's perichoretic communion. The Spirit is the principle both of

---

[76] Moltmann, *God for a Secular Society*, 105.
[77] Moltmann, *Theology of Hope*, 209.
[78] Moltmann, *Theology of Hope*, 309.
[79] Moltmann, *Theology of Hope*, 7.
[80] Moltmann, *God in Creation*, 101.

every creature's ongoing life and of every creature's eternal life to come. The *novum* of a future of peace in which all creatures will participate in God and one another is dawning onto all time in the eschatological *adventus*. Human beings, especially as the church, are called to be the proleptic witnesses of that dawning by practicing peace within the encounter between history and the eschatological future.

I have attempted to put these pieces together in a consistent framework, as Moltmann himself does not. Even with this framework constructed, however, we must ask the questions of ethics: Who should we be, and what then should we do? Moltmann is vague and inconsistent regarding what types of animal ethics might come of this theology. Here, I examine Moltmann's ethics and offer what I perceive to be a moral vision consistent with his theology.

The Cosmic Community Based on Law

Moltmann's ethic is favorable toward nonhumans, but not at the expense of concern for humanity, for "the dignity of human beings is unforfeitable."[81] Yet the dignity of humanity is not categorically unique. It is rather a manifestation of the dignity of the cosmos:

> We can talk about special human dignity if the premise is our recognition of *the creation dignity* of all other creatures—not otherwise. As the image of the Creator, human beings will love all their fellow creatures with the Creator's love. Otherwise, far from being the image of the Creator and lover of all the living, they will be his caricature. Consequently, special human rights to life and existence are valid only as long as these human beings respect the rights of the earth and of other living things.[82]

In the cosmic community, each individual member has his or her own intrinsic dignity as part of the whole. For Moltmann, "life is an end in itself . . . it is beyond utility or uselessness."[83] Hence, no creature is simply a chain in evolutionary emergence—a steppingstone for another creature of true worth. Furthermore, no creature is merely a resource for human use. Moltmann

---

[81] Moltmann, *Trinity and the Kingdom*, 233.
[82] Moltmann, *God for a Secular Society*, 132.
[83] Moltmann, *Ethics of Hope*, 59.

thus rejects anthropocentrism in favor of biocentrism. "It is not the human being that is at the center of the earth; it is life."[84]

For Moltmann, the cosmic community requires laws intended to safeguard the integrity of its members, especially those who cannot legally protect themselves. Thus, Moltmann's theology calls for legal solidification of the rights of the various parts of the cosmos, including nonhuman animals, for their own sakes.[85] This solidification must reflect these creatures' worth before God as part of the cosmic community. That is, it must reflect God's cosmic law, the manner in which God cares for the community. As I see it, Moltmann offers two basic dimensions of this cosmic law: conservationism and transfiguration.

The Conservationist Dimension of Cosmic Law

The present order of creation is open to God's future by the presence of the Spirit. When using creation instrumentally, humans must do so within the purview of the Sabbath. Moltmann develops this point, writing,

> In the sabbath stillness men and women no longer intervene in the environment through their labour. They let it be entirely God's creation. They recognize that as God's property creation is inviolable; and they sanctify the day through their joy in existence as God's creatures within the fellowship of creation. The peace of the sabbath is peace with God first of all. But this divine peace encompasses not merely the soul but the body too; not merely individuals but family and people; not only human beings but animals as well; not living things alone, but also, as the creation story tells us, the whole creation of heaven and earth.[86]

In line with the Sabbath, Moltmann advocates a form of conservationism.

> The first ecological law is that for every intervention in nature there must be a compensation. If you cut down a tree you must plant a new one. . . . If your city builds a power station, it must plant a forest which produces just as much oxygen as the power plant uses up.[87]

---

[84] Moltmann, *Ethics of Hope*, 61–62.
[85] Moltmann, *God for a Secular Society*, 131.
[86] Moltmann, *Trinity and the Kingdom*, 277.
[87] Moltmann, *God for a Secular Society*, 94.

Concretely, Moltmann delineates four general conservationist rights of the inanimate creation. First, it has the right to existence, which Moltmann defines as "preservation and development."[88] Second, it has the right to the integrity of its ecosystems. Third, it has the right to its own development apart from human intervention with the exception of justified and legitimate cases. Finally, rare ecosystems are under absolute protection.

Regarding nonhuman animals, Moltmann advocates animal rights, claiming that "a Universal Declaration of Animal Rights should be part of the constitutions of modern states and international agreements."[89] However, he is vague in his description of these rights.[90] He maintains that they must include a prohibition on factory farming.[91] He wavers on animal experimentation, calling for reduction through the development of alternative methods but not cessation.[92] Generally, Moltmann claims that every animal has the right to "preservation and development of its genetic inheritance" and "a species-appropriate life."[93]

The Transfigurative Dimension of Cosmic Law

The conservationist dimension of cosmic law suggests that humans must respect the integrity of creation as it is. However, this integrity is not static but dynamic. The cosmos is open for *creatio nova*. Thus, there is also a transfigurative dimension to Moltmann's ethics.

Because Moltmann does not separate *creatio continua* from *creatio nova*, "Christian ethics are eschatological ethics."[94] These ethics derive from *creatio anticipavita*—the prolepsis of *creatio nova* in the presence of the Spirit.[95] In the wake of the Christ-event, "resurrection has become the universal 'law' of creation, not merely for human beings, but for animals, plants, stones and all cosmic life systems as well."[96] There are therefore new possibilities within

[88] Moltmann, *Ethics of Hope*, 144.
[89] Moltmann, *God for a Secular Society*, 131.
[90] Celia Deane-Drummond notes this vagueness in conjunction with Moltmann's theological claims of a maximally inclusive and death-free eschatological vision. See Deane-Drummond, *Eco-theology* (Winona, MN: Anselm Academic Press, 2008), 173.
[91] Moltmann, *Ethics of Hope*, 156–57.
[92] Moltmann, *God for a Secular Society*, 131.
[93] Moltmann, *Ethics of Hope*, 144.
[94] Moltmann, "Liberation of the Future," 289.
[95] Moltmann, *God in Creation*, 209.
[96] Moltmann, *The Way of Jesus Christ*, 258.

history for all creation because of the *adventus* of *novum* through Christ and the Spirit.

This theological vision leads Moltmann to claim, "The hope for God's eschatological transformation of the world leads to a transformative ethics which tries to accord with this future in the inadequate material and with the feeble powers of the present and thus anticipates it."[97] With this claim, Moltmann distinguishes his eco-theological ethics from that of Teilhard and Thomas Berry, for example, and from certain strands of ecofeminism that champion mere conservationism. In a critique of the latter, he writes, "Deep respect for 'the good earth' does not mean that we have to give ourselves up for burial with the consolation that we shall live on in worms and plants. It means waiting for the day when the earth will open, the dead will rise, and the earth together with these dead will 'be raised' for its new creation."[98]

The point to be emphasized here is that conservation in the present does not do justice to the *adventus* of *novum* in history. Preservation is important and pertains to a realistic worldview. But it does not exhaust human responsibility to the cosmos, which includes witnessing to new possibilities and hopes through proleptic, transforming action. Human beings bear a role in witnessing to the eschatological future for the sake of the nonhuman creation. Moltmann thus claims that "creation is to be redeemed through human liberty."[99]

Constructing an Ethics Consistent with Moltmann's Animal Theology

Moltmann maintains that both the Jewish and Christian traditions are "at their best" when they "are movements of practical hope for peace for all peoples and all creatures."[100] Yet the exact meaning of this peace is unclear when it comes to concrete ethics, particularly in reference to individual nonhuman animals. In earlier writings, Moltmann acknowledges this point: "It is not yet fully clear what it means to withdraw from human beings the right of disposal over the creatures which they are in a position to dominate [i.e., nonhuman animals]. But it quite certainly includes the protection of species."[101]

---

[97] Moltmann, *Ethics of Hope*, xiii.
[98] Moltmann, *The Coming of God*, 276–77.
[99] Moltmann, *God in Creation*, 69.
[100] Moltmann, *Ethics of Hope*, 65,
[101] Moltmann, *The Way of Jesus Christ*, 311.

In the preceding quote, it appears that Moltmann is willing perhaps to settle on conservationist ethics when it comes to individual nonhuman animals. However, based on the new law of resurrection, I believe that his theology supports a further-reaching law. Neither suffering nor death pertains to the eschatological future of *any* individual creature. If such is the case, then no one can justify killing by appealing to the naturalness of death. Neither can one cause suffering to any creature by appealing to nature. Rather, death and suffering should cause lament because such transience is antithetical to God's kingdom, which "is also the kingdom of the universal 'sympathy of all things.'"[102] In this sense, all nature that dies is drawn into the scope of human concern. However, sentient creatures are drawn into that scope in a special manner, for Christ took *their* suffering into the triune life and redeemed *their* suffering in the resurrection. For this reason, the church must evince special concern for sentients, witnessing to the future by seeking not simply to avoid killing, but also to avoid causing suffering.

But even more can be said. For Moltmann, eternity is the fullness of time—all time gathered up into a present.[103] As such, the resurrection of a creature into eternity is the gathering of all times from that creature's life into the fullness of a moment. Hence, eschatologically, all cosmic times will perichoretically participate in God's eternity and, in that eternity, also in one another.[104] This point suggests that *every moment of every individual creature's life* bears eternal significance. Therefore, each moment of every individual creature's life is sacred. To cause one creature even a moment of suffering is at once to deny the eternal significance of that moment before God and to embrace the order of transience. While at times such actions might be necessary within the contradictions of history, they should never be considered unequivocally good. As Moltmann writes, "Anyone who lives in necessary contradiction to the laws and powers of 'this world' hopes for a new world of correspondences. The contradiction suffered is itself the negative mirror-image of the correspondence hoped for."[105]

When humans evince the new community of creation through anticipation of the eschatological future by treating animals peacefully, and/or by suffering with and on behalf of animals, they render the future present *for those animals*. This proleptic witness ought to be most evident in the church, which

[102] Moltmann, *God in Creation*, 213,
[103] See Moltmann, *Sun of Righteousness*, 62–63; Moltmann, *The Coming of God*, 280–81, 291.
[104] Moltmann, *The Coming of God*, 306.
[105] Moltmann, *The Coming of God*, 200.

recognizes the eschatological (i.e., new) community of creation. In this recognition, "the suffering of weaker creatures is the church's suffering too."[106]

So the church's first act of eschatological witness is fellow suffering. But this fellow suffering leads to a second act of witness—resistance:

> We have got used to death, at least the death of other creatures and other people. And to get used to death is the beginning of freezing into lifelessness oneself. So the essential thing is to affirm life—the life of other creatures—the life of other people—our own lives . . . the people who truly affirm and love life take up the struggle against violence and injustice. They refuse to get used to it. They do not conform. They resist.[107]

This resistance begins with a refusal to accept and benefit from the suffering and death of nonhuman animals. Humans must witness to the dignity of all creatures in living with them as common members of the cosmic community—members for whom Christ died to loose the Spirit that facilitates the burgeoning of cosmic transfiguration—sighing in the contradictions of history.

> Unless *the whole* cosmos is reconciled, Christ cannot be the Christ of God and cannot be the foundation of all things. But if he is this foundation, then *Christians cannot encounter other creatures in any way other than the way they encounter human beings*: every creature is a being for whom Christ died on the cross in order to gather it into the reconciliation of the world. . . . None of these other creatures has been destined to be "technologically manipulated" material for human beings.[108]

In my view, Moltmann's theology grounds two practices in particular.[109] If the eschatological future is seriously a category of *novum*, then every anticipation of it is simultaneously an act of rebellion toward some reality pertaining to the present. Thus, "living up to the future . . . means *resisting and anticipating*."[110] Both anticipation and resistance serve as means of

---

[106] Moltmann, *God for a Secular Society*, 32.

[107] Moltmann, *The Spirit of Life*, xii.

[108] Moltmann, *The Way of Jesus Christ*, 307; emphasis added.

[109] These two examples do not exhaust the possibility of concrete ethics from Moltmann's theology. Many other practices, such as animal experimentation and trapping, would appear much less justified as well.

[110] Moltmann, *Ethics of Hope*, 8.

preparation for the eschatological future. Through these means, the "eschatological future becomes present without ceasing to be future."[111]

Now, if "an ethics of hope sees the future in light of Christ's resurrection" and "points the way to transforming action so as to anticipate as far as possible, as far as strength goes, the new creation of all things,"[112] and if this new creation entails a cosmic peace between humans and animals that precludes predation, and if so many humans on the planet today hunt and eat meat out of luxury and not necessity, then it seems to me inevitable to conclude that both refusing to hunt and practicing vegetarianism are higher forms of Christian living. That is, these responses are *better* anticipations of the eschatological future than their counterparts. The same reasoning that Moltmann applies elsewhere (e.g., regarding fair trade prices) applies here. Just prices in a global economy are not "already the kingdom of God itself; but . . . they correspond to the kingdom more closely than unjust prices."[113] Following the same logic, refusing to hunt and practicing vegetarianism better correspond than hunting and meat-eating to an eschatological kingdom in which death will be no more.[114]

Conclusion

Moltmann does not set out to construct a systematic animal theology. However, he provides a framework that bears great potentiality for constructing one. There is an inclusive space for animals in all his theological loci. Furthermore, this space bears outcomes for morality—who we should be and what we should do in relation to animals.

While Moltmann does not develop an ethics that is thoroughly consistent with his framework, his eschatological orientation coupled with his inclusion of every single moment of every individual creature who has ever lived

[111] Moltmann, *Ethics of Hope*, 38.
[112] Moltmann, *Ethics of Hope*, 41.
[113] Moltmann, "Liberation of the Future," 288.
[114] Moltmann does not make this link between the eschatological future and vegetarianism explicitly. He does claim that vegetarianism is a better way to live, but this claim seems more about preservation than about eschatological witness. "It is . . . useful not to eat the foods which top the food chain but to move away from meat to vegetarian dishes. How much grain has to be used in order to produce one kilo of meat? It is not just cheaper to eat vegetarian food but fairer too, and healthier in addition. No one must suddenly become a vegetarian if his body cannot cope with the changeover to vegetarian food, but everyone can reduce his consumption of animal food to some extent, as long as this is not distasteful." Moltmann, *Ethics of Hope*, 157. For a critique of this claim, see McLaughlin, *Preservation and Protest*, 231–32.

into the scope of God's redemptive work suggests that the church's role as eschatological witness ought to include the cessation of violence toward non-human animals to the greatest extent possible. The phrase "the greatest extent possible" is wrought with ambiguity, but at the very least it entails more than preservation and conservation. It calls for the complete resistance of violence, even in some cases where there is luxurious benefit to humanity. In my view, such a position implies a move toward protecting animals from being hunted and eaten except in areas where such practices are necessary for sustaining human life and/or maintaining a healthy ecology. In doing so, the church witnesses to the eschatological future within the contradictions of history.

Acknowledgment

This chapter draws heavily upon and develops the following previously published article: Ryan Patrick McLaughlin, "Anticipating a Maximally Inclusive Eschaton: Jürgen Moltmann's Potential Contribution to Animal Theology," *Journal of Animal Ethics* 4, no. 1 (Spring 2014): 18–36.

Bibliography

Bauckham, Richard. "Eschatology in *The Coming of God*." In *God Will Be All in All: The Eschatology of Jürgen Moltmann*, edited by Richard Bauckham, 1–34. Minneapolis: Fortress Press, 2001.

Bauckham, Richard. *The Theology of Jürgen Moltmann*. Edinburgh: T&T Clark, 1995.

Bauckham, Richard. "Time and Eternity." In *God Will Be All in All: The Eschatology of Jürgen Moltmann*, edited by Richard Bauckham, 155–226. Minneapolis: Fortress Press, 2001.

Beck, David. *The Holy Spirit and the Renewal of All Things: Pneumatology in Paul and Jürgen Moltmann*. Eugene, OR: Pickwick, 2007.

Deane-Drummond, Celia. *Eco-theology*. Winona, MN: Anselm Academic Press, 2008.

McLaughlin, Ryan Patrick. "Anticipating a Maximally Inclusive Eschaton: Jürgen Moltmann's Potential Contribution to Animal Theology." *Journal of Animal Ethics* 4, no. 1 (Spring 2014): 18–36.

McLaughlin, Ryan Patrick. *Preservation and Protest: Theological Foundations for an Eco-eschatological Ethics*. Minneapolis: Fortress Press, 2014.

Moltmann, Jürgen. *The Church in the Power in the Spirit: A Contribution to Messianic Ecclesiology*. Translated by Margaret Kohl. Minneapolis: Fortress Press, 1993.

Moltmann, Jürgen. *The Coming of God: Christian Eschatology*. Translated by Margaret Kohl. Minneapolis: Fortress Press, 1996.

Moltmann, Jürgen. *The Crucified God: The Cross of Christ as the Foundation and Criticism of Christian Theology*. Translated by R. A. Wilson. Minneapolis: Fortress Press, 1993.

Moltmann, Jürgen. *Ethics of Hope*. Translated by Margaret Kohl. Minneapolis: Fortress Press, 2012.

Moltmann, Jürgen. *God for a Secular Society: The Public Relevance of Theology*. Translated by Margaret Kohl. Minneapolis: Fortress Press, 1999.

Moltmann, Jürgen. *God in Creation: A New Theology of Creation and the Spirit of God*. Translated by Margaret Kohl. Minneapolis: Fortress Press, 1993.

Moltmann, Jürgen. *History and the Triune God: Contributions to Trinitarian Theology*. Translated by John Bowden. New York: Crossroad, 1992.

Moltmann, Jürgen. *In the End—the Beginning: A Life of Hope*. Translated by Margaret Kohl. Minneapolis: Fortress Press, 2004.

Moltmann, Jürgen. "The Liberation of the Future and Its Anticipations in History." In *God Will Be All in All: The Eschatology of Jürgen Moltmann*, edited by Richard Bauckham, 265–89. Minneapolis: Fortress Press, 2001.

Moltmann, Jürgen. *The Spirit of Life: A Universal Affirmation*. Translated by Margaret Kohl. Minneapolis: Fortress Press, 1992.

Moltmann, Jürgen. *Sun of Righteousness, Arise! God's Future for Humanity and the Earth*. Translated by Margaret Kohl. Minneapolis: Fortress Press, 2010.

Moltmann, Jürgen. *Theology of Hope: On the Ground and Implications of Christian Eschatology*. Translated by James W. Leitch. London: SCM Press, 2002.

Moltmann, Jürgen. *The Trinity and the Kingdom: The Doctrine of God*. Translated by Margaret Kohl. Minneapolis: Fortress Press, 1993.

Moltmann, Jürgen. *The Way of Jesus Christ: Christology in Messianic Dimensions*. Translated by Margaret Kohl. Minneapolis: Fortress Press, 1993.

Polkinghorne, John. "Jürgen Moltmann's Engagement with the Natural Sciences." In *God's Life in Trinity*, edited by Miroslav Volf and Michael Welker, 61–70. Minneapolis: Fortress Press, 2006.

24

Andrew Linzey (1952–)

Animal Theology

Ryan Patrick McLaughlin

Andrew Linzey has both forged and shaped the field of animal theology.[1] Although his earliest work, *Animal Rights*, is not as deeply theological as his later works, it marks an important moment in the development of animal theology.[2] It was the first step toward a systematic exploration concerning the extent to which Christianity can speak positively about the well-being of nonhuman animals. For Linzey, this ongoing exploration has yielded the following conclusion: "The best the Christian tradition has to offer cannot . . . be bettered elsewhere."[3]

Linzey's work is situated within the general framework of the animal welfare and animal rights movement.[4] His theology and ethics find sources as diverse as Rosalina Godlovitch,[5] Karl Barth,[6] Albert Schweitzer,[7] Dietrich Bonhoeffer,[8] Tom Regan,[9] and Eastern Christianity.[10] By drawing upon these sources, Linzey highlights something deeply pro-animal buried beneath the more visible Christian traditions of anthropocentrism and these traditions' resulting exclusion of animals from the status of direct moral concern. In this

---

[1] For a much fuller exploration of Linzey's theology and its implications for animals (and the rest of the nonhuman creation), see Ryan Patrick McLaughlin, *Preservation and Protest: Theological Foundations for an Eco-eschatological Ethics* (Minneapolis: Fortress Press, 2014), especially chaps. 10–12. Some of the current chapter draws from this source.

[2] See Andrew Linzey, *Animal Rights: A Christian Assessment* (London: SCM Press, 1976).

[3] Andrew Linzey, *Christianity and the Rights of Animals* (New York: Crossroad, 1987), 5.

[4] Linzey, *Animal Rights*, viii.

[5] Andrew Linzey, *Why Animal Suffering Matters: Philosophy, Theology, and Practical Ethics* (New York: Oxford University Press, 2009), 158.

[6] Andrew Linzey, *Animal Theology* (Urbana: University of Illinois Press, 1994), 9–12.

[7] Linzey, *Animal Rights*, 42.

[8] See Andrew Linzey, "C. S. Lewis's Theology of Animals," *Anglican Theological Review* 80, no. 1 (Winter 1998): 60–81.

[9] Linzey, *Christianity and the Rights of Animals*, ix.

[10] See Linzey, *Christianity and the Rights of Animals*, 17–18, 32.

Ryan Patrick McLaughlin, *Andrew Linzey (1952–)* In: *Animal Theologians*. Edited by: Andrew Linzey and Clair Linzey, Oxford University Press. © Oxford University Press 2023. DOI: 10.1093/oso/9780197655542.003.0025

chapter, I aim to delineate the foundations of Linzey's animal theology by examining his understanding of God in relation to God's creation.

Trinitarian Love as the Ground for Creation

The heart of Linzey's animal theology is the divine rapport with the world. Two key concepts establish this rapport. First, God is a trinitarian community of love. Second, God's love is the foundation for creation, from its origin to its eschatological redemption.

The importance of the doctrine of the Trinity is evident in Linzey's personal creed in *Animal Gospel*. This creed affirms the creative role of the Father, the incarnational and redemptive role of the Son, and the vitalizing role of the Spirit.[11] Linzey furthermore notes the unique roles of the trinitarian persons vis-à-vis the cosmos:

> God the Father gives life; God the Son in his passion, death, and resurrection rescues this life from its own folly and wickedness, thereby reconciling it again to the Father; and God the Spirit indwells in this life preserving it from dissolution, working towards the redemption and consummation of all created things.[12]

These claims notwithstanding, however, Linzey does not often draw out the doctrine's implications in any detail. That is, while Linzey claims that the trinitarian persons play different and vital roles in the creation and redemption of the cosmos, he does not clearly develop why God's trinitarian nature is meaningful for creation.

Even so, that Linzey considers the love between the trinitarian persons an essential component of the doctrine of creation is implicit. He writes, "God is *for* creation. I mean by that that God, as defined by trinitarian belief, cannot be fundamentally indifferent, negative or hostile to the creation which is made."[13] Somehow, though the idea is not here developed, the fact that God is Trinity denotes that God is *for* creation. But how so?

---

[11] Andrew Linzey, *Animal Gospel* (Louisville, KY: Westminster John Knox Press, 2000), 7.
[12] Linzey, *Christianity and the Rights of Animals*, 71.
[13] Linzey, *Animal Theology*, 24.

I suggest that Linzey maintains that God's very nature is evident in the loving relationship between the Father, Son, and Spirit. This nature is one of other-embracing love. In *After Noah*, Linzey describes God as a "community of love."[14] Prior to this phrase, he writes that "the unity of creation is but a showing forth of that already existing unity of Father and Son."[15] Linzey's exclusion of the Spirit here is likely due to his focus on Christology and creation. Regardless, the claim suggests that God's trinitarian nature, which is love, is the foundation for the entire created order. Moreover, Linzey maintains that this love constitutes the destiny of the entire created order: "The Trinity is that community of love which has already taken creation to itself, to bind it, and heal it, and make it whole."[16] God's love is the true end of creation, and this end entails a thorough healing of creation's wounds.

In line with this reading, I suggest that for Linzey the doctrine of creation is fundamentally, from the original act of creation to the eschatological consummation, a love story in which the Trinity pursues the world with the same love that exists within the divine community. Thus, the Trinity's nature, as love, is the foundation for the economy of salvation for the created order.[17] In this sense, trinitarian love has a central role in theology.

An Empowered Creation and a Suffering God

For Linzey, creation is neither finished nor static. It is necessarily incomplete and dynamic because creation "cannot be anything other than less than divine."[18] On this ground, Linzey argues, "To be a creature is necessarily to be incomplete, unfinished, imperfect."[19] Creation is on its way to a destination—participation in God's triune love.

Why does God make the world in this manner? Linzey's understanding of divine love suggests that God does so for the sake of establishing a genuine rapport with creation. If creation were merely an extension of God, God could not pursue it in love. It is necessary that creation be other-than-God

---

[14] Andrew Linzey, *After Noah: Animals and the Liberation of Theology* (Herndon, VA: Mowbray, 1997), 77.

[15] Linzey, *After Noah*, 77.

[16] Linzey, *After Noah*, 77.

[17] Linzey, *Christianity and the Rights of Animals*, 71. See also Andrew Linzey, *Creatures of the Same God: Explorations in Animal Theology* (New York: Lantern Books, 2009), 53.

[18] Linzey, *Animal Theology*, 81.

[19] Linzey, *Animal Theology*, 81.

in order for God to have a loving relationship with it.[20] Hence, God creates the cosmos as the other-*than*-God so that it is free to become the other-*with*-God. And it can become the latter only if it is the former.

Because creation, if it is to be other-than-God, is necessarily dynamic, incomplete, and imperfect, the act of creation entails a risk for God. Because creation is other-than-God, "the very nature of creation is always ambiguous . . . it affirms and denies God at one and the same time."[21] Linzey is not here suggesting that evil is *necessary* for creation (in this context, he is focusing on the parasitic dimensions of nature). Rather, creation entails the necessary *risk* of evil obtaining. If there were no risk, creation would not be a genuine other whom the Trinity could pursue in love.

In the discussion that follows, I examine how this claim speaks to Linzey's understanding of the violent state of nature and eschatological redemption. Here, I simply note that for Linzey, creation is other-than-God and therefore imperfect and dynamic. This point is significant because it suggests that God must be perpetually willing to suffer the existence of the other-than-God as well as the risk that this existence entails for God. Thus, Linzey writes that the

> "for-ness" of God towards creation is dynamic, inspirational, and costly. It is dynamic because God's affirmation of creation is not a once-and-for-all event but a continual affirmation[;] otherwise it would simply cease to be. It is inspirational because God's Spirit moves within creation—especially within those creatures that have the gift of a developed capacity to be. It is costly because God's love does not come cheap.[22]

Out of God's own love, God inaugurates a dynamic creation and chooses perpetually to affirm its dynamic existence. Because creation necessitates a God who is willing to suffer the cosmos its own integrity, creation must begin with an act of grace—divine kenosis (self-emptying). This kenosis continues throughout creation's narrative because the Trinity continuously safeguards the integrity of the cosmos. In this sense, the act of creation witnesses to God's possibility (a point to which I will subsequently return).[23]

The previously quoted passage also points toward the manner of God's presence in the world: the Spirit of God. For Linzey, the Spirit is the breath

[20] The phrase "other-than-God" is my own, but I believe it represents Linzey's view of creation well.
[21] Linzey, *Animal Theology*, 81.
[22] Linzey, *Animal Theology*, 25.
[23] Linzey, *Animal Theology*, 57.

of all sentient life. In the Spirit, God embraces the harrowing narrative of the world and feels its twists and turns. It is this divine sympathy that leads Linzey to emphasize the significance of sentience. In the Spirit, God experiences the *pathos* of the world. The Spirit is thus uniquely present in those life forms who can suffer. Although God empowers the entire creation with its own integrity as the other-than-God, for Linzey there is a special manner in which the Spirit empowers and embraces sentient creatures. It is here that we begin to see that Linzey's theology is neither anthropocentric nor biocentric; it is sentience-centric.[24]

Creaturely Rights as Theos-Rights

Because creation is fundamentally an act of God for the sake of love, for Linzey God is the ultimate stakeholder in creation. Thus, the rights of creatures are in actuality theos-rights—the rights of God as Creator. This approach provides the foundation for a theological theory of rights that is ontologically relational—that is, one that recognizes the essentiality of relationships. Creatures are always and already creatures of God. Therefore, the interests of these creatures are simultaneously the interests of God. Conversely, the interest of God is the interests of these creatures. As Linzey states, "while rights are grounded in the existence of Spirit-filled lives, what constitutes their rights is the will of God who desires that they should so live."[25]

The concept of theos-rights avoids two significant pitfalls. First, it is not predicated on an essentialist reduction of creatures. Linzey does not construct a hierarchy of beings in which moral worth exists only above the line of rationality.[26] Rather, whatever hierarchical arrangement of the cosmos exists with regard to characteristics such as rationality is of secondary moral relevance to the notion that *everything* in this hierarchy comes from God. God is the Creator and therefore has a stake in all that exists. The moral worth of a creature, then, cannot be reduced to human judgments concerning insuperable lines based on ontological qualities. Every creature is a creature-in-relation-to-God because God, as Creator, is a God-in-relation-to-every-creature.

---

[24] See McLaughlin, *Preservation and Protest*, 279–84. Linzey defines his theological ethics with the term "mammalocentricity." See Linzey, *Christianity and the Rights of Animals*, 84–85.

[25] Linzey, *Christianity and the Rights of Animals*, 75.

[26] Indeed, Linzey maintains that rationality is not a morally relevant distinction. On rationality and other distinctions that are not morally relevant, see Linzey, *Why Animal Suffering Matters*, 10–29.

While there may be morally relevant distinctions in the cosmos—Linzey holds that sentience is such a distinction—such issues are subsequent to the theological claim that God has a stake in God's creation. Thus, rights do not derive from the innate qualities of creatures but rather are grounded relationally.

The second pitfall avoided by the concept of theos-rights is the procurement of concern for animals on *only* a relational ground. That is, the rights of nonhuman animals, though predicated fundamentally on God's rights, are at once the rights *of those creatures*. They have value in and of themselves because they are creatures of God. Significantly, then, Linzey is not arguing that creatures have value only indirectly (i.e., he does not argue that violating a creature is morally wrong only because it violates God). Such an argument would amount to nothing more than a position of divine property rights. The value of creatures is not based on an indirect concern, as it was for Aquinas and Kant. Nor is God's love for creatures based on their productivity. It is rather a love of the creatures in themselves. In this sense, to say that theos-rights are relationally grounded is not to say that they are not the rights of the creatures in question. Theos-rights belong to animals because God has created them and cares for their well-being for their own sake.

The concept of theos-rights is central to Linzey's work. However, in and of itself, the concept is not sufficient to ground the type of moral concern for animals that Linzey has in mind. After all, God could have created a world in which humans alone have intrinsic value and therefore enjoy, by divine right, supreme reign over all other creatures. Indeed, I have elsewhere argued that such is the theocentric vision of Aquinas.[27] In such a scenario, harming a creature would not violate theos-rights because God would have created those creatures for the sake of humans' well-being. Hence, no harm would be done in harming them. The point here is that the significance of theos-rights depends on the nature of the *theos* (God) who establishes them.

In this sense, the true heart of Linzey's *theological* contribution is not only theos-rights but also his particular vision of theos. The theos-rights of the trinitarian God who creates and empowers all creation to be, and who is uniquely entangled in the sufferings of sentient creatures, establish a powerful paradigm of moral concern for sentient nonhuman animals. But to appreciate Linzey's understanding of theos adequately, we must examine

---

[27] See Ryan Patrick McLaughlin, *Christianity and the Status of Animals* (New York: Palgrave Macmillan, 2014), chap. 1.

(1) how God's suffering becomes acutely present in history with the Christ-event and (2) how this Christ-event points toward an eschaton in which all creation will experience redemption. Before examining these concepts, however, we must consider how Linzey addresses the violent state of nature as it` currently exists.

The Mysterious Fallenness of Creation

Linzey is adamant that creation is good and blessed by God. However, he is equally adamant in claiming that the entire cosmos is, in some sense, fallen and incomplete.[28] Linzey affirms that notion that "the wickedness of man throws the system of intending order into disorder"—that "harmony becomes engulfed in meaninglessness and teleology lapses into futility."[29] He goes as far as to suggest that denying the Fall—a denial that he links to accepting the world as it is—is tantamount to the denial of Christianity itself. In a manner very similar to Jürgen Moltmann, Linzey writes, "The Gospel truth is that we do not have to accept the world as it is. We must distinguish creation from nature."[30]

Linzey maintains the distinction between creation and nature on strictly theological and moral (as opposed to scientific) grounds. He lists a number of problems that would arise should the doctrine of the Fall disappear from theology.[31] First, morally speaking, "predation and parasitism [become] either morally neutral or, even worse, positive aspects of nature to be tolerated or even emulated."[32] It follows that humans would not be ethically obliged to witness against the mechanisms of evolution but rather should participate in the "one inexorable law of the universe," which is "eat and be eaten."[33] Second, there would no longer be any need for the eschatological redemption of the nonhuman world.[34] If creation is fine as it is, then there need be

[28] Linzey, *Christianity and the Rights of Animals*, 33.
[29] Linzey, *Christianity and Rights of Animals*, 11.
[30] Linzey, *Animal Gospel*, 15. On Moltmann, see Jürgen Moltmann, *God in Creation: A New Theology of Creation and the Spirit of God*, trans. Margaret Kohl (Minneapolis: Fortress Press, 1993), 37–40.
[31] Linzey, *Animal Gospel*, 28–31; Linzey, "C. S. Lewis's Theology," 70–71.
[32] Linzey, *Animal Gospel*, 28.
[33] Linzey, *Animal Gospel*, 30.
[34] Linzey, *Animal Gospel*, 29. Christopher Southgate challenges Linzey on this point, writing, "There is no reason to believe that just because God used a long evolutionary process to give rise to the biosphere we know, God may not have inaugurated a redemptive movement that will heal that process." See Christopher Southgate, *The Groaning of Creation: God, Evolution, and the Problem of Evil* (Louisville, KY: Westminster John Knox Press, 2008), 179 n. 1.

no overturning of nature in an act of new creation.[35] However, for Linzey, rejecting "a transformed new heaven and earth in which all sentients will be redeemed is logically tantamount to denying the possibility of a morally good God."[36] In short, a God who affirms nature as it is and therefore leaves the many victims of nature in their graves is not a God who loves or does justice by those individual victims.

Of course, the difficult issue here is the science. Nature's tragedies and violence—including predation, parasitism, and disease—are an inevitable outcome of the very structures of the cosmos that make life possible.[37] Furthermore, certain disvalues such as pain are essential for the survival and development of sentient creatures.[38] In this sense, if nature's violence is the result of a Fall, then the structure of the cosmos itself (including the life within the cosmos) must be a result of the Fall. But it would then follow that the Fall is the reason that life (including the *blessings* of life) as we know it exists. This issue has led many theologians to reject or question deeply the doctrine of the Fall.[39]

How does Linzey address this issue? Ambiguously. He acknowledges that evolutionary suffering seems integral to life processes and burgeons from nonmoral sources (e.g., natural selection).[40] But he cannot accept that God *intended* the world to be this way. He draws on Genesis 1 to argue that "parasitical existence is incompatible with the original will of God."[41]

So who is responsible? Again, there is ambiguity. In *Christianity and the Rights of Animals*, Linzey writes, "Humans alone are properly responsible" for the curse, including "suffering and predation," apparent in the present condition of nature.[42] In *Animal Theology*, he suggests that evil arises out of creation's status as "incomplete, unfinished, [and] imperfect."[43] In the same

[35] For example, see Holmes Rolston III, "Does Nature Need to Be Redeemed?," *Zygon* 29 (1994): 205–29.

[36] Linzey, *Animal Gospel*, 31.

[37] See Nancey Murphy, "Science and the Problem of Evil: Suffering as a By-Product of a Finely Tuned Cosmos," in *Physics and Cosmology: Scientific Perspectives on the Problem of Natural Evil*, ed. Nancey Murphy, Robert John Russel, and William R. Stoeger (Notre Dame, IN: University of Notre Dame Press, 2007), 131–52.

[38] See John Polkinghorne, *Reason and Reality: The Relationship between Science and Theology* (London: SPCK, 1991), 98.

[39] See Southgate, *The Groaning of Creation*, 28–29; Polkinghorne, *Reason and Reality*, 98; Arthur Peacocke, *Theology for a Scientific Age: Being and Becoming—Natural, Divine and Human* (Minneapolis: Fortress Press, 1993), 222–23.

[40] Linzey, *Animal Rights*, 70; Linzey, *Christianity and the Rights of Animals*, 61.

[41] Linzey, *Animal Theology*, 80.

[42] Linzey, *Christianity and the Rights of Animals*, 18.

[43] Linzey, *Animal Theology*, 81.

text, he also argues for the possibility of an angelic disobedience as the root of the Fall.[44] Elsewhere, he embraces C. S. Lewis's reasons for appealing to an angelic fall: (1) human sin cannot account for the suffering of dinosaurs in a post-Darwin worldview, and (2) predation cannot be a result of God's will if God is good.[45] In *Animal Gospel*, Linzey maintains that God's creative processes must be morally justifiable, but he excludes "parasitism and predation" from this category because they are "unlovely, cruel, evil aspects of the world ultimately incapable of being reconciled with a God of love."[46]

Linzey's ambiguity notwithstanding, he is consistent in his claim that nature's violence is not compatible with God's love. While he struggles to explain the origin of this violence (and the structure of the cosmos that renders it inevitable and/or necessary), he is also consistent in his claim that God seeks to rescue nature from its current state. For Linzey, the Christ-event is the ultimate rescue mission of God, and this mission points toward the redemption of all sentient creatures in an eschatological future.

God the Suffering Redeemer

As already noted, Linzey rejects God's impassibility. As Creator, God must suffer creation its unique identity as other-than-God. In order to relate to a dynamic creation, God must be dynamic. God the Spirit is present in creation, bearing the full force of its many contradictions. God's co-suffering is exhaustive. That is, God suffers *all* the suffering of all sufferers.[47]

Linzey's rejection of divine impassibility is fundamental to his animal theology. He writes, "Only the most tenacious adherence to the passibility of God may be sufficient to redeem us from our own profoundly arrogant humanistic conceptions of our place in the universe."[48] In other words, God's suffering helps us to move beyond our anthropocentric tendencies—theological and otherwise. If we can understand God's suffering as embracing the suffering of all sufferers, the meaning of the word "us" expands immensely. God does not simply suffer with "us" (i.e., humans); God suffers with *all of us* (i.e., all sentient life). With this expansion, theology and ethics shift dramatically.

---

[44] Linzey, *Animal Theology*, 167 n. 8.
[45] See Linzey, "C. S. Lewis's Theology," 64.
[46] Linzey, *Animal Gospel*, 27–28; see also Linzey, *Creatures of the Same God*, 36.
[47] Linzey, *Animal Theology*, 52.
[48] Linzey, *Animal Theology*, 57.

The suffering of the animal whom humans eat is also the suffering of the God who created both her and those who eat her.

For Linzey, God continues to suffer (and in unique ways) in the unfolding narrative of God's pursuit of the other-than-God, particularly with reference to sin and redemption.[49] The fallen cosmos, immersed as it is in violence, needs redemption. Christ is the definitive divine response to this cosmic need.

Linzey's Christology is as sentience-centric as his wider theology. He is thus quite critical of Karl Barth's Christology, in which the incarnation is the divine "yes" to humanity.[50] For Linzey, Christ is the incarnate Logos, "the origin and destiny of all created things."[51] As such, the incarnation cannot simply be "God's 'Yes' " to humanity. Because "the *ousia* assumed in the incarnation is the *ousia* of all creaturely being, it is difficult to resist the conclusion that what is effected in the incarnation for man is likewise effected for the rest of the non-human creation."[52]

While this claim appears to be biocentric (if not cosmocentric), elsewhere Linzey limits his focus, writing, "The incarnation is God's love affair with all fleshy creatures."[53] The term "fleshy" here points toward sentience for Linzey. The Spirit's unique presence in certain creatures as *ruach* ("breath"), coupled with the Spirit's redemptive role for individual suffering creatures, permits a distinction between sentient (fleshy) creatures and other life forms.[54] Thus, although all creation has value in God's eyes, sentient creatures have unique value.[55] Following this pattern, Linzey notes that in the incarnation God takes on not simply matter and energy but also all the travails of those who suffer. Christ's suffering envelops the suffering of all sentient creatures.

It is only because the Trinity is open to the suffering of the entire cosmos that there can be any hope that "*all* suffering can be transformed by joy."[56] In particular, Jesus's resurrection points toward the redemption of all creaturely suffering. For Linzey, it follows that we cannot establish morality with

---

[49] Linzey avoids the question of how God's suffering might be reconciled with attributes such as omnipotence or impassibility. Linzey, *Animal Theology*, 50.

[50] See Linzey, *Animal Theology*, 68.

[51] Linzey, *Creatures of the Same God*, 14.

[52] Linzey, *Christianity and the Rights of Animals*, 34. For a similar position, see David Clough, *On Animals* (New York: Bloomsbury, 2014), 84–86. However, Clough is more generous to Barth than Linzey. See Clough, 16–17.

[53] Linzey, *Creatures of the Same God*, 14.

[54] See Linzey, *Christianity and the Rights of Animals*, 79–80.

[55] See Linzey, *Christianity and Rights of Animals*, 9; Linzey, *Why Animal Suffering Matters*, 10–11.

[56] Linzey, *Christianity and the Rights of Animals*, 45.

reference to nature's laws.[57] Indeed, the true "natural law" is better under-stood as "trans-natural law"—a law that accounts for God's eschatological in-tention for nature.[58] Such a law recognizes that creation remains unfinished "until all violence is overcome by love."[59]

God and God's Images

While Linzey rejects anthropocentrism, he does not deny that humans are unique in God's creation. In fact, his theology *depends* on human unique-ness.[60] It is the unique constitution and status of human beings that grounds human responsibility for the well-being of creation and, in a special way, sen-tient animals.

For Linzey, humans alone bear the image of God. However, Linzey rejects the view that this image creates a dividing line between the privileged moral status of humans and the deficient (or only indirect) moral status of *all* nonhumans.[61] Instead, he embraces the vision of modern biblical scholar-ship, also represented in Christian history, that the image constitutes a func-tional task for humans.[62] In other words, although Linzey rejects a *moral* anthropocentrism (in which humans alone have moral value), he embraces a *functional* anthropocentrism (in which humans bear a special responsibility in the created order). God endows humans with the divine image (noun) *so that* they can image (verb) God within and for the sake of the nonhuman creation.

It follows that humans have an important role in Linzey's theology. He writes, "Christian animal rights advocates are not interested in dethroning humanity. On the contrary, the animal rights thesis requires the reenthroning of humanity. The key question is, what kind of king is to be reenthroned?"[63]

[57] Neil Messer makes a similar point in his discussion of Aquinas's appropriation of Aristotelian biology. Neil Messer, "Humans, Animals, Evolution and Ends," in *Creaturely Theology: On God, Humans and Other Animals*, ed. Celia Deane-Drummond and David Clough (London: SCM Press, 2009), 215.

[58] Linzey, *Animal Theology*, 83–84.

[59] Linzey, *After Noah*, 76.

[60] See Linzey, *Animal Gospel*, 38.

[61] See Linzey, *Christianity and the Rights of Animals*, 61; Linzey, *Animal Theology*, 58–59; Linzey, *Animal Gospel*, 49; Linzey, *Creatures of the Same God*, 11. See also McLaughlin, *Preservation and Protest*, 265–70.

[62] See Linzey, *Why Animal Suffering Matters*, 28–29. On biblical scholarship, see J. Richard Middleton, *The Liberating Image: The Imago Dei in Genesis 1* (Grand Rapids, MI: Brazos Press, 2005).

[63] Linzey, *Animal Gospel*, 38.

The answer is humans who embody a dominion that reflects the character of the God whose image they bear.

For Linzey, this character is most fully revealed in Christ, who sacrificed himself for the sake of others.[64] In *Animal Gospel*, Linzey expounds this claim in his creed, writing that Jesus is "the true pattern of service to the weak," "the Crucified" in whom are "the faces of all innocent suffering creatures."[65] Christ expresses the nature of divine rule, which in turn expresses the intended nature of human rule. In Christ, "God's power is expressed in powerlessness, in condescension (*katabasis*), humility and sacrificial love."[66] It is this kind of power and dominion that humans must image to the nonhuman creation.[67]

In *Animal Theology*, Linzey describes humanity's proper dominion (i.e., Christlike dominion) with the notion that humans are the "servant species."[68] Humans should use whatever exceptional qualities we have for the well-being of all God's creatures, especially sentient ones. Linzey writes, "Humans are the species uniquely commissioned to exercise a self-sacrificial priesthood, after the one High Priest, not just for members of their own species, but for all sentient creatures."[69]

Human uniqueness is thus that of a priest—a unique status for a unique task for the sake of others. But Christlike priesthood is for the sake of the *radically* other—the nonhuman other. As priests, humans are to follow Christ's example, sacrificing their own peace by entering into the suffering of all those who can suffer. In this sense, there can be no genuine human priesthood of creation that is not for the sake of nonhuman animals. One must also suggest that just as God creates the other-than-God for the sake of love, humanity must learn to view the otherness of nonhumans as an opportunity to love, not an opportunity to exploit.

Being for the radically other in this sense is no easy task, and Linzey knows as much. Based on the divine call for humans to image God, Linzey develops the "Generosity Paradigm," which "rejects the idea that the rights and welfare of animals must always be subordinate to human interests, even when vital

---

[64] See Linzey, *Animal Theology*, 32–33.
[65] Linzey, *Animal Gospel*, 7.
[66] Linzey, *Christianity and the Rights of Animals*, 28.
[67] Although Linzey notes that the image has been marred by human sinfulness, he also maintains that Christ restores—or at least begins the process of restoring—the divine image and thereby enables humans to assume their role as keepers of the peace in the cosmos. Linzey, *Animal Gospel*, 149.
[68] See Linzey, *Animal Rights*, chap. 3; Linzey, *Creatures of the Same God*, 3.
[69] Linzey, *Animal Theology*, 45.

human interests are at stake."[70] Generosity requires a willingness to be for the other even when doing so is costly—perhaps *especially* when it is costly. Just as God's love for the other-than-God costs God so much (most notably in Christ's crucifixion), so also will humanity's call to love the other-than-human cost humanity.[71] Priestly humans should be willing to pay this cost for the very fact that we are "greater" than other animals.

Linzey furthermore maintains that humanity's role as the image of God is "an extension of the suffering, and therefore also redeeming, activity of God in the world."[72] Thus, there is an eschatological dimension to Linzey's functional anthropocentrism. Human beings are to act in light of God's ultimate desire for the cosmos, which entails its redemption from suffering and death. "New creation is man-centered . . . but it cannot logically be man-monistic, i.e., for man only."[73] The new creation is centered on humanity "precisely because of [humanity's] unique ability to co-operate with the Spirit."[74] On account of this ability, "humankind is essential in order to liberate animals."[75]

Part of humanity's eschatological role entails being moved by the suffering of sentient creatures and acting to alleviate such suffering. Linzey sees this activity in the monastic tradition, including the hagiographies in which saints protect animals and make violent animals peaceful.[76] When humans act peacefully toward other creatures, the eschatological future of the world becomes present by means of anticipation. Humans "become anticipatory signs of the kingdom."[77] Thus, Linzey proposes a balance between a realizable and a fully transcendent eschatology.[78] In his view, the doctrine of the Trinity—including the Trinity's economic interaction with the world—requires humans to cooperate with the redemptive movement of God within history without lapsing into a political program of completing the kingdom within history.[79]

---

[70] Linzey, *Animal Theology*, 44.
[71] Linzey, *Animal Theology*, 55.
[72] Linzey, *Animal Theology*, 52.
[73] Linzey, *Animal Rights*, 75.
[74] Linzey, *Christianity and the Rights of Animals*, 76.
[75] Linzey, *Animal Theology*, 72.
[76] Linzey, *Christianity and the Rights of Animals*, 45.
[77] Linzey, *Creatures of the Same God*, 52.
[78] See Linzey's critique of Barth's transcendent eschatology in Linzey, *Christianity and the Rights of Animals*, 93.
[79] Linzey, *Christianity and the Rights of Animals*, 93.

Being God's Images in a Fallen World

The eschaton is a matter of God's activity because the contradictions of the present state of reality are intrinsic to reality.[80] Linzey recognizes this point. It is simply not possible, given the world in which we live, to avoid causing suffering completely.[81] Human sin makes it so that "no human being can live free of evil."[82] (I would add to this point that the very lawlike structure of our cosmos also makes it so that "no human being can live free of evil.") Indeed, Linzey acknowledges that even a vegan lifestyle results in the death of animals during the farming process.[83] Eden is an impossibility given our current state of existence.[84] As Linzey is fond of expressing, "there is no pure land" in a fallen world.[85] Only an eschatological redemption can definitively end evil. However, empowered by the Spirit in the wake of the Christ-event, humans can live in solidarity with other creatures caught up in the same "structures of disorder."[86]

Linzey thus seeks a balance. On the one hand, we must recognize that life as we know it necessitates suffering and death and therefore leads to moral conflicts for someone who seeks to alleviate and prevent such realities. On the other hand, there is a divine calling to avoid normalizing suffering and death institutionally on the basis that they are, in certain situations, necessary for either human existence or the ongoing well-being of the cosmos.[87] Said theologically, humanity's Spirit-filled and imaginative witness to the eschatological future remains only a witness.[88] It is not the province of humans to construct the kingdom; but neither is it the luxury of humans to ignore its ideal for the sake of luxurious self-gratification.

---

[80] Linzey, *Creatures of the Same God*, 34–35.
[81] Linzey, *Christianity and the Rights of Animals*, 19–20; see also Linzey, *Why Animal Suffering Matters*, 24–25.
[82] Linzey, *Christianity and Rights of Animals*, 101.
[83] Linzey, *Animal Theology*, 132; Linzey, *Animal Gospel*, 77–79; Linzey, *Creatures of the Same God*, xiv–xv.
[84] Linzey, *Animal Theology*, 58.
[85] See Linzey, *Animal Theology*, 132, Linzey, *Animal Gospel*, 90; Linzey, *Creatures of the Same God*, xiv.
[86] Linzey, *Animal Theology*, 58.
[87] Linzey, *Animal Rights*, 33–42.
[88] Linzey, *Christianity and the Rights of Animals*, 35.

Ethical Implications

Humanity cannot construct the eschaton but can witness to it through non-violent living. What might such a witness entail? Linzey goes into great detail on this point.[89] He addresses issues such as animal experimentation, hunting, trapping and farming for fur, and vegetarianism. On each issue, Linzey provides convincing arguments, drawing upon theology, scripture, and facts about institutionalized forms of suffering. He typifies animal experiments as "Un-Godly Sacrifices," hunting as the "Anti-Gospel of Predation," genetic engineering as "Animal Slavery," and vegetarianism as "a Biblical Ideal."[90] He advocates for an eschatological vegetarianism, writing, "By refusing to eat meat, we are witnessing to a higher order of existence. . . . By refusing to go the way of our 'natural nature' . . . by standing against the order of unredeemed nature we become signs of the order of existence for which all creatures long."[91]

These contributions are all important. However, where Linzey makes one of his most significant contributions (in my view) is his rejection of the general societal practice of *institutionalizing* these forms of suffering. Even if causing suffering and death to nonhumans is at times a sad necessity, it does not follow that causing harm and death should be the norm of society. Hence, Linzey targets legal justifications for the common practices that cause millions of animals an immense amount of suffering. First and foremost, he aims to restrict such practices. Ultimately, he seeks to eliminate them.

In *Animal Gospel*, Linzey advocates six steps toward this end.[92] First, humans must be provided with a "space for an ethical appreciation of living creatures."[93] For Linzey, this step entails encouraging the childlike intuition to protect nonhuman animals. Second, advocates must expose the various forms of institutionalized suffering. Revealing institutionalized evil is an important step in combating it. Third, animal rights scholars must engage in interdisciplinary dialogues and debates concerning their positions. Linzey rightly notes that ideas matter. They form our practices. As such, "we shall not change the world for animals without also changing people's ideas about the world."[94] Fourth, as consumers animal advocates must seek

---

89   For a full exploration, see McLaughlin, *Preservation and Protest*, chap. 12.
90   Linzey, *Animal Theology*, table of contents.
91   Linzey, *Animal Theology*, 90–91.
92   Linzey, *Animal Gospel*, 126–39.
93   Linzey, *Animal Gospel*, 127.
94   Linzey, *Animal Gospel*, 130.

to institutionalize practices of peace through their purchasing decisions.[95] Humans must engage in just peace-making with regard to nonhuman animals. We cannot be passive pacifists. We must be active pacifists. On the one hand, this step requires accurate labeling of products and transparency about how the products are produced. For instance, what are the specific conditions in which egg-laying hens and chickens raised for meat live? How much space do they have? Are they genetically modified? Are they permitted other natural tendencies (e.g., vegetarian feed)? These questions help consumers make informed choices concerning the animal products they purchase. On the other hand, consumers must be willing to pay more for their products. Ethics are costly because we can almost always turn a greater profit if we ignore the dignity of the other, whether human or otherwise. We must also be willing to consume *less*. Paying more for less? Being a "servant species" is thus costly in the most literal sense. Fifth, there must be legislation that is both gradual (i.e., not "all or nothing" for animals) and truly progressive (i.e., laws that entail more than cosmetic changes to institutionalized suffering). Laws are an extremely important aspect of the effort to end institutionalized suffering. After all, institutionalized abuse calls for an institutional response. Furthermore, as Linzey notes, "only changes in laws secure lasting protection."[96] Sixth, though Linzey is critical of capitalism in general, he argues that there are enough people who would seek alternative (cruelty-free) products if such products were available.[97] In other words, there is a demand for cruelty-free products. Businesses would do well to supply products for this demand.

Collectively, Linzey's aim is to embody eschatological hope through nonviolent living on both a personal and communal level. Personally, we ought to be responsible consumers. We ought to engage in harmful practices only out of vital necessity—and even then with a healthy dose of penitence. We ought to seek the most life-affirming (or at least sentient life–affirming) practices in our particular contexts. Communally, we should seek to pass laws that address current institutional abuses of animals. We should reevaluate, as a species, the ways of thinking that have permitted (and even encouraged) practices such as factory farming, hunting for sport, and fur trapping. In these ways, we can lessen the gratuitous evils that so many animals face.

---

[95] Linzey, *Animal Gospel*, 131; Linzey, *Why Animal Suffering Matters*, 66–67.
[96] Linzey, *Why Animal Suffering Matters*, 66.
[97] See Linzey, *Animal Gospel*, 136–37.

Conclusion

Linzey's animal theology draws on central theological loci in order to construct a practically relevant ethics for today's world. The God whose nature is love creates out of and for the sake of love. To this end, God empowered creation to be an other-than-God—a separate way of being with its own integrity. This creative move entailed the risk that creation would not develop as God desired it to develop. In some mysterious way, this risk came to fruition, as the creation experienced a cosmic Fall into destructive violence. Such violence is now embedded in the way of "nature." But God has never abandoned creation. In the Spirit, God is ever-present in the cosmos, empowering its life and experiencing its sufferings. Furthermore, in the incarnation God took all of creation's torturous harms into the life of the Trinity. But God also transformed those harms. In the resurrection, God established a new "transnatural" law. This law points to the eschatological redemption of all sentient life. In the wake of the resurrection of Christ, we can no longer equate "nature" with "creation." The former is the current state of the cosmos. The latter is the eschatological end of nature—the renewal of all things.

Humans bear the image of the God who has done nothing less than suffer alongside and die for the sake of God's creatures. Hence, when humans image God, the deep love of God for all creation revealed in God's activity with the cosmos should be evident in that imaging. When humans fail to image this God—when we harm without adequate reason or without penitent remorse—we both besmirch the nature of God and reject God's desire for peace for all creatures. It is in this sense that we violate God's rights as the loving Creator when we fail to love. In light of the Creator's love for the entire creation, all creatures enjoy the morally relevant status of "God's beloved." As God's image, humans ought to honor this status by practicing ways of love to whatever extent possible. This call to love excludes the exploitation of animals for food, for hunting, for recreation, and for experimentation.

With his theology, Linzey has contributed a great deal to animal theology. Indeed, he has forged the field in many ways. His work reminds us that God cares for all of God's creatures. Any anthropology that calls for less from humans fails to embody this care. For these contributions, Linzey is to be greatly commended.

Bibliography

Clough, David. *On Animals*. New York: Bloomsbury, 2014.

Linzey, Andrew. *After Noah: Animals and the Liberation of Theology*. Herndon, VA: Mowbray, 1997.

Linzey, Andrew. *Animal Gospel*. Louisville, KY: Westminster John Knox Press, 2000.

Linzey, Andrew. *Animal Rights: A Christian Assessment*. London: SCM Press, 1976.

Linzey, Andrew. *Animal Theology*. Urbana: University of Illinois Press, 1994.

Linzey, Andrew. "C. S. Lewis's Theology of Animals." *Anglican Theological Review* 80, no. 1 (Winter 1998): 60–81.

Linzey, Andrew. *Christianity and the Rights of Animals*. New York: Crossroad, 1987.

Linzey, Andrew. *Creatures of the Same God: Explorations in Animal Theology*. New York: Lantern Books, 2009.

Linzey, Andrew. *Why Animal Suffering Matters: Philosophy, Theology, and Practical Ethics*. New York: Oxford University Press, 2009.

McLaughlin, Ryan Patrick. *Christianity and the Status of Animals*. New York: Palgrave Macmillan, 2014.

McLaughlin, Ryan Patrick. *Preservation and Protest: Theological Foundations for an Eco-eschatological Ethics*. Minneapolis: Fortress Press, 2014.

Messer, Neil. "Humans, Animals, Evolution and Ends." In *Creaturely Theology: On God, Humans and Other Animals*, edited by Celia Deane-Drummond and David Clough, 211–27. London: SCM Press, 2009.

Middleton, J. Richard. *The Liberating Image: The Imago Dei in Genesis 1*. Grand Rapids, MI: Brazos Press, 2005.

Moltmann, Jürgen. *God in Creation: A New Theology of Creation and the Spirit of God*. Translated by Margaret Kohl. Minneapolis: Fortress Press, 1993.

Murphy, Nancey. "Science and the Problem of Evil: Suffering as a By-Product of a Finely Tuned Cosmos." In *Physics and Cosmology: Scientific Perspectives on the Problem of Natural Evil*, edited by Nancey Murphy, Robert John Russel, and William R. Stoeger, 131–52. Notre Dame, IN: University of Notre Dame Press, 2007.

Peacocke, Arthur. *Theology for a Scientific Age: Being and Becoming—Natural, Divine and Human*. Minneapolis: Fortress Press, 1993.

Polkinghorne, John. *Reason and Reality: The Relationship between Science and Theology*. London: SPCK, 1991.

Rolston, Holmes, III. "Does Nature Need to Be Redeemed?" *Zygon* 29 (1994): 205–29.

Southgate, Christopher. *The Groaning of Creation: God, Evolution, and the Problem of Evil*. Louisville, KY: Westminster John Knox Press, 2008.

Index

For the benefit of digital users, indexed terms that span two pages (e.g., 52–53) may, on occasion, appear on only one of those pages.
Figures are indicated by *f* following the page number